SOCIOLOGY:
AN INTRODUCTION

SOCIOLOGY: AN INTRODUCTION
FOURTH EDITION

CHRISTOPHER BATES DOOB
SOUTHERN CONNECTICUT STATE UNIVERSITY

THE HARCOURT PRESS

HARCOURT BRACE COLLEGE PUBLISHERS

Fort Worth   Philadelphia   San Diego   New York   Orlando   Austin   San Antonio

Toronto   Montreal   London   Sydney   Tokyo

Editor-in-chief	Ted Buchholz
Acquisitions editor	Chris Klein
Developmental editor	Karee Galloway
Project editor	Steve Norder
Production manager	Cynthia Young
Art director	Burl Sloan
Picture editor	Greg Meadors

Address for editorial correspondence: Harcourt Brace College Publishers, 301 Commerce Street, Suite 3700, Fort Worth, TX 76102.

Address for orders: Harcourt Brace & Company, 6277 Sea Harbor Drive, Orlando, FL 32887. 1-800-782-4479 or 1-800-433-0001 (in Florida).

ISBN: 0-15-500771-8

Printed in the United States of America

4 5 6 7 8 9 0 1 2   032   9 8 7 6 5 4 3 2

*Once again, to Eveline Bates (Doob)
and Leonard William Doob who,
besides being my parents,
have always been my best teachers.*

Preface

In recent years the Soviet Union has been dissolved, and what were once its satellite nations have undergone massive changes. Meanwhile most developing nations face formidable challenges to bring themselves into the modern world, with poverty, limited resources, overpopulation, and hunger invariably threatening them. While most U.S. citizens face less drastic threats, a declining economy, poverty, political corruption, environmental pollution, crime, racism, sexism, delinquency, and family problems are common realities lacking simple solutions. Before these problems can be solved, people must better understand how the society works, or fails to do so. Never has the need to provide introductory sociology been more urgent. With that thought in mind, I enthusiastically tackled the preparation of the fourth edition.

Colleagues teaching introductory sociology, editors at Harcourt Brace, and students have all helped to shape this book. Their comments have been invaluable. Those involved with the fourth edition have proposed a number of specific changes, but there has been general support for the basic structure established in previous editions. Thus the text has retained certain general features, although they have been systematically revised and updated:

■ A streamlined format, now involving sixteen chapters, permits comprehensive coverage comfortably within a semester.
■ A built-in study guide, updated for this edition, enables students to review the material they have just read.
■ Six updated or new "Research in Sociology" sections provide concrete illustrations of what sociological research involves. These sections are placed at the end of their respective chapters, immediately before the study guide.

NEW TO THIS EDITION

Throughout the preparation of the fourth edition, there has been a relentless effort to supply new source material—new studies and statistics, in particular.

■ Material from the previous chapter on gender roles and sexuality has been integrated into existing chapters on emerging minorities and the family and alternative lifestyles.
■ Two new research sections—one about race-relations studies and the other about religious cults—appear at the end of Chapters 9 and 12 respectively.
■ Nine new features provide sociological analyses of contemporary topics such as confronting gender inequality in the classroom, the impact of Hurricane Andrew on southern Florida, and Nelson Mandela's leadership in South Africa.
■ About 450 new references ensure coverage that accurately reflects both society and the state of sociology in the 1990s.
■ Numerous updates of tables and figures, photos that capture recent events, and chapter openings contribute to the book's contemporary character.

ORGANIZATION

I remain convinced that a fairly traditional organization is best for an introductory textbook. Thus the five parts of the original edition have been retained. Part I examines the particular features, contributions, and theories that distinguish the sociological point of view and surveys the major methods and problems of doing research. Part II launches into the variety of influences, conditions, and pressures that help make individuals part of the larger social environment. Part III examines the nature of inequalities in modern society and the processes that affect specific minorities in the United States. Part IV brings the student to the next level of complexity in social arrangements by surveying a range of social institutions, how (and how well) they meet the collective needs of American society, and how and why they are changing. The final section of the book examines the forces and issues that have affected and often changed each level of our social order, from relationships between institutions to small-group interactions.

The textbook, which previously had seventeen chapters, now has sixteen, maintaining the approximate length of the third edition. Many instructors who have used the book indicate that they are comfortable with that length. They also have confirmed that the best way to economize is in the coverage of social institutions. Thus six institutions are presented in combination chapters, which illustrate the respective relationships between religion and education, the political and economic institutions, and science and medicine.

STYLE OF PRESENTATION

Many introductory sociology students, even potential majors, have little background in the social sciences and even less familiarity with the way scientists and academicians think. For this reason textbooks that make assumptions about the students' reach can easily slip beyond their grasp. In spite of a subject matter that is inherently interesting and relevant, student motivation can quickly subside when there are too many hurdles to learning. Students need to feel successful about understanding and interpreting what they read. This means that a textbook must spell out the implications of the material presented in straightforward language, interrelate facts and ideas so that they make sense together, and anchor concepts and theories within familiar experiences and events.

To help the student experience success—and, I hope, excitement—in learning about sociology, I have tried to provide the following:

■ Careful attention to vocabulary and sentence length, consistent presentation of basic terminology, and a personalized, informal

style that speaks with, instead of at, the student.

■ An orderly presentation of topics, moving—especially in Part IV—from large-scale theoretical and substantive issues to small-group and individual experiences.

■ A special emphasis on contemporary issues and examples with which students already have some familiarity and personal interest.

■ Careful integration of all visual supplements to the text—figures, charts, tables, and photographs—through well-developed in-text references, explanations, and captions.

■ Comprehensive coverage that addresses all major topics, research, and trends without being overly detailed.

■ A balanced presentation of the major theoretical perspectives, with careful attention to both their contributions and their limitations. Up-to-date statistical information is drawn from government and survey data, with special care given to explaining the relevance of these facts and figures to the issues and trends under discussion. Topics analyzed include fear of AIDS, sexual harassment, teenage suicide, the effectiveness of public education, the relationship between economic development and population control, and the American drug problem.

SPECIAL AIDS TO TEACHING AND LEARNING

It is easy to fill a textbook with an assortment of pedagogical devices. In fact, it is sometimes difficult to know when to stop. I have, however, carefully put together a variety of aids that I feel work together in the scope of an introductory book and genuinely enhance teaching and learning.

Built-In Study Guide   Study-guide materials are included after each chapter, so students will have immediate, economical access to features that can aid their review of material. The sections contain:

■ Learning objectives   A list of major issues outlines the basic material that must be learned within each chapter.

■ Summaries   Numbered paragraphs at the end of each chapter provide a framework for review of important material.

■ Key Terms   Concepts that are boldfaced

and defined in the textbook proper are regrouped alphabetically and redefined for easy reference and review. For further assistance an alphabetized glossary containing all key terms is provided at the end of the book.

■ Tests   True–false, multiple-choice, and essay questions offer opportunities to determine how well one has assimilated the material. Answers to the true–false and multiple-choice questions are provided at the end of each chapter study guide.

■ Suggested readings   Each chapter of the study guide contains eight incisively annotated readings drawn from a variety of categories: novels, essays, case studies, articles, critiques, theoretical analyses, biographical and autobiographical accounts, practical guides, historical and cross-cultural documents, and literature surveys.

■ Additional assignments   These projects, which require students to analyze, synthesize, and evaluate material in the chapter or conduct some kind of simple study, can be assigned by instructors to give students a chance to apply the knowledge contained in the chapter.

"Research in Sociology"   I believe that one of the most difficult tasks teachers of introductory sociology face is conveying a concrete sense of the challenges and problems involved in doing sociological research.

To make this task easier, the text contains six sections which examine sociological research into the topics of culture, rape, racism, cults, charisma, and prison riots. It is my intention that the "Research in Sociology" sections will reinforce many of the methodological issues discussed in Chapter 2, and, most importantly, that they will bring sociological research to life for the student.

Feature Sections   The following features provide recent illustrations of many issues and topics discussed in the text. Each chapter contains two of these different features, each of which is tied to discussions within the body of the chapter.

■ Social Applications   These sections provide recent illustrations of issues and topics discussed in the text and include such subjects as drugs in America, privatizing executions, and freedom of the press.

■ Cross-Cultural Perspectives   To provide an invaluable counterperspective to issues and trends in American society, these inserts examine such topics as socialization in Samoa, the impact of major-league baseball on the Dominican Republic, and education for black South Africans after *apartheid*.

■ American Controversies   These sections provide opposing positions on such issues as sociologists' preferences for particular theories, affirmative action for minority groups, and abortion. As students evaluate, discuss, and debate these issues, the stimulation they receive will undoubtedly produce insights into the related social processes.

SUPPLEMENTS TO THE TEXT

No textbook can address all the particular needs of each student and instructor, and so the quality of the supplementary materials is nearly as important as the textbook itself. The following supplements provide a comprehensive and easy-to-use package of materials suitable for different paces and styles of teaching and geared to both the motivational and learning needs of various students.

Instructor's Manual and Test Bank   Prepared by Robert Thompson of Minot State University, each chapter of the instructor's manual contains a chapter synopsis, teaching objectives, a list of key concepts and terms, lecture ideas with references, topics for class participation and debate, and an annotated list of films and videos. The manual also includes advice for using the built-in study guide and other features of the textbook.

Each chapter of the test bank contains more than 100 multiple-choice, true-false, short answer, and essay questions. All test items are page referenced to the textbook.

Computerized Test Banks   A computerized version of the text bank is available for use with IBM, Macintosh, and Apple computers. This powerful program is capable of randomly generating tests within the parameters specified by the instructor. The program also allows instructors to modify existing questions or to create new ones. A telephone hotline is available for anyone who experiences difficulty with the program. Harcourt Brace provides a customized test construction service for users of *Sociology: An Introduction*, fourth edition. Exams can be generated within forty-eight hours

x

and dispatched by either mail or facsimile machine.

Interactive Computer Program   Users of this book also will be able to obtain a newly revised version of *The Social Scene*, an interactive computer program specifically designed for sociology students. This program lets students put their newfound knowledge to work in surveying data analyses and manipulating data sets drawn from the General Social Survey.

Overhead Transparencies   A recently revised set of fifty color transparencies helps to enhance classroom lectures. These transparencies contain information that supplements—rather than duplicates—important material in the textbook.

Sociology Videos   Harcourt Brace & Company offers twelve videos—based on the popular telecourse, the "Sociological Imagination"—to accompany this edition of *Sociology: An Introduction*. All programs are twenty-six minutes long and are accompanied by a video instructor's manual written by Glenn Currier, the project sociologist for the "Sociological Imagination."

ACKNOWLEDGMENTS

As with any project of this size, it cannot be accomplished by one person alone. To all those who contributed to the success of this textbook, I thank you.

Once again my debt to Teresa Carballal is large. Because of her busy life, I was inclined to involve her less than in the past. Still, many times I consulted her, and so for the fourth time, her mark on the book is readily apparent.

I enjoyed working with Karee Galloway at Harcourt Brace College Publishers. She always seemed relaxed and as a result relaxed me. At the same time, she demanded the best I could provide and, in turn, supplied important ideas and criticisms throughout the period of manuscript creation. Also at Harcourt Brace, steve Norder's

efficient, thorough direction of the process of converting the manuscript into a book made that lengthy, often arduous activity nearly painless. He was helped by the book team of Cynthia Young, Burl Sloan, and Greg Meadors.

Reviewers are an essential part of a project of this scope and magnitude; I simply do not know what I would have done without them. Reviewers of this edition as well as those who participated in previous editions have provided many general insights, specific evaluations, and commentaries that have proved nothing less than invaluable. For their contributions to this book, I would like to thank Robert S. Anwyl, Miami-Dade Community College; James A. Glynn, Bakersfield College; E. M. Griggs, Abraham Baldwin Agricultural College; Robert P. Snow, Arizona State University; Marcelle Williams, San Joaquin Delta College; Robert Alexander, North Hennepin Community College; Paul Brasky, Ulster Community College; Lois Easterday, Onondaga Community College; Laura Hartman, University of Texas at Austin; Margaret Park Haun, St. Louis Community College at Florissant Valley; Clinton McCurdy Lipsey, Tennessee State University; Vicki Pate, Fayetteville Technical Community College; Richard Phillips, Kalamazoo Valley Community College; Stephanie Shanks-Meile, Indiana University Northwest; Stephen Spitzer, University of Minnesota at Minneapolis; Metaleen Thomas, Caldwell Community College; and Robert Thompson, Minot State University.

Recognizing how interesting and valuable people's commentaries can be, I want to encourage any faculty colleague or student with a commentary or question to contact me in writing at the following address:

Sociology Department
Southern Connecticut State University
501 Crescent Street
New Haven, CT 06515

This practice began with the third edition, and I received many interesting inquiries. Once again I promise to answer all letters.

Christopher Bates Doob

CONTENTS IN BRIEF

CONTENTS

FEATURES CONTENTS

Social Applications

Cross-Cultural Perspectives

American Controversies

Research in Sociology

About the Author

Christopher Bates Doob has been teaching Introductory Sociology as well as courses in Social Problems, The Family, Social Change, The City in Western Civilization, and Environmental Sociology for twenty-three years. He is currently professor of sociology at Southern Connecticut State University. He has been a Senior Research Scientist for the New York State Department of Mental Hygiene. He also served as a consultant to the Roper Organization in New York City.

In addition to *Sociology: An Introduction*, Dr. Doob has written *The Open Covenant: Social Change in Contemporary Society* published by Praeger Publishers in 1987 and *Racism: An American Cauldron* published by HarperCollins in 1993. He is currently working on a social problems text for Harcourt Brace and serving as a member of the steering committee for the New Haven Child Plan.

Dr. Doob received his bachelor's and master's degrees in sociology from Oberlin College and his Ph.D. in sociology from Cornell University.

Photo by Joy Bush.

SOCIOLOGY:
AN INTRODUCTION

The Contribution of Sociology

1
SOCIOLOGY: THE KEY TO UNDERSTANDING THE SOCIAL WORLD

2
DOING RESEARCH IN SOCIOLOGY

Sociology: The Key to Understanding the Social World

THE SOCIOLOGICAL PERSPECTIVE

THE DEVELOPMENT OF SOCIOLOGY
Karl Marx
Émile Durkheim
Max Weber
American Sociology

CONTEMPORARY SOCIOLOGICAL THEORIES
Conflict Theory
Structural-Functional Theory
Symbolic-Interaction Theory
Choosing and Using Theories

STUDY GUIDE

1

On the afternoon of April 30, 1992, Tim Rutten, a columnist for the *Los Angeles Times*, stood with his wife on his front lawn and watched "the worst urban riot in modern American history" making its way toward them. Instead of the usual April smell of jasmine and mock orange, there was the heavy odor of burning. By late afternoon the columns of smoke were much closer, and Rutten went inside, got the shotgun he had used to shoot game birds as a child, loaded it with shells from a twenty-five-year-old box of ammunition, and stationed himself inside by the bedroom window. At one point a neighbor dropped by to say that a liquor store two blocks away was being looted. But the Ruttens and their neighbors were fortunate as the columns of smoke moved past their area and toward the hills (Rutten 1992).

The Los Angeles riots started the day after an all-white jury acquitted four white policemen of assault, ending a seven-week trial involving the widely publicized videotaped beating of Rodney King, a black man. The immediate impetus to the riots was the defendants' surprise acquittal in a trial where most observers felt that the evidence made a guilty verdict a foregone conclusion. Behind that issue, however, lay the anger, frustration, and rage suffered by the city's poor people, who had long experienced severe unemployment and underemployment, inferior education, and rundown housing. The rioters came from varied ethnic and racial backgrounds as the arrest record confirms. In the four days following the verdict when most of the property damage occurred, the Los Angeles police department and the county sheriff's department arrested more than 7,000 people. Hispanic-Americans, African-Americans, whites, and Pacific Islanders were all represented in the arrests, with Hispanic-Americans providing 49 percent and African-Americans 40 percent of the total (Rutten 1992, 53). While Los Angeles's celebrated gangs participated, they received plenty of assistance. Ed Turley, a field coordinator for Community Youth Gang Services in the south-central section of the city where the riots occurred, explained that the verdict was "like a 10.0 earthquake that woke everyone up"—a "real slap in the face whether you're a gang member or Joe Citizen" (Terry 1992, A25). A gang member also emphasized the significance of the social context in which the riots occurred. He explained:

> Rodney King? Shit, my homies be beat like dogs by the police every day. This riot is about all the homeboys murdered by the police, about the little sister killed by the Koreans, about twenty-seven years of oppression. Rodney King just the trigger.
>
> (Davis 1992, 745)

The riots affected many people's lives. Homes and businesses were destroyed; damage totaled $785 million; and many minority businesses either were not insured or were underinsured (Rutten 1992, 52). Some people suffered serious psychological damage. At Queen Anne Place Elementary School near the riot area, attendance was light the week after the riots because many children were afraid to go to school or their parents were afraid to let them. Those who did show up were often very nervous as they adjusted to life after what many referred to as "the war." In the nurse's office, Christopher Romero, a third grader wearing a Boston Celtics sweatshirt and faded jeans, lay rigidly on a small cot. "I don't feel so good. I got a fever," he explained. Asked how long he had been sick, he said, "When the fire came, the fire that came with the war" (Wilkerson 1992, A24).

How does this account make you feel? Are you angry that thousands of people would engage in rioting and looting? Or, are you inclined to focus on the fact that local citizens, already oppressed by economic and political conditions, were driven to violence by the King verdict? Perhaps you are simply confused.

If you are even somewhat confused, don't feel

too bad. Sociologists have dedicated their lives to studying social issues, and they recognize that both effective sociological analyses and solutions to social problems are usually complex and debatable. Throughout this book we discuss a range of social issues. We hope that at the end of the course you will understand more about the issues themselves as well as the tools for analyzing them.

Let's begin with a basic idea—that sociologists stress that people are affected by their social world. In the situation just described, for instance, they appreciate that Tim Rutten, a middle-class journalist, and Christopher Romero, a poor inner-city resident, are living in socially diverse contexts that significantly affect their perceptions and actions. Sociology focuses on the belief that a scientific analysis of the factors in the social world is one of the most effective and interesting ways to understand human behavior. To restate this, **sociology** is the scientific study of human behavior in groups and of the social forces that influence that behavior.

The various information sources with which we come into contact constantly suggest questions or problems about social issues. Why did the Los Angeles riots occur? How were residents affected? What can be done to prevent such outbreaks in the future? Sociologists are well-equipped to conduct research and analysis that systematically tackle such questions. Sociology, in fact, can examine social issues involving groups of all sizes as well as all phases of people's lives. If more effectively understanding the social world interests you, then this course should be valuable

to you. But even if your enthusiasm about social issues is limited, you can learn a great deal that may prove helpful for living in our complex modern society.

Sociologists do not simply declare their beliefs indisputable truth—they do research to determine whether those beliefs are supported by facts. Their investigations are rooted in the scientific method. It is this method that distinguishes the sociological perspective from a "commonsense" interpretation of the world.

A **science** is a systematic effort to develop general principles about a particular subject matter, based on actual observations and stated in a form that can be tested by any competent person. Sciences are usually divided into two main branches: the **natural sciences**—older sciences such as astronomy, chemistry, physics, and biology that study the physical world—and the **social sciences**—the sciences that focus on various aspects of human behavior. Besides sociology, the social sciences include anthropology, economics, history, political science, and psychology.

In the first section of this chapter, we look at the group settings of human behavior and describe the scientific nature of sociology. Our focus then shifts to a discussion of early sociologists who have contributed significantly to the development of sociological thought. In the final section, we survey the three most prominent contemporary theories of sociology, and in that discussion we return to the Los Angeles riots as illustrations for those theories.

The Sociological Perspective

The sociological perspective emphasizes that people's thoughts and actions are strongly influenced by the groups to which they belong as well as by other social factors, such as values, beliefs, practices, and institutions. Of course, individuals often have the opportunity to choose among alternative courses of thought and action. They are not entirely independent beings, however. From birth until death, individuals are imbedded within and influenced by groups and larger structures. Groups are often small and immediate, for example, fami-

lies and friends. Larger structures, called "institutions" and discussed in Chapter 4, "Groups," can be enormous and remote—the economy and government, for instance.

Think about what you have just read because it is fundamental to understanding what sociology involves. The basic idea of the sociological perspective is that people's behavior is affected by the groups and other social forces with which they come in contact. The fact is that many U.S. citizens—and perhaps you are one of them—

6

resist this idea, feeling that individuals control their destiny. Certainly sociologists do not deny individuals' ability to affect what happens to them, but more than most Americans, they emphasize the impact of group forces on their behavior. The idea of the sociological perspective is so important that it will be continually emphasized throughout this book.

The ways groups influence their members can be surprising, even for sociologists. In the late 1930s, for example, a young sociologist named William Foote Whyte was conducting a lengthy study of a group of young men in Boston. One evening Whyte and a number of the men went bowling. Before the game started, some of the group leaders predicted that they would score higher than the other men, and as a close associate of the leaders, Whyte was included in the prediction. At first Whyte paid little attention, because such an outcome made little sense. Why, for example, should Frank Bonnelli, the best athlete in the entire group, finish well down the list? Why did Frank himself say that he did not expect to score well, not when he was "playing with fellows I know like that bunch" (Whyte 1955, 318)?

After some thought Whyte realized that he was observing the influence of a group upon each of these men. The expectations and support of the group leadership strongly affected each man's bowling scores, regardless of his ability. Even Whyte himself was affected. That evening he felt strong group support, and as he stepped up to bowl, he was entirely confident that he would hit the pins at which he aimed. He had never felt that way before. Whyte later wrote, "It was a strange feeling, as if something larger than myself was controlling the ball as I went through my swing and released it toward the pins" (Whyte 1955, 319). When the bowling was over, Whyte checked the scores. He was pleased to discover that the predicted order of finish was almost entirely correct. Whyte now had evidence to support his idea that the group was influencing its individual members.

About a half-century later, Eric L. Hirsch (1990) conducted another sociological study, which also sought to determine a group's impact on its participants. In this case the researcher was interested in learning what factors help explain recruitment and commitment in social movements. To determine the sources of these behav-

Like the bowlers in William Foote Whyte's study, accomplished athletes realize that people's scrutiny can affect their performance.

iors, Hirsch focused on a protest which occurred in April 1985 when Columbia University and Barnard College students sat down in front of the chained doors of Columbia's principal classroom and administrative building. Blockading the entrance, the students stated that they would not leave until the university divested itself of stock in corporations doing business with South Africa.

Hirsch conducted nineteen extended interviews, which averaged one-and-a-half hours each, with members of the steering committee that organized and led the protest as well as others taking part in the building blockade. From the interviews he obtained information about the students' political backgrounds, their activities during the three weeks of protest, and their feelings about the personal impact of participation. In addition, the sociologist distributed 300 surveys to a randomly chosen sample of Columbia and Barnard students, and had 181 or 60.3 percent of the surveys returned. Besides giving basic demographic information and commenting on their political values, respondents indicated attitudes toward those on both sides of the protest and their personal involvement in the divestment campaign.

Hirsch's overall conclusion was that the protest developed among a close-knit group of politically committed activists using carefully planned strategies and tactics. For instance, protest leaders recruited active supporters by putting themselves on the line. A half-dozen members of the steering committee fasted nearly two weeks just to get a meeting with the university president and trustees. Another member of the protest group indicated that the fasters' willpower increased his own. He added:

> To have to go into the hospital because you were off food for fifteen days, and the Trustees won't even speak to you. It really made me angry at the Trustees, so I was determined that this was not something that was just going to wimper off. At least I was going to be there, and I know others felt the same way.

> (Hirsch 1990, 248)

Furthermore lengthy discussions within the group tended to increase members' commitment. At one point university officials wrote letters to some of the participants, threatening them with dismissal. One blockader who was three weeks from graduation received one of these letters and "was petrified, especially since Columbia has not been fun for me but rather painful." He wanted to leave the protest, but at the group's meetings he learned that other students had received threatening letters and were committed to continue. He added, "One other factor was the fasters, the fact that there were South Africans involved in it, and that these people had more on the line than I did" (Hirsch 1990, 249).

These two studies help illustrate the meaning of the sociological perspective. The nearby Social Application on C. Wright Mills provides a prominent sociologist's analysis of why this perspective is both important and useful.

In the next section, the sociological perspective is applied to the science of sociology, with an examination of the social conditions and prominent individuals contributing to its formation and expansion.

The Development of Sociology

The growth of science contributed to the development of sociology. In 1687 Isaac Newton, an Englishman, published his famous *Mathematical Principles of Natural Philosophy*, about the laws of motion and the law of gravity. He concluded that the universe was logical and operated itself and was not, as had been believed for centuries, under divine influence. During the next century, leading French intellectuals came to accept the idea that science and reason, not religion, should shape their thinking.

Perhaps nobody took this idea more strongly to heart than the French theorist Auguste Comte (1798–1857). Living during the era when the Industrial Revolution was transforming some European societies from feudal, agricultural states to capitalist, urban powers, Comte believed that the same practices of observation and experimentation used

to produce advances in the physical sciences could be employed in the study of human beings.

Often referred to as "the father of sociology" because he initiated the application of scientific principles to the study of society and coined the word *sociology*, Comte felt that systematic knowledge about group behavior would provide the basis for rational social planning, with sociologists as the operating elite. While Comte's notions about the relationship between knowledge and social change turned out to be naive and utopian, he was the first writer to propose a role for social scientists in the development of industrial society (Coleman 1990, 613–14). However, the work of three other nineteenth-century European thinkers—Karl Marx, Émile Durkheim, and Max Weber—has had a more significant impact on modern sociology.

SOCIAL APPLICATION
C. Wright Mills on Private Troubles and Public Issues

When should the sociological perspective be applied to individuals' problems? In his book *The Sociological Imagination* (1961), C. Wright Mills offered a clear answer: when the problem ceases to be what he called "a personal trouble" and becomes "a public issue."

Consider the topic of unemployment. If a small number of men and women are unemployed, that is their personal trouble. We can examine their character and skills and probably find deficiencies that make them incapable of holding a job. However, if more than 9.7 million people representing over 8.1 percent of the labor force are unemployed—the situation in the United States in 1992—then sociological analysis produces a different conclusion. Such a high unemployment rate represents a "public issue." Sociologists, economists, and other an-

alysts cannot focus only on individuals and their inadequacies to understand why so many people are unemployed. They must examine the U.S. economic system and assess the various reasons why such a substantial percentage of Americans are unable to find jobs.

Consider another topic. If a few American couples seek divorce, we might conclude that these individuals are suffering from personal trouble. Perhaps they lack the skills and motivation necessary to make a marriage succeed. However, current statistics reveal an unprecedentedly high divorce rate—about one-half of first marriages formed in the past decade will end in divorce. Sociologists must analyze a number of relatively new social conditions to understand why such a high rate of divorce now exists.

Mills realized that in times of rapid social change, most

people find it difficult to look beyond personal troubles to the public issues that affect them and people they know. He emphasized, however, that the more capable one becomes in using the sociological imagination, the more insight one develops into many problems in one's own life and the more effectively one will be able to deal with them.

After more than two decades of being a sociologist, I am deeply impressed by the contribution the sociological perspective makes. In particular, one becomes aware that a range of social problems are not simply individuals' personal traps but result from difficult or destructive conditions beyond ordinary citizens' control. This insight is important because once one begins to understand the process producing a social problem, the possibility of confronting and resolving it are greatly increased.

Source: C. Wright Mills. The Sociological Imagination. New York: Oxford University Press, 1959.

KARL MARX

Karl Marx (1818–1883) was born in the Rhineland district of Germany. The young Marx attended local schools and then went to the University of Bonn and later the University of Berlin, where he associated with a group of socialist philosophers whose ideas influenced his later writings. In 1841 Marx received a doctorate from the University of Jena (also in Germany) but was unable to obtain a university post because of his political connec-

tions. Instead he took a position with a socialist newspaper. When the paper was closed down by the authorities in 1843, he moved to Paris, where he became acquainted with some of the leading French socialists. While in Paris Marx also met Friedrich Engels (1820–1895), with whom he frequently collaborated throughout the rest of his life. Engels, the son of a wealthy textile manufacturer, often provided financial support for Marx and his family when no other source of income was available. Marx was expelled from France in 1845 because of his socialist activities. He was subsequently deported from Germany and again from France. In 1849 Marx and his family moved to London, where he spent the rest of his life.

Marx was not a sociologist, and yet, in several ways, his ideas have had a significant impact on sociology. First, throughout his work, he emphasized the importance of economic factors in determining social life. In particular, he stressed that the capitalist economic system was responsible for the injustices and inequalities of the modern social-class structure. As we will see in the upcoming discussion of sociological theories, many modern sociologists are sympathetic to this conclusion.

Another of Marx's key ideas was that systems of belief and thought are the products of the era in which they occur. This position asserts that even cultural and religious ideas are products of economic and social conditions and that, as these conditions change, so do the ideas. Once again,

Karl Marx, who was a major figure throughout the world, particularly in socialist or former socialist countries, has strongly influenced both theory and research in American sociology.

many contemporary sociologists back the Marxist position.

A third main idea that has emerged from Marx's writings is the concept of work alienation—that modern workers have lost control over their work routines as well as what happens to the products of their labor. A century after Marx wrote on the subject of work alienation, sociologists continue to explore and refine this concept.

ÉMILE DURKHEIM

Émile Durkheim (1858–1917) was born in Lorraine, on the northeastern border of France. The son of a rabbi, Durkheim received his basic education in France and then studied economics, folklore, and cultural anthropology in Germany. In 1887 he returned to France as a professor of sociology at the University of Bordeaux, where he taught the first sociology course offered at a French university. In 1896 Durkheim founded *Année Sociologique*,

Émile Durkheim was an important early influence on American sociology, with his study of suicide making a formidable contribution to the development of systematic sociological research.

which was for years the leading journal of sociological thought and research in France. In 1902 he joined the faculty of the University of Paris.

In response to France's disastrous defeat in the Franco-Prussian War (1870–1871) and the chaotic era which followed this defeat, Durkheim, like Comte, developed an overriding concern for social order. He believed that the scientific study of society could provide a sense of how to establish and maintain social order in modern industrial societies. Durkheim believed that one way to learn about social order was to study a situation in which order appeared to be absent—suicide. Durkheim's book *Suicide*, published in 1897, was a careful investigation of suicide rates in various European countries. It was also the first prominent study conducted by a sociologist.

Durkheim's project had two goals. First, he intended to refute the various popular theories that tried to explain the differences in group suicide rates in terms of racial, genetic, climatic, or geographical factors. Second, he wanted to develop a theoretical approach that would better explain the suicide rates in different places. Durkheim's findings supported his first goal. His data clearly invalidated the old theories about suicide rates. The evidence also suggested a new theory—that suicide was produced by three basic social conditions. One condition was the individual's lack of group support. Durkheim's investigation showed that single people were more likely than married people to commit suicide and that married individuals with children were even less likely to kill themselves. A second condition promoting suicide, according to Durkheim, was the disruption of social life. He found that depression, revolution, war, or even sudden prosperity within a society can increase that society's suicide rate. Finally Durkheim suggested that in some preindustrial societies, as well as in some modern armies, people would be called on to commit suicide for the common good. In Japan, for example, the practice of hara-kiri—ritual suicide traditionally committed by nobility when they felt they had performed a dishonorable act—assured that the family and community would be spared disgrace.

A century later the book remains a significant contribution to the field because it was the first effective attempt to test sociological theories by conducting scientific research. In addition,

With prominent works on bureaucracy and formal organizations, religion, political systems, caste and class, economic activity, and cities, Max Weber might have been the person with the greatest concrete impact on American sociology.

Durkheim demonstrated that suicide, which is an individual act, can be explained by sociocultural factors. Thus the study both justifies and illustrates the usefulness of the sociological perspective.

MAX WEBER

Max Weber (1864–1920) was a member of a wealthy German family. As a young man, Weber received training in law and economics. He earned a doctorate in law from the University of Berlin in 1889 and joined the bar a short time later. In 1891 he became a member of the law faculty of the University of Berlin, and in the following years, Weber earned several full-time appointments at leading German universities. Over the course of his life, Weber published a large number of books and essays. He also traveled widely, including a visit to the United States.

No sociologist has had a more profound impact on the field of sociology than Max Weber. His contributions to sociological thought are apparent throughout this book. The areas of study to which he made extensive contributions include bureaucracy and formal organization, religion, political authority systems and political organization, caste and class, economic activity, and the city.

One of Weber's most significant contributions was the **principle of *verstehen*** (understanding), which describes an effort to grasp the relationship between individuals' feelings and thoughts, and their actions. To Weber the principle of *verstehen* involved a three-step process. First, a sociologist observing a situation tries to imagine the emotions people are feeling. Second, that observer attempts to figure out the participants' motives. Third, the sociologist's explanation of any activity that occurs includes his or her interpretation of the participants' feelings and motives.

Consider the following illustration. A young man and a young woman are walking arm in arm while chatting loudly and smiling at each other. Suddenly the young woman says, "I don't want to climb mountains for my vacation." The young man stops walking, pulls his arm away from hers, jams his hands into his pockets, and without a word turns and walks stiffly and quickly in the direction from which they had come. A sociologist who employs the principle of *verstehen* might conclude that the young man is angry with the woman's statement; his motive is to communicate that anger; therefore he acts in a way that shows her that he is angry.

The principle of *verstehen* was an important contribution to sociology because it helped "humanize" the field by emphasizing that people's feelings and motives, and not just their behavior, must be studied.

AMERICAN SOCIOLOGY

Although Marx, Durkheim, Weber, and other Europeans made the initial contributions to sociology, the field has been most widely accepted in the United States. Social problems arising in the early twentieth century encouraged the growth of sociology in the country. Rapid industrialization and urbanization made poverty, violence, crime, and vice painfully apparent in American cities. Like their European predecessors, early American sociologists believed that an effective study of society could promote an understanding of major social problems and their solutions.

In 1892 Albion W. Small (1854–1926) became the head of a newly formed department of sociology at the University of Chicago. He retained this position until 1925. During that era the department was the unchallenged leader in American sociology. Until 1930, in fact, the University of Chicago produced more Ph.D.s in sociology than all other American sociology departments combined. Among them was Lester F. Ward (1841–1913), another important early American sociologist. Like Comte, Ward believed that the discovery of the basic principles of social behavior could lead to effective social reform. In the 1920s Robert Ezra Park (1864–1944), a former journalist, organized an ambitious research program at the University of Chicago designed to promote the understanding and the elimination of such major urban problems as juvenile delinquency, crime, divorce, and social disorganization.

From the 1940s through the 1960s, leadership in sociology spread from Chicago to such universities as Harvard, Columbia, and Michigan. The focus of sociology also shifted. The dominant concerns were no longer specific social problems but rather the development of theory and advances in research techniques. Talcott Parsons (1902–1979)—the most significant figure in the discipline from the early 1940s until the late 1960s—emphasized the need to develop a systematic general theory of social action. He believed that until such a theory was constructed, the empirical research conducted by sociologists would lack overall coherence and sociology would never become a mature science. Robert Merton (b. 1910), a student of Parsons, has also emphasized that the growth of sociology can occur effectively only if theory and research promote each other's development.

In the 1990s sociologists' professional contributions are diverse. For fifty years they have helped refine survey research methods, which make it possible to provide vital information for

12

government, business, and the general public. Studying all major social issues and social problems of modern society, American sociologists have produced a substantial body of professional writings. But increasingly their impact has extended beyond the discipline, with books and articles of general interest, local newspaper columns, and radio and television programs. Recognizing the central importance of course offerings, the American Sociological Association (ASA) has emphasized the importance of upgrading undergraduate curricula. Perhaps in part because of this effort, a 1990 survey of 100 sociology departments showed a 10 to 15 percent increase in enrollments and majors over the 1985 figures (Babbie 1992; D'Antonio 1992).

About 13,000 American sociologists belong to ASA, which is a professional organization maintained by and for sociologists (Levine 1992, 2). ASA sponsors some of the discipline's most prominent journals and produces a yearly national meeting, at which the field's latest theoretical and research findings are presented. The ASA office is located in Washington, D.C., where officials frequently inform government personnel about the contributions made by sociological research and seek to negotiate increased opportunities for the discipline's future research efforts.

Contemporary Sociological Theories ∎

A **sociological theory** is a combination of observations and insights that offers a systematic explanation of social life. All people make use of informal theories about social behavior. Parents and educators, for instance, support different ideas about proper child rearing. The old saying "Spare the rod and spoil the child" is one informal theory about this topic. Americans also have different theories about the best strategy to maintain world peace. Some favor the development of increasingly powerful nuclear weapons that will make other nations avoid nuclear war for fear of massive retaliation. Opponents of nuclear weaponry consider this theory insane, emphasizing that a continuing nuclear-weapons buildup increases the possibility of accidental nuclear war. They offer a contrasting theory that proposes bilateral nuclear disarmament as the best way to prevent such a war.

A major difference between the theories constructed by practicing sociologists and those developed by the majority of the public is that sociologists, like other scientists, are expected to subject their theories to continuous scrutiny and testing. They conduct extensive research to determine whether or not their theories provide effective explanations of social behavior, and they carefully examine other studies published in professional journals and books to further evaluate relevant sociological theories.

Sociologists have produced a wealth of fine theories. In this section we focus on three important theories that sociologists continue to examine and reevaluate: conflict theory, structural-functional theory, and symbolic interaction. The discussion of each theory includes material about the Los Angeles riots. Table 1.1 summarizes these three theories.

CONFLICT THEORY

Conflict theorists argue that groups are inevitably organized to compete against one another. Change is a continuous element in this theory. Karl Marx's perspective on class conflict is the foundation upon which modern conflict theory has been built. Marx observed that each of the major industrial societies of his day maintained capitalism, in which a ruling class controlled the means by which goods were produced and constantly sought to extend its wealth and power. For the working class, Marx argued, economic and working conditions would steadily worsen. Yet out of this desperate situation, workers would be able to seize the opportunity to produce a dramatic

Table 1.1 Three Contemporary Sociological Theories

Theory	Definition	Contributor
Conflict theory	A theory contending that the struggle for power and wealth in society should be the central concern of society	Karl Marx; C. Wright Mills
Structural-functional theory	A theory suggesting that groups in interaction tend to influence and adjust to one another in a fairly stable, conflict-free pattern	Talcott Parsons; Robert Merton
Symbolic-interaction theory	A theory that emphasizes the importance of symbolic communication—the use of gestures and, above all, language—in the development of the individual, group, and society	Herbert Blumer

change in their lives. Eventually they would recognize that they shared a common plight—because of the oppressions imposed by the ruling class, their only hope for a better life was to organize themselves and overthrow their oppressors. According to Marxist theory, the defeat of the ruling class and the economic system it controls would create extensive change because economic systems significantly affect all other elements within any society. Although Marx's predictions about revolution have not come to pass, many of his ideas have influenced modern sociologists.

Some American sociologists have developed conflict perspectives that share Marx's focus on the centrality of both conflict and the role of the ruling class. In *The Power Elite*, C. Wright Mills (1956) argued that an upper-class group of politicians, business people, and military leaders effectively controls American society, placing the top priority upon their own political, economic, and military interests and subordinating those of the general citizenry. In *Class and Class Conflict in Industrial Society*, Ralf Dahrendorf (1959) also used a conflict approach, and like Mills considered the scarce commodity of power the focus of conflict. Dahrendorf examined the conditions that promote and diffuse conflict. Although he concluded that the more violent manifestations of conflict can be toned down, to him conflict seemed inevitable in society. Conflict, he argued, always produces

change, and since conflict would be continuous, societies are in constant flux.

G. William Domhoff has been a modern disciple of Mills, adapting his theory to current U.S. society but maintaining Mills's central idea that "the upper class, rooted in the ownership and control of large corporations, rules or governs through a leadership group called the power elite at the national level" (Domhoff 1990, 17).

In brief, **conflict theory** contends that the struggle for power and wealth in society should be the central concern of sociology. Many people are restricted or controlled by limits placed upon them by the powerful, and this restriction creates or at least encourages conflict. In turn, conflict generates change. According to this theory, there is never enough wealth and power to satisfy everyone within a given society. Those who have the wealth and power, the chief beneficiaries of the existing system, will attempt to control the general citizenry in order to protect their own privilege. The wealthy, for instance, will contribute heavily to the campaigns of politicians who support legislation to protect the economic interests of the wealthy.

People with limited power often engage in conflict in order to reduce or remove restrictions placed on them by the powerful. For example, since the late 1960s, many groups of people—in particular, racial and ethnic minorities, and women—have begun resisting the restrictions

14

traditionally placed on them. These groups have initiated the long and difficult process of changing social arrangements that have denied them equal opportunities to seek wealth, power, and prestige in American society. Since the goals of these groups require the pursuit of scarce resources, conflict is usually one consequence of their efforts. Sometimes such conflict has been violent, as in the killings of black leaders and other activists during the 1960s, but more often it has been nonviolent, as in the lobbying for or against legalized abortion. Arguments, debates, legal suits, picketings, and strikes are all nonviolent activities that involve conflict. Within modern sociology there is widespread support for conflict theory's theme that the struggle for wealth, power, and other scarce resources is a dominant reality of modern societies. Conflict theory seems to more effectively explain social events involving change and conflict than other sociological theories.

Using a conflict perspective, consider two points about the Los Angeles riots of 1992—first, that rioters, who were victims of limited job opportunities, poor schools, and possible police repression and abuse, were spurred to action by the verdict in the King trial, which they considered the most recent injustice against poor minority-group members. Then, second, those deprived individuals saw the situation as a "call to participate in the general redistribution of wealth in progress" (Davis 1992, 743).

During the Los Angeles riots, many people looted stores. This demonstrated conflict theory's claim that people seek diverse ways to obtain a larger share of society's scarce resources.

Sometimes conflict erupts because of more specific conditions—such as longstanding hostilities between two groups. During the riots nearly 2,000 Korean businesses were destroyed—in large part it appeared because the previous year a Korean grocer shot and killed a 15-year-old black girl over a dispute about a bottle of orange juice. Shortly after the riots, speakers at a meeting of formerly warring gangs emphasized that out of the ashes of Korean businesses, black capitalism could arise. Summarizing the situation, one gang member declared, "After all, we didn't burn our community, just *their* stores" (Davis 1992, 745).

The conflict perspective makes an important contribution to sociological analysis by focusing on issues of struggle and change. This theory, however, tends to ignore some aspects of society. In particular, it fails to take into account the topics of cooperation and stability addressed by the structural-functional perspective.

STRUCTURAL-FUNCTIONAL THEORY

In sharp contrast to the conflict perspective, **structural-functional theory** suggests that groups in interaction tend to influence and adjust to one another in a fairly stable, conflict-free pattern. The theory most readily applies to either traditional, static societies or to the more stable parts of modern society. A structural functionalist might note that the American work world contains more than 20,000 types of jobs, with people in each kind of job interdependent with those in other work roles. Nurses, for instance, provide direct care for sick or injured people, and in turn they depend on other workers for food, clothes, transportation, entertainment, and many other needs.

The focus of this theory is the concept of **function**—an adjustive or stabilizing consequence produced by an item, individual, or group and affecting a particular group or society. Traditional structural functionalism would emphasize that functions performed by nurses help restore the sick and injured workers in various occupational categories to health (an "adjustive consequence"). Nurses, in short, function to maintain the stability of the American occupational system, according to structural-functional theory.

Robert Merton (1968) developed some important refinements of the structural-functional theory. He defined a **manifest function** as a function that is intended and openly recognized by members of the group producing it. A **latent function** is a function that is not intended and that often goes unrecognized by members of the group producing it. A **dysfunction** is a disruptive or destabilizing consequence produced by an item, individual, or group and affecting a particular group or society. Like a function a dysfunction can be manifest or latent. The Los Angeles riots can illustrate the four types of functions and dysfunctions.

A manifest function of the riots was that in this unusual situation where police often stayed conspicuously absent, participants had a chance both to release pent-up anger and frustration and to obtain useful items without paying for them. One middle-aged lady told a writer, "Stealing is a sin, but this is like a television game show where everyone in the audience gets to win" (Davis 1992, 743). Looters tended to focus on such practical items as cockroach spray and Pampers.

Unlike this manifest function of the L.A. riots, latent functions were not obvious. One notable illustration of a latent function was the truce in gang wars that followed shortly after the riots started. As rioting spread through the south-central section of the city, 1,600 members of the two largest gangs, which had been warring for more than twenty years, met to discuss their common interests, including the possibility of black economic self-determination. One social worker observing the truce explained, "It took the Watts riots [of 1965] to start the gangs. It took another riot to get them to see that they're all in this together" (Terry 1992, A21). Obviously ending gang warfare was not on rioters' minds, and yet their actions contributed to this possibility.

A manifest dysfunction of the L.A. riots is readily apparent. Individuals who burned down businesses and homes were often consciously striking back at those they considered enemies. Less than a day after the rioting began, 90 percent of the Korean-owned businesses in the south-central part of the city had been burned down (Davis 1992, 744).

Latent dysfunctions of the rioting are also clear. It seems unlikely that participants were trying to frighten local children, and yet that was a dis-

From the beginning of the Los Angeles riots, which started on April 29, 1992, *there was evidence, such as this graffiti, that the two largest African-American gangs—Crips and Bloods—had established a truce in their lengthy, bloody conflict. Thus the truce represented a latent function of these riots.*

tinct impact of the riots as we saw in this chapter's opening, which referred to a child who had felt sick ever since "the war" started. In addition, many black-owned businesses were destroyed when consumed by fires spreading from Korean-owned neighbors (Mydans and Marriott 1992).

The nearby American Controversy analyzes why one prominent sociologist supported structural-functionalism and another conflict theory. The discussion indicates that the supporters of these two theories differ in more than their theoretical preferences.

SYMBOLIC-INTERACTION THEORY

I couldn't find my scotch tape, and based on previous performance, the prime suspect was my six-year-old daughter. "Gabriella, did you steal my tape?" I asked her kiddingly.

"No, daddy," she replied earnestly. "I didn't *steal* it. I *needed* it." Gabriella believed that the negative action of stealing was avoided as long as she put the tape to good use. While hardly a position widely endorsed in the social and legal worlds, her statement was a clear reminder that all

AMERICAN CONTROVERSY
Why Sociologists Prefer Particular Theories

 The approaches of structural functionalism and conflict theory differ significantly. Sociologists often have a strong preference for one theory or the other. Why is that?

Two prominent sociologists provide excellent illustrations. Why, for example, did Talcott Parsons support structural-functional theory? Why did C. Wright Mills adopt a conflict perspective?

Sociologist Alvin Gouldner argued that one specific condition in Parsons's upbringing most strongly supported his preference for a theory that downplayed conflict and change— his year of birth, 1902. Actually year of birth seems to combine with several other factors. Parsons grew up in an upper-middle-class family during an era of affluence. He attended Amherst College in Massachusetts and later Heidelberg University in Germany. He was a faculty member at Harvard University before the stock market crash of 1929 signaled the beginning of the Great Depression. Distant from Parsons's own life, then, were the poverty, misery, and inequality that encouraged other sociologists to embrace conflict theory.

C. Wright Mills grew up in a different time and place. Roughly sixteen years younger than Parsons, he was a college student during the 1930s. In those depression years, brutal economic conditions encouraged sociologists to launch strong criticisms of American society. Furthermore Mills did not leave his native state of Texas until he became 21. Mills himself believed that growing up outside of major urban centers made it easier for him to become a critic of the political and economic activity that was concentrated in those cities. Thus some factors in Mills's background seem to have encouraged him to become a conflict theorist.

The protests of the 1960s convinced many sociologists that the structural-functional perspective did not effectively analyze the conflict and change that were widespread at that time. During that era conflict theory gained support.

What about in the 1990s? As you examine modern society, which theory seems to provide a more effective analysis? In your response you might include references to important political and economic issues in the news. It is often difficult to analyze personal reasons for reaching a particular conclusion, but, nonetheless, try to explain why you prefer one of the two theories. In other words try to determine which factors in your own background encourage you to support one of these perspectives instead of the other. You might find it interesting to discuss with other students your respective preferences and the reasons for those preferences.

Sources: Alvin Gouldner. The Coming Crisis of Western Sociology. New York: Equinox Books, 1970; Irving Louis Horowitz (ed.). The New Sociology. New York: Oxford University Press, 1964.

words, which are symbols, are invariably open to interpretation.

This episode illustrates a type of social analysis that is the focus of a theory known as symbolic interaction. **Symbolic-interaction theory** emphasizes the importance of symbolic communication—the use of gestures and, above all, language—in the development of the individual, group, and society. Human beings are unique in their capacity to use symbolic communication. Knowledge of what a symbol is will help to clarify the significance of this form of communication.

A **symbol** is an object or event whose meaning is fixed not by the nature of the item to which it is attached but by the agreement of the people who use it in communication. For example, words such as *book* or *shoe* are symbols. We use those words because people who speak the English language have agreed to associate the particular word with the particular object; there is nothing inherent in the objects themselves requiring the choices that have been made. Moreover, by using words, people communicate with one another in a way that otherwise would be impossible.

The symbolic-interaction theory appreciates the subtlety of human communication. Even at age 6, Gabriella knew that a stronger inflection of the words *steal* and *needed* would emphasize their significance. The supporters of this theory also emphasize that communication is not entirely verbal. Gestures and body language also play an important part.

Sociologists who favor the symbolic-interaction approach tend to focus on the more minute, personal aspects of social interaction occurring in small groups. Frequently this theory is used to analyze situations involving socialization, where people, often children or young people, are learning the rudiments of their culture. Chapter 5, "Social Interaction," further discusses symbolic interaction, including analysis of ethnomethodology and dramaturgic sociology, which are both versions of symbolic interaction. Although the practice has been to apply this theory to small-group situations, some proponents have argued that all human behavior involves symbolic communication, and thus no inherent reason restricts symbolic interaction from analyzing the larger topics that structural-functional and conflict theories have traditionally monopolized (Lyman 1988).

One of the major proponents of symbolic interaction was Herbert Blumer. According to Blumer the symbolic quality of social interaction centers on the meanings individuals ascribe to other people and things. These meanings do not simply exist in the social world but derive from people's judgments in the course of their daily experience; a major contributor to these meanings is contact with other people. Sometimes as individuals interpret their experience, however, meanings change. Whether meanings change or remain the same, they affect people's behavior (Blumer 1969, 2–10).

As Americans watched the Los Angeles riots on television and read about them in newspapers, this remote contact with rioters helped develop their judgments about what was happening. A *New York Times*/CBS poll indicated that 60 percent of respondents viewed the riots as a warning, indicating that too little money was being spent on problems of large cities, while only 31 percent felt that too much or the right amount was being spent. Seventy-eight percent believed that more jobs and job training would help to reduce racial tensions and prevent riots (Toner 1992).

For many people living near the riot area, their experience of either seeing the rioting personally or viewing it on television caused a new interpretation—a growing fear that police might be incapable or unwilling to defend citizens during a period of civil unrest. For the first eleven days of May 1992, California residents bought 50 percent more guns than over the same time period the previous year. Sean Collinsworth, the owner of a gun-training service in Los Angeles, explained, "I always thought if there was a serial rapist or murderer loose my business would go up, but nothing beats a race riot. People are really scared" (Egan 1992, A20).

CHOOSING AND USING THEORIES

The previous discussion of contemporary sociological theories indicates that there is no such thing as the "best" sociological theory. As the American Controversy suggests, background factors can determine the theoretical approach a sociologist prefers. One individual might feel most comfortable studying what appear to be the inevitable sources of conflict, while another chooses to focus on how social groups provide support and continuity within society. No theory is inherently correct or incorrect. In some situations a particular theory is more appropriate or is well-matched with a sociologist's personal tastes. Within the field of sociology and within individual sociology departments, people recognize that their colleagues differ in their theoretical preferences. Sometimes disagreements are sharp and well publicized. Often, however, preferences for different theories lead to useful discussions and debates. One quality all sociological theories share is their unrelenting emphasis on the sociological perspective.

Now that you have read about the theories, you might find that you too have a preference. To

18

help determine your preference, look back at Table 1.1, which lists the major features of each theory, and use the table to help evaluate them. Does one theory make the most sense to you? In other words does one of the three seem most consistent with your own outlook on the social world? On the other hand, does one theory seem particularly distasteful? Discuss what seem to be the respective strengths and weaknesses of the different theories with classmates or friends.

STUDY GUIDE

Learning Objectives

After studying this chapter, you should be able to:

1. Define sociology.
2. Discuss the sociological perspective.
3. Define science; distinguish between natural sciences and social sciences; and discuss problems that sociology faces in the scientific study of human beings.
4. Describe the social conditions of the era in which sociology originated and identify Auguste Comte's contributions to the field.
5. Summarize the contributions to sociology made by Karl Marx, Émile Durkheim, and Max Weber.
6. Discuss the twentieth-century development of American sociology.
7. Define sociological theory, and compare and contrast it with informal theory.
8. Define conflict theory, structural-functional theory, and symbolic-interaction theory; provide examples of each; and discuss their respective strengths and weaknesses.
9. Explain why there is no one "best" sociological theory.

Summary

1. Sociology is the scientific study of human behavior in groups and of the social forces that influence that behavior.

2. The sociological perspective emphasizes that people's thoughts and actions are strongly influenced by the groups to which they belong, as well as by other social factors, such as values, beliefs, practices, and institutions. Sociology is one of six social sciences.

3. Auguste Comte coined the word *sociology* and founded the field. Marx, Durkheim, and Weber also made major contributions to the development of sociology in Europe. In the United States, the University of Chicago was the first center of sociology, with research focusing on major urban social problems. In the 1990s sociologists' contributions are diverse, involving not only professional writings but also including books and articles of general interest, local newspaper columns, and radio and television programs.

4. A sociological theory is a combination of observations and insights that offers a systematic explanation about social life. Conflict theory contends that the struggle for power and wealth in society should be the central sociological concern.

In contrast, structural-functional theory

suggests that groups in interaction tend to influence and adjust to one another in a fairly stable, conflict-free pattern.

Symbolic interaction is a theory emphasizing the importance of symbolic communication—gestures and above all language—in the development of the individual, group, and society.

There is no such thing as the "best" sociological theory. A sociologist uses a particular perspective because it seems most appropriate for a particular analysis or because it matches his or her personal tastes.

Key Terms

conflict theory a theory contending that the struggle for power and wealth in society should be the central concern of sociology

dysfunction a disruptive or destabilizing consequence produced by an item, individual, or group and affecting a particular group or society

function an adjustive or stabilizing consequence produced by an item, individual, or group and affecting a particular group or society

latent function a function that is not intended and that often goes unrecognized by members of the group producing it

manifest function a function that is intended and openly recognized by members of the group producing it

natural sciences older sciences such as astronomy, biology, chemistry, and physics that study the physical world

principle of *verstehen* Max Weber's concept that involves an effort to grasp the relationship between individuals' feelings and thoughts, and their actions

science a systematic effort to develop general principles about a particular subject matter, based on actual observations and stated in a form that can be tested by any competent person

social sciences the sciences that focus on various aspects of human behavior

sociological theory a combination of observations and insights that offers a systematic explanation about social life

sociology the scientific study of human behavior in groups and of the social forces that influence that behavior

structural-functional theory a theory suggesting that groups in interaction tend to influence and adjust to one another in a fairly stable, conflict-free pattern

symbol an object or event whose meaning is fixed not by the nature of the item to which it is attached but by the agreement of the people who use it in communication

symbolic-interaction theory a theory that emphasizes the importance of symbolic communication—the use of gestures and above all language—in the development of the individual, group, and society

Tests

True • False Test

_____ 1. William Foote Whyte's study of young men in Boston suggests that the expectations and support of the group, especially its leaders, influence individual members.

_____ 2. Eric L. Hirsch's study of the protest at Columbia demanding the university's divestment of stock in corporations doing business with South Africa concluded that most students joined the social movement because they were lonely and seeking a personal sense of direction.

_____ 3. Auguste Comte was the first writer to propose a role for social scientists in the development of industrial society.

_____ 4. Durkheim found that in some preindustrial societies, as well as in some modern armies, people will be called upon to commit suicide for the common good.

_____ 5. The principle of *verstehen* has helped to humanize sociology.

_____ 6. From the 1940s through the 1960s, the University of Chicago dominated the field of sociology.

_____ 7. Conflict theory asserts that conflict inevitably leads to violence.

_____ 8. A manifest dysfunction of the Los Angeles riots involved the fears produced in children.

_____ 9. Symbolic-interaction theory never analyzes face-to-face social situations.

_____ 10. Symbolic interaction is concerned with the meanings individuals give to other people and things.

Multiple-Choice Test

_____ 1. The sociological perspective:
   a.   indicates that people are seldom influenced by the groups to which they belong.
   b.   can be used to explain the bowling performances of the young men described in Whyte's study conducted in Boston in the 1930s.
   c.   is not relevant to Hirsch's study of student protest.
   d.   a and b

_____ 2. Which of the following is a natural science?
   a.   biology
   b.   economics
   c.   history
   d.   sociology

_____ 3. Isaac Newton's scientific work:
   a.   increased the influence of religion in seventeenth-century Europe.
   b.   inhibited the development of sociology
   c.   emphasized that the universe was logical and not under divine influence.
   d.   a and c

_____ 4. Karl Marx's theory was based in part on which of the following ideas?
   a.   The socialist economic system is responsible for injustice and inequality in the modern social-class structure.
   b.   Systems of belief and thought are independent of the era in which they occur.
   c.   Modern workers have more control over their work routines than did preindustrial workers.
   d.   Economic conditions determine what happens in the social world.

_____ 5. Durkheim's study of suicide theorized that suicide was produced by three basic social conditions. Which of the following is NOT one of these basic conditions?
   a.   the disruption of social life
   b.   the individual's lack of group support
   c.   certain personality characteristics
   d.   the individual's call to commit suicide for the common good

6. The principle of *verstehen* is a three-step process. Which of the following actions is NOT part of the process?
   a. The sociologist tries to figure out the participants' motives.
   b. The observer tries to imagine the emotions people are feeling.
   c. The sociologist makes recommendations to improve the situation.
   d. The observer's explanation includes an interpretation of the participants' feelings and motives.

7. According to conflict theory, the central sociological concern should be:
   a. the legal system.
   b. politicians' bids for election.
   c. physical violence.
   d. the struggle for wealth and power.

8. According to structural-functional theory, a function that is intended and openly recognized by members of the group producing it is called a:
   a. manifest function.
   b. latent function.
   c. manifest dysfunction.
   d. latent dysfunction.

9. In this chapter the gang truce declared after the Los Angeles riots is classified as a
   a. manifest function.
   b. latent dysfunction.
   c. latent function.
   d. manifest dysfunction.

10. Symbolic-interaction theory:
   a. cannot be used to analyze large groups.
   b. emphasizes that the meanings of things and people are obtained in interaction with others.
   c. is identical to conflict theory in most respects.
   d. emphasizes that the meanings individuals give to people and things seldom affect behavior.

Essay Test

For each essay carefully choose your words so that you capture and develop the basic idea or ideas in question. Make an effort to stay on the topic at hand and provide as much detail as possible. When you have finished, turn to the relevant section in the book and compare your answer with the material there.

1. Discuss the sociological perspective, giving an example that demonstrates its usefulness.
2. Summarize the contributions to early sociology made by Marx, Durkheim, and Weber.
3. Define sociological theory. Give an example of an informal theory of social behavior and indicate how such a theory differs from the sociological type.
4. What is conflict theory? Discuss a social situation where this perspective seems particularly relevant.
5. Define structural-functional theory. Describe situations that demonstrate the workings of a manifest function, a latent function, a manifest dsyfunction, and a latent dysfunction.
6. Define symbolic interaction. Describe a group context that illustrates the symbolic-interaction process.
7. Discuss in detail the theory you like best.

Suggested Readings

Bateman, Nils I., and David M. Petersen (eds.). 1990. *Social Issues: Conflicting Opinions*. Englewood Cliffs, NJ: Prentice-Hall. Articles offering conflicting views on sixteen sociological issues, involving the broad topics of becoming a human being, inequality, social institutions, and change.

Cargan, Leonard, and Jeanne H. Ballantine (eds.). 1991. *Sociological Footprints: Introductory Readings in Sociology*. 5th ed. Belmont, CA: Wadsworth. An excellent combination of classical and recent essays, covering all the major topics addressed in introductory sociology.

Finsterbusch, Kurt (ed.). 1992. *Sociology: 92/93*. Guilford, CT: Dushkin. An array of articles from magazines and popular journals supplying supplementary material for most topics covered in an introductory sociology course.

Gans, Herbert J. (ed.). 1990. *Sociology in America*. Newbury Park, CA: Sage. Well-known sociologists' essays examining the relationship between the United States and sociology, with topics including sociology's effect on America, America's effect on sociology, sociology and social criticism, and sociology and critical American issues.

Henslin, James M. (ed.). 1991. *Down to Earth Sociology: Readings*. New York: Free Press. A set of interesting, easy-to-read articles providing introductory students access to a combination of classical and contemporary sources.

Mills, C. Wright. 1959. *The Sociological Imagination*. New York: Oxford University Press. A conflict-perspective analysis of American society that makes some thought-provoking proposals about the role that ought to be played by modern sociologists.

Richlin-Klonsky, Judith, and Ellen Strenski (eds.). 1991. *A Guide to Writing Sociology Papers*. 2nd ed. New York: St. Martin's. A concise little book, leading the reader through the various practical steps of writing a sociology paper and including good chapters on ethnographic field research and quantitative research.

Westby, David L. 1991. *The Growth of Sociological Theory: Human Nature, Knowledge, and Social Change*. Englewood Cliffs, NJ: Prentice-Hall. A thorough introduction to classical sociological theory, with two chapters each on the contributions of Marx, Weber, and Durkheim.

Additional Assignments

1. Take a topic of interest to you that deals with human behavior—for example, the effects of war, male-female differences, or violent crime. After learning about the subject through books, magazines, and other sources, write about the social forces that produce this behavior and also the effects that this particular activity has upon different groups in American society. Share your report with other students and obtain their reactions to your conclusions.

2. Consider a current social problem—for example, unemployment, violent crime, family tensions. Indicate why this problem has occurred and continues to occur, using the three major sociological theories—structural-functional, conflict, and symbolic-interaction. Does any theory seem more or less effective than the others for explaining the behavior? Does any theory do more to suggest actions that might solve the problem?

Answers to Objective Test Questions

True • False Test

1. t
2. f
3. t
4. t
5. t

6. f
7. f
8. f
9. f
10. t

Multiple-Choice Test

1. b
2. a
3. c
4. d
5. c

6. c
7. d
8. a
9. c
10. b

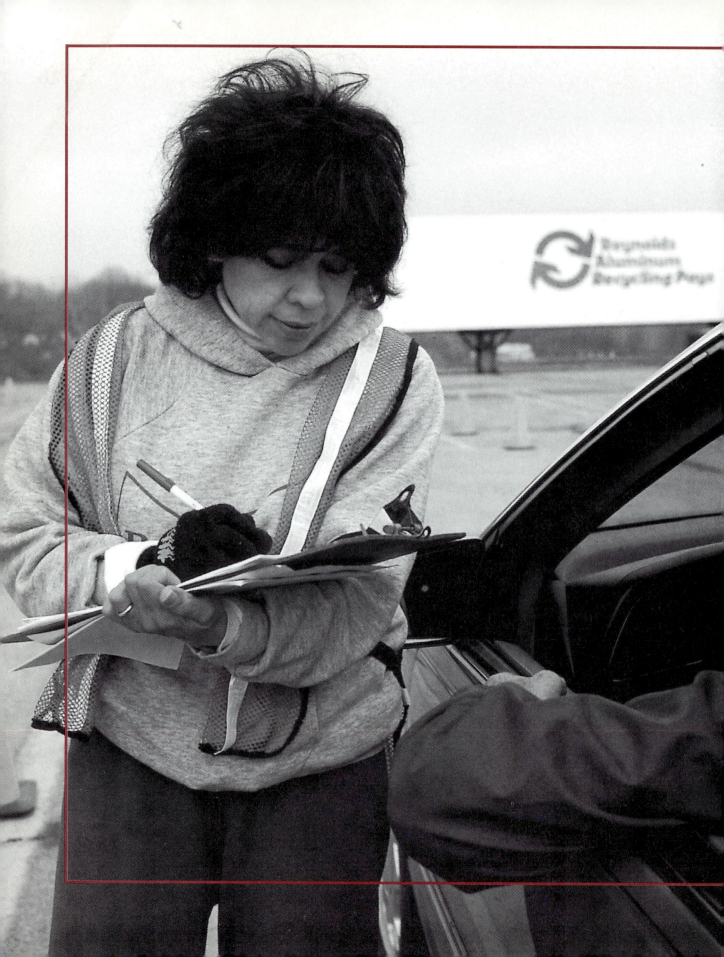

Doing Research in Sociology

2

From the 1960s through the early 1990s, Soviet sociologists struggled to establish the independence of their discipline, telling political leaders that thorough investigations of social structure, public opinion, and changes in labor patterns and lifestyle would provide information they could use in the process of changing society.

The problem was that Soviet leaders were resisting change and felt threatened by the data and analysis their sociologists provided. In spite of this opposition, many sociologists had the courage both to pursue their research and make every effort to publicize their findings. The best known of these so-called "constructive dissidents" was Tatiana Zaslavskaya, who in 1983 provided a paper based on her research declaring that Soviet society was ridden with contradictions, that the Soviet economic system was obsolete, and that the Soviet bureaucracy was a major impediment to necessary changes. Eventually Mikhail Gorbachev endorsed her analysis of these problems.

During the 1970s and 1980s, however, Soviet sociologists received little official support and faced great uncertainty, even danger from an administration that did not support their work. Communist Party officials sharply criticized Zaslavskaya's paper, branding it criminal activity and declaring her ideas divisive.

Confrontations often occurred, especially when the topic was an issue like social class, where research had been extensive and the administration felt particularly threatened by frank analysis. In 1970 at the Seventh World Congress of Sociology, a Soviet sociologist produced a blackboard sketch of his conception of the future class structure of Soviet society. As he was about to explain his sketch, a Soviet official, who was a well-known opponent of unrestricted research, leaped to his feet, reprimanded the sociologist, and erased the drawing, declaring it was nothing but conjecture (Weinberg 1992).

But clearly Soviet sociologists were on track, studying the changes that were occurring in their society and seeking to contribute research findings that would provide vital information for that process. Sociologists have produced such studies in many countries. Throughout this chapter we see numerous illustrations of the contributions American sociologists' research has made to a better understanding of our society.

Sociologists speak of **methodology,** the set of principles and procedures that guides sociological research. The effective use of methodology permits sociologists to do research that produces systematic, convincing results.

This chapter is fundamental. The substance of sociology comes from articles, monographs, and books that present research findings. Such research, however, is impossible without specific principles and procedures. We discuss them in this chapter. The first section focuses on sociology as a science, including the stages in the research process. Then the four principal types of social research are analyzed. The final section examines two significant issues involving the researcher's role.

The Scientific Approach of Sociological Research

In medieval Europe there was a popular belief that the devastating epidemics that occasionally swept across the continent were caused by gases or mists originating somewhere in the East. Medical research has discredited this theory, establishing that a variety of microorganisms were responsible for these diseases. In another case, however, folk wisdom proved correct. In the late eighteenth century, Edward Jenner investigated English peasants' claims that people who had contracted cowpox, a relatively mild disease, would be immune to smallpox. After determining that the peasants' claim was accurate, Jenner developed a vaccine that used cowpox bacteria to immunize people against smallpox, one of the most potent diseases ever suffered by humanity.

SCIENTIFIC PRINCIPLES

Scientists seek the truth systematically. To understand the process requires knowledge of a number of basic concepts, which, like the letters in the alphabet, might be dull but must be understood if you wish to become "literate" as a researcher. To begin, we should realize that sociologists study the relationship between or among variables. A **variable** is a factor that has two or more categories or measurable conditions. Common sociological variables are social class (that is, working class, middle class), political affiliation (that is, Democrat, Republican), and sex (that is, male, female). An **independent variable** is a variable that influences another variable—the dependent variable. Thus the **dependent variable** is a variable that is the consequence of some cause. In sociological research dependent variables are frequently attitudes and activities. As these definitions suggest, a central concern in this process is **causation,** a situation in which one variable can produce the occurrence of another.

Sociologists agree that causation is present if three conditions are met (Cole 1980). First, causation can only occur if the independent variable exists before the dependent variable. For example, people's political affiliation (Democrat or Republican), which exists when they enter the polls, often strongly influences their voting behavior. In other words the affiliation—the independent variable—exists *before* the voting behavior—the dependent variable. Second, if causation exists, then change in the independent variable affects the dependent variable. Thus if causation occurs, then Democrats and Republicans would generally vote for different candidates. Finally causation cannot be established until researchers have ruled out the influence of other possible independent variables. Their method is to analyze the effect of each possible independent variable on the dependent vari-

able, while keeping constant all other possible independent variables. To establish the impact of political affiliation as an independent variable, for example, researchers would need to make certain that their Republicans and Democrats were matched on such factors as age, sex, race, education, and occupation. If, following such a matching, Democratic and Republican respondents do support different candidates, then the researcher can conclude that political affiliation has influenced their choice.

Sociologists recognize that in the situations they study, causation is difficult to determine. It is seldom possible to specify that a or b is the sole independent variable influencing c. Sociologists generally must settle for a **correlation**—that is, a statistical description of the relationship between variables. A positive correlation of +1.0 indicates the strongest possible statistical relationship. It means that an increase in an independent variable is associated with a corresponding increase in the dependent variable. A negative correlation of −1.0 is a perfect inverse relationship. It means that an increase in the independent variable is associated with a corresponding decrease in the dependent variable. A correlation of 0 indicates no relationship at all between the two variables.

Correlations almost always fall somewhere between the two extremes. For example, sociologists undertaking the political study mentioned above might find that in a certain presidential election, a correlation of +.82 exists between citizens' political affiliation and their support for their party's respective presidential candidate. Thus the chances are a little better than eight out of ten that in this election voters back the candidates nominated by their party. One more point: By squaring a correlation, a researcher can determine how much of the total variation in the dependent variable is associated with the independent variable. If we square the figure of +.82, we obtain a value of about .67. That figure signifies that party affiliation accounts for about 67 percent of the variation in voters' support for presidential candidates. Other independent variables, such as the candidates' personal appeal and the major issues in that election, account for the other 33 percent of the variation.

When researchers find correlations, they should not leap to the conclusion that causation exists. Consider, for instance, a study that found

28

an inverse correlation between marijuana smoking and grade-point average—thus those who smoked marijuana had lower grades than those who did not. While the investigator might be tempted to conclude that marijuana smoking lowered grades, the mere existence of an inverse correlation provides insufficient evidence to support that conclusion. Recall that one requirement of causation is that the independent variable exists before the dependent variable, but there is no such supportive evidence in this case. In fact, an alternative explanation reversing the sequence of variables is distinctly possible—that low grades was the independent variable causing students to despair and turn to marijuana smoking as an escape. Another reason for not assuming causation here is that the data have not ruled out other possible relevant independent variables—such as emotional problems. One can plausibly argue that emotional problems could be the independent variable producing either marijuana smoking or lowered grades (Bonney 1989, 66–67). This example illustrates that making claims of causation based on correlation evidence is very tricky business and should be pursued cautiously.

STAGES IN THE RESEARCH PROCESS

The following analysis considers the major activities of sociologists in the course of their research. The stages are presented here in an ideal, logical pattern that does not necessarily summarize the sequence of events in an actual study.

It also should be emphasized that sociological theory has a powerful effect on researchers while they work, from the choice of topic to the reporting of their findings. Sociologists are likely to be influenced by the ways different theories encourage them to analyze the social world. They also tend to keep in mind the possibility that their findings can contribute to existing theories, by supporting certain theoretical positions or by suggesting new ones.

1. ***Choosing a topic.***   Several factors are likely to determine a sociologist's choice of a topic to study. The factors include the researcher's personal interest in the topic, its current popularity, the potential contribution such a study would make to sociological literature, and the availability of government or private funding for research in that area.

   Realizing that there is a widely held belief, especially among critics of the welfare system, that women on welfare have an above-average number of children, sociologist Mark R. Rank (1989) did research to find out whether this claim was actually true.

2. ***Reviewing the literature.***   As sociologists start a research project, they are aware that others have done work that may help them. It is likely that a theory or set of theories can help map out the questions their studies should attempt to answer. In addition, previous investigations might provide researchers with some specific aids for their own study.

   For example, in his literature review, Rank found no competent investigations that compared the number of children produced by women on welfare with the number of children produced by women in the general population. Thus he realized that his study would provide unique information.

3. ***Formulating a hypothesis.***   Researchers are looking for answers to questions. To guide their searches, they present their expectations in a form that permits them to be researched. A **hypothesis** is a scientifically researchable suggestion about the relationship between two or more variables. Most sociological studies are devised to test hypotheses—that is, to find out whether or not they are true. Thus hypotheses are central to the development of sociological investigations. Hypotheses contain both independent and dependent variables.

   Rank's study tested the following hypothesis: Women on welfare tend to have more children than women in the general population. In this instance the independent variable is source of support—welfare or some other source; the dependent variable is the number of children.

4. ***Picking the research design.***   In order to do research, sociologists must choose a method. (The four major methods of

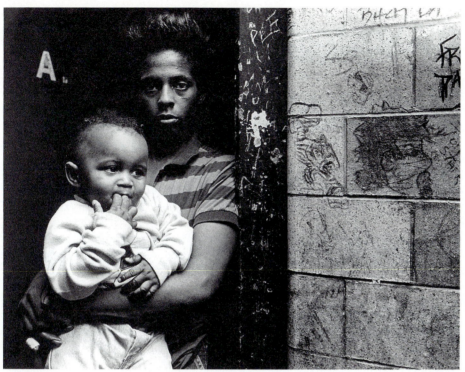

Research often provides valuable insights about people from varied backgrounds. A face-to-face interview with this woman, who lives on welfare in public housing in New Haven, Connecticut, is likely to reveal significant information about the difficult, demanding world in which she lives.

social research are discussed in the following section.) A researcher's preference for one particular method might help determine the choice. In many situations, however, the particular hypotheses to be tested will require a certain type of design.

Certainly Rank could have engaged in original research to obtain the information he sought. However, the relevant data were already available in state and federal records, to which Rank was able to obtain access. As we see later in this chapter, this type of research design is called secondary analysis. In addition, to gather in-depth information not available from these sources, Rank conducted interviews with fifty welfare families.

5. **Gathering the data.**   Data are the substance of a study. Thus even though collecting and recording data sometimes strike those who perform the tasks as

tedious work, it is essential that they do these jobs conscientiously. Researchers for large sociological projects often hire graduate students, undergraduates, or other people to conduct interviews. In training interviewers, team leaders must help their workers develop the requisite skills. In addition, they must convince them that conscientious job performance is essential for effective completion of the study.

Rank's data on welfare women came from two sources in Wisconsin—welfare records for welfare recipients and Department of Health and Social Services information for nonwelfare subjects—and also from U.S. Bureau of the Census information for the national population of women.

6. **Analyzing the data.**   Sociologists examine their data to find out whether the information supports the hypotheses or

whether new hypotheses need to be developed to account for the data. Frequently sociological theories as well as related research can help complete the analysis.

Rank's central finding was that in 1980 women on welfare in the prime childbearing years (18 to 44) had about 46 children per 1,000 women, while women of comparable age in the general Wisconsin population had about 75 children per 1,000 women and those in the U.S. population had 71 children. Thus the hypothesis Rank proposed was rejected. According to this study, women on welfare have fewer—not more—children than the general population.

7. ***Producing a report.***   Organizations that sponsor research require researchers to write a report summarizing their findings. In addition to fulfilling such a formal requirement, researchers belong to a scientific community, and they realize that a monograph or an article in a professional journal is an effective way to make their peers aware of their research results. In this format sociologists are likely to emphasize implications that their findings have for sociological theory. Furthermore they probably discuss the directions that future research could take.

Having obtained the results of his study, Rank wrote an article, which was published in the *American Sociological Review*, one of the most distinguished, widely read sociological journals. Many sociologists subscribe to this journal and are likely to read the article and evaluate its contribution. In particular, those doing research on related issues will find it a useful source in their own review of the literature.

Figure 2.1 summarizes the stages of the research process.

When a sociologist's peers read a report of findings, they evaluate their validity. **Validity** is the condition in which a research item accurately measures what it claims to measure. For example, a group of workers might express satisfaction with their work to a researcher, but is this investigator obtaining valid information? Perhaps not. The workers' statements might reflect their knowledge of a false rumor indicating that the investigator will pass on all dissatisfactions to their boss, who then plans to fire any discontented employees.

Besides considering validity, sociologists assessing their peers' work are concerned with reliability. **Reliability** is consistency in measurement. Researchers want to know whether a research item produces a similar result when it is used as a measurement in one situation and then used again in another. Is what the ruler designates an inch in the first instance the same as what the ruler designates an inch in the second case? In the example used to illustrate validity, evidence in favor of reliability would be obtained if the researcher conducted the same study in a different setting with people of similar background, and those individuals expressed a comparable level of job satisfaction to those interviewed in the original study.

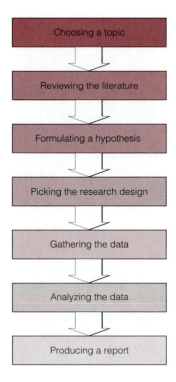

Figure 2.1

Stages in the Research Process

The stages of the research process tend to follow each other in this order. Other sequences are possible, but researchers find that this arrangement is the most convenient.

Types of Research Design

Even though sociological research generally passes through the same sequence of stages, the research process can vary considerably. One major reason is that the different research methods pose particular demands and challenges. We explore these differences in the upcoming discussion of the four major techniques of social research—surveys, experiments, observation studies, and secondary analysis.

SURVEYS

A **survey** is a research technique that uses carefully constructed questions to obtain a variety of facts about people's thoughts and behavior. One type of survey is an **interview**—a set of questions that are delivered face-to-face or over the telephone. The other type of survey is a **questionnaire,** in which a respondent writes the answers to a list of questions. The questions contained in a survey can either be closed-ended, requiring responses that fall into two or more categories provided by the researcher, or open-ended, permitting respondents to speak or write whatever they want. Surveys are administered in a variety of natural settings, such as in homes, offices, restaurants, and even on park benches or beaches.

Researchers conduct surveys by taking a sample from a population. A **population** is the entire category of people possessing the characteristics that interest a researcher undertaking a particular study—for example, the female students at a certain college, male blue-collar workers in a midwestern city, or the entire American electorate. A **sample** is a limited number of individuals chosen from a population for the purpose of conducting research.

A sociologist chooses a sample because a population is usually much too large to study in its entirety. Forced to use a sample, a researcher wants to make certain that respondents obtained are representative—that the characteristics of sample members closely resemble those of the entire population. Survey research has demonstrated that if a sample is representative, then the information individuals within it provide will be very similar to what could be produced by the population itself. Thus the trick is to choose a representative sample.

A basic principle for choosing a sample is that it will be representative of the population from which it is drawn if biases favoring some individuals are excluded, allowing each member of the population an equal chance of being selected in the sample. Such a **random sample** is a sample drawn from a population by a process that assures that every individual in that population has an equal probability of being included. A sociologist often uses a **stratified random sample**—a sample broken into segments that correspond in number to their respective proportions in the population. For instance, researchers selecting a stratified random sample from a college population composed of 28 percent freshmen, 26 percent sophomores, 22 percent juniors, and 24 percent seniors will maintain those same percentages in their sample. The use of stratified random sampling recognizes that the members of a stratified group tend to be more similar to each other than to individuals outside of their category. If the sample can be stratified by key factors, then it can more accurately represent the population than random sampling that excludes stratification.

In modern presidential polls, the results of using stratified random sampling are impressive. Responses from 1,500 respondents come within a few percentage points of those that would have been obtained from the adult population of over one hundred million people. But presidential polls have not always been satisfactory in this regard.

Before World War II, sampling techniques were crude. The widespread belief was that the best way to predict the outcome of a national election was to sample as many people as possible. In 1936, for example, the staff of the *Literary Digest*, a prominent magazine, used this approach. These researchers mailed out about 10 million postcard ballots, obtaining their list of respondents from telephone directories and auto-registration records. The results of their survey indicated that Alfred Landon, the Republican candidate, would win easily, with about 56 percent of the vote.

The *Literary Digest* poll was proved dramatically wrong when Franklin Roosevelt, the Democratic

32

candidate, obtained 56 percent of the popular vote and carried forty-six of the forty-eight states. The problem with the *Literary Digest* poll was that it drew its sample only from people who had cars and telephones. In other words its sample consisted of relatively affluent people in the 1930s— and the affluent tend to vote Republican. There was, in short, a distortion, or bias, built into the *Literary Digest*'s sampling procedure. A young pollster named George Gallup used a random sample to predict that Roosevelt would win the election, and he also predicted the precise outcome of the *Literary Digest* poll. Gallup's triumph in 1936 helped convince the American public that by using a stratified random sample of about 1,500 people surveyed a few days before the election day, pollsters can be very confident that predictions about the outcome of presidential contests will fall within three percentage points of the eventual outcome (Gallup 1972).

In modern political polls, different survey firms usually get almost the same results. If they do not, then the observer has reason to be suspicious about distortion in either the sampling procedure or in the tallies of the numerical results. In July 1992 when President Fernando Collor de Mello of Brazil was widely accused of corrupt practices, two surveys were conducted to assess voters' confidence. The results were sharply different, with one indicating that 67 percent of those interviewed believed that Collor should remain in office and the other concluding that 53 percent of the respondents felt that the president should resign. What makes the results particularly suspicious is that the first survey was done by a firm that counts the federal government among its largest clients and the second was sponsored by an anti-Collor newspaper (*Buenos Aires Herald* 1992, 3).

Undoubtedly you are aware of many other modern uses of surveys. Television, radio, newspapers, and magazines frequently report the results of public-opinion polls on a range of subjects. Big businesses conduct surveys in order to learn how consumers or potential consumers react to their products. Political candidates or parties sponsor survey research in order to determine politicians' popularity or the electorate's dominant needs and interests. The principal difference between sociological surveys and other surveys is that the sociological variety involves more extensive analysis of patterns and relationships in the social world.

Steelman and Powell's study of parents' attitudes about subsidizing their children's college education is a case in point.

A Study of Parents' Willingness to Support Children's Higher Education

It has been long recognized that a significant factor affecting people's status advancement has been parents' ability and willingness to support their children's higher education. However, this important investment has seldom been directly investigated. This is a particularly significant deficiency in a society where a college degree has become increasingly important in permitting people to get good jobs.

Lala Carr Steelman and Brian Powell's (1991) study of the traits of parents paying for their children's higher education seems very timely. The researchers used data from a mailed questionnaire developed by the National Opinion Research Center (NORC), a major firm conducting large national surveys. The questionnaire was sent to 2,327 high-school seniors' parents, randomly chosen from the parents of about 30,000 high-school seniors interviewed by NORC. In its choice of schools included in the study, NORC made an effort to represent the nation's geographical, ethnic, racial, and income diversity. To preserve this diversity, an effort was made to interview any parents who did not answer the firm's mailed questionnaire. Ultimately 91 percent of the specified respondents were included in the survey.

The data produced some decisive findings. The factor most clearly related to parents' ability to pay was the number of children: As the number of children in a family increased, the likelihood that parents felt they could subsidize college decreased. Parents with just one child were almost four times more likely to believe in subsidizing children's higher education than letting the children pay for themselves. In contrast, families with nine children were slightly less likely to feel that the responsibility for this funding lay with parents than with children.

The questionnaire indicated that resources seemed to be the key to parents' willingness to support children's advanced schooling. Steelman and Powell found that in addition to their number of children, parents were more likely to feel they could support a child's college education when their income was higher, when they had more extensive education, and when they had few children younger than the child in question.

Some of the study's findings provided practical information for policy makers. For instance, the survey results indicated that few parents, including those with college-aged children, expected much governmental support for higher education. Unless a push from the citizenry develops, the federal government is unlikely to provide much financial help to low-income people seeking higher education. Steelman and Powell concluded, "Without governmental intervention, it would appear that family membership will continue to confer advantages or disadvantages on an individual's college opportunities and therefore on his or her life-time prospects" (Steelman and Powell 1991, 1528). This final point hardly supports the traditional image of a society where ample opportunity exists for members of all social classes to achieve successful and productive lives.

Critical Evaluation

A major strength of surveys is that they are a quick means of gathering information from large numbers of respondents. In the study by Steelman and Powell, the results of data obtained from 2,327 respondents to mailed questionnaires were analyzed. This analysis provided extensive information about which characteristics of prospective college students' parents make them willing to subsidize their children's college education.

A disadvantage of surveys is that they do not directly measure what people have done but only what they say they have done or would do. No assurance emerges from Steelman and Powell's study that all respondents would be consistent with their attitudes. When it actually came to paying for their children's higher education, some parents might back out; on the other hand, others might provide the money when they indicated in the questionnaire that they would not. Survey analysts must take people at their word, and sometimes respondents are unable or unwilling to provide information consistent with their behavior. While sometimes people intentionally give false information about their actions, often the inconsistency between statements and deeds is quite innocent. In the spring of 1992 in a Con-

While parents seem to uniformly rejoice when their children graduate from college, the willingness to help them pay the bills varies considerably.

necticut classroom, the teacher asked her combination of first graders and kindergarteners how many wanted to do both the shore and woods walks during their nature outing. Initially twenty-three of twenty-six students chose to do both. However, heat, humidity, and boredom took a toll, and only eighteen of twenty-six completed both walks.

EXPERIMENTS

An **experiment** is a research technique in which the investigator manipulates conditions so that the effects produced by one independent variable can be isolated and observed. Experimenters seek to establish causal connections. The most basic procedure is to select two groups of respondents whose social characteristics are similar, duplicate to the extent possible the conditions affecting the two groups, and then introduce the expected independent (experimental) variable to one group (the experimental group) and not to the other (the control group). Experiments can be conducted either in laboratories or in natural settings.

A well-known study of aggression conducted by Albert Bandura and his colleagues (1963) illustrates the basic experimental model. In Bandura's study a number of children who had similar social characteristics were randomly divided into two groups. Both groups were placed in a room that contained a large plastic doll, a punching-bag toy.

34   In the experimental group, the children observed an adult hitting the doll, and when the adult stopped doing it, the children started to hit the doll themselves. In the control group, in which no adult hit the doll, the children were much less likely to do it themselves. Since the only difference between the two groups was the presence of the experimental variable in one group and its absence in the other, the researchers were in a strong position to assert that the presence of the experimental variable—the adult's hitting of the toy—caused the greater amount of children's hitting in the experimental group (Bandura et al. 1963).

Sometimes experimenters decide that circumstances do not require a control group—that with two groups of subjects possessing similar backgrounds exposed to two or more experimental variables, any behavioral differences that the subjects exhibit are very likely to result from the different experimental variables. The following study offers such an illustration.

Experiment on the Evaluation of Sexual Harassment

The highly publicized confrontation between Judge Clarence Thomas and Professor Anita Hill dramatically brought the issue of sexual harassment to public attention, but some feminist researchers had been focused on the topic for many years.

For instance, an experimenter sought to understand more fully the factors influencing people's judgments about a complaint of sexual harassment. After examining the literature on the subject, Russel J. Summers (1991) produced several hypotheses:

1. Men would respond less favorably than women toward complaints of sexual harassment.
2. A second set of hypotheses was based on the so-called "attribution principle," emphasizing that if a distinct quality was associated with the woman complaining, then this attribute might distract those analyzing the situation, adversely affecting support for the complaint. Specifically:
    a. If the woman was described as a feminist, then support for her complaint would be reduced.

b. If the woman was competing for a job with the man harassing her, support for her complaint would also be lessened.

The experiment involved a fairly homogenous group of students—eighty female and eighty male students, who either were enrolled in an MBA program or were senior-level undergraduates. The average age of the group was 24.8 years old. These students were randomly divided by sex into four groups, and each group was provided a statement about sexual harassment, which was typed, doubled-spaced, and one-and-a-half pages long. In each case the statement indicated that a female employee accused a male employee of persisting with jokes and comments involving sexual innuendo even after he had been told repeatedly to stop. The four accounts emphasized the following specific details: In the first the accuser was a feminist; in the second she was a member of the Heart and Lung Association; in the third the accuser and the accused were in direct competition for a better job; and in the fourth, the statement indicated that the woman and man performed different jobs and that only the man was being considered for promotion.

The subjects in the experiment read the statements, and then answered thirteen multiple-choice questions, providing data for the researcher's conclusions.

Summers learned that the subjects in his research concluded that the perpetrator's actions were primarily responsible for the complaint of sexual harassment. However, support for his hypotheses also was apparent. Specifically there was a decline in belief of the male employee's guilt when the research subject was a male, when the victim was a feminist, and when the victim was in competition with the perpetrator for a job.

Critical Evaluation

Both of the experiments we have discussed indicate a distinct strength of the experimental method—the likelihood of establishing a causal link. The researcher sets up an experiment that seeks to eliminate the influence of other independent variables. If this influence is effectively removed, then the dependent variable—the manner in which the subjects respond—can be attributed to the influence of the experimental variable. In Bandura's experiment the control and experimental groups were similar except for the experimental manipulation of hitting the plastic doll. Thus differences between subjects' responses in the two groups can reasonably be attributed to the presence of that manipulation in the experimental group and its absence in the control group. While other experiments are often more complicated than Bandura's, they all provide an opportunity to establish a clear causal connection between the independent and dependent variables.

Experiments, however, also have weaknesses. One issue is the problem of whether or not they are realistic. Would Summers's results have been produced in "the real world"? Perhaps in the fairly brief written accounts read by the research subjects, the attributes of feminism and competition with a man for a job were highlighted more than they would have been in an actual situation, where people would have had more extensive information about the individuals. As a result the impact of these attributes in the experiment might have been exaggerated. Another criticism of many experiments involves an ethical issue—whether it is right to engage in deception in the course of doing research. Does the end, which in this case is the investigator's quest for information, justify the means, the use of deceit? In Summers's study this is not an issue, but in other experiments it can be a significant consideration. As we see in the section about research ethics at the end of this chapter, sometimes experimenters engage in major deceptions.

OBSERVATION STUDIES

To some people it might seem a bit strange that individuals can do research simply by observing others. "All right," an individual might say, "I can understand that conducting surveys and experiments is hard work. But just people watching!?" Actually that can be quite hard work. It is true that sociologists who conduct observation studies do not enter the research situation with a carefully developed survey or experiment, but they must be prepared to be active investigators, who conscientiously observe their research subjects over a fairly lengthy period of time (months, sometimes even years), analyze what they observe, and relate their conclusions to concepts and theories in their field.

There are two types of observation research. Some studies use **nonparticipant observation,** a method of observation in which an investigator examines a group process without taking part in the group activities. In many instances, however, researchers believe that they will obtain a more detailed knowledge of their topic if they use **participant observation,** a method of observation in which an investigator becomes involved in the activities of the group being studied.

Participant-Observation Study of Peer-Group Development

Between 1966 and 1967, I conducted a year-long participant-observation study of the development of peer groups among adolescent Puerto Rican males (Doob 1970). The principal finding was that the young men's peer groups reflected their family of origin in two significant respects: shared interests and activities, and range of contacts. For instance, respondents who came from families that shared many interests and activities and participated in large social networks tended to belong to peer groups with these same two traits.

During the study I lived on the block where the research was focused and spent considerable time observing, talking to, and playing a variety of sports with the boys who were the research subjects. A tape recorder was my constant companion, and I took extensive notes.

What these observations produced was detailed, often subtle information about the process by which family patterns become peer patterns. One striking example was how one 13-year-old boy, whose father and mother shared few interests and activities, was being slowly but relentlessly pressured to give up peer contacts and become his mother's frequent companion. The result? The boy was steadily withdrawing into a fantasy life featuring a half-dozen television cartoon characters. In contrast, I had ample opportunity to observe the process by which a local 18-year-old became involved in a peer group composed of ambitious, hard-working students, whose activities, interests, and contacts were much like those of his family and were systematically encouraged by his parents.

Could this richly detailed information have

36 been obtained with any other research technique? I doubt it.

Critical Evaluation

The research section at the end of Chapter 3, "Culture," discusses the use of participant observation for studying culture. The strength illustrated by the previous study of peer-group activity is demonstrated there again: The researcher has the opportunity to obtain detailed information about individuals and groups over time in a natural setting. Neither surveys nor experiments obtain the same rich detail available to the participant-observation investigator, who spends a fairly lengthy period of time studying a small number of subjects.

On the other hand, because of the lengthy involvement with their subjects, observation researchers, particularly participant observers, risk the possibility of emotional involvement—attraction, dislike, or some other distinct reaction—that will distort their observations. Did my personal feelings about the research subjects affect my analysis of their activities? This was often a major concern, which I tried to relieve by comparing my assessments of individuals and groups to those of other outsiders with some social-research training. Observation studies have another weakness: They usually involve a single or a small number of group situations. As we have observed, sociological inquiries are seeking to uncover patterns and generalizations. Researchers who study a single or small number of cases might encounter distinct or unusual characteristics in the situations they are studying, and these qualities might encourage the investigators to produce misleading or downright incorrect generalizations. I wondered, for instance, whether the particularly heavy drug trafficking on the block where I focused my study had a distinct impact on local behavior, producing peer-group activity for the block's adolescent boys that was significantly different from the peer-group activity on other blocks in the locale.

Whether they have conducted observation studies or some other type of research, sociologists writing up their investigations often use tables as a means of presenting their data. The nearby Social Application is a lesson in how to read a table.

SECONDARY ANALYSIS

Sometimes researchers may use **secondary analysis,** a study using data banks available to researchers but produced by other individuals and organizations for their own purposes. The United States Bureau of the Census, for example, obtains large quantities of data that sociologists frequently use as sources for research. In some cases researchers find that they can employ earlier studies as sources of data. Other secondary sources include diaries, letters, court records, biographies, autobiographies, and novels. They can also use various visual media sources, such as television programming.

Increasingly social researchers appreciate the impact of the mass media on modern citizens. Marvin L. Moore indicated that if television is truly the influential medium it is widely claimed to be, then "one can hardly assume that the patterns of family life being presented on a regular basis are not influencing the family patterns of real households" (Moore 1992, 42).

For this study the researcher analyzed successful family television series between 1947 and 1990, designating as successful the series that were included in the prime-time schedule for more than one broadcast season. Moore categorized families as "conventional" or "nonconventional." Conventional families were either couples with children or couples without children, while nonconventional families were either single-parent families or so-called "contrived" families, containing individuals operating as a family unit in spite of the absence of a blood relationship. A variety of other family characteristics were also considered, such as social-class membership and race.

The data showed that over the four decades, prime-time television made increasingly more equal presentations of conventional and nonconventional families. For instance, in the 1950s, only 12 percent of series presented single-parent families, but in the 1960s nearly 45 percent of the prime-time family shows featured single-parent families, with the percentage falling slightly in the two succeeding decades. It is notable, however, that throughout the 43-year time period, the majority of single-parent families represented in prime-time family shows were male-headed, with the number of successful female-headed family shows only outnumbering the male-headed ones

SOCIAL APPLICATION
Reading a Table

 Anyone studying sociology needs to read tables. In this exercise carefully follow the sequence of steps, concentrating on each step as you reach it.

1. Examine the title, which indicates the topic to be analyzed. Many people plunge into tables and other reading matter without even a glance at the title, which is a succinct summary of the information the writer is supplying. In Table 2.1 the topic involves reducing the spread of AIDS, a current major crisis issue. The data appear in percentage form. Sometimes tables present the number of people instead of percentages.

2. Read captions and footnotes. It is probably even easier to disregard captions, footnotes, and source notes than the titles of tables—since their placement is less prominent—but such omissions are often critical. The caption is likely to offer a brief substantive statement about the data. With Table 2.1 the caption supplies the precise wording of the question. Footnotes are likely to provide such facts as the source of the data and the means by which the information was obtained. In both cases the reader learns something about the quality of the research. As our discussion on surveys indicated, a national random sample of 1,000 men and women offers an accurate representation of the entire adult American population on a given question. Gallup Poll is a well-established commercial survey firm.

3. Identify the variables. When researchers devise tables, they frequently put the independent variable across the top and then arrange the dependent variable or variables along the left-hand side. Sociologists are likely to assume this arrangement exists when they first examine a table. However, anyone reading a table must be aware that for emphasis or convenience researchers may reverse the pattern. Table 2.1 maintains the convention. The independent variable—age of respondents—is horizontal, and the dependent variable—choices about educational focus to stop the spread of AIDS—appears vertically.

4. Study the labels to understand the data in the table. Researchers call each vertical list of data a "column" and each horizontal list a "row." Read the labels for each column and row and try to set them firmly in mind. You will need to consider both column and row headings simultaneously when you read the table. The variable across the top—age—has three breakdowns in years: 18–29, 30–49, and 50 and older. Thus there are three columns of data. The four categories of the dependent variable—"safe sex," abstinence, both equally, and no opinion—run down the side. So there are four rows of data.

5. Analyze the information presented in the table. In a table that presents the independent variable across the top, you should examine the column headings to see whether the various categories of the independent variable establish distinct patterns in relation to the categories listed down the side. The accompanying table does indicate some distinct differences

Table 2.1 [*Title*] Efforts to Reduce the Spread of AIDS[1]

[*Data labels*]	[*Independent variable*] AGE [*in years*]		
	18–29	30–49	50 & older
[*Dependent variable*]			
"Safe sex"	72%	57%	38%
Abstinence	26	38	55
Both equally	2	5	5
No opinion	0	0	2

[1] [**Footnote**] *The data presented here were obtained from 1,000 men and women 18 years of age and over. The sample was obtained nationwide, and a complicated sampling procedure insured the randomness of the respondents chosen. Interviews were conducted by telephone.*

[**Source note**] *Source: Adapted from the Gallup Poll. Gallup Poll Monthly. (November 1991).*

[**Caption**] *The following message was read to respondents over the telephone. "Do you think public education efforts to reduce the spread of AIDS among young people should focus more on encouraging them to practice safe sex or more on encouraging them to abstain from sex?"*

38

among the respondents of different ages. The older the respondents, the less approval of "safe sex." The specific figures on approval of "safe sex" were 72 percent for people aged 18–29, 57 percent for those aged 30–49, and 38 percent for those 50 and older.

6. Consider how further analysis can expand the central conclusions. As you examine the table, the relationship between age and approval of "safe sex" is clear. Additional analysis could determine the impact of a number of other independent variables, such as race, religion, ideology, and income, on people's attitudes toward educational efforts to reduce the spread of AIDS. Once statistical relationships are established, you need to reach beyond the data to explain them. Why does approval of "safe sex" decline with age? One relevant factor seems to be the changing cultural climate over the past two or three decades—a growing trend in business, educational and political circles, and the mass media to support a sexually permissive lifestyle. Unlike many Americans who are 50 and older, younger people reached maturity in this more sexually tolerant atmosphere.

during the 1970s. In real life about 90 percent of single-parent families are female-headed.

In addition, families in these prime-time programs tended to be white and middle-class, and were disproportionately contrived compared to the real world. Commenting on these trends, Marvin Moore suggested that those controlling television programming have always tried to find the most appealing material to promote a large viewing audience. Perhaps these people believe "that the world in which the great majority of us live is somehow not entertaining. Instead, it is the male single parent, the wealthy family, the contrived family . . . that draws an audience" (Moore 1992, 58). Feeling concerned, Moore wondered about the implications of so many people regularly viewing gender-role representations so out of step with modern reality.

Secondary sources can serve as future resources. One researcher wrote, "The best of this information should be preserved, not only so that contemporary colleagues may use it, but also so that we leave a legacy for posterity describing what we were like, we of a particular period and place" (Card 1989).

Table 2.2 summarizes the four types of research design discussed in this section.

In the 1950s the conventional family, such as that presented in "Father Knows Best," dominated prime-time programming. However, unconventional families, such as that represented in the recent show "Full House," where three men and one woman have been bringing up three girls, started becoming much more common in the 1960s.

Table 2.2 Types of Research Design

Type	Varieties	Strengths	Weaknesses
Surveys	Telephone or face-to-face interviews, questionnaires	A great deal of information can be gathered easily and efficiently	Possibility of distorted findings since data involve people's words and not their actions
Experiments	Laboratory or field experiments	Distinct possibility of establishing a causal link	Possible artificial influence of experimenters operating in a laboratory setting; ethical issues associated with experimenters' deception
Observation studies	Nonparticipant observation, participant observation	Detailed observations of groups over time in a natural setting	Danger of emotional involvement and loss of objectivity; problems of generalizing from a single case
Secondary analysis	Earlier studies, diaries, court records, biographies, novels	Procurement of data in situations where the use of other methods is either impractical or infeasible	The diverse limitations imposed by researchers not gathering data themselves: for example, the inability of secondary sources to answer some questions of particular significance to the study at hand

Issues in Sociological Research ■

We now turn to some general issues in research which often pose major challenges to sociologists and other social scientists. Each of the issues discussed involves controversy. In some instances, such as the question of objectivity in the research process, debate occurs primarily among social scientists; in other cases the disputes tend to pit social researchers against individuals outside of social science, such as law-enforcement officials or government bureaucrats.

OBJECTIVITY IN THE RESEARCH PROCESS

Objectivity is the ability to evaluate reality without using personal opinions and biases. Researchers try to maintain objectivity in their work—that is, to report the facts in the situations that they study without reflecting their personal feelings. If two investigators conducted the same piece of research independently of each other and produced the same or almost the same findings, then we would have strong reason to believe that they had achieved objectivity.

Loss of objectivity can occur for several reasons. Some research areas might provoke intense personal feelings in entire groups of investigators. As an extreme case, it would be unreasonable to expect an African-American or Jewish sociologist to do an objective study of the Ku Klux Klan, a group which has had a history of brutally terrorizing both ethnic groups, especially blacks. Furthermore the majority of American sociologists are white, middle-class, and politically liberal, and each of these qualities could be a source of bias in a research situation.

Another reason for the loss of objectivity is a researcher's commitment to a fixed theoretical or idealogical position. Researchers sometimes

40   approach their studies not as open-minded observers, but as individuals selectively seeking evidence for a particular position.

A third factor is the researcher's relations with his or her respondents. During a participant-observation study, an investigator might develop such a close relationship with research subjects that he or she might begin to accept the subjects' definitions of critical situations—their analyses of community events, their assessments of the "good people" and the "bad people," and more. Such a situation can seriously endanger the objectivity of a project.

Sociologists can take several steps to avoid the loss of objectivity. First, recognizing that both their topics and their techniques are affected by their own values, they can attempt to carefully analyze how their values apply to their studies. Once they have determined the impact of their values, they are probably less likely to let personal inclinations undermine the objectivity of their investigations. Second, sociologists might seek the assistance of colleagues who can visit the research site and make independent assessments of the people under study. The colleagues' assessments, though based on brief observations, might provide the investigators with clues indicating whether or not they are losing their objectivity.

A researcher's objectivity can also be assessed by another person's follow-up investigation. After reading a report about a particular study, a second sociologist might want to evaluate the accuracy of the findings. He or she will conduct a **replication**—a repetition or near repetition of an earlier study to determine the accuracy of its findings.

The loss of objectivity can occur in any social scientific study. As the nearby Cross-Cultural Perspective indicates, even famous social researchers can be vulnerable to this criticism.

ETHICS IN THE RESEARCHER'S ROLE

All sociologists agree that research must be conducted in an ethically sound manner. Exactly what the ethical limits should be, however, is often a topic for debate. The American Sociological Association's Committee on Professional Ethics has provided the association's Code of Ethics, submitting proposed changes in the code every five years to the association's governing body

(*Footnotes* 1992). In this section we consider three possible areas where ethical problems can arise—issues of confidentiality, painful self-revelation, and use of findings.

Problem of Confidentiality

There are different aspects to the issue of confidentiality. Occasionally sociologists publish data that prove embarrassing or irritating to subjects who believe that their confidentiality has been violated. On the other hand, sociologists like Mario Brajuha sometimes find themselves acting to protect informants' confidentiality.

In 1982 Mario Brajuha, a graduate student in sociology at the State University of New York at Stony Brook, began his dissertation research, a participant-observation study of a restaurant where he was employed as a waiter. Brajuha had collected about 700 pages of notes when a suspicious fire destroyed the restaurant.

A few days later, local police and fire investigators contacted Brajuha demanding the release of his records. Brajuha refused, saying that this move would violate the confidentiality he had promised his subjects. The assistant attorney general threatened to have Brajuha jailed for contempt. On the day that he was expected to surrender his records, Brajuha appeared before the judge presiding over the case. Upon examination of Brajuha's records, the judge agreed that the researcher's claim that people would be embarrassed if his records were revealed was realistic. Nonetheless, the judge eventually ruled that Brajuha should surrender his notes. The pressure on Brajuha increased when the federal district attorney issued a subpoena for the research records. Attorneys for both sides presented their cases to a federal judge who ruled that serious scholars must be permitted the same confidentiality as journalists. At the same time, the Brajuha case was sent back to the lower court for additional information. One unanswered question was whether or not as a graduate student Brajuha could claim to be a serious scholar.

This question was never answered in court. Following a reorganization of the federal attorney's office, there was an out-of-court settlement in which Brajuha supplied federal investigators with some carefully edited information from his notes.

CROSS-CULTURAL PERSPECTIVE
Margaret Mead in Samoa: Objectivity in Participant-Observation Research

Objectivity is a priority in research, but sometimes investigators fail in this regard. This example illustrates some of the conditions that might undermine objectivity.

In 1925 Margaret Mead, a 23-year-old anthropologist, arrived in Samoa. After nine months of research, she produced a book that became the first anthropological bestseller, *Coming of Age in Samoa.* Nearly sixty years later, after her death, a New Zealand anthropologist named Derek Freeman completed a book, *Margaret Mead and Samoa,* indicating that Mead's participant-observation study lacked objectivity and that its conclusions were largely incorrect.

Before Mead left for Samoa, she had been a graduate student of the anthropologist Franz Boas. At the time Boas was deeply involved in the debate about whether human development is primarily the result of biological influence or of cultural influence. According to Freeman, Boas wholeheartedly supported the latter idea, and, to bolster the cultural position, he sought evidence to counter his opponents' contention that the turmoil of adolescence was a biological necessity. In Samoa Mead hoped to find a culture free of adolescent stress, and this discovery would have given Boas valuable ammunition in

his debate with the biological determinists. Freeman contended that Boas was pleased with the study that Mead planned to undertake. Freeman wrote, "In Margaret Mead there was at hand a spirited young cultural determinist ideally suited to the project he had in mind" (Freeman 1983, 60).

If Freeman is correct, then Mead's objectivity was already seriously tarnished even before she left the United States. Independent support for Freeman's claim does exist. Robin Fox, an English anthropologist, indicated that Mead characterized the relationship of Boas with his graduate students in the following fashion: "He told us what to look for and we went and found it" (Leo 1983, 69).

Freeman concluded that because Mead's research lacked objectivity, she produced blatantly inaccurate findings. In *Coming of Age in Samoa,* Mead described a culture in which people had a pleasant, relaxed attitude toward sex. Before marriage, she contended, adolescents could engage in free lovemaking, and marriage itself was not a major hindrance to free love. Mead's overall sense of the Samoans was that they were an amiable, relaxed, and peaceful people. Freeman disagreed with her on both points. His own recent study concluded that Samoan adolescents were sub-

jected to authoritarian control. The adults did not encourage youthful sex; in fact, they explicitly prohibited it. In addition, Freeman did not believe that the Samoans he observed were an amiable, peaceful people. His impression was that they were competitive, jealous, and frequently violent. While Mead reported that forcible rape was unknown to the Samoans, Freeman offered data indicating that the incidence of forcible rape was high, twice that of the United States and twenty times that of England. He claimed that all Mead had needed to do to learn about the frequency of rape among the Samoans was to read the local newspaper, which regularly reported rape cases during her stay.

Freeman claimed throughout his book that biological factors have as much impact in the shaping of human development as cultural factors do. Freeman's critics, however, contended that, like Mead, he forsook objectivity in an effort to convey an ideological position. Bradd Shore, another anthropologist who has done field work in Samoa, suggested that the Samoans fall somewhere between the Mead and Freeman characterizations. They are neither as amiable and peaceful as Mead described nor as competitive and violent as Freeman claimed.

Sources: Derek Freeman. Margaret Mead and Samoa. Cambridge: Harvard University Press, 1983; John Leo. "Bursting the South Sea Bubble," Time. vol. 121 (February 14, 1983), pp. 68–70; Eliot Marshall. "A Controversy on Samoa Comes of Age," Science. vol. 219 (March 1983), pp. 1042–45; John Noble Wilford. "Customs Check: Leave Your Ideological Baggage Behind," New York Times. (February 6, 1983), sec. 4, p. 8.

42

Because of the settlement, this case did not establish a legal precedent (Hallowell 1985). For those who know about it, however, it is a testimony of one young sociologist's commitment to high ethical research standards.

The issue of confidentiality is often complicated. Sociologists and other social scientists engaged in research often can not anticipate sensitive findings. Does an investigator who learns that an HIV-infected respondent is engaging in unprotected sex with unsuspecting partners report this activity to officials? Anticipating such difficult situations, the British Sociological Association Code of Practice specified that sociologists "should not give a guarantee of confidentiality of a kind they may not be able to fulfill" (Robinson 1991, 281). Researchers may face the difficult challenges of weighing the public good versus the need for confidentiality and reaching some manageable course of action.

Problem of Inflicting Mental Suffering

When research subjects are manipulated, painful self-revelations are sometimes produced. Stanley Milgram (1963), a psychologist, did a series of experimental studies in which his subjects believed that they were applying a sequence of increasingly powerful shocks to hypothetical subjects in a learning experiment. Milgram's elaborate "shock machine" did not actually administer any shocks to the supposed victims, who had been instructed by the researcher to express surprise, pain, and sometimes even pleas for mercy after the subject pushed one of the shock buttons. Yet for the purposes of the experiments, which focused on the subjects' willingness to obey an authority figure (the experimenter), it was essential that the people who pushed the buttons on the machine believed that it was producing real shocks. The following exchange illustrates how a typical subject responded to this experimental situation.

The subject began the experiment calmly but became increasingly nervous as he proceeded. After believing that he had administered a 180-volt shock, this man pivoted in his chair and addressed the experimenter in an agitated voice.

SUBJECT: I can't stand it. I'm not going to kill that man in there. You hear him hollering

EXPERIMENTER: As I told you before, the shocks may be painful, but—

(Milgram 1974, 73)

As the voltage increased, the subject became even more agitated.

SUBJECT: What if he's dead in there? . . . I mean, he told me he can't stand the shock, sir. I don't mean to be rude, but I think you should look in on him. All you have to do is look in on him. All you have to do is look in the door. I don't get no answer, no noise. Something might have happened to the gentleman in there, sir.

EXPERIMENTER: We must continue. Go on, please.

(Milgram 1974, 76)

The subject did go on, pushing the voltage buttons until the experimenter finally indicated that the exercise was over.

Milgram (1963) explained that before subjects left, a "friendly reconciliation" occurred between them and their imagined victims. Furthermore the experimenter made a distinct effort to reduce any tensions that had arisen during the experiment. But could he actually succeed in this regard? One critic was very doubtful. She noted that Milgram himself conceded that the reaction produced in subjects was "traumatic to a degree . . . nearly unprecedented in sociopsychological experiments," and so "his casual assurance that these tensions were dissipated before the subject left the laboratory is unconvincing" (Baumrind 1964, 422).

Some psychologists and sociologists have defended Milgram's research. Several have pointed out that his experiments revealed startling, important findings about people's tendencies to obey authority figures. But does the importance of the findings justify the emotional disruption that many subjects suffered? If researchers accept that the ends justify the means, then they have adopted a frightening ethical position.

Use of Findings

At the beginning of the twentieth century, social scientists considered mental retardation the most serious problem in the United States.

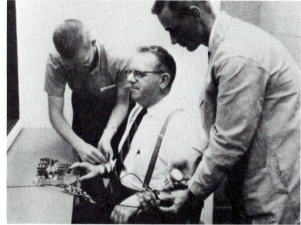
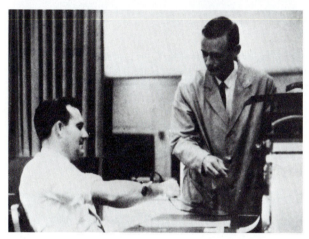

In the above series of photos taken form the film Obedience *by Stanley Milgram, one can see the "shock machine," the "victim" (seated, upper right), the researcher (in lab coat), and the subject (bottom photos).*

Policy-makers were warned that unless retarded individuals were prevented from reproducing, mental retardation would assume frighteningly larger proportions and that significantly more crime, prostitution, alcoholism, poverty, and delinquency would accompany the increase.

Two developments in the field of psychology promoted that concern. The first was fragmentary research concluding that mental retardation is inherited; the second was the adaptation of Alfred Binet's intelligence test to classify mentally handicapped individuals. In the early 1920s, a prominent researcher gave IQ tests to delinquents, criminals, members of ethnic and racial minorities, and prostitutes and found that many received low scores. Instead of considering that most of these people lacked the cultural background to do well on such tests, the investigator simply concluded that low scores were attributable to genetic inferiority. Impressed by these findings, a host of prominent social scientists advocated the institutionalization and involuntary sterilization of mentally handicapped people. Between 1910 and 1923, such institutionalization more than doubled and twenty-six states passed sterilization laws.

By the 1930s new research caused some scientists to question the wisdom of the earlier policies, and gradually the policies began to change, but institutionalization of mentally handicapped people capable of functioning in the social world has continued to the present. This historical case illustrates that in areas of sensitive research, findings need to be applied with great care and a sense of social responsibility (Sieber and Stanley 1988).

STUDY GUIDE

Learning Objectives

After studying this chapter, you should be able to:

1. Define methodology and explain its importance in scientific research.
2. Define causation, distinguish between an independent variable and a dependent variable, and identify the conditions necessary for causation.
3. Define correlation, indicating its relationship to causation and distinguishing between positive and negative correlations.
4. List the stages in the research process, describing the sociologist's task at each stage.
5. Define hypothesis and explain the contribution that hypotheses make in the research process.
6. Distinguish among the following concepts—population, sample, and random sample—and explain the importance of random sampling in sociological research.
7. Define and discuss the four major types of research design—surveys, experiments, observation studies, and secondary analysis—and evaluate the strengths and weaknesses of the first three types.
8. Define objectivity, explain its importance in scientific research, identify factors that may hinder objectivity, and indicate how the loss of objectivity may be prevented.
9. Identify and discuss ethical issues involved in sociological research.

Summary

1. Methodology is the set of principles and procedures that guides sociological research.

2. The stages of the research process include choosing a topic, reviewing the literature, formulating a hypothesis, picking the research design, gathering the data, analyzing the data, and producing a report.

3. The four main types of sociological research design are surveys, experiments, observation studies, and secondary analysis. A survey uses carefully constructed questions to obtain large amounts of information about people's thoughts and behavior. The two principal types of surveys are interviews and questionnaires. An advantage of surveys is that they permit researchers to gather a great deal of information easily. A disadvantage is that they measure people's anticipated or reported behavior and not their actual behavior, and sometimes inconsistencies occur.

In an experiment the investigator manipulates conditions so that the effects of one variable can be observed, while other variables are held constant. An advantage of experiments is that they can indicate a causal link. They also have weaknesses. Critics question whether experimental results would materialize in the "real world." Another criticism involves an ethical issue—whether it is right to deceive subjects in the course of research.

The two types of observation research are participant observation and nonparticipant observation. Participant observation, in particular, offers the special opportunity to study individuals and groups over time in a natural setting. On the other hand, participant observers can lose their emotional detachment, and such a loss might impede a full and balanced understanding of the group process under investigation.

Secondary analysis involves the use of sources available to researchers but produced by other individuals and organizations for their own purposes. The United States Bureau of the Census obtains large quantities of data that can serve as the principal or exclusive source for sociological research.

4. Researchers are expected to be objective.

A number of factors influence their success in this regard.

Research has raised serious ethical questions. Issues arising in major social-scientific studies involve confidentiality, the problem of inflicting mental suffering on research subjects, and the use of findings.

Key Terms

causation   a situation in which one variable can produce the occurrence of another

correlation   a statistical description of the relationship between variables

dependent variable   a variable that is the consequence of some cause

experiment   a research technique in which the investigator manipulates conditions so that the effects produced by one independent variable can be isolated and observed

hypothesis   a scientifically researchable suggestion about the relationship between two or more variables

independent variable   a variable that influences another variable—the dependent variable

interview   a type of survey composed of questions that are delivered face-to-face or over the telephone

methodology   the set of principles and procedures that guides sociological research

nonparticipant observation   a method of observation in which an investigator examines a group process without taking part in the group activities

objectivity   the ability to evaluate reality without using personal opinions and biases

participant observation   a method of observation in which an investigator becomes involved in the activities of the group being studied

population   the entire category of people possessing the characteristics that interest a researcher undertaking a particular study

questionnaire   a type of survey in which a respondent writes the answers to a list of questions

random sample   a sample drawn from a population by a process that assures that every individual in that population has an equal probability of being included

reliability   consistency in measurement

replication   a repetition or near repetition of an earlier study to determine the accuracy of its findings

sample   a limited number of individuals chosen from a population for the purpose of conducting research

secondary analysis   a study using data banks available to researchers but produced by other individuals and organizations for their own purposes

survey   a research technique that uses carefully constructed questions to obtain a variety of facts about people's thoughts and behavior

validity   the condition in which a research item accurately measures what it claims to measure

variable   a factor that has two or more categories or measurable conditions

Tests

True • False Test

_____   1. In sociological research, dependent variables are frequently attitudes and activities.
_____   2. A correlation of "0" indicates no relationship at all between two variables.
_____   3. Surveys usually use samples instead of populations.
_____   4. Steelman and Powell's study of the traits of parents paying for their children's higher education indicated that a strength of surveys is that they demonstrate the relationship between people's claims and their actions.

_____ 5. In Russel J. Summers's experiment, research subjects' judgment about the occurrence of sexual harassment was unaffected by whether or not the complainant was portrayed as a feminist.

_____ 6. The loss of objectivity is less likely to occur in an observation study than in an experiment or survey.

_____ 7. Sociologists often use data produced by the United States Bureau of the Census as a secondary source.

_____ 8. The British Sociological Association Code of Practice specified that sociologists must always give their respondents guarantees of confidentiality.

_____ 9. Stanley Milgram's experiments were controversial, with some social scientists saying his work was unethical and others indicating that his startling, important findings served to justify the research.

_____ 10. Research about mentally handicapped people early in the twentieth century immediately produced progressive policies making the lives of these individuals more rewarding.

Multiple-Choice Test

_____ 1. Scientists' central concern is:
   a. causation.
   b. the systematic pursuit of the truth.
   c. the effective use of random samples.
   d. correlation.

_____ 2. Causation cannot be established until researchers have *ruled out* the:
   a. existence of other possible dependent variables.
   b. influence of other possible independent variables.
   c. possibility that the independent variable existed before the dependent variable.
   d. inverse relationship between variables.

_____ 3. "The higher people's social class, the fewer children they have" is an example of a:
   a. theory.
   b. dependent variable.
   c. hypothesis.
   d. logical pattern.

_____ 4. Organizations that sponsor research demand that the researchers:
   a. gather data.
   b. analyze their findings.
   c. summarize their findings in a report.
   d. demonstrate the importance of their findings for sociological theory.

_____ 5. The *Literary Digest* poll of 1936 demonstrated that:
   a. random samples don't work.
   b. biases in sampling can produce disastrous research results.
   c. very large samples are necessary for predicting elections.
   d. several other types of samples work as well as random samples.

_____ 6. In Albert Bandura's experiment with a punching-bag toy:
   a. there was no independent variable.
   b. there were no children in the experimental group.
   c. the adult's hitting of the toy occurred in the control group.
   d. the adult's hitting of the toy occurred in the experimental group.

_____ 7. Participant-observation studies:
   a.   make it possible to observe individuals and groups over time in a natural setting.
   b.   are usually done with surveys.
   c.   require a set of no fewer than six hypotheses.
   d.   use a control group.

_____ 8. In examining the family membership of prime-time family television programming, Marvin L. Moore analyzed:
   a.   experimental design.
   b.   primary sources.
   c.   secondary sources.
   d.   nonparticipant observation.

_____ 9. The loss of objectivity may occur because:
   a.   some researchers are not intellectually equipped for the studies they do.
   b.   some topics provoke intense feelings in entire groups of investigators.
   c.   researchers do not have a fixed theoretical or ideological position.
   d.   investigators are too detached from their subjects.

_____ 10. Milgram's "shock-machine" studies focused social scientists' attention on the ethical issue of:
   a.   confidentiality.
   b.   painful self-revelation.
   c.   validity.
   d.   replication.

Essay Test

1. Describe the stages in the research process, indicating the major activity occurring at each stage.
2. What is a survey? Indicate a major strength and a major weakness of this approach.
3. Define experiment and indicate how the experimental process works. Discuss an important strength and an important weakness of this technique.
4. Write about observation studies, defining participant observation and pointing out a significant strength and a significant weakness of this research form.
5. What are secondary sources? Under what conditions might a sociologist decide to use them?
6. Define objectivity and discuss conditions that can undermine it during research. What steps can researchers take to avoid the loss of objectivity?
7. Discuss two areas in which ethical problems can arise in the course of social-scientific studies.

Suggested Readings

Babbie, Earl. 1989. *The Practice of Social Research*. 5th ed. Belmont, CA: Wadsworth. An entertainingly written, thorough introduction to the study of research methods. Babbie has presented what could be difficult, tedious material in a form that makes it readily understood and interesting.

Hammond, Phillip E. (ed.). 1964. *Sociologists at Work*. New York: Basic Books. Sociologists involved in eleven methodologically varied studies candidly analyze their research experiences in detail. These accounts offer a concrete discussion of issues and problems which can arise at different steps in the research process.

Huff, Darrell. 1954. *How to Lie with Statistics*. New York: W. W. Norton. A revealing, entertaining discussion of the problems and limitations of statistical material.

48   Menard, Scott. 1991. *Longitudinal Research*. Newbury Park, CA: Sage. A brief but fairly comprehensive analysis of the now widely recognized topic of longitudinal research—studies conducted with the same body of respondents over an extended period of time.

Sieber, Joan E. 1992. *Planning Ethically Responsible Research: A Guide for Students and Internal Review Boards*. Newbury Park, CA: Sage. A detailed introduction to the background knowledge necessary for evaluating the complicated ethical issues often confronting social researchers.

Singleton, Royce, Jr. et al. 1988. *Approaches to Social Research*. New York: Oxford University Press. A thorough, effectively organized, well-written introduction to the principles and practice of social research.

Sociological Abstracts. A report issued five times a year and containing summaries of the latest articles and books in sociology.

Webb, Eugene J., Donald T. Campbell, Richard D. Schwartz, and Lee Sechrest. 1966. *Unobtrusive Measures*. Chicago: Rand McNally. A discussion of a large variety of ingenious ways in which social researchers can gather information about individuals and group members through nonparticipant observation.

Additional Assignments

1. Assume that you have been hired to study a problem of job satisfaction and dissatisfaction where you work. You have recently developed the following hypothesis: The better the workers are paid, the greater their job satisfaction. In your library find articles and books on job satisfaction and use these sources for developing a study to test this hypothesis. Are you able to discuss effectively all the stages in the research process? (Hint: *Sociological Abstracts* and *Psychological Abstracts* will help you find articles.)

2. In a newspaper or magazine find a questionnaire or a self-test. Make a list of the variables asked about, such as age, sex, level of education, and occupation. What is the questionnaire trying to determine? Sort the variables into two categories—independent and dependent variables. Now using these variables, construct what seem to be reasonable hypotheses about the subject in the questionnaire.

Answers to Objective Test Questions

True • False Test

1. t	6. f
2. t	7. t
3. t	8. f
4. f	9. t
5. f	10. f

Multiple-Choice Test

1. b	6. d
2. b	7. a
3. c	8. c
4. c	9. b
5. b	10. b

The Individual in Society

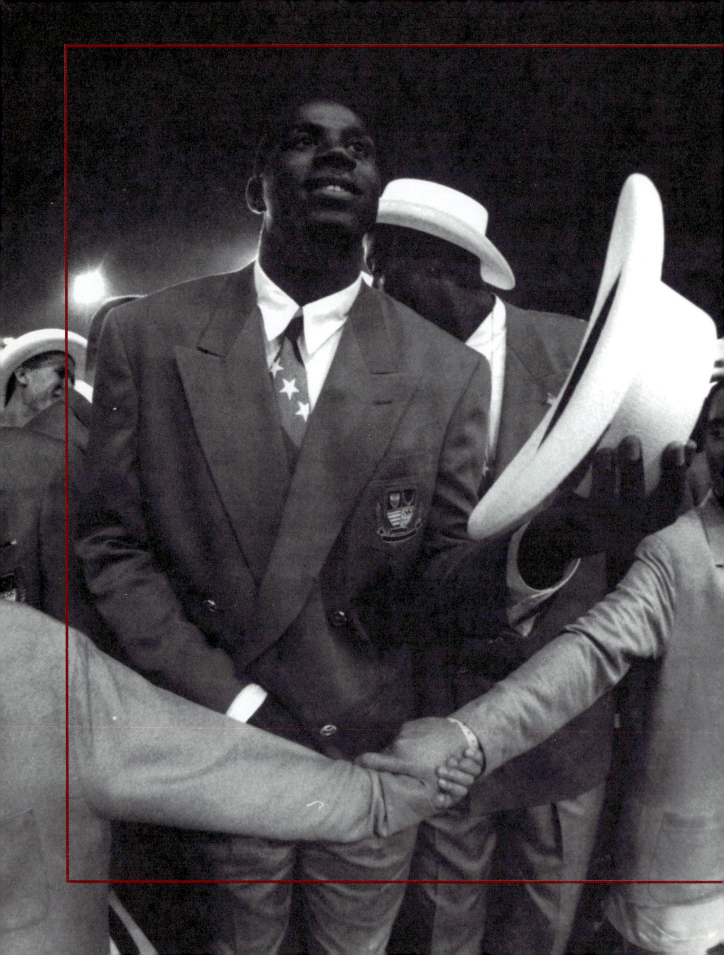

Culture

3

everal years ago Maureen Giovannini, an anthropologist, started conducting fieldwork in the Sicilian town of Garre. After arriving in Garre, she introduced herself to four leading town officials, all of whom were male. When they had examined her letters of recommendation, Giovannini asked about the possibility of renting a small apartment. In a cold and suspicious voice, the vice-mayor asked, "And what would a young girl like you want with her own aparment?"

Realizing that she had blundered into making a suggestion that was highly inappropriate within the local culture, Giovannini quickly overcame the blunder by saying, "Well, of course I don't *want* to live alone, but I didn't think that any other arrangement was possible. If I had my choice I would certainly prefer to live with a family where I could feel safe and secure" (Giovannini 1992, 28). Now the four officials' tense expressions gave way to smiles, and one of them indicated that he and his wife had a spare room that they would be happy to rent. Right away Giovannini accepted the offer, realizing that as a young woman in Sicilian society, she simply would not be permitted to live alone.

Cultural differences also appeared as the research progressed. Giovannini struck up a friendship with a man named Franco, who proved an invaluable informant about male Sicilians' customs—information that as a woman the anthropologist was unable to obtain. But a problem arose. Franco told Giovannini that several of his friends had found out about their meetings and that they had mercilessly teased him about his relationship with l'Americana, saying that if he didn't manage to get her into bed, then he wasn't really a man. Circumstances, Franco explained, required that he end their association. The alternatives were to lie about the relationship, thus maintaining his image as a "predatory" male while destroying both her reputation and research project, or to tell the truth, thereby safeguarding Giovannini's reputation but undercutting his own social worth in that community. So regretfully for the two participants, Sicilian cultural standards forced the end of a relationship that was quite ordinary in American culture but outside of the local rules.

Culture consists of all the human-made products associated with a society. Basically two types of cultural products exist—the material and the nonmaterial. Material products consist of the physical objects people make and use—ranging in size from laboratory-developed microorganisms to skyscrapers and in complexity from the crudest stone or wood tools and weapons to the most sophisticated computers. Nonmaterial products are intangible, and yet they are the foundations of culture, providing information essential for interpersonal behavior and for the development of material culture. Beliefs, technology, values, norms, and symbols are important components of culture, which we discuss in this chapter.

Culture is one of the most basic yet profound realities of people's lives. Culture provides them with a shared framework to guide them as they solve their everyday problems. If this statement seems abstract to you, try applying it to yourself. Imagine that you are sitting alone, just thinking. Note that the process of thought involves language and that language is a shared component of culture. You feel hungry. You might think that hunger is simply a biological urge, but a person's sense of hunger is inevitably affected by cultural standards. Perhaps you find yourself looking at your watch wondering if it is "time" to be hungry. Many, perhaps most, Americans are geared to three meals a day at fairly fixed times. However, people in other cultures often follow different arrangements; and, of course, differences also exist in food preferences. Americans would probably find their culturally prescribed sense of hunger rapidly receding if they were offered a few staples of some different cultures—such delicacies as lice, lizards, snakes, ants, worms, animal eyes or brains, wasps, and beetles.

The AT&T Telephone Story

Alexander Graham Bell, 1876

The story of the telephone is the story of change, of the relentless search for new methods and materials to better transmit the human voice. For well over a century, AT&T has pursued this goal. Much of the progress has been achieved in switching and transmission equipment that is invisible to users who are more interested in the instrument they see. This is what AT&T's telephones looked like as they evolved over the years.

1876 Liquid Telephone
On March 10, Alexander Graham Bell spoke the first words over his invention, this telephone: "Mr. Watson, Come Here I Want You."

1876 Bell's Centennial Telephone
Bell used this set for his first public demonstrations at the Centennial Exposition in Philadelphia. Emperor Dom Pedro of Brazil reacted typically, exclaiming, "My God, It Talks!"

1878 "Butterstamp"
The first set with a hand-held receiver/transmitter was in service when the first switchboard opened in New Haven, CT.

1878 "Coffin"
Switching the same instrument from mouth to ear caused confusion, so a second receiver/transmitter was added with this set.

1877 First Commercial Set
This set went into service in 1877, connecting a banker's office with his home. The opening served as both receiver and transmitter.

1880 Blake
The telephone attracted many inventors. This carbon transmitter, invented by Francis Blake Jr., quickly became standard equipment.

1892 Desk Set
This Gay 90s classic shows that decorator sets are hardly a recent idea. It also has a newly designed compact receiver.

1886 Long Distance Transmitter
Early long distance service required special receivers connected to special circuits. By 1910, the system was rewired for long distance compatibility.

1896 Common Battery
Electricity from the exchange powered this phone, providing uniform power for the talking circuit.

1897 Desk Set
With this model, the desk set assumed the basic design it would carry for thirty years. This set is cast brass; later versions were usually black.

1882 Magneto Wall Set
The first "standard" set combined Blake's transmitter, Bell's receiver and a side-mounted crank for signalling the operator.

1921 Dial Telephone
Invented in 1896 by Almon Strowger, it took until 1921 for AT&T to begin to manufacture dial systems and add them to its telephone network.

1937 "300" Type Desk Set
The "300" had its bell in the base instead of in a separate sub-set. In the 1940s, it became the first model with a plastic body.

1938 Key Set
Business systems took a major step forward with this first telephone to provide buttons for multiple lines and "hold" as part of the set.

1907 Magneto Wall Set
Similar sets were produced from the late 1890s to the 1930s. They were used where the phone was locally powered by cranks and dry cells.

1928 Desk Set
This is the first AT&T set to combine the receiver and transmitter in a handset. It came in both manual and dial versions.

1949 "500" Type Desk Set
This completely redesigned set remained the standard for decades. It featured an adjustable bell and, beginning in 1954, a choice of colors.

1968 Trimline® Telephone
This set, with "dial" in handset, evolved from years of research. It had a then-new 12 button key pad, for access to advanced services.

1964 Touch-Tone Telephone
Pushbuttons and electronic tones replaced dials and clicks. Calling was speeded and a host of new features became possible.

1959 Princess® Telephone
The desk set received a smart new look—and an illuminated dial. This telephone was widely used as a bedroom extension.

1958 Speakerphone
Hands-free telephoning arrived with the speakerphone, which also permitted conference calls between groups at different locations.

1956 Wall Telephone
The telephone returned to the wall with this companion to the "500." It was popular in kitchens where counter space was at a premium.

1969 Picturephone Set
A technological tour-de-force, this telephone let you see as well as hear. Its successors provide video teleconferencing service.

1974 Design Line Telephones
Telephones became designer accessories in the 1970s as AT&T offered sets to complement a wide range of decor.

1983 Touch-a-Matic® 1600
This all electronic residential "feature phone" stored 15 numbers for one-touch dialing and had a digital display.

1973 Touch-a-Matic® Telephone
The first telephone with a solid state memory, it could store and automatically dial 31 numbers.

1976 Transaction Telephone
This telephone read the magnetic strip on credit cards, introducing automatic verification of credit information from remote computers.

1984 Merlin® System
This digital system brought to small businesses advanced features previously available only in large switchboard-type systems.

1988 System 2000
This is the first system to provide access to 2 telephone lines and an intercom without extensive rewiring or separate control boxes.

1990 1532 Two-Line Remote Answering System
AT&T has been producing answering machines since 1993. This system serves 2 lines at once, and allows remote retrieval of messages from both rotary and Touch-tone phones.

1989 Merlin® Cordless Telephone
This is the first set to offer cordless convenience as a fully-integrated part of a multi-line business system.

1987 5000 Series Cordless Telephones
Continuing innovation at AT&T Bell Laboratories brought advances such as the first cordless telephones with corded sound quality.

As modern material culture has developed, some items, like the telephone, have become more sophisticated, capable of performing increasingly complex functions.

54

Perhaps you take culture for granted, but like air, which you might also take for granted, culture plays a fundamental part in your life. Consider politics. Americans frequently complain about the corruption and ineffectiveness of their politicians, and as a kind of impotent protest, many people often fail to vote. Most of us seem to accept our existing political system with relatively little thought. But imagine how you would respond if the political leadership suddenly declared that you could never vote again and that as an ordinary citizen you could never participate at all in the political process—the case in many nations.

A distinction needs to be made between "culture" and "society." Culture involves the human-made products associated with a group, and **society** consists of the interacting people who share a culture. The two concepts are closely interrelated. A culture cannot exist without a society to implement it, and a society cannot exist unless a culture provides guidelines for its activities. In one sense culture is like a game plan developed by a coach for an athletic team, which represents society. The team needs the game plan to guide the strategy for its upcoming contest. However, without the players to put it into action, the game plan is no more than an idea. Thus people and the groups that they form are components of a society; in order to interact, these individuals and groups require the guidance of their culture. Given the close relationship between the terms "culture" and "society," it is not surprising that they are often used interchangeably, but you must realize that a distinction between the two can be made.

In this chapter we will examine the components of culture, the diversity and unity of culture, and American culture. One additional point: Are you familiar with the following use of "culture"? Someone says, "She's a really cultured person." Or another person contends, "He ain't got no culture." In these instances "culture" means classy, polished, or stylish—in short, a quality of someone a "cut" above the average. We are not concerned with this meaning of "culture." Whether we are classy or not, all of us have culture.

Components of Culture

Since the arrival of modern humanity, culture has developed very rapidly. About 100,000 years ago, the ancestors of modern human beings started wearing clothes, constructing shelters, and learning to survive in climates ranging from the tropical to the subarctic. The domestication of animals and the cultivation of crop plants began about 10,000 years ago, producing a profound effect on human life. People no longer needed to move constantly from place to place in search of big game. With improved production of crops and domestic animals, the environment could support increasingly larger populations, permitting a growing number of people to move into specialized occupations. Towns and cities started to develop. About 200 years ago, the Industrial Revolution began, eventually producing worldwide communication systems, effective mass transportation, and a vast assortment of technological advances.

Throughout human history technological changes have affected the content of culture. That trend continues in modern times as we see in the present section. We examine the following components of culture: beliefs, technology, values, norms, and language.

BELIEFS

A **belief** is a statement about reality that people accept as true. Beliefs are based on observation, logic, tradition, other people's opinions, or faith. Thus we can speak about scientific and nonscientific beliefs.

People who share a culture do not necessarily share beliefs. When asked in a national survey to express their view about the creation of human beings, 47 percent of adult Americans supported the biblical position that God created humanity in the present form within the last 10,000 years, 9 percent indicated that the process had developed over millions of years without God's intervention, 40 percent professed that human evolution occurred over millions of years with God guiding the process, and 4 percent had another or no clear opinion. As Table 3.1 indicates, women, people over 50, individuals who had not graduated from high school, conservatives, respondents with income under $20,000 a year, and Protestant Evangelists were more likely than members of other social categories to believe that God created humanity in the present form within the past 10,000 years (Gallup and Newport 1991, 34).

Beliefs can produce deadly effects. For nineteenth-century Americans, the doctrine of Manifest Destiny reflected the belief that the Europeans and their descendants were the properly dominant race in North America; thus they were supposed to be the guardians of American Indians, the land, and other natural resources. This popular nineteenth-century belief was a rationalization for the settlers' violent takeover of Native-American lands and for a pattern of violating treaties once they were signed.

Beliefs supply the framework for people's perceptions. Many Americans believe that people are

Table 3.1 How Was Humanity Created?

THE CREATION PROCESS			
By God in last 10,000 years	*Evolved without God*	*Evolved with God*	*No opinion*
47%	9%	40%	4%

By God in last 10,000 years
SEX
Female	53%
Male	39
EDUCATION
College graduates	25
College not completed	40
High-school graduates	52
Not high-school graduates	65
IDEOLOGY
Liberals	39
Moderates	33
Conservatives	51
INCOME
$50,000 and over	29
$30,000–49,999	44
$20,000–29,999	46
Under $20,000	59
RELIGION
Protestant	53
Protestant Evangelist	70
Catholic	42
None	10

Source: Gallup Poll Monthly. (*November* 1991), *p.* 34.

People who are female, have not graduated from high school, are conservative, have income under $20,000 a year, and are Protestant Evangelists are more likely than members of other social categories to believe that God created humanity in the past 10,000 years.

56

generally untrustworthy, that only locks, bolts, and bars can protect personal property. Thus it surprised a newsman accompanying President Richard Nixon's tour to China in 1972 to find that his camera was still sitting on the bus seat where he had forgotten it. Americans abroad can also encounter foreigners' beliefs about the United States. To the poor people of many African, Asian, and Latin American countries, all people from the United States seem fabulously wealthy. These poor would find it difficult to believe that poverty, malnutrition, and hunger exist in the United States.

Furthermore the widespread exposure of American movies and television has contributed to a glamorous, violent image of the country. Todd Gitlin, a sociologist, noted that films like *Die Hard*, *Lethal Weapon*, *Terminator*, and their respective sequels are huge moneymakers abroad, solidifying American movies' reputation "for speed, savagery [and] ethical emptiness." Realizing that international viewers are developing an addiction to the violence, movie makers seek "new ways to savage and kill, . . . with [d]irectors draw[ing] pride from their ability to surpass the previous round of abominations" (Gitlin 1992, 30). An emphasis on competition, in short, appears to contribute to the growth of American films' violent image.

TECHNOLOGY

Technology is any repeated operation that people use to manipulate the environment to achieve some practical goals. Technology ranges in complexity from such simple activities as the construction of crude digging tools or weapons to the production of the most sophisticated, modern computers. Perhaps it is the technology of modern cultures that most dramatically sets them off from earlier cultures. Since Mark Twain wrote *A Connecticut Yankee in King Arthur's Court* in 1889, many writers and filmmakers have dramatized the tremendous power and influence that time travelers could exercise if they could move backward to ancient cultures. One can argue that such a "step backward in time" was in effect made by European explorers and settlers when they used advanced weaponry, communication forms, and means of transportation to subdue or annihilate the native inhabitants of five continents.

Technology profoundly affects people's everyday lives in various ways, such as compelling the development of new occupations. A hundred years ago none of the following occupations existed: radiologist, astronaut, computer programmer, professional race-car driver, or deep-sea diver. These occupations could not exist because the respective technologies that make them possible had not yet been invented. Technology can also influence existing occupations. Today a doctor's job is often simplified by modern equipment. Does the leg have a fracture or the brain contain a tumor? X-rays and brain scans can provide definitive answers that could not be obtained in the past.

To many observers the robotics industry seemed to represent the epitome of technological development. Encouraged by novels like Isaac Asimov's I, *Robot* and *The Robots of Dawn*, researchers and business people were fired by the belief that it would be only a few years "before scientists successfully married computer brains to powerful, mobile machinery that would do mankind's bidding" (Feder 1992, D1). This was an overly optimistic response.

As robots began pouring into the marketplace in the early 1980s, many proved unreliable as manufacturers often spent too little to produce effective equipment. In other instances robots did not integrate well with human beings and other machinery. For instance, the fast-food industry was long felt to be an obvious area for robotics, but the machines have been unable to deal with sudden surges in customers, and with the intricacies of serving human beings. While robots can spot-weld fenders, they have trouble holding the mayo while adding extra pickles.

Robots currently seem most effective performing tasks too dangerous or boring for human beings. In nuclear-power plants, they prove useful for tank cleaning, looking inside pipes, and retrieving loose parts. Another service area for robotics seems to be hospitals. Transitions Research Corporation's Helpmate robot can carry patients' food trays from the third-floor dietary department to the twelfth-floor nursing unit, crossing several corridors and operating an elevator without human assistance, and then give directions to a nurse or attendant: "Please unload compartment one. Press the green button."

But, in addition, robots have capabilities to perform some tasks better than people. Integrated

Surgical Systems, Inc., has been seeking clearance from the Food and Drug Administration to start human trials using robots to remove hip bones for replacement by titanium implants. Programmed with the dimensions and exact location for the implant and operating under a doctor's instantaneous control, the robot can make cuts so precise that the gaps between the replacement and the remaining bone are about 50 microns—about half the width of a human hair and one-twentieth the gap surgeons normally produce (Feder 1992). Some other countries already use computers for delicate surgery. At the University of Grenoble in France, for instance, surgeons often perform computer-assisted brain surgery and recently started to explore the possibility of robotic involvement in spinal operations. At the Hospital for Sick Children in Toronto, James M. Drake, a neurosurgeon, receives help from industrial robots to remove brain tumors from gravely ill children (Corcoran 1992).

Like many products of modern technology, the famed Swiss Army Knife, which was first delivered to the Swiss Army in 1891, has become more intricate over time. This recent version, called "Super Timer," comes with twenty-two miniature implements, including a Swiss quartz watch, and sells for $140.

NORMS

For a moment imagine that you are small enough to fit into an anthill or a beehive. Standing out of the flow of traffic, you would observe thousands of insects unerringly moving about their tasks, each a tiny cog in a complicated organizational structure. Such behavior is a magnificent testimony to the finely tuned genetic programming of these little organisms. Human beings, however, function very differently from ants and bees. People are primarily directed or controlled not by instinctive genetic guidelines but by learned norms.

A **norm** is a standard of desirable behavior. Norms are the rules people are expected to follow in their relations with each other. Norms not only provide guidelines dictating appropriate behavior in a given situation but also supply people with expectations of how others will respond to their actions. Norms often vary widely from society to society. In many respects English and American cultures are similar, and yet numerous normative differences exist—for example, the English drive on the left-hand side of the street, and they always hold their forks in the left hand while eating. Norms also change over time. In the early twentieth century, bathing suits were ridiculously modest by current standards. Skimpy modern models would have been viewed with horror.

Norms are often situational—that is, they are associated with certain contexts and not with others. It is considered appropriate to express problems and fears to therapists but not to bank tellers, whose embarrassment or irritation would indicate that they expect only "small talk" when transacting bank business. During a football game, the players are supposed to block and tackle each other, but they are penalized for continuing such action after the whistle has been blown to stop play. In some situations people find it difficult to forsake previously relevant norms after they have become inappropriate or even criminal. After returning to the United States, some Vietnam veterans found it difficult or impossible to forsake their violent lifestyles and either got into trouble with the law or signed on as mercenaries in foreign wars. In all societies most people follow important norms, but individuals violate some of them. Chapter 7, "Deviance," explores norm-violating behavior.

Sociologists make some basic distinctions about norms. The following classifications were developed to demonstrate specific qualities of norms and represent simplifications of reality. Keep in mind that actual norms often fail to fit neatly into one category or the other.

58

Folkways and mores. **Folkways** are norms that specify the way things are customarily done; they are concerned with standards of behavior that are socially approved but not considered morally significant. Violation of folkways seldom leads to punishment. Folkways leave room for eccentric or harmless behavior. Picking one's nose in public, littering, or arguing loudly with one's spouse at a party would be considered violations of folkways.

Violations of mores are much more serious. Child abuse, forcible rape, torture, murder, and cannibalism are prominent examples of violations of mores. **Mores** (pronounced "morays") are norms people consider vital; they are embedded in what members of a society believe to be morality. Unlike folkways, mores involve clear-cut distinctions between right and wrong. Punishment for the violation of mores will range from avoidance and ridicule to imprisonment and death.

Many mores and some folkways are supported by **laws,** which are norms recorded by political authorities and maintained by police or other enforcement officials. Often mores violations are crimes, and American society has a large body of criminal law, which is discussed in Chapter 7, "Deviance." Examples of folkways transgressions for which laws exist include parking violations, littering, and public drunkenness.

Explicit and implicit norms. Within a culture some norms are **explicit,** out in the open. Explicit norms are learned formally. For example, parents tell their children, "Don't speak with your mouth full, Sally" or "Stop that, Frank! Don't hit your sister." Because explicit norms are formally learned, almost everyone can explain them. Other norms are **implicit,** not normally discussed and not easily stated. Often these norms are most easily identified when violated. In many American households, parents enforce an implicit norm about nudity. The family members are not supposed to see each other naked. In most families this norm is probably never stated, but the children learn it when mom or dad hurriedly turns around or closes the bedroom door so as not to be seen unclothed.

Ideal norms and real norms. **Ideal norms** are standards requiring strict obedience to the guidelines provided. In everyday life, however, some "slippage" occurs because the standards are often too lofty, impractical, or demanding. As a result **real norms** emerge: the adjustment of standards to the practical conditions of living. Small deviations from norms are expected, even tolerated, but limits to the deviations are set.

Public figures often endorse ideal norms but then fail to live up to them. During his 1988 campaign for the presidency, George Bush described himself as an environmentalist (Vig 1990, 33), but his most notable environmental activity was providing various corporations opportunities to evade existing environmental-protection standards. Broken campaign promises, a frequent reality of modern American politics, often result from politicians' failure to achieve their previous claims about ideal norms as they settle for real norms that personally prove more beneficial.

When people find it unpleasant or awkward to acknowledge that their responses fall short of an ideal norm, they are likely to offer rationalizations to explain why they are not responsible for the violation of the ideal norm. The Hindu religion prohibits Indian farmers from killing cattle. Through the centuries farmers have developed means of avoiding direct slaughter. For example, to "kill" unwanted calves, owners place a triangular wooden yoke around the calves' necks so that when they try to nurse they jab the cow's udder and get kicked to death. Farmers then rationalize that the cows, not they, were responsible for the calves' deaths (Harris 1974, 28).

VALUES

Fierceness is a very important value to the Yanomamö of the South American jungle. When a Yanomamö wife has been caught in an affair with another man, a club fight, which emphasizes the value of fierceness, is arranged. In these duels one man holds a ten-foot club, steadies himself by leaning on the club, and then exposes his head for a blow from the opponents's club. After that the positions are reversed. The majority of duels end up as free-for-alls, with everyone clubbing everyone else. Fatalities sometimes result but not very often because the headmen of the different groups stand by with bows drawn ready to kill anyone who delivers an intentionally lethal blow. The scalps of the older men often contain as many as a dozen enormous, angry scars, which are fully displayed on the possessors' proudly shaved heads (Chagnon 1977). Around the planet Americans are considered aggressive and prone to violence. Yet they are amateurs compared to the Yanomamö, who strongly emphasize the values of fierceness and violence.

As this illustration suggests, values vary from one culture to another, but all cultures have them. A **value** is a general conviction about what is good or bad, right or wrong, appropriate or inappropriate. Values are abstract, stating broad behavioral preferences, while norms guide behavior in specific situations. Americans tend to embrace the value of patriotism. Norms associated with patriotism specify that adult citizens should vote and that they should stand up, face the flag, and sing when the national anthem is played in public. Values concern what people regard as good or desirable, while beliefs focus on what they consider true and factual. The members of a family or community attend regular religious services and donate heavily to their religious organization; a prominent value in their lives is the importance of religion. A significant belief for these same people is the existence of God.

Values are important because they influence the content of norms. If a culture such as the Yanomamö values fierceness and violence, its norms will provide such opportunities as club fights, that permit members to demonstrate fierceness and engage in violence.

While values influence the development of norms, the "fit" between the two is not always a neat, one-to-one relationship. By definition, values are abstract and norms are specific. Thus it is not surprising that different norms can be derived from a given value. The American emphasis on competition is a case in point. Evidence suggests that some top college football programs have been so determined to develop winning teams that they have made under-the-table payments to

Among the Yanomamö, for whom fierceness is an important value, disputes about extramarital affairs are often settled with fights using these long clubs.

60

players; other programs have not resorted to this illegal (norm-violating) practice. Allen L. Sack, a sociologist, surveyed 1,182 active or retired National Football League players, finding that about a third (32 percent) received illegal payments during their college years. These under-the-table payments were most prominent in the Sunbelt, with factors encouraging illegal payments to players including intense southern interest in football, the willingness of wealthy boosters to provide illegal payments, and vast sums of money from televised games funds for these payments to university programs (Sack 1991).

LANGUAGE

Alice and Bill are an elderly couple with an elderly dog. They tell people that their dog is just like a member of the family. "He listens to everything I say," Bill reports, "and I can tell by the look in his eye if he agrees with me." Alice concurs. "Ralph is nothing short of brilliant," she explains. "He must understand what I say, because he seems to know what I plan to do almost before I've made the decision myself." Undoubtedly Ralph is very sensitive to his owners' wishes and plans, but is he actually using language?

Ralph is responding to signs. A **sign** is an object or event that stands for something else. Many signs provide a fixed interpretation. The smell of smoke suggests that a fire is in the vicinity, the taste of a particular beverage indicates that it is coffee. Ralph's capacity to interpret signs is aided by hearing and a sense of smell that are well-developed. Thus no matter how quietly Bill or Alice opens the refrigerator door, Ralph will dash to the kitchen, hoping for a snack.

Although Ralph can detect certain signs, he has a limited capacity to understand symbols. A **symbol** is a sign with a meaning that is not fixed by the nature of the item to which it is attached but by the agreement of the people who use it to communicate. In American culture a wave of the hand stands for "hello" or "good-bye," a whistle blown by a referee means "to stop," and the color black represents mourning.

A **language** is a system of symbolic communication that uses words, which are sound patterns that have standardized meanings. Like all symbols, words for items are not choices fixed by the

nature of the items themselves. The four-legged piece of furniture on which a teacher writes papers and letters is called a "desk," but no inherent quality of the object requires it to be so labeled. The desk could just as easily be called a "glump." In this case the word is "desk" because the members of English-speaking cultures recognize and accept the word to represent the particular object. Language has two prominent traits as a communications system. First, there is its symbolic quality, which we have just discussed. Second, the symbols of language are combined in ways prescribed by a set of norms called "grammar"—for instance, the grammatical norm of word order. Thus "Marilyn smiled at Frank" has a different meaning from "Frank smiled at Marilyn."

We have considered some of the qualities of language. How should we describe its purpose?

The Social Construction of Reality

Basically language supplies meaning to cultures in a couple of ways. First, language can be used to accumulate human experience. When animals die, everything they have learned from experience perishes with them. But language lets human beings develop a history. Through written or oral accounts, people can gain access to the knowledge and experience of those who have come before them. No matter how intelligent human beings might be, without language each generation would possess no greater advantage over its ancestors than do geese, rabbits, or donkeys over their predecessors.

Second, language organizes our perception of the world. We can use language to refer to the past ("I went yesterday"), the present ("I am going now"), or the future ("I will go next week"). Language permits us to speak about single cases ("It was hot yesterday") or make general statements ("Summers are always hot around here"). Without language we would not be able to interpret the evidence of our own senses, but with language we are even capable of describing subtle thoughts and perceptions.

The last point raises an interesting question. Do the people of all cultures see the world the same way, or do their respective languages organize their perceptions in different ways? The

linguistic-relativity hypothesis, also referred to as the Sapir-Whorf hypothesis, contends that the unique grammatical forms and vocabulary of a language actually shape the thoughts and perceptions of its users (Sapir 1921; Sapir 1929; Whorf 1956). According to this concept, language is much more than just another element of culture.

The issue of time provides an example. Americans and other Westerners tend to think of time as something that can be broken into segments—years, days, hours, minutes, and seconds—and used for their own purposes. "Time is money," says a businessperson in the typical American tradition. Someone asks a friend to stay and talk. "Can't," the other replies. "I haven't got the time." To Americans time is scarce, elusive, and therefore precious. In contrast, the Hopi Indians have no words for "time," "late," "day," "hour," and "minute." They live in the present, emphasizing that all forms of life are working on their own time schedules and that things simply happen when they happen and will take as long as they take (Whorf 1956). Inevitably these different orientations to time have created conflicts between the Hopi and their white neighbors. For instance, Hopi who were expected to show up for appointments at certain hours or to make mortgage payments by specific dates simply did not understand the system of time measurement the whites used and often would not show up at all or would be outrageously late by whites' standards. Table 3.2 shows how a grammatical difference between English and Spanish illustrates the linguistic-relativity hypothesis.

The more involved the members of a culture are with a particular activity or thing, the more detailed their language becomes. Arabs have hundreds of words to describe camels and camel equipment, and in many societies where grazing animals are a prominent feature, there is a variety of terms for different textures of hay. Americans do the same thing with cars, distinguishing a number of types—station wagons, sports cars, compacts, subcompacts, and sedans—as well as companies and finally models produced by a given company: Buick's Riviera, Electra, Lesabre, Regal, Skylark, and other models.

These examples suggest that some relationship exists between language and people's thoughts and perceptions. However, the examples do not necessarily confirm the linguistic-relativity hypothesis, which indicates that language shapes thought and perception. Which is it? Does language shape people's view of reality, or is it really the other way around? The problem is somewhat like the old question: Which came first—the chicken or the egg? Since the formation of new languages cannot be observed, such issues simply cannot be resolved by research. What an assessment of the available facts suggests is that language develops as a means of enabling people to describe and explain their experiences. Then once a particular language has evolved, it shapes the world view of those brought up with its usage.

Table 3.2   The English and Spanish Use of the Pronoun "You": An Illustration of the Linguistic-Relativity Hypothesis

ENGLISH USE OF "YOU"	SPANISH USE OF "YOU"[1]	
	"Tu" (*Informal*)	"Usted" (*Formal*)
For all people, regardless of the type of relationship or age	Family members Friends Children and adolescents God Animals	Individuals with whom formal relations exist (one's doctor, teacher, or plumber)

[1]*Usage varies to some extent from one Spanish-speaking country to another. Furthermore there is a distinct tendency for younger people to use the informal form more readily.*

The use of the two "you" forms in Spanish affects people's perceptions and behavior. Young people know that they are considered adults when strangers begin using the formal form when addressing them. On the other hand, when adults start addressing each other with the familiar form, they have crossed the boundary from acquaintance to friend. The fact that modern English has only the single "you" form means that similar perceptions are not built into the language.

62

Thus moderate support for the linguistic-relativity hypothesis seems justified: Language does appear to influence certain perceptions and thoughts. This relationship is apparent in everyday life. For example, consider the function of a word like "un-American." Such a term establishes a clear boundary, indicating that any outlook or activity not traditionally American is traitorous. In particular, it is "un-American" to be "soft" on "Commies." These terms rigidly outline the idea that Americans are good and that they, the "Commies," are bad. Such uses of the language predispose many Americans to accept indiscriminately negative evaluations of the People's Republic of China, Vietnam, or Cuba and to ignore or at least to tolerate the U.S. government's support of anticommunist dictatorships, the injustices of the U.S. economic system, and the enormous financial emphasis the government places on defense. Furthermore research offers some support for the linguistic-relativity hypothesis; for instance, one study discovered that Chinese-speaking respondents and English-speaking respondents possessed significant, language-related differences in their perceptions and memory (Hoffman, Lau, and Johnson 1986).

Table 3.3 summarizes the components of culture presented in this section.

From the previous discussion, you have learned that all cultures contain the same basic components. In fact, anthropologists have discovered that cultures always have a fairly large number of **cultural universals**—traits believed to exist in all cultures. George Murdock (1965), an anthropologist, listed over sixty cultural universals, including cooking, family, feasting, folklore, funeral rites, gift-giving, greeting forms, housing, incest taboos, laws, medicine, music, sport, toilet-training, and toolmaking.

A major reason that cultural universals develop is the need to resolve the issues that all human beings face in the common effort to survive and, whenever possible, to enjoy life. Thus new members must be reared; guidelines for behavior must be developed; goods and services must be produced and distributed; sick people must receive care; people must be given opportunities to escape the daily "grind."

Often elements of one culture are transmitted to another. The nearby Cross-Cultural Perspective demonstrates the effect that American baseball has had on one of this country's Caribbean neighbors.

Table 3.3   Culture

Component	Brief definition	Examples
1. Belief	1. A statement about reality that people accept as true	1. "The earth is round."
2. Technology	2. Any repeated operations people use to manipulate the environment for practical goals	2. A wooden club or a computer
3. Norm	3. Standard of desirable behavior	
a. Folkways	a. Norms that specify the way things are customarily done	a. Norms about public nose-picking or street littering
b. Mores	b. Norms people consider vital	b. Norms about murder and rape
c. Laws	c. Norms that are officially recorded and supported by political authorities	c. Laws about murder, rape, or street littering
4. Value	4. A general conviction about what is good or bad, right or wrong, appropriate or inappropriate	4. Equality or a sense of racial superiority
5. Language	5. A system of symbolic communication using words, which are sound patterns that have standardized meanings	5. English, Spanish, and Hottentot

CROSS-CULTURAL PERSPECTIVE
Impact of Major-League Baseball on the Dominican Republic

When officials of a multinational corporation enter a third-world nation, their aim often is to obtain raw materials that elsewhere can be developed into commercially profitable products. The principal difference between major-league baseball and other large corporate interests in this regard is that in baseball the products are human beings, not commodities. Consider how this process has unfolded in the Dominican Republic.

The first Dominican major leaguer was Ozzie Virgil in 1955. During the following quarter century, the number of Dominicans in the major leagues grew steadily and included such prize catches as San Francisco's Juan Marichal and the three Alou brothers. By 1980 there were forty-nine Dominican major leaguers, but the number has increased impressively since then. For the 1990 baseball winter meetings, sixty-five Dominicans were protected members of major-league rosters, meaning that the team management considered them core players. In addition, by that time 325 players were in the minor leagues, where future major leaguers are developed.

As increasing numbers of Dominican players have been taken on to major-league rosters, Dominican baseball has been steadily subjected to the negative impact of competition with major-league interests. First, the Dominican leagues switched from summer play, where there was direct competition against the major leagues, to winter. In addition, as the connection to the North American professional leagues became closer, Dominican baseball began to lose its cultural autonomy—its heroes, style, and traditions. Third, as Dominican players attained success in the major leagues, both they and American team officials became consistently more opposed to their playing in the Dominican winter leagues, where modest pay could not remotely compensate for the ever-present possibility of serious injury. Thus most Dominicans could no longer see their baseball heroes play in person.

In the late 1970s, two major-league teams formed their own island-based academies, where players have been signed, fed, clothed, and trained by the organization from the age of 17. With thirteen academies now established, amateur baseball on the island has been greatly weakened. If young players are talented, they are much more likely to seek out academies, and if dismissed from one, they simply move on to another.

Because of the impact of major-league baseball, the Dominican game has been drastically changed. Does evidence suggest that the local people are resisting the cultural invasion? Not really. A principal reason is that a great deal of pride for the Dominican players' accomplishments has developed. Alan Klein noted that on the sports pages of the local newspapers, the emphasis was almost always on Dominican players' achievements, with other aspects of individual contests subfeatured. Thus a typical sports account read this way:

> For Toronto the *Dominican* Tony Fernandez was 1 for 5, his *countryman* George Bell was 2 for 4 . . . The other *Quisqueyena* [expression for Dominican] Manny Lee hit a single in three trips and scored a run, while his *compatriot* Nelson Liriano went 1 for 4. (Klein added emphasis to indicate national pride.)

> (*Klein* 1991, 83)

But while pride in Dominican players' accomplishments overshadowed anger and resentment about major leagues weakening Dominican baseball, Klein found that Dominicans were still emotionally invested in their own baseball tradition. Evidence came from a survey item, where Klein asked 164 Dominicans to indicate whether they would prefer to wear the hat of their favorite major-league team or the hat of their favorite Dominican team. Given the general preference for American products, Klein expected that the dominant choice would be the major-league team, especially ones with Dominican players.

He was wrong. One hundred and twenty-eight (78 percent of his respondents) opted for the Dominican team, giving a clearly nationalistic reason for the response. For instance, one person said, "I am a Dominican.

64

This is my country, so I'll take Licey [a local team]."

Baseball is very important to Dominicans, representing perhaps the only area in which the local people can assert their sense of equality, even superiority to the United States. They might have felt huge anger and resentment that the major-league teams have virtually destroyed their local baseball teams. However, because a sufficient number of their players have been successful at the major-league level, pride in their continuing accomplishments has largely overshadowed those negative emotions.

Source: Alan M. Klein. "Sport and Culture as Contested Terrain: Americanization in the Carribean," Sociology of Sport Journal. vol. 8 (March 1991), pp. 79–85.

We and They: Cultural Diversity and Conflict

While cultural universals do exist, considerable variety occurs in the ways different societies carry out a given universal. For instance, Americans often greet each other informally, while the Baganda of the East African country of Uganda exchange a standardized set of questions and answers.

This section focuses on cultural differences. Within a given culture, groups often make a "we-they" distinction—an emphasis on being culturally separate from and superior to other groups. That same distinction can also occur when the members of different cultures make contact.

DIVERSITY AND CONFLICT WITHIN CULTURES

So far we have discussed culture as if all its elements were shared equally by everyone within the society. This is not always the case. In most societies subcultures exist.

Subcultures and Countercultures

A **subculture** is the culture of a specific segment of people within a society, differing from the dominant culture in some significant respects, such as in certain norms and values or in language. When do sociologists determine that a particular segment of the population possesses its own subculture and when do they decide that people merely have a number of relatively unimportant differences with the dominant culture? Frankly this distinction is hard to make with actual cases. As we saw in the discussion about types of norms, concepts do simplify reality. We can learn from studying concepts but must realize that reality is usually more complicated than they suggest.

In modern, industrialized societies, many subcultures exist. They are based on such factors as occupation, racial and ethnic status, disadvantaged condition (such as being blind, deaf, or mentally handicapped), or deviant or previously deviant lifestyle (such as being a criminal, a drug addict, an alcoholic, a former criminal, a recovering drug addict, or a recovering alcoholic).

Subcultures are usually useful for their members because they provide emotional and social support and help them to cope with their life situations. Typically an American with a strong ethnic affiliation might say, "I was born in this country, raised here, and most of the time I feel like an American. But also, deep down, I'm Greek. And when I'm back in Baltimore having a Greek meal, surrounded by family and friends and speaking Greek, then I'm really home." Or a former drug addict might explain, "After going through this drug program, I'm convinced that the only people who should work with junkies are ex-junkies. After all, we've been through the whole thing ourselves. We know all the tricks, and so they won't pull anything with us."

Subcultures are generally supportive for their members, but let us consider whether they are beneficial for the society as a whole. One might argue that a society that allows subcultures to develop extensively—that, in essence, lets people "do their own thing"—gives those people a chance to feel self-fulfilled. Furthermore members of such tolerated groups probably would be unlikely to rebel because they are permitted to live much as they like. However, sometimes rebellion may seem to be the only way that members of a subculture can accomplish their most cherished goals.

A case in point involves the escalation of the protests of the 1960s. In the early years of the decade, some middle-class white students formed a subculture that worked with Southern blacks to promote the racial integration of buses, restaurants, and other public facilities. Others actively sought nuclear disarmament. The number of students involved in this protest-oriented subculture was fairly small, and their tactics were nonviolent.

By the late 1960s, however, the situation had changed. Small but determined groups of primarily young people, both on college campuses and elsewhere, began to actively oppose dominant American economic and political policies. Members of the different protest groups made speeches, wrote pamphlets and articles, and participated in sit-ins and building take-overs. These and other actions were supposed to dramatize to the American public the need to oppose the Vietnam War, the capitalist economic system, civil-rights injustices, and also local economic and political inequities.

The protest groups in this example were a counterculture. A **counterculture** is a subculture whose members consciously and often proudly reject some of the most important cultural standards of the mainstream society. Countercultures require extensive, sometimes full-time, commitment of members' time and energy and tend to have relatively few members. Under certain conditions, particularly during major protests on college campuses, countercultural groups have received larger, subcultural support.

The countercultural activity of the 1960s created considerable disruption and conflict, and one might argue that it was harmful to the society as a whole. However, as a legacy of those protests, a number of previously unquestioned social, economic, and political conditions have been challenged, and new perspectives and, in some cases, laws have been introduced, promoting equal access to education, jobs, and other prized resources for racial minorities, women, the disabled, and the elderly. In addition, the protests against the Vietnam War contributed to the Nixon administration's withdrawal of troops from Vietnam.

Countercultural members resist the values and beliefs within the dominant culture. However, some forms of resistance are more acceptable than others. In the spring of 1969, a few student protesters at Cornell University emerged from a building occupation carrying guns. There was widespread surprise and shock, and photos like this one were displayed on the front pages of newspapers across the country.

In the 1980s some public figures began sharply criticizing the drug abuse and sexual behavior that sometimes accompanied countercultural activity in the 1960s. It needs to be appreciated that the freedoms advocated by members of the 1960s countercultural groups have not been a pure blessing. Self-indulgent, confused behavior was often intermingled with activities that have produced significant progressive trends (Gitlin and Rosen 1987). Instead of simply condemning or praising this era as a whole, sociologically oriented citizens of the 1990s need to study what happened and assess the distinct effects of that era on the present culture.

A LOOK AT OTHER CULTURES

Americans are often surprised and sometimes confused when they are introduced to some common practices of other cultures. In a number of societies, children may watch their parents engage in acts of sexual intercourse. In one culture all males must perform explicit homosexual acts before adopting heterosexual roles in adulthood. In another society all males at puberty go through

66

a ritual in which the penis is cut to the urethra and sliced the entire length of the organ. Are these people "crazy"? No, they simply have cultural patterns that differ from those of Americans.

Observing such practices, Americans might experience **culture shock,** the psychological and social maladjustment many people suffer when they visit or live in another society. Foreign students in the United States often find American customs are unsettling. At Southern Connecticut State University, Rigoberto Vernon explained that "the people are not so open here as in Panama. There the people welcome you into their homes easily. Here you have to call ahead." JingJing Hsee, a graduate student from the People's Republic of China, expressed a related complaint. "When I was first in New England, I discovered a coldness. The general feeling was not very welcoming. One thing, I never know when people say hello. Sometimes they just pass you by" (Cahow 1992, 7).

When people of one culture assess the standards and practices in another, two distinct possibilities exist. One alternative is that people view the customs of the other culture as inferior; the other prominent possibility is that they simply consider them different. Let us examine both possibilities.

Ethnocentrism

Ethnocentrism is the automatic tendency to evaluate other cultures by the standards of one's own, ultimately finding them inferior. Ethnocentrism is often innocently performed. Traveling abroad, Americans and other Westerners can readily fail to consider that their behavior might prove offensive. For many cultures sensitive topics include taking pictures of police, military installations, or industrial sites; or wearing clothing considered inappropriate—for instance, women with pants or short skirts in Muslim nations (U.S. Department of State 1990, 6). In addition, observing members in developing nations, some Americans are likely to condemn their residents for failing to emphasize "getting ahead"—working long hours every week day in a competitive context to earn large amounts of money permitting an affluent lifestyle.

Many people spend their entire lives without ever leaving their own culture. It is hardly surprising that such people tend to view their particular cultural standards as the only acceptable way to live. Consider Laura Bohannon's experience. Bohannon (1975), an anthropologist, attempted to tell the story of Shakespeare's *Hamlet* to a group of old men of the Tiv tribe in Nigeria. It was her chance, she felt, to make *Hamlet* "universally intelligible." However, she failed because the story aroused the old men's ethnocentrism, and they constantly interrupted Bohannon to emphasize that the cultural practices she was describing were unacceptable. For instance:

> The elders could not understand why Hamlet was upset when his mother remarried quickly. After all, if she had not done so, there would have been no man to hoe the land.
>
> The old men could not accept the claim that a ghost appeared before Hamlet and spoke to him. They explained to Bohannon that no such things as ghosts exist. It was an omen, but omens, the men contended, cannot talk.
>
> Furthermore it was not appropriate for Hamlet to avenge his father's death. Since the killer was a generation older than he, the task should have been performed by an older man.

Like the members of many other cultures, the Tiv elders were ethnocentric because they had been immersed in their own cultural tradition from infancy, with little exposure to any other.

An additional factor helps explain the occurrence of ethnocentrism: It can be functional for those who practice it. First, ethnocentrism can establish and sustain group loyalties, especially under stressful conditions. Warfare would be a case in point. If soldiers are going to fight well, they should believe that their cause is just, and ethnocentric slogans and inspirationally titled policies promote such a belief. For instance, World War I was sold as "the war to end all wars" and "the war to make the world safe for democracy." In World War II, Americans and their allies believed that they were fighting for the "Four Freedoms"— freedom of speech and expression, freedom of worship, freedom from want, and freedom from fear. The Four Freedoms slogan was first presented to Americans by President Franklin Roosevelt in the course of his message to Congress in January 1941, shortly after the United States entered the war. During the Korean War, ethnocentric passions centered on "stopping the spread of the Red menace," and the policy designed to accomplish this task was called "containment." In the Vietnam War era, the target of the most prominent slogan was not the enemy but antiwar protesters. "America, your country, love it or leave it" was an outright demand that people be ethnocentric.

Ethnocentrism has another function: to help an already dominant group maintain its position of superiority. In many American cities of the 1830s, Protestant groups distributed large amounts of strongly anti-Catholic literature. The most notorious of these publications was Maria Monk's *Awful Disclosures*, an account of atrocities experienced by a young woman in a Catholic convent. The book was eventually exposed as the work of anti-Catholic propagandists; yet it went into twenty printings and sold more than 300,000 copies. Anti-Catholic ethnocentrism contributed to the development of a movement of native-born Protestant Americans who strongly resented the masses of newly arrived Irish immigrants. This anti-Catholic movement developed because the Protestant workers feared competition over jobs with the Irish, because they saw Catholicism as a threat to established values, and because they wished to maintain the northern European homogeneity of the nation's large cities (Shannon 1966, 41–43).

Cultural Relativism

When people are ethnocentric, they view other cultures as inferior. On the other hand, if they practice cultural relativism, they see them as just different. **Cultural relativism** is the principle that a culture can be effectively evaluated only when analyzed by its own standards and not by those of any other culture. A custom is not good or bad or right or wrong, in and of itself. The cultural-relativistic point of view requires that any element of a culture be evaluated in relation to the entire culture. People who adopt this point of view recognize that while the lifestyle in another culture might make no sense at first, a careful study will reveal a distinct, understandable pattern.

The fact that Indian Hindus are often desperately poor and yet refuse to eat beef, while cows wander where they wish, dumbfounds many Americans. Marvin Harris, an anthropologist, noted that during lectures students would often ask for an explanation:

"But what about all those cows the hungry peasants in India refuse to eat?" The picture of a ragged farmer starving to death alongside a big fat cow conveys a reassuring sense of mystery to Western observers. In countless learned and popular allusions, it confirms our deepest conviction about how people with inscrutable Oriental minds ought to act.

(*Harris* 1974, 11)

Harris studied the relationship between cows and the Hindu culture. Indeed he did find out that in the Hindu religion the cow is the symbol of all living creatures and that there is no greater sin than killing one.

Harris also uncovered other important information. He found out that cows generally give about 500 pounds of milk a year—an important, sometimes critical part of the family diet. In addition, the cows' manure is the only fertilizer that poor farmers can afford, and when dried it also serves as a primary cooking fuel. Furthermore the possibility exists that a cow can give birth to a male calf that, when castrated, will develop into an ox, the scarce, highly prized animal used by Indian farmers for dry-field plowing. Certainly Hindus' religion requires them to revere cattle, but a careful analysis of the culture shows that some very practical reasons reinforce their conviction that cattle should not be killed.

Are there situations where social researchers and other outside observers of a culture find that cultural relativism no longer serves as a productive tool for analysis? One possibility is that very difficult economic or political circumstances can undermine cultural standards so that the members of a culture begin thinking and acting in ways that are significantly different from their cultural tradition. For instance, I would argue that severe poverty in Germany following World War I made German citizens responsive to Adolf Hitler's effort to rally citizens in support of an effort to return the country to past prominence and glory. The positive, often fervent response to Hitler included widespread willingness to support or overlook the persecution and eventual murder of millions of European citizens. The willingness to abuse or kill innocent people is not apparent in an analysis of traditional German culture; it seems to have been the result of unusual, culture-disrupting circumstances.

68

But possibly one can venture even further, criticizing or condemning some traditional practices in cultures that are not crumbling. For example, throughout much of Africa and in parts of the Middle East, an estimated 84 million women were circumcised in childhood. Most commonly without anesthesia, the clitoris was partly or completely removed, with little or no precaution against infection. Resulting problems included tears between the wall of the rectum or bladder and the vagina, the development of cysts, scars, and infected abscesses, and the retention of menstrual blood (Jacobson 1992, 86). Women perform these rites, justifying the operations by explaining that they reduce female sexuality, promote cleanliness, prevent rape, or have some religious significance. Reviewing a book which examined this practice, Melvin Konner, an anthropologist, noted that like many anthropologists, the writer was soft on the ritual. He responded:

> These procedures are mutilations. And since they are done to children, they are also child abuse, [with] millions of little girls . . . [being] deprived of the only human organ whose sole function is pleasure, and in the process . . . being subjected to pain, infection, and death. Cultural relativism has limits, and this is one place where we ought to draw the line.

(*Konner* 1990, 6)

American Culture ■

As our focus shifts from the contacts between different cultures to the analysis of American culture, your first reaction might be to suspect that cultural variation and conflict will be much less prominent issues. But do not forget our discussion of counterculture. American culture has always included conflicting elements, and that tendency is especially clear in this era of rapidly changing values.

TRADITIONAL AMERICAN VALUES

Robin Williams, Jr. (1970, 452–500), an American sociologist, has produced a well-known analysis of American values. Williams has described fifteen values, which have been evident in American culture. These values include freedom, achievement and success, progress, equality, democracy, humanitarian goals, and racism and other themes of group superiority.

Some studies suggest that a number of these values are more strongly emphasized in American culture than in most other cultures. For instance, looking at the topic of individual freedom, researchers found that individuals and groups involved in commercial-development projects in cities faced far less government regulation in the United States than in Japan or Italy (Molotch and Vicari 1988). Research supports the conclusion that an emphasis on achievement and success are particularly strong in American culture. In the United States, men in higher occupational positions reported greater self-confidence than other men, while in Poland, where the emphasis on achievement and success is probably weaker, men in higher occupational positions actually expressed lower levels of self-confidence than other men (Slomczynski et al. 1981). In addition, in a study on the ideal qualities respondents associated with the performance of their gender roles, a researcher learned that compared to their counterparts in six European countries, young American women and men were more likely to emphasize assertiveness and ambition as part of the gender-role ideal—qualities that generally are associated with an emphasis on achievement and success (Block 1973).

The last two studies indicate that Americans are unusually emphatic about the individual's role in achievement and success. In *Blaming the Victim*, William Ryan (1976) concluded that Americans are also inclined to focus on the individual's contribution when failure occurs—for example, he or she is poor, does badly in school, has illegitimate children. While sociologists are not suggesting that individuals be freed of all responsibility for their actions, they consistently emphasize the sociological perspective, that is, that social forces—

CHANGING AMERICAN VALUES

During the opening game of the 1992 World Series between the Atlanta Braves and the Toronto Blue Jays, a member of the U.S. Marine color guard accidentally held the Canadian flag upside down. When the third game was played in Toronto, some Canadians reacted good-humoredly but decisively, with signs and shirts clearly sending the message that a country's flag is a patriotic item that must always be treated respectfully.

parents, teachers, friends, available professional help, and various impersonal resources such as books, computers, and other educational aids—play a crucial role in determining who succeeds and who fails.

In a society that emphasizes achievement and success, people are likely to be very competitive. The nearby American Controversy presents two positions about competition and encourages you to think about and evaluate them.

One conclusion is clear about Americans' values—they change over time. To illustrate this reality, we examine a few selected topics.

Americans have become increasingly tolerant of various groups and lifestyles. A national survey indicated that in 1963 if African-Americans moved next door, 45 percent of whites might have moved or definitely would have moved while in 1990 the figure dropped to 5 percent for those two options. In 1963, 78 percent of whites might have moved or definitely would have moved if large numbers of blacks entered their neighborhood while in 1990 the number fell to 26 percent (Gallup and Hugick 1990, 27).

On the issue of whether sex before marriage is wrong or not wrong, the percent declaring it wrong fell from 68 percent in 1969 to 40 percent in 1991. The most significant respondent characteristic seemed to be age, with 23 percent between 18 and 29, 31 percent between 30 and 49, and a whopping 62 percent 50 and older declaring sex before marriage wrong (Hugick and Leonard 1991, 69). Clearly many of the older people had reached adulthood before the so-called "sexual revolution" of the 1960s encouraged a liberalized approach to sexuality.

On a number of issues, Americans take a strong position when they feel threatened. Let's consider two significant topics. Over time support for the death penalty for people convicted of murder has increased. In 1936 the figure was 61 percent, falling to a low of 42 percent in 1966 and then gradually rising to a high of 79 percent in 1988 before dropping slightly to 76 percent in 1991. Over half (51 percent) felt that the death penalty served as a deterrent (Gallup and Newport 1991, 42–43). In an era of rising crime, including murder, capital punishment appears to a majority to be a reasonable response to the threat provided by murderers.

To many Americans environmental destruction poses another significant threat. In 1984 when asked whether protection of the environment should be given priority, even at the risk of curbing economic growth, 61 percent of the sample responded affirmatively. Seven years later the figure had risen to 71 percent (Hueber 1991, 6). Table 3.4 provides further details of these survey items.

AMERICAN CONTROVERSY
Competition in American Society

 Whether it is sports, business, or school, Americans stress the importance of defeating the competition. Their language is filled with expressions that make this point. "In business it's kill-or-be-killed," an urban professional says when returning from work. "Honey," his wife replies, "it's a dog-eat-dog world out there." Talking to his sister on the telephone, Betty's father says: "Yes, Judy, we're so proud of our little girl. Year after year she's at the top of her class!" An emphasis on competition exists in American society, but is it desirable?

Those who strongly emphasize competition are likely to say that an emphasis upon it is "the American way"—separating winners from losers in head-to-head competition. The proponents of competition will often contend that the process is character-building. They will argue that in the course of competition, individuals will be encouraged to do better; as the well-known phrase goes, they will "strive for excellence." Sport, many backers of competi-

tion will argue, is so popular in the United States because it is a theatre in which competition appears in a pure form. Football, in particular, is competition with an especially crude yet deeply appealing style, where magnificent physical specimens use both brawn and brains to try to defeat each other in a nearly no-holds-barred situation of team-to-team combat.

The opponents of an emphasis on competition might accept part of the last point. While they would probably concede the impact of spectator sports in the United States, they would be critical of its impact. There's no need to glorify violent competition, they would argue. With limited emphasis on competition, children can grow up to be intelligent, skilled, and sensitive to the needs of others. The opponents of competition would suggest that when competition is very intense, participants are encouraged to "cut corners" to win. For instance, according to Allen Sack's research, the more popular college football becomes within an athletic conference, the more likely quality

players are illegally paid to join and remain members of a given team.

What do you think? Do you strongly favor one position or the other? Or do you find yourself somewhere in the middle, supporting competition under some circumstances and not others?

Evaluate and discuss the following statement: In many competitive circumstances, it is possible to avoid a focus on competition by, instead, striving to do one's best. While discussing the issue of competition, try to understand more fully the position of those who think differently from you. Attempt to figure out what were the circumstances that led to your respective positions on the issue. One way to analyze the topic would be to reverse positions with someone whose stance is different from your own. See if you can state that individual's outlook convincingly to him or her, and then have that person try to perform the same task.

Source: Allen L. Sack. *"The Underground Economy of College Football,"* Sociology of Sport Journal. *vol.* 8 *(March* 1991), *pp.* 1–15.

• •

Young people's views often change over time. A recent study compared samples of students from Ohio State University drawn in 1958, 1968, and 1988. Of the three sets of students, those from 1958 were the most morally severe while those from 1988 were the least. In particular, the most

recent group was least severe in judgments about selfishness and misrepresentations of truth for financial gain, perhaps reflecting the influence supplied by political and business leaders over the past two decades (Bovasso, Jacobs, and Rettig 1991).

Table 3.4   Selected Illustrations of Americans' Changing Values over Time

WOULD MOVE IF BLACKS MOVED NEXT DOOR		
	1963	1990
Yes, definitely	20%	1%
Yes, might	25	4
No, would not	55	93
No opinion	0	2

WOULD MOVE IF BLACKS ENTERED NEIGHBORHOOD IN GREAT NUMBERS		
	1963	1990
Yes, definitely	49%	8%
Yes, might	29	18
No, would not	22	68
No opinion	0	6

WRONG TO HAVE SEXUAL RELATIONS BEFORE MARRIAGE		
	1969	1991
Wrong	68%	40%
Not wrong	21	54
No opinion	11	6

DIFFERENT AGE GROUPS' RESPONSE TO THIS QUESTION IN 1991		
	18-29 *years*	30-49 *years*	50 & *older*
Wrong	23%	31%	62%
Not wrong	72	64	30
No opinion	5	5	8

FAVORING DEATH PENALTY FOR PEOPLE CONVICTED OF MURDER		
	1936	1966	1991
Yes	61%	42%	76%
No	39	47	18
No opinion	0	11	6

PROTECTION OF THE ENVIRONMENT A PRIORITY, EVEN AT RISK OF CURBING ECONOMIC GROWTH		
	1984	1991
Priority of environmental protection	61%	71%
Priority of economic growth	28	20
No opinion	11	9

Sources: Adapted from Alec Gallup and Frank Newport. "Death Penalty Support Remains Strong," Gallup Poll Monthly. *(June 1991), pp. 40–45; George Gallup, Jr. and Larry Hugick. "Racial Tolerance Grows, Progress on Racial Equality Less Evident,"* Gallup Poll Monthly. *(June 1990), pp. 23–32; Graham Hueber. "Americans Report High Levels of Environmental Concern, Activity,"* Gallup Poll Monthly. *(April 1991), pp. 6–12; Larry Hugick and Jennifer Leonard. "Sex in America,"* Gallup Poll Monthly. *(October 1991), pp. 60–73.*

RESEARCH IN SOCIOLOGY: SECTION I

The Participant-Observation Study of Culture

Participant-observation studies, which we examined in Chapter 2, "Doing Research in Sociology," have represented an effective technique to uncover the subtlety and complexity of individual cultures. Certainly this type of research has produced more accurate information about cultures than the earliest efforts to understand them.

To modern Americans it is clear that to understand cultures one must conduct research—careful research. But 150 years ago, such a conclusion was not obvious. In that era scholars were more inclined to read and reflect and then produce abstract conclusions. It was the era of "armchair anthropology," and one of the best-known scholars of that time was Lewis Henry Morgan. Morgan and other "armchair anthropologists" often provided interesting, logical analyses. However, they were not scientific; little or no supportive research had been done.

Early in the twentieth century, the anthropological approach changed. At this time one of the most renowned participant-observation studies of culture was done by Bronislaw Malinowski in the Trobriand Islands of New Guinea in the South Pacific. At first Malinowski found the research difficult. He had few guidelines on how to conduct this kind of research. Furthermore he was an outsider, he did not speak the language, and there were no other Europeans around. Malinowski wrote, "I had periods of despondency, when I buried myself in the reading of novels, as a man might take to drink in a fit of tropical depression and boredom" (Malinowski 1922, 4). Certainly Malinowski was implying that "armchair" anthropology would have been easier. In the end, however, his persistence paid off. Malinowski developed several procedures for conducting participant-observation research: to have clearly set research goals; to isolate oneself from members of one's own culture by immersing oneself in the local culture; and to develop techniques for obtaining thorough information about the entire culture.

Besides helping to refine the participant-observation technique, Malinowski uncovered some significant information about the Trobriand Island culture. Particularly interesting were his conclusions about magic. Malinowski learned that magic played an important part in the tribespeople's daily lives. They believed that magical rites and spells would insure the success of gardening and fishing throughout the society. This research helped reject what was then a widely held but erroneous view that magic was used only for such personal and vicious purposes as causing harm to enemies.

Sociologists' Use of Participant Observation

Eventually sociologists began to adopt the participant-observation technique. Their use, however, tended to occur in modern cultures, which generally are much more complex and diversified than those studied by anthropologists. As a result sociologists have not studied entire cultures but focused on subcultures. Perhaps the best-known of all such sociological investigations has been William Foote Whyte's *Street*

These two sociologists are conducting participant-observation research in East Harlem, New York City. Sometimes, as in this case, participant observers obtain information from informal interviews, but usually they just accompany their subjects, observing what they say and do.

Corner Society discussed in Chapter 1. Like Malinowski, Whyte had a problem of entry into the community he studied—Cornerville, an Italian-American slum district of Boston. On a friend's advice, he tried going to a bar and buying drinks for a woman; this, he had been told, was an effective way of obtaining a woman's life story. For his effort, however, he almost got himself thrown down a flight of stairs. Finally Whyte met a local young man known as Doc, who became interested in the study and promised to do everything he could to advance the research.

The book that Whyte eventually wrote included some important conclusions about American slum communities. Just as early anthropologists made unsupported generalizations about culture, some social scientists of Whyte's era produced undocumented statements about the culture and structure of slum communities. In particular, they believed that slums were completely disorganized. Whyte's three-year study compelled him to disagree.

Cornerville's problem is not lack of organization but failure of its own social organization to mesh with the structure of the society around it. This accounts for the development of the local political and racket organizations and also for the loyalty people bear toward their . . . [ethnic group] and toward Italy.

(*Whyte* 1955, 273)

Whyte documented this point at length, showing that in spite of their involvement in local organizations, most of the young people he studied failed to succeed in the larger society.

Through the years sociologists have continued to use the participant-observation technique to clarify the workings of subcultures. In the late 1950s, Blanche Geer found that only three days of research during the orientation of freshmen at the

74   University of Kansas gave her and her co-workers new, revealing information about them. Geer wrote:

> Before entering the field, I thought of them as irresponsible children. But as I listened to their voices, learned their language, witnessed gesture and expression, and accumulated the bits of information about them which bring people alive and make their problems real, I achieved a form of empathy with them and became their advocate.

> *(Geer 1964, 341)*

Geer suddenly found herself immersed in her subjects' lives; she obtained information about college student subculture, which she was able to pass on to her readers.

Studying organizational subcultures, participant-observation researchers often find it useful to work with technical specialists whose expertise often supplements their own, leading to innovative ideas and practices. In the 1960s the Norwegian Work Research Institutes developed a collaborative project in which behavioral scientists, ship owners, and unions produced major changes in the architecture of ships and in the social systems involved in ship operation. The innovations developed in this project eventually affected ship architecture and organizational systems throughout the world, producing a much closer working relationship between the engine room and the deck crew; reduced status barriers between officers and seamen; and provided major improvements in accomodations for living and recreation aboard ship.

Could research teams combining participant-observation researchers and problem specialists develop innovative, exciting approaches to environmental protection and reduced racism?

Conclusion

These studies have produced important information about cultures that was not previously known. But are the results of these investigations unquestionably correct? Certainly not! As we saw in Chapter 2, one of the principal difficulties with participant-observation research is the problem of generalizing from a single case. Could Malinowski claim that in all technologically simple societies magic would be used in just the same way that it was in the Trobriand Islands? Could the researchers at the Norwegian Work Research Institutes be confident that the reduced status barriers between officers and seamen produced on one ship would also develop on other ships? In both situations the answer is no. But that does not detract from the significance of these studies. They produced powerful ideas that later researchers could investigate.

Sources: Blanche Geer. "First Days in the Field," In Phillip E. Hammond (ed.), Sociologists at Work. New York: Basic Books, 1964, pp. 322–45; Bronislaw Malinowski. Argonauts of the Western Pacific. London: Routledge and Kegan Paul, 1922; Lewis H. Morgan. Ancient Society. Cambridge, MA: Belknap Press, 1964 (Originally published in 1877); William Foote Whyte. Street Corner Society. Chicago: University of Chicago Press. Revised ed. 1955; William Foote Whyte. "The Social Sciences in the University," American Behavioral Scientist. vol. 34 (May/June 1991), pp. 618–33.

STUDY GUIDE

Learning Objectives

After studying this chapter, you should be able to:

1. Define culture and describe its importance in human life.
2. Define the major components of culture—beliefs, technology, norms, values, and language—and discuss their respective activities.
3. Examine the different types of norms, defining and discussing folkways, mores, and laws; explicit norms and implicit norms; and ideal norms and real norms.
4. Distinguish between sign and symbol, define language, and explain how language supplies meaning to culture.
5. Define and illustrate the linguistic-relativity hypothesis.
6. Define subculture and counterculture, providing examples of each.
7. Distinguish between ethnocentrism and cultural relativism and explain two functions of ethnocentrism.
8. List several traditional American values and summarize research comparing Americans' values with those of individuals in other cultures.
9. Discuss Americans' changing values, indicating why the changes are occurring and what new commitments are emerging.

Summary

1. Culture consists of all the human-made products associated with a society. The products of culture include material products and nonmaterial products.

2. The different components of a culture—beliefs, technology, norms, values, and language—are all products of their respective cultural traditions, and each, in turn, also affects the culture from which it develops.

3. Within cultures and between cultures, distinctive differences often exist, and sometimes these differences produce conflict. In modern societies various subcultures arise based on such factors as occupation, racial and ethnic status, disadvantaged condition, and deviant or previously deviant lifestyle. Some subcultures, namely countercultures, reject many of the standards of the mainstream society. As the members of one culture contact those of another, ethnocentrism frequently develops. Although the members of all cultures are ethnocentric, the practice is most dominant in isolated societies. To offset ethnocentrism, one can use a cultural relativistic approach to viewing other cultures.

4. Sociologists have extensively studied American values. Research suggests that Americans strongly emphasize individual freedom, achievement and success, and focusing on the individual's contribution when failure occurs.

5. Over time Americans' values constantly change. Survey items on diversity and threat serve to illustrate two trends that have been occurring. A study indicated that of three sets of students sampled over time, the most modern group was least severe in judgments about selfishness and misrepresentations of truth for financial gain.

Key Terms

belief   a statement about reality that people accept as true

counterculture   a subculture whose members consciously and often proudly reject some of the most important cultural standards of the mainstream society

cultural relativism   the recognition that a culture should be evaluated by its own standards and not by those of any other culture

cultural universals   traits believed to exist in all cultures

culture   all the human-made products associated with a society

culture shock   the psychological and social maladjustment many people suffer when they visit or live in another culture

ethnocentrism   the automatic tendency to evaluate other cultures by the standards of one's own, ultimately finding them inferior

explicit norm   a standard that is out in the open

folkway   a norm that specifies the way things are customarily done. Folkways are concerned with standards of behavior that are socially approved but not considered morally significant.

ideal norm   a standard requiring strict obedience to the guidelines provided

implicit norm   a standard that normally is not discussed and is not easily stated

language   a system of symbolic communication that uses words, which are sound patterns that have standardized meanings

law   a norm that is recorded by political authorities and supported by police or other enforcement officials

linguistic-relativity hypothesis   the contention that the unique grammatical forms and vocabulary of a language actually shape the thoughts and perceptions of its users

mores   norms people consider vital

norm   a standard of desirable behavior. Norms are the rules people are expected to follow in their relations with each other.

real norm   adjustment of a standard to the practical conditions of living

sign   an object or event that stands for something else

society   the interacting people who share a culture

subculture   the culture of a specific segment of people within a society, differing from the dominant culture in some significant respects

symbol   a sign with a meaning not fixed by the nature of the item to which it is attached but by the agreement of the people who use it to communicate

technology   any repeated operation people use to manipulate the environment to achieve some practical goals

value   a general conviction about what is good or bad, right or wrong, appropriate or inappropriate

Tests

True • False Test

_____   1. Society cannot exist without culture, but culture exists independent of society.

_____   2. People who share a given culture can disagree about some beliefs.

_____   3. In modern societies real norms and ideal norms tend to be identical.

_____   4. Values are important because they influence the content of norms.

_____   5. The smell of smoke signifies the presence of fire; in this case smoke is a sign but not a symbol.

_____   6. Evidence suggests that Americans no longer experience culture shock.

_____   7. Bohannon's experience in trying to bring Shakespeare's _Hamlet_ to the Tiv tribe suggests that this universal story actually eliminated ethnocentrism.

_____ 8. People who take a cultural-relativistic perspective believe that the lifestyles of other cultures have understandable patterns.

_____ 9. A recent study has concluded that the levels of self-confidence expressed by American and Polish men in high-status jobs are strikingly similar.

_____ 10. When modern sociologists have used the participant-observation technique to study cultures, they have tended to focus on subcultures rather than entire cultures.

Multiple-Choice Test

_____ 1. Material culture includes:
   a. beliefs.
   b. physical objects people make and use.
   c. values.
   d. b and c

_____ 2. Which of the following is NOT a component of culture?
   a. language
   b. values
   c. technology
   d. group

_____ 3. Which statement about technology is NOT true?
   a. It has profound effects on people's everyday lives.
   b. It can contribute significantly to the development of new occupations.
   c. It cannot be dysfunctional for specific groups.
   d. It involves manipulation of the environment.

_____ 4. Which of the following is (are) true about folkways?
   a. They specify the way things are customarily done.
   b. They are considered to be morally significant.
   c. Violation always leads to punishment.
   d. All of the above

_____ 5. The idea of adjustment of a standard to practical conditions of living is found in which one of the following concepts?
   a. explicit norm
   b. implicit norm
   c. real norm
   d. ideal norm

_____ 6. Values:
   a. are abstract, stating broad behavioral preferences.
   b. are becoming rare in modern societies.
   c. have little or no relationship with norms.
   d. are a type of material culture.

_____ 7. The linguistic-relativity hypothesis:
   a. does not apply to modern languages.
   b. indicates that some ethnic groups have a greater in-born tendency to use complex language forms than other ethnic groups.
   c. has been used to explain body language but not spoken language.
   d. contends that the unique grammatical forms and vocabulary of a language actually shape the thoughts and perceptions of its users.

78

_____   8. The members of a certain occupational group develop a common set of beliefs, values, and activities that are different in significant respects from those in the general culture. These people share a:
a.   counterculture.
b.   subculture.
c.   cultural-relativistic approach.
d.   ethnocentric outlook.

_____   9. Ethnocentrism can be functional for those who practice it because it:
a.   encourages people to become more tolerant.
b.   helps dominant groups retain positions of superiority.
c.   establishes how much influence different mores maintain.
d.   helps make explicit norms more implicit.

_____   10. According to the discussion in this chapter:
a.   modern Americans' values are remarkably similar to the values of people in other industrialized nations.
b.   traditional values no longer affect modern Americans.
c.   all Americans consider an emphasis on competition highly desirable.
d.   modern Americans seem to feel more threatened by both murderers and environmental destruction than they did about a decade ago.

Essay Test

1.   What is culture? Why does culture have a profound impact on people's lives?
2.   Discuss five cultural components, indicating how each affects social activity.
3.   Define the different types of norms and illustrate each type.
4.   Discuss the linguistic-relativity hypothesis, giving examples that demonstrate its usefulness.
5.   Define the concepts of subculture and counterculture, emphasizing their impact on societies.
6.   Define ethnocentrism and cultural relativism and give examples of each.
7.   How have Americans' values changed over the past twenty years? Discuss reasons for the changes.

Suggested Readings

American Anthropologist. Official journal of the American Anthropological Association published four times a year and containing up-to-date articles and research reports about culture.

Bellah, Robert, N., Richard Madsen, William M. Sullivan, Ann Swidler, and Steven M. Tipton. 1986. *Habits of the Heart: Individualism and Commitment in American Life*. New York: Harper & Row. A provocative study of past and present American values.

Brim, Gilbert. 1992. *Ambition: How We Manage Success and Failure throughout Our Lives*. New York. Basic Books. Reliance on extensive social research to demonstrate how people deal with winning and losing, concluding that happiness has little to do with concrete achievement and success.

Giles, Howard, and W. Peter Robinson (eds.). 1990. *Handbook of Language and Social Psychology*. New York: John Wiley & Sons. Articles examining social-psychological perspectives on language, language in interpersonal settings, verbal and nonverbal communication, and the use of language in applied social-scientific situations.

Guttmann, Allen. 1991. *Women's Sports: A History*. New York: Columbia University Press. A comprehensive historical account of women's sports, divided into two sections—the first providing a detailed coverage of women's sports from ancient to modern times and ranging across the Middle East,

Europe, and North America; and the second analyzing significant changes in the state of women's sports during the 1970s and 1980s.

Harris, Marvin. 1974. *Cows, Pigs, Wars and Witches*. New York: Random House. A captivating series of essays demonstrating how to apply the concept of cultural relativism to a variety of cultural situations where Americans' ethnocentrism is likely to be aroused.

Slater, Philip. 1976. *The Pursuit of Loneliness*. Revised ed. Boston: Beacon Press. A critical examination of American value conflict: the longing for engagement, dependence, and community that is often frustrated by emphasis on individualism and competition. The family, the political structure, and the economy are examined.

Williams, Robin M., Jr. 1970. *American Society: A Sociological Interpretation*. 3rd ed. New York: Random House. A well-known analysis of American culture and society containing a comprehensive classification and examination of American values.

Additional Assignments

1. Select some aspect of federal-government activity, such as military spending, foreign aid, relations with Russia, welfare programming, or civil rights. Read the editorial pages of a major daily newspaper for two or three weeks and then list the expressed values you find related to your topic. Can you conclude that there is a consistent set of values presented in the editorials?

2. Choose a holiday celebrated in American culture, such as Halloween, Easter, Passover, Christmas, Thanksgiving, or the Fourth of July. List the norms frequently associated with celebrating the holiday. Do the "norms of celebration" suggest any value conflicts? Find information in the library about the origins of the holiday. Which value(s) seem(s) to have inspired its development?

Answers to Objective Test Questions

True • False Test

1. f	6. f
2. t	7. f
3. f	8. t
4. t	9. f
5. t	10. t

Multiple-Choice Test

1. b	6. a
2. d	7. d
3. c	8. b
4. a	9. b
5. c	10. d

Groups

4

In early June of 1991, it appeared certain that in order to eliminate a $460 million budget deficit before the end of the fiscal year, the governor of Massachusetts would close down the state, putting government employees on furlough. Then something unexpected happened.

Kathleen Betts, a part-time employee of the state's Department of Public Welfare, indicated that after studying a new federal regulatory document, she was convinced that the state could qualify for additional federal Medicaid reimbursements to cover poor people's medical bills. Thanks to Betts, Massachusetts officials made their case successfully to federal government personnel. She explained, "The Feds went down kicking and screaming on this one, but this issue is of great importance to me" (Tabor 1991, 1).

It was also very important to state workers, who, according to Betts, "say to me, 'Thank you, good work, now we don't have to take our furlough'" (Tabor 1991, 10).

The governor, who during his campaign had vowed to cut state government and had referred to state employees as "walruses," now found that one of those "walruses" had helped him immensely. Instead of a huge budget deficit, he had a $29 million surplus, making it unnecessary either to make unpopular spending cuts or break his campaign vow not to raise taxes. Gratefully the governor asked the legislature to allot a $10,000 reward for Betts.

This incident demonstrates how an obscure member of one group—the Massachusetts Department of Public Welfare—significantly affected a very large group—in this instance the entire Massachusetts state government. While our everyday group activities seldom produce such spectacular results, our actions as group members invariably affect other people.

A **group** consists of two or more interacting people who share certain expectations and goals. When people share group membership, there is a feeling of unity, a set of common goals, a number of collective norms, and a direct or indirect communication among the members based on their common rights and obligations.

Everyone participates in groups. Families and school classes are groups. So are army units, baseball teams, corporate boards of directors, debating organizations, and exotic dance troops. It would be easy to move through the alphabet and provide a long list of groups to which people belong.

We can distinguish groups from two closely related clusters of people—aggregates and categories. An **aggregate** consists of two or more people who share physical space but lack the interaction of group members. Aggregates can sometimes become groups. For example, a number of people might be waiting for a bus. Since they are not interacting, they do not consititute a group. However, a group might form if an approaching person fainted and several individuals rushed forward to provide assistance. A **social category** consists of a number of people who have one or more social characteristics in common, such as age, sex, marital status, income, or race. Like members of an aggregate, people belonging to a social category do not invariably interact with one another. Sometimes, however, they have common values, interests, or grievances that can provide a foundation for the development of such groups as women's rights organizations, taxpayers' associations, and ethnic support groups.

Ever since you were born, you have been involved in group activity. Most likely this awareness started in the family, where even in infancy you began to have some sense of how you would fit in. You probably learned what behavior would please a parent or older sibling and what behavior would displease such people. Very quickly others' body language and words made it clear when you could get away with imposing your own will in a situation involving family or peers. As you have grown older, you have extended your range of group involvement. It should be easy to name a number of groups to which you belong—for instance, your family, a group of close friends, the classroom portion of this introductory sociology course, some extracurricular club or team, and an organization for which you work. It is also likely that within a year or two years, some of your group affiliations will change, and since all people are strongly influenced by the groups to which they belong, you also will change.

The group is the most basic unit of sociological analysis. In this chapter we first analyze several important types of groups. Then we look briefly at institutions and societies, which are large structures containing numerous groups. The chapter concludes with an assessment of some of the prominent problems facing Americans in everyday group activity.

Types of Groups

The group is one of the most significant concepts in sociology, and sociologists have designated many varieties. Primary and secondary groups, in-versus out-groups, membership and reference groups, and formal organizations and bureaucracies are among the most prominent types. The first three types of groups involve the **micro-order**—the structure and activity of small groups.

PRIMARY AND SECONDARY GROUPS

The terms primary group and secondary group are not widely known in U.S. society, but we are all aware of their significance in the everyday social world. For instance, a woman comes home from work and says to her husband, "It was awful, Ted. The boss called me into his office and just spilled his guts—all the problems he's having with his wife and children. Then he started to cry. I was so embarrassed." She pauses to draw a deep breath. "This was a man I've been on formal terms with for five years. The most intimate thing I knew about him was that he'd get really excited over last year's marketing reports. And now this. . . ." Clearly the boss had violated a standard secondary-group norm, requiring group members to avoid in-depth discussion of personal feelings and problems.

As members of both primary and secondary groups, we all learn what is appropriate behavior in each group setting. Generally speaking, primary group behavior is more personal and less specialized than secondary group behavior. Let's examine both types.

Primary Groups

A **primary group** is a group in which relationships are stable over long periods of time, members are able to expose many facets of their personality, and a strong sense of affection and identity (a "we feeling") develops (Cooley 1962, 23). Primary groups are small, permitting face-to-face contact. The family is the most important primary group. Other primary groups to which many Americans belong include peer groups, neighborhood circles, social clubs, and informal groups within complex organizations, such as cliques within factories or offices. Research and analysis of primary groups have extended from early in the twentieth century to recent years (Scott and Scott 1981).

Primary-Group Norms Primary-group norms are sometimes consistent with the standards that exist elsewhere in society and sometimes are not. Consider the issue of disciplining children within the family. In preindustrial societies most family norms were widely shared. Modern societies are less consistent in this respect. Many modern parents are permissive, putting few limitations on their children's behavior and seldom punishing them when they break existing family rules. Children whose families have lenient primary-group norms are likely to have a difficult and confusing time if they encounter teachers who set exacting limits on their behavior.

Within a given type of primary group, members' relationships can vary distinctly. A study of families found that in father-child dyads

84 (two-person groups), interaction patterns involving such issues as vocal exchange and child compliance were similar to the patterns involving both parents and the child, but the patterns created in mother-child dyads were different from the other two group situations. The reseachers suspected that since mothers spend more time with their children, they are able to develop unique relational patterns that do not appear in other social contexts (Liddell, Henzi, and Drew 1987).

Since primary groups involve extensive, intimate relations, their members have ample opportunity to observe each other and assess the group's norms. "You know, Mommy," a little girl says. "Every time I talk about the money for dancing lessons, Daddy starts wrinkling his nose and sniffing. Then he hardly talks to me for the next couple of hours." With no more than a facial expression or a few words, primary-group members can let each other know whether their behavior is desirable or undesirable. Frequently people in these groups conform to each other's expectations because they value their membership and do not want to risk altering its quality.

Primary groups, most notably families, are critical settings for people's development and sense of well-being. When their activity is cooperative, individuals benefit greatly, but, on the other hand, if conflict within them is frequent, then their members can be adversely affected. For instance, as we see in Chapter 6, "Socialization," if parents neglect or abuse their children, the long-term effects frequently are extensive.

Solidarity and Primary-Group Membership As people work together, a sense of primary-group membership can emerge. A study of a seventy-member planning department in an eastern U.S. city indicated that it had distinct overtones of a family. Members often referred to the unit as a "family" and engaged in extensive activities with colleagues, eating with each other, celebrating birthdays and other events together, dating one another, organizing athletic teams, and providing mutual support in a variety of ways. The caring atmosphere of this "family" provided staff members a variety of opportunities to act aggressively with one another, including their superiors, with an unusually limited concern about dangerous consequences and the distinct hope for creative

In military units, which are secondary groups, strong primary groups are likely to develop because of the members' critical dependence on each other. In this photo taken during the Vietnam War, soldiers are carrying a wounded buddy, who was shot in the leg by a sniper.

solutions. The primary-group quality of the planning department declined when two events occurred—rivalry for promotions increased, and the unit's director, who was the organization's father figure, retired (Baum 1991).

Primary groups also emerge in the course of warfare. Most of us probably have seen the vintage World War II films that portray the fighting men as motivated primarily by patriotism and a fervent belief in "the American way." In contrast, research has shown that during war American soldiers are primarily motivated by loyalty to their buddies. For instance, a soldier wounded while fighting in Sicily commented:

> You know the men in your outfit. You have to be loyal to them. . . . They depend on each other— wouldn't do anything to let the rest of them down. They'd rather be killed than do that. They begin to think the world of each other. It's the main thing that keeps a guy from going haywire.

> (*Stouffer et al.* 1949, 136)

Captain John Early, a veteran of Vietnam and a former mercenary, called the association between men in combat "a love relationship." He emphasized the importance of this relationship among professional soldiers. "And you'll find that people who pursue combat . . . are there because they're friends, the same people show up in . . . wars time and again" (Quoted in Dyer 1985, 104).

In secondary groups, to which we now turn, such strong personal commitments are less common.

Secondary Groups

A **secondary group** is a group of people who cooperate with each other for distinct, practical reasons and generally maintain few if any strong emotional ties within the group. Face-to-face contact between secondary-group members is normally limited, with the individuals relating to each other exclusively on the basis of specific roles they are playing—secretary and boss, student and teacher, or senator and constituents. However, primary relations sometimes arise within secondary groups. The members of a college class or of a work team are initially secondary-group members, but,

in the course of their activity together, they may develop genuine friendships.

Analyzing the distinction between primary and secondary groups, some students become fixated on the fact that secondary groups normally lack the emotional intensity of primary groups. Certainly this is true, but it is *not* the only feature of a secondary group. Secondary groups develop so that people can work together to achieve distinct, practical goals. Don't forget this important point as we examine the significance of emotion within secondary groups.

In a secondary group, the strong emotions that normally accompany primary-group relations can impede effective decision making. For example, presidents and their advisers have sometimes made very poor decisions on crucial issues because of the emphasis on cohesiveness and unanimity (primary-group feelings) that have crept into their secondary group. In 1961 John Kennedy had just been elected president, and his immediate advisers were convinced that with Kennedy leading the country "the world was plastic and the future unlimited" (Janis 1972, 36). They believed, in short, that with Kennedy in command anything could be accomplished. There was a powerful sense of united purpose, a "we feeling" shared by the circle of advisers around the president. Some of these advisers had personal misgivings about the administration's plan to overthrow the Fidel Castro regime in Cuba. Like Kennedy these advisers feared having a communist government so close to their own shores, but they questioned whether the plan to invade Cuba would work. However, because of the strong "we feeling" that filled this secondary group, their misgivings were mildly expressed or not expressed at all. When the Bay of Pigs invasion occurred, it was a humiliating failure for Kennedy and his administration.

In spite of the fact that primary-group feelings can hamper secondary-group relations, people sometimes regret the absence. Early in Thomas Mann's novel, *Confessions of Felix Krull Confidence Man*, Krull was travelling to Paris. During the trip he watched the conductor—how each time he punched a ticket he remained silent and emotionless. The repeated scene reminded Krull of "the standoffishness, amounting almost to lack of interest, which one human being, especially an official, feels compelled to manifest toward his

86 fellows" (Mann 1955, 119). Krull noted the wedding ring on the man's finger and realized that he had a wife and children. Krull, in turn, had a private life that was hidden from the conductor. None of this was supposed to be revealed, however. Their relationship should remain focused on the conductor's inspection of Krull's ticket. The arrangement struck Krull as unnatural, and yet to abandon the impersonal system, he realized, would create confusion and embarrassment. While Krull was analyzing secondary-group relations, the conductor returned, examined the ticket once again, and perhaps inspired by Krull's youth noted that he was bound for Paris. Krull replied cordially, and a brief conversation developed. At the end they wished each other luck and Krull asked the conductor to convey his regards to the man's wife and children. The conductor replied, "'Yes, thanks—well, what do you know!' He laughed in embarrassment, mixing his words up oddly, and hastened to leave. But on his way out he tripped over a nonexistent obstacle, so competely had this human touch upset him" (Mann 1955, 120).

Secondary-group activity can be upsetting in other ways. A sociological analysis of the sport of bicycle racing suggested that a prominent reason why this sport has never become popular in the United States is that in the course of races, members of different teams (secondary groups) often cooperate with each other in breakaways from the main field of riders. Such cooperation, the author argued, opposes the standard American sport norm emphasizing that members of one team always remain united in an unrelenting conflictful effort to defeat members of another team (Albert 1991). This argument stresses that in American sporting events, members of one team invariably consider members of another team an out-group.

IN-GROUPS AND OUT-GROUPS

Even some nonhuman species establish group boundaries. For instance, among wolves, when a family wants to designate its territory, the members mark it off with a trail of urine (Mowat 1965, 60). Human beings can be just as explicit about boundaries, marking them with such things as family names, passports, team uniforms, or employee membership cards.

The idea of group boundaries is central to the distinction between in-groups and out-groups. An **in-group** is any group characterized by a strong sense of identification and loyalty and by the exclusion of nonmembers. An **out-group** is composed of people who do not belong to an in-group, outsiders who are viewed with hostility and even contempt by the in-group members (Summer 1906, 12–13). Research on both concepts still continues (Wilder 1990; Wilder and Shapiro 1991).

In sociology, concepts often oversimplify the social world. For instance, the previous discussion presented a conceptual distinction between primary and secondary groups, and yet often the distinction becomes somewhat muddled, with work units, or parts of work units taking on many of a primary group's characteristics. However, in the case of in-groups and out-groups, the process of group formation eliminates any middle ground, compelling people to belong to one group or the other. Few if any individuals have a choice. A 1960s protest leader illustrated this reality when he stated, "You're either with us or against us." The in-group/out-group distinction, in short, often requires the same clarity in the real world that the concepts themselves suggest.

In-group/out-group hostility occurs frequently in small groups. The struggle for scarce resources is one way to produce it. Muzafer and Carolyn Sherif (1956), two social psychologists, studied friction and competition between two groups of twelve-year-old boys, with a dozen to a group. The Sherifs conducted experiments in which the members of each group were required to cooperate with their respective group members in order to win a tournament of competitive games. The competition was keen because the boys on each team had been promised a four-bladed jackknife if they won, and these knives were highly valued. Competition soon led to bad feelings between the two groups, and cheers like "2-4-6-8, who do we appreciate" deteriorated to "2-4-6-8, who do we apprec*ihate*." Throughout the experiment hostility between the two groups remained at a high level, and retaliatory acts occurred on both sides.

In contrast to the Sherifs' experiment, changing social conditions can sometimes make it less likely that certain individuals are considered an out-group. Through the late 1980s and into the 1990s, mass-media coverage on AIDS was extensive. It appeared that as Americans learned more about the problem, they became more compassionate toward AIDS victims, less willing to label them members of an out-group. National survey data indicated that between October 1987 and May 1991, the percentage of respondents believing that it is people's own fault if they get AIDS declined from 51 to 33 percent. During that same time period, those who said they would refuse to work alongside someone who has AIDS dropped from 25 to 16 percent, and those saying people with AIDS should be isolated from the rest of society went from 21 to 10 percent (Gallup and Newport 1991, 26).

As this material suggests, situations in which the concepts in-group and out-group apply are situations in which people's feelings are strong and often conflicting. The nearby American Controversy provides an opportunity to address this emotional issue personally.

Jim Stiles, a retired credit manager, belongs to the AIDS Buddy Program in Fairfield, Connecticut. In providing emotional support and practical help to AIDS patients, individuals like Stiles are refusing to accept that people suffering from AIDS are out-group members.

MEMBERSHIP AND REFERENCE GROUPS

One day Lin came into my office looking a bit perplexed. We had spent the semester working on his master's thesis, which emphasized that young adults in the People's Republic of China had developed distinctly different values and beliefs from their parents, a reality that Lin himself strongly endorsed. "Let me tell you what just happened," he said. "I was talking to this Chinese friend of mine, and she was telling me how she is becoming more and more serious about her American boyfriend and that they were starting to talk about getting married." He frowned. "Well, I listened for a while, and then suddenly I just blurted out, 'What would your parents think?' I can still hear my tone. It was accusatory. I sounded like a representative of the elder generation."

Like Lin most of us find that our family is more than just a **membership group**—a group to which an individual belongs. To his surprise Lin discovered that his family still acted as a **reference group**—a group whose standards a person uses to help shape his or her own values, beliefs, and behavior.

The illustration above suggests that the impact of a person's reference group is often subtle and difficult to anticipate. Reference groups affect people's behavior in a variety of areas. For example, recent studies examining the influence of reference groups on behavior have included West African political leaders' policies (Agyeman-Duah and Ojo 1991), adolescents' drug problems (Barrett, Simpson, and Lehman 1988), and citizens' support of the two major American political parties (Miller, Wlezien, and Hildreth 1991).

It is important to recognize that a group can be a reference group even if an individual does not belong to it. **Anticipatory socialization** is the acceptance of a group's standards preparatory to becoming a member of the group. When little children talk and behave like older children, they are preparing themselves for their later roles. Adolescents, college students, and older adults engage in similar, if more sophisticated, behavior—for instance, in preparation for jobs or careers. Anticipatory socialization can provide benefits for individuals. Research conducted during World War II suggested that privates who accepted the formal army standards valued by officers were more likely to be promoted than were privates who did not accept those standards (Merton 1968, 319). A significant contribution this concept makes is the recognition that people

AMERICAN CONTROVERSY
In-Group Membership: Healthy or Unhealthy?

 Americans vary considerably in their feelings about in-groups and out-groups. Let's consider a number of different issues.

To begin, there are people who are strongly inclined to designate their own in-group superior. For instance, members of the American Nazi Party or of the Ku Klux Klan believe in what they call "racial superiority"; they claim that members of certain racial groups are superior to members of other racial groups. Whites, primarily whites of northern European backgrounds, are considered the in-group, and blacks, Asians, and Jews are members of the out-group. This kind of in-group/out-group distinction is particularly inflexible because there is nothing people can do to move from the in-group to the out-group: They are locked in by superficial biological characteristics. While our society officially discourages using racial characteristics as a way of making an in-group/out-group distinction, such activity continues to be widespread.

Other uses of in-groups and out-groups are generally considered more acceptable—claims of patriotism, for example. Historically politicians, business leaders, and others have suggested that the United States is the greatest country in the world. In both times of war and peace, it has been widely claimed that anyone who opposes the interests of the United States is misguided at best and downright evil at worst.

In the past few decades, however, this outlook has begun to change. At the time of the Vietnam War, a large number of Americans took the position that their government was making a mistake—a tragic mistake—by involving itself in a war with a little country in Southeast Asia. Slogans were the order of the day as youthful opponents of the war shouted, "Hell no! We won't go!" From the perspective offered by the in-group/out-group distinction, these protesters were turning their backs on traditionally patriotic (in-group) standards which demanded that all young men be willing to serve and die for their country in its wars. Traditional patriots were horrified by such a stance, and often their reply was: "America, your country, love it or leave it!" In other words as in-group members, traditional patriots were telling the antiwar protesters that either they played by the rules of the in-group or got out—left the country and joined the (communist) out-group.

Drawing in-group versus out-group distinctions promotes psychological distance, tension, and conflict between or among groups, but it fails to effectively gain insight from the sociological perspective. For instance, consider the issue of homelessness. Marta Elliott and Lauren J. Krivo, a pair of researchers, observed that nearly everyone addressing the topic, including most investigators, have focused on homeless people's characteristics, thereby emphasizing their differences from the general population and maintaining a victim-blaming point of view that establishes homeless people as an out-group. A more productive approach, Elliott and Krivo concluded, would be to recognize the structural conditions promoting homelessness, particularly limited availability of low-income housing and of mental-health care. A fairly modest investment in increasing these services would be the most productive method to reduce the size of the out-group composed of homeless people.

Now comes the chance to discuss and argue a little. Get together with a group of your friends or fellow students and examine the following questions:

1. Are you a member of any in-groups? What are they? What are their positions about their respective out-groups?

2. Do you approve of patriotic in-groups? Does the present presidential administration effectively express your patriotic views? Discuss.

3. Do you have a strong sense of ethnic or racial in-group membership? Indicate whether or not your feelings on this topic have altered in recent years and if they are likely to change in the future.

Source: Marta Elliott and Lauren J. Krivo. "Structural Determinants of Homelessness in the United States," Social Problems. vol. 38 (February, 1991), pp. 113–31.

do not need to belong to a reference group for it to have a significant impact upon them.

Theodore Newcomb's analysis of the attitudes and beliefs of women at Bennington College in Vermont is a well-known investigation of reference-group behavior. The original research, which occurred in the 1930s, took place over a four-year period so that Newcomb could study changes in his subjects' attitudes and beliefs during their college careers. He found that most of the freshmen reflected their well-to-do parents' conservative views on political and economic issues. As they moved through college, however, the women tended to adopt the much more liberal attitudes of their teachers. The faculty members served as a reference group for the students. The teachers did not deliberately try to change their students' values, but they did "think of their students . . . as having led overprotected lives, and they included among their teaching responsibilities that of introducing students to the rest of the world" (Newcomb et al. 1967, 4). A sizable minority of the students resisted the teachers' liberal values. These students tended to be relatively isolated at college, very dependent on their parents, or rebellious toward prevailing community values. In a follow-up study, Newcomb and his associates (1967) learned that the women who were liberals when they left college in the late 1930s were still liberal in 1960, while those who were conservative in the 1930s were usually still conservative over twenty years later. This research suggests that the impact of reference groups on a person's standards can persist over long periods of time.

A reference group establishes values and norms for guiding its members' activities. When women become cadets at West Point, they are expected to meet the behavioral standards required of the male cadets.

Figure 4.1 represents the different kinds of groups that are found in the micro-order. Formal organizations and bureaucracies tend to be larger.

FORMAL ORGANIZATIONS AND BUREAUCRACIES

Throughout our lives all of us are in regular contact with schools, hospitals, courts, corporations, and

Figure 4.1
Shared Outlooks of Group Members in the Micro-Order

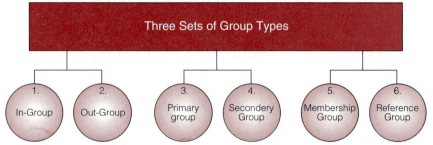

In this figure the members of each group type share a common outlook. Thus, if we consider the groups in the numerical order shown, we see the following patterns: (1) a feeling of exclusiveness; (2) a feeling of exclusion; (3) a "we" feeling; (4) cooperation for distinct, practical reasons; (5) a recognition of belonging to a group; (6) a willingness to accept the influence of group standards to shape one's own values, beliefs, and behavior.

90   government agencies. These are **formal organizations,** groups characterized by formally stated rules, clearly defined members' roles, and distinct objectives. As formal organizations become larger and more complex, they need **bureaucracies**— the administrative sections of formal organizations that have the task of controlling their operation. Students, for example, are part of the formal organization of a school, but they are not part of its bureaucracy because they have no administrative duties.

Bureaucracies often evoke a negative image in people's minds. In its least negative form, a stereotype of bureaucracy includes masses of paperwork, inefficiency, and taut nerves. More negatively individuals might visualize mental patients or prison inmates incarcerated for years, perhaps for decades, because of some "bureaucratic slip-up," or Adolph Eichmann claiming that he was a guiltless cog in the Nazi bureaucracy when he "just followed orders" to execute millions of Jewish concentration camp victims.

Bureaucracies existed in preindustrial times— in ancient Egypt, China, and Rome, for instance— and the impressive monuments and buildings those ancient civilizations produced are in part a result of the organized use of labor and materials that their bureaucracies helped promote. With its highly practical emphasis on maximizing profit, the Industrial Revolution encouraged business leaders to establish large-scale bureaucratic structures that used workers efficiently and gave business owners increased control over both their employees and the work process. Eventually bureaucratic procedures came to be used in public institutions, such as government, education, the penal system, and facilities for mentally handicapped people.

As bureaucracies became prominent in modern societies, Max Weber produced what is now considered the classic analysis of this type of structure.

Weber's Analysis of Bureaucracies

Weber developed an ideal-type model of bureaucracy. An **ideal type** is a simplified description of some phenomenon based on an analysis of concrete examples, emphasizing those characteristics that best help us to understand its essential nature. Weber analyzed bureaucracies as the most efficient means of structuring employees' time and energy. His ideal-type model emphasized the following points (Gerth and Mills 1946, 196–98).

Specialization.   Within a bureaucracy it is most efficient to have each worker specialize in a task, thus becoming an expert in its performance. When faculty members at a college or university have questions concerning their salaries, they call the payroll office and speak to the person in charge of the faculty payroll, the specialist on this subject within the college bureaucracy.

Formal qualifications for bureaucratic roles. The members of bureaucracies are hired on the basis of merit, not favoritism; they have the appropriate educational credentials, experience, or both. Much of the training for bureaucratic positions, of course, occurs before a person actually enters an organization. However, within many large-scale bureaucracies, training for medium-status roles is common today. Personnel are often expected to complete intensive training programs that may vary in length from a few days to many months and are sometimes carried on at special centers built by the organization. American Telephone and Telegraph, several fast food chains, and many of the major insurance companies have developed such centers. Successful completion of these programs makes employees eligible for higher salaries and promotion. In addition, graduates are provided with certificates that resemble diplomas and are meant to increase the sense of personal pride resulting from affiliation with their organization.

Full-time employment.   In modern bureaucracies the amount of work that must be completed generally requires that staff members be hired on a full-time basis. During formally prescribed hours, they are expected to be on the job devoting their time and energies to their tasks. How employees spend their time when they are off the job is not the concern of the bureaucracy; a clear distinction is drawn between work and personal lives.

Impersonality.   Officials remain impersonal with their clients, treating them as "cases" and not as individuals. They adopt the same formality in their relations with fellow staff members. As a result personal preferences and biases are excluded from the work process and are unlikely to affect the decisions bureaucratic officials must make.

Files, providing written documentations of precedents.   The decisions of a bureaucratic staff are based on precedent, and so in order to make decisions, they must be sure that all prior actions of the bureaucracy are recorded and retained indefinitely for reference. Specialists receive the task of organizing and updating these files. Since Weber's era computers, microfilm, and other types of modern technology have greatly increased the efficiency with which these records can be maintained.

Hierarchy of authority.   Within bureaucracies people receive orders or directives from their superiors and are directly accountable to them. Majors give orders to captains in the army, just as deans issue commands to departmental chairpersons in colleges and universities. In both situations the "chain of command" is a distinct, efficient means for the transmission of orders and information.

Elaborate formal norms.   There are clear-cut rules governing all possible contingencies. These rules tend to remain stable over time and must be learned by employees of the organization. Try to imagine what a bureaucracy would be like without such an emphasis on rules. Consider, for instance, college registration. For many students and college administrators, this is a difficult, time-consuming period at the beginning of each semester. If there were no rules covering matters such as reimbursement of funds, numerical limitations on class size, or prerequisites for entry into certain courses, administrators would need to deliberate on each case as it arose, making the long lines students sometimes must face during registration move very slowly indeed.

As we have noted, Weber's description of bureaucracy offers a simplified version of its struc-ture and activities—an ideal type. Modern analysts of bureaucracies have continued to use Weber's ideas in their own work (Jacobs 1990; Redner 1990; Warren 1988). At the same time, researchers recognize that bureaucracies contain some important characteristics he did not consider.

Informal Structure of Bureaucracies

"Things are not always what they appear to be." This well-known saying can apply to Weber's analysis of bureaucracies. He suggested that bureaucracies are formal structures, with clearly designated lines of authority and fully specified rules. In any particular organization, however, one individual frequently exercises much more influence in reality than does another occupying a comparable position in the formal organizational structure. Similarly workers frequently recognize that some rules are much more important than others, despite the fact that in the organizational handbook all rules appear equally important. As Figure 4.2 suggests, the informal organization within a bureaucracy frequently decreases the significance of the formal structure. Cliques, grapevines, and informal power alliances are among the factors contributing to this outcome.

An important set of studies demonstrating the impact of the informal structure within bureaucracies was conducted at the Hawthorne plant of the Western Electric Company in Illinois (Roethlisberger and Dickson 1939). One of the principal Hawthorne studies was completed by some observers sitting in a room with fourteen workers wiring telephone equipment. The researchers learned that the workers had developed group norms often in opposition to the official norms established by management. For instance, if someone worked more quickly than the standard, fellow workers designated that person a "ratebuster," while someone who worked more slowly than the norm was called a "chiseler." The punishment for minor violations, such as working quickly, was often "binging"—hitting the offender on the upper arm—or ridicule. The worst violation of the informal group norms occurred when a worker "squealed" on fellow workers to the foreman. In this case the punishment was exclusion;

Figure 4.2

Informal Activities of a Bureaucracy: Commentary on Weber's Model

Partial organizational chart. When the informal activities of a hypothetical computer company are examined, exception can arise to each of the points contained in Weber's model of bureaucracies.

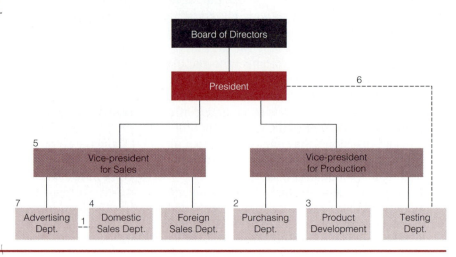

Weber's characteristics	Informal activities in the computer company providing exceptions to Weber's model
1. *Specialization*	1. Booming domestic sales neccessitates a temporary shift to sales of one-third of the advertising specialists.
2. *Formal qualifications*	2. The manager of the purchasing department has advanced rapidly because he is an expert at "playing politics"; in fact, he has very little experience in the area of purchasing.
3. *Full-time employment*	3. A 20-year-old computer wiz is paid a full-time salary for part-time work.
4. *Impersonality*	4. Some customers receive distinctly preferential treatment. It is well known that a number of mayors obtained huge discounts on high-priced models in exchange for their cities signing large contracts with the company.
5. *Written documentation of precedents*	5. The vice-president for sales has been so busy directing the hiring and training of sales staff that she has not kept records on the procedures she has used.
6. *Hierarchy of authority*	6. The president, who has a strong background in product testing, frequently bypasses the production vice-president to give orders to the testing department.
7. *Elaborate formal norms*	7. Members of the advertising department recognize that some of the rules relating to their duties are more important than others. Many members of this department, for example, break an office rule about taking office supplies for personal use.

the other workers simply pretended that the person did not exist.

Informal group norms defined "a fair day's work" as less than the amount of production desired by management. In order to conform to group norms, the fastest members simply stopped working earlier than did the others. These workers seemed to realize that voluntary restriction of output was useful for the group as a whole since increased production would probably have encouraged the company to initiate layoffs. In addition, if the workers had increased their production level, cutthroat competition and massive disruption of the group might well have occurred. The informal norms restricting productivity prevented the occurrence of both possibilities (Blau and Scott 1963, 92–93).

Besides his failure to analyze the informal workings of bureaucracies, Weber also overlooked their weaknesses.

Weaknesses of Bureaucracies

It appears that Weber simply saw bureaucracies as a positive force, establishing cooperative patterns contributing to a smooth-running industrial society (Gerth and Mills 1946). He did not consider that their weaknesses could cause conflict and disruption.

While efficiency is one of the most obvious assets of bureaucracy, placing an excessive emphasis on it can violate humanitarian standards. For example, in public mental hospitals, the laundering process is easier if patients are issued institutional clothes. This procedure eliminates the necessity of individually marking each piece of clothing and returning it to its owner. The emphasis on efficiency, however, overlooks the fact that wearing one's own clothes can be very meaningful, providing continuity with one's previous life and perhaps helping combat mental illness.

On the other hand, bureaucracies can be inefficient. This attribute has provoked a number of satirical analyses, including the Peter Principle, which contends that within bureaucracies officials continue to rise until they reach a level at which they are incompetent. If people do their jobs well, they are promoted; only when they do their jobs badly do they stop advancing, and there they remain. According to the author, Lawrence Peter, the only reason bureaucracies function at all is, because at any given time, a certain number of individuals have not yet reached their level of incompetence (Peter and Hull 1968).

Another possible weakness of bureaucracies is their frequent focus on self-perpetuation. Staff members are likely to stress the importance of their group operation, whether or not they are providing a demonstrably useful service; the obvious collective motive is that members' jobs are their source of livelihood. Governmental agencies are

Bureaucracies are the administrative arms of formal organizations, and as the looks on these people's faces suggest, bureaucratic officials often perform tasks that are routinized and not highly stimulating.

particularly notorious for maintaining long-term survival. A study of the Environmental Protection Agency's enforcement of clean-air standards indicated that officials invariably acted to promote the agency's survival. At times this meant restraining clean-air enforcement in order to avoid budget reductions, while at other times an aggressive stance was intended to show politicians and the public that the agency had a crucial role in cleaning up the nation's air (Wood 1988).

Communication problems can also be a weakness of bureaucracies. Within the construction industry, for example, managers used to hold meetings over a cup of coffee at the work site. However, these organizations have grown larger and more complex, and their different activities have become more separate. One observer wrote:

> On our present job, our engineer-managers are paper-oriented. . . . Their working styles consist of spending days and weeks studying details on plans or researching specifications before they are ready to help our people who are doing construction work. Many or most consider neat files more important than getting involved in meeting deadlines, making decisions which might be risky, and taking abuse for failures or mistakes.

> (*Applebaum* 1982, 231)

94

This statement suggests that the growth of bureaucracies isolates managers and encourages a more aloof, less communicative style than they generally maintained when the structures were smaller.

An additional weakness of bureaucracies is that they produce the development of a type of personality widely regarded as abnormal. The **bureaucratic personality** emphasizes rules and procedures and tends to lose track of organizational goals (Merton 1968). This type of person enforces "rules for rules' sake." Most of us have probably encountered such an approach when dealing with certain bureaucratic personnel: The college official who never "bends" the rules to help students; the motor vehicles department clerk who makes a host of trivial corrections on a car registration application; or the hospital administrator who will not admit a patient, even one in considerable discomfort, until the proper forms are completed in triplicate. On the other hand, some evidence suggests that in reality bureaucratic personalities are not common in modern bureaucracies. For example, Melvin Kohn (1971), a sociologist, studied a sample of more than 3,000 men engaged in a wide variety of civilian occupations. He discovered that men working in bureaucracies more readily think for themselves, are more open to new experiences, place greater emphasis on self-direction, and maintain more responsible moral standards than do nonbureaucratic personnel. Kohn suggested that the fact that bureaucratic organizations often hire people with higher educational qualifications than those found in many other types of jobs helps to explain the differences.

We have seen that bureaucracies often have dysfunctional tendencies, but is the modern picture primarily negative? The nearby Cross-Cultural Perspective provides one response to this question.

COMMUNITIES

As the young man reached the center of the park, his dog ran up to an elderly man sitting on a bench. "Here. I've got something for him," the old man said. Stiffly he reached into his pocket and took out a cookie.

"I'm sure she'll like it."

"You know, these days many people your age don't have enough time to stop and talk."

"Well, I guess I rush around, too, but I'm not in that big a hurry. Besides I'm living right over there on Court Street, and I'm interested in the community."

"The community." The old man nodded and smiled as if the phrase were the punchline to a quiet joke. "This ain't no community no more. Back in the thirties, back then it was a community. People of all ages used to be out on the street till midnight. There'd be vendors selling food anddrinks. Back then you could sit in the park and watch the whole show. It was better than a Jimmy Cagney thriller." He paused to look at a man walking by. "Do you know him?"

"I don't think so."

The old man nudged his listener with an elbow. "You should. That's Barry Garcia. He's got that little factory over on Sweet Street. Right now he's paying twenty-five workers, but he's moving out to Shortland Hills into a large, new plant. That guy's really going places, and Barry's from right here—the community." He nodded proudly.

Like this man many Americans yearn for a sense of community they once knew or perhaps they know only from hearsay, and at the same time they respond positively to the very social conditions—the emphasis on individual achievement and on industrial development—that have undermined communities in the United States and other Western countries. For many Americans it has been difficult to come to grips with their changing communities.

To begin, a **community** is a settlement of people living in a specific geographical area and maintaining a system of interrelationships that satisfies many of the people's physical and social needs. Because of the interrelationship among its inhabitants, a community is normally a source of group identification.

Early in the twentieth century, Robert Ezra Park and other members of the Chicago School of Sociology undertook an extensive set of community studies that helped transform sociology from an "armchair" discipline into an empirical science. Park, a former newspaper reporter, retained his sharp curiosity for facts; when he became a professor at the University of Chicago, he outlined an extensive program of research into the sociology of

CROSS-CULTURAL PERSPECTIVE
The Human Factor in Bureaucracies: The Japanese Case

William Ouchi (1981), a management specialist, developed Theory Z, a model for organizing bureaucracies that is based on Japanese management practices and emphasizes long-term planning, decision making by consensus, and the development of intense loyalty between workers and management. Ouchi has contended that Theory Z can help many American firms with serious problems of high employee turnover, declining productivity, and profound worker alienation. Some American corporations, including IBM, Proctor and Gamble, and Hewlett-Packard, now use Theory Z techniques.

The theory commands attention because Japanese production has become legendary in Western societies. Between 1975 and 1981, the annual sale of Japanese cars in the United States rose from 800,000 to 1.9 million; Japanese products control about a quarter of the American car market. Japanese cameras, radios, televisions, microwave ovens, and motorcycles have also proven popular in the United States and other Western nations. In recent years, admittedly, the Japanese economy has fallen on hard times, and some of the practices discussed in this section have had to be restricted. Yet these bureaucratic practices are still worthy of Americans' attention.

The central idea of Theory Z is the importance of establishing a powerful bond between workers and their firms. Japanese managers take a number of steps to maintain and strengthen this bond. Among them:

1. **Lifetime employment.** Over 35 percent of the Japanese work force is covered by this practice, which requires sacrifice by all company employees when recession or other problems threaten layoffs. Instead of dismissing workers, management will cut everyone's paychecks, including its own, or will defer payment of the large, twice-yearly bonuses all employees normally receive.

2. **Promotion and payment policies.** Many Japanese companies provide promotions as infrequently as once every ten years. Yet since all employees receive the same treatment, no one must fear falling behind. In the 1990s as difficult economic conditions descended on Japan, leading executives have done something unknown in the United States: They have competed with each other to absorb the deepest pay cuts.

3. **Nonspecialized careers.** Unlike American managers, who generally specialize in one area of company business (sales, finance, or production), Japanese executives regularly move from one corporate department to another and eventually become experts in the entire structure and all of the activities of their firms.

4. **Collective decision making.** In comparison with American executives, who are often expected to act quickly and decisively and to accept the consequences of their individual decisions, Japanese management makes major decisions by means of a collective compromise process that may involve sixty to eighty people. The Japanese call this process of establishing consensus *nemawashi* (root building). In the same way that a gardener carefully wraps all the roots of a tree together before planting it, Japanese business leaders must bring together all the members of a company before finalizing a decision. This process may be tedious, but when it is completed everyone is likely to feel committed to the collective goal.

96

Because the Japanese approach to business differs from that of the United States, one might suspect that it would be ineffective in the United States. It has, however, been fairly successful in some cases. In a Sony plant in San Diego, which employs 1,800 workers, 700,000 color television sets were produced in 1981, a level of productivity that approaches the one achieved in the Japanese plants. The Japanese factory manager said, "Americans are as quality conscious as the Japanese. But the question has been how to motivate them." Managers have tried to build strong ties with workers, expecting that they will then reciprocate. During the recession of 1973–1975 when television sales dropped and production plummeted, no one was fired. Workers stayed busy with plant maintenance and other chores. In fact, since the plant opened in 1972, no workers have been laid off. This personnel policy has been a success. Several attempts to unionize the work force have been defeated by margins as high as three to one. A parts dispatcher who was a former member of the Retail Clerks Union explained, "Union pay was better, and the benefits were probably better. But basically I'm more satisfied here."

Sony has not forced Japanese customs on its American workers. The use of lemon-colored smocks for assembly-line workers is optional, and most of the employees prefer jeans and running shoes. An attempt to establish an exercise period similar to those common in the Japanese plants was dropped when managers saw that it was not popular. Inevitably differences in customs cause some misunderstandings. American workers often interpret the Japanese system of managing by consensus as reflecting an inability to make decisions. One employee complained, "There is a lot of indecision. No managers will ever say do this or do that."

In general, however, most of the workers like the Japanese management style and do not feel that it is particularly foreign. An American supervisor said, "A long time ago, Americans used to be more people-oriented, the way the Japanese are. It just got lost somewhere along the way" (Coutu 1981). The Japanese approach to employee-management relations appears to contain some valuable lessons for Americans.

Sources: Christopher Byron. "How Japan Does It," Time. vol. 117 (March 30, 1981), pp. 54–60; D. L. Coutu. "Consensus in San Diego," Time. vol. 117 (March 30, 1981), p. 58; William Ouchi. Theory Z: How American Business Can Meet the Japanese Challenge. Reading, MA: Addison-Wesley, 1981; David E. Sanger. "In Japan's Bad Times, Chiefs Say Sorry and Cut Their Pay," New York Times. (April 11, 1991), p. 1+; Takahiro Suzuki. "A Hollow Future for Japan?" Futurist. vol. 22 (May/June 1988), p. 33.

• •

the community. Park emphasized that sociologists studying communities should analyze them as social systems, characterized by shared attitudes toward morality, business, the law, politics, and the future of the area (Krause 1980).

Currently sociologists find that communities in the traditional sense are an unusual, even rare item. In *Habits of the Heart*, Robert Bellah and his coauthors made a distinction between communities and lifestyle enclaves. While defining community in much the same way as we have, they distinguished it from a *lifestyle enclave*, a group of people who emphasize similarities in private life, especially similarities involving leisure and consumption patterns. Lifestyle enclaves are narrower than communities in two respects. Instead of including all residents within a locale, they are composed of selected individuals; in addition, instead of encouraging their members to relate to each other in diverse ways, lifestyle enclaves involve highly focused shared interests. Frequently, these sociologists argued, when people use the word "community" in specific contexts—referring to the youth community, the Hispanic community, or the gay community—their conception of community closely resembles the idea of lifestyle enclave (Bellah et al. 1986, 72–75).

Certainly many investigations that are considered to be community studies focus on the fact that the interrelatedness of supposed community members is limited. For example, research on low-income, female workers for federally funded anti-poverty agencies concluded that their ability to mobilize extensive local support to protest for

Some modern urban residents are deeply involved in community activities. This photo shows residents of Cincinnati's Over the Rhine district cleaning up a debris-filled lot in preparation for a neighborhood garden.

government-subsidized programs to improve their communities was limited by a variety of economic and political conditions, including threats of funding cutbacks if the workers' efforts to mobilize the local poor were not curtailed (Naples 1991). A study of farm communities concluded that farmers tended to consider relations with their neighbors as exchanges, and thus if neighbors were so crippled financially that they showed no prospects of reciprocating favors, then future relations were broken off (Wright and Rosenblatt 1987).

Table 4.1 measures peoples' reaction on two related community issues—their sense of whether or not their neighborhoods have developed increased criminal activity and whether or not they have become more unsafe to walk in at night. In March 1992, 54 percent of a national sample indicated that their residential areas had more crime than a year ago, and 44 percent concluded that there were places within a mile of where they lived that would be unsafe to walk in at night. With respective figures of 51 and 42 percent in 1972, respondents' evaluations have remained stable over a twenty-year period (Hugick 1992).

The Macro-Order: Institutions and Societies ■

We have just examined the principal types of groups sociologists distinguish. All groups are visible to the naked eye; they exist in a concrete sense. The same claim, however, cannot be made about institutions and societies, even though they contain a visible element—groups. In this section our focus is the **macro-order**—the large-scale structures and activities that exist within societies and even between one society and another. We begin with institutions.

Table 4.1   Community Crime and Safety

INDIVIDUALS' PERCEPTION OF THE AMOUNT OF CRIME IN THEIR RESIDENTIAL AREAS COMPARED TO A YEAR EARLIER

	More	Less	Same	No opinion
NATIONAL	54%	19%	23%	4%
SEX				
Female	58	17	21	4
Male	49	22	25	4
COMMUNITY SIZE				
Large city	64	15	16	5
Medium city	57	21	17	5
Suburbs	46	21	28	5
Small town	47	23	27	3
Rural area	58	14	24	4
RACE				
Racial minorities	66	23	6	5
Whites	52	19	25	4

UNSAFE TO WALK WITHIN A MILE OF RESIDENTIAL AREA AT NIGHT

	Yes	No	No opinion
NATIONAL	44%	56%	0%
SEX			
Female	59	41	0
Male	28	72	0
AGE			
18–29 years	48	52	0
30–49 years	40	60	0
50–65 years	46	53	1
65 and older	55	44	1
COMMUNITY SIZE			
Large city	60	40	0
Medium city	56	44	0
Suburbs	42	57	1
Small town	36	63	1
Rural area	31	69	0
INCOME			
$50,000 and over	33	67	0
$30,000–$49,999	42	58	0
$20,000–$29,999	37	62	1
Under $20,000	57	43	0

Source: Larry Hugick. "Public Sees Crime Up Nationally," Gallup Poll Monthly. (March 1992), pp. 51–53.

Certain social characteristics correlated to respondents' response on both issues. People who were female, from larger communities, and members of racial minorities were more likely to have perceived an increase of crime in their locales in the past year. Individuals who were female, older, from larger communities, and had lower incomes were more inclined to believe that there were unsafe places to walk at night within a mile of where they lived.

An **institution** is a system of statuses, roles, groups, and behavioral patterns that satisfies a basic human need and is necessary for the survival of a society. Industrial societies always contain a well-developed set of institutions, while preindustrial societies often have limited or no development in many institutional areas.

The chapters in the third part of this book examine major institutions. The family is an institution that supplies a host of functions, including sexual regulation, reproduction, child-rearing, and the provision of food, shelter, and emotional support. Religion develops group cohesion (a common sense of purpose), maintains social control, and provides an ethical design for living. Education serves a variety of purposes, including the transmission of culture, the teaching of knowledge and skills, and the sorting of students into vocational and college-preparatory programs. The political institution maintains social order and exerts changes in the legal structure, while the economic institution controls the production, distribution, and consumption of goods and services. Medicine is concerned with the prevention and treatment of disease and the treatment of injury, and science supplies systematic knowledge that can be used to produce progress in a variety of technological and social areas. Institutions not discussed in this text include the military, which can either attack the enemies of a society or defend against them, and sport, which provides recreation, exercise, and entertainment.

Institutions tend to be relatively stable because members of society, especially those who are wealthy and powerful, generally do not feel that social change supports their interests. Consider the political institution. For almost the entire history of the United States, there have been only two political parties in most elections. The majority of the citizens, especially influential people, find that their political interests are well enough represented by the principal parties that they are not motivated to support third parties. Thus third parties have almost always lacked the wealth and influence to launch successful political campaigns, even at the local level. In the 1992 presidential campaign, H. Ross Perot's great wealth permitted him to conduct a well-advertised campaign for the presidency, but in spite of ideas and plans many voters found appealing, he received only 19 percent of the popular vote.

Institutions do not change readily, but when they do, they are likely to alter one or more other institutions. The reason is that the institutions are intimately tied to one another. Changes in the economic institution, for instance, can affect families. In an agricultural society, children generally represent a source of wealth for their parents—more hands to work the land. However, in an industrial society, in which people live off wages, children represent an economic liability. It makes sense, therefore, to restrict the number of children. This appears to be one important reason that families in industrial societies are smaller than families in agricultural societies.

Across time and space, the form of a particular institution and the kind of activities it produces will often vary considerably. Recreation and sport, for instance, have changed over time in U.S. society. In the first permanent American villages, the Puritans opposed play, games, and sport for two reasons. First, they emphasized that it was a full-time task simply to survive—to wrest a living from the wilderness and to protect themselves from the Indians. Second, religious rules prohibited leisure, branding such activities as idle and wasteful. But as the frontier moved westward, religious restrictions weakened. Gambling on horse races, cock fights, fist fighting, wrestling, and rifle shooting were popular activities. In the taverns, drinking, cards, billiards, bowling, and rifle and pistol shooting provided both competition and entertainment (Leonard 1980, 23–24). As the country grew, leisure also expanded. Industrialization, transportation growth, and the expansion of mass media all contributed. Eventually leisure and spectator sport became big business.

Other societies often have institutions very different from those in the United States. Americans have a variety of spectator sports but none like the following examples. In Merida, in western Spain, the people once walled off an enormous plain to a height of four feet, creating a small lake on which model ships could engage in simulated naval battles. In less technologically advanced societies, citizens use natural structures as settings for spectator sports. In a remote island of the New Hebrides, the entire community would gather at the bottom of a cliff to watch young male villagers throw themselves headlong toward the cliff floor, confident that the vine ropes attached to their heels would bring them to a halt just before

100 they smashed into the rocks (Michener 1976, 11–12). Like their institutions, societies are varied.

Recall from Chapter 3 that a **society** is the interacting people who share a culture. Sociologists have classified societies into different types. Émile Durkheim (1946), for instance, divided societies into those maintaining mechanical solidarity and those featuring organic solidarity. The former were preindustrial societies, in which a simple division of labor and limited social roles encouraged people's integration into a system featuring shared values and behavior along with highly conformist behavior and loyalty to tradition. In modern societies, Durkheim argued, the social order is very different—not based on shared values and behavior or respect for tradition but on an interdependence of many highly specialized roles, where different groups contribute to society, much like the individual organs of an organism. Robert Redfield (1941) and Ferdinand Tönnies (1957) are among a number of social scientists who have developed similar distinctions between preindustrial and industrial societies.

Social scientists, particularly anthropologists, have found that food production is a reasonable means by which to classify societies. Fifteen thousand years ago, all the earth's inhabitants lived by hunting, fishing, and the gathering of wild plants. Gradually the cultivation of domesticated plants and the rearing of domesticated animals began to replace hunting and gathering. By 2,000 years ago, the number of people engaged in hunting and gathering dropped to about 50 percent, and about 500 years ago when Christopher Columbus arrived in the New World, only about 15 percent of the planet's population lived by hunting and gathering. Today fewer than 30,000 people, less than 1/1000th of the earth's people, are still engaged in this pattern of subsistence. Recognizing that this way of living is fast disappearing, anthropologists continue to study hunting-and-gathering societies very thoroughly (Colinvaux and Bush 1991).

In classifying societies, sociologists now recognize that a new kind of society has been developing—the postindustrial type. In such nations as Canada, England, France, Germany, Japan, Sweden, and the United States, societal characteristics are similar, featuring a shift from a mass industrial society to one producing information. In

The modern world is highly diversified, with some people, like these bank officers at computer terminals in New York City's financial district, involved in postindustrial activity, while others, like this farmer in Hong Kong, are still pursuing a preindustrial lifestyle.

the United States, the shift has been dramatic, with the number of people involved in the creation, processing, and distribution of information in such occupational areas as banking, the stock market, insurance, education, and government rising from 17 percent in 1950 to 55 percent three decades later.

A central feature of postindustrial societies is their membership in a global economy in which modern technology permits information to be instantaneously shared world wide and the proportion of world economic output involved in international trade has steadily increased. As technologically advanced societies have entered the postindustrial age, industrial activity has increas-

ingly shifted to developing nations, where corporations' wage payments are much lower.

The dramatic shift to a postindustrial economy has been producing a redistribution of American income. Overall the wealthy have benefitted greatly while the poor have suffered significantly. Data from the Congressional Budget Office indicated that between 1977 and 1989, the top 1 percent of families received 70 percent of the gains from the nation's economic growth. In striking contrast the middle 20 percent gained only 2 percent of that total while the poorest 20 percent lost the equivalent of 11 percent of the total gain (McCracken 1992; Naisbitt 1982; Nasar 1992).

Humanization of Group Activity

On July 3, 1988, the commander of a U.S. Navy warship mistook an Iranian passenger plane for an Iranian F-14 fighter, fired two surface-to-air missiles at the plane, and killed 290 civilians. Admiral William J. Crowe, Jr., the chairman of the Joint Chiefs of Staff, said that he regretted the loss of life but that "the commanding officer had a very heavy obligation to protect his ship, his people" (Halloran 1988, A1). This incident emphasizes what we have seen in several sections of this chapter, especially the discussions of in-groups and out-groups, bureaucracies, and communities—that modern group activity is aggressive, self-centered, and not especially humane.

Sociologist Philip Slater (1976) contended that Americans must choose between an emphasis on community, in which the wish to live in trust and cooperation in a collective setting is the chief concern, and a focus on conflict, in which the advancement of the individual at the expense of others is given top priority. American culture, Slater noted, did not invent competition, but he claimed that, compared to most other societies, the United States is extraordinarily competitive.

And yet it should be remembered that a desire for community was very strong in many of the earliest American settlements—in particular, among the Puritans. Just before landing in Salem harbor in 1630, John Winthrop, the governor of the colony, gave a famous speech describing the "city upon a

hill" that he and his fellow Puritans intended to found. He said, "We must delight in each other, make others [sic] condition our own, rejoyce [sic] together, mourn together, labor and suffer together, always having before our eyes our community as members of the same body." In *Habits of the Heart*, Bellah and his coauthors noted that the Puritans' fundamental criterion of success was "the creation of a community in which a genuinely ethical and spiritual life could be lived" (Bellah et al. 1986, 28–29).

To implement humanitarian reform in modern institutions, we would do well to start with some basic questions. In the case of the crisis-ridden public-education system, for instance, we might first ask, "Why are most students learning so far below their actual potential?" And then: "What sorts of citizen workers does our society need in the future, and how can our education system best help to prepare them?" (Kay 1991). Thoughtful, thorough answers to these and related questions could provide foundations for implementing a dramatically improved education system.

You could extend discussion of this issue in class, suggesting what seem to be the most significant group reforms that could be implemented in such major institutional areas as the family, politics, work, the military, and medical and health care.

STUDY GUIDE

Learning Objectives

After studying this chapter, you should be able to:

1. Define group and distinguish among group, aggregate, and social category.
2. Compare and contrast primary groups and secondary groups.
3. Define in-groups and out-groups and indicate circumstances encouraging their development.
4. Distinguish between membership and reference groups and define anticipatory socialization.
5. Define formal organization, bureaucracy, and ideal type and discuss Weber's analysis of bureaucracies.
6. Describe informal activities within bureaucracies.
7. Identify weaknesses of bureaucracies.
8. Define community and discuss lifestyle enclaves.
9. Define institution and describe the activities of the major institutions.
10. Define society, discuss Durkheim's distinction between societies maintaining mechanical solidarity and those having organic solidarity, and summarize the nature of postindustrial society.
11. Indicate major problems of group life in modern society and offer some suggestions about how these problems might be solved.

Summary

1. A group consists of two or more interacting people who share certain expectations and goals. Groups can be distinguished from aggregates and social categories, which are related concepts.

2. Sociologists have defined many different types of groups. Primary groups entail stable, long-lasting relationships, permitting members to exercise many facets of their personality and to develop strong ties of affection and identity. By contrast, secondary groups are composed of people who join a group for distinct, practical reasons and generally maintain few, if any, powerful emotional ties.

Another important conceptualization involves in-groups and out-groups. An in-group is any group characterized by a strong sense of identification and loyalty and a feeling of exclusiveness toward outsiders. The out-group consists of people who do not belong to the in-group and are viewed with hostility and even contempt by in-group members.

Reference groups, groups that a person uses to help shape his or her own values, beliefs, and behavior, are influential in the socialization of people. The concept of anticipatory socialization suggests that groups can serve as reference groups even if people do not belong to them.

Another significant type of group is the bureaucracy—the administrative section of a formal organization that has the task of controlling its operation. Max Weber analyzed the bureaucracy as an ideal type, indicating the bureaucratic features that make it the most efficient structure for using employees' time and energy within an organizational structure. Later sociological analysis modified Weber's conclusions, identifying the informal group activities within bureaucracies and weaknesses of bureaucracies.

The community is a settlement of people living in a specific geographical area and maintaining a system of interrelationships that satisfies many of the people's physical and social needs.

3. An institution is a system of statuses, roles, groups, and behavioral patterns that satisfies a basic human need and is necessary for the survival of a society. Institutions include the family, religion, education, the political order, the economy, medicine, science, the military, and sports. A society is composed of the interacting people who share a culture. Social scientists have developed different schemes for classifying societies into types. Postindustrial societies, like the United States, are deeply involved in the production and use of information and participate extensively in international trade.

4. In an industrial age, people often find themselves confronting two opposing demands—one pulling them toward efficiency and achievement and the other toward intimacy and community. People can take decisive steps to offset the impersonal tendencies of modern life.

Key Terms

aggregate   two or more people who share physical space but lack the interaction maintained by group members

anticipatory socialization   the acceptance of a group's standards preparatory to becoming a member of the group

bureaucracy   the administrative section of a formal organization that has the task of controlling its operation

bureaucratic personality   a type of personality that emphasizes rules and procedures and tends to lose track of organizational goals

community   a settlement of people living in a specific geographical area and maintaining a system of interrelationships that satisfies many of the people's physical and social needs

formal organization   a group characterized by formally stated rules, clearly defined members' roles, and distinct objectives

group   two or more interacting people who share certain expectations and goals

ideal type   a simplified description of some phenomenon based on an analysis of concrete examples, emphasizing those characteristics that best help us to understand its essential nature

in-group   any group characterized by a strong sense of identification and loyalty and a feeling of exclusiveness toward nonmembers

institution   a system of statuses, roles, groups, and behavioral patterns that satisfies a basic human need and is necessary for the survival of a society

macro-order   the large-scale structures and activities that exist within societies and even between one society and another

membership group   a group to which an individual belongs

micro-order   the structure and activity of small groups

out-group   people who do not belong to an in-group; outsiders who are viewed with hostility and even contempt by the in-group members

primary group   a group in which relationships are usually stable over long periods of time, members are able to expose many facets of their personality, and a strong sense of affection and identity develops

reference group   a group whose standards a person uses to help shape his or her own values, beliefs, and behavior

secondary group   a group of people who cooperate with each other for specific, practical reasons and maintain few, if any, strong emotional ties within the group

social category   a number of people who have one or more social characteristics in common

society   the interacting people who share a culture

Tests

True • False Test

_____   1. The family is a major primary group.

_____   2. In the wars following World War II, American soldiers' fighting units failed to develop the qualities associated with primary groups, such as a strong sense of loyalty among members.

_____   3. Analysis of bicycle racing demonstrates that this activity can produce both cooperation and competition among members of different secondary groups.

_____   4. Anticipatory socialization occurs only when people already belong to a reference group.

_____   5. Theodore Newcomb's study of college women's political attitudes and values over time indicated that teachers' influence had little or no lasting effect on attitudes and values.

_____   6. Bureaucracies do not exist separately from formal organizations.

_____   7. In analyzing bureaucracies, Weber produced major insights about their informal structures.

_____   8. Weber's ideal type for bureaucracies does not assess the weaknesses of these structures.

_____   9. Lifestyle enclaves are closely knit, traditional communities, such as those which existed in preindustrial America.

_____ 10. Industrial societies always have a set of well-developed institutions, while preindustrial societies often have limited or no development in many institutional areas.

Multiple-Choice Test

_____   1. A number of people who have one or more social characteristics in common, such as age, sex, or race, would be a(n):
   a.   group.
   b.   aggregate.
   c.   social category.
   d.   secondary group.

_____   2. Compared to a primary group, a secondary group tends:
   a.   to have less face-to-face contact.
   b.   to have more of a "we feeling."
   c.   to be inferior.
   d.   to involve a more intimate kind of relationship.

_____   3. When a person accepts a group's standards preparatory to becoming a member of the group, this behavior is called:
   a.   a membership group.
   b.   aggregate behavior.
   c.   anticipatory socialization.
   d.   an ideal type.

_____   4. Which statement is true of bureaucracies?
   a.   They have existed for less than a century.
   b.   They are informal organizations.
   c.   They do not exist in economic or political structures.
   d.   They are found in large formal organizations.

_____ 5. Which of the following characteristics is included in Weber's analysis of bureaucracies?
   a.   an informal system of authority
   b.   hiring based on formal qualifications
   c.   a blending of work and personal lives
   d.   self-perpetuation as a goal

_____ 6. Which of these factors is an important weakness of bureaucracies?
   a.   an excessive emphasis on efficiency
   b.   the discouragement of the bureaucratic personality
   c.   specialization
   d.   unwritten traditions

_____ 7. Communities:
   a.   have not been studied by sociologists in recent decades.
   b.   no longer contain lifestyle enclaves.
   c.   are now revitalized in most large cities, according to a recent study.
   d.   have been studied by sociologists since early in the twentieth century.

_____ 8. Which of the following statements is true of institutions?
   a.   In some societies many institutions simply exist without any apparent functions.
   b.   They tend to be unstable.
   c.   Their structure and activities tend to be very similar across time and space.
   d.   When they change, they tend to affect other institutions.

_____ 9. Societies are:
   a.   part of the micro-order.
   b.   part of the macro-order.
   c.   not considered postindustrial if they engage in extensive international trade.
   d.   b and c

_____ 10. Postindustrial societies:
   a.   belong to a global economy.
   b.   have a declining percentage of poor people.
   c.   have fewer members working in occupational areas related to information than indus-
        trial societies.
   d.   a and b

Essay Test

1. Evaluate the following statement: Primary groups and secondary groups serve the same purposes for people.
2. Describe a situation presented in the text illustrating how in-group/out-group hostility is produced.
3. Distinguish between formal organizations and bureaucracies and summarize Weber's analysis of bureaucracies. Then examine the informal structure and weaknesses of bureaucracies, indicating why this material represents a criticism of Weber's work.
4. Define community and discuss modern sociologists' conclusions about communities.
5. Summarize the basic characteristics of postindustrial societies, illustrating each point with specific information about the United States.

Suggested Readings

Anderson, Elijah. 1990. *Streetwise: Race, Class, and Change in an Urban Community*. Chicago: University of Chicago Press. A rich description of two city communities—one a poor, black area and the other a racially mixed district undergoing gentrification—providing readers basic information about the realities of street life.

Gerth, H. H., and C. Wright Mills (eds.). 1946. *From Max Weber*. New York: Oxford University Press. A well-known collection containing an informative biography of Max Weber and compelling excerpts from his major works, including a chapter devoted to his analysis of bureaucracies.

Morgan, Glenn. 1990. *Organizations in Society*. New York: St. Martin's Press. A well-written overview of the sociological analysis of organizations, including theories of organizations, different organizational types, cross-cultural analysis and comparison, and the economic and political context in which organizations are located.

Shkilnyk, Anastasia M. 1985. A *Poison Stronger than Love: The Destruction of an Ojibwa Community*. New Haven: Yale University Press. The moving account of how a forced move to a reservation and industrial waste in the local river combined to destroy a Native-American community.

Skolnick, Jerome H., and Elliott Currie (eds.). 1991. *Crisis in American Institutions*. 8th ed. New York: HarperCollins. A popular, effective set of readings dividing forty-eight articles into twelve categories addressing major problems in the principal American institutions.

Warren, Roland L., and Larry Lyon (eds.). 1988. *New Perspectives on the American Community*. 5th ed. Belmont, CA: Wadsworth. The latest edition of a successful book of readings containing both classical perspectives and studies on the community and a substantial up-to-date list of contemporary contributions.

Whyte, William Foote, Jr. 1991. *Social Theory for Action: How Individuals and Organizations Learn to Change*. Newbury Park, CA: Sage. Drawing from the author's research experiences, this book analyzes the development of sociological theory that will help provide solutions to organizations' practical problems.

Additional Assignments

1. Interview three people, preferably of different ages, who have been residents of your community for at least five years. Ask them what significant changes they have seen in their community, why they consider these changes significant, and whether they feel optimistic or pessimistic about the impact of the community changes. Then seek information about your community in a local newspaper. (Hint: At the end of the year, many newspapers contain sections reviewing the year's events.) Did your respondents highlight the same changes as those discussed in the newspaper? Does what you learned about your own community correspond with information in the text? Discuss.

2. Keep a diary for a week which logs a) your formal activities at work and school and b) your social activities. At the end of the week, use your diary to answer the following questions:
    a. How much involvement occurred in primary groups and in secondary groups? Was one type of involvement more rewarding than the other? Explain.
    b. Did you experience any in-group/out-group tensions or hostilities? From which sources?
    c. Did you obtain significant support from any reference group(s)?
    d. Did your contact with bureaucracies suggest that they are efficient, inefficient, or both?
    e. How often did you feel your activities were affected or controlled by others? Explain.

Answers to Objective Test Questions

True • False Test

1. t	6. t
2. f	7. f
3. t	8. t
4. f	9. f
5. f	10. t

Multiple-Choice Test

1. c	6. a
2. a	7. d
3. c	8. d
4. d	9. b
5. b	10. a

Social Interaction

5

The general managers, who build basketball teams in the National Basketball Association, are astute judges of talent, and yet judging talent is not all that is required. They also need to be amateur sociologists, anticipating what the loss of a current player or the addition of a new player will mean for the team's chemistry.

Al Bianchi, the former general manager of the New York Knicks, observed:

> The word chemistry has come into vogue in recent years, but it has always been important. It seems almost ludicrous that you have to worry about chemistry these days when guys are being paid millions to play basketball. Who wouldn't be happy doing that? But some guys aren't. And yes, there are certain players I would not draft or trade for, largely because of their reputation.

> (Brown 1989, *sec.* 8, *p.* 4)

In the spring of 1989, the Detroit Pistons made a controversial trade, sending Adrian Dantley, a high-scoring forward to Dallas in exchange for Mark Aguirre, another high-scoring forward. Both men were fine players; the question, as Bianchi observed, was whether they would be able to fit in with their new teams, get along with teammates and effectively contribute their talents to win ball games. Aguirre was especially questionable—the leading scorer at Dallas but at odds with his teammates and coaches and going to a team with two players to whom he would be expected to subordinate his talents. At the time of the trade, Detroit had the best record in professional basketball. Had the front office badly misjudged the situation?

Three months later the answer was clear. Detroit completed the regular season with the best record in professional basketball and won four play-off rounds, sweeping four games from the former champion Los Angeles Lakers in the finals. Obviously Aguirre's acquisition had not hurt the team.

Whether it is the issue of a basketball player relating to new teammates or a greeting as two people pass each other on the street, human contacts involve **social interaction**—the basic process through which two or more people use language and gestures to affect each other's thoughts, expectations, and behavior. Through social interaction people obtain the knowledge and skills that make them functioning members of society. Social interaction is essential for all organized life. No social activity could take place in the political, educational, religious, economic, or familial structures without the process.

In this chapter we explore social interaction. The first section examines three important theories in this area. Next the major components of social interaction are considered. The chapter concludes with an analysis of what happens when patterns of social interaction are disrupted.

Theories of Social Interaction ■

This section examines three theoretical perspectives that help explain social interaction and social relationships: symbolic interaction, ethnomethodology, and dramaturgic sociology.

SYMBOLIC INTERACTION

Symbolic interaction is a theory that emphasizes the importance of symbolic communication—gestures and, above all, language—in the development of the individual, group, and society. A large body of research related to this theory has been produced. For instance, studies using this theoretical approach have examined the impact of social-interaction patterns on agricultural production in Ifugao society (Brosius 1988); two opposing symbolic-interaction perspectives on humor (Flaherty 1990); the relative worth accorded to self ratings and others' ratings of self (May 1991); and psychologist William James's use of symbolic interaction (Schellenberg 1990).

As we noted in Chapter 1, a major proponent of symbolic interaction was Herbert Blumer (1969), who emphasized that the nature of the theory could be summarized in the following manner. Blumer observed that the symbolic quality of social interaction centers on the meanings individuals give to people and things. The meanings do not simply exist in the social world but derive from people's judgments in the course of their daily experience; a major contributor to these meanings is contact with other people. Sometimes as individuals interpret their experience, meanings change. Whether meanings change or remain the same, they affect people's behavior. Figure 5.1 illustrates responses and meanings associated with some symbols.

We continue this analysis, using as illustration a discussion of fathers' changing roles. Blumer noted that one of the basic elements in symbolic interaction is the nature of the objects with which people must interact. These objects are of three types—physical objects such as chairs or trees, social objects such as parents or friends, and abstract objects such as ideas or philosophical principles. People's conceptions of the significant objects in their environment can differ vastly and are shaped by the interpretations they develop when interacting with others. For instance, a progressive father was expertly changing his baby's diaper on a park bench. While he was laboring, an older gentleman, who clearly had a different perception of fatherhood, stopped to watch. As the father slipped the plastic bag containing the diaper into a small pack, the gentleman said with a slight accent, "In my country I have never seen such a thing." The father smiled and replied, "Welcome to America" (Fort 1989, 79).

Symbolic interaction also perceives the individual as an acting organism. In Chapter 6, "Socialization," the summary of George Herbert Mead's version of symbolic interaction develops this issue, and so at this time, we only need to discuss the point briefly. Blumer observed that most other social theories consider people the passive objects of others' behavior; by contrast, symbolic interaction emphasizes people's ability to function as independent entities in the social world—to analyze and note the impact of significant events

Figure 5.1

A Comparison of Signs and Symbols

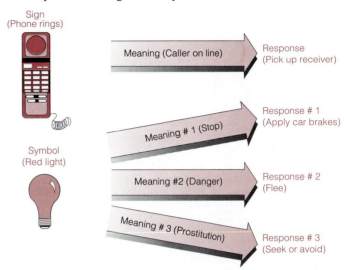

Signs have fixed meanings and fixed responses. When the telephone rings, people know that a caller is on the line, and they will generally pick up the receiver. Symbols, however, have neither fixed meanings nor fixed responses. A red light, for instance, can mean to stop one's car at an intersection, to recognize danger when a jammed valve is creating a buildup of pressure that will soon produce an explosion within a furnace, or to realize that one has entered a so-called "red-light district," where houses of prostitution are located. As the figure indicates, each meaning of a symbol requires a particular response.

in their own lives (Blumer 1969, 14). Frequently other individuals and groups can help in this assessment process. For over a decade, Mark Podolner has been counseling individual fathers and groups of fathers, helping them to understand that in most cases they were raised to repress their feelings and that for both themselves and their children it will be beneficial if they can express their feelings openly. Podolner helps his clients understand what he believes are the destructive effects of this repression on both the men themselves and their children. For instance, he explains that because boys are largely raised by women and yet are expected to use fathers as role models, they often become insecure as adults and seek to oppress women, feeling their mothers had too much control over them.

Once individuals have analyzed the impact of events on their lives, they take action. According to Blumer, the factors people take into account include their goals, the means to achieve those goals, their self-images, and the likely result of the

Like the man pictured here, many modern fathers are more actively involved in their children's upbringing than fathers tended to be in the past.

course of action (Blumer 1969, 15). A substantial number of modern fathers have embarked on a course of action where, as Podolner phrased it, their goal is "to become the father they wish they had." These men realize that they have not been brought up to be emotionally expressive, and so their self-image includes the recognition that they are likely to experience an inner struggle as they attempt to give emotional support to and receive it from their children. They appreciate, however, that the likely result of such a course of action will be release from a chain of emotional repression that has existed for generations, with significant improvement in the emotional lives of all directly involved (Fort 1989, 80–82).

ETHNOMETHODOLOGY

Two mothers are sipping coffee and talking. One turns to the other and says, "Carrie, I don't know what it is. You seem to have such an effortless time with your children."

"It's really pretty straightforward, Lucy," the other replies. "I have a set of simple rules, and come hell or high water I stick to them. The kids and I really understand each other."

Carrie seems to have some grasp of the ethnomethodological perspective. **Ethnomethodology** is the study of the sometimes recognized but often unrecognized social order, the set of underlying shared norms and expectations that promote harmony in most everyday social interactions. That "often unrecognized social order," you might realize, suggests that ethnomethodology is concerned more with implicit than with explicit norms; both types of norms were discussed in Chapter 3, "Culture."

While one can consider ethnomethodology a form of symbolic interaction, this approach focuses on the process by which the social order develops and not on social interaction itself. In contrast to symbolic interaction, ethnomethodology has received limited attention in sociology. Nonetheless discussion about its contribution to the discipline is apparent in the modern sociological literature (Boden 1990; Hilbert 1990).

Harold Garfinkel, a leading proponent of ethnomethodology, summarized the special contributions he feels the theory can make to sociology (Garfinkel 1988). Garfinkel's studies emphasized that an effective way of grasping the significance of shared norms and expectations is to violate them. As people express their irritation, anger, or confusion in response to the violation, the functions performed by the underlying norms will become apparent.

In one informal study, Garfinkel asked undergraduate students to create informal experiments that would reveal the implicit norms that existed in their families. Members were horrified as the students acted like boarders or guests in their homes rather than family members. The students' reports were filled with accounts of anger, astonishment, bewilderment, anxiety, and embarrassment. Parents demanded explanations. What was wrong? Was the student sick? Had he or she flunked a test at school? Garfinkel wrote, "One student acutely embarrassed his mother in front of her friends by asking if she minded if he had a snack from the refrigerator. 'Mind if you have a little snack? You've been eating little snacks around here for years without asking me. What's gotten into you?'" (Garfinkel 1967, 47–48).

Eventually the students told their families what had been happening. Most were neither amused nor intrigued by the study. To them the underlying social order was not a subject of interest. The aroused emotions of family members demonstrated, however, that they became acutely concerned when there was a disruption of the established patterns.

Garfinkel's studies all involved contrived experimental situations. Under natural circumstances people may also find themselves facing challenges to the existing social order that reveal its unstated but nonetheless great significance. In the winter of 1846, the Donner party, a group of travelers heading westward, was trapped by a blizzard in the Sierra Nevada Mountains. Slowly the party began starving to death. Just before he died, F. W. Graves urged his weeping, grief-stricken daughters to take any measure possible to keep themselves alive. With his last breaths, Graves insisted that the living use his flesh to sustain themselves. Soon the deed was done. An historian provided the following account. "The men finally mustered up courage to approach the dead. With averted eyes and trembling hand, pieces of flesh were severed from the inanimate forms and laid upon the coals. It was the very refinement of torture to taste such food, yet those who tasted lived." But eating human flesh was not the only horror of the situation. The historian explained:

> Although no person partook of kindred flesh, sights were often witnessed that were blood curdling. Mrs. Foster . . . fairly worshipped her brother Lemuel. Has human pen power to express the shock of horror this sister received when she saw her brother's heart thrust through with a stick, and boiling upon the coals?
>
> (McGlashan 1879, 69–70)

It is obvious that cannibalism represents a serious violation of cultural standards. However, why this is true is not immediately self-evident. After all, few if any of us receive parental advice urging us to refrain from eating human flesh. However, we do encounter an unrelenting if often implicit emphasis on the spiritual value of human beings. To eat people is to unspeakably violate underlying normative standards: to reduce human beings to something repulsively material. The woman who saw her brother's heart roasted and eaten was witnessing a prime symbol of love and emotion turned into mere food. Thus the survivors of the Donner Party faced a gruesome dilemma on the issue of social order. They could die, clearly violating the social order. On the other hand, they could stay alive by eating human flesh—an act that invariably defiled the social order by reducing human beings to nothing more than a source of protein.

DRAMATURGIC SOCIOLOGY

Wearing sunglasses, Marilyn Monroe could usually appear in public without being recognized. One day she was walking down a city street with a close friend. Marilyn turned to the friend and asked, "Do you want to see me be her?" At first the friend did not understand the question. Then she saw that something was happening, something difficult to explain. It was as though a light bulb were being turned on—an inner adjustment was occurring— and suddenly the people around began to notice that the world's most famous actress was in their midst (American Broadcasting Company 1988).

As this illustration suggests, social interaction involves people playing parts. **Dramaturgic sociology** is a theoretical approach that analyzes social

The dramaturgical sociological approach seems appropriate for analyzing many human encounters. When John P. Imlay, Jr., wrested the chairmanship of Dun & Bradstreet Software Holdings from Frank H. Dodge, Dodge gave Imlay this mask of Imlay's face. Dodge had used the mask to motivate his staff at sales meetings.

114

interaction as if the participants were actors in a play. For example, a recent study of magazine advertisements, which can be considered photos of carefully posed theatrical roles, concluded that these advertisements represent current cultural ideals for both sexes, with women's representations in the ads often demonstrating distinct subordination to men (Belknap and Leonard 1991).

Erving Goffman (1959), the creator of dramaturgic sociology, suggested that actors perform their parts, follow the script most of the time, and improvise whenever the script is unclear. People's daily performances are generally given in distinct settings. Rooms, furniture, food and drink, and so forth constitute props, the physical context of social interaction. Furthermore, as in an actual play, the setting tends to be immobile, and often the interaction cannot begin until the actors reach the setting. Even if all the people scheduled to participate in a meeting happened to meet by chance on the street a few minutes before the meeting was due to begin, they would probably not conduct their business right there. Customary procedures as well as efficiency would likely dictate that they head for the conference room.

Many performances are straightforward. Garage mechanics fix cars and dentists take care of teeth. Salespeople in clothing stores sell dresses, suits, shirts, socks, and underwear. But sometimes, Goffman emphasized, people's performances are deceptive, involving a form of activity that remains concealed from the public because of its incompatibility with a respectable, honest image. For instance, there is the cigar store or barber shop owner who secretly runs a bookie joint, or workers who routinely rob their employers by stealing tools, reselling food and other supplies, or traveling on company time. Another type of deceptive performance involves the concealment of errors and mistakes, a practice that provides the impression of infallibility so important in many performances. There is a well-known saying that doctors bury their mistakes. One of the discomforting features of a malpractice suit is its clear implication that doctors are definitely not infallible.

Frontstage versus Backstage

Like a theater performance, social interaction may be thought to have a frontstage and a backstage.

The **frontstage** is the physical area or region where people present a performance. On the frontstage people are expected to maintain certain behavioral standards toward those with whom they interact: their audience. These standards fall roughly into two categories. One category involves the treatment of the audience; Goffman designates these standards as "matters of politeness." Waiters or waitresses are supposed to be pleasant, respectful, and attentive when they attend to customers. The second category concerns performers' behavior when they are within visual or hearing range of the audience but not necessarily in direct communication; Goffman uses the term "decorum" here. Often people within a given social context fail to appreciate the significance of standards of decorum until someone violates them. Most people would readily accept the necessity of being quiet during a funeral service. The fact that this quiet signifies respect for the deceased and his or her family would strike those present forcefully only if someone entered the service speaking in a loud, boisterous manner.

Unlike the frontstage, the backstage lies outside the audience's view. The **backstage** is the physical area or region where people construct the illusions and impressions they will use in a performance. Frequently the frontstage and backstage lie close to each other. This arrangement permits the performer to receive assistance from backstage if necessary and also allows him or her to spend brief periods of rest and relaxation in the back region, where members of the audience are unlikely to intrude. A waiter, for instance, passes through a swinging door into the kitchen, picks up "props"—the food and drink for customers—and then returns to the dining hall, which is the frontstage. In many restaurants, including the fanciest, it is essential that the audience—the customers—be kept out of the backstage, where they would probably discover conditions and practices that could destroy their appetites. The British author George Orwell, who worked in the kitchens of many French restaurants, observed that most kitchens were insufferably dirty. The cook, he conceded,

> . . . is an artist, but his art is not cleanliness. To a certain extent he is even dirty because he is an artist, for food, to look smart, needs dirty treatment. When a steak, for instance, is brought up for the head cook's inspection, he does not handle it with

a fork. He picks it up in his fingers and slaps it down, runs his thumb around the dish and licks it to taste the gravy, runs it round and licks again, then steps back and contemplates the piece of meat like an artist, judging a picture, then presses it lovingly into place with his fat, pink fingers, every one of which he has licked a hundred times that morning.

(*Orwell* 1959, 59)

As people move from backstage to frontstage, they engage in **impression management**: the attempt to control others' evaluations by presenting themselves in the most favorable light. In some instances impression management is relatively easy, especially when the actor can anticipate others' reactions and can visualize a way to behave that will be mutually acceptable to everyone involved. However, in other situations the appropriate style of presentation is not readily apparent or is difficult to execute. Sometimes performers must be simultaneously concerned with impression management and with the effective maintenance of valued relationships. For instance, chief surgeons are likely to make joking comments if subordinates commit minor mistakes during operations. Such observations reflect well on the surgeons—clearly they retain a distinct yet relaxed control over their team—and, at the same time, they ease the tension among team members anticipating punishment for their mistakes (Goffman 1961, 122).

We have examined three perspectives on social interaction. None of these three theories can claim to be inherently superior to the others. Sometimes one perspective might seem more effective for analyzing a given social interaction. Often a sociologist chooses a particular approach because he or she simply favors it, feeling that the issues it emphasizes are more interesting and thought-provoking than those raised by the other perspectives. Table 5.1 compares the three theories of social interaction.

The nearby Social Application illustrates the usefulness of dramaturgic sociology.

The Structure of Social Interaction

The theoretical perspectives discussed in the previous section indicate that social interaction uses symbolic communication, that it contains an underlying social order, and that it can be analyzed like the action of a play. In each case the theory reveals certain patterns that occur in social interaction. If we examine such concepts as status and role, leadership, conformity, and decision making, other patterns will become apparent, and our understanding of social interaction will increase.

Table 5.1 Three Theories of Social Interaction

Theory	View of human behavior	Example
Symbolic Interaction	The meanings individuals give people and things determine human behavior and are learned in interaction with others.	An appreciation and understanding of the father role can be learned from a variety of sources, including individual or group counseling.
Ethnomethodology	An often unrecognized social order underlies everyday social activity.	Through informal research Garfinkel's students discovered some implicit norms about appropriate behavior existing in their families.
Dramaturgic Sociology	The participants in social interaction behave like actors in a play.	When interviewed for a job, an effective candidate will engage in impression management.

SOCIAL APPLICATION
Privatizing Executions: A Use of Dramaturgic Sociology

In addressing significant social problems, writers can use an approach similar to dramaturgic sociology to characterize an issue in ways that would be less emphatic with ordinary prose. When the celebrated playwright Arthur Miller wrote about the delegation of executions to the private sector, he was able to use his dramatic power to highlight both the brutality of executions and the modern tendency to commercialize an extensive range of situations.

At the moment, Miller indicated, everyone loses with an execution—the convicted person, the family, and society. Since executions are only one illustration of government's inability to do anything right, the best bet is to turn this activity over to private business.

Executions would be conducted in the largest sports stadiums, with current enthusiasm for capital punishment suggesting that there would be huge crowds willing to pay $200 to $300 for ringside seats and only slightly less for those with a less intimate view. Certainly condemned criminals would receive a percentage of the gate, to be worked out by their agents or promoters in backstage negotiations before the great performance occurred.

As with all sporting events, a certain theatrical ritual would develop in the frontstage area. The principal prop would be the electric chair, set on a platform like a boxing ring without the

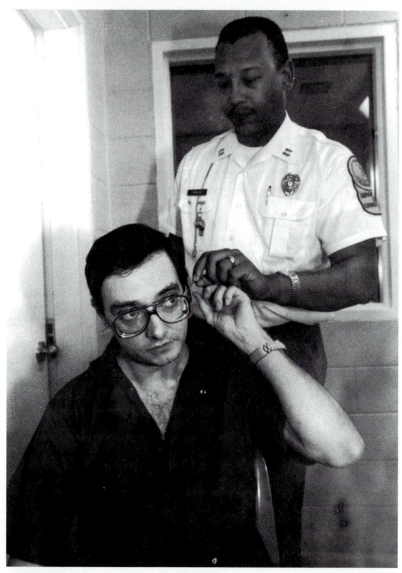

While executions will never become the full-fledged media events described in this Social Application, television sometimes plays a significant role. Roger Keith Coleman, who was convicted of murder and rape, appeared on "Donahue," claiming his innocence and unsuccessfully seeking an appeal for his scheduled execution, which was carried out the following day.

rope, near the stadium's second base.

A standard sequence of acts (with each carefully planned to obtain the full benefit of impression management) would then unfold—first, a soprano singing the national anthem; followed by the governor, with microphone in hand, providing a thorough description of the condemned murderer's list of crimes and failed appeals; then the featured performer's entrance announced by a military band's trumpet fanfare or other musical accompaniment; next a minister or priest's blessing on the execution; then as an option, a short statement from the condemned person; and finally the executioner, hooded to protect himself from possible retaliation, approaching a console and, after receiving the governor's signal, pulling the switch.

Miller wrote:

> The condemned man would instantly surge upward against his bindings, with the smoke emitting from his flesh. This by itself would provide a most powerful lesson for anyone contemplating murder. For those not contemplating murder, it would be a reminder of how lucky they are to have been straight and honest in America.

> (*Miller* 1992, A31)

Everyone involved, the playwright concluded, would benefit. The state would obtain additional income; the audience would have an intense, meaningful experience, so meaningful that parents might consider bringing their children. Even the condemned people would gain, realizing that their lives had not been for nothing. In fact, some critics might argue that the staged execution would prove so compelling that some individuals might consider committing murder just to become the featured actor—an element to his plan, Miller admitted, that illustrated that no solution to a social problem is completely without drawbacks.

Perhaps after seeing several dozen privatized executions, people might begin to grow tired of the spectacle. With the fervor gone, the public might start appreciating that capital punishment merely adds to the number of untimely deaths without limiting the number of murders committed. Americans might also start wondering why the U.S. murder rate is higher than in other countries. But, because we never get to witness executions, Miller argued, we are not yet bored enough with them to ask this question. He concluded, "My proposal would lead us more quickly to boredom and away from our current gratifying excitement—and ultimately perhaps to a wiser use of alternating current" (Miller 1992, A31).

Source: Arthur Miller. "Get It Right. Privatize Executions," New York Times. (May 8, 1992), p. A31.

STATUS AND ROLE

Imagine that two 20-year-old women—Jan and Jill—meet at a bus station. Both are on the way home from college for the spring break, and soon they are talking about their school experience. Jan has been studying over fifty hours a week ever since her freshman year. "It's the only way I can keep a high average," she explains. Jill, in contrast, is relaxed about her grades and spends a lot of time socializing, drinking, and going to parties. "We're certainly having a very different time at college," Jan says.

These two women occupy a common status: that of college student. A **status** is a position that indicates where a person fits into a group or society and how he or she should relate to others in the structure. Any particular status stands in a definite relationship to other statuses because of the rights and obligations associated with it. As college students both Jan and Jill have the right to take courses for credit, and they are expected to pay for their schooling and to complete their assignments.

Whereas both Jan and Jill occupy the status of student, they perform the role of student differently. A **role** is a set of expected behaviors associated with a particular status. Several roles may be "attached" to one status. An individual occupying the status of student may emphasize academic performance; extracurricular activities such as student government, clubs, and athletics; or social life, particularly parties and friendships. As Figure 5.2 indicates, Jan and Jill visualize the student status very differently. Jan concentrates on the academic role while Jill's main concern is the social role.

In modern societies people play many roles, and often two roles played by an individual will

Figure 5.2
Statuses and Roles

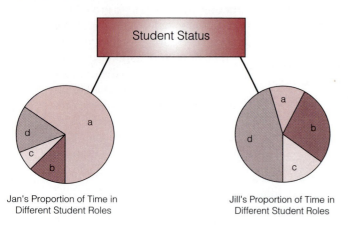

"a" represents time doing schoolwork (studying, attending classes, speaking
   to professors, etc.).
"b" is time at work to pay for schooling and basic expenses.
"c" stands for extracurricular activities (school clubs, athletic teams, etc.).
"d" represents social activities.

*These two students differ profoundly in their interpretation of
their student status. Knowledge of their respective priorities permits some predictions about role strains. Jill, for instance, would
be much more likely to interrupt studying to socialize with her
friends. The resolutions to role conflicts would be difficult to predict without more knowledge of the women. For instance, how
would a conscientious student like Jan respond to the pressing
needs of a sick relative at exam time?*

clash. **Role strain** is an incompatibility between
two or more roles associated with the same status.
For example, students experience role strain when
they must decide whether to study for a test or go
to a party.

Role conflict refers to incompatibility between two or more roles associated with different
statuses. For instance, a certain man has the statuses of husband and businessman. In the role of
husband, he recognizes that he should be concerned about his wife's happiness—he knows that
she is attached to the town they live in—and thus
as a husband the man wants to remain in town. In
the role of businessman, however, he receives an
offer for a better paying, more prestigious job with
a company in another state, and so as a businessman he wants to leave town. Therefore this man's
two role expectations are in direct conflict, and the
decision on what to do will mean that either as a
husband or as a businessman he will fail to meet
that role's expectation.

In the past twenty years, a large body of
research has developed on one topic involving role
conflicts. What is the topic? Keep in mind that a
rapid growth in social research tends to reflect
events within the society. Have you got the
answer? The topic is the role conflicts faced by current adults, who must meet the often conflicting
demands on their time and energy made by family
members and work obligations. Many studies
focus on role conflicts of working women with children (Hock and DeMeis 1990; MacEwen and
Barling 1991; Reifman et al. 1991), but some investigations examine the role conflicts both women
and men face in reconciling the demands of family
and job (Burley 1991; Duxbury and Higgins 1991;
Wiersma and van den Berg 1991).

LEADERSHIP

A man pridefully watches his son playing with a
group of children in his backyard. His wife walks
over, and he puts his arm around her. "That kid of
ours, Judy, is giving orders like a shop foreman.
He's one heck of a leader. You know what I think? I
think some day Pete's going to be elected president." Like many people Pete's father apparently
believes that leadership is simply the ability to
issue commands. As we see in this section,
research has indicated that leadership is more
complicated than that.

Leadership is the exercise of influence or
authority within a group by one or more members.
Studies in the early 1990s investigated leadership
and ethics in law enforcement (King 1991), the crisis of leadership in modern organizations (Krantz
1990), and the identification of opinion leaders
(Weimann 1991). Since early in the twentieth century, researchers have recognized that activities
seem to follow a systematic pattern or, at any rate,
that problem solving might be simplified if they
did. In spite of this early interest, a thorough effort
to map out small-group activities did not begin
until after World War II. In the late 1940s, Robert
Bales and his associates (Bales 1953; Bales and
Strodtbeck 1968) set out to analyze all the basic
types of interpersonal relations that occur in small
groups.

Bales studied twenty-two small groups
involved in a wide variety of tasks, and he identified two types of communication—those that are
instrumental, intended to promote the pursuit of

group goals, and those that are **expressive,** concerned with emotional or social issues. Expressive communications frequently are meant to restore the harmony disrupted in the pursuit of group goals. If a group is to function effectively, the competent performance of both types of tasks is essential. Laboratory studies indicate, however, that a single person seldom provides both expressive and instrumental leadership in a group (Bales and Slater 1955). The skills required of each type of leader are different, and furthermore the considerable time and energy that must be devoted to providing one type of leadership often precludes actively pursuing the other type of leadership.

Small-group researchers have also assessed the consequences of different styles of leadership. One investigator studied the behavior of groups of boys subjected to three different adult leadership styles. **Authoritarian leaders** controlled all aspects of group activity yet stayed somewhat aloof from the group. **Democratic leaders** permit-

ted group members to determine many policies and took an active role in discussions. In contrast, **laissez-faire leaders** left group members free to reach their own individual or group decisions. The research showed that:

> Authoritarian leadership tended to be ineffective because the group members became bogged down in internal conflicts.

> Democratic leadership proved to be efficient. The quality of work in democratically led groups was better than that performed by groups with authoritarian leadership, and work motivation was stronger in a democratically led group than in an authoritarian setting. In addition, originality was more common, and greater group-mindedness and friendliness prevailed.

> Under laissez-faire leadership, the group members did less work, and the quality of the work accomplished was poorer than was the case in democratic contexts. More time was spent playing.

One provocative way to analyze the impact of leadership is to focus on followers' actions, often revealing inconsistencies between the leader's claims and followers' behavior. In the 1990–1991 Persian Gulf conflict, President George Bush and other prominent Americans frequently pointed to the U.S. leadership role, asserting that their country was heading a broadly based coalition of thirty-five countries in the war against Iraq. But beyond a United Nations Security Council resolution requiring Iraqi withdrawal from Kuwait by any means necessary, the U.S. received limited support. With the exception of Great Britain, U.S. allies participated modestly or not at all in the military effort, undercutting the Bush administration's frequent claim that the war was an American-led multinational effort. Analysis of followers' actions, in short, can reveal a great deal about a leader's performance (Cooper, Higgott, and Nossal 1991).

The nearby Cross-Cultural Perspective examines a significant leader's rise to prominence.

Many leaders, including presidents, experience emotional roller-coaster rides. This photo catches a triumphant moment for Bill Clinton — his reception by followers on election night.

CONFORMITY

Conformity is behavior that supports the norms of a certain group. Society could not survive without considerable conformity, and yet excessive conformity suggests mindlessness, an inability to think

CROSS-CULTURAL PERSPECTIVE
Nelson Mandela's Leadership in South Africa

Sociologists tend to downplay the importance of single individuals. In some instances, however, a key person at the right time and place has an enormous impact on the lives of millions of people. Though not an elected official, Nelson Mandela has been such a rare person—someone whose half-century record of handling enormous stress and conflict with great wisdom and dignity have propelled him into the center of political decision making in South Africa. We consider Mandela's development as a leader, and the role that he currently plays.

In 1944 at the age of 26, Mandela joined the African National Congress (ANC), an organization dedicated to obtaining rights for black Africans in a country where the *apartheid* system of segregation of racial groups meant that racial minorities were profoundly oppressed politically, economically, and socially. For the next eighteen years, Mandela was an active member of the ANC, protesting against the racist restrictions imposed on Africans. In spite of several bannings, which prevented him from attending public meetings, and brief imprisonment, he continued his protest activities. In 1961 acting independently of the ANC, Mandela and a group of ANC members decided that authorities' resistance to the elimination of *apartheid* was so unrelenting that they would precipitate change through acts of sabo-

tage, making certain that no lives would be endangered. In December 1961 homemade bombs were exploded in three South African cities. At that point Mandela went underground, but in August 1962 following an informer's tip, he was arrested.

Sentenced to life imprisonment in 1963, Mandela began serving his sentence. Already famous and respected when arrested, Mandela's years in prison turned him into a nearly legendary figure. He was the epitome of commitment to the fight against *apartheid.* In 1973 the government promised to release him if he would stay in the remote Transkei region—obviously out of harm's way, from an official point of view. Mandela refused. In 1980 a movement called the "Release Mandela Campaign" started and then grew the next year, with six French organizations, including the ruling Socialist Party of France, delivering a petition with 17,000 signatures calling for Mandela's release to the South African Embassy in Paris.

Recent Events   As the 1990s approached, Mandela's fame continued to increase. In the minds of both sympathetic South Africans and foreigners, he had come to embody the most noble image of black South Africans' fight for the end of *apartheid.* When the so-called "Eminent Person Group" was permitted to visit him, they indicated that while Mandela longed to be permitted to con-

tribute to solving his country's racial strife, he remained "unmarked by any bitterness despite his long imprisonment" (Meer 1990, book jacket). When she saw him the year before his release, Mandela's biographer wrote, "[His] face is unwrinkled; he smiles readily and often, his eyes crinkling at the corners; his laughter is deep-throated and spontaneous" (Meer 1990, xviii).

But beneath his relaxed demeanor, Mandela's commitment to his cause was unwavering. When released from prison in 1990, Mandela was asked whether *apartheid* was dying. Mandela replied that when he was sent to prison in 1963, he could not vote. He added, "Twenty-seven years later, I still have no vote and that is due to the color of my skin. You can then decide whether *apartheid* is alive or dead" (Wren 1990, 6).

In March 1992 South Africa's whites voted an official end to *apartheid,* permitting citizens of all races to vote. While certainly progressive, this action has not solved the situation, because the political machinery ending *apartheid* still must be set in motion. Mandela's role in this process is important and complicated by the diversity now existing in the country.

Mandela's power base, the ANC, to which he has belonged for fifty years, is hardly a unified organization. Its members vary in age and experience. Some are former political prisoners or exiles while others are trade unionists or members of community organizations within South Africa. In addition, Mandela faces competition for political control of the African population from such organizations as Inkatha and Pan Africanist Congress. The latter group, which has a strong appeal to frustrated young Africans, emphasizes black consciousness, dismissing cooperation with whites and expressing confidence that eventually their organization will win support of the majority of the African population.

Furthermore, while Mandela has been trying to establish cooperative relations among all four racial groups—blacks, Coloreds (people of mixed black and white ancestry), Indians, and whites—he has found that *apartheid* has entrenched difficult, often bitter relations between racial groups. For instance, in Natal province, where the majority of Indians live, there has been a long history of tensions between black Africans and Indians, who are better educated, control most of the trade, and hold a much higher proportion of white-collar jobs.

Although relations among

all racial groups are important, Mandela has recognized that whites still control political power and that while a decision to end *apartheid* has been reached, he and members of other racial minorities remain unable to vote.

Mandela and members of the ANC want a government of majority rule, meaning that blacks, who represent nearly two-thirds of South Africa's population, will numerically dominate the electorate. The National Party, which has run the country since 1948, is determined to make certain that in spite of representing only about a fifth of the population, whites will retain a significant share of power. Furthermore President F. W. de Klerk and members of the National Party proposed that there be an interim constitution to set up a transitional government, with a final constitution to be thrashed out in the future. Mandela and his associates have opposed this idea, saying that for them an interim constitution represents a trap with which whites could comfortably live forever.

While significant differen-

ces persist, important progress has been made. Both sides support the creation of a new democratic constitution, insuring political equality for all racial minorities and individual safeguards for whites, and they are also generally agreed about the structure of the new parliament.

At the center of all deliberations stands Nelson Mandela. While often others disagree with him, all groups contributing to the new South Africa recognize what he has done and what he still can do. Mandela has developed a cordial, mutually respectful relationship with President F. W. de Klerk, and while he has remained a tough, demanding negotiator for black Africans' rights, he has refused to resort to threats of violence when talks have broken down. A well-known specialist on South Africa indicated that since his release from prison, Mandela "has handled himself with great dignity and, I believe, in nearly every respect with remarkable political wisdom. His survival seems crucial for the prospects of peaceful transformation in South Africa" (Thompson 1990, 18).

Sources: Economist. *"The ANC's New Faces,"* vol. 320 (June 29, 1991), *p.* 38; *Fatima Meer.* Higher Than Hope: The Authorized Biography of Nelson Mandela. New York: Harper & Row, 1990; *Leonard Thompson.* "South Africa: The Fire This Time?" New York Review of Books. vol. 37 (June 14, 1990), *pp.* 12+; *Christopher S. Wren.* "South African Talks Yield Outlines on an Agreement on Basic Political Changes," New York Times. (May 5, 1990), *pp.* 1+; *Christopher S. Wren.* "South African Foes Struggle to Be Partners," New York Times. (May 24, 1992), *sec.* 4, *p.* 4.

and act on one's own. In Hans Christian Andersen's fairy tale "The Emperor's New Clothes," all the subjects watching the king were excessive conformists, acting in line with the official norm that their ruler was wearing beautiful new clothes even though he was actually naked. Finally a little girl commented loudly that the king was wearing nothing. As soon as the little girl had spoken, her father

said, "Just hear what the innocent says." Quickly the word spread through the crowd of conformists that the king was indeed naked.

A wide range of research has been conducted on the topic of conformity. Studies have examined noncoercive means of producing conformity to the law (Curtis et al. 1991), situational factors affecting group members' reactions to conforming or

122 deviant opinions (Kruglanski and Webster 1991), and the relationship between shame and conformity (Scheff 1988).

Solomon Asch's experiments are among the best known investigations of conformity.

The Asch Experiments

Some years ago Asch (1963), a social psychologist, devised an experiment to explore how group pressure affects judgment. The original study featured a control group and an experimental group. In the control situation, people sat in a room without talking and examined two set of cards. As Figure 5.3 indicates, there was one line on the card on the left, and the card on the right held three lines, only one of which exactly matched the length of the line on the first card. Each person recorded the number of the line on the second card that seemed to be the same length as the line on the first card. Altogether there were twelve sets of cards, and in each case there was one obvious match between the single line on the first card and the three lines on the second. Virtually no mistakes were made, indicating that normally people had no difficulty accomplishing this task.

In the experimental group, there were eight men. Seven of them were confederates, who had met previously with the experimenter, who had instructed them to respond at certain points with unanimous, incorrect judgments. The eighth per-

Figure 5.3

A Sample Comparison of Lines in the Asch Experiment

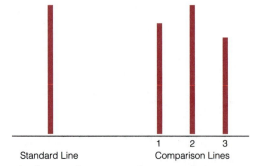

Standard Line   Comparison Lines

Control subjects made correct matchings more than 99 percent of the time. Experimental subjects conformed to incorrect matchings one-third of the time when faced with the unanimous matchings of seven confederates.

Source: Solomon E. Asch. *Social Psychology.* Englewood Cliffs, NJ: Prentice-Hall, 1952, p. 452.

son, the actual subject, who confronted this unanimous majority, was the real focus. Asch wrote, "He faced, possibly for the first time in his life, a situation in which a group unanimously contradicted the evidence of his senses" (Asch 1963, 179).

The results from the experimental group were very different from those that emerged from the control group. In the experimental context, a third of the total number of matchings made by the subject were factually incorrect, conforming to the prearranged stated judgment of the confederates.

Variations in the experimental setup produced different results. When the actual subject received the support of another person who provided correct matchings, the incidence of conformity to the group opinion dropped sharply. If, however, this "true partner" suddenly stopped giving accurate answers and sided with the majority, then the incidence of conformity rose to 28.5 percent, nearly as high as in the original experiment. Asch also varied the group size of confederates. When there was only one person who had been instructed to give incorrect answers, conforming responses by the subjects practically disappeared. With two confederates 12.8 percent of the naive subjects' responses were conforming. Conformity rose to the one-third level when there was a majority of three opposing the subject. Larger groups of confederates (four, eight, and sixteen) did not significantly increase the level of conformity.

Subsequent experiments have tried to refine Asch's results. For instance, in experiments similar to those conducted by Asch, Luther Jennings and Stephen George (1984) sought to determine the extent to which the distortion of judgment produced by group influence was conscious or unconscious. They found that conscious distortion of judgment occurred four to five times more frequently than unconscious distortion. Since the research subjects were aware of their incorrect judgments, it can be assumed that they felt that it was more important to support the group judgment than to be correct.

While some people are probably disturbed by the mindlessness often accompanying conformity, conforming behavior generally does not arouse strong reactions until cases are revealed in which people felt compelled to obey orders to commit brutal acts. If a person is already inclined to commit such acts, then the support of authority figures simply makes such behavior easier, as the

In extreme form conformity is frightening and dangerous. The deputies of the German Reichstag saluting in unison Adolf Hitler's arrival represent a vivid illustration of such a phenomenon.

following illustration suggests. In January 1942, Adolf Eichmann, head of the Jewish Office in the German Secret Police (Gestapo), met with a group of top-level Nazi civil servants to coordinate efforts to the "Final Solution," Adolf Hitler's plan to exterminate the Jews of Europe. Eichmann still had some doubts about "such a bloody solution through violence," but when he observed this group of elite civil servants competing against one another to take the initiative in the genocidal effort, he felt freed of guilt. As Eichmann told the court at his trial in Jerusalem, he not only obeyed orders but also was following the new law of the land (Berkowitz 1980, 316–17). We well might wonder whether the members of modern societies can eventually eliminate the conditions producing Eichmanns.

DECISION MAKING

There is an old saying that two heads are better than one. This proverb is certainly valid if the "two heads" are trying to make a decision that can be based on factual knowledge. For instance, a team of people do better at a crossword puzzle than a single individual. Similarly a clinic that employs a

variety of medical specialists is likely to be better equipped than a single physician to diagnose and treat a wide range of illnesses.

In other situations it is less clear whether an individual or a group will make better decisions. One researcher first asked individual subjects to reach decisions on hypothetical problems and then combined the individuals into groups and instructed them to reach group decisions. The latter decisions often displayed a "risky shift," a move toward a more daring course of action (Stoner 1961). One reason this occurred is that a group decision diffuses responsibility among the members, particularly if the decision turns out to be bad.

The vast literature on decision making includes research analyzing the impact of eyewitness evidence on plea-bargain decisions by defense attorneys and prosecutors (McAllister 1990), the factors affecting treatment decisions for breast cancer (Siminoff and Fetting 1991), and the conditions determining alliance decisions for twentieth-century democracies (Siverson and Emmons 1991).

The following study of the management of public input into foreign policy revealed that sometimes decision making emerges as a process

124

with a distinct set of steps. The first significant factor was government officials' impression about the public's approach to foreign policy—that both their interest in the topic and their knowledge about it was quite limited.

Nonetheless the second step indicated that among foreign-policy officials there has developed a strong feeling that a successful foreign policy must incorporate the public's views—that otherwise the government can find itself with staunch opposition that can make policy implementation difficult or impossible and threaten careers. One official noted that recognition of public influence was a fairly new condition. He added, "I think if you discussed these kinds of questions with people in the [State] Department 20 years ago, you would get very different answers" (Powlick 1991, 625).

After taking into account public opinion, government officials implement policy, recognizing that if it is sufficiently different from the dominant public position to produce public opposition, then explanation will be necessary. An official in the Inter-American Affairs Bureau explained that in formulating policy, he and his colleagues normally "put [public opinion] aside and decide what is the best reaction to these circumstances—what does the policy dictate that we do—and afterwards say, 'OK, how can this be explained to the public?'" (Powlick 1991, 623).

The Disruption of Patterns of Social Interaction

In the last two sections, we examined theories and concepts that demonstrate how the social-interaction process works. These analyses have emphasized the central role that social interaction plays in human relations. Further support for that conclusion becomes apparent if we examine situations where there is a breakdown in the normal social-interaction patterns. The absence of such patterns will suggest their importance in maintaining people's sense of well-being.

Frequently people experience stress when isolated. Research indicates that there are several stages isolated people are likely to pass through (Schachter 1959). In the beginning these people often experience full-blown anxiety attacks that increase with time and then decrease sharply in many cases. As the sense of isolation diminishes, there is apathy or even withdrawal and detachment. Finally the isolated individual may dream, fantasize, or even hallucinate about other people.

Many human beings are highly adaptive in a solitary condition. A small number of hearty individuals have sailed alone around the world, in small boats, apparently without suffering significant psychological damage. Admiral Richard Byrd, an experienced polar explorer, spent the winter of 1933 completely alone in his camp in Antarctica. Such people have been able to withstand their isolation because they have had activities to keep them busy. Individuals in situations of forced isolation seem to do better when they invent tasks for themselves such as solving puzzles, reciting poetry, or performing exercises.

Whether natural or produced by human beings, disasters involve a significant disruption of

When the World Trade Center was bombed by terrorists in February 1993, seven people were killed and thousands injured. As the distress on this woman's face indicates, being present during a disaster can be a traumatic experience.

social interaction. On the afternoon of July 19, 1989, a DC-10 crashed while attempting an emergency landing at Sioux City, Iowa. Despite the destruction of the airplane and a fire that followed, 184 of 296 passengers survived. While the medical response to this air disaster was effective, there was no coordinated effort to meet people's mental-health needs.

A team of social scientists (Jacobs, Quevillon, and Stricherz 1990) concluded that competent handling of situations like the Sioux City crash requires a mental-health disaster plan, minimizing chaos by reducing stress for individuals involved in the disaster. The greatest need for mental-health services is immediately following the occurrence of the disaster, thus requiring the plan to be produced ahead of time.

Many predictably difficult issues should be considered in this plan—for instance, an unrelenting emphasis on obtaining accurate information related to the disaster while recognizing that in such situations information is often inaccurate and subject to frequent changes. The morning following the Sioux City disaster officials were told that a group of 100 family members would be arriving in ninety minutes, and quickly eighty counselors were assembled to deal with them. Several hours later an official explained that there had been a misunderstanding and that only seven family members were showing up, and half the counselors were immediately dismissed. However, a half hour later an airline representative said that the original estimate of 100 family members was accurate. Then ten minutes later amidst hasty efforts to reassemble the large group of counselors, only seven family members appeared. While some communications problems are probably inevitable in disasters, the better coordinated the different organizations involved in providing mental-health services, the smaller the amount of misinformation.

Another issue requiring planning is the mental-health personnel's relationship to the organization most central to the disaster. In this case that organization was the airline, whose representatives at first interacted minimally with mental-health personnel. This situation changed significantly when one individual was appointed official liaison to the head of the mental-health team, facilitating coordination between the two groups and, in particular, permitting mental-health service personnel to provide various kinds of support, including stress management, for airline staff.

AIDS or other lethal diseases, homelessness, divorce, or death of a loved one—these are common disruptive events in current Americans' lives. The sociological perspective can be applied to each of them. One can examine the social and nonsocial factors that have produced the disruptive situation, analyze the sequence of events that occur as the individual or group confronts the problem, and speculate about people's adaptation after the crisis has passed.

STUDY GUIDE

Learning Objectives

After studying this chapter, you should be able to:

1. Define social interaction and discuss its significance in people's lives.
2. Discuss symbolic interaction, ethnomethodology, and dramaturgic sociology, defining each theory and offering clear, detailed examples of all three.
3. Define status and role, distinguishing between the two concepts by using clear illustrations.
4. Discuss role strain and role conflict, clarifying their differences and providing an example of each.
5. Define leadership, examine the leadership styles of authoritarian, democratic, and laissez-faire leaders, and identify the factors determining leadership effectiveness.

126

6. Analyze conformity, defining the concept and summarizing the major findings of the Asch experiments.
7. Examine the factors that affect group decision making.
8. Indicate how social-interaction patterns may become disrupted and how people may react or adapt to such disruption.

Summary

1. Social interaction is the basic process through which two or more people use language and gestures to affect each other's thoughts, expectations, and behavior. Social interaction provides the foundation of people's development.

2. Theories of social interaction include symbolic interaction, ethnomethodology, and dramaturgic sociology. Symbolic interaction is a theory that emphasizes the importance of symbolic communication—gestures and, above all, language—in the development of the individual, group, and society. To understand symbolic interaction, researchers must study the meanings of social interaction.

Ethnomethodology is the study of the sometimes recognized, often unrecognized social order. Harold Garfinkel's informal experiments have supplied the pioneer research in this area.

Dramaturgic sociology is a theoretical approach that analyzes interaction as if the participants were actors in a play. The actors perform their parts, follow the script if possible, and improvise whenever the script is unclear or nonexistent. Dramaturgic sociology emphasizes that like a theater performance, social interaction involves a frontstage and a backstage. Performers also engage in impression management: an attempt to control other people's evaluations of them by presenting themselves in the most favorable manner.

3. Concepts that play a significant part in social interaction include status and role, leadership, conformity, and decision making. A status is a position that indicates where a person fits into a group or society and how that person should relate to others in the structure. A role is a set of expected behaviors associated with a particular status. Role strains and role conflicts also influence group activities.

Leadership is another important component of the social-interaction process. Studies of leadership demonstrate that two broad sets of leadership tasks exist: the instrumental and the expressive; and that different kinds of leadership develop: the democratic, authoritarian, and laissez-faire varieties.

In examining social interaction, some researchers have studied conformity, behavior that supports the norms of a certain group. The well-known Asch experiments have demonstrated how group pressure affects judgment.

Decision making is another prominent social-interaction process. An analysis of the management of public input into foreign policy revealed that in this instance the process contains three distinct steps.

4. Whether people are experiencing the stress of being alone or are surviving following a disaster, behavioral adjustments will occur. Research has indicated the usefulness of a well-conceived plan for mental-health services to be implemented following a significant disaster.

Key Terms

authoritarian leader   a leader who controls all aspects of group activity yet stays somewhat aloof from the group

backstage   the physical area or region where people construct the illusions and impressions they will use in a performance

conformity   behavior that supports the norms of a certain group

democratic leader   a leader who permits group members to determine many policies and takes an active role in discussion

dramaturgic sociology   a theoretical approach that analyzes social interaction as if the participants were actors in a play

ethnomethodology   the study of the sometimes recognized, often unrecognized social order, the set of underlying shared norms and expectations that promote harmony in most everyday social interactions

expressive   concerned with emotional or social issues

frontstage   the physical area or region where people present a performance

impression management   the attempt to control others' evaluations by presenting oneself in the most favorable light

instrumental   intended to promote the pursuit of group goals

laissez-faire leader   a leader who does not take an active role in group discussions, leaving group members free to reach individual or group decisions

leadership   the exercise of influence or authority within a group by one or more members

role   a set of expected behaviors associated with a particular status

role conflict   an incompatibility between two or more roles associated with different statuses

role strain   an incompatibility between two or more roles associated with the same status

social interaction   the basic process through which two or more people use language and gestures to affect each other's thoughts, expectations, and behavior

status   a position that indicates where a person fits into a group or society and how that person should relate to others in the structure

symbolic interaction   a theory that emphasizes the dominant part played by symbolic communication—gestures and above all language—in the development of the individual, group, and society

---

Tests

True • False Test

_____   1. Researchers using the symbolic-interaction theory are concerned with the meanings individuals give to people and things.

_____   2. Garfinkel's ethnomethodological study of his students' families showed that to most family members the underlying social order was not a very interesting subject.

_____   3. Arthur Miller's account of a privatized execution focuses on a major weakness to dramaturgic sociology.

_____   4. Several statuses may be "attached" to one role.

_____   5. In a role-conflict situation, the fulfillment of one role expectation means that another role expectation will not be met.

_____   6. In recent years there has been almost no research done on role conflicts.

_____   7. Instrumental leaders are concerned with emotional or social issues.

_____   8. Soon after Nelson Mandela's release from prison, he voted in South Africa's national election.

_____   9. In the Asch experiments that explored how group pressure affects judgment, the behavior in the experimental group was sometimes very different from the behavior in the control group.

_____ 10. After studying a DC-10 crash in Sioux City, Iowa, a team of social scientists concluded that the greatest need for mental-health services is immediately following the occurrence of a disaster, thus requiring a plan to be produced ahead of time.

Multiple-Choice Test

_____   1. According to the discussion of the changing father role:
         a.   most men find it easy to be open emotionally.
         b.   some men try to become the father they wish they had.
         c.   group counseling cannot change men's conception of the father role.
         d.   a and b

_____   2. The Donner party described in this chapter faced a challenge to the social order when its members had to choose between death or survival by committing:
         a.   war atrocities.
         b.   cannibalism.
         c.   violations against animals they worshipped.
         d.   incest.

_____   3. Using a dramaturgic sociological perspective, Goffman suggested that the performances people give are:
         a.   independent of the social setting.
         b.   only done in the backstage.
         c.   always done without impression management.
         d.   sometimes based on deception.

_____   4. An incompatibility between two or more roles associated with the *same* status is a:
         a.   role conflict.
         b.   role strain.
         c.   anticipatory status.
         d.   conformity conflict.

_____   5. Bales and Slater studied communication in task-oriented groups. They found that:
         a.   instrumental and expressive leadership skills are similar.
         b.   the typical leader has well-developed instrumental and expressive skills.
         c.   only very nervous people have instrumental skills.
         d.   both sets of skills are necessary for a group to function effectively.

_____   6. In the Persian Gulf conflict:
         a.   President Bush emphasized the U.S. leadership role as head of a coalition of thirty-five countries.
         b.   the United States received troop support from two dozen nations.
         c.   besides Great Britain, U.S. allies participated modestly or not at all in the military effort.
         d.   a and c

_____   7. Jennings and George's experiments that sought to refine Asch's research on conformity found that:
         a.   surprisingly, Asch's results were incorrect.
         b.   conscious distortion of judgment occurred four to five times more frequently than unconscious distortion.

   c.   unconscious distortion of judgment occurred four to five times more frequently than conscious distortion.

   d.   Americans are much less likely to conform than people in other countries.

_____ 8. A study about the management of public input into foreign policy indicated that a successful policy must incorporate:

   a.   the public's views.

   b.   backstage activities.

   c.   the influence of control groups.

   d.   role strain.

_____ 9. Foreign-policy officials have found that:

   a.   a successful foreign policy must incorporate the public's view.

   b.   a high level of public interest in foreign policy now exists.

   c.   since the end of World War II, they have needed to take into account the public's position on foreign-policy issues.

   d.   b and c

_____ 10. A plan for mental-health services following a disaster should include:

   a.   the establishment of martial law to prevent civil disorder.

   b.   a blackout of all local mass media to prevent false rumors and mass hysteria.

   c.   a strong emphasis on officials' obtaining accurate information related to the disaster.

   d.   a and b

Essay Test

1. List and discuss two theories of social interaction, providing definitions of each and your own examples (*not* those in this chapter) representing the major issues and concepts of each theory.
2. Define status and role, drawing a clear distinction between the two terms. Write about a social situation that demonstrates the meanings of the two concepts. Use this same situation to illustrate the meanings of role conflict and role strain.
3. Define leadership and also three different leadership styles. Discuss the leadership style in two groups in which you participate. Are the styles effective in both cases? Explain.
4. Define conformity and discuss in detail the findings of the Asch experiments.
5. Discuss how people are likely to respond to the disruption of social-interaction patterns.

Suggested Readings

Blumer, Herbert. 1969. *Symbolic Interactionism: Perspective and Method*. Engelwood Cliffs, NJ: Prentice-Hall. A thorough, thoughtful, if somewhat abstract introduction to symbolic interaction by an authority on the subject. The opening essay is particularly informative.

130 Erikson, Kai. 1976. *Everything in Its Path: Destruction of Community in the Buffalo Creek Flood.* New York: Simon & Schuster. A nicely written, well-documented account of what happened to the interaction patterns of a tightly knit mining community when it was ravaged by a flood.

Garfinkel, Harold. 1967. *Studies in Ethnomethodology.* Englewood Cliffs, NJ: Prentice-Hall. A set of eight challenging articles outlining Garfinkel's informal studies of the social order underlying all social interactions.

Goffman, Erving. 1959. *The Presentation of Self in Everyday Life.* Garden City, NY: Doubleday. An introduction to some of the intricacies and subtleties of social interaction. Goffman discusses the devices people use to influence others' perceptions of them. The illustrative material is colorful, wide-ranging, and thought-provoking.

Golding, William. 1954. *Lord of the Flies.* New York: Coward-McCann. A classic novel describing how a group of boys gradually deteriorates into savagery following an airplane crash. Group decision making, leadership, and the influence of groups on individuals are important themes throughout the account.

Janis, Irving L. 1972. *Victims of Groupthink.* Boston: Houghton Mifflin. Use of case studies of the Bay of Pigs invasion, the escalation of the Vietnam War, the Cuban missile crisis, and other important international confrontations to illustrate the process by which top governmental leaders make both foolish and effective decisions.

Macionis, John J., and Nijole V. Benokraitis (eds.). 1992. *Seeing Ourselves: Classic, Contemporary, and Cross-Cultural Readings in Sociology.* 2nd ed. Englewood Cliffs, NJ: Prentice-Hall. A book of sociological readings, with the majority of them examining small-group interactional patterns involving a variety of sociological topics.

Orwell, George. 1959. *Down and Out in Paris and London.* New York: Berkeley Medallion. Originally published in 1933. The youthful adventures of the well-known writer when he was cleaning pots in Paris restaurants and living as a tramp in England. The book reads like a gripping novel and is filled with insights about social-interaction patterns.

Additional Assignments

1. Select a place to eat—a fast food restaurant, a student cafeteria, or a fairly expensive restaurant. As you eat, make mental notes (to be recorded as soon as you leave) regarding the physical layout, behavior of patrons, interaction of waiters and waitresses, or other important features of the setting. When you are alone, try to visualize the activity as if you were going to write and produce a play. Would social interaction flow more smoothly if any of the actions, settings, or props were changed? Did you detect any failures in impression management? Did any actions occur in the frontstage that more appropriately should have occurred backstage? Compare your findings with those obtained by other students.

2. Among people you like and trust (such as friends, family members, or roommates), violate a fairly minor social norm. Note people's immediate reactions. After the violation behave as though you had done nothing wrong or unusual and observe others' reactions for the next few minutes. Do they seem to be encouraging you to maintain conforming behavioral patterns? Complete this informal experiment by explaining what you have done and what sociologists seek to learn from such research. How did you feel during the experiment? Did this experience give you insight about the Garfinkel and Asch studies presented in the text?

Answers to Objective Test Questions

True • False Test

1. t   6. f
2. t   7. f
3. f   8. f
4. f   9. t
5. t   10. t

Multiple-Choice Test

1. b   6. d
2. b   7. b
3. d   8. a
4. b   9. a
5. d   10. c

Socialization

6

Now John Coleman would begin ten days of living as a homeless person, learning firsthand what the experience involved. He went to Penn Station and changed into the old clothes he had bought the day before. He stowed his normal clothes in a locker and went outside into the winter cold. Were people looking at him differently? He felt that men, especially the successful ones in their forties, saw him and wondered about him. The others, he felt, didn't even notice him.

By the second day, being homeless had started to change John Coleman. He walked much more slowly, seeing no need to beat a traffic light or be the first through a revolving door. From force of habit, he'd check his watch once in a while, but no watch was there. Even if there had been, it was now much less significant than another measuring device—the thermometer. Squatting with a companion in a doorway on 29th Street during his third day of homelessness, Coleman heard the other man say, "The onliest thing is to have a warm place to sleep. That and having somebody care about you. That'd be even onlier" (Coleman 1992, 84).

On his eighth night, Coleman decided to stay in a Brooklyn shelter for the homeless. At about ten o'clock, an official herded a bunch of newcomers into a corner of the auditorium, where he delivered an abusive speech outlining the horror that lay ahead in the long night. Coleman wrote, "It's illustrative of what the experience of homelessness and helplessness does to people that all of us—regardless of age, race, background, or health—listened so passively" (Coleman 1992, 89). It turned out that the man was a minor official with almost no authority, who was simply grabbing an opportunity to assert himself.

On his last day, Coleman went to the Pavillion restaurant, where he had eaten five times previously. The man at the cash register didn't recognize him and said, "Get out." Coleman explained that he had money, but the man repeated the order.

"That man knows me," Coleman replied, pointing to the owner, who nodded.

"Okay, but sit in the back," said the man at the register. Coleman concluded that if his life on the streets had been real, he'd have departed with the first order. And the impact of the order would have left its mark, making him feel unworthy of being served at the restaurant and thus preventing him from returning there (Coleman 1992, 89–90).

In adjusting to the homeless life, John Coleman was undergoing **socialization,** the process by which a person becomes a social being, learning the necessary cultural content and behavior to become a member of a group or society. Socialization is most apparent in childhood when the basic elements of culture are learned, but the process continues throughout people's lifetimes as they change their group affiliations and thus must learn new ways of thinking and acting. As John Coleman discovered, people experiencing socialization often encounter difficult, stressful conditions. In fact, throughout this chapter, we will see that the occurrence of stress is a frequent reality in the socialization process.

You are in many ways a product of socialization. For one thing you have been significantly influenced by your parents. Perhaps you do not even recognize the extent to which you have adopted their beliefs, values, and behavioral patterns as your own, but if you analyze your family life, you will recognize that many things you were taught and the patterns you observed in your family influenced the development of your standards and behavior. For this reason you are probably different from your friends or classmates. You get angry faster or perhaps slower, you drink more or perhaps less, or you study many more hours or perhaps fewer. You can recognize that others have also contributed to your socialization: friends, neighbors, and teachers. Furthermore socialization continues throughout the entire life span. Perhaps you have older parents, grandparents, or other elderly acquaintances, and you can observe the extent to which modern values and lifestyle and perhaps retirement have affected them. In American society people often pride themselves on being independent and self-reliant, but we are social animals and we require socialization in order to function competently in group situations.

In examining socialization, this chapter is concerned with the process of the individual's growth in the social world. The following section assesses the factors that determine human development. Next we consider the effects of deprived childhood socialization, followed by a summary of four important theories of socialization. Our fourth topic concerns sources of socialization, and the chapter closes with a look at certain common socialization experiences people find difficult.

The Origin of Human Development

The late Isaac Asmimov, a writer of more than 500 books on a wide range of subjects, explained his success by saying that he was "fortunate to be born with a restless and efficient brain, with a capacity for clear thought and an ability to put that thought into words." Asimov added, "None of this is to my credit. I am the beneficiary of a lucky break in the genetic sweepstakes" (Rothstein 1992, B7). Others would disagree, suggesting that Asimov's socialization contributed significantly to his success. For over a century, controversy has raged on the issue of nature versus nurture. Are human beings the product of their **nature** (their inborn biological characteristics or heredity), their **nurture** (their socialization), or some combination of both?

The "nature" position dominated the thinking of most scholars in the nineteenth century. For example, the renowned biologist Charles Darwin emphasized "natural selection": the view that in the struggle for space, food, and shelter, the most adaptable members of a species will live and the less adaptable will perish. In sociologist Herbert Spencer's words, this is the principle of "the survival of the fittest." This principle proved useful to many elitist nineteenth-century political and economic leaders. They could justify their positions of dominance by arguing that the fact that they held such exalted posts was merely an indication of their natural superiority. Such people would say that there was nothing wrong with exploiting the poor in the United States and elsewhere in the world. They would say that individuals' poverty and deprivation were clear indications of innate inferiority, and like beasts of burden, inferior human beings should be exploited.

Some social scientists who shared the heredity-oriented approach began to focus their analysis on **instincts:** unalterable behavior complexes that parents transmit genetically to their children. In the late nineteenth century, psychologists started to compile lists of what they believed to be human instincts and went on to attribute many behavioral patterns to them. Thus warfare was supposedly the result of an "aggressive" instinct, capitalism of an "acquisitive" instinct, and society of a "herding" instinct. These simplistic analyses overlooked the massive evidence suggesting that such types of behavior are principally learned. If these behaviors were instinctual, then they would occur in all societies, but they do not. Societies exist where most people are nonaggressive and nonacquisitive, and under certain circumstances people will voluntarily isolate themselves.

By the early twentieth century, the "nature" perspective had begun to lose support. Ivan Pavlov, a Russian physiologist, proved that he could train or "condition" dogs to exhibit an involuntary response such as salivation when they heard the ringing of a bell. The writings of John B. Watson, an American psychologist, emphasized the same general conclusion: that nurture is the most important factor in human development. According to Watson (1924), children can be turned into anything: doctors, lawyers, artists, beggars, or thieves, depending on how they are raised. The well-known American psychologist B. F. Skinner (1972) made a similar point, claiming that such environmental influences as parental approval and social custom lead us to want to do certain things.

In the past two decades, a new school of thought emphasizing the importance of heredity

136 has emerged. Proponents of **sociobiology** argue that through the evolutionary process, human beings have acquired tendencies that determine much of their behavior. Edward Wilson (1978), a zoologist, has claimed that among human beings, behaviors such as aggression, selfishness, territoriality, and the tendency to form dominance hierarchies are both innate and universal. According to Wilson and other sociobiologists, government officials planning public policy should take into account certain alleged inflexible tendencies in human nature.

Many sociologists have sharply criticized sociobiology, arguing that little supportive evidence has been presented in defense of this perspective and that unlike sociologists, sociobiologists pay almost no attention to the effects of social, political, and economic factors on the societies about which they generalize. However, a number of social scientists have asserted support for a modified sociobiological position (Caporael and Brewer 1991; Ellis 1991; Oyama 1991; Rushton and Nicholson 1988). Thus these specialists argue that human behavior will be enhanced if both genetic and cultural factors are examined.

Our focus will be on the cultural aspect of socialization as we see in the nearby Cross-Cultural Perspective.

The Results of Deprived Socialization ▪

Both nature and nurture affect human development, but the sociological perspective decidedly emphasizes nurture. The present section implicitly supports the nurture position, which suggests that from early infancy an intimate relationship between child and caretaker establishes a child's sense of well-being and permits the child to develop the social and intellectual skills necessary for effective participation in society. When children are deprived of such relationships, their development is seriously affected.

Three decades ago Harry Harlow and his associates at the University of Wisconsin conducted research on the effects of extreme isolation on young rhesus monkeys (Harlow and Harlow 1962; Harlow and Zimmerman 1959). Harlow found that the monkeys isolated in his labs showed behavior similar to that of human psychotics: They were afraid of and hostile toward other monkeys, and, in general, they acted sluggish and reclusive. In one experiment Harlow built two artificial "mothers." One was produced from wire mesh and dispensed milk while the other, which was similar in size and shape, was made from a terrycloth bath towel and offered the comfort of soft contact but not milk. During the 165-day period that the infant monkeys spent with both "mothers," they showed a marked preference for the cloth substitute, spending an average of sixteen hours per day clutching the cloth figure compared to one and a half hours on the wire mesh. Apparently the need for contact with a soft object proved more compelling than the need to reduce hunger.

Of course, researchers cannot devise experiments where children are purposefully deprived of nurture. One investigator, however, discovered a situation in which caretakers for children were very scarce. René Spitz (1945) conducted a study that compared infants raised by their own mothers with infants of the same age raised in an orphanage. The first group of children had extensive social involvement with their mothers while the orphans were kept isolated in small cubicles, with no human contact beyond feeding, clothing changes, and doctoring. After eighteen months the two groups showed dramatic differences. One third of the orphans were dead, and the remainder were physically, intellectually, and emotionally handicapped. The children raised by their mothers were physically and mentally healthy.

Kingsley Davis's (1948) case studies of two isolated girls provide further evidence for the harmful effects of depriving children of conventional socialization. The first girl, an illegitimate, unwanted child named Anna, had been kept isolated in an upstairs room for nearly six years. When Anna was discovered, her clothing and bedding were filthy, and she had received no instruction or friendly attention whatsoever. She could not walk, talk, feed herself, or do anything that showed intelligence. She was emaciated, with skeletonlike arms and legs and a bloated stomach. Anna made

CROSS-CULTURAL PERSPECTIVE
Socialization in Samoa

Many social scientists have accepted the idea that parents' transmission of cultural standards to their children is a fairly clear, straight-forward process. That, however, is often not the case. Within most cultures the transmission process is often difficult and stressful, with individuals frequently struggling to resolve how to respond to traditional cultural expectations. In Samoa, a group of South Pacific islands, this struggle is embodied by the term *loto,* which refers to dual ways an individual can approach a given situation—with one disposition being blameworthy and the other praiseworthy. We consider two illustrations.

After children are about six months old, parents are expected to distance themselves emotionally from their children as a means of teaching them culturally supported emotional control. Often parents find this requirement stressful, wanting to pick up crying babies but reluctant to do so because it is believed that such behavior simply encourages the child to seek greater parental attention. Should the child become sick, this reticence disappears, and parents carry their children about, constantly massaging them and displaying attentiveness discouraged for a healthy child.

Samoans apply the concept of *loto* to this situation by making a distinction between *lotovaivai,* which refers to an excessive display of private emotion,

While Samoans believe that individuals should control their emotions, this photo demonstrates that it is considered appropriate to show happiness and contentment.

and *lototele,* which is a courageous display of self-control. While Samoans recognize that people often become *lotovaivai* when either a journey or a death occurs, such displays are viewed negatively. Instead the individual who possesses *lototele* is greatly admired because that person has sufficient self-mastery to appear in command regardless of what happens. For example, when the village virgin performs the final and most important dance on ceremonial occasions, young men, old women, and various chiefs try to distract her, but epitomizing the person with *lototele,* she remains poised and unaffected.

A second important Samoan socialization issue involves the family's age-grade hierarchy, in which children are expected to show respect for their elders—parents, grandparents, and even

older siblings. Ample evidence suggests resistance to this principle. Interviews with adults about their childhood and children about their current experiences indicated that there is a widespread belief that one "cannot control the *loto.*" Because of this negative form of *loto,* called *lotofaamaualuga,* Samoans believe that children are stubborn rather than deferential and must be subjected to parental punishment.

But while this belief exists, *lotofa'amaualalo,* an ever-present respect for elders, receives more emphasis. In fact, people who are *lotofa'amaualalo* have their emotions sufficiently under control that they remain relaxed about the status they may rightfully expect, forgoing it and thereby undercutting rebellion against the social hierarchy by those below them.

138

In both emotional distancing and in the age-grade hierarchy, the Samoan culture poses a clear ideal but recognizes with the two-part division of *loto* that a negative option is always possible. Certainly Samoan culture is hardly unique in this regard. Can you find parallels in the socialization experience of U.S. culture?

Source: Jeannette Marie Mageo. "Samoan Moral Discourse and the Loto," *American Anthropologist. vol.* 93 (June 1991), *pp.* 405–20.

considerable progress after she was discovered. She learned to follow directions, to string beads, to identify a few colors, and to build with blocks. Eventually she also learned to talk (though in phrases and not full sentences), to wash her hands, and to brush her teeth. Anna died before she was 11, but the progress she made demonstrates that it is possible to teach many things to a child totally isolated during the first six years of life. At her death Anna's social and cognitive development was equivalent to that of a normal 2- or 3-year-old. The possibility that Anna was mentally handicapped might have prevented more extensive progress.

Davis's other case study involved a girl named Isabelle, who also was found at about the age of 6. Her mother was a deaf-mute, and the two of them had spent most of their time together in a dark room. They communicated by gestures, not by speech. Because of lack of sunshine and poor diet, Isabelle was in poor health. At first she seemed incapable of forming relationships, and it was not clear whether or not she was deaf. When it was established that she could hear, specialists started working with her. People first believed she was feebleminded, but under a program of skillful guidance, she began to show signs of a rapidly expanding intelligence. A little more than two months after speaking her first words, Isabelle started making sentences. Nine months later she could read and write quite well, add to ten, and retell a story after hearing it. Seven months later she had a vocabulary of between 1,500 and 2,000 words and was asking complicated questions. By the age of eight-and-a-half, she had reached a normal level of knowledge, covering in two years the development that usually requires six. The case of Isabelle suggests that, with conscientious and skillful effort, specialists can overcome the deficiencies produced by highly deprived socialization.

The Spitz research and the Davis case studies show the devastating effect of isolation on children. These are extreme situations, and yet one might wonder whether some negative impact is apparent in less extreme situations.

Without doubt the answer is affirmative. A study of abused toddlers concluded that some impact of the abuse they had received was revealed when other children cried. Toddlers from nonabusive households responded with interest, empathy, or sadness when their agemates were distressed. By contrast, toddlers from abusing homes reacted to agemates' crying with physical

While it is clear that this child was the victim of physical abuse, the emotional impact of this mistreatment cannot be detected.

attacks on the distressed children, fear, or anger. For instance, Thomas, an abused 1-year-old, was playing when he heard a child crying in the distance. The researchers wrote:

> Suddenly, Thomas becomes a statue. His smile fades and his face takes on a look of distress also. He sits very still, his hand frozen in the air. His back is straight, and he becomes more and more tense as the crying continues. The fingers on his hand slowly extend a bit. . . . The [distant] crying diminishes. Suddenly Thomas is back to normal, calm, mumbling and playing in the sand.
>
> (*Main and George* 1985, 410)

Research has also indicated that either abused or neglected adolescents experience more attention problems and more daily stress about such concerns as school, health, and finances than do nonmaltreated peers (Williamson, Borduin, and Howe 1991).

A related topic is sexual abuse of children. It is not known how widespread its occurrence is, but it is more frequent than many specialists realize. For instance, when a mental-health treatment center started to offer treatment to sexually abused children, the social-work clinicians expected to receive about three referrals each month; the first month they obtained fifteen referrals, and by the sixth month, sexual abuse accounted for 40 percent of their cases. Child victims of sexual abuse frequently feel stigmatized, filled with shame and guilt, and consider themselves "damaged goods"; they also consider themselves betrayed, because in their view parents failed to protect them; finally they feel powerless, subjected to the all-powerful will of another who has treated them vilely (Patten et al. 1989).

Often the impact of sexual abuse is traumatic—so traumatic, in fact, that victims can repress memories of the incidents for many years. A case in point involved Susan Schick, a 28-year-old woman who was sexually abused by a neighbor for six years, beginning when she was 8. Fourteen years later she began having flashbacks of the attacks. Schick said, "For me, the main point of this is to deal with a sense of rage, and not to turn it inside" (Lueck 1992, B2).

Theories of Socialization

The **self** is one's perception of his or her own person, which forms as a result of other people's response in the course of socialization. In the last section, we noted that children who are neglected often possess an undeveloped sense of self while those who are abused develop a confused or painful sense of self.

This section examines four theories that analyze the growth of the self. Two of the theories were developed by sociologists and two by psychologists.

SOCIOLOGICAL THEORIES OF SOCIALIZATION

Charles Horton Cooley's and George Herbert Mead's theories have distinct differences, but on one point they agree—that the self is the product of a learning process that occurs in interaction with others. Both theories, in short, are distinctly sociological.

Cooley and the Looking-Glass Self

The professor can't wait for introductory sociology to start today. The joke is not only funny but a perfect illustration of the concept to be discussed that morning. The class begins, the teacher tells the joke, and following the punchline waits for laughter. Nothing. Desperately she searches the faces for a glimmer of a smile. Nothing, a complete bomb. At least for the moment, the professor questions her ability to tell a joke, and perhaps in the future will be reluctant to tell another joke, at least with this class.

This situation illustrates a concept Charles Horton Cooley (1864–1929) called the **looking-glass self:** Our understanding of what sort of

The looking-glass self develops in many social contexts, including the classroom. Whether or not this child feels comfortable performing before classmates in the future is likely to be influenced by their reaction to this performance.

person we are is based on how we think we appear to others. Cooley wrote, "We always imagine, and in imagining share, the judgments of the other mind" (Cooley 1964, 185).

According to Cooley, there are three steps in the development of the looking-glass self:

1. Our perception of how we appear to another person.
2. Our estimate of the judgment the other person makes about us.
3. Some emotional feeling about this judgment, such as pride or shame.

Looking back you can see that the professor in the previous example experienced these three steps.

Of course, one person does not have direct contact with another's thoughts or feelings; an individual only makes guesses from other people's responses. Faulty communication or confusion sometimes happens: A disapproving expression might be mistaken for an approving smile; or a person may receive mixed messages from different people. Some of the professor's students might frown or scowl while others might laugh. With such a reaction, she is uncertain about trying to tell a joke in the future. If such mixed messages continue, this individual might develop a confused sense of whether she is a funny person, at least in class. Children who grow up with a constant supply of mixed messages are likely to become adults who are confused and unsure of themselves.

Mead's Conception of the Development of Self

George Herbert Mead (1863–1931) accepted the idea of the looking-glass self theory. However, he believed that the development of the self-concept is the product of more than people's perceptions of others' reactions to them (Mead 1930). According to Mead, the socialized individual has learned to read complicated social situations before taking whatever actions are judged the most appropriate.

Mead visualized the development of the self as a three-stage process:

1. The preparatory stage occurs in early childhood. In the course of their second and third years, children imitate others' behavior. They copy the way that their parents or older siblings hold a spoon, do a dance step, or make an obscene gesture. Children do learn some useful skills through imitation but discover little about how roles work.
2. Children enter the play stage at the age of 4 or 5. **Play** is the process of taking the role of specific individuals and thereby starting to learn the rights and obligations that particular roles entail. Mead wrote, "A child plays at being a mother, at being a teacher, at being a policeman; that is, it is taking different roles" (Mead 1934, 150). At this stage children's role performances begin to give them an understanding of their significance. But these performances are definitely "play" in the sense that children are not committed to these roles and are able to make up the rules as they proceed.
3. The final stage is the game stage. According to Mead, a **game** is a group activity in which each participant's role requires interaction with two or more individuals. In order to take part in

games, a person must have a **generalized other**: an image of the role expectations for all the game participants with whom a person must interact. Mead noted, "The fundamental difference between play and the game is that in the latter the child must have the attitude of all the others involved in that game" (Mead 1934, 153–54). Unlike the play stage, the game stage is serious business. Children are expected to commit themselves to the roles they perform, and to perform effectively they must learn the rules governing all participants' behavior. Not following the rules can lead to a sense of personal failure.

An actual game provides an illustration. In baseball, for instance, the infielders must be aware of not only their own role expectations but also those of their fellow infielders. The first baseman must realize that without a runner on base, he must take the throw on a ground ball to the shortstop. With a runner on first base, the first baseman knows that the shortshop's throw will go to the second baseman, who then will throw to first.

The concept of game also applies to social situations. Let us imagine, for example, that Jackie is having problems with her boyfriend. She wants to discuss the situation with her friend Angela, and so she gives her a call. They agree to meet an hour later at the college cafeteria. Angela arrives, however, with her younger sister Peggy. "Mom had to go shopping," Angela says apologetically, "and she asked me to bring Peggy along." Peggy is 10 years old, always curious, and is likely to pass on any information she hears to her mother, who in turn will tell Jackie's mother. In this situation the Meadian game includes the following facts: Both Jackie and Angela are aware of how Peggy is likely to act in this situation, and each knows that the other is aware. Thus the two young women engage in a careful conversation, avoiding references to certain issues: that Jackie frequently spends the night with her boyfriend, that most of their friends drink liquor and use drugs, and that Jackie has seriously considered dropping out of school. They also convey some information with facial expressions and gestures when Peggy is not looking. As they are leaving, Jackie whispers to Angela, "Ma's pretty

understanding about my personal life. She really tries not to ask too many questions. She knows she'll just get upset and that I'll end up doing what I want anyway."

The two young women understand how the generalized other applies here. They know what behavior to expect from Peggy, their mothers, and each other. With this knowledge they perform their roles smoothly in this Meadian game. The skills demonstrated by Jackie and Angela involve a level of social sophistication that far exceeds what is necessary to develop a looking-glass self.

PSYCHOLOGICAL THEORIES OF SOCIALIZATION

In general, psychologists are more inclined than sociologists to focus on individuals and their experiences and less on the group contexts affecting people. This difference is apparent when Sigmund Freud's and Jean Piaget's theories are compared to Cooley's and Mead's. These two psychological theories have had a profound impact on scholars in diverse fields concerned with socialization.

Freudian Theory of Socialization

Sigmund Freud (1856–1939), certainly one of the most prominent theorists in psychology, described the different impulses to which we are subjected. All of us experience impulses pulling us in different directions: Our wish to have another piece of pie conflicts with concern for our waistline; the wish to sleep through an early morning class clashes with concern that the material covered in lecture will be featured on the next test. Freud's theory, more than the other three theories in this section, highlights the stress that people encounter during socialization.

Freud (1952) contended that socialization is a process that requires people to sacrifice personal impulses and desires for the common good. Without such a sacrifice, society would disintegrate as people pursued their most selfish goals. According to Freud, the energy inherent in these impulses and desires is redirected along socially acceptable paths by the socialization process. As you read about this theory, recognize that the struggles Freud analyzed can also be considered either role strains or role conflicts discussed in Chapter 5, "Social Interaction." Do you recall the distinction between the two terms? If not, you might look up the concepts in Chapter 5.

Freud identified three distinct parts of the personality that exist as concepts, not in a physical form. One part is the **id,** which is unconscious, primitive, and constantly pleasure-seeking. The second part is the **superego,** which has internalized standards of right and wrong, a conscience. Parental influence is strong in the development of the superego, but other authority figures such as teachers or the police also affect its development. Struggle between the superego and id is not inevitable, but Freud suggested that in modern life almost continuous warfare will occur between them. In short, there is an ongoing conflict between basic impulses produced by the id and standards of society supplied by the superego. Generally the superego tries to force the id to modify or renounce its urges or at least to postpone them. The final part of the personality is the ego. The **ego** is Freud's conception of the self. It must cope with pressures from three often contradictory forces: the outside world, the id, and the superego.

In everyday life one can easily visualize the struggle among the three parts of the personality Freud described. Suppose that a student has an important test scheduled the next day. That evening, however, a party will take place at a friend's apartment. The party promises to be a lot of fun—plenty to drink and eat—and many of the student's friends will be there. The id urges, "There's only one way to handle a party like this one—go early and stay late!" The superego takes the opposite tack. It argues, "This test could make or break your grade. You must study all evening and then turn in early. Parties are for weekends, after all." The ego is forced to evaluate both arguments. Which decision will be reached? The party? Studying? Perhaps the ego will compromise: Study most of the evening, then spend two hours at the party, and have only one or two drinks. From a Freudian point of view, the decision reached will reflect the relative abilities of the id and the superego to "convince" the ego

Piaget's Theory of Cognitive Development

Jean Piaget (1896–1980) was a Swiss psychologist and a leading expert on children's thought pro-

cesses. Piaget's work has complemented Mead's analysis, with the latter focusing on the child's growing understanding of social relations and Piaget emphasizing **cognitive ability**: the capacity to use perception, thought, memory, and other mental processes to acquire knowledge. Piaget (1970) contended that a child's cognitive ability develops through four principal stages. These stages are age-related because the brain must develop physically over time in order to allow certain types of cognitive processes to occur and because passage into a given stage requires a successful experience in the preceding one. Indeed people are generally aware that cognitive abilities are age-related. We would be shocked to hear a six-month-old infant speaking in full sentences or an 8-year-old discussing the theory of relativity or symbolic interaction. The four stages cover the time period from birth to the age of 15.

1. ***The sensorimotor stage.*** This phase involves the first two years of life. During these years infants learn to coordinate sensory experiences (such as seeing objects) with motor activities (such as touching objects). Infants discover that if they reach for bright-colored objects like mobiles or rattles, they can touch, grasp, or even jiggle them. They are starting to distinguish themselves from the surrounding environment, an ability an infant does not possess for the first three or four months of life. Eventually infants develop **object permanence,** the childhood recognition that specific objects still exist after they are removed from one's line of vision. A child of four months might play with a toy but will not seem to notice when it is taken away. However, a child of nine months will start looking for the same toy if removed. The older child has developed object permanence, recognizing that the toy has an existence independent of his or her own perception.

2. ***The preoperational stage.*** This phase is named from the fact that a child between 2 to 7 years old does not yet fully understand certain basic concepts one must grasp in order to function effectively in

the everyday world. These concepts include weight, volume, speed, and cause and effect. Children's abilities at this stage can be deceptive, sometimes dangerously so. For instance, a baby sitter is with Jamie, a 4-year-old, in the child's yard. "I'm thirsty," Jamie says. "I'd like a glass of milk." The sitter stands up, and as he heads for the kitchen door he says, "Now you stay right here, Jamie. I don't want you going into the street." Just to check, he might add, "Now tell me what you're supposed to do, Jamie," The little girl will be able to explain—she seems to understand danger—but in reality she does not yet comprehend the speed of cars nor does she grasp the process of cause and effect (that is, that if hit she will be injured or killed). Thus even though she has understood her baby sitter's words, she is too young to grasp their significance, namely the personal danger that speeding cars represent.

3. **The concrete operational stage.** This phase involves children approximately 7 to 11 years of age, and in the course of it, they master the cognitive skills necessary for everyday life. They come to understand measurement, speed, weight, time, and cause and effect. Unlike younger children they are able to appreciate other people's outlooks and, as Mead suggested, to coordinate other people's viewpoints and actions with their own. Children at the concrete operational stage, however, lack the ability to think abstractly.

4. **The formal operational stage.** Children's responses to the following set of sentences display the difference between the concrete operational and the formal operational stages:

   1. All children like spinach.
   2. Boys are children.
   3. Therefore boys like spinach.

   Younger children, especially if they do not like spinach, will focus on the content of the syllogism, while adolescents are much more likely to examine the argu-

ment because they are impressed by its logical form (Phillips 1969). This stage occurs from ages 11 to 15. Children develop the ability to think abstractly, to manipulate concepts not linked to experience in the immediate environment. In the formal operational stage, children are beginning to explore the vast capacities of the mind, and education is a prominent vehicle for these explorations.

Piaget's theory has some interesting implications for education. Because expanded cognitive abilities are the result of both the physical maturation of the brain and intellectual experiences, it would be difficult and counterproductive to force children to think abstractly before they are intellectually ready. On the other hand, once they have developed their full intellectual capacities, there is no reason to move slowly. A child of 14 has completed the formal operational phase, suggesting that most high-school students are fully capable of the same sort of abstract thinking college students must perform.

COMPARISONS OF THE FOUR THEORIES

The four theories of socialization we have discussed all recognize the changing nature of the self. Three of the theories contend that social interaction determines the development of the self while Piaget's theory claims that brain maturation is the major source. Furthermore each theory has its own particular focus. Cooley's approach concludes that a person's perception of how other people evaluate his or her behavior determines the content of the self. Mead's analysis accepts Cooley's central point but emphasizes that the development of the self requires an understanding of how roles work. Unlike the two sociological theories, the Freudian perspective suggests that there is a conflict-laden relationship between the individual and society in the on-going struggle between the id and superego. Finally Piaget's theoretical contribution involves an entirely different aspect of socialization, focusing on children's development of cognitive abilities and not on their increasing understanding of social relations. Table 6.1 compares these three theories.

144   **Table 6.1**   Four Prominent Theories of Socialization

Theorist	*Principal concept(s)*	*Central idea(s)*	*Individual's relationship to society*
Charles Cooley	Looking-glass self	That people's sense of self is based on how they imagine they appear to others	Continuous effort to adjust one's behavior to one's perception of others' desires and expectatons
George Mead	Play, generalized other, and game	That the development of the self is a three-stage process, where each stage represents a more sophisticated understanding of the world	The necessity to understand the generalized other for each game in which one participates
Sigmund Freud	Id, ego, and superego	That there is an ongoing conflict between a person's primitive impulses and societal controls, with the ego (self) serving as negotiator	Requirement that the ego places heavy restraints on the id in line with the demands of the superego
Jean Piaget	Cognitive abilities	That the acquisition of knowledge is a four-stage process occurring in childhood and featuring a particular set of mental operations at each stage	Expectation that at each stage a child meets socially approved cognitive demands, such as in school performance

Sources of Socialization

The focus now shifts from an examination of theories which analyze the entire process of socialization to a discussion of specific influences in the process—key sources of socialization. One of these sources, the family, received some attention in the previous section.

THE FAMILY

Children are born into families, and it is within the family context that they obtain their first exposure to the values, norms, beliefs, and knowledge char-

acteristic of their society. Research has shown that parents significantly affect their children on such wide-ranging issues as involvement in crime (Dunaway and Cullen 1991), marital conflict (Guttman 1991), social skills (Jones and Houts 1992), and self-esteem (Whitbeck et al. 1991). Furthermore the socialization experience within the family continues for many years. Most American children live with their parents until they are in their late teens, and many continue living with them much longer. As the Cooley and Mead theories emphasize, parents and other family members have a tremendous impact on children. Sometimes family influences involving distinctive patterns of facial and bodily expression or behavioral patterns are readily apparent. In other cases these traits are not obvious, and yet the parental influence remains equally pervasive.

Americans usually think of childhood as a distinct period of time in people's lives, but such a conception has not always been accepted. Let's examine how it has changed.

The Changing Conception of Childhood

During the Middle Ages, children were treated as little adults. Parents had no distinct perception of themselves as people involved in child-rearing, and the family was generally thought of as an institution for the transmission of a name and inheritance. Between the thirteenth and the seventeenth centuries, this outlook gradually changed. Religious groups began to take an increasingly important part in the education of children, and the members of these groups started to emphasize that parents were the guardians of their children's souls. From the seventeenth through the nineteenth centuries, the growing involvement of parents showed itself in increasingly stricter codes of discipline. This trend became particularly apparent in the early nineteenth century when the Industrial Revolution encouraged a sharp role distinction between men and women, forcing many wives to remain in the home where they were expected to concentrate much of their energy on rearing their children. By the end of the nineteenth century, the combined forces of the family and the school had firmly established the concept of childhood (Ariès 1962).

With the existence of childhood confirmed, people have disagreed about which child-rearing patterns are appropriate. Before the 1920s a restrictive approach to parenting generally prevailed. There was a widespread belief that it was critical to maximize children's obedience to the social norms. Most parents felt that the use of punishments and rewards was the best means of securing this obedience. During the 1920s the increasing acceptance of the ideas of Sigmund Freud, educator John Dewey, and others led to an almost complete reversal of the earlier approach. Parents became aware that children have their own individual perceptions and needs and that bad experiences suffered in childhood can pro-

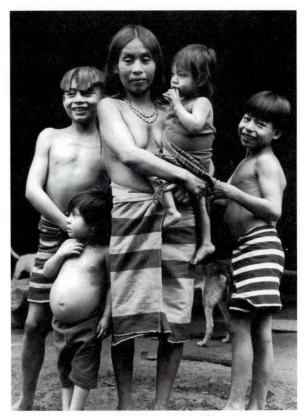

While socialization among Ecuador's Colorado Indians and in the United States is very different, both sets of children are prepared to become adults in their respective cultures.

duce psychological damage that will carry into adulthood. Different opinions regarding discipline also have become apparent. Some critics of the student protests of the 1960s, for example, suggested that a major cause of the unrest was the supposedly overly permissive child-rearing typical of the post–World War II era.

People often believe that a particular approach to rearing children is best. However, many social scientists argue that there is no single "right approach." Americans are inclined to believe that infants are inherently helpless and must establish strong emotional bonds with their caretakers. The ethnocentrism within many Americans arises when they learn that traditional Japanese mothers believed that their young children were uncivilized creatures whose emotions needed to be soothed and tamed—quite the opposite of the Americans' approach. It further strains Americans' capacity for cultural relativism to discover that many Indian mothers in the highlands of

146   Guatemala believe that their children's day of birth will determine their dispositions and therefore make no effort to shape their personalities. However, in all three of these societies, most children grow up to be relatively well-adjusted, productive adults; research indicates that children do not need exposure to a particular set of socialization patterns to develop properly. Beyond meeting a child's basic physical needs and providing minimal social contact, there appear to be no universal needs among children. One psychologist has concluded, "To ask what a child needs is to pose half a question. We must always specify the demands the community will make upon the adolescent and young adult" (Kagan 1983, 411). Thus the child-rearing of American children will prepare them for American society, not for traditional Japanese or Guatemalan societies.

DAY-CARE CENTERS AND SCHOOLS

For working parents of younger children, day care is often necessary. Of the 14 million preschool children in 1990, slightly less than half—48 percent or 6.7 million—were in a day-care program. With about 15 million preschool children projected for 1995, the number of day-care children is currently increasing (Hofferth and Phillips 1991, 3).

An examination of 150 children, ages 2 to 4, in six different child-care arrangements concluded that children who attended day-care centers part or full time had more advanced social and intellectual development than children in home care. The advanced development in centers resulted from lessons fostering social and intellectual skills, instruction in recognizing and obeying rules, opportunities to practice skills and follow rules with various peers and adults, and encouragement at developing self-direction and independence. The opportunities provided by day care can be enhanced by experiences at home, particularly those initiated or supplemented by the child (Clarke-Stewart 1991).

Martha J. Zaslow (1991) indicated that recent research has made it clear that the type of day care provided is less important for children's social and intellectual development than its quality, with the central features of quality being a warm emotional climate, frequent personal interaction with care givers, and extensive interaction with care givers involving information sharing.

While day care in the United States is growing, we should recognize that almost all the major advanced industrialized nations are ahead of the U.S. in the supply, quality, and affordability of child-care services. For instance, in France, all children aged two years and three months or more are eligible to participate in a program that emphasizes cognitive development within a developmentally appropriate curriculum. The activity goes from 8:30 A.M. to 4:30 P.M., with lunch available at school. Many preschools and primary schools also have after-school programs. The basic preschool program is free, with parents paying income-related fees for lunch and for the after-school program (Kamerman 1991).

Although many children now receive day care, all children are exposed to schooling, where they receive formal knowledge from teachers and from books but also much more. In some of their courses, they are likely to obtain more distinct emphasis on patriotism than is normally provided at home. In addition, children in school will learn how to behave in group settings. They learn to sit quietly and to obey teachers providing instructions, whether the instructions make sense or not. Children are also encouraged to compete, to attempt to produce higher quality work than do their classmates. A body of criticism has developed concerning the regimentation that occurs in the early school years. One writer, for instance, suggested that kindergarten is "an academic boot camp," in which the system of routines and orders prepares young children for blind obedience over the next dozen years of schooling and also within the large-scale occupational bureaucracies of current society (Gracey 1977).

Parents, educators, politicians, and others are well aware that schools are a critical means of socialization in modern society, but as Table 6.2 indicates, most Americans provide low grades for the country's public schools.

A few schools, however, have produced excellent results. In a film entitled "Why Do These Kids Love School?," filmmaker Dorothy Fadiman showed young children in nine schools representing diverse populations around the country. The children shared one thing—a love of school. One clear message was that in contrast to schools that impose a rigid, highly controlled approach, these

Table 6.2 Public Schools as a Socialization Agent

GRADE FOR THE PUBLIC SCHOOLS NATIONALLY

	National sample	Public-school parents
A	2%	2%
B	16	17
C	48	48
D	18	18
F	4	4
Don't know	12	11

WILLINGNESS TO SERVE AS AN UNPAID VOLUNTEER IN LOCAL PUBLIC SCHOOL

	National sample
Yes	59%
No	34
Don't know	7

	Different categories answering yes
SEX	
Male	54%
Female	64
AGE	
18–29 years	65
30–49 years	65
50–64 years	54
65 and over	36
EDUCATION	
College graduate	70
High-school graduate	57
Grade school	45
COMMUNITY SIZE	
1 million and over	53
2500–49,999	71
CHILDREN IN SCHOOL	
No children in school	51
Public-school parents	72
Nonpublic-school parents	49

Source: Stanley M. Elam, Lowell C. Rose, and Alec M. Gallup. "The 24th Annual Gallup/Phi Delta Kappa *Poll of the Public's Attitudes toward the Public Schools,*" Phi Delta Kappan. *vol.* 74 (*September* 1992), *pp.* 41–53.

schools stress freedom in league with cooperation. Children are encouraged to act independently, but at the same time, their actions should promote trust, community, and collaboration. A second message apparent in the film was that "good education is doable"—in opposition to the widespread feeling that the United States is "incapable of offering education that is simultaneously effective, high in quality, equitable, and appealing" (Raywid 1992, 632).

The ultimate, currently elusive challenge is to make day care and school kids can love available to all American children. Such a perspective on schooling and day care can be related to theories examined earlier in this chapter. An ideal day care or school is one that can promote relationships with caretakers, teachers, and peers that will establish and maintain a positive looking-glass self; that will most effectively develop the social skills needed in Mead's preparatory, play, and game stages; and that will facilitate children's development in Piaget's sensorimotor, preoperational, concrete operational, and formal operation stages.

PEERS

In a scene from the film *Diner,* one young man was complaining that since he was getting married, all the good times would be over. His male companion, whom everyone regarded as knowledgeable about sexuality, suddenly looked strangely at the other young man. Then he smiled confidently and said, "You're a virgin." The other, acutely embarrassed, admitted that his friend was "technically" correct.

Research indicates that American males are likely to face strong peer pressure to become sexually experienced and that virgins are sometimes made to believe that they are not demonstrating proper masculinity and that something must be wrong with them (Kirkendall 1968).

Sex is hardly the only activity over which peers exert influence. Articles have shown that peers

While Americans generally do not feel that public schools have done a good job, the majority would be willing to serve as unpaid volunteers in local public schools. Women, younger people, college graduates, individuals from small or moderate-sized communities, and public-school parents are most likely to offer their services.

148

affect such issues as alcohol consumption (Mitic 1990), political attitudes (Straits 1991), and involvement in juvenile delinquency (Warr and Stafford 1991). The fact that young people of school age spend an average of twice as much time with their peers as they do with parents, and that they like that arrangement, underlines the significance of teenage peer groups (Bronfenbrenner 1970).

Whether we applaud or condemn the influence of young people's peer groups, we might wonder why they have become so important. The sociological perspective examines the social world in which modern young people live, observing that in a highly complex industrial society the family turns over many of its primary functions, such as moral training, to the schools. Within the school, however, a close, emotional relationship is unlikely to develop between adolescent students and their teachers. Thus students must look to

their own age group for much of their emotional support and guidance (Coleman 1961).

By grouping students of similar academic level, schools can contribute to dysfunctional peer relations (Dishion et al. 1991). Children whose academic performance is low find themselves with peers of a similar academic profile. From the perspective of Mead's game stage, we can see a developing interactional pattern where the youthful participants recognize that they are officially considered inferior to other students, and so influenced by this perception, they collectively resort to delinquent activity. Were tracking systems eliminated, this problem would be undercut.

MASS MEDIA

The **mass media** are the instruments of communication that reach a large audience without any

Figure 6.1

Media Use in the Last Twenty-Four Hours.

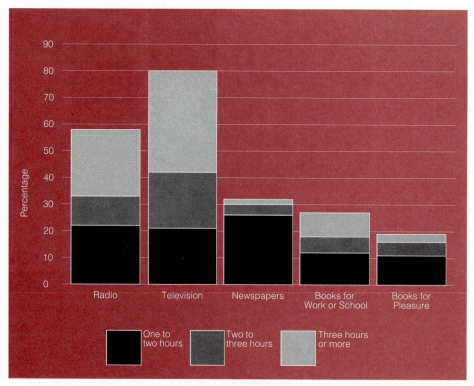

While substantial numbers of Americans read various types of written material, television is the most popular medium.

Source: *Gallup Poll.* Gallup Poll Monthly. (*February* 1991), *p.* 50.

personal contact between the senders and the receivers. Books, records, newspapers, magazines, television, radio, and movies are the most prominent mass media. Figure 6.1, based on national survey data, indicates how extensively Americans employ various types of media information during the typical day.

As Figure 6.1 indicates, in the United States, television is the most popular form of mass media. One study indicated that by the age of 18, the average American child will have spent more time watching television than performing any other waking activity (Liebert and Poulos 1972). But while Americans enjoy watching television, many believe they overdo it. In 1990, 49 percent of a national sample felt they saw too much television while only 18 percent believed they saw too little. In comparison, only 7 percent felt they read too much for pleasure, and 73 percent concluded that that they did too little recreational reading (*Gallup Poll Monthly* February 1991, 51).

Television and other commercial media are profit-oriented. Television networks and local channels, radio stations, newspapers, and magazines sell time or space to advertisers, whose investment proves worthwhile only if a large audience pays attention to the medium. A team of experts noted, "The purchase of a thirty-second spot on CBS or a page in *Time* is a meaningless act—and a poor business decision—unless there are audiences involved. In reality, advertisers buy the audience, which is a byproduct in the mass communication process" (Hiebert, Ungurait, and Bohn 1974, 39). Television programming involves vast sums of money, and thus competition for the audience is intense. The producers of most major network shows attempt to develop programs that will "hook" the viewers, reel them in like fish. So the central concern is audience appeal; any consideration of artistic merit is distinctly secondary.

One of the most effective ways to hook an audience is with violent activity. It has been estimated that an average American child will see more than 13,000 killings on television by age 15. There is twice as much violence in American television as there is in British programming. Yet it is difficult to assess the effects of television violence. A rigorous study of the relationship between violent programming and violent behavior has determined that previous research claiming a relationship is inconclusive (Baron and Reiss 1985).

Still certain developments appear possible: that audiences that have had extensive contact with violence in the mass media are relatively likely to perform violent acts in situations in which they expect to be rewarded for such behavior or when they encounter a situation similar to the one presented by the media (National Commission on the Causes and Prevention of Violence 1969).

In other topical areas, mass media can also exert destructive effects. A recent study found a statistical association between respondents' unrealistic beliefs about intimate relationships (such as the conviction that disagreement is always destructive, or the belief that sex will automatically be perfect) and exposure to such popular romantic media as rock music, TV drama, romantic films, and romantic novels. While the research did not discover a clear causal connection, the investigators suspected that a circular pattern developed, with romantic media disproportionately drawing people with unrealistic beliefs and that once these people were exposed to the romantic media those beliefs were enlarged (Shapiro and Kroeger 1991).

The nearby Social Application considers one of the perplexing current issues of the mass media—the freedom of the press.

ADDITIONAL AGENTS OF SOCIALIZATION

Parents, the media, teachers, and peers are important sources, or agents, of socialization. But are there others as well? Several types come to mind.

Institutional "caretakers." Staff members provide significant socialization for orphans, juvenile delinquents, and mentally and physically handicapped children. However, the fact that these staff members are frequently overworked generally means that the quality of socialization they can provide would be considered quite inadequate by most people.

Social workers. Individuals of various ages often receive help from such organizations as child-abuse centers; programs for the elderly; centers for the treatment of drug abuse, alcoholism, or gambling; and social-welfare departments. In some cases a kindly, insightful staff person (or the opposite—a cold, uncaring individual) can have an impact seemingly out of proportion to the time and

SOCIAL APPLICATION
What about Freedom of the Press?

As we have noted, the mass media are the instruments of communication that reach a large audience without any personal contact between the senders and receivers. The lack of personal contact, however, does not prevent people from having strong feelings about the press—newspapers, magazines, TV, and radio—and their personnel. For instance, in 1973, 39 percent of a national sample of Americans expressed a great deal or quite a lot of confidence in newspapers; that figure rose to 51 percent in 1979 and then dropped steadily, reaching 32 percent in 1991. For television 37 percent expressed a great deal or quite a lot of confidence in 1973, and then a steady decline in confidence developed, with the number dropping to 24 percent in 1991. William Greider, a well-known journalist, concluded that following the Watergate scandals, the press made its peace with big business and politicians, and that the "dull monotone" that emininates from all major media occurs because they "now cant [incline] themselves toward those in authority" (Greider 1992, 12).

Joseph Kopec, a public-relations specialist, suggested that the American public perceives the press as arrogant, unnecessarily intrusive, and as distant from the everyday struggles of average citizens as big business or big government. Kopec proposed ways for press officials to reform this situation: policing themselves; using whatever means necessary to correct errors and establish credibility with the public; and reestablishing contact with the people, holding meetings where reporters and editors can candidly communicate with local citizens.

But other observers of the press would suggest that Kopec's reforms are insufficient. The problem, some critics observe, is that the mass media are a prime portion of the corporate world. Michael Parenti noted that just ten major companies control fifty-nine major magazines (including *Time* and *Newsweek*), fifty-eight important newspapers (including the *New York Times* and the *Washington Post*), the three major TV and radio networks, thirty-four TV stations, 201 cable systems, and twenty record companies. The owners of the major media have diversified business involvements, and they emphatically do not see it as in their interest to examine big-business activities in depth, especially when those businesses have significant problems. Thus an investigation of the media coverage of a major oil spill at Santa Barbara in 1969 showed that the local news media, which were not owned by large corporations, were about equally likely to provide coverage to environmental groups and oil companies. In sharp contrast the nonlocal press, which was considerably more likely to be controlled by large corporations, generally excluded the environmental groups, giving six times as much coverage to the oil companies.

Is the central issue in freedom of the press simply a question of power and influence? Do powerful corporations control mass media in line with their interests? While some apparently believe this is the basic question, others don't. Leo Szilard, a Hungarian-born scientist and writer who lived in the United States, contended that Americans are subtly socialized to censure themselves. In a short story, he described the process by which a brilliant dolphin was taught the workings of modern societies. What he learned about American society was often complicated and perplexing.

> Thus, on one occasion, Pi Omega Ro [the dolphin] asked whether it would be correct to assume that Americans were free to say what they think, because they did not think what they were not free to say. On another occasion, he asked whether it would be correct to say that in America honest politicians were men who were unable to fool others without first fooling themselves.
>
> (*Szilard* 1961, 42–43)

Herbert Marcuse, a philosopher, agreed with Szilard's dolphin, indicating that even members of the press will monitor and control themselves. Why do members of the press respond this way? The reason, Marcuse claimed, is because they are all playing the samee game: They want to become rich and successful and revel in the good life, glorifying in material wealth. The press is no different from any other sector of American society in this respect. Thus mass media are not a particularly significant factor shaping Americans' perceptions and views. "The preconditioning does not start with the mass production of radio and television and with the centralization of their control. The people enter this stage as preconditioned receptacles of long standing" (Marcuse 1964, 8).

So what do you think? Do we have freedom of the press? If your answer is wholly or partially negative, what do you believe is the source of the restriction?

Sources: George Gallup and Frank Newport. "Confidence in Major U.S. Institutions at All-time Low," Gallup Poll Monthly. (October 1991), pp. 36–40; William Greider. "The Betrayal of Democracy," National Public Television (Frontline). (April 15, 1992); Joseph A. Kopec. "The Big Chill," Vital Speeches. vol. 50 (June 1, 1984), pp. 528–30; Herbert Marcuse. The One-Dimensional Man. Boston: Beacon Press, 1964; Harvey Molotch and Marilyn Lester. "Accidental News: The Great Oil Spill as Local Occurrence and National Event," American Journal of Sociology. vol. 81(September 1975), pp. 235–60; Michael Parenti. "The Moneyed Media," Economic Notes. vol. 51 (October 1983), pp. 7–12; Leo Szilard. The Voice of the Dolphins and Other Stories. New York: Simon & Schuster, 1961.

energy spent with the person needing help. ***Miscellaneous influences.*** Sometimes people will encounter individuals whose guidance or example may lead them to decisions about their best future course of action. For example, a charming, articulate professor or physician may inspire a young woman or man to prepare for the same profession. Or, in a different vein, a pleasant, kindly representative of the Unification Church ("Moonies") may offer what seems to be a message of hope to a confused, unhappy young man or woman who relinquishes control over his or her destiny in exchange for the promise of happiness and fulfillment.

Figure 6.2 represents the possible impact of different agents of socialization on two individuals.

TOTAL INSTITUTIONS

Unlike the other socializations agents discussed in this section, total institutions are concerned with **resocialization**—a systematic effort to provide an individual new cultural content, permitting him or her to become a smoothly functioning member of a group or society. A **total institution** is a place of residence where inhabitants experience nearly complete restriction of their physical freedom in an attempt to effectively resocialize them into a radically new identity and behavioral pattern. Frequently such barriers as locked doors, high walls, water, cliffs, or barbed wire are used to prevent unrestricted contacts with outsiders. Psychiatric hospitals, prisons, monasteries, boarding schools, and some army camps are examples.

Inhabitants' resocialization in total institutions is a two-step procedure: The old identity

Figure 6.2
Agents of Socialization

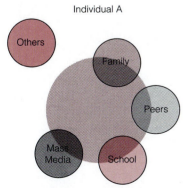

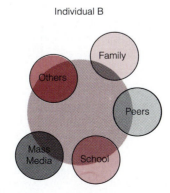

In the course of socialization, different agents exert varying degrees of influence. For Individual A the family and peers were especially significant. In contrast, Individual B received much less influence from these two agents. In this case the school, particularly two teachers, and others—a couple that owned a local small business—were the most influential.

152   must be stripped away and replaced with a new one. This change begins with a **mortification process,** a series of degradations and humiliations of inhabitants that is systematically carried out by staff members of total institutions. The mortification process begins the moment an individual enters the total institution. Erving Goffman wrote:

> We very generally find staff employing what are called admission procedures, such as taking a life history, photographing, weighing, fingerprinting, assigning numbers, searching, listing personal possessions for storage, undressing, bathing, disinfecting, haircutting, issuing institutional clothing, instructing as to rules, and assigning to quarters.
>
> (*Goffman* 1961, 16)

Obviously the mortification process in a psychiatric hospital will be different from the one in a boarding school. In both cases, however, significant portions of inmates' former identities are systematically stripped away by admissions procedures and other new, often deeply disturbing situations they must experience. As the mortification process continues, inmates are gradually exposed to the **privilege system**: a framework for inmates' resocialization. The three parts of the privilege system are the "house rules," norms that indicate the main requirements of inmate conduct; punishments for breaking the rules; and rewards or privileges provided in exchange for obedience to staff. Goffman noted:

> The building of a world around these minor privileges is perhaps the most important feature of inmate culture, and yet it is something that cannot easily be appreciated by an outsider, even one who has previously lived through the experience himself. This concern with privileges sometimes leads to generous sharing; it almost always leads to a willingness to beg for such things as cigarettes, candy, and newspapers.
>
> (*Goffman* 1961, 50)

The mortification process strips away people's identities as a first step toward attempting to resocialize them to useful social roles. We can wonder whether the process will succeed with these men, whose convictions for criminal violations led to their placement in a "shock" camp in New York.

Does the resocialization that occurs within total institutions prepare people to function effectively in the greater society? While the question is so general that neither "yes" nor "no" would be an adequate answer, a negative response often seems more appropriate. A central problem is that officials within total institutions often become fixated on control, taking extensive measures to prevent rebellious behavior and reacting with harsh punishment when rules are broken. In such a system, inmates become hardened, not resocialized. In a study of five British prisons, one respondent who was often punished by being put in isolation explained:

> All the time I've spent in segregation has made me hard. You put on a mask to protect yourself and then your mask becomes who you are yourself. When my family visit me they tell me how much harder and colder I've become.

(*King and McDermott* 1990, 468)

Total institutions have also failed in the mental-health field. Articles indicate that in western Europe (Prior 1991) and the United States (Sutton 1991) mental hospitals have generally proved ineffective and that new, much more effective mental-health programs that truly rehabilitate people need to be devised and implemented.

Perhaps part of the problem with total institutions is the concept itself. Motivated by the comforting belief that the best way to fight crime is to isolate and rehabilitate dangerous criminals in prisons, American criminal-justice policy has consistently supported harsher laws, producing longer sentences for more citizens. But such a system simply does not work. Prisoners are neither fully isolated nor are they rehabilitated, and each year both crime and the prison population rise substantially (Farrington 1992). Philip Slater (1976, 15–16) took a similar position, indicating with his "toilet assumption" that problems involving criminals or mental patients can not be effectively treated like feces—simply flushed out of sight.

Tough Times: Transitions in the Socialization Process ■

In the last two sections, we have learned something about how socialization works. Most of the time the process runs smoothly. However, when people make major transitions in their lives, they must undergo resocialization, and at these times they can have difficulties learning or accepting the new cultural standards or modes of behavior. Adolescence, job loss, divorce, and the death of a spouse are significant "tough times"—clearly situations in which individuals must confront high levels of stress.

ADOLESCENCE

When Susan Smith of Mystic, Connecticut, talks about her son Joshua, she often brings out a photo album, with pictures of Joshua sitting under the Christmas tree surrounded by gifts, washing the car, or mugging into the camera with dark glasses. "I want them to think of Josh as a person, not just a statistic," she said. "He grew up, he had dreams" (Collins 1992, sec. 13, p. 8).

Unfortunately Joshua also became a statistic.

Following therapy for alcoholism, loss of his job, and a bout of mononucleosis, Joshua killed himself. "I didn't even think of suicide," his mother explained. "I didn't know this was something a child would even consider. But when I look back I say, yeah, there were signs" (Collins 1992, sec. 13, p. 8).

A 1991 survey conducted by the Centers for Disease Control indicated that 27 percent of teenagers interviewed said they had thought about suicide while 8 percent indicated that they had actually attempted it (Collins 1992). Between 1970 and 1986, the rate of suicide for teens aged 15 to 19 nearly doubled. Why, one might wonder. James M. Henslin, a sociologist, suggested that young people face a fast-changing, confusing world with little sense of community or overall purpose. Henslin indicated that the modern emphasis on the importance of material goods is "simply not an adequate substitute for God, or for heroes that instill allegiance and make the blood run hot in dedication to larger causes" (Henslin 1990, 106).

Numerous investigations document the fact that adolescence is a confusing time. Research

Each year thousands of teenagers try to kill themselves, and some, like this young man, are prevented from accomplishing the act.

conducted by Roberta Simmons, Florence Rosenberg, and Morris Rosenberg (1973) of nearly two thousand urban school children in grades three through twelve found that the most disturbed sense of self developed among early adolescents. Compared with the other children, these early adolescents tended to be more self-conscious, less stable in their self-image, less positive in their self-esteem, and less confident about the evaluations of them maintained by parents, teachers, and peers of the same sex. The researchers suggested that the move from the relatively protected, personalized atmosphere of the junior high school to the more impersonal environment of the high school contributed significantly to their informants' disturbed sense of self.

Another source of adolescent confusion in modern cultures is the failure to provide youths with a clear indication of their status. In preindustrial cultures a rite of passage is normally provided: a formal ceremony initiating both boys and girls into adulthood. Such ceremonies contribute to young people's socialization, giving them strong assurance that their status has truly changed and that in the future people will regard them differently. No such assurance is provided to teenagers in modern societies. In the United States, boys and girls gradually emerge from childhood into adolescence, putting away childish things and taking up adult activities—drinking, drugs, sex, and more mature types of entertainment—but not yet assuming full adult responsibilities. When does one actually become an adult? We have no generally accepted way of marking the transition. Adolescence in America can be considered a "big waiting room" (Davison and Davison 1979).

Some young people are better able to cope with the stresses of adolescence than others. Research has indicated that the family setting, support networks, and the adolescent's personality characteristics are the three factors best predicting an ability to confront adolescent stress successfully. The families most helpful for adolescent children are those simultaneously emphasizing warmth and respect for individuality along with the firm maintenance of rules and discipline—a combination summed up by psychologist Laurence Steinberg as "demandingness." Support systems can be very significant, particularly in poor single-parent households. Studies have indicated that low-income urban adolescents who cope effectively with stress have one significant adult role model, not necessarily a parent. Finally adolescents who are sensitive, cooperative, socially responsible, active, and emotionally stable are able to confront stressful situations well, retaining self-confidence and a sense of personal power as they learn to be self-reliant and in control of their lives (*Carnegie Quarterly* Winter/Spring 1990, 10).

Adolescents burdened by stressful problems often lack the motivation and skills to discuss them. Can anything be done to encourage disclosures? Research has indicated that adolescents were more encouraged to discuss their problems if the conversation started off with such easily approached topics as music or hobbies than if it began with an analysis of such emotionally demanding subjects as unhappy or happy moments in their lives. Furthermore disclosure of personal problems was more extensive in group than in individual interviews. In the former context, adolescents used each other as models; once one individual disclosed his or her problems, others were encouraged to do so, too (Mills 1983).

JOB LOSS

Most people value their jobs, and this is revealed

when they lose them. Research has concluded that loss of job produces such reactions as a diminished self-esteem and sense of well-being, increased anxiety and depression, and more physical illness (Brand and Pullen 1991; Hoffman et al. 1991; Kessler, Turner, and House 1988; Reynolds and Gilbert 1991).

Douglas Powell and Paul Driscoll (1979) studied seventy-five male scientists and engineers who lost their jobs. The subjects averaged 41 years of age, had a mean of sixteen years of education, and had experienced 9.5 months of unemployment. As they were gradually socialized to the unemployed status, these men generally passed through four stages that involved the learning of new values and norms.

Stage I: *Period of relaxation and relief.* In most cases the men were aware of the layoffs in advance, and they were relieved when they finally took place. There was a sense of being "between jobs," and while most of the men made a definite effort to look for work, they tended to treat this period like a vacation at home, spending time with their families, sleeping late, and reading or tinkering in their workshops.

Stage II: *Period of concerted effort.* After about twenty-five days, the men usually felt rested and sometimes also bored. At this point they generally initiated a systematic effort to find new work, using such well-established strategies as calling friends, sending out resumés in response to ads, and going to job-placement centers. This phase averaged about three months, but the length varied considerably depending on such factors as the individual's ability to sustain his morale in the face of repeated rejection letters from potential employers, the amount of savings or other financial resources available to tide over the family, and the extent to which the wife provided moral support and handled the secretarial chores that accompany job seeking. During this stage the men often avoided others who were unemployed. "I'm not like them," one engineer said. "They are out of a job. I am waiting for an offer from Corning Glass."

Stage III: *Period of uncertainty and doubt.* At this point the men had been unemployed longer than they had ever been before. After

repeated unsuccessful encounters with the job market, their optimism began to erode. During this stage many men lost a clear sense of their occupational competence, often starting to feel that they were losing to younger men in the job competition or that their own knowledge and skills had become obsolete. Depression and rage often set in, with the rage frequently directed inward because there was no suitable external object on which to vent it. Toward the end of this period, a decline in job-hunting activity took place. The men made comments like the following: "I've stopped using certain approaches like sending out resumés. I push a little harder only when an opportunity comes up."

Stage IV: *Period of cynicism.* The transition to this stage was fairly smooth. The intervals between efforts to secure a job became longer and longer. The researchers concluded that a man was socialized to the status of unemployed person when he went two months without personally contacting a potential employer or job counselor. At this time many of the men in the study started to lose the conviction that they were in control of their occupational lives. The following statement was typical. "No matter what I do it just doesn't make any difference. It's just a throw of the dice, whether I'll get the job or not." A strong sense of powerlessness and pessimism appeared. "Why go in for an interview?" a physicist asked. "I'll never get past the secretary anyway." This cynicism seemed to be a way of avoiding a confrontation with the reality that a return to work would require a major change in lifestyle—in particular, that any jobs the men would be able to obtain would pay much less than the ones they had previously. Once in this stage, men were likely to spend more time at home and to associate less with friends. While financial limitations played a part in this change, the major reason seemed to be a deliberate avoidance of people whose lifestyle now differed sharply from their own. With their husbands out of work, wives frequently sought full-time employment, and husbands assumed a more active role on the domestic front. Further developments would depend

156

on changes in the job market and on the willingness of the man to accept a more modest position than the one he previously held.

In the modern economy, where job instability has become a widespread phenomenon, the likelihood that individuals will remain with a single firm throughout their lives has declined sharply. Jim Murphy, a chemical engineer who was recently laid off by a Houston firm specializing in cleaning of chemical equipment, told a reporter that his father had been with one company for fifty years and that he had been with two firms for fifteen years each. Murphy told his 20-year-old son that "[t]hey're not going to be loyal to you. Don't be loyal to them" (Barringer 1992, sec. 4, p. 6). Recognizing the job instability in modern society, the son has been preparing for two careers—one in Navy submarines and the other in general engineering.

DIVORCE

Do you think that divorce tends to be a difficult experience? A study of stressful life events ranked the relative impact of forty-three issues. The death of one's spouse was placed first, and divorce was second. But a pair of researchers have asserted that these findings have actually minimized the impact of divorce. They concluded that the impact of divorce is "often much more disruptive, both immediately and in the long term, than losing one's spouse" (Counts and Sacks 1985, 151).

Paul Bohannon (1970) suggested that divorce is especially difficult because it encompasses six different dimensions simultaneously and because American society does not yet possess effective means of helping people cope with these experiences. What Bohannon has called the "six stations of divorce" include:

1. **The emotional divorce.** The spouses withhold emotion from each other—they grow apart—because their trust in and attraction for each other has ended.
2. **The economic divorce.** When the household is broken up, an economic settlement is necessary, separating the shared assets into two portions.
3. **The legal divorce.** In the courts the formal termination of the marriage takes place, along with bestowal of the right to remarry.

4. **The coparental divorce.** Decisions are made about such issues as the custody of the children, visitation rights, each parent's financial and child-rearing responsibilities, and so forth.
5. **The community divorce.** Changes occur in the way friends and acquaintances react to the former couple when they learn about the divorce. Like property, friends too are often divided, becoming "her friends" or "his friends."
6. **The psychic divorce.** When marriage partners break up, an uncoupling occurs, and the sense of self alters. Each spouse must fully realize that he or she is no longer part of a couple. Once again the person is single, and for many this is a shock.

On the psychic dimension, Alan Booth and Paul Amato (1991) studied divorced people's psychological stress, measuring this factor with questions about happiness and emotional distress. Using a national sample of people married in 1980, the researchers found that compared with those who remained married, individuals who divorced experienced sharp rises in psychological distress both before and after divorce occurred, with stress levels dropping down close to those of married people two years after divorce took place. Respondents' stress reduction occurred more quickly when family income was high, the wife's education went beyond high school or she was employed, and when the former spouses accepted that their marriage was troubled and also that divorce was a morally appropriate response to a troubled marriage.

Like divorces, remarriages can be unsettling, especially when children are involved. In such cases the socialization of the step-parent includes learning how to build a relationship with his or her spouse's children. At present our society lacks clear standards on how step-parents should treat their spouses' children. Even the terms to use are unclear. What do children call their parents' new spouses—"Dad," "Mom," or do they refer to them by their first names? One obvious problem is that the missing biological parent is likely to resent the new spouse being called "Dad" or "Mom": It symbolizes a seizure of the parental role (Cherlin 1983). Additional questions arise: For instance, does the new spouse have a parent's full rights and obligations—the right to discipline the children or the obligation to become a full partner in the lengthy list of tasks that accompany parenthood?

A study of 232 remarried couples and 102 first-married couples found that the remarried respondents reported greater financial pressures in the preceding six months and more disagreements about rearing and disciplining children. In addition, remarried wives tended to report extensive difficulties with their step-children. Nevertheless remarried people's scores on measures of marital adjustment were quite similar to those produced by first-married individuals. One possible explanation supported by data in the study is that remarried husbands give into their wives more frequently than first-married husbands. The researcher concluded that the "implication is clearly that wives have more leverage in remarried than in first married situations, or that husbands have greater needs in remarriages than in first marriages, or both" (Hobart 1991, 84).

DEATH OF SPOUSE

Research has indicated that elderly citizens who had lost a spouse in the past two months were more likely to report a newly developed or worsened illness, greater use of medication, and generally poor health than a comparison group of elderly citizens who had not suffered such a loss (Thompson et al. 1984). On the other hand, a large study that followed subjects' lives over a ten-year period found that widowed people showed little or no differences from married individuals in self-rated health, daily activities, social-network size, openness to new experiences, psychological well-being, and depression (McCrae and Costa 1988). Thus while it is undeniable that people suffer when a spouse dies, most of them fully recover.

People inevitably undergo a period of adjustment after the loss of their spouse. This socialization experience is often referred to as **grief work**: the process by which people attempt to establish a new identity after the death of a loved one. Grief work involves several stages. First, numbness and disbelief dominate. In the beginning surviving spouses often cannot accept the fact that their husbands or wives have actually died. This stage frequently continues for several weeks beyond the funeral. Second, longing for the lost spouse

In dealing with the loss of a spouse, elderly people benefit from friends' social support, engaging with them in a variety of activities, including, for a select few, vigorous rowing.

becomes obsessive. Constant crying, psychosomatic symptoms such as headaches and insomnia, feelings of guilt about failing to prevent the spouse's death, hostility toward doctors, and other strong emotional reactions occur at this time. Third, depression is likely; sadness and loneliness become incapacitating. The surviving spouse no longer follows his or her normal routine and often expresses no motivation to keep living. A study starting with 350 widows and widowers found that 24 percent of the respondents experienced depression two months after the spouse's death; that 23 percent were depressed seven months after the loss; and that thirteen months afterwards 16 percent still had depressive episodes. Finally recovery occurs, with the surviving husband or wife recognizing that, with adjustments, life can continue. When people reach this point, they have completed the grief work (Hiltz 1980; Hultsch and Deutsch 1981; Zisook and Shuchter 1991).

Because American women average about seven more years of life than do American men and also tend to be younger than their husbands, wives generally survive longer. At any given point in time, in fact, there are about five times more American widows than widowers. Studies on women suggest that several factors determine how difficult they will find the acceptance of the new role. One consideration involves the circumstances of the husband's death. If there is a long illness, then the wife has some opportunity to prepare for her new role. On the other hand, if death arrives unexpectedly,

158

then she finds herself thrust suddenly into the widow's role despite being utterly unprepared to meet the psychological, economic, and social problems looming before her; the impact of this factor is increased if the woman has little general sense of control over life events. A related condition is the character of the relationship between the husband and wife. A wife who was dependent upon her husband to make decisions and to handle practical matters is in a more difficult situation than is a wife who has taken a more active part in family affairs. Another factor is the woman's marital role orientation. Research indicates that women who have given their highest priority to the wife role have more difficulty accepting the death of their husbands and assuming the widow role than do those who have emphasized the mother role as their strongest priority (Loether 1975; Stroebe, Stroebe, and Domittner 1988).

But perhaps the most significant factor involves the widow's social network. If a widow is greatly distressed one month after her husband's death, the most frequently associated condition is the absence of support from friends. Close friends often intimately share the sense of loss, permitting the widow to feel that she is not forced to suffer the stress and pain alone. A 56-year-old widow, who had lost her husband several weeks earlier, explained, "This friend of mine said the other day, 'I just can't believe this is happening to *us*.' That told me a lot. She just felt it was happening to her too, you know" (Lund et al. 1990, 67). Besides friends, family members, neighbors, service agencies supplying help in transportation, housekeeping, legal aid, and sick care, psychotherapy groups, and mutual self-help groups can contribute to widows' support systems (Lopata 1988; O'Bryant and Morgan 1990; Vachon and Stylianos 1988).

Losing one's spouse is difficult, and yet, according to one team of researchers, "the majority, it appears, see themselves stronger for having undergone the experience. We do them a disservice if we insist on focusing upon potential pathology associated with this transition period" (Thomas, Digiulio, and Sheehan 1988, 238).

CONCLUSION

In discussing the loss of a spouse, we have seen that in spite of the pain and stress involved, widowed people generally recover. Critical to their recovery is the support of social networks, and seeking support from these networks often requires individuals to act differently than in the past.

An instructive conclusion seems to emerge here: As the sociological perspective emphasizes, people are influenced by surrounding social forces, but, as in the case of widowed individuals, modern Americans face options and thus can make some choice about what forces should influence them.

Might it be possible for a variety of modern Americans to do something similar—resocialize themselves to some degree to more productive, cooperative patterns? A pair or researchers suggested that Americans could learn a great deal from people in developing nations. For instance, the people in Papua, New Guinea, have a concept of land that is different from the prevailing standard in the Western world: People have specific rights to the same piece of land; one individual has the fishing rights, another the living rights, a third the ceremonial rights, and so forth (Ellis and Ellis 1989).

This is simply an illustration of how different cultural standards might be instructive. The crucial idea is that maybe our lives could be made more tranquil, more stress-free, safer, and, in some ways, more productive if we sought to socialize ourselves to new, cooperative cultural standards.

STUDY GUIDE

Learning Objectives

After studying this chapter, you should be able to:

1. Define socialization and discuss its importance for human life.
2. Discuss the interplay of nature and nurture in human development.

3. Describe the effects on human development of deprived socialization in childhood.
4. Discuss in detail the different socialization theories developed by Cooley, Mead, Freud, and Piaget.
5. Examine the family as an agent of socialization, indicating how conceptions of childhood have changed over time.
6. Discuss day care and schools, peers, and the mass media as sources of socialization.
7. Define total institution and describe the two-step process of inmate resocialization.
8. Analyze the following "tough times," major transitions in the socialization process: adolescence, job loss, divorce, and death of spouse.

Summary

1. Socialization is the process by which a person becomes a social being, learning the necessary cultural content and behavior to become a member of a group or society. The most fundamental socialization occurs in childhood, but the process continues throughout people's lifetimes.

2. Sociologists address the question of whether human beings are the product of their nature (their innate biological characteristics or heredity) or their nurture (their socialization). While recognizing the significance of the nature issue, sociologists emphasize the importance of nurture or socialization.

3. When children grow up in very isolated circumstances or are the victims of deprived socialization, their sense of self is likely to be underdeveloped, confused, or unusual in some other respect. Studies of isolated infant monkeys, isolated children, and abused children have demonstrated these patterns of development.

4. Several well-known theories analyze the development of the self: Cooley's looking-glass self and George Herbert Mead's discussion of "play" and "game" indicate how the self develops as a result of interaction with others. Freudian theory divides the self into three parts, with one of the parts—the ego—acting as a mediator between the conflicting demands of the other two. Jean Piaget's theory of cognitive abilities involves four age-graded stages, where progressive knowledge builds from the experience obtained in the previous stage or stages. The four theories of socialization we have examined all recognize the changing nature of the self.

5. Sources of socialization include the family, day care and the school, peers, and the mass media. The family is a prominent source of socialization because within it children receive their first exposure to the cultural standards of their society. The concept of childhood and appropriate child-rearing practices vary in different eras and social settings. Day care and schooling are other prominent sources of socialization. With a substantial proportion of mothers in the work force, day care, especially high-quality day care, has become a national priority. The content of children's schooling often arouses controversy. Peers are another agent of socialization. In industrialized societies peer groups appear to have assumed some of the socialization functions performed by the family in the past. The mass media, especially television, are also a modern agent of socialization for people. The influence of television in the area of violent programming is a source of widespread concern. Besides the previous agents of socialization, a variety of others can be important influences on individuals. Inhabitants in total institutions experience resocialization, with the mortification process and the privilege system contributing to that outcome.

6. In the course of their lives, people encounter certain "tough times," transitional periods when new standards and new activities affect them. Some "tough times" are adolescence, job loss, divorce, or the death of a spouse. Adolescence is a difficult, confusing time period because it involves a shift from childhood to adult roles. Job loss can be a disturbing experience. People who suffer it can pass through four stages that involve a gradual socialization to their unemployed status. Divorce also involves a significant readjustment. Bohannon described six levels on which divorce occurs. The loss of a spouse also involves new socialization experiences. Learning to live without one's spouse can be described as a four-step process.

Key Terms

cognitive ability   the capacity to use perception, thought, memory, and other mental processes to acquire knowledge

ego   Sigmund Freud's conception of the self that must cope with pressures from three often contradictory forces

game   according to George Herbert Mead, a group activity in which each participant's role requires interaction with two or more individuals

generalized other   an image of the role expectations for all the game participants with whom a person must interact

grief work   the process by which people attempt to establish a new identity after the death of a loved one

id   according to Sigmund Freud, the part of the personality that is unconscious and primitive

instincts   unalterable behavior complexes that parents transmit genetically to their children

looking-glass self   according to Charles Cooley, our understanding of what sort of person we are is based on how we imagine we appear to other people

mass media   the instruments of communication that reach a large audience without any personal contact between the senders and the receivers

mortification process   a series of degradations and humiliations of inhabitants systematically carried out by staff members of total institutions

nature   inborn biological characteristics or heredity

nurture   socialization

object permanence   according to Jean Piaget, the childhood recognition that specific objects still exist after they are removed from one's line of vision

play   according to George Herbert Mead, the process of taking the role of specific individuals and thereby starting to learn the rights and obligations those particular roles entail

privilege system   a framework for inmates' resocialization

resocialization   a systematic effort to provide an individual new cultural content, permitting him or her to become a smoothly functioning member of a group or society

self   one's perception of his or her own person, formed as a result of other people's response in the course of socialization

socialization   the process by which a person becomes a social being, learning the necessary cultural content and behavior to become a member of a group or society

sociobiology   a field in which the proponents contend that through the evolutionary process, human beings have acquired tendencies that determine much of their behavior

superego   according to Sigmund Freud, the part of the personality that has internalized standards of right and wrong, a conscience

total institution   a place of residence where inhabitants experience nearly complete restriction of their physical freedom in an attempt to effectively resocialize them into a radically new identity and behavioral pattern

Tests

True • False Test

_____   1. Socialization continues throughout the entire life span.

_____   2. In the Samoan culture, the sense of stress that accompanies the socialization process in most cultures has been eliminated.

_____   3. Cooley and Mead both believed that the self is the product of a learning process that develops through interaction with others.

_____   4. Piaget's theory is concerned with children's increasing understanding of social relations.

_____   5. During the Middle Ages, children were treated as little adults.

_____   6. Most major advanced industrialized nations are ahead of the United States in the supply, quality, and affordability of child-care services.

_____ 7. While television remains very popular in the United States, about half of American adults believe they watch too much.

_____ 8. The resocialization of patients in mental hospitals has been surprisingly effective.

_____ 9. Grief work is a process that elderly people do not experience.

_____ 10. While losing one's spouse is difficult, a research team indicated that people see themselves as stronger for having undergone the experience.

Multiple-Choice Test

_____ 1. Darwin's idea of "natural selection" is consistent with the idea of:
   a. nurture.
   b. the id.
   c. instinct.
   d. survival of the fittest.

_____ 2. Cooley's concept of the looking-glass self:
   a. was rejected by George Herbert Mead.
   b. involves an image of the role expectations for all the game participants with whom a person must interact.
   c. suggests that our understanding of what sort of person we are is based on how we imagine we appear to other people.
   d. is closely related to Freud's concept of the superego.

_____ 3. All but one of the following are stages in the development of the self as described by Mead. Which is NOT a stage?
   a. play
   b. game
   c. generalized
   d. preparatory

_____ 4. In Freud's theory of the self, the internalized standards of right and wrong (conscience) exist in the:
   a. superego.
   b. id.
   c. ego.
   d. instinct.

_____ 5. In Piaget's theory of cognitive development, the ability to think abstractly occurs in which stage?
   a. concrete operational
   b. formal operational
   c. sensorimotor
   d. preoperational

_____ 6. On the topic of child-rearing, it now seems apparent that:
   a. children in all societies should be reared the same way.
   b. there are few universal needs beyond a child's basic physical needs and minimal social contact.
   c. Americans have developed the best approach to child-rearing for all societies.
   d. non-Westerners rear their children more effectively than Westerners do.

_____ 7. The main factors helping young people cope with the stresses accompanying adolescence include:
   a. support systems.
   b. the family setting.
   c. religious training.
   d. a and b

_____ 8. Powell and Driscoll studied scientists and engineers who had lost their jobs. Depression and rage occurred during which stage of response to job loss?
   a. period of relaxation and relief
   b. period of concerted effort
   c. period of uncertainty and doubt
   d. period of cynicism

_____ 9. A study of remarried and first-married couples found that remarried respondents reported:
   a. greater financial pressures in the preceding six months.
   b. a greater tendency for remarried husbands to oppose wives' decisions.
   c. much more extensive marital adjustment.
   d. a, b, and c

_____ 10. It is easier for widows to accept their new roles if:
   a. the husband died suddenly.
   b. the woman gave highest priority to the wife role.
   c. the wife had been dependent on her husband to make decisions and handle practical matters.
   d. the widow is imbedded in a supportive social network.

Essay Test

1. Define socialization. Why is this process important?
2. Distinguish between nature and nurture and discuss the development of the "nature" position, including sociologists' reaction to it.
3. How does deprived socialization affect young children? Discuss the different issues raised in the section on this topic.
4. What is the self? Describe Cooley's, Mead's, Freud's, and Piaget's analyses of the self. Indicate significant similarities and differences between and among the theories.
5. Discuss the impact of three important sources of socialization on American college students.
6. Describe three difficult transitions that can occur in the socialization process, referring to relevant concepts and studies.

Suggested Readings

Axline, Virginia. 1968. *Dibs: In Search of Self*. New York: Ballantine. A vivid account of a withdrawn child's effort to clarify his sense of self with the aid of a highly skilled therapist.

Burkitt, Ian. 1992. *Social Selves: Theories of the Social Formation of Personality*. Newbury Park, CA: Sage. An analyis of the development of the social self, focusing on the relationship between the individual and society and using a variety of theoretical frameworks, including symbolic interaction, Marxism, and developmental psychology.

Fiske, Marjorie, and David A. Chirboga. 1990. *Change and Continuity in Adult Life*. San Francisco: Jossey-Bass. The results of a twelve-year study, indicating how working-class and lower-middle-class respondents at different age stages of adulthood adjust to the pressures and stresses of modern life.

Goodman, Paul. 1960. *Growing Up Absurd*. New York: Vintage. A sociologist's uncompromisingly critical account of the frustrations and confusion that all children face growing up in American society where, according to Goodman, useless, destructive, and above all absurd standards and activities are dominant.

Kagan, Jerome. 1984. *The Nature of the Child*. New York: Basic Books. A noted psychologist's highly readable analysis of what is known about children. A wealth of cross-cultural references are included. Frequently traditional theory and research is challenged.

Lerner, Richard M., Anne C. Petersen, and Jeanne Brooks-Gunn (eds.). 1991. *Encyclopedia of Adolescence*. Hamden, CT: Garland. A review of recent research findings, facts, and figures drawing from diverse disciplines and examining over 200 topics involving modern adolescents' challenges and problems.

Roth, Henry. 1932. *Call It Sleep*. New York: Cooper Square. A novel sensitively describing the fear, confusion, and loneliness encountered by a young Jewish immigrant boy living in early twentieth-century New York City.

Spock, Benjamin, and Michael B. Rothenberg. 1985. *Dr. Spock's Baby and Child Care*. 6th ed. New York: Pocket Books. A book originally published in 1945, which continues to be the country's leading guide to parents seeking practical knowledge about how to care for their children.

Additional Assignments

1. In the course of an ordinary day at school or work, observe the behavior of someone (without being noticed), noting how often and under what circumstances this person seems to alter his or her behavior in order to fit in with others' expectations. Alternatively you might make mental notes on your own behavior, recording your own behavioral changes when you are with other people. Discuss your findings with other class members. How do your observations fit with Cooley's and Mead's theories? How do your findings fit with Goffman's theory (dramaturgic sociology) discussed in Chapter 5?

2. Make a list of the different agents of socialization with which you have been in close contact today. Then ask yourself which of these agents of socialization you would consult regarding the following issues: problems with school, difficulties in interpersonal relations (such as your love life), career choices, self-improvement goals, and the need to release strong emotions (such as love, hate, or fear). What does this exercise suggest about the varied influences of different agents of socialization? Would you have made the same consultations five years ago?

Answers to Objective Test Questions

True • False Test

1. t	6. t
2. f	7. t
3. t	8. f
4. f	9. f
5. t	10. t

Multiple-Choice Test

1. d	6. b
2. c	7. d
3. c	8. c
4. a	9. a
5. b	10. d

Deviance

7

In the summer of 1992, Gabe Pressman, a long-time reporter for WNBC-TV, complained that collectively the television news programs in New York City were "a ton of garbage." He concluded, "The whole thing is: Can we be more outrageous and sensationalist than the next guy? Can we tease people into the 10 o'clock news?" (Manegold 1992, 41, 50). Violent crime plays a prominent part in the teasing process. Chuck Scarborough, the local anchor at WNBC-TV, explained that besides being dramatic, violent crime is "reasonably easy to shoot, and the cast of characters is readily available. So we do a lot of it" (Manegold 1992, 50).

Increasingly viewers are complaining about the ugly image of the city they see represented. Liz Smith, a nationally syndicated gossip columnist and a resident of the city, said that while admittedly New York City has problems, there is no reason why TV news reporters should keep viewers in "this state of horrifying anxiety." She added, "If they do a story about someone putting a baby in an oven, I don't want to see it four times before bedtime and then again when I get up in the morning." Such reporting "just makes people feel really sick" (Manegold 1992, 50).

Besides affecting people's outlook, the portrayal of violent crime might affect individuals' behavior. For instance, researchers found that exposure of college-aged males to films portraying violence against women in sexual contexts encouraged insensitive attitudes toward victims of sexual and spousal violence. Perhaps the influence might go a step further, encouraging these viewers to engage in sexual violence (Linz, Wilson, and Donnerstein 1992).

While illegal and widely considered immoral, violent crime has an appeal to many modern people. They are interested, even fascinated by it, just as they often are by other types of deviance. As we discuss violent crime and other forms of deviance in this chapter, we see that the way they are viewed is not fixed but determined by the existing social standards.

What is deviance? Sociologist Albert Cohen suggested that it includes "knavery, skulduggery, cheating, unfairness, crime, sneakiness, malingering, cutting corners, immorality, dishonesty, betrayal, graft, corruption, wickedness, and sin . . ." (Cohen 1966, 1). But simply listing types of deviant activities, colorful though they may be, does not indicate precisely what qualifies them as deviant. **Deviance** is any behavior that violates social norms considered sufficiently significant that the majority of a group or society responds negatively to their violation. The word "deviance" conveys the strong feeling that the people who engage in this behavior—the "deviants"—are different or even inferior and generally set apart from the rest of us.

Because social groups determine whether a thought or action qualifies as deviant, it should be apparent that what is considered deviant behavior will vary widely across time or space. About thirty years ago, I was watching a recent film, and to my surprise the heroine said "damn"—a word my tender ears had not previously encountered in a movie theatre. Apparently the censors of the early 1960s decided that prevailing standards of decency permitted the word "damn" to be used— that its use was not deviant. Obviously in the intervening three decades, standards of deviance have changed dramatically, with film censors permitting much greater freedom in the use of what traditionally was considered obscene language and the representation of sexually explicit scenes.

Deviance is a broad and interesting topic. In American society such legal activities as alcoholism, compulsive gambling, lying, radical political behavior, the refusal to bathe regularly, the sale or purchase of pornography, and transvestism are widely considered deviant. In the following section, we examine some of the most useful sociological theories of deviance, followed by a discussion of crime. The chapter closes with an examination of the social control of deviance. Admittedly the chapter strongly emphasizes crime and offers relatively little material on noncriminal deviant behavior. The reason, unfortunately, is the space limitations of an introductory text. It seems important to pay considerable attention to the type of deviant behavior that creates extensive concern and fear for most Americans, including students.

Sociological Theories of Deviance

Over the past half-century, a rich body of theory involving deviance, especially criminality, has developed. The following four theories are among the most prominent.

ANOMIE THEORY

Anomie is the confusing situation produced when norms are either absent or conflicting. Societies that experience widespread anomie risk disintegration because their members no longer possess guidelines for achieving common purposes. The individual members often feel isolated and disoriented.

Robert Merton (1968) used the concept anomie more specifically, suggesting that it is a discrepancy between a socially approved goal and the availability of means to achieve that goal. Merton indicated that the attainment of wealth has been a strongly emphasized goal all Americans have been encouraged to seek. However, he also noted that many strivers for wealth and success, especially members of minority groups, have found the channels to achievement relatively closed. Either these individuals have lacked easy access to the culturally acceptable means to attain wealth or, because of their socialization, they have not possessed the appropriate personality qualities that would have allowed them to become achievers.

This photo illustrates a central idea of anomie theory—that access to wealth and income varies widely for American citizens.

Merton described five courses of action or adaptations to being in such a condition of blocked opportunity. Only in the case of conformity does the individual continue to accept both the pursuit of culturally prescribed goals and to feel favorable toward using solely legitimate means. The other four adaptations are regarded as deviant. They involve the nonacceptance of legitimate means, goals, or both. Table 7.1 summarizes Merton's theory.

Table 7.1 The Five Modes of Adaptation in Merton's Anomie Theory

Modes of adaptation	Culturally approved goals	Culturally approved means
I. Conformity	Accepts	Accepts
II. Innovation	Accepts	Rejects
III. Ritualism	Rejects	Accepts
IV. Retreatism	Rejects	Rejects
V. Rebellion	Seeks to create new goals	Seeks to create new means

Source: Adapted from Robert K. Merton. Social Theory and Social Structure. 3rd ed. New York: Free Press, 1968, p. 194.

When people are blocked from culturally approved activities to obtain wealth, they pursue one of five adaptations. Either they endorse conformity, accepting the culturally approved means and goals, even though it is unlikely they will obtain their goals, or they pursue one of four deviant adaptations, rejecting either the culturally approved means, the culturally approved goals, or both the culturally approved means and goals, or seeking to create new means and goals.

168

1. **Conformity.**   This is a nondeviant adaptation. Individuals pursue legitimate goals and the culturally accepted means to achieve them, even though it is likely they will not attain those goals. In the 1920s a young black person who went to college with the hope of eventually becoming a wealthy professional was pursuing a culturally legitimate means to a legitimate goal. However, with the widespread discrimination that existed, it was unlikely the goal would have been achieved.

2. **Innovation.**   This common deviant adaptation develops when a person seeks legitimate goals but is blocked from effectively using culturally accepted means to achieve them. If the drive to become wealthy cannot be satisfied through legitimate means, some people turn elsewhere. For instance, some poor but ambitious members of economically deprived ethnic groups have turned to organized crime. There has been a definite pattern of ethnic succession in this activity. In the nineteenth century, organized crime was initially dominated by the Irish, followed by Jews and then Italians. African-Americans and Puerto Ricans are the latest in line. As each ethnic group has found conventional channels of success becoming increasingly available to them, they have moved gradually out of the underworld (Bell 1962, 148).

     Organized criminals are not the only success-oriented people who display innovative behavior. Merton observed that most great American fortunes were accumulated at least in part by techniques generally considered culturally illegitimate and even illegal. The respect most Americans show toward those who have accumulated such wealth indicates that the goal itself—the achievement of wealth—usually is considered more important than the legitimacy of the means by which it is achieved (Merton 1968, 195–203).

3. **Ritualism.**   This pattern occurs when culturally prescribed success goals are no longer actively sought, but the legitimate means for achieving those goals are conscientiously pursued. The ritualist avoids the dangers and possible frustrations of open competition and simply follows safe and easy routines of living and working. The ritualist qualifies as deviant because he or she fails to address goals which are strongly supported within the society. Merton mentioned a number of well-known clichés that apply to the ritualist—"I'm not sticking my neck out," "I'm playing it safe," and "Don't aim high and you won't be disappointed." As a prime example of ritualism, Merton cited the "zealously conformist bureaucrat" (Merton 1968, 203–205). Such a person accepts the organization's goals or rules as personal goals or rules and is characterized by an unquestioning allegiance to the organization.

4. **Retreatism.**   A person is a retreatist if he or she pursues neither the culturally prescribed goals of success nor the means for achieving these goals because of limited opportunities or a sense of personal inadequacy. Among the types of deviants who may be regarded as retreatists are "psychotics, . . . outcasts, vagrants, vagabonds, tramps, chronic drunkards, and drug addicts" (Merton, 1968, 207). In short, retreatists are dropouts, and they are frequently condemned by many people because of their inability or unwillingness to lead normal, productive lives.

5. **Rebellion.**   This deviant adaptation happens when an individual decides that the existing society imposes barriers preventing the achievement of success goals. Therefore that individual strikes out against the society, seeking to change its goals and also the existing means for achieving goals. According to Merton (1968, 210), people who engage in rebellion withdraw their allegiance from the existing society and develop "a new myth." This myth or set of beliefs claims that the source of frustration lies in the organizational and cultural patterns of the present society. Thus the myth proposes new cultural arrangements that do

not display the problems emphasized by the people involved in the rebellion. In the past fifteen years, women, African-Americans, students, welfare recipients, antiwar activists, antinuclear protestors, work groups, and environmentalists have been prominent groups initiating social movements that support rebellious activity.

Critical Evaluation

A major contribution of the anomie perspective is that it allows us to interpret a wide variety of deviant behavior by means of a single theory. As one writer noted, the scheme includes such diverse deviant personality types "as Cubists, alcoholics, lone-wolf inventors, religious martyrs, executives, and beggars" (Hunt 1961, 59). Furthermore this theory contributes significantly to an understanding of deviance by taking a distinctly sociological perspective, indicating that social forces play an important role in encouraging people to behave in a deviant manner and opposing the widely held belief that all responsibility for deviant acts should be placed on the individuals in question. Using a national sample of 1,146 adult Americans, a team of researchers found general support for the theory's emphasis on the role played by social forces in the development of deviant behavior (Huang and Anderson 1991).

On the other hand, Merton's analysis has been sharply criticized. Some individuals have claimed that the scheme provides no more than a general idea of how anomie can contribute to deviance; the precise process by which people learn deviance, including the motivation to learn deviance, needs to be mapped out much more thoroughly and systematically (Agnew 1985; Messner 1988). Merton (1976, 32) himself admitted that his theory addresses only selected issues as it analyzes sources of deviance and contributes nothing about how people learn to be deviant. That task is left to other theories, in particular the differential-association perspective.

DIFFERENTIAL-ASSOCIATION THEORY

What is the process by which criminal behavior is learned? Edwin Sutherland's theory of differential association addresses this issue. Essentially this perspective emphasizes that people's behavior is largely determined by the company they keep. The concept of reference group, which is discussed in Chapter 4, "Groups," is closely related to this theory. The following four steps summarize the differential-association process.

1. Criminal behavior, like most other behavior, is learned in interaction with others, mostly in intimate groups.
2. Learning criminal behavior consists of acquiring both criminal techniques and the motives, drives, and attitudes appropriate for criminal behavior.
3. A person becomes a criminal "because of an excess of definitions favorable to violation of law over definitions unfavorable to violation of law." Therefore someone is likely to become a criminal if that person's values and the values of the individuals who have the greatest influence over him or her more strongly support criminal activity than noncriminal activity.
4. A person's criminal associations can vary in certain respects. In particular, the frequency, length, and intensity of these contacts will help determine the impact of these associations on the individual (Sutherland and Cressey 1978, 80–83).

The differential-association theory can be applied to diverse forms of criminal and delinquent behavior. For example, a detailed study indicated that in Nazi Germany many doctors joined the Nazi party and enthusiastically promoted Adolf Hitler's program for racial "purity" by murdering Jews, handicapped children, psychiatric patients, and other designated undesirables with a variety of techniques (Proctor 1988). Thus these doctors encountered an excess of definitions favorable to widespread murder of supposed undesirables over those unfavorable to such a course of action.

One of the latent dysfunctions of prisons is that they provide a learning context for budding criminals. Young, fairly inexperienced people arrive in prison, and from the more experienced inmates they may obtain critical information for a successful criminal career. In the mid-1970s, a young man was sent to a minimim-security federal

170   prison, where he served a short sentence for selling marijuana. In prison he learned the intricacies of the system, using small airplanes to smuggle hundreds of pounds of marijuana into the country at a time. While still in prison, he realized that the same approach could be used with cocaine, and upon release he began setting up such a system and soon became one of the most successful drug traffickers (Massing 1989).

During the first half of this century, juvenile gangs were often the context in which young men could learn the values, skills, and motivation necessary for a criminal career in association with others (Shaw and McKay 1942; Thrasher 1926). The process has continued into modern times. For instance, some youthful immigrant Chinese males drop out of school when their limited knowledge of English forces them to fall behind. Finding little support from parents who are working long hours or are themselves poorly educated, they are likely to join youth gangs and start hanging out around Chinese gambling clubs. At these clubs alienated youth start performing errands, help protect the club from outsiders, and execute other services for the organized criminals running the gambling establishments. While so engaged these young men learn the values and norms of criminal life from professionals whose own painful rejection from schools and mainstream society makes them both sympathetic and effective transmitters of criminal standards (Chin 1993).

Critical Evaluation

Critics of the differential-association perspective have charged that some of the terminology of the theory is vague, making verification through research difficult. For example, it is not entirely clear how the phrase "excess of definitions favorable to violation of law over definitions unfavorable to violation of law" can be tested (Sutherland and Cressey 1978, 83–92). Certainly researchers will continue to scrutinize this phrase. For example, a recent study of national survey data on delinquency suggested that peers' behavior serves as a greater influence than their attitudes (Warr and Stafford 1991).

Over all differential-association theory has made a significant contribution: It emphasizes the fact that the development of criminal behavior can be understood only by examining the particular needs and values that specific criminal groups provide for their members.

CONFLICT THEORY

Criminologists Ian Taylor, Paul Walton, and Jock Young (1973) produced a book called *The New Criminology*. While their analysis offered little that was actually new, it did give increased prominence to the social-critic role of criminologists examining the failure of modern society to promote a truly just social-justice system. The book applied Marxist thinking to the analysis of criminal justice, emphasizing that complete social freedom for most citizens is severely limited by the fact that laws are enacted and maintained by people at the upper socioeconomic levels—the ruling class—whose intention is to keep those who are not wealthy and powerful in their place.

Proponents of conflict theory offer somewhat different explanations of why the situation they describe has arisen in modern societies. William Chambliss and Robert Seidman (1971) contended that such a condition will occur in any complex society that has a multilevel class system. On the other hand, Richard Quinney (1974) argued that Western capitalism is the prime source of these inequities.

Quinney's (1975, 37–41) version of the conflict theory of deviance has focused on "the social reality of crime." He described four conditions that help explain high U.S. crime rates and also the prevailing system of criminal justice. First, the ruling class defines as criminal those behaviors that threaten its existence. Second, the elite uses these definitions of criminal behavior to protect its own interests. Third, because of the limited life chances available to them, members of the subordinate classes are virtually compelled to engage in the sorts of behaviors defined as criminal. Finally the ruling class develops an ideology that explains criminal behavior and that, in effect, downgrades the subordinate classes or groups, which are said to contain a disproportionate number of dangerous people.

Critical Evaluation

Conflict theory suggests that those defined as criminals are generally members of subordinate classes; this suggestion is an oversimplification. Consider the crimes of the prominent politicians, business people, and labor leaders who have been indicted in the post-Watergate years.

Conflict theory has also been criticized for its failure to describe the causes of deviant behavior. However, the theory makes no claim to do so; it pursues a specific task. The theory attempts to explain why certain standards for criminal behavior are established and not others. For instance, why are homosexuality, excessive drinking, the habitual use of powerful prescription drugs, and uncontrolled gambling frequently considered deviant but not classified as criminal? According to the conflict perspective, the reason is that it is not in the interests of the ruling class to establish a criminal definition for these activities.

LABELING THEORY

Labeling theory is based on symbolic interaction, and because it falls within this theoretical tradition, the perspective is centrally concerned with interaction between deviants and conformists. In addition, since the interaction is symbolic, labeling theory is concerned with the meanings the participants derive from each other's actions and reactions. Labeling theory emphasizes that behavior itself does not distinguish deviants from nondeviants. Instead the distinction is provided by the actions of the conforming members of society. These members interpret certain behavior as deviant and then apply the deviant label to individuals. Like conflict theory the labeling perspective does not seek the causes of deviance but raises such questions as who applies the deviant label to whom and what are the consequences for the people labeled.

Labeling theory emphasizes that labels are applied by people powerful enough to impose their standards on society—for instance, police, judges, prison guards, and psychiatrists. Those labeled include criminals, juvenile deliquents, drug addicts, alcoholics, prostitutes, homosexuals, mental patients, and retarded people (Thio

Arrested for suspicion of committing a crime, this young man is experiencing secondary deviance, finding himself labeled a criminal and, quite possibly as a result, either already considering himself a criminal or soon accepting that status.

1978, 56–58). Recent studies have examined labeling in the development of juvenile delinquency (Kaplan and Johnson 1991), social workers' evaluations of possible child abusers (Margolin 1992), and the reaction to deviance in the U.S. military (Stevenson 1990).

If labeling theory were concerned only with the issue of who imposes labels on whom, it would be closely related to conflict theory. However, labeling theory also examines another important issue: the consequences of being labeled deviant.

Consequences of Labeling

The labeling process can be divided into two stages, primary deviance and secondary deviance (Lemert 1951, 75–76). With **primary deviance** individuals violate a social rule but are not labeled and so do not see themselves as deviant. **Secondary deviance** occurs when authorities label individuals deviants and those individuals accept that status. The label seems to fit. "Yes," the person admits, "I am an alcoholic," or "I did

172 commit a crime by embezzling the company funds." Perhaps you see the relationship between these two concepts and the concept of the looking-glass self. If not, turn to Chapter 6.

Why does primary deviance tend to become secondary deviance? Edwin Lemert (1951, 77) suggested that there is a process of interaction between the person and various forces of social control. Primary deviance is followed by the imposition of social penalties. Additional primary deviance happens, followed by stronger penalties and rejections. Further hostilities and resentment occur, perhaps with a hostile focus on those penalizing. The community now takes formal action, labeling the individual as a deviant. Eventually the person accepts the deviant role and incorporates an awareness of being deviant into his or her life pattern. At this point secondary deviance has taken place.

In a study of two groups of white male high-school students, William Chambliss (1973) demonstrated the selective nature of the labeling process. Both groups were frequently involved in delinquent acts—truancy, drinking, petty theft, vandalism, and (for one group) wild driving. The members of one group, however, were never arrested, while the members of the other were in constant difficulty with the police. The boys who were never in trouble—in the study they were called the "Saints"—came from respectable families. They had established good, sometimes excellent reputations in school; tended to have good grades; and were careful "to cover their tracks" so that they would not be caught following their misdeeds. If confronted by the police, the Saints were polite and apologetic, and if necessary their parents would intervene on their behalf. These boys engaged in primary deviance but carefully avoided run-ins with the authorities. In other words they escaped the labeling process that would have led them to see themselves as deviants.

The other group, whose members were called the "Roughnecks" in the study, came from much lower-status families. The Roughnecks had poor reputations and grades in school; they were less likely to have cars than the Saints, and so if they got into trouble they were less easily able to escape the situation. Being without cars also encouraged the Roughnecks to stay in the center of town where everyone, including teachers and the police, could see them. Unlike the Saints the Roughnecks appeared hostile and disdainful if confronted by the police. The parents of the Roughnecks, feeling powerless, were unlikely to intervene with the police on behalf of their children. In short, various social forces in the community propelled the Roughnecks toward secondary deviance.

It proved difficult to make an accurate comparison of the relative severity of the deviance engaged in by members of the two groups. The Saints took part in a greater number of deviant acts and may have caused greater damage with their drunken driving. The Roughnecks were much more inclined toward physical violence. From the point of view of the community, however, the comparison was easy. Selective perception operated. As the products of upper-middle-class families, the Saints were perceived to be "good"; the lower-class Roughnecks were seen as "bad." The police frequently took action against the Roughnecks and never against the Saints, setting the secondary deviance process in motion for the Roughnecks.

Critical Evaluation

There are several limitations to the labeling perspective. First, this theory applies only to a relatively small range of deviant behavior. The majority of the people who take part in deviance are never caught or labeled. This generalization applies to types of deviance as diverse as stealing, homosexuality, extra-marital sex, marijuana use, drunken driving, and crimes committed by business people or politicians. Second, sociologists who employ the labeling perspective tend to focus primarily on lower-class people, who are relatively easily labeled, and to ignore middle- and upper-class individuals, who have considerable ability to resist labeling. This situation seems unavoidable. After all, the labeling process is initiated by middle- and upper-class people in positions of authority, and these people are not likely to permit themselves or their children to be labeled deviants (Thio 1978), as the Chambliss study on high-school boys illustrates. Furthermore in recent articles, sociologists have indicated that the concepts in this theory are "murky" and thus difficult to test in studies (Dotter and Roebuck 1988; Tittle 1988). Under precisely what circumstances, for instance, has an individual crossed the line from primary to secondary deviance?

Table 7.2 Four Sociological Theories of Deviance

The theory	Its basic question	The answer
1. Anomie theory	1. What are the social conditions that produce deviance?	1. Limited access to culturally approved goals, the means to achieve them, or both
2. Differential-association theory	2. How do people learn deviant norms, values, and behavior?	2. By the influence of the company they keep
3. Conflict theory	3. What is the primary motivation behind a society's definitions of deviance and crime?	3. That the definitions protect wealthy and powerful people's needs and interests
4. Labeling theory	4. What happens to a person who is labeled deviant?	4. A two-part process that is likely to produce a deviant career

Despite such limitations labeling theory does contribute substantially to our understanding of many kinds of deviant activity. In particular, the theory emphasizes that a force other than the deviant act itself—namely, the reactions of oth-ers—frequently contributes to the development of deviance (Clinard 1974, 25–27).

Table 7.2 summarizes all four theories of deviance.

Crime

In the previous section, we encountered a number of references to crime. The majority of crimes are, in fact, generally regarded as deviant activities—for instance, murder, rape, assault, robbery, bur-glary, embezzlement, and a host of others. On the other hand, people who talk to themselves in pub-lic or who do not bathe would qualify as deviant but not criminal in U.S. society. In addition, some technically illegal behaviors are often not regarded as deviant. There is widespread violation of some outdated laws, such as restrictions against pre-marital sexual relations or Sunday sports.

Crime is simply an act that violates criminal law. Criminal laws generally reflect the prevailing standards of deviant behavior, and when those standards change, the laws are likely to be altered or disregarded. Punishment for crime is provided by the criminal-justice system of a society. Behavior is likely to be defined as criminal when it is too disruptive to be permitted and cannot be controlled by informal means.

In this section we examine the limitations of criminal statistics, the different types of crime, and criminals' characteristics.

LIMITATIONS OF CRIMINAL STATISTICS

Official crime statistics drawn throughout the United States are reported in the FBI's annual *Uniform Crime Report*. We will see that serious biases can affect these data when we examine four sources of these biases.

From Complaints to Official Statistics

One of law enforcement officials' chief tasks is to respond to people's complaints. The officer must decide whether or not to file a formal report of the complaint, thereby making it a crime known to police. One study indicated that the major variable affecting the reporting and recording of a crime is its perceived seriousness—most important is the victim's perception and less significant is the offi-cer's view—and that unlike earlier research this investigation found that offenders' and victims' personal characteristics seem to have a minor impact on reporting and recording crimes (Gove et al. 1985). Besides the perceived seriousness of a crime, some crimes pose particular problems

174

for reporting. Arson is probably underreported, because before a report of arson can be made, it must be established that a fire has been "willfully or maliciously set," and that can be difficult to determine (Jackson 1988).

Issues Involving the Victim's Willingness to Cooperate

The victim's willingness to cooperate can be a critical factor affecting crime statistics. Consider the case of rape. For many years experts on this topic have asserted that official statistics on rape, such as the Justice Department figure of 130,260 rapes for 1990, represented a vast underreporting. After being emotionally devastated by the assault, they pointed out, victims were often unwilling to face the added turmoil of reporting this crime. This assertion was validated when 0.7 percent of a stratified random sample of 4,008 women indicated that they had been raped in the previous twelve months. Projected to the 96 million women in the United States, the estimate would be that 683,000 women, more than five times the Justice Department number, were raped in the previous year (Johnston 1992). It appears that the survey figure was much higher than official government statistics because many women being interviewed found it much easier to tell an interviewer that they had been a rape victim than to make an official report to the police.

Administrative Distortions

Sometimes crime rates appear to increase because a police force has become more professional. For example, in 1950, under pressure from the FBI, the New York City Police Department changed its system of reporting crime, and in one year the city's reported robbery rate increased 400 percent and the burglary rate rose 1,300 percent (Zeisel, cited in Reid, 1982, 50–51).

More than four decades later, in 1992, reported crime in New York City declined from the previous year, with recorded drops in every major category of crime. While some politicians triumphantly declared that the shift showed a decline in the city's lengthy crime wave, some criminologists suggested that a change in the department's administrative operations, especially less emphasis on reporting various types of

crime, might have played a significant role (James 1992).

Absence of White-Collar Crime

Later in this chapter, we discuss white-collar crimes, which are crimes committed by people of higher socioeconomic status in the course of their business activities. White-collar crime is omitted from the annual *Uniform Crime Report*. As a result high-income individuals, who are more likely to engage in white-collar crimes than other types of criminal activity, are significantly underrepresented in criminal statistics.

TYPES OF CRIME

The people who commit different types of crime are likely to vary in their background characteristics, lifestyles, and subcultures. However, all are probably affected by some of the social forces referred to in the theories we have examined. Many are, in Merton's terminology, innovators: seeking wealth through crime because legitimate access to its pursuit has been blocked. Furthermore as differential-association theory indicates, most lawbreakers are exposed to criminal reference groups, providing an excess of definitions favorable to violation of the law. And in line with conflict theory, most criminals engage in behavior that influential citizens have—to their advantage—designated as criminal. Finally many lawbreakers experience the process of being labeled as criminals and, especially if sent to prison, enter the phase of secondary deviance.

Crime against Persons and Property

The crime statistics presented in the FBI's *Uniform Crime Reports* are divided into two categories, Part I offenses and Part II offenses. Part II offenses are less serious crimes, such as drunkenness, fraud, prostitution and commercialized vice, and disorderly conduct. Part I offenses are further divided into two subcategories: (1) violent crimes, namely murder, negligent manslaughter, rape, robbery, and aggravated assault; and (2) property crimes, specifically burglary, larceny (theft), motor vehicle theft, and arson. The *Uniform Crime Reports* focus on these two sets of offenses because they have consistent definitions throughout the states and because they occur frequently enough to be statistically significant.

Violent Crime As the chapter opener indicated, television and other mass media are never at a loss for accounts of new violent crimes. In 1990 a violent crime known to the police took place every seventeen seconds on the average. An aggravated assault occurred every thirty seconds, a robbery every forty-nine seconds, a rape every 5.1 minutes, and a murder every 22.5 minutes. Of the nearly 14.5 million total Part 1 crimes reported by the police in 1990, over 1.8 million (13 percent) were violent crimes. However, law-enforcement officials place special emphasis on violent crime, arresting suspects in 29 percent of the known violent crimes compared to 14 percent of the suspects in property crimes (U.S. Bureau of the Census, *Statistical Abstract of the United States: 1992*, No. 287 and No. 302).

Many Americans today fear being murdered. Americans often think of murderers as deranged people like Jeffrey Dalmer, the Son of Sam, Charles Manson, the Boston Strangler, or Jack the Ripper, who strike quickly and entirely unexpectedly, murdering and sometimes raping victims they have never met. Although such murders are often well publicized, they represent only a small portion of the total. Most murders occur after social interaction between the murderer and the victim. In a substantial number of cases, the victim precipitated the violence, perhaps by striking the first blow or by attempting to use a deadly weapon. Furthermore most people who kill lack apparent psychotic tendencies.

Murders, in fact, tend to occur in the course of ordinary behavior. A recently developed theory— the "routine activities" approach—suggests that most murders are committed in the midst of people's everyday routines, which tend to vary according to such personal characteristics as age, sex, race, marital status, and employment status. For example, one study found that the very young and the very old are more likely to have their routine activities centered in the home than are other people. Subsequently these two age categories are more likely to be murdered at home than are others (Messner and Tardiff 1985).

Studies suggest that men kill and are killed four to five times more frequently than women;

that there is no actual season for murder but that December, July, and August are the most common months; that murders are most likely to occur in warmer and rainier cities; that most murders take place on weekends, particularly on Saturday night between 8:00 P.M. and 2:00 A.M.; and that in nearly two-thirds of all murders, either the victim or the offender (or both) has been drinking (Cheatwood 1988; Lester 1991; Wolfgang 1967).

Americans generally support the death penalty in murder convictions. As Figure 7.1 indicates, 76 percent of a national sample provided support for the death penalty in murder convictions, and only 18 percent opposed it. Those supporting the death penalty were asked to give one or more reasons. Fifty percent indicated that their reason was "a life for a life," 22 percent cited the idea of deterrence, 16 percent indicated that further killing was prevented, and 10 percent mentioned the cost of prison maintenance (Gallup and Newport 1991). These findings are interesting, suggesting that while some social scientists have forcibly argued against the death penalty as a deterrent (Bayles 1991; Peterson and Bailey 1991), the majority of death-penalty supporters are not seeking deterrence: They want revenge and are quite willing to seek legal violence to obtain it.

Rape is another type of violent crime. It is a crime that, according to feminist writer Andrea Dworkin, plays out the essence of the "sexual colonialization of women's bodies," graphically demonstrating the reality that women are no more than men's property, to be used in any way men see fit (Dworkin 1989, 229).

Many social critics have argued that widespread attention, even glorification of violence has encouraged rape. Speculation exists that pornographic material, particularly sadomasochistic pornographic material displaying both sex and violence, can produce a combination of sexual arousal and a denigrated image of women as sexual property. While researchers have not been able to establish that pornography directly stimulates rape, analysts conclude that a sexist approach to women and sexually aggressive behavior might result from the accumulated impact of multiple exposures (Lindsey 1990, 173; St. Lawrence and Joyner 1991, 50).

Although the factors influencing rape might be somewhat obscure, little doubt exists about its prevalence. As we noted, a recent study has

Figure 7.1

Support of Death Penalty for Individuals
Convicted of Murder

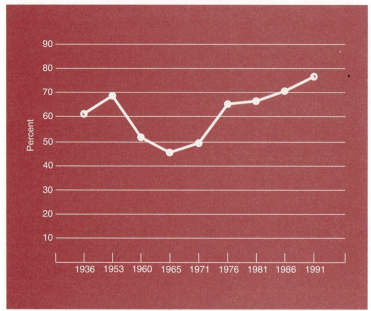

For the past thirty years, Americans have been increasingly willing to support the death penalty for murder.

Source: Gallup Poll Monthly. (June 1991), p. 43.

indicated that this violent crime is much more common than earlier statistics suggested. In fact, since the study provided no statistics on female children and adolescents as well as boys and men, its estimate of 683,000 rapes in 1990 is probably about half the actual figure (Johnston 1992).

Some problems researchers studying rape must confront are discussed in the research section at the end of this chapter.

Crime against Property People who know little about correctional institutions might assume they are overflowing with murderers and rapists. Actually, of the nearly 1.5 million individuals under some form of correctional supervision, by far the greatest number are held for offenses against property. In short, the prisoners have stolen or damaged something that belongs to someone else. Property crimes are much more common than violent crimes. In fact, a property crime known to the police occurs in the United States every 2.5 seconds, more frequently than most of us blink. About one in five households experiences theft, burglary, or motor-vehicle theft each year (U.S.

Bureau of the Census, *Statistical Abstract of the United States: 1992*, No. 294).

In 1990 people under 25 accounted for 56 percent of larcenies, 74.5 percent of motor-vehicle thefts, and 65 percent of burglaries (U.S. Bureau of the Census, *Statistical Abstract of the United States: 1992*, No. 302). Finally some current social conditions seem to promote increasing rates of property crime. Americans are living in a "ripoff society," one critic asserted. He suggested that impersonal urban conditions, the cost of adequate security in businesses and homes, the ability of the mass media—especially television—to stimulate an intense desire for worldly goods, and the lessening impact of organized religion have all encouraged an increase in property crime (Bacon 1979).

In addition, use of computers has permitted a new type of property crime—"computer crime." Anyone with a small computer and a modem (a device costing approximately $100 that converts a computer's digital pulses into electromagnetic waves that can be transmitted over a phone line) can employ a relatively easy trial-and-error procedure to hook into thousands of business and military computers. One prominent computer scientist suggested that the low level of security at many computer centers is "like leaving the keys in the ignition of an unlocked car" (Broad 1983, 1). It is now widely acknowledged that the most sophisticated computer systems cannot be protected from penetrators who have high-level skill, knowledge, and resources. A recent estimate indicated that computer crime costs American companies about $5 billion a year (Sessions 1991).

One of the unusual aspects of computer crime is that since widespread use of computers is recent, the formation of criminal laws in relation to them is also recent. It appears that the mass media have played a major role in the development of computer law. The media decided that computer abuse was a newsworthy issue and thus provided the public detailed accounts of instances in which individuals used computers to embezzle large sums of money or to break into strategic information systems. By showing that such abuses were quite frequent, the mass media contributed to the public's sense of threat and encouraged widespread support for the development of criminal laws related to computer abuse (Hollinger and Lanza-Kaduce 1988).

Victimless Crime

A **victimless crime** is defined as the willing (hence "victimless") exchange among adults of strongly desired but illegal goods or services. As the term suggests, those who engage in victimless crimes are generally not preying on others. The list of victimless crimes includes gambling, illicit drug use, prostitution, loansharking, vagrancy, and public drunkenness.

Prostitutes, vagrants, and drunks are public eyesores who often draw police complaints. Arrests are frequent. It might be surprising to learn that in 1990, 6 percent of all arrests were for public drunkenness, with about 717,000 people arrested. There were also 869,000 arrests for drug abuse, 580,000 for disorderly conduct, 138,000 for (juveniles) running away from home, 91,000 for prostitution and commercialized vice, and 65,000 for juvenile curfew violations and loitering (U.S. Bureau of the Census, *Statistical Abstract of the United States: 1992*, No. 302).

Defining the types of behavior just discussed as crimes has a couple of negative consequences.

First, when highly desired goods and services are made illegal, black-market activities develop to supply users. If these operations are profitable enough, organized crime is likely to step in. It is hard to deny that in the 1920s the Volstead Act, which made the sale of alcoholic beverages illegal, helped organized crime to flourish and that the continuing illegal status of drugs, prostitution, and to some extent gambling have also strongly benefited organized crime. Second, the illegal status of these goods and services keeps quality questionable. In Washington, D.C., and New York City, where prostitution is illegal, the current estimate is that half of the prostitutes there are HIV-positive. In stark contrast, in Nevada's thirty-six legal brothels, where condom use is required and prostitutes are regularly examined by doctors, no prostitute has tested positive for AIDS, even though the volume of business is heavy—about 600,000 "dates" in 1990 (*Economist* 1991).

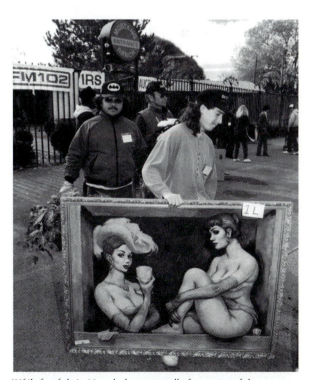

While brothels in Nevada have generally been successful commercial activities, the Internal Revenue Service forced the Mustang Ranch, the state's best known house, to close in 1990. To compensate itself for unpaid federal taxes, the IRS conducted an auction, with more than 1,000 people turning up to bid on items like this painting.

178   Crime by the Powerful and Affluent

As we noted in the discussion of Merton's anomie theory, organized-crime leaders have been highly successful innovators, achieving great wealth and power through illegitimate channels when legitimate channels have been blocked for members of their particular ethnic group. The earliest organized-crime leadership was dominated by WASPs (white Anglo-Saxon Protestants). Their domination was followed by Irish, Jewish, and the present Sicilian-Italian leadership. As each successive ethnic group has found legitimate channels to achievement, they have moved into the middle class and out of organized crime. For Italian-Americans, who still are the most powerful group in organized crime, a middle-class base is now firmly established, and replacement by African-Americans and Hispanic-Americans, who currently find limited opportunities through legitimate channels, seems likely (Ianni 1973). Organized crime exists not only in the United States but also in western Europe, where its scope of operations is narrower, focused on traditional criminal operations and not yet entering legitimate business (Fijnaut 1990).

Organized crime activities in the United States fall roughly into three categories:

1. Illegal activities, such as gambling, prostitution, and narcotics. Public opinion varies widely on the morality of these different activities.
2. Legitimate businesses. Organized crime has infiltrated many ordinary businesses, such as the vending-machine and the solid-waste disposal industries; such activities provide significant income and some measure of respectability to the participants.
3. Racketeering, which is the systematic extortion of funds over a period of time. For instance, if owners pay for "protection," their businesses will not be destroyed by the mob (Clinard and Quinney 1973, 390).

The consequences of some of organized crime's activities have been devastating. For instance, organized crime has the cash to finance the drug trade, which frequently employs expensive and elaborate equipment such as computers, processing laboratories powered by electric generators, and radar-equipped private planes.

What are the effects of organized crime's control of illegal drugs? For one thing the drive to get the money necessary to pay for illegal drugs has created an army of muggers, who are estimated to initiate over half the violent crime in major cities. Courts and prisons are overloaded with addicts. Many billions of tax dollars are spent on efforts to combat and treat addiction. Furthermore government officials estimate that drug-related murders and overdoses account for some 15,000 deaths a year. Finally in order to keep law-enforcement officials from interfering in the drug trade, organized crime has corrupted the police departments of many large cities (Newfield and Dubrul 1979).

In recent years government officials have been making extensive efforts to fight organized crime. At times they have resorted to novel measures, including the confiscation of attorneys' fees from those defending individuals accused of being involved in organized crime. Prosecutors have argued that a person should be permitted to purchase neither a Rolls Royce nor a "Rolls Royce class of attorney" with the profits of criminal activity (Dombrink, Meeker, and Paik 1988).

Certainly organized crime has produced tremendous profits. Estimates indicate that organized crime is the second largest business in the United States, with gross revenues of about $150 billion in 1978 compared to the automobile industry's $125 billion. White-collar crime produced about $100 billion (Fox 1985, 252).

White-collar crime is crime committed by people of higher socioeconomic status in the course of their business activities. The list of white-collar crimes includes bribery, embezzlement, sale of dangerously defective products (such as cars, military equipment, and pharmaceuticals), illegal dumping of toxic waste, criminal price-fixing, serious consumer fraud, Medicare theft, deliberate shipping of defective products to unsuspecting foreign markets, and systematic violation of safety and pollution-control standards. Consumer advocate Ralph Nader wrote, "By almost any measure, crime in the suites takes more money and produces far more casualties and diseases than crime in the streets—bad as that situation is" (Nader 1985, 3). According to Nader, corporations, like fish, rot from the head down. To attack white-collar crime in corporations, law-enforcement officials need to start at the top.

Some prosecution for white-collar crime has occurred, and those prosecuted experience highly varied impacts upon their careers. Professionals (lawyers, in particular), government workers, and people in licensed occupations (for instance, accountants) tend to suffer a negative response from their occupational group and frequently are barred from continued activity in their field. On the other hand, business people generally encounter few such negative responses (Benson 1984; Grasmick, Bursik, and Cochran 1991).

Generally Americans think of white-collar crime as individuals or small groups involved in secretive, illegal money-making schemes. But a broader outlook seems necessary. A prime case in point' would be the Iran-Contra affair, which became public in 1987: Members of the National Security Council engaged in several major illegal acts, selling arms to Iran and transferring funds from the sale to the Contra rebel forces fighting the Sandinista government in Nicaragua. Both of these acts were illegal because they occurred without congressional approval, which is required in each case. What makes such political examples of white-collar crime unusual is the ideological quality associated with the criminal acts. Some of the participants, in fact, claimed that while their activities were illegal, the behavior was justified because it represented the participants' willingness to do what the president felt was best for the country. Testifying before a Senate investigating committee, Lieutenant Colonel Oliver North became a hero to many Americans with statements like this one:

> This lieutenant colonel is not going to challenge a decision of the Commander in Chief for whom I still work, and I am proud to work for that Commander in Chief, and if the Commander in Chief tells this lieutenant colonel to go stand in the corner and sit on his head, I will do so.
>
> (*Draper* 1989, 40)

In the nearby Social Application, which examines illegal drugs in America, the role of wealthy, powerful people is apparent. Because of the

Even though Colonel Oliver North committed white-collar crimes, many Americans considered him a hero, fervently supporting his claim that the illegal acts in which he engaged were conducted in the country's best interest.

increasingly serious nature of the problem, the discussion is longer than normally found in these sections.

WHO COMMITS CRIME?

A number of years ago, I was speaking with a man who had spent fully half his life in prison. "You know, Chris," he said, "you and your friends grew up aware that you'd be going to college. For me and my friends the college we saw ahead was the slammer." Several of the theories we have discussed, most obviously the anomie and differential-association perspectives, support the conclusion that certain types of people are especially susceptible to becoming involved in crime. The speaker in the example just cited was African-American, male, of urban origin, as well as young

SOCIAL APPLICATION
Drugs in America

In 1989 the American government's war on drugs was in disarray. Eleven federal departments and thirty-seven federal agencies were involved in the war, and Congress had seventy-four committees and subcommittees with jurisdiction over narcotics issues. To consider that a coordinated attack on the drug problem will occur soon requires courage which perhaps borders on the psychotic.

Nonetheless, at times governmental efforts have been valiant. In the longest, most expensive trial in American history, the U.S. attorney in New York City and his assistants presented evidence against twenty-two defendants indicating that they had conspired to import one-and-a-half tons of pure heroin into the United States and then had distributed it through pizzerias in the East and Midwest. In February 1987, after a trial that lasted nearly eighteen months, the government was rewarded with convictions and long prison terms for all but two defendants. But drug trafficking was not affected.

The problem is that the traffickers are too well organized and powerful. They include individuals like the immensely successful "Kojak" (so called because of his shaved head), who runs a fleet of speedboats that travel at ninety miles an hour between remote islands in the Bahamas and drop-off points on the Florida coast. Because of the Coast Guard's limited resources, an elaborate radio network for warning his boatmen, and his intimate knowledge of the waters off Miami, about 98 percent of Kojak's shipments reach their destination. Another prominent participant has been Carlos Lehder; he took over a small Bahaman island with an airstrip, driving out the inhabitants with guns and dogs, and then hired a half-dozen pilots who flew to hidden airstrips in Columbia, loaded their planes with cocaine, refueled on Lehder's island, and under cover of darkness slipped into the United States.

The drug war is distinctly international, with government officials in the Bahamas, Cuba, Mexico, Nicaragua, and Panama accepting bribes for their participation. A study by the RAND Corporation concluded that even if the American government made a much greater commitment of personnel to stopping the entrance of illegal drugs, the effect would be no more than a 5 percent cutback on the current supply. In the late 1970s, cocaine was arriving a few kilos at a time; now the shipments are measured in *tonnage*—often three or four tons in size. Francis C. Hall, the former chief of the police department's narcotics division in New York City, explained, "There is so much cocaine in New York today, it is beyond measure. Beyond measure. When I look at 5,000 pounds, I say to myself, how many more of these stash houses are there around?" (Hall 1989, 9). But even if all supplies were cut off, synthetic cocaine and heroin, which are cheap and fairly easy to make, would be available in a few months. The problem, it seems, is less rooted in the supply of drugs than in the demand for them.

In 1988, for the first time, Congress seemed to accept the idea that cutting the drug supply should not be the only priority, allotting as much funding for treatment, prevention, education, and research as for restricting the supply. At the same time, the American public took a related stance. Forty-seven percent of a national sample indicated that educating young people would be the best strategy for halting the drug epidemic, and 35 percent chose the option of making it harder for drugs to enter the country.

Educating young people might be a fine general goal, but how can program developers go about implementing it? To date most educational programs have emphasized that the best way of fighting drugs is to increase young people's knowledge of the subject. But very little data indicates how successful drug-education and drug-treatment programs have been, and without such information experts have little basis for choosing how most effectively to use funds to restrict illegal drug use.

One good thing is now happening. Because of the current efforts to publicize the

Victims of the modern drug problem include infants, such as this six-month-old boy who is suffering withdrawal symptoms produced as a result of his mother's cocaine addiction.

destructive effect of drugs, it appears that most middle-class young people are getting the message and cutting back or eliminating hard drug use. The problem is that drug addiction has increased dramatically among the young, urban poor, and the distinct possibility exists that if drugs are no longer a problem among middle-class youth, the governmental education and treatment efforts will decline or cease.

The result of the current trend will be massive destructive effects in poor, urban districts. Hall explained, "The social problems associated with drugs are mind-boggling—crack babies, babies born with AIDS. The death rate in Harlem among infants is as high at it gets in third world countries. It's outrageous, a national disgrace" (Hall 1989, 9).

There will be other effects of increased drug use among the poor. Individuals who use illegal drugs must pay for their supply, and those with little or no money will readily turn to crime. Examining the careers of male and female drug addicts, sociologists have found that increased involvement in property crime accompanies addiction.

Perhaps the most frightening legacy of the relationship between poverty and drugs is the distinct possibility of higher levels of violence, with crack, a fairly cheap, increasingly popular cocaine derivative, playing a central role. A half-dozen sociologists doing research projects in East Harlem, an area where a young female jogger was raped by a gang of young adolescent boys in a highly publicized case in April 1989, all agreed that the

district had changed dramatically in a few years. For decades heroin and cocaine had been prominent there, but with the advent of crack, young adolescents and even children had become dealers. Their involvement in selling this prized commodity has meant a shift in power from adults to adolescents, and along with the shift the feeling that a young person has the right to take anything he wants as long as he can get away with it. Furthermore to be respected among his drug-selling peers, a young male frequently has to prove that he can be brutal. One of the sociologists explained, "There has been an extraordinary resurgence of violence since crack. Violence is up throughout the community and the types of crimes that are committed are more violent" (Kolata 1989, C1).

182

In the early 1990s, the division of the country into two separate nations was becoming increasingly apparent. While middle-class citizens continued a decade-long trend of cutting back on drug use, inner-city addiction kept rising, with a 30-percent increase in cocaine-related visits to hospital emergency rooms occurring between 1990 and 1991. While the federal anti-drug budget nearly doubled between 1989 and 1992, little governmental effort was made to reach such high-risk groups as school dropouts, gang members, abused children, and teenage mothers. Mark A. R. Kleiman, a drug specialist at Harvard, suggested that if treatment programs permitted formerly drug-using thieves and robbers to stay out of jail by passing frequent urine tests, crime could ultimately drop appreciably, and as much as half the cocaine market might dry up.

Researcher Michael Massing concluded that without more forceful intervention among those hardest hit by drugs, "the problem is certain to get worse. What to do about long-term, hard-core drug use is the key element missing in the current drug debate" (Massing 1992, 46).

Sources: M. Douglas Anglin and Yih-ing Hser. "Addicted Women and Crime," Criminology. vol. 25 (May 1987), pp. 359–97; M. Douglas Anglin and George Speckart. "Narcotics Use and Crime: A Multisample, Multimethod Analysis," Criminology. vol. 26. (May 1988), pp. 197–233; George Gallup, Jr. Gallup Reports. (March 1988); Francis C. Hall. "Report from the Field on an Endless War," New York Times. (March 12, 1989), p. 1+; Gina Kolata. "Grim Seeds of Park Rampage Found in East Harlem Streets," New York Times. (May 2, 1989), p. C1+; Michael Massing. "Dealing with the Drug Horror," New York Review of Books. vol. 36 (March 30, 1989), pp. 22–26; Michael Massing. "What Ever Happened to the 'War on Drugs'?" New York Review of Books. vol. 39 (June 11, 1992), pp. 42–46; David N. Nurco et al. "Differential Criminal Patterns of Narcotic Addicts over an Addiction Career," Criminology. vol. 26 (August 1988), pp. 407–23; Joseph B. Treaster. "20 Years of War on Drugs, and No Victory Yet," New York Times. (June 14, 1992), sec. 4, p. 7.

when he started in crime. All these are factors associated with a high likelihood of being arrested. By no means, however, is it being suggested that the mere presence of these factors predestines a life of crime and arrest. We are simply addressing statistical probabilities here. Moreover, even these probabilities may reflect biases in how crime statistics are compiled and also in arrest patterns.

Age

According to official statistics, in 1990 people under 25 accounted for about 56.5 percent of all arrests for Part 1 crimes and 45.7 percent of all arrests (U. S. Bureau of the Census, *Statistical Abstract of the United States: 1992*, No. 302). Table 7.3 lists some relevant percentages. A number of factors contribute to this high rate of arrests among young people. For one thing the police are much more inclined to arrest those under 25 than they are to arrest older people. In addition, the rate of serious crime committed by those under 25 has apparently risen more sharply than has the rate for older persons (Cohen and Short 1976, 59–60). Finally, until recent years, the number of young people had been increasing. This meant an increase in the number of crimes committed by youths, whether or not their crime rate rose. Since the youthful group has begun to decline in size, it seems likely that the number of crimes committed by youths will start to decrease.

Sex

Men are considerably more likely to be arrested than are women. In 1990, 82 percent of the people charged were male, meaning that over four-and-a-half times as many men as women were arrested. Table 7.3 indicates that for serious crimes males are considerably more likely to be arrested than females. The only categories of crime in which men are arrested less frequently than women are prostitution and running away from home. However, the general trend over time has been for the female arrest rate to rise more rapidly than the male rate. In the past quarter-century, the ratio of males to females appearing before juvenile courts has dropped to four to one, probably the lowest of any Western society. At the turn of the century, ratios of fifty to sixty to one prevailed. In the past two decades, arrests of females for property crime have increased more rapidly than arrests of males for property crime, but a similar trend has not occurred for violent crime. One fact that might help explain these findings is that women are generally socialized to restrain their emotions and especially their violent tendencies much more effectively than are men. Furthermore women's inclination toward property crimes may be partially related to expectations associated with the contemporary female role, especially in difficult economic times—the female shopper becomes a shoplifter or the female casher of good checks

Table 7.3 Arrests for Serious (Part I) Crimes: Males and Different Age Groups in 1990

| | | AGE GROUPS | | | |
	Males	Under 18	18–24	25–44	45 and over
Murder and manslaughter	89.6%	14%	37.7%	40.8%	7.5%
Rape	98.9	14.9	29.3	48.7	7.1
Robbery	91.7	24.2	37.4	36.8	1.7
Larceny (theft)	68	30	26	37	7.0
Motor-vehicle theft	90	43.3	31.2	23.9	1.6
Arson	87	43.8	19.7	30.6	6.0

Source: U.S. *Bureau of the Census*. Statistical Abstract of the United States: 1992, No. 302.

Males and younger people are more inclined to be arrested for violent crimes than females and older individuals.

turns into a passer of bad checks. It seems apparent that there are no simple, broad patterns of female criminality and that the variety of existing patterns will be most effectively revealed by detailed studies of the lives of women engaged in different criminal behaviors (Box and Hale 1984; Simon 1975; U.S. Bureau of the Census, *Statistical Abstract of the United States: 1992*, No. 302).

Ethnicity and Race

When ethnic and racial groups have limited access to mainstream economic opportunities, a disproportionate number of individuals will turn to crime, becoming—in the language of anomie theory—innovators. African-Americans, Native Americans, Mexican-Americans, and Puerto Ricans are prominent cases in point. Some ethnic groups, such as the Jews and the Irish, were once very active in crime, but as they have gained some access to the legitimate channels that may be used to obtain economic success, they have tended to move out of crime. On the other hand, certain Asian-American groups, once relatively crime free,

have become more actively involved because of lessening economic opportunities and partial community disintegration.

Place of Residence

The extent to which an area is urbanized is definitely related to its arrest rate. Specifically, the larger the population of a community, the higher its arrest rate is likely to be. For instance, in 1990, cities of 50,000 or more had an arrest rate for violent crime that was nearly twice as high as that of cities with populations of under 50,000 and more than four times as high as the rate in rural areas (U.S. Bureau of the Census, *Statistical Abstract of the United States: 1992*, No. 288). Arrest rates are higher in more urbanized areas because larger cities are more likely to house high percentages of low-income people and to be characterized by physical deterioration and high population density. It is also possible that large cities, which tend to have professionalized police forces, place more emphasis on a high arrest rate than the police in small cities. Table 7.4 compares violent crime rates in selected American cities.

The Social Control of Deviance   ■

A young child disobeys a parental command and is sent to his or her room. An adult breaks a law and must pay a fine or go to prison. Both individuals are punished by means of **social control**—the

application of systematic behavioral restraints intended to motivate people to obey social expectations. Most people usually obey the rules because they have **internalized** cultural standards.

Table 7.4   Violent Crime in Selected American Cities: 1990[1]

	Total	Murder	Forcible rape	Robbery	Aggravated assault
Chicago[2]	2843+	31	———	1335	1477
Washington, DC	2458	78	50	1214	1117
Dallas	2438	44	134	1049	1211
Baltimore	2438	41	93	1288	1015
Los Angeles	2405	28	58	1036	1283
New York	2384	31	43	1370	941
San Francisco	1711	14	58	974	665
Houston	1388	35	82	792	479
Philadelphia	1349	32	6	808	463

[1]*Violent-crime arrests per 100,000 people of all ages, with cities listed according to their respective total of violent crime.*
[2]*Chicago, which does not use Uniform Crime Reporting guidelines for its rape statistics, comes first in this table based on the other statistics.*

Source: U.S. Bureau of the Census. Statistical Abstract of the United States: 1992, No. 290.

This means that through socialization, social expectations have become part of the personality structure. People therefore feel guilty when they deviate. For some people in certain situations, however, these internalized standards are not sufficient to ensure conformity. In such situations informal or formal social control is necessary.

INFORMAL SOCIAL CONTROL

Most of the time people obey the norms, but sometimes the rules are violated, and informal social control is unleashed. **Informal social control** consists of unofficial pressure intended to convince potential deviants to conform to social norms. Consider a student who has recently transferred to a new college. He wants to be accepted by the other students in the dormitory, but he is too pushy. He jumps into conversations and then monopolizes them. When two close friends go out for a beer, he forces his company on them. Informal social control is soon applied. The new arrival gets the "cold shoulder." Everyone says, "I'll see you later" whenever he appears. Perhaps the newcomer will eventually realize his behavior is unacceptable, and will tone down his efforts to gain acceptance. If, on the other hand, he fails to come to this realization, he may continue to be shut out by the others.

Use of Informal Social Control

Most people are very responsive to informal social control. Few of us pick our noses publicly, make frequent obscene gestures, or speak loudly at weddings and funerals. We fear others' disapproval.

Informal social control is also commonly exercised in occupational settings. Numerous studies suggest that a certain kind of person is especially likely to be in business—the "organization man" (Whyte 1956). Such people realize that the best way to get ahead and to escape the disapproval of their superiors is to be first and foremost a conformist. They subscribe to the organizational leadership's prevailing values and interests, displaying total loyalty to the organization and avoiding, at all costs, creative suggestions or pursuits. But it is not just people's superiors who impose informal social control. One investigation concluded that informal social control initiated by one's co-workers can be a powerful deterrent to committing deviant acts on the job (Hollinger and Clark 1982).

Effects of Ignoring Informal Social Control

Sometimes people risk a great deal when they ignore others' wishes. Loss of support from one's family and severed friendships are possible. Even bodily harm can result. A case in point is the "maverick," the person who in many situations stubbornly refuses to conform. Americans often have mixed feelings toward mavericks. Such people tend to be highly individualistic, a trait Americans widely admire. Yet their individualism, if uncontrolled, frequently triggers the disapproval of others and restricts their access to such highly valued items as wealth and power. Mavericks generally risk disapproval or even stronger reactions because they are unusually moral. They follow the dictates of their own internalized sense of right and wrong and not the external directives that bring material success. "Whistle-blowers"—people who expose the existence of defective merchandise, cost overruns, client-harming bureaucratic policies, and safety and health violations in the companies or government agencies for which they work—are a case in point (Parmerlee, Near, and Jensen 1982; Rosecrance 1988). Common reactions to whistle-blowing include colleagues' and superiors' anger and hostility, dismissal, and even lawsuits. Recently when a dedicated scientist blew the whistle on her boss for falsifying data, she was fired, lost her house, and was confronted with a wide-range of accusations. The most painful accusation, she said, was that as a nursing mother, she was simply irrational. However, she persevered, and eventually officials at the National Institutes of Health supported her claims and praised her courage (Hilts 1991, B6).

While the crime or crimes for which this young man was convicted will affect his sentence, his economic status also is likely to have an impact.

FORMAL SOCIAL CONTROL: THE CRIMINAL-JUSTICE SYSTEM

Formal social control is official pressure intended to convince potential deviants to conform to social norms. Besides the criminal-justice system, a variety of federal, state, and local bureaucracies enforce legally binding regulations involving health, environmental protection, child care, disabled people's rights, and a host of other issues.

The American image of justice shows a woman blindfolded to ensure equal treatment for all people who appear before her. However, many feel that the blindfold must have holes in it because in practice the American criminal-justice system is clearly biased. From arrest to sentencing, the likelihood of being ignored, released, or lightly treated improves as the accused person's affluence increases. This relationship will be apparent

as we examine the different steps in the process: arrest, trial, and sentencing. Prisons will also be discussed.

Arrest

For any particular crime, the poor are more likely than the affluent to be arrested. A study of 3,475 delinquent boys in Philadelphia compared middle-class and lower-class boys with similar arrest records detained for equally serious offenses. It concluded that the police were considerably more likely to refer lower-class youth to juvenile court (Thornberry 1973).

How can we explain these findings? A number of factors seem relevant. For one thing poor people have less privacy. More affluent people can engage in certain illegal activities—gambling or drug use, for example—in the seclusion of their homes. The poor, however, are more likely to be forced into the public arena where they can be directly observed by the police or where the complaints of others are likely to draw the attention of law-enforcement officers. Second, in some cases the police are less likely to arrest affluent youth than poor youth

186 because they believe that middle-class parents will take a more active, effective role in disciplining their children. In addition, many researchers feel that police training and experience tend to make officers especially inclined to attribute criminality to certain groups—in particular, lower-class youth, African-Americans, Puerto Ricans, Mexican-Americans, and Native Americans. Finally some evidence indicates that law-enforcement officers often are most willing to arrest those least able to bring political pressure to bear in their own behalf—in short, the poorest members of society (Reiman 1979, 104).

Pretrial and Trial

Poor people usually have little hope of raising bail. Being in jail during the pretrial period means that defendants are unable to work actively for their own defense. Furthermore defendants out on bail are able to walk into court off the street, like anyone else. By contrast, defendants not released on bail are likely to be led into court from a nearby detention center and thus give the appearance of being guilty, probably influencing juries and judges. Research indicates that among defendants accused of the same offenses, those who post bail are more likely to be acquitted than those who do not (Foote 1954).

Besides bail another issue that can influence the outcome of a defendant's case is the quality of the legal assistance. Since the *Gideon v. Wainwright* decision in 1963, all defendants must be provided with a lawyer. But the effectiveness of legal assistance varies considerably. The poor often receive "assembly-line" legal aid from a public defender or a private attorney assigned by the court. In both instances the lawyer's payment is likely to be modest, and public defenders' case loads are usually much larger than those of private criminal lawyers. Because of these facts, poor people's lawyers tend to be strongly motivated to bring cases to a quick conclusion. They may work out a deal with the prosecutor whereby the defendant pleads guilty to a somewhat reduced charge.

In business time is money, and defendants without funds are normally unable to command more than a minimum of a lawyer's time. By contrast, wealthy, white-collar defendants are able to hire a battery of skilled lawyers with sufficient resources to make it in the prosecutor's interest to settle quickly and leniently out of court. When white-collar criminals appear before judges, they frequently find themselves in friendly surroundings. The judge often sees the defendant as someone whose style of dress and general behavior are much like his own—a prominent, wealthy man who may well belong to the same country club as he does and who is the kind of person whom the judge represented when he was in private practice. One corporation lawyer explained that ". . . it is best to find the judge's friend or [former] law partner to defend an antitrust client—which we have done" (Green, Moore, and Wasserstein 1979, 543).

Sentencing

The poor experience a double bias when they appear before a judge for sentencing. First, as we noted, the crimes usually committed by poor people generally receive harsher penalties than do the "crimes in the suites" of the more affluent. For instance, a *New York Times* story on the fate of twenty-one business executives found guilty of making illegal campaign donations during the Watergate scandal indicated that most of these men were still presiding over their companies. Only two went to prison, serving no more than a few months each. Upper-class criminals, in short, were punished leniently for their attempts to undermine the independence of the electoral process and to endanger the basic vitality of our democratic form of government (Jensen 1975).

Furthermore the poor are likely to be the objects of discrimination. They more frequently receive long prison terms than do more affluent people convicted of the same crimes. Research has suggested that even when equitable standards of sentencing are established and stressed, subtle ways to affect the lengths of sentences can be found. For instance, African-Americans are more readily charged than whites with the use of a weapon in the course of committing a crime (Miethe and Moore 1985; Reiman 1979).

A study of 504 cases eligible for capital punishment concluded that the victim, not the offender, was the critical factor affecting the sentence. Those killing whites were twice as likely to receive a death sentence as those killing African-Americans, regardless of the offender's race (Smith 1987).

Prisons

What purposes are served by prisons? Retribution is certainly one of them. Prisons are supposed to bring suffering to people who have made the lives of other people unpleasant. A common interpretation of the Old Testament doctrine of "an eye for an eye and a tooth for a tooth" has often been the justification for putting people in prison.

Second, prison life is expected to act as a deterrent, encouraging individuals not to return to crime once they are released. But some research suggests that the kinds of criminals generally incarcerated, such as drug addicts and sex offenders, are less likely to be deterred by prison sentences than are such criminal types as shoplifters and white-collar criminals who normally manage to avoid prison (Chambliss 1969; Pittman and Gordon 1968). There has also been the widespread belief that punishment can deter the noncriminal public from engaging in crime. This might be an accurate claim, but there is limited research evidence to support it (Reid 1985, 88).

Third, prisons are supposed to isolate criminals, thus protecting the law-abiding public. Incarceration does produce this effect for the period of time that the individual is imprisoned. An important question, however, is whether or not the person still pursues crime after being released. If so, the protection provided is only temporary.

The final purpose of prisons is rehabilitation, the effort to reform inmates so that they will become productive citizens and no longer commit crimes. Vocational education and psychotherapy have been used sporadically in attempts to rehabilitate inmates.

Prisons have quite successfully isolated and punished their inmates, but they have been much less effective at deterrence and rehabilitation.

The prison population has grown rapidly. As Figure 7.2 suggests, the number of people held in federal and state prisons more than tripled in nineteen years—from 196,429 in 1970 to 738,894 in 1990 (U.S. Bureau of the Census, *Statistical Abstract of the United States*: 1992, No. 329). Many prisons are severely overcrowded, with their inmate populations suffering high rates of hypertension, cardiovascular disease, mental disorders, and suicide. For whites crowded prisons also offer the additional discomfort of being members of the minority groups and therefore suffering the racial oppressions that minority-group members encounter in the outside world. Among specialists, overcrowding is generally recognized as one of the two or three most serious problems involving modern prison systems (Clayton 1987; Klofas, Stojkovic, and Kalinich 1992; Leger 1988; Lein et al. 1992).

To learn how to improve their prisons, Americans can profit from cross-cultural information—such as the study on Dutch prisons described in the nearby Cross-Cultural Perspective.

Although the American prison population steadily increases, the amount of crime does not drop; in fact, as we noted earlier, it too increases. Considering this sorry situation, you might ask why strong support for continued prison construction exists. The following propositions offer a number of reasons:

1. The American tradition, in fact the tradition of all Western nations, is to put law breakers in prison or to punish them some other way.

2. Politicians find such an approach useful, because the construction of new prisons gives the sense that something practical and tangible is being done to protect constituents' personal safety and property. An appeal to the public's fear of violent crime is often an effective political strategy.

3. In line with the general approach of conflict theory, throwing people in prison is particularly easy to do if those people are different and can be considered inferior. Many politicians are white and affluent, and the majority of actual voters are white and somewhat more affluent than average; in federal and state prisons, the proportion of black inmates is four times greater than their proportion of the population, and they represent nearly half the total; whether minority-group members or white, prison inmates tend to come from low-income backgrounds.

4. In supporting the prison system, both politicians and the general public are much more concerned with short-term "solutions"—locking up those who are dangerous, desirable, or troublesome—than sensitive to the destructive impact

Figure 7.2

Number of Federal and State Prison Inmates
over 20 Years

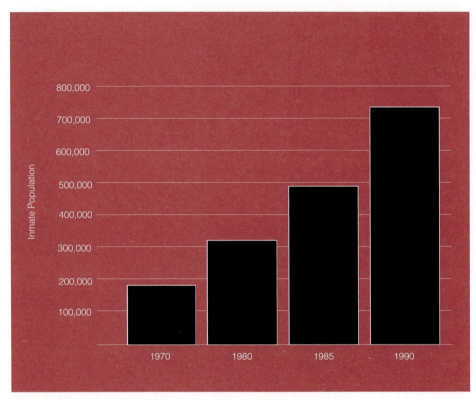

Over the past two decades, the prison population has sharply increased.

Source: *U.S. Bureau of the Census. Statistical Abstract of the United States: 1992, No. 329.*

prison can have on individuals. As the processes described by both differential-association and labeling theories indicate, prison systems tend to produce hardened criminals.

The American prison system has serious problems and certainly does not reduce crime. In particular, violent crime and the public's fear of violent crime appear to be relentlessly increasing. With these realizations in mind, I conclude this chapter with a difficult question. By what measures could crime be significantly reduced in this society? Systematic study and experimentation to answer this question seem to be activities worthy of major federal funding. Positive programs developed from these efforts would not only improve the lives of prospective victims and offenders but would benefit all citizens in various ways. Do you agree or disagree with these ideas? Discuss your reactions with classmates.

The chapter finishes with the second of six research sections; this one discusses research on rape.

CROSS-CULTURAL PERSPECTIVE
The Case for Going Dutch: Penal Policy in Holland

All in all, there seems to be nothing mystical about establishing a prison system that is humane and truly oriented to rehabilitation. Prisoners need to be treated well—permitted to be somewhat comfortable in their surroundings and, as a result, to have the chance to feel fairly good about themselves. In this regard the Dutch system has been quite successful.

A series of interviews were conducted with twenty-seven prisoners, thirteen of whom were British prisoners in the Dutch system and fourteen of whom were Dutch in the British system. Thirteen had experienced both British and Dutch prisons. The respondents suggested that in most ways the Dutch system was better.

A significant factor for prisoners is visits and home leave, which can help keep relationships alive and reduce the sense of inhumanity created by confinement. In Holland these were much more liberally available than in Britain. Inmates in the Dutch prisons spoke emotionally about the significance of frequent conjugal visits, indicating that these occasions permitted an intimate self-expression

not possible during a regular visit. One explained, "Sometimes we just cuddle each other and weep." Another noted, "Here, you can have private visits, you can have sex, you can plan a family, you've got something to come out to."

Overcrowding was another distinct difference between the two systems, with the British facilities always containing more prisoners than had been planned. One respondent pointed out that in the British system there was "not a minute, not a second, privacy—never . . . Here it is terrible." In the Dutch prisons, inmates always received a private cell.

Another factor involved the enforcement of rules, with guards in the British prisons often imposing unaccountable, arbitrary punishments for violation. One inmate observed, "Some screws treat you like shit, trip you up on little rules." For instance, this man received a much larger punishment for going to the dining room at the wrong time than other prisoners he knew. Such petty, arbitrary enforcements tended to add up emotionally over time, creating in prisoners' minds a sense of a very oppressive system.

Generally Dutch inmates

had more rights than their British counterparts. For example, prisoners' wages were over four times higher in Holland than in Britain, permitting the Dutch prisoners the chance to purchase much more tobacco and other valued commodities than could those in the British system.

While life in Dutch prisons is hardly idyllic, it tends to be a much more pleasant experience than that obtained in British facilities. It appears that a central difference in the systems is that the Dutch system has been planned with inmates' needs in mind. Consider the issue of space. In Holland, unlike Britain, no individual is brought into the prison system unless there is an empty cell. To make certain cells are available, Dutch officials have an array of devices they can use, including noncustodial sentences, grants of home leave, interruptions of sentences, and early release of prisoners with less serious charges. If a heavy influx of inmates occurs in the future, then it is likely that the well-run Dutch system will be eroded.

Source: David Downes. "The Case for Going Dutch: The Lessons of Post-War Penal Policy," Political Quarterly. vol. 63 (January–March 1992), pp. 12–24.

Research on Rape: A Progressive Struggle

In the early and middle 1970s, social scientists' papers about rape were often strongly worded statements demanding greater societal concern with the issue. During the intervening years, as the modern women's movement has received stronger support, the issue of rape has become defined as a significant social problem worthy of scientific investigation. As a result the quality of research has steadily improved. However, research on rape is still in its infancy, and investigators face some special problems when they do studies on this topic.

Let us consider the meaning of the statement that research on rape is in its infancy. For the most part, investigators have not yet approached the subject matter systematically. As we noted in Chapter 1, the relationship between research and sociological theory is an intimate one, with sociologists developing concepts and theories to guide research, and investigators, in turn, refining these tools based on their conclusions. For instance, investigators recognize that "date rape" and "stranger rape" differ in the conditions under which they occur, in responses produced by victims' friends and family members, and in the victims' own response, but they have not clearly defined these differences.

Besides the fact that researchers studying rape are charting new territory, they find themselves facing some special problems—in particular, bias in the reporting of rape and difficulties with studies of offenders.

Bias in Reporting Rapes

A significant problem with research on rape is that the victims studied represent a biased sample. As we noted earlier in this chapter, the majority of rapes go unreported. The recent National Women's Study indicated that their projection of the number of women raped in 1990, based on a national stratified sample of 4,008 respondents, was five times the official estimate based on rapes reported to the police. Thus a serious sampling problem exists, since studies of rape victims usually draw their respondents from rape-crisis centers or other organizations where rape victims have made their victimization known. How do women who report rapes differ from those who do not? The troubling fact is that we really do not know. And since we do not know, any generalizations made about rape victims based on those who report the rape are biased in unknown ways.

Another body of rape victim research involves follow-up studies. Here too the conclusions that are drawn are affected by biased sampling; in this case the bias results not only from limited reporting but also because some subjects cannot be tracked down at a later date. For instance, researcher Carol Nadelson and her associates initially interviewed 130 women in a general hospital emergency room after they had been raped. One to two-and-a-half years later, the investigators were only able to track down forty-one of those women—just 32 percent. Once more one does not know to what extent those interviewed in the follow-up were typical or not typical of the original set of respondents.

Researchers of rape have been concerned about the sampling bias among victims and have tried to figure out who has reported and who has not in order to learn about differences between the two groups. Studies have suggested that the victim's age, race, marital status, and relationship to the rapist are the factors that most strongly influence whether or not the crime is reported. However, until recently studies have produced inconsistent, seemingly unrelated information on the impact of these different factors.

After a number of studies of rape victims had been published, sociologist Linda Williams did a systematic investigation, highlighting several steps in the research process discussed in Chapter 2, "Doing Research in Sociology." First, in the course of her literature review, she read the various studies on reporting rape and noted their different, often inconsistent conclusions. Then based on the information obtained from those studies, she formulated a hypothesis, which seemed to resolve the major inconsistencies: that a woman was more likely to report a rape if it approximated a classic rape than if it did not. What she meant by a classic rape was a situation in which a woman was raped in public by a stranger who threatened or used a high degree of force and frequently produced injury. After developing the hypothesis, Williams tested it. The results of systematic research paid off; the hypothesis was generally supported. In an article on the subject, Williams emphasized that the most significant factor related to reporting the crime was whether or not the victim had known the rapist. If she had known him, Williams concluded, then the woman found herself in a difficult, self-blaming situation. Many woman have been socialized to believe that they should control all female-male interaction. If such women are raped, then they are likely to believe that it is largely or wholly because they failed to control the situation. Williams wrote, "This study . . . shows that those circumstances in a classic rape which discourage the woman from blaming herself also increase the probability that she will report the crime to the police" (Williams 1984, 265).

Difficulties with Research on Offenders

The limited reporting of rapes is a prominent reason why the samples of offenders in rape studies are also biased. If only about 20 percent of rapes are reported, then about 80 percent of rapists are never caught. Furthermore, even when a rape is reported, a sizable percentage of offenders are not apprehended.

But wait! The sampling bias problem can be even greater. Consider sociologists Diana Scully and Joseph Marolla's study of convicted rapists. In this study the researchers' subjects were drawn from the approximately 25 percent of rapists incarcerated in seven maximum or medium security prisons in Virginia who volunteered to be included in the investigation. Were the 25 percent who volunteered significantly different from the 75 percent who didn't? Again, we simply don't know.

The Scully and Marolla research also raises another research problem in rape-offender studies—a question about validity. In Chapter 2 we briefly discussed validity—the condition in which a research item accurately measures what it claims to measure. In this case did the researchers receive valid answers to their questions? The authors did not examine this question, but they conceded that since the offenders talked more about their feelings and emotions when the interviewer was female, the interviewer's sex may have affected the information received. It is possible, for instance, that some of the harsh, brutal statements these men made about women could have been aroused by a woman's presence. On the other hand, one might argue that when the interviewer was a male, the offender might have been inclined to

192   feel competitive with him and that he (the offender) might have asserted this competitiveness by demonstrating what he considered his mastery of women. While the researchers did not discuss the issue of the relationship between interviewers' sex and validity, they did acknowledge a general concern with validity, indicating that because prison inmates are known for "conning" outsiders, they had taken the researcher's normal precaution of comparing the data from their interviews with presentence reports on file at the prisons. For the most part, no significant discrepancies were found with rapists' earlier explanations of their crimes.

Recognizing the sampling problems of research on rapists, psychologist David Lisak used a different approach to investigate the topic. Interviewing male college students at a major southeastern university, he studied men who had not been indicted but were revealed as rapists during a screening interview in which they provided detailed descriptions of physical force used to compel women to have sexual intercourse or oral sex. These fifteen rapists were compared to a group of fifteen controls whose primary social characteristics were similar but whose screening interviews disclosed that they had never engaged in rape.

Lisak's study revealed that compared to the controls, rapists had the following combination of characteristics—mothers whom they considered nagging, overbearing, weak, and ineffectual and fathers described as cold, even hostile, distant, and often absent. Differences between rapists and controls were particularly dramatic with fathers. While members of the control group often considered their fathers affectionate and caring and providing ample opportunities for identification with them, the rapists comments were overwhelmingly negative, emphasizing fathers' remoteness.

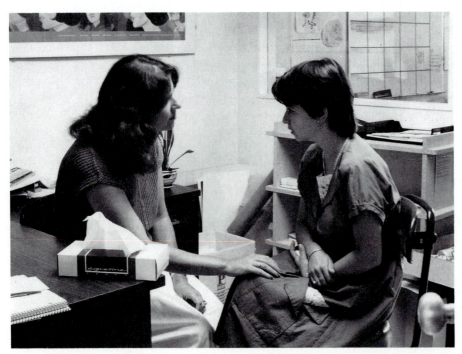

At rape crisis centers, which are located in many cities and towns throughout the country, victims receive counseling and support. Researchers on rape have sometimes obtained subjects from these centers.

Lisak concluded that the rapists had been raised in an atmosphere where relationships with parents compounded in a lethal way. From interaction with their mothers, the boys had developed a sense of women as potentially hostile, troublesome adversaries who needed to be controlled, perhaps dominated. Their fathers had exacerbated the situation, completely failing to provide the sense of male gender role that a developing boy most readily receives from a warm, supportive father. With a blurred sense of self, the boys developed into men who sought to resolve their ambiguous sense of gender by a decisive yet highly destructive act—rape.

Conclusion

Several decades ago research on rape represented a small set of studies, but in recent years that situation has changed. As competent studies on this topic increase, some investigatory problems are likely to decline. For example, as research on rape helps publicize the issue, a higher proportion of women are likely to report the crime and decrease the sampling biases that currently exist. Eventually, based on modern research, a sophisticated body of theory will develop. It is hoped that from this theory there will emerge powerful insights for taking legal and social steps to curtail, and some day eliminate, this dreadful form of behavior.

Sources: Mary Beard Deming and Ali Eppy. "The Sociology of Rape," Sociology and Social Research. *vol.* 65 (July 1981), *pp.* 357–80; David Johnston. "Survey Shows Number of Rapes Far Higher than Official Figures," New York Times. (May 24, 1991), *p.* A14; Mary P. Koss. "The Underdetection of Rape: Methodological Choices Influence Incidence Estimates," Journal of Social Issues. *vol.* 48 (1992), *pp.* 61–75; David Lisak. "Sexual Aggression, Masculinity, and Fathers," Signs. *vol.* 16 (Winter), 238–62; Carol C. Nadelson et al. "A Follow-Up Study of Rape Victims," American Journal of Psychiatry. *vol.* 139 (October 1982), *pp.* 1266–70; James D. Orcutt and Rebecca Faison. "Sex-Role Attitude Change and Reporting of Rape Victimization, 1973–1985," Sociological Quarterly. *vol.* 29 (Winter 1988), *pp.* 589–604; Diana Scully and Joseph Marolla. "Convicted Rapists' Vocabulary of Motive: Excuses and Justifications," Social Problems. *vol.* 31 (June 1984), *pp.* 530–44; Diana Scully and Joseph Marolla. "'Riding the Bull at Gilley's': Convicted Rapists Describe the Rewards of Rape," Social Problems. *vol.* 32 (February 1985), *pp.* 241–63. Linda S. Williams. "The Classic Rape: When Do Victims Report?" Social Problems. *vol.* 31 (April 1984), *pp.* 459–67.

STUDY GUIDE

Learning Objectives

After studying this chapter, you should be able to:

1. Define deviance and discuss changing definitions of deviance across time and space.
2. Define, discuss, and evaluate the anomie, differential-association, conflict, and labeling theories of deviance.
3. List and describe the limitations of criminal statistics.
4. Examine the following prominent types of crime: violent crime, property crime, victimless crime, and crime by the powerful and affluent.
5. Determine who is likely to commit crimes and why by examining the following factors: age, sex, ethnicity and race, and place of residence.
6. Define informal social control, indicate how it is achieved, and describe the effects of ignoring it.
7. Define formal social control. Then identify and discuss the four steps of the criminal-justice process, examining the discriminations suffered by poor people at each stage.

194

Summary

1. Deviance is behavior that violates social norms considered sufficiently significant that the majority of a group or society responds negatively to their violation.

2. Sociology provides a number of theories of deviance. Merton's anomie perspective indicates that U.S. culture strongly emphasizes monetary success for all, without placing an equally strong emphasis on the legitimate means to achieve that success. The theory describes five individual adaptations to cultural values, four of which are deviant.

The differential-association perspective claims that someone is likely to become a criminal if that person's values and the values of the influencing individuals show greater support for criminal activity than for noncriminal activity.

According to the conflict theory of deviance, a ruling class uses its strategic location to develop and maintain the legal standards the group desires, to the advantage of higher-class and the disadvantage of lower-class people.

Labeling theory contends that certain people are labeled as deviant by those powerful enough to impose their standards on society. The labeling process can be divided into two stages, primary and secondary deviance.

3. Crime is simply an act that violates criminal law. Limitations to criminal statistics occur because many complaints are never reported, some victims refuse to cooperate, administrative distortions happen, and white-collar crime is missing from the official statistics. Among the different types of crime are crime against persons and property, victimless crime, and crime by the powerful and affluent. People with certain social characteristics—the young, males, minority-group members, and city dwellers—are more likely to be arrested.

4. The social control of deviance is the application of systematic behavioral restraints intended to motivate people to obey social expectations. Both informal and formal means of social control exist. The criminal-justice system is one of the most visible examples of formal social control. More affluent suspects fare better with the criminal-justice process at all stages—arrest, pretrial and trial, and sentencing. Prisons are supposed to serve the functions of retribution, deterrence, isolation, and rehabilitation. Prisons are seriously overcrowded, and the penal system in general needs major reform.

Key Terms

anomie   the confusing situation produced when norms are either absent or conflicting

conformity   a nondeviant adaptation, where individuals pursue legitimate goals and the culturally accepted means to achieve them, even though it is likely they will not attain those goals

crime   an act that violates criminal law

deviance   behavior that violates social norms considered sufficiently significant that the majority of a group or society responds negatively to their violation

formal social control   official pressure intended to convince potential deviants to conform to social norms

informal social control   unofficial pressure intended to convince potential deviants to conform to social norms

innovation   a deviant adaptation that develops when a person seeks legitimate goals but is blocked from effectively using culturally accepted means to achieve them

internalized   through socialization, social expectations have become part of the personality structure

primary deviance   individuals in question have violated a social rule but are not labeled and so do not see themselves as deviant

rebellion   a deviant adaptation displayed when a person decides that the existing society imposes barriers preventing the achievement of success goals. Therefore that individual strikes out against the society, seeking to change its goals and also the existing means for achieving goals.

retreatism a deviant adaptation in which an individual pursues neither the culturally prescribed goals of success nor the means for achieving these goals because of limited opportunities or a sense of personal inadequacy

ritualism a behavioral pattern that occurs when culturally prescribed success goals are no longer actively sought, but the legitimate

means for achieving those goals are conscientiously pursued

secondary deviance authorities label individuals deviants and the individuals accept that status

social control the application of systematic behavioral restraints intended to motivate people to obey social expectations

victimless crime the willing (hence "victimless") exchange among adults of strongly desired but illegal goods or services

white-collar crime crime committed by people of higher socioeconomic status in the course of their business activities

Tests

True • False Test

_____ 1. The evaluation of what constitutes deviant behavior does not change across time and space.
_____ 2. Robert Merton uses the concept of anomie to designate a discrepancy between a socially approved goal and the availability of means to achieve the goal.
_____ 3. Using the differential-association theory, one can appreciate that prisons can serve as places where criminal practice can be learned.
_____ 4. Labeling theory analyzes primary but not secondary deviance.
_____ 5. It is possible to engage in behavior that is considered deviant but not criminal.
_____ 6. Recent research suggests that about 85 percent of rape victims report the crime to police.
_____ 7. Most commonly murderers are strangers to the people they kill.
_____ 8. The majority of people under correctional supervision are held for offenses against property.
_____ 9. The Iran-Contra affair can be considered a situation that involved white-collar crime.
_____ 10. In the past decade, the construction of many new prisons has reduced the crime rate.

Multiple-Choice Test

_____ 1. According to anomie theory, the only nondeviant adaptation one can make to a condition of blocked opportunity is:
    a. innovation.
    b. ritualism.
    c. retreatism.
    d. conformity.

_____ 2. Critics of the differential-association theory contend that it:
    a. fails to appreciate that criminal behavior is learned in interaction with others.
    b. can be used only to analyze juvenile gangs.
    c. overemphasizes criminals' involvement in violent activity.
    d. contains some vague terminology.

_____   3. Quinney's "social reality of crime" version of the conflict theory of deviance emphasizes:
   a.   definitions of criminal activity by the ruling class.
   b.   socialism as a cause of crime.
   c.   that the social-class system has no relationship to criminal standards or behavior.
   d.   learning criminal skills from peer associations.

_____   4. Labeling theory:
   a.   is a form of symbolic interaction.
   b.   analyzes causes of deviance.
   c.   does not explain consequences of being labeled deviant.
   d.   demonstrates how behavior distinguishes deviants from nondeviants.

_____   5. Biases exist in official crime statistics because:
   a.   official reporting of misdemeanors is more likely than is reporting of felonies.
   b.   of administrative distortions in reporting crimes.
   c.   officers are more likely to report complaints made by low-income groups.
   d.   of the widespread reporting of crimes when actually no crimes occurred.

_____   6. Which of the following statements is true of a Part I offense?
   a.   It is less serious than a Part II offense.
   b.   It does not have a uniform definition throughout the states.
   c.   It is either a violent crime or a serious property crime.
   d.   It is not likely to occur often enough to be statistically significant.

_____   7. Organized crime:
   a.   is confined to illegitimate business activities.
   b.   has not been attacked by the federal government.
   c.   is no longer in the prostitution business.
   d.   is involved in such illegal activities as gambling and narcotics, legitimate businesses, and racketeering.

_____   8. Between 1989 and 1992:
   a.   the war against drugs lost most of its federal funding.
   b.   little government effort was made to reach such high-risk groups as school dropouts, gang members, and teenage mothers.
   c.   middle-class citizens started to increase their drug use.
   d.   a, b, and c

_____   9. Which of the following statements is true of the arrest process?
   a.   The poor are more likely than the rich to be arrested.
   b.   Since middle-class people have less privacy than do the poor, their crimes are more readily observed.
   c.   There is no evidence suggesting that police officers are more likely to arrest those least capable of exerting political pressures on their own behalf.
   d.   Police are strongly inclined to arrest middle-class adolescents because they believe that their permissive upbringing has encouraged delinquent behavior.

_____   10. To avoid the sampling problems faced by other researchers studying rapists, David Lisak:
   a.   interviewed only men who during their trial confessed to committing rape.
   b.   gave up studying rapists and switched his research to an examination of rape victims.
   c.   studied men who were not indicted but were revealed as rapists during a screening interview.
   d.   none of the above

1. What is deviance? Discuss the variations of standards of deviance across time and space.
2. Define, discuss, and evaluate two theories of deviance.
3. Is there bias in the reporting of criminal statistics? What factors seem to contribute most substantially to this bias?
4. Which categories of people are more likely to be arrested for crimes? Discuss.
5. Define informal social control and assess the effects of ignoring it.
6. By examining the four steps in the criminal-justice process, indicate whether or not this system truly provides justice.
7. Why is so much emphasis placed on building new prisons?

Suggested Readings

Dilulio, John J. 1987. *Governing Prisons: A Comparative Study of Correctional Management.* New York: Free Press. A persuasive, optimistic analysis of modern prisons arguing that the key to prisons that rehabilitate inmates is effective management.

Erikson, Kai T. 1966. *Wayward Puritans.* New York: John Wiley and Sons. A study of deviance among Massachusetts Puritans. Erikson explains how the activities of the Puritan era contributed to the development of American standards of deviance and crime.

Kelly, Delos H. (ed.). 1990. *Criminal Behavior.* 2nd ed. New York: St. Martin's Press. A set of effectively introduced classical and contemporary essays acquainting students with the field of criminology.

Kennedy, William. 1983. *Legs.* New York: Penguin Books. A powerfully written fictional account of the last years in the life of "Legs" Diamond, the famous gangster. The novel is particularly effective in conveying a sense of why many people have admired, even glorified major crime figures.

Scully, Diane. 1990. *Understanding Sexual Violence: A Study of Convicted Rapists.* Boston: Unwin Hyman. A powerful, eye-opening study based on interviews with 144 convicted rapists, indicating why some men rape and what they feel are the gains from doing it.

Shoemaker, Donald J. 1984. *Theories of Delinquency: An Examination of Explanations of Delinquent Behavior.* New York: Oxford University Press. A text that effectively describes the principal bodies of theory seeking to interpret delinquent behavior.

Spiegel, Don, and Patricia Keith-Spiegel (eds.). 1973. *Outsiders USA.* San Francisco: Rinehart Press. Twenty-four well written, effectively documented analyses of different types of deviance.

Trebach, Arnold S., and Kevin B. Zeese (eds.). 1991. *New Frontiers in Drug Policy.* Washington, DC: Drug Policy Foundation. Advocates to reform drug laws and policies examine such issues as the right to use drugs, the morality of the drug war, dealing with pregnant drug users, and the deadly combination of drugs and AIDS.

Additional Assignments

1. The following list contains a combination of noncriminal deviant forms and criminal behaviors:
    a. alcoholism
    b. assault
    c. dependence on legally available drugs
    d. embezzlement
    e. behavior demonstrating mental illness

198

    f.   murder
    g. nonviolent student protesting
    h. organized crime
    i.   rape
    j.   theft
    Ask five people (not in your sociology class) to rank these activities from one to seven, with one being the most serious. Compare and discuss your results with other students in the class. Is there strong consensus about the seriousness of the different activities? In particular, are the crimes always considered more serious violations than the noncriminal deviant activities?

2.   Select an interesting prominent person, such as a celebrity, political figure, or religious leader. Prepare a short biography which outlines this person's well-known deviant and nondeviant activities. On the whole, can you conclude that this person's prominence occurred because of deviant or nondeviant behavior? Ask other students to name something famous this person did. Which did students name more frequently—deviant or nondeviant activities?

Answers to Objective Test Questions

True • False Test

1. f	6. f
2. t	7. f
3. t	8. t
4. f	9. t
5. t	10. f

Multiple-Choice Test

1. d	6. c
2. d	7. d
3. a	8. b
4. a	9. a
5. b	10. c

Social Stratification

8

In July 1988, when asked which is more often to blame if a person is poor—lack of individual effort or circumstances beyond his or her control—40 percent of a national sample indicated lack of effort, 37 percent circumstances, and 17 percent a combination of both factors. Four years earlier 33 percent of a sample had opted for lack of effort (George Gallup, Jr., *Gallup Poll*, September 1988). The rise is hardly surprising, considering that during the intervening years the country was exposed to the Reagan administration's fervent rhetoric emphasizing that people's failure or success is determined by individual effort.

Ronald Reagan and his associates, to be sure, were consistent with an American tradition analyzing behavior in strictly individual terms and avoiding consideration of the sociological perspective that social forces beyond individuals' control largely shape their opportunities and destiny. Many modern economists endorse the sociological perspective, declaring that the present economy has become increasingly less hospitable to the young, the unskilled, and less educated. Gary Solon, a University of Michigan economist, found that a child whose father is in the bottom 5 percent of earners has only one chance in twenty of making it into the 20 percent of families with the highest income; however, the same child has better than two chances in five of staying poor or near poor (Solon 1992). Solon concluded, "It's not that you inherit the same position, but there's a substantial correlation." And referring to the rage and frustration vented by some poor residents of Los Angeles during the 1992 riots, David M. Cutler, a Harvard economist, said, "All you have to do is look at L.A. to decide that there are lots of people who think their permanent prospects are pretty crummy" (Nasar 1992b, A1).

Such social conditions as family prospects affect individuals' economic opportunities, but a sizable proportion of Americans, including many poor people, do not appreciate the existence of these social forces, placing the responsibility for individuals' poverty squarely on the individual's shoulders.

The social forces discussed here are part of the macro-order. Do you recall the distinction between the macro-order and the micro-order? If not, turn to the Key Terms in Chapter 4, "Groups." When sociologists analyze social stratification, they appreciate that the social forces of the macro-order significantly affect people's lives.

Social stratification is the structured inequality of access to rewards, resources, and privileges that are scarce and desirable within a society. "Structured inequality" means that because of their roles and group memberships, some people have a better opportunity than others to obtain rewards, resources, and privileges. The sociological perspective emphasizes that social forces determine people's location within a social-strati-fication system. By contrast, the sociobiologists discussed in Chapter 6, "Socialization," contend that through the evolutionary process, some people have acquired biologically linked traits of aggressiveness, ruthlessness, and intelligence that make them the most likely candidates to seek and obtain highly valued rewards and privileges.

You undoubtedly realize that because of family income, parental connections, and other factors some people have better opportunities to obtain these rewards and resources than others. At the same time, you probably are also aware that for most of us little of value simply drops into our laps. If you are going to obtain the benefits of the U.S. stratification system, then you must plan your life and, in particular, your career. It is likely that you have decided that a college education will help you in this effort.

Throughout this chapter I emphasize the sociological perspective—that social forces largely beyond individuals' control help to determine their opportunities, successes, and failures. This chapter examines four major topics, beginning with three theories of social stratification; the following subject involves the prominent dimensions of social stratification—wealth, power, and prestige; then analysis focuses on the American social-class system, indicating how stratification enters the everyday activities of Americans; the chapter closes with an examination of social mobility in American society.

Theories of Social Stratification

The conflict and structural-functional theories always offer different perspectives on a particular issue. In this instance conflict theory emphasizes that social classes emerge out of the production process, in which the rewards and privileges of social stratification are passed from one generation to the next. By contrast, the structural-functional theory focuses on the supposed contribution different jobs provide, contending that their respective contributions determine the rewards and privileges individuals receive; but it ignores the advantages that well-placed parents can pass on to their children.

MARXIST CONFLICT THEORY

Karl Marx believed that the struggle between economic classes was the central feature in the development of societies. In his famous *Communist Manifesto*, he wrote, "The history of all hitherto existing society is the history of class struggles."

Marx was convinced that classes arise out of the productive system within a society. In an agricultural society, the principal positions are landowner and serf or tenant. In an industrial society, the principal positions are the **bourgeoisie**— the class of modern capitalists who own the means of economic production and employ wage labor— and the **proletariat**—the class of modern wage laborers who possess no means of production and thus must sell their own labor in order to survive.

According to Marx, the interests of the bourgeoisie and the proletariat are inevitably opposed. Those who own the means of economic production—the factories and the farms—are primarily interested in maximizing their profit, and the workers, in turn, invariably want to increase their wages and benefits. But capitalists' wealth gives them enormous power. Because of their economic prominence, the bourgeoisie are able to exert political influence to control legislation, education, religion, the press, and the arts and also to prevent any organized expression of workers' discontent.

Marx contended that even though the members of the proletariat are disorganized and often unaware that they constitute a social class, they nonetheless share class membership because of two common experiences. First, they are all victims of the capitalist production process since they perform essential physical labor but receive minimal pay for their efforts. Second, all workers are powerless to confront the political strength of the state, which prevents them from expressing their discontent.

According to Marx, the proletariat gradually begins to develop **class consciousness**: recognition by the members of a class of the role they play in the production process. The workers' class consciousness involves an awareness of their relation to the bourgeoisie, especially a recognition of the owners' determination to prevent them from receiving a fair share of company profits. Marx believed that industrial conditions invariably encourage the development of class consciousness. He wrote:

> But with the development of industry the proletariat not only increases in number; it becomes concentrated in greater masses, its strength grows, and it feels that strength more. The various interests and conditions of life within the ranks of the proletariat are more and more equalized, in proportion as machinery obliterates all distinctions of labor and nearly everywhere reduces wages to the same low level. . . . Thereupon the workers begin to form combinations [trade unions] against the bourgeois; they club [join] together in order to keep up the rate of wages. . . .

(*Marx and Engels* 1959, 16)

204   Marx believed that in the final stage of class consciousness, the members of the proletariat recognize that the only way they will receive payment commensurate with their work efforts is to organize themselves into an army, overthrow the capitalists, and eliminate private ownership of the means of production.

Critical Evaluation

One point of contention involves Marx's claim that once a class of individuals recognizes its common interests and is willing to act on them in the public arena, it will always try to overthrow the existing system. This conclusion fails to recognize that most politically disenfranchised people usually want to become part of the system rather than to overthrow it. Prominent American cases in point have been the labor movement, a variety of racial and ethnic movements, and the women's movement. In the specific case of industrial workers, Marx underestimated the improving opportunities many of them have historically gained—in particular, good pay, pensions, social security, tenure and seniority, trade unionism, and the chance for some individuals, especially potential leaders, to move from lower- to higher-status positions. Thus, as one writer noted, were Marx to return to earth a century after his death, he would discover "that, in the most advanced capitalist countries, the proletariat had gained in many ways, despite the continuing exploitation against it, and that new middle classes had arisen, contrary to his expectation of class polarity" (Gurley 1984, 112).

In addition, the Marxist scheme takes a highly oversimplified view of the human personality. For Marx people seemed to be little more than the products of a uniform class experience, shifted around in large numbers in response to general social conditions. Thus Marx minimized the extent to which individuals are capable of making their own decisions (Beeghley 1978, 22–24; Rossides 1976, 423–27).

While stimulated by Marx's insights, many modern scholars have recognized that his analysis needs reevaluation—either because a concept like social class has not been used consistently (Katz 1992) or because the development of modern society has altered the social and economic conditions Marx analyzed (Wright and Martin 1987). In his well-known version of conflict theory, sociologist Eric Olin Wright (1985; Steinmetz and Wright 1990; Wright and Martin 1987) has highlighted one particularly significant aspect of changing class structure that did not exist in Marx's era—corporate managers' entrance into the elite class, occurring because their expertise in running huge business organizations provides them considerable power and wealth.

In Kashmir, where a caste system is firmly in place, this poverty-stricken man has no realistic opportunity to obtain a more affluent life.

STRUCTURAL-FUNCTIONAL THEORY

In 1945 sociologists Kingsley Davis and Wilbert Moore (1945) produced a structural-functional theory of stratification that attempts to explain the unequal distribution of rewards, resources, and privileges. Davis and Moore contended that all societies must face the problem of getting people to fill different positions and, once in those positions, to perform the duties associated with them. Some positions, however, are more critical to fill than others. The most critical jobs are those functionally important for the survival of society and those that require highly qualified personnel.

Davis and Moore suggested that functional importance alone will not assure job holders that they are well-rewarded. Some positions make a major contribution, but their ranks are so easy to fill that high salaries are not necessary. Police, fire fighters, and sanitation workers are examples.

Other positions are both functionally important and require highly qualified personnel. The promise of rewards will increase the likelihood that a fairly large number of people will endure the long, costly training that will qualify them for these positions. The potential to be a physician, for example, probably falls within the mental capacity of most people, but the training is so expensive and demanding that it is unlikely that many individuals would seek to enter the profession without the promise of a high income.

Davis and Moore concluded that differences between one system of social stratification and another exist because of conditions affecting the two determinants of differential reward—namely, functional importance and scarcity of personnel. Doctors, for instance, would not receive a high income in a society in which the members do not believe that modern medical techniques will work or the training for medical personnel is fairly brief and inexpensive.

Critical Evaluation

Conflict theorists who have criticized Davis and Moore's theory have claimed that this perspective does not establish a convincing link between the rewards provided by the stratification system and the contributions people make. According to Davis and Moore, the people who fill all high-paid positions are making an important, even necessary contribution to the society. But it seems impossible to argue that such individuals as underworld crime leaders, baseball superstars, and corrupt but wealthy business people are performing essential, important services. Furthermore many affluent individuals have neither special talents nor special training. Children of wealthy parents or people who marry the wealthy are cases in point. Sociologist Melvin M. Tumin (1953) argued that the American stratification system restricts rather than facilitates the selection of talented people for prestigious, high-paying positions. The structural-functional theory provides a perspective which justifies, even praises a stable social order with sharp social-class distinctions, while it does not explicitly praise the successful nor condemn the unsuccessful. However, it offers little insight into the social forces determining people's social stratification.

LENSKI'S THEORY

Gerhard Lenski (1966) was convinced that neither conflict theory nor structural-functional theory offers a complete and effective analysis of social stratification. He borrowed from both approaches in developing his own theory. This theory is compatible with the flexible approach of the previously cited, modern Marxist researchers.

Lenski noted that structural-functionalists believe that people are generally self-serving—that when individuals must choose between their own group's interests and the interests of others, they almost always choose the former. By contrast, the conflict theorists are much more likely to conclude that many people, especially members of the proletariat, are "good," putting the interests of their entire class above their own and their family's interests. On this issue Lenski agreed with the structural-functionalists.

On the other hand, Lenski supported conflict theorists' observation that societies contain individuals and groups that constantly struggle to obtain precious, scarce goods. Lenski was critical of Davis and Moore's conclusion that "perfect" systems of social stratification develop in order to meet the precise needs of the societies in which they are located. He asserted that since

> there is no such thing as a perfect social system, we should stop spinning theories which postulate their existence and direct our energies toward the building of theories which explicitly assume that all human organizations are imperfect systems. Second, social theorists (and researchers too) should stop trying to find social utility in all the varied behavior patterns of men; they should recognize that many established patterns of action are thoroughly antisocial and contribute nothing to the general good.
>
> (*Lenski* 1966, 34)

Lenski has suggested that on some issues the accuracy of the structural-functional or the conflict perspective varies with the type of society. For instance, structural-functionalists have contended that consensus (shared agreement) maintains

206

social-stratification systems, and conflict theorists have concluded that coercion plays the dominant part. Lenski's analysis of societies led him to the conclusion that consensus is considerably more important in societies with little or no economic surplus while coercion is more significant in societies that possess a substantial economic surplus. Unlike the simpler societal forms, the latter kinds of societies have inevitably developed a small governing class that controls the political process and requires the people outside the elite to turn over most of their economic surplus; the use of force or the threat of its use has been the only way to ensure such compliance.

Structural-functionalists are generally committed to the existing stratification system, and Lenski's analysis offers some evidence favoring such an outlook. He noted that until the advanced industrial age, major technological innovations tended to increase social inequality within societies. In recent decades, however, this trend has reversed. The United States and other major industrialized nations show somewhat more equitable distribution of power, privilege, and prestige than was apparent in less advanced industrial societies. On the other hand, Lenski's analysis has provided evidence in support of the conflict theorists' criticism of the current stratification system. In particular, he noted that the gap between the wealthy and the poor nations has been growing since the beginning of industrialization. One expert has estimated that between 1860 and 1960, the wealthiest quarter of nations increased their share of the world's income from 58 to 72 percent, and during the same period, the income of the poorest quarter dropped from 12.5 to 3.2 percent (Lenski and Lenski 1982; Zimmerman 1965, 38).

The chief difference between Lenski's theory and the other two is that Lenski's analysis does not take a firm ideological position into which facts are fitted. Instead basic theoretical conclusions are determined by available evidence. The Lenski theory, in short, is a more effective scientific endeavor than its predecessors.

Dimensions of Social Stratification

Max Weber (Gerth and Mills 1946, 180–95) emphasized that there are three dimensions of social stratification, which we will refer to as wealth, power, and prestige. The relationship among these dimensions is not self-evident. Sometimes they are highly interdependent. For instance, a person with great wealth might be able to exert considerable power in the political process by making substantial contributions to legislators' campaign funds. In other situations no apparent relationship exists. Members of long-time wealthy families in the locale of the wealthy individual just mentioned might feel that the person is low in prestige, lacking the education and social contacts that would make that individual an acceptable member of their set of friends.

Keep in mind that while we are analyzing these dimensions of social stratification as broad, somewhat abstract social forces, they profoundly affect individuals' lives. As you read this section, you might consider whether the facts you encounter are more consistent with structural-functional theory or with conflict theory.

WEALTH AND INCOME

Wealth is people's economic assets—their cars, homes, stocks, bonds, and real estate—which can be converted into cash. A disproportionate share of economic assets belong to the wealthy, and that share has been increasing. While in 1983 the wealthiest 1 percent of American families received 31 percent of the total net worth of American families, their share had risen to 39 percent by 1989. Meanwhile the least affluent 90 percent of American families found that their share of families' total net worth declined from 33 to 32 percent (Nasar 1992a).

Data on **income,** which is people's earnings obtained through wages, salaries, business profits, stock dividends, and other means, are more accessible and easily measured than data on wealth. For this reason researchers study income more frequently than wealth. However, a study of income fails to acknowledge various sources that are not reported or are indirect, such as professors' research grants and business executives' use of company cars and recreational facilities. Figure 8.1 represents the distribution of income in the United States.

Absolute versus Relative Wealth and Income

Analysts often make a distinction between two types of wealth—absolute and relative. **Absolute wealth** is the cash value of an individual's economic assets. **Relative wealth** is the value of an individual's economic assets compared to the assets possessed by other citizens in that society.

Through most of American history, rising industrial productivity, the tax structure, and various supplemental income programs have produced an absolute increase in wealth for all classes. However, over time the relative inequality of class income has remained stable. One sociologist suggested that modern stratification systems are like "a fleet of ships in a harbor: an incoming tide—rising productivity and a rising standard of living—does not diminish the difference between rowboats, cabin cruisers, cargo vessels, and giant ocean liners" (Rossides 1976, 112).

These two assessments of income distribution focus on different issues. For instance, absolute income figures indicate that in 1960, 22.2 percent of American citizens were classified as below the poverty level, meaning they had insufficient income to purchase basic goods and services. That figure dropped gradually, reaching 11.4 percent in 1978, then rising to 15.2 percent in 1983 before once again declining. In 1990 absolute income figures indicated that 33.6 million or 13.5 percent of the national population had insufficient income to purchase basic goods and services (U.S. Bureau of the Census, *Statistical Abstract of the United States:* 1992, No. 717).

Relative income figures highlight the fact that over time the distribution of income has remained

Figure 8.1

Percentage of Households in Different Income Categories, 1990

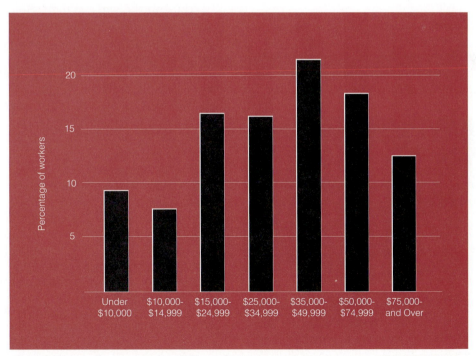

The median income for American households was $35,353 in 1990.

Source: U.S. *Bureau of the Census.* Statistical Abstract of the United States: 1992, No. 707.

208   fairly stable. Thus in 1947 the lowest fifth of the American population received 5 percent of all income and the highest fifth 43 percent. In 1990 the respective figures were 5.2 percent and 41.5 percent (U.S. Bureau of the Census, *Current Population Reports*, Series P-60, *Money Income of Households, Families, and Persons in the United States*: 1983, 1984, Table 17; U. S. Bureau of the Census, *Statistical Abstract of the United States*: 1992, No. 704).

The United States has about a half-million millionaires, or—in 1990—about one in every 497 citizens. The largest number reside in big business centers—in New York, California, and Illinois—while Idaho, Maine, and North Dakota have the highest per capita ratio of millionaires. Historically the majority of millionaires have had inherited wealth, but in the past two decades, that proportion has diminished, with entrepreneurs in such high-tech businesses as computer software, skilled professionals in fields like neurosurgery and the law, and corporate executives being among the most prominent new entries.

The nearby American Controversy should encourage you to analyze an important issue related to whether or not people's success is predetermined or self-determined—inheritance.

Effect of Taxes

The tax structure is a prominent means by which unequal economic distribution is kept fairly stable. Certain taxes—those on property, sales, and on

While the income-tax system is technically progressive, the availability of loopholes increases as people's incomes rise. Wealthy individuals can afford to hire high-priced accountants, whose detailed knowledge of how to use the income-tax system to best advantage can save clients large sums of money.

behalf of social security—are regressive, meaning that all people pay the same percentage of a product's value, regardless of their income. Therefore if the state sales tax is 7 percent, any person making a purchase must pay an additional 7 percent beyond the cost of the item.

On the other hand, income taxes are supposedly progressive, apparently taking a greater percentage of people's income as it increases. If income taxes truly were progressive, then economic inequality might be significantly reduced. However, the tax system is progressive only for low-income and middle-income people. For those with high and very high income, a range of available tax loopholes permits them to keep significant portions of their income untaxed or taxed at sharply reduced rates. For example, people financially involved in the search for such exhaustible resources as oil or natural gas receive tax breaks because they are investing in the procurement of scarce but essential resources. In addition, people in various businesses and professions are able to "write off" a wide range of activities as business expenses. Sometimes these meals, travel costs, rented cars, hotel rooms, and villas will represent legitimate business costs, and sometimes they will not.

Thus on the surface, the U.S. tax structure is progressive, but the more significant fact is that the number and size of tax loopholes increase as people's income increases. In 1972 a person with an income under $3,000 a year averaged a $15 yearly benefit from tax loopholes, but at high income levels (over $500,000 per year) the savings provided by loopholes rose sharply, reaching an average of $726,198 for people with incomes over $1 million per year (Surrey, 1973: 71).

The installation of tax loopholes is an example of the close relationship between wealth and power. As we see in Chapter 13, "The Political and Economic Institutions," interest groups attempt to influence politicians to pass favorable legislation, and wealthy interest groups tend to be more successful than their less affluent counterparts. In the last couple of decades, there has been rising citizen dissatisfaction about the tax breaks available to the wealthy. For example, in 1969, Congress passed a seemingly major tax reform. However, in spite of the apparently sweeping changes that this law enacted, wealthy people have continued to find multiple tax loopholes. Furthermore in 1971,

AMERICAN CONTROVERSY
What Should Be Done about Inheritance?

 Let me tell you about the very rich. They are different from you and me. They possess and enjoy early, and it does something to them, makes them soft where we are hard, and cynical where we are trustful, in a way that, unless you were born rich, it is difficult to understand. They think, deep in their hearts, that they are better than we are because we had to discover the compensations and refuges of life for ourselves. Even when they enter deep into our world or sink below us, they still think that they are better than we are. They are different.

F. Scott Fitzgerald

In this chapter we encounter some information backing Fitzgerald's position: that the wealthy not only have more valued material resources than others but they also think of themselves as different, in significant ways superior. Should our society permit conditions encouraging people to maintain such a sense of superiority? A critical issue underlying this question is the subject of inheritance. After all, it is the opportunity to inherit that allows wealth to be passed from one generation to another. Let us consider different positions on inheritance.

A position in favor of inheritance: We live in a capitalist society which rewards an individual's intelligence and perseverance. One of the most satisfying rewards that can be bestowed upon successful business people is the knowledge that their families will be able to inherit the wealth that they have accumulated. The existence of wealthy families serves as an incentive to others to produce similar achievements. Were inheritance eliminated or severely restricted, it is distinctly possible that many potentially excellent business ventures would not be pursued. Not only would individual families suffer but the society would not obtain the benefits provided by these enterprises. In particular, the diverse foundations wealthy individuals and families establish to assist various scientific, artistic, educational, and social programs would be eliminated, thereby restricting or ending numerous activities that have made a significant contribution to the enrichment of American society.

A position against inheritance: We live in a society which emphasizes equality. One of the most effective ways to achieve equality is to place a priority on economic equality, and the elimination of inheritance would be a significant step toward such an achieve-ment. The government could use the enormous wealth that it obtained from taking over all inheritance to eliminate poverty, hunger, and disease and to reorganize and revamp a vast range of public structures and facilities, including the education system, health care, antiquated public buildings, highways, and other public works. It is unlikely that the elimination of inheritance will significantly discourage business people from pursuing commercial ventures: Immediate economic success and glory are considerably more important to those who engage in such activities than a consideration of their children's inheritance. Finally one might argue that for the wealthy, inheritance weakens or even kills the work ethic, a highly prized value in our society. Most of us work because we have no alternative means to purchase goods and services. Those born wealthy, however, have no such incentive

What do you think? Do you strongly support one of the positions presented here, or do you find yourself somewhere in between? Discuss the issues in class or outside of class with several others in the course. In particular, try to assess the impact different policies would have on various groups as well as on the society over all.

---

after the furor over tax reform had died down, Congress passed a law restoring some of the loopholes plugged in 1969. Therefore wealthy people influence Congress through their interest groups, which act in a carefully planned series of maneuvers. A pair of sociologists noted, "Rarely is a

210

frontal assault undertaken, lest the self-interest of the wealthy be exposed. Rather, the progressivity of the tax structure is eroded by a persistent series of skirmishes" (Turner and Starnes 1976, 113).

Efforts to reform the income-tax system continue. In September 1986, Congress passed a tax reform bill, which enacted some important changes. About 6 million low-income people were removed from the tax rolls, and about 60 percent of taxpayers faced reduced payments. Many corporations taxed at or close to the maximum received a tax cut, while others, especially those formerly benefitting from special tax subsidies that were repealed, were compelled to pay more. Over all it was estimated that business-tax payments would increase by about $120 billion over six years to counterbalance an equivalent amount of tax cuts received by individuals (Egan 1986; Koepp 1986). Four years later a national survey indicated that the new legislation did not affect Americans greatly. While 7 percent indicated that their taxes had gone down a lot or a little, 34 percent said they had increased a little, 22 percent claimed they had increased a lot, and 27 percent declared they had remained the same. When asked to evaluate the impact of this tax reform, a distinct majority—56 percent—concluded it had made little difference (Newport 1990).

Some critics have emphasized that the issue of tax cuts receives too much attention, simply failing to address the society's dominant economic problem—a distinct slowdown in the growth of American productivity since 1970 (*Economist* 1992).

POWER

Power is the ability of an individual or group to implement wishes or policies, with or without the cooperation of others. A young girl who forces a smaller child to bring her a cookie is exercising power. A special kind of power is **authority,** which is power that people generally recognize as rightfully maintained by those who use it. A college teacher who assigns two tests, three quizzes, and two short papers at scheduled intervals through the semester is exercising authority. However, it is in the realm of politics that sociologists most frequently study power; we focus on the topic in Chapter 13, "The Political and Economic

Institutions." At this time we briefly consider two sharply opposed theories on the operation of power in the American political process: the pluralist perspective and the power-elite approach.

The two theories differ in their assessment of whether or not political authority is concentrated. The pluralist perspective emphasizes that authority is not concentrated, that it is dispersed to different centers that must represent their constituents' needs and interests or lose their access to political authority (Dahl 1967). The pluralists contend that the only way elected officials can effectively represent their constituents' interests on different issues is to form a separate alliance on each issue. Thus a state legislator might be aligned with one set of politicians on a tax reform bill and be working with an entirely different set on an antipollution measure. In both cases the legislator is seeking to promote constituents' interests.

The power-elite perspective popularized by C. Wright Mills (1956) opposes the pluralist approach. This theory claims that there is a group of high-status men who are well educated, often wealthy, socially prominent, and located in occupational positions where they can exert considerable power. Members of the elite control basic governmental policy in the political, economic, and military realms. If, in fact, Mills was correct, then our political system is not really a democracy. We, the people, might elect our political representatives, but these individuals are not attuned to the majority's interests; instead they are controlled by the power elite behind the scenes.

Mills visualized three levels of society. At the top is the power elite. Then there is a middle class of politically unorganized white-collar employees dominated by the corporations and government agencies for which they work. At the bottom are the masses, whose access to channels of power and influence is entirely cut off.

Examining the relationship between economic and political activity across time and space, sociologist G. William Domhoff concluded that "the upper class, rooted in the ownership and control of large corporations, rules or governs through a leadership group called the power elite at the national level" (Domhoff 1990, 17). In Domhoff's view the relationship between the upper class and the power elite is intimate and mutually beneficial, but no foregone conclusion exists that the two are in full harmony: Each new political issue must be examined to determine the influence exerted by the upper-class group on the political process. It seems that what makes this theory particularly attractive is that it combines a clear conflict perspective with an appreciation of the importance of some empirical flexibility.

Over all neither the power-elite view nor the pluralist perspective provides a fully accurate picture of the role of authority in American society. The power-elite thesis probably exaggerates the extent to which upper-class people operate as a group with strongly shared interests. Competition sometimes exists among the rich and powerful for limited resources like government contracts or political offices. On the other hand, the pluralist thesis fails to recognize that exploitation, privilege, corruption, and powerlessness are deeply rooted in American politics. Both theories seem to provide part of the truth.

PRESTIGE

Prestige is the possession of attributes that elicit recognition, respect, and some degree of deference. Generally Americans tend to be fairly consistent in their assessments of prestige. A study found that two groups of respondents—one from the working class and the other from the middle class—were very similar in their prestige rankings for eighty-four Long Island communities (Logan and Collver 1983). A similar consistency occurs with occupations, which are frequently linked with prestige. Figure 8.2 shows the prestige ranking of selected white-collar occupations. In 1947 the National Opinion Research Center at the University of Chicago (NORC) used a national sample of 2,920 respondents to rank ninety occupations in relation to each other, and across the nation there was remarkable consistency obtained from the subjects. The NORC study was repeated in 1963, and with minor variations the occupational rankings were strikingly similar (Hodge, Siegel, and Rossi 1966). Research in other industrialized as well as nonindustrialized countries reveals a very similar pattern (Treiman 1977).

The fact that Americans are highly consistent in the occupational rankings they provide suggests that for high-status jobs there is a nationally shared respect, which legitimates the performance

Figure 8.2
Prestige of Selected White-Collar Occupations

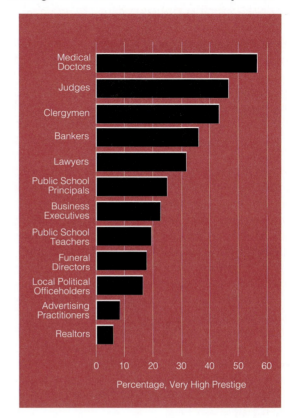

As this assessment of twelve occupations illustrates, Americans consider some white-collar positions much more prestigious than others.

Source: George Gallup, Jr. Poll. (October 7, 1981).

of people in these positions. On the other hand, those ranked low are consistently valued in a negative way, an evaluation that tends to legitimate their economic failure and justify their placement at the bottom of the occupational prestige structure. Evidence suggests that the American public is particularly inclined to maintain generalized negative images of low-status occupational groups, not recognizing that such categories as farm workers contain people with diversified personal characteristics and lifestyles (Whitener 1985)

People in low-status positions obviously feel the brunt of their prestige rankings. Taxi drivers, for example, do not possess an unusual or specialized skill. Sometimes drivers will try to convince their passengers that they do indeed have a special talent and "will resort to darting nimbly in and out of traffic, making neatly executed U-turns and

212

leaping smartly ahead of other cars when the traffic light changes" (Davis 1959, 160). Tenants generally believe that custodial work is low in prestige. Custodians usually recognize the tenants' estimations of their work and sometimes attempt to enhance their image by representing themselves as similar to professionals, especially doctors. Some custodians tell their tenants to call only during daylight hours except for emergencies, or like some doctors they charge their tenants on a sliding scale for any extra jobs that their tenants might request (Gold 1952).

In the comedy series "Cheers," Cliff, the postal worker, demonstrates a similar drive for prestige recognition. Surrounded by primarily white-collar workers, he often asserts his supposed professional status. When an admiral in uniform entered the bar, Cliff, also in uniform, approached him his hand extended, referring to them both as uniformed government professionals.

In the first section, we looked at theories that consider why social stratification exists in societies. We continued an analysis of the macro-order in this section, examining the distribution of wealth, power, and prestige throughout the society. Now the focus narrows, with an analysis of the micro-order in the everyday lives of people belonging to various social classes.

Whether it is his occupational status or something else, Cliff, the postal worker in "Cheers," seldom seems happy. Here he is shown glowering at his mother, who in his estimation prefers Woody, the man whose hand she is holding, to her own son.

Social Class in America ■

A **social class** is a large category of people who are similar in income level, educational attainment, and occupational prestige-ranking. The members of a social class share a set of values and also similar opportunities to obtain desired goals and experiences.

Sometimes people speak about "the social class structure" as if a single, distinct way of determining an individual's social-class placement exists. In reality a number of approaches have been used (Kohn et al. 1990; Runciman 1990).

The **subjective definition of social class** is a measuring technique that requires people to indicate the social class to which they belong. In some cases the investigators provide a range of choices, and in other cases they do not. One problem with this approach is that research suggests that some people are not sure to which class they belong.

One sociologist has reported that a substantial number of Americans have been unable to decide whether they are middle or working class (Kahl 1957).

Research suggests that working women and men differ in their subjective definition of social class. Men's class identification tends to be based on whether they do manual or nonmanual work while women's subjective view of social class is determined by whether or not they are self-employed, work in a primarily female occupation, or have union membership. The two sets of results might have been produced by different work histories, with men's current work patterns developing during industrial times and women's in the postindustrial, service-oriented era (Simpson, Stark, and Jackson 1988).

The **reputational definition of social class** is

a measuring technique in which researchers use resident experts from the community—"judges"—to assess their neighbors' social-class position. This approach works well in residential areas that have a population that is sufficiently small and stable to permit the researchers to find judges who know all the local citizens well enough to place them in social classes. In the majority of modern American communities, the population is too large and physically mobile to make the use of this technique possible.

Finally the **objective definition of social class** is a measuring technique that uses certain quantifiable factors—income, occupational prestige level, or level of education, for example—as the basis for determining an individual's social-class position. Investigators sometimes employ a single factor, and in other cases they use a combination of several. Among sociologists the objective approach is the most popular one, but what factors to use and how much weight each should receive is not an issue on which unanimity exists. Table 8.1 summarizes the three approaches.

As we study social class, we should keep in mind that there is not unanimous agreement about how the American class system is structured. Most sociologists, however, would accept some approximation of the following scheme:

1. A capitalist class, with considerable wealth, whose members, if working, maintain executive positions, have been educated at prestigious universities, possess a family income of about $500,000 a year, and represent about 1 percent of the population. (All the income figures presented in this discussion were calculated for the United States in 1991.)

2. The upper-middle class, containing people who are managers and professionals, have an annual income of about $50,000 or more, have attended college and perhaps done postgraduate study, and constitute about 20 percent of the population.

3. The lower-middle class, with members who work as lower-level managers, semi-professionals, salespeople, craft workers, and foremen, earn $25,000 to $50,000 or more a year, have at least a high-school education, and comprise about 33 percent of the population.

4. The working class, who are operatives, clerical and sales workers, or low-paid craftspeople, receive $15,000 to $25,000 a year or more, have graduated from high school, and represent about 19 percent of the population.

5. The working poor, employed as service workers, laborers, and low-paid operatives, have some high-school education, make below $10,000 to $15,000 a year, and are about 10 percent of the population.

Table 8.1 Three Ways to Measure Social Class

The approach	Who determines the respondents' social class?	A problem with the approach
Subjective definition	The respondents themselves	Some people's uncertainty about their own class membership
Reputational definition	Local "judges"	Modern, urbanized living making it impossible for any citizen to have sufficient knowledge of all fellow residents to serve as judges
Objective definition	Researchers using certain quantifiable factors, such as occupational evaluations, income, or educational level	Limited agreement about which factors to use or how much weight to provide each given factor

6. The underclass, who are unemployed or underemployed and sometimes are maintained by welfare, tend to have a primary-school education, receive $10,000 a year or less, and comprise about 17 percent of the population (Gilbert and Kahl 1982, 348).

People within a particular social class share a common sense of outlook and experience. Those in various social classes, for instance, have different opportunities and lifestyles (Tumin 1967).

OPPORTUNITY AND SOCIAL CLASS

As we analyze the issue of opportunities, we consider once again whether some people's chances in life are predetermined to be better than those available to others. We find that the higher people's social class, the longer their life expectancy, the less likely they will suffer mental illness, the more effective their capacity to communicate, and the higher their self-esteem.

Life Expectancy

People can pay to lengthen their lives in a number of ways. In particular, the higher classes benefit from longer life expectancy in situations in which death is preventable since, because of income and other advantages, they have greater access than lower-class people to effective means of prevention. For example, when the *Titanic* struck an iceberg and sunk, sufficient lifeboats for everyone were not available. Only 4 of 150 women and children in first class (3 percent) went down with the ship compared to 13 of 117 in second class (11 percent) and 141 of 244 in third class (58 percent). It appears that third-class passengers suffered two distinct disadvantages; they were much more likely to be denied entrance to the life boats, and their residential areas were much farther from the boat deck (Hall 1986).

A variety of more general conditions promote greater life expectancy for people in higher social classes. For example:

> Front-line troops have tended to come from the lower social classes. A researcher who studied combat soldiers in Vietnam found that about two-thirds of the soldiers in

the units with which he stayed were from working-class backgrounds and the remainder had lower-middle-class origins. Nearly two-thirds had graduated from high school, and most of the others were high school dropouts. Several had attended college, but none were college graduates (Moskos 1969).

Studies conducted in twenty European countries indicated that people with higher social-class ranking were less prone to such life-threatening but either avoidable or treatable conditions as infant death, infectious disease, respiratory disease, and alcoholism than individuals of lower social-class ranking (Illsley 1990; Lahelma and Valkonen 1990).

Evidence suggests that in the past coronary heart disease was disproportionately suffered by the affluent. With the development of mechanized transportation and a variety of labor-saving devices, emphasis on low-cholesterol food among the educated, and the growing predominance of smoking among low-income citizens, coronary heart disease has increasingly become a disease of the poor (Wing 1988).

Mental Illness

Sociologists Robert Faris and Warren Dunham (1939) examined more than 30,000 people admitted to hospitals in Chicago for the treatment of mental illness. They found an inverse relationship between social-class position and the rate of mental illness. Another study, which assessed the psychiatric condition of a random sample of 1,600 New Yorkers, reached a similar conclusion (Srole et al. 1962). Later research has produced consistent results, concluding that people in higher social classes have lower rates of schizophrenia, depression, unhappiness, and anxiety (Syme and Berkman 1981).

We might wonder why. People in higher social classes generally have greater educational and occupational opportunities, which can promote a positive sense of self and decrease the likelihood of mental illness. Furthermore less affluent people's general life condition, in which most items that are highly prized are in short supply, is likely to encourage a negative, even fatalistic outlook on reality. Such an outlook makes it difficult to deal resourcefully with stress in the course of everyday life (Kessler and Cleary 1980; Kohn 1976). In addition, the perception of type of mental illness in different social classes is to some extent in the eye of the beholder. Growing evidence indicates that mental-health specialists develop preconceptions of the kinds of mental illness associated with different social classes (Landrine 1987). They also might have preconceptions about frequency in different social classes.

All of these conditions can adversely affect homeless people. They are likely to have had limited opportunities to promote a positive self-image, to have a negative outlook on life fostered by their limited opportunities, and to be viewed adversely by mental-health specialists, who are likely to conclude that the homeless are a difficult and unrewarding group to treat. Still there have been many calls to treat homeless mentally ill people, who compose about a third of homeless individuals. The majority, declared psychiatrist H. Richard Lamb, need supervised housing since they cannot effectively care for themselves. Lamb wrote, "The time for action is overdue. We must be prepared to mount a large-scale operation that will give relief to all of the homeless mentally ill" (Lamb 1990, 651).

Communication Effectiveness

The higher the social class of the family, the earlier and the more effectively speech will develop (Berelson and Steiner 1964, 69). Sociologists Leonard Schatzman and Anselm Strauss (1972) conducted 340 interviews with witnesses of tornados. They found that the social class (especially the amount of education) of the individuals involved in these disasters significantly influenced the effectiveness of the accounts they gave. In particular:

> The working-class participants could see the events only through their "own eyes." By contrast, the middle-class witnesses could also offer explanations from the point of view of another person or a group of other people
>
> The working-class respondents often did not anticipate what the listener who had not been present during the disaster knew about the course of events. The result was that the accounts from working-class people were often so undeveloped that

they were hard to follow beyond the description of individuals' personal reactions. On the other hand, the middle-class person stood "between his own images and the hearer and . . . [implicitly said], 'Let me introduce you to what I saw and know.'"

> The working-class respondents could describe individuals, but they were not able to discuss effectively the activities of categories of people (the rich or the poor, the hurt or the unhurt) or organizations. Seemingly without effort middle-class people tended to analyze their perceptions in relation to these different categories and to convey information about them in an effective, coherent manner.

Quite possibly communications effectiveness is related to intellectual flexibility—the ability to produce a variety of options to resolve complex tasks and a more prevalent characteristic in higher-class individuals according to a study of Japanese, Polish, and American men (Kohn 1990).

Self-Esteem

An important consideration in analyzing the relationship between self-esteem and social class is the significance of work in people's self-evaluation. A study of 228 employed men found a close connection between their occupational placement and self-esteem if work were central in their self-evaluation but little relationship when the family was more central than work to respondents' self-evaluation (Gecas and Seff 1990).

For many Americans their emphasis on work or work prospects leads to a negative self-evaluation. A case in point is the "hidden injury" of class, the fact that working-class people are denied a sense of worth in the eyes of others and of themselves. This lack of esteem, sociologists Richard Sennett and Jonathan Cobb (1973) suggested, has two sources: first, the idea that class placement is the result of ability, and second, the often futile pursuit of efforts to improve one's class position. Sennett and Cobb undertook a study in Boston, conducting 150 in-depth interviews of working-class men and women ranging in age from their late teens to their sixties. The study offered many illustrations of working-class people's low self-esteem.

For example, a respondent told the researchers about his sense of inferiority in the presence of middle-class people.

Research has indicated that some working-class people suffer the "hidden injury of class," but others, such as the men on the right side of this table, are able to take significant steps to overcome this problem. These men are factory workers who serve on the negotiating team for the local chapter of the United Auto Workers at Ford's Louisville assembly plant. The handshake signals that they have just completed negotiations with management for a new contract.

[W]henever I'm with educated people, you know, or people who aren't my own kind . . . um . . . I feel like I'm making a fool of myself if I just act natural, you know? See, it's not so much how people treat you, it's feeling like you don't know what to do.

(*Sennett and Cobb* 1973, 110)

The man went on to describe a time when he had appeared at a meeting of middle-class people and felt entirely out of place and isolated.

It seems that children's sense of relationship between their social-class position and self-esteem develops gradually. A study concluded that among children ranging from fifth to eighth graders, the perceived relationship between social class and self-esteem rose with age. Apparently as children become older, they pay more attention to social class, increasingly allowing their own position within the system to determine their self-image (Demo and Savin-Williams 1983).

LIFESTYLE AND SOCIAL CLASS

People from different social classes tend to demonstrate variations in lifestyle, as indicated in the following discussion of fertility, child-rearing patterns, sexual behavior, and clubs and friendships.

Fertility

In a chart that attempts to represent humorously the relationship between family life and social class, researchers William Simon and John Gagnon (1972, 86–87) suggested that upper-class couples tend to have one child each by previous marriages or as many as God provides; upper-middle-class couples produce 2.4 children; lower-middle-class couples usually have three children; and lower-class couples have as many as God provides.

In fact, this summary is somewhat accurate. With the exception of some upper-class couples, an inverse relationship—in this case the higher the social class, the fewer the number of children—often exists between social class and family size. Blacks generally have more children than whites, and this pattern is apparently class-linked. When researchers compare black and white families of the same social class, the difference in family size disappears.

Several factors explain the statistical relationship between social class and family size. The higher the social class, the greater the tendency for women to be extensively educated and career-oriented and thus to want to control family size. Furthermore people in the middle or upper-middle class are more likely than lower-class individuals to plan their lives in accord with the dominant value patterns of the day as represented in the media, and having a modest number of children is such a prevailing value pattern (Reiss and Lee 1988, 315).

Between 1900 and 1970 in Sicily, the higher couples' social-class position, the fewer children they generally produced, even though the most prominent form of birth control involved *coitus interruptus*, the removal of the penis from the vagina before ejaculation. Gradually a standard endorsing a small number of children spread through the entire social-class structure, and nowadays, regardless of social class, couples with six or more children are likely to be called "mice" or "rabbits" (Schneider and Schneider 1991).

Approaches to Child Rearing

Middle-class and working-class parents' child-rearing techniques are similar in many respects. In the United States and several western European countries, however, some distinct differences are apparent: In particular, middle-class parents place more emphasis on self-direction and working-class parents on conformity to external authority. One factor which seems to contribute to the different child-rearing values is the influence of respective work environments. Working-class individuals' jobs are much more supervised and routinized than those of middle-class people, whose occupations involve more autonomy and task variety (Kohn et al. 1990; Reiss and Lee 1988, 328–30).

During the Vietnam War, different class attitudes toward raising children became a political issue. Vice-President Spiro Agnew, a man of working-class origins, made a number of speeches in which he sharply criticized the behavior of upper-middle-class antiwar activists. Agnew suggested that these young people were products of "permissive" child-rearing practices, practices that allowed or even encouraged the activists not to respect their parents and their political leaders.

Sexuality

Researcher Wardell Pomeroy (1972, 469) suggested that by comparing adolescent boys' sexual histories one can conclude which individuals will be more likely to attend college. For instance, one boy has intercourse with a number of girls, does not remove his clothes for sexual relations, disap-

proves of oral sex, masturbates less often at 18 than in his early teens, and has few "wet dreams." The sexual history of a second boy shows that if he has sexual intercourse, he has less than the other boy, engages in a great deal of petting and may try oral sex, and considers sexual activity more enjoyable in the nude. The first boy, according to Pomeroy, displays sexual behavior typical of a lower-class background, and coming from this background he is unlikely to attend college. On the other hand, the sexual behavior of the second boy is typically middle-class, and middle-class adolescents are likely to attend college.

Lower-class people tend to begin their sexual lives somewhat earlier, but their sexual activity tends to be less frequent and less fulfilling, especially for women (Howell 1973). A study of low-status marriages in four places—the United States, Puerto Rico, Mexico, and England—suggested that the belief frequently exists that "sex is a man's pleasure and a woman's duty." This particular attitude seems to be a product of segregated gender roles, which permit a very limited sharing of interests and activities between women and men (Rainwater 1964). On the other hand, middle-class or upper-class spouses are quite likely to share common interests and a sense of closeness, openly discussing their sexual relations and remaining sensitive to their partners' needs (Reiss 1980, 275–85).

The modern era of sexual permissiveness can be particularly confusing for working-class women. Like many modern men, most working-class men recognize the value placed on women's orgasm. Many of them now believe that unless their wives achieve orgasm, they have failed as lovers. The women, on the other hand, have often been raised by mothers who stress "a grin-and-bear-it" approach to sex, and they are unlikely to enjoy sex and achieve orgasm (Rubin 1983).

Social-class ranking and sexuality relate in another way. When college women and men were shown photographs of members of the other sex to determine whether or not they would consider sexual intimacy with them, women were more interested than men in the prospective partner's social-class level. This finding is consistent with a pattern indicating that women are more concerned than men with assessing an individual's marital potential before engaging in sexual intercourse (Townsend and Levy 1990).

People are more likely to choose friendships and associations among their own class. Ethnic and racial similarities may also affect the choice of organizations and clubs people join.

Friendships and Clubs

An upper-middle-class man spoke to a researcher about the prospect of having working-class friends. He said, "I am not a snob, but it is a fact of life that in most of those occupations we would have nothing in common" (Laumann 1966, 28).

Many people would agree with this man. When classes are defined on the basis of occupation, people are more likely to choose friends from among their own or adjacent classes. In one study the pattern was most distinct at the extremes, with unskilled and semiskilled workers finding more than three-quarters of their friends close to their own class level and with the professional and business classes doing the same (Laumann 1966, 65).

Recent research done in Canada, Norway, Sweden, and the United States indicated that the extent of interclass friendship patterns depends on the measure of social class used. For instance, if class placement is determined by property ownership—dividing individuals into the categories of self-employed with employees, self-employed

without employees, or not self-employed—then relatively few friendships across class lines occurred. People who are business owners with employees tend to find their friends from among their own property class, and a similar development occurs with employees. However, when social class was based on authority—separating respondents into management, supervisory, or nonmanagement positions—there was considerably more interclass friendship. For example, supervisors and individuals they supervised often became friends (Wright and Cho 1992).

The members of different social classes tend to join certain kinds of organizations, and the prestige of the organizations depends on the prestige of the members. There are upper-class and upper-middle-class social clubs: athletic clubs, men's clubs, women's gardening clubs, and charitable organizations. These same classes support professionally oriented clubs: chambers of commerce, business and professional associations, and service clubs. These organizations can serve a variety of purposes for their members. Typically men's professional organizations provide the opportunity to make valuable contacts, to obtain useful information, and to engage in interesting, stimulating discussion. In contrast to men's clubs, women's organizations are more likely to be local than national, and upper-middle-class women usually belong to more clubs than their husbands and to place greater emphasis on clubs as a source of status advancement (Hodges 1964; Lerner 1982).

Clubs and friendships can be effectively used to help people "get ahead." In the following section, we discuss Americans' efforts to improve their social-class position.

Social Mobility in American Society

At the end of the nineteenth century, Horatio Alger's novels about poor boys who rose from rags to riches through hard work sold more than 30 million copies. These novels underlined the American belief that the United States is an open society in which enormous opportunity for personal success exists and that people will receive rewards of wealth, power, and prestige in correspondence with the effort they make. Actually how open is the social-class system? Does the American system permit success for anyone willing to push hard enough, or are people's opportunities largely structured by conditions outside their control? To address such questions, we must examine the concept of social mobility.

Social mobility is the movement of a person from one social class or status level to another, either upward or downward with accompanying gains or losses in wealth, power, and prestige. In the past couple of decades, there have been many studies of mobility processes (Bridges and Villemez 1991; Landale and Guest 1990) and debates on how this complex topic should be conceptualized (DiPrete and Grusky 1990; Wong 1990).

Sociologists generally study two kinds of social mobility. **Intergenerational mobility** is a comparison of a parent's and a child's social-class positions. This comparison indicates whether the child's social-class position is higher or lower than the parent's or has remained the same. Most prominent studies of intergenerational mobility have compared fathers' and sons' social-class position, using occupational status as its measure. An increasing number of intergenerational mobility studies on women seems inevitable as they enter the work world in rapidly increasing numbers. Recent cross-cultural research has indicated that in spite of some differences among industrial nations, patterns of intergenerational mobility are basically similar (Grusky and Hauser 1984; Ishida, Goldthorpe, and Erikson 1991).

Intragenerational mobility is an analysis of an individuals's occupational changes in the course of a lifetime. Thus a researcher might observe that a particular woman started as a bank teller, advanced to management status, and eventually retired as the bank president. One recent study of intragenerational mobility in three countries—Austria, France, and the United States—found that because of different conditions governing the move from lower-status to higher-status jobs, the three cultures differed significantly in their intragenerational mobility patterns (Haller et al. 1985).

Let us consider current evidence of social mobility, the causes of social mobility, some of the effects produced by it, and prospects for upward mobility.

EVIDENCE

Perhaps you have participated in a conversation like the following. A group of friends are having lunch together. Jane says, "Last night I spoke with my grandfather, and all he talks about these days is how much things have changed. Yesterday he kept harping on the fact that you can't work your way up from the bottom anymore. The big corporations run the whole show, and they keep people pretty much locked in. If your family has got money and power it's one thing, but for the rest of us. . . ." She shakes her head unhappily.

Ron smiles. "I don't agree. It seems to me that if you have a good idea and can market it, you can still make a pile and gain all the power and prestige that go with it. My mom and dad went to high school with Frank Trudeau. In his early twenties, he had a simple idea for a household device, and he turned it into a multimillion dollar business."

Many Americans have bits and pieces of opinion and knowledge that suggest that U.S. society is either more or less open than it was in the past. We need to look beyond bits and pieces and see if we can detect a broad pattern. In the first place, we must be aware that it is difficult to make meaningful comparisons of social-mobility rates over long periods of time. It is misleading, perhaps impossible, to compare people in an agrarian society with those in an industrial one. If the grandson of a blacksmith who earned $500 a year becomes an automobile worker making $10,000 per year, he is likely to be downwardly mobile in a relative sense, in spite of a sizable increase in income. In this case "relative sense" means that the automobile worker will be proportionately lower in the modern stratification system. When agrarian societies become industrial, most people become "wealthier, healthier, more skilled, better educated, and the like than their forebears, but modern populations are just as unequal, relative to their own societies, as people were in the past" (Rossides 1976, 99).

Comparisons over short periods of time involving a society with a fairly stable economic system are easier to understand. In 1962 sociologists Peter Blau and Otis Duncan (1967) conducted a study that David Featherman and Robert Hauser (1978) repeated a decade later. In both cases the investigators arranged with the Bureau of the Census to add two pages containing questions on career history and parental background to the regular monthly survey of employment and unemployment. Blau and Duncan received data on 20,000 fathers and sons, and Featherman and Hauser obtained information on 33,000 fathers and sons.

The researchers focused on their respondents' occupations. They divided the men into five categories based on their type of job—white-collar, lower white-collar, upper manual, lower manual, and farm. In the 1973 study, Featherman and Hauser found that 49 percent of sons moved up, 32 percent stayed in the same general category, and 19 percent went down. The Blau and Duncan findings from eleven years earlier were just slightly different. The percentage of upward mobility was the

same, but 2 percent more stayed the same, and thus 2 percent fewer went down.

Blau and Duncan examined findings from some older studies that allowed them to make comparisons back to 1947. They found that between 1947 and 1962 an increasing percentage of men moved from manual origins into white-collar jobs and that no corresponding downward move occurred. Furthermore in that fifteen-year span, an increasing proportion stayed at the same occupational level as their fathers (Blau and Duncan 1967, 103).

Thus the American occupational structure has shown a trend toward upward mobility. However, some distinct limitations to that pattern occur.

Cases of Limited Access

In the first place, it is very difficult for lower-class people to move up. Many sociologists contend that millions of poor people are trapped in a **vicious cycle of poverty,** a pattern in which the parents' minimal income significantly limits the educational and occupational pursuits of the children, therefore keeping them locked into the same low economic status. Does such a cycle of poverty actually occur? Researcher Bradley Shiller (1970) studied 1,017 men who grew up in families receiving Aid to Families with Dependent Children. Sixty-three percent of the respondents were in some kind of unskilled jobs, and only 8 percent achieved a white-collar position. Therefore a few men did succeed in breaking the vicious cycle of poverty, but nearly two out of three remained in marginal job slots, leaving them likely candidates to carry the cycle into the next generation. For high-school graduates, breaking the cycle has become increasingly difficult. Data from a University of Michigan study indicated that in the 1970s 93 percent of white men and 84 percent of black men graduating from high school were able to earn more than a poverty-level income, but the respective figures fell to 88 and 75 percent in the 1980s (Nasar 1992b).

People caught in the cycle of poverty have very limited opportunities to break the cycle. The head of the household in many poor families is often a young woman, perhaps a teenager, who has few skills to prepare her children to be successful in modern society, or to earn an above-poverty

SOCIAL APPLICATION
The Vicious Cycle of Poverty: A Case Study

The vicious cycle of poverty consists of the transmission of limited opportunity from one generation to the next. But how does the process actually occur? One concrete answer comes from looking at case studies of individuals, such as the life account of José Alvarez, who grew up in East Harlem, a Puerto Rican district of New York City. For José and other people caught in the cycle of poverty, the opportunity to obtain affluence, good jobs, and prestige has been remote.

At the time of the research, José was 18 years old, a dropout from high school. He had a host of interests and talents including photography, electrical gadgetry, and sports. His photographs were widely acclaimed by local residents and outsiders who saw them. After studying a stack of José's photos, one expert declared that the young man had a rare knack of "catching that special moment." José was also mechanically inclined; he could put together a television from spare parts or repair serious automotive problems without even a manual.

In spite of José's talents, a number of factors made his future bleak, beginning with his family. When José was young, his mother died and his father remarried. The new wife was not enthusiastic about raising her husband's son, and soon he was shipped to his grandmother. This small, white-haired woman, always dressed in black, had come to New York

City before José was born. She survived on public assistance, living an almost reclusive existence, and she forced the same lifestyle on her grandson. José explained, "I never got to go downstairs and play outside like the kids now. So on the way home from school I'd sometimes stop at the library and pick up a book. All I ever did was read."

Although he read constantly, José generally did not take school seriously. As a boy he failed to grasp its relation to occupational success. Neither his grandmother nor his counselors ever encouraged him to do anything but "just get by." He went to a vocational high school, but several of his friends explained to him that the best he could hope for in the future with a vocational degree was a job as a factory worker. As a result of this advice, he transferred to an academic high school, but then another hurdle appeared in front of him. He became involved with Maria Pagan.

Maria was divorced with two children, and soon after she and José started going together, she was pregnant again. José explained, "I quit school and got myself a job. Like the people say, when the woman gets pregnant you've got to forget about school and go to work!"

Several years later José returned to school, but his attendance was irregular, and he seldom did his homework. I met José at this time, and he would speak enthusiastically about school, about the teachers who

stimulated him, and about friends applying to college. The way he spoke made it clear that he felt that college and the good jobs that would come from higher education were fascinating but not attainable.

I told José that if he wanted to go on to college, he could. José pointed out to me that it was easy for me to say that. My life, after all, had been simple. I admitted that José had a point but still persisted. If José really wanted to go to college, he would be able to in spite of the difficulties involved. José laughed bitterly and gave me a paper he had written. One paragraph read in part:

> POVERTY: WHO KNOWS WHAT IT REALLY IS? You have to know from experience what it is like to be poor. You have to learn about a life where you can't afford to pay $1.25 for a hair cut. You have to get to know the smell of second-hand mattresses after too many babies have lain on them.

When I returned the paper to José, he told me that this was true, that you couldn't learn about poverty from books, only from experience. I agreed but added that José could still go to college. He stared blankly and said nothing.

Fifteen years later José had a long list of menial jobs, a lengthy involvement with hard drugs, a short jail sentence, two broken marriages, and five children. Not surprisingly he never went to college. Certainly there

222

were economic and practical problems, but for José the cycle of poverty seems to have set its most vicious trap at the interpersonal level. As Cooley's looking-glass-self concept suggests, we see ourselves as others see us. It appears that no one ever visualized José as a college student, or for that matter as any kind of consistent success. So he never visualized himself in any successful roles either, and his talents have simply gone to waste.

Source: Christopher Bates Doob. The Development of Peer Group Relationships among Puerto Rican Boys in East Harlem. Unpublished Ph.D. dissertation. Cornell University, 1967.

income. Furthermore studies indicate that even when poor mothers obtain jobs, they will not necessarily remove their families from poverty because their positions are often low-paying, they are vulnerable to layoffs and other work interruptions, and they face fairly high expenses for child care (Petersen 1992).

The nearby Social Application demonstrates how the cycle of poverty can develop. Once more we consider the extent to which people's success is predetermined.

African-Americans are another category of people who encounter special difficulties when they try to advance themselves in social-class position. On the average African-Americans have certain distinct disadvantages compared to whites—poorer parents, fewer years of education, less sympathetic and thorough supervision early in their careers, and extensive discrimination. Yet in spite of these disadvantages, the black community is no longer lower class occupationally. Employed black males divide roughly into thirds, with one-third in the underclass or among the working poor, another third in working-class jobs, and the final third in some level of middle-class positions.

Advancement problems are particularly acute for the African-American underclass, which experiences high unemployment rates, high welfare rates, and a decrease in movement out of poverty—in short, the vicious cycle of poverty. About 31.9 percent of African-Americans compared to 10.7 percent of whites—three times the proportion—are living in poverty (U.S. Bureau of the Census, *Statistical Abstract of the United States*: 1992, No. 722). An editorial in *The Economist*, a British journal, offered a distinctly non-American viewpoint on the plight of the African-American underclass in the "land of opportunity," where upward mobility tends to be a dominant national concern. It was suggested that unlike Europeans, who are obsessed with the idea of people ending up relatively equal in wealth and income, Americans only want to ensure that people start out equal. However, "with the emergence of a huge . . . largely black, underclass, that belief is now impossible to sustain" (*Economist* March 15, 1986, 29).

A highly relevant factor in social mobility is social networks—in this case the individuals or groups who have job contacts—and minority-group members often suffer in this regard. A study of 4,078 employers indicated that black high-school graduates who used segregated networks averaged $5.69 per hour, those who did not use any networks averaged $5.74 per hour, and, in contrast, those who had access to integrated networks averaged $6.45 per hour (Braddock and McPartland 1987). The networks issue helps explain employment problems for minority groups at different levels, suggesting why poor minority-group members are likely to have access to no jobs at all while middle-class individuals, especially among African-Americans, tend to serve their own consumers and communities.

Poor families, like this homeless mother and children put up in a cheap motel at state expense, have very limited opportunities to break the vicious cycle of poverty and achieve a higher economic status.

Women also face special problems attaining upward mobility. One difficulty is the sex-typing of occupations. Traditionally people in occupations classified as "male" have considered women who tried to enter them as deviants and have placed obstacles in their paths. In the past couple of decades, women have managed to join many previously exclusive male professions, but in certain high-status positions, they are still nearly absent: for instance, architecture, surgery, engineering, commercial piloting, and top business management.

Another difficulty is the informal, sex-linked "old boy" network that prevails in most professions. Like women, men often form a subculture. They talk about sports, about women, and about other "masculine" topics at lunch or over drinks in situations that implicitly or explicitly exclude women. This exclusion can be a serious problem for women, because career advancement often emerges out of these informal contexts. For the few women who possess the social skills to function in these male-oriented situations, this informal colleague system can prove to be an asset for career advancement.

Another problem women encounter is an outgrowth of the "old boy" network. In many situations men's occupational advancement results from the sponsorship of an established professional. The younger man serves an apprenticeship in which he "learns the ropes." Established professionals are less likely to develop such relationships with women because they are often incapable of or unwilling to visualize women as their successors. Furthermore an apprentice relationship with a woman is likely to be awkward—to raise questions in people's minds about the possibility of a personal relationship between the two of them. Thus women frequently do not have the opportunity to participate effectively in male-dominated professional structures. The result of this exclusion is limited representation at the top levels (Farr 1988; Hagan 1990; Morrison and Von Glinow 1990).

CAUSES

If one starts with the assumption that a society has a closed social-class system, in which children inevitably fill the same occupations as their parents, one can suggest four types of social mobility that would alter that static condition.

First, there is circulation mobility. Some people are downwardly mobile, opening up positions for others moving up. Second, reproductive mobility can occur. As we noted earlier in the chapter, a relationship between social class and number of children exists—the higher the social class, the fewer the children. Before World War II, estimates indicated that professional men were not producing a sufficient number of sons to replace themselves—870 sons to every 1,000 professional fathers. Farmers, however, were averaging nearly double that number—1,520 sons to every 1,000 farmers. Estimates suggest that if fathers of all status levels, including professionals, had produced families of equal size, then the upward mobility of blue-collar sons would have decreased by 7 percent.

Third, immigration mobility can encourage upward mobility. If immigrants fill a large number of the unskilled labor jobs, then opportunities increase for native-born citizens to move up the status ladder. For example, at the turn of the century, a strong demand existed for workers in the mines and factories. During those years the arriving immigrants provided a major source of unskilled and semiskilled labor, allowing native-born citizens, including the sons of foreign-born parents, to move into skilled manual and white-collar positions.

Finally a significant factor affecting upward mobility is occupational or structural mobility—a type of upward social mobility that occurs because technological innovation or organizational change creates more new jobs at the middle or upper levels of the occupational structure than at the lower levels. For instance, from 1940 to 1970, professional and technical jobs for men increased 192 percent while jobs for farm laborers dropped by 75 percent (Gilbert and Kahl 1982, 170–74).

EFFECTS

Fifty million fans watch as the television coverage shifts to the locker room. The announcer moves through the crowd of players, coaches, and media personnel until he reaches the game's hero, whose hair and face are glistening with a combination of champagne and perspiration.

224

"How does it feel?" the announcer asks.

"I . . ." The player shakes his head. "I don't have the words to explain it. I've waited so long for this moment . . ."

Some semblance of this scene has occurred many times in American professional sport. The television camera catches the sporting hero at the moment of glory. Professional sport stars have been upwardly mobile—they have achieved wealth and prestige—and yet many have drug, alcohol, gambling, or other serious personal problems. Other upwardly mobile people do, too.

Sociologist Melvin Tumin (1957) has suggested that upward mobility can produce "diffusion of insecurity." The upwardly mobile have departed from their original social-class position and thus feel lost, no longer firmly grounded in a social-class tradition with its associated family, friends, and lifestyle. Other sociologists make a similar assessment (Ellis and Lane 1967; Sorokin 1927).

One study indicated that upwardly mobile people are more likely to show high levels of anxiety and psychosomatic illness than the socially stable whereas downwardly mobile individuals exceed the average on serious forms of psychotic illness (Kessin 1971). The last conclusion receives support from another investigation, where the major finding was that higher suicide rates occur among downwardly mobile men (Breed 1963). Some social conditions can offset such tendencies. An investigation of upwardly mobile African-American families has concluded that the family (generally with the mother serving as a full-time homemaker) has played a significant role in blunting the impact of stress in members' lives (McAdoo 1982).

In spite of the difficulties involved, a strong incentive exists for many Americans to improve their social-class position. Let us consider the current prospects for continuing upward mobility.

PROSPECTS FOR UPWARD MOBILITY

Many Americans apparently believe that opportunities still exist to enter the higher social classes. Studies conducted in Boston and Kansas City indicate that Americans feel that getting ahead depends on four things: parental encouragement, an effective education, ambition to get ahead, and plenty of hard work. In particular, when the respondents in these studies talked about upward mobility "the phrases they most freely applied in explaining how it happened were 'pure effort,' 'perseverance,' 'just plain hard work,' 'sheer work,' 'work, work, and more work,' and 'he wasn't ever afraid of working' (Coleman and Rainwater 1978, 240). In addition, recent research has revealed a specific attribute that seems to contribute to upward mobility: the ability to keep one's emotions under control in situations which could easily provoke anger or irritation. This quality makes people easier to work with and more socially acceptable than individuals without it (Snarey and Vaillant 1985).

Today if people are planning to move into the middle- or upper-middle class, they must be aware of the choices they are making. They must realize that in a slumping economy certain occupations offer prospects for affluence and others do not. People who have jobs in which salary advances have been running behind inflation include middle-level managers, secretaries and other office personnel, salespeople, retail clerks, college professors, public employees, construction laborers, and factory workers. Those who have stayed ahead include top-level managers, doctors, dentists, lawyers, and computer programmers. Because they lose their jobs or because they are looking for a position that is more appealing in some respect, about 10 million American workers change their occupation each year (Mergenhagen 1991).

In the past two decades, many people have not only found themselves entering occupations with receding incomes, but many others also discovered no work available. In the last decade, a third of male college graduates and two-thirds of female college graduates had to accept work outside their chosen field, often in jobs not requiring any college training.

Certain lifestyle choices are also likely to promote a middle-class affluence or to prevent it. The employment of wives can substantially increase family income. The decision to have one or two children instead of three or more children will mean significant savings, particularly in an era when the cost of food, clothing, higher education, and many other goods and services paid for by parents has been skyrocketing. Finally the avoidance of divorce can be a decisive factor affecting family affluence. The capacity to support or partially support two families is simply beyond the economic scope of most modern citizens (Maloney 1981).

Some Americans, including many college students, are in a situation that permits them to move from the working class into the middle class. For many Americans, however, upward mobility simply involves an escape from poverty or near poverty. For the 6.8 million families living below the poverty level, significant advance in their social position will probably not occur without some changes in federal policies.

Such changes would include a reallocation of federal spending to meet basic needs of the poor and near poor. Student loans or subsidies would seem particularly useful since educational opportunity could help people obtain jobs that would permit them to escape poverty.

In these closing paragraphs, we have been discussing practical steps to produce upward mobility for middle-class and lower-class people. But another line of thought, already anticipated by the brief discussion on the effects of social mobility, should also be mentioned.

Over the past two generations, the rate of depression, with symptoms of hopelessness, passivity, low self-esteem, and possible suicide, has risen about tenfold. Frequently those who experience depression are upwardly mobile and, by income, education, and prestige measures, successful or very successful.

What observations can the sociological perspective offer on this widespread problem? At the core of the problem seems to be the rootlessness of modern American society, where support and direction provided by local communities, religion, and the family frequently no longer are effective. Instead for many people work is expected to supply meaning and direction, but major deficiencies exist here. First, while occupational success is emphasized in American society, what actually constitutes it is often unclear. High income and the conspicuous display of expensive consumer goods serve as the only fixed indicators of success, but their effectiveness in convincing observers that individuals truly are successful is questionable. Generally people develop their own sense of what constitutes success, and then if they don't get the raise or promotion, the result is likely to be severe disappointment or depression. Second, when Americans become "career-oriented," the intrinsic worth of the job can become submerged in the quest for income, power, and prestige. Thus while individuals might become "successful," their sense of self-esteem can still diminish if the job has lost value to them (Bellah et al. 1986, 148–50; Seligman 1988).

In the past many Americans had more sources of support. They could go to church and hear that there was a power greater than themselves. Or, they could talk to members of their extended family or neighbors and receive friendly advice or encouragement. And while all of their doubts and concerns might not have been removed, a sense of belonging and self-enhancement could have been produced.

With few emotional ties to kin, friends, and community, many modern people expect to obtain similar profound emotional meaning from work, and when the work fails in this regard, they have no place else to turn. It seems that as we move toward the twenty-first century, one of the great challenges will be to develop social systems on the job and elsewhere that encompass both people's need for meaning in their work and the need for support and belonging.

STUDY GUIDE

Learning Objectives

After studying this chapter, you should be able to:

1. Define social stratification and consider its significance in modern life.
2. Discuss and evaluate the three theories of social stratification examined in the text—Marxist conflict, structural-functional, and Lenski's.

3. Identify and analyze the three dimensions of social stratification.
4. Define social class, identify and define the three principal ways of measuring social class, and list and briefly discuss the American social-class structure.
5. Describe the impact of social class on people's opportunities and lifestyle.
6. Define social mobility, distinguish between intergenerational and intragenerational mobility, and summarize current evidence on the social-mobility issue, including cases of limited access.
7. Identify and discuss four causes of social mobility, examine its effects, and discuss prospects for upward mobility.

Summary

1. Social stratification is structured inequality of access to rewards, resources, and privileges that are scarce and desirable within a society.

2. The Marxist conflict and structural-functional theories take very different approaches. The conflict theory of social stratification emphasizes the inequity of the rewards which are passed from one generation to the next. The structural-functional theory of stratification does not consider the advantages parents pass to their children, focusing instead on the supposed relationship between the importance of people's jobs and the rewards they receive. Both theories have received extensive criticism, and Gerhard Lenski's theory is an effort to use their respective strengths and avoid their weaknesses.

3. Three prominent dimensions of social stratification are wealth, power, and prestige. Wealth is people's economic assets that can be converted into money. Over time Americans have experienced an increase in absolute wealth, but relative wealth has remained fairly stable. The current tax system contributes to the sharp economic inequalities that persist in U.S. society.

Power is the ability of an individual or group to implement wishes or policies, with or without the cooperation of others. Authority is power that people generally recognize as rightfully maintained by those who use it. Sociologists have tended to use two approaches to examining authority: the pluralist and the power-elite perspectives.

Finally prestige is the possession of attributes that elicit recognition, respect, and some degree of deference. Survey research indicates that Americans show some consistency on ranking the prestige of a range of occupations.

4. A social class is a large number of people who are similar in income level, educational attainment, and occupational prestige-ranking. Sociologists have used a number of different approaches to measure social class. The members of different social classes vary in life expectancy, occurrence of mental illness, communication effectiveness, and self-esteem.

People from various social classes also differ in lifestyle. Fertility, approaches to childrearing, sexuality, and friendships and clubs are lifestyle activities that vary among the social classes.

5. The topic of social mobility, which is the movement of a person from one social class or social status to another, addresses the issue of the openness of the American social-class system. A comparison of two studies conducted in 1962 and 1973 suggests that the amount of social mobility varied little at those two times. Certain people—the poor, African-Americans, and women—have below-average opportunities for upward mobility.

Upward mobility occurs because of circulation mobility, reproductive mobility, immigration mobility, and occupational or structural mobility. The effects of social mobility include the "diffusion of insecurity," anxiety, psychosomatic illness, and high rates of suicide.

Upward mobility into the higher social classes is still possible, with the choice of profession and lifestyle serving as significant determinants. Changed governmental policies could help more people escape the poor or near-poor categories. In spite of the rewards upward mobility brings, serious psychological problems can accompany it.

Key Terms

absolute wealth the cash value of an individual's economic assets

authority power that people generally recognize as rightfully maintained by those who use it

bourgeoisie the class of modern capitalists who own the means of economic production and employ wage labor

class consciousness recognition by the members of a class of the role they play in the production process

income people's earnings obtained through wages, salaries, business profits, stock dividends, and other means

intergenerational mobility a comparison of a parent's and a child's social-class positions

intragenerational mobility an analysis of an individual's occupational changes in the course of a lifetime

objective definition of social class a measuring technique that uses certain quantifiable factors—income, occupational prestige rank, or level of education, for example—as the basis for determining an individual's social-class position

power the ability of an individual or group to implement wishes or policies, with or without the cooperation of others

prestige possession of attributes that elicit recognition, respect, and some degree of deference

proletariat the class of modern wage laborers who possess no means of production and thus must sell their own labor in order to survive

relative wealth the value of an individual's economic assets compared to the assets possessed by other citizens in that society

reputational definition of social class a measuring technique in which researchers use batteries of resident experts from the community to assess their neighbors' social-class position

social class a large category of people who are similar in income level, educational attainment, and occupational prestige-ranking

social mobility the movement of a person from one social class or status level to another

social stratification structured inequality of access to rewards, resources, and privileges that are scarce and desirable within a society

subjective definition of social class a measuring technique that requires people to indicate the social class to which they belong

vicious cycle of poverty a pattern in which the parents' minimal income significantly limits the educational and occupational pursuits of the children, thereby keeping them locked into the same economic status

wealth people's economic assets—their cars, homes, stocks, bonds, and real estate—which can be converted into cash

Tests

True • False Test

_____ 1. Marx believed that in the final stage of class consciousness, members of the proletariat would be able to use negotiations to resolve their differences with capitalists.

_____ 2. Evidence that many affluent people have neither special talents nor special training supports the structural-functional theory of social stratification.

_____ 3. Gerhard Lenski's theory of social stratification accepts some ideas from both the structural-functional and the Marxist conflict theories.

_____ 4. Relative income figures highlight the fact that over time the distribution of American income has changed little.

_____   5. Survey research indicated that Americans felt that the 1986 tax reform was progressive.
_____   6. Women and men differ in their subjective definitions of social class.
_____   7. A study of 228 employed men found a clear pattern—that respondents' occupational placement determined their self-esteem.
_____   8. Between 1900 and 1970 in Sicily, the higher couples' social-class position, the fewer children they generally produced.
_____   9. A recent study of respondents in four cultures found that if class placement is determined by authority, then interclass friendships are uncommon.
_____   10. Research done in sixteen countries has concluded that the patterns of intergenerational mobility are strikingly different.

Multiple-Choice Test

_____   1. Marx suggested that the members of the proletariat share class membership because of the following characteristic:
a.   They are disorganized.
b.   They are unaware of their class position.
c.   They are victims of the capitalist production process.
d.   They are profit-oriented.

_____   2. The theory of social stratification which emphasizes the need to fill jobs critical for the survival of society with highly qualified personnel was developed by:
a.   Marx.
b.   Davis and Moore.
c.   Steinmetz and Wright.
d.   Lenski.

_____   3. Lenski's theory of social stratification is different from the structural-functional and conflict theories in which respect?
a.   It is more scientific.
b.   It is less scientific.
c.   It emphasizes social mobility to a greater extent.
d.   It demonstrates less commitment to the existing stratification system.

_____   4. People's earnings obtained through wages, salaries, business profits, stock dividends, and other means are called:
a.   wealth.
b.   income.
c.   relative income.
d.   relative wealth.

_____   5. In C. Wright Mills's power-elite theory, the politically unorganized white-collar employees of corporations and government agencies belong to the social class known as:
a.   the power elite.
b.   the pluralist class.
c.   the proletariat.
d.   the middle class.

_____ 6. When researchers use community judges to assess their neighbors' social-class position, the approach is called:
   a.   the reputational definition of social class.
   b.   the subjective definition of social class.
   c.   the power definition of social class.
   d.   the objective definition of social class.

_____ 7. The higher one's social class, the better his or her chances are for:
   a.   mental illness.
   b.   a combination of interracial marriage and intergenerational mobility.
   c.   avoidance of both infant death and alcoholism.
   d.   religious satisfaction.

_____ 8. Which statement about the relationship between social class and sexuality is true?
   a.   The statement that "sex is a man's pleasure and a woman's duty" has become increasingly applicable to upper-middle-class marriages in the last decade.
   b.   Working-class wives tend to enjoy sex and easily achieve orgasm.
   c.   Working-class boys tend to begin their sexual lives earlier than middle-class boys.
   d.   a and b

_____ 9. For middle-class African-Americans:
   a.   integrated social networks have been readily available.
   b.   employment is concentrated in areas serving African-American consumers and communities.
   c.   the vicious cycle of poverty is often a reality.
   d.   a and c

_____ 10. The situation in which some people are downwardly mobile, encouraging upward mobility for others, is called:
   a.   occupational or structural mobility.
   b.   immigration mobility.
   c.   reproductive mobility.
   d.   circulation mobility.

Essay Test

1.   Define social stratification and discuss the general significance of social stratification in American society.
2.   Summarize and evaluate the three theories of social stratification discussed in this chapter.
3.   What are three major dimensions of social stratification? List and discuss them, focusing on recent evidence about each dimension.
4.   Define social class and discuss two issues citing social-class differences in opportunity and two issues indicating social-class differences in lifestyle, using studies and examples described in the chapter.
5.   What is social mobility? Discuss the causes and effects of social mobility as well as prospects for and problems of upward mobility in the years ahead.

Suggested Readings

Breiger, Ronald L. (ed.). 1990. *Social Moblity and Social Structure*. New York: Cambridge University Press. An effective, if somewhat technical introduction to current research and analysis of social mobility, presenting thirteen articles written by some of the leaders in the field.

230

De Vos, George A., and Marcelo Suarez-Orozco. 1990. *Status Inequality: The Self in Culture*. Newbury Park, CA: Sage. Analysis of the processes by which people adapt to minority statuses of class, caste, ethnicity, and gender.

Dreiser, Theodore. 1953. *An American Tragedy*. New York: Random House. Originally published in 1925. A gripping novel about a young man with aspirations to marry into the upper class. The sharp contrast between lower-middle-class and upper-class lifestyles appears throughout the book.

Gilbert, Dennis, and Joseph A. Kahl. 1987. *The American Class Structure: A New Synthesis*. 3rd ed. Homewood, IL: Dorsey Press. The newest edition of Kahl's leading sociological text on American social class first published over thirty-five years ago. The current edition is fairly comprehensive and easy to read.

Rubin, Lillian Breslow. 1976. *World of Pain: Life in the Working-Class Family*. New York: Basic Books. A study based on intensive interviews with fifty blue-collar couples and a comparison group of twenty-five upper-middle-class couples. Rubin concluded that norms that originated in the upper-middle class are filtering to working-class people and are producing huge strains in their marriages.

Sennett, Richard, and Jonathan Cobb. 1973. *Hidden Injuries of Class*. New York: Vintage Books. An account of the pain, disappointment, and lack of confidence associated with American working-class life. This book is based on competent sociological research, and yet its poignant, well-written material makes readers feel they are caught up in a novel.

Sidel, Ruth. 1990. *On Her Own: Growing Up in the Shadow of the American Dream*. New York: Penguin Books. A survey-based examination of the social context facing American women, who are misleadingly pressured by the mass media to accept that the right packaging will produce wealth, fame, and glory.

Warner, W. Lloyd, J. O. Low, Paul S. Lunt, and Leo Srole. 1963. *Yankee City*. New Haven, CT: Yale University Press. A single, slim volume presenting the principal conclusions of the historic, five-volume Yankee City study, the earliest analysis of the American class structure.

Additional Assignments

1. Interview a dozen people with varied social characteristics—age, sex, race, and occupation. Ask them the following questions:
    a. Is there a difference in the contributions to the welfare of society made by people in high-status or low-status jobs?
    b. What substantial differences, if any, exist between people who are successful economically and socially and those who are not?
    c. Does class consciousness exist in the United States? Should it?
    d. Is America the "land of opportunity"? Explain.
    From the answers to these questions and perhaps others you might wish to add, try to construct a simple theory, or perhaps several theories of social stratification. What are the similarities to and differences from theories examined in this chapter?

2. From the local chamber of commerce or some other source, obtain a street map of the city or town in which your college or university is located. Then choosing a sample of people who appear to be from varied social-class backgrounds, place them in the six social classes discussed in this chapter, basing the placement on information about occupation, education level, and income level obtained from interviewing a selected number of people on every block or in every neighborhood. For an interesting comparison, it would be instructive to also ask people's subjective view of their class membership. Then using different colors to designate different social classes, fill in the map. Did the two approaches to measuring social class produce similar or different results? Did some people refuse to answer all or some of the questions?

Answers to Objective Test Questions

True • False Test

1. f
2. f
3. t
4. t
5. f

6. t
7. f
8. t
9. f
10. f

Multiple-Choice Test

1. c
2. b
3. a
4. b
5. d

6. a
7. c
8. c
9. b
10. d

Racial and Ethnic Groups

9

Look," said Jim, turning to Mary and Jake with a quick apologetic smile right after they had toasted the evening. "I hope you don't mind mixing a little quick business with pleasure. Let me ask you something."

"Go ahead," said Mary.

"I just wondered whether you folks have any positions opening up."

"Things are pretty tight, but next month we'll probably have an opening in the mail room."

"Well, I've got a guy for you."

"He's 19, energetic, intelligent, and finished in the top quarter of his high-school class; he plans to go to college as soon as he can raise some money."

"Where's he live?" Jake asked.

"Over on Everett Street."

"That's a black area, isn't it?"

"Yeah, so what?"

"Look, Jim," Mary said, patting him on the wrist. "We're not prejudiced about race. It's just that Jake and I would rather not hire black workers."

"Why not?"

"It's just a feeling."

"Have you had any difficulty with them?"

"No, it's nothing I can exactly put my finger on," said Jake, shaking his head.

"I'd sum it up as a motivation problem," Mary added. "Many blacks simply aren't motivated enough."

Although this dialogue is fictional, it is based on fact. Analysis of recent national survey data shows that between 1977 and 1989, white Americans have generally indicated declining prejudice toward African-Americans, but there has been a fairly stable percentage of respondents who have stated that blacks' inferior jobs, income, and housing are wholly or in part due to individual failure, particularly insufficient motivation (Kluegel 1990). As the above exchange suggests, the next step is likely to involve opposition to an equal opportunity for African-Americans and perhaps also other minority-group members.

Throughout this chapter we see many references to the fact that minority status is harmful to individuals in many respects, that as a result of it people lose valued resources—power, wealth and income, and prestige and respect. If you are the member of a racial or ethnic group that has been badly treated, then you might have experienced the anger and frustration produced by discrimination in a country that professes to treat all its citizens equally. On the other hand, if you belong to the so-called dominant group, you also suffer the effects of American racial and ethnic problems. You are likely to feel confusion and fear—fear of talking seriously and honestly with members of certain groups, and fear of walking or even driving through their neighborhoods.

Anger, frustration, and fear are certainly emotions that traditionally have been part of the American racial and ethnic picture. However, people of different heritages can also frequently have positive relations, and colleges and universities are places for such contacts. In these settings students of different backgrounds can meet on essentially neutral grounds, where the fears and prejudices they might have grown up with are likely to be muted. On campuses and elsewhere in many American communities, different ethnic and racial groups sometimes sponsor festivals, fairs, plays, dances, and other activities that can help make the American public aware of their particular cultural experiences. Quite possibly more of those kinds of activities occur in your locale than you realize. Local mass media, both on campus and in the surrounding towns and cities, will reveal the events that different groups sponsor.

In this chapter we consider a number of important issues involving racial and ethnic groups. The next two sections concern basic concepts—first, an analysis of racial, ethnic, and minority groups and then the important processes of prejudice and discrimination. The third section is a discussion of the diverse array of behavioral patterns that can emerge when different racial and ethnic groups encounter each other. Finally a look at major American ethnic and racial groups is followed by a brief analysis of race and ethnic relations in the decades ahead.

Throughout these discussions remain aware that while incidents involving racial and ethnic prejudice are ugly realities involving individuals and small groups, our principal task is not to focus on those individuals or small groups. Instead we aim to analyze the social forces producing both disruptive and harmonious ethnic and racial relations in American society.

Racial, Ethnic, and Minority Groups ■

In Chapter 3, "Culture," we examined the linguistic-relativity hypothesis, which emphasizes that language influences people's perceptions and behavior. As far as the present topics are concerned, language allows people to place themselves and others in distinct categories that focus on differences considered significant.

RACIAL GROUP

The call reaches the patrol car from police headquarters. "Liquor store robbed at the corner of Hudson and Grove. The suspect is a . . ." Usually the next word is a reference to the person's race. Americans and the citizens of many other Western nations often use a person's race as a basic means of identification. Race and sex are the two most prominently used status characteristics for identification, but while people fall into either the male or female category, race does not divide as neatly.

Superficially a basis for classification of races seems to exist. Westerners designate three broad racial categories: Caucasoid, Mongoloid, and Negroid. The Caucasoids, who originally lived in western Europe, northern Africa, and western Asia, have light skin pigmentation, frequent male balding, prominent chins, and fairly long trunks. The Mongoloids, who first inhabited northern and eastern Asia, have brown to yellow skin, black hair, broad cheekbones, low nose bridges, and eye folds, which produce the sense of slanting eyes. Negroids, the first residents of Africa, have dark pigmentation, low-bridged noses, and kinky or curly hair.

This three-part classification scheme is well known, but many groups, including some large groups, do not fit easily into the categories. Specialists have developed nearly 200 categories to account for discrepancies like the following. The Australian aborigines have Negroid skin but straight hair and are sometimes classified as a fourth race. Among Native Americans, who are a subrace of Mongoloids, there are great differences in height and head shape. The tallest people in the world, the Watusi, and the shortest, the Pygmy, are both in the Negroid category and live within a few miles of each other.

Racial classifications are imprecise, and their practical significance seems modest. Admittedly certain biological adaptations have probably been useful. The original inhabitants of areas with high solar radiation appear to have received protection from their dark skin, and Negroids apparently have developed a much greater resistance to malaria forms than the Caucasoids and Mongoloids arriving later in Africa. But no evidence suggests that one racial group is more intelligent, more creative, more athletic, more ferocious, in fact "more anything" involving brain power, personality, or capability than other groups. Sometimes the behavior of different racial groups suggests otherwise, but that is because one group receives better opportunities than another. Human beings are simply a single species, with all members possessing the same skeletal structure, the same complex nervous system, the same intricate sensory organs, and the same intellectual capacity.

If the classification of races has limited usefulness, one must wonder why racial distinctions are

236 so important. In a sentence the answer is that race is significant because people consider it thus. No matter what its biological meaning, therefore, race has social significance. Sociologically **race** refers to distinct physical characteristics, such as skin color and certain facial features, used to divide people into broad categories. Thus a **racial group** is a number of people with the particular physical characteristics that produce placement into a broad category.

ETHNIC GROUP

An **ethnic group** is a category of people that is set apart by itself or others because of distinct cultural or national qualities. Ethnic groups differ on such issues as values, religion, ideas, food habits, family patterns, sexual behavior, beauty standards, political outlook, work orientation, and recreational behavior, and the culture of an ethnic group creates a sense of identity among the members. Outsiders recognize ethnic-group membership, and hostilities between different ethnic groups have been a major source of conflict in human history.

In U.S. society ethnicity is often synonymous with national group membership. Thus there are Chinese-Americans, Irish-Americans, Italian-Americans, Mexican-Americans, Polish-Americans, and other groups. Then there are linguistic groups that maintain their own cultural identity, such as the English-speaking Canadians and the French-speaking Canadians. Sometimes religious groups develop as ethnic groups—for instance, the Amish and Hutterite religious communities in the United States.

In many situations ethnic and racial groups have minority-group status, which is analyzed in the upcoming discussion.

MINORITY GROUP

A **minority group** is any category of people with some recognizable trait that places it in a position of inferior status so that its members suffer limited opportunities and rewards. Racial and ethnic traits are prominent characteristics for determining minority-group membership, but as we see in Chapter 10, sex, age, and disability are other traits that can be used to establish minority-group status. The members of a minority group are inevitably aware of the unequal treatment they all share, and this awareness helps create a sense of belonging to the group. It is important to understand that minority status has no intrinsic relationship to group size. Sometimes a minority group is hundreds of times larger than the dominant group in the society. Such a situation existed when the European countries established colonies in Africa, Asia, and the Americas. In other cases—African-Americans in the United States, for instance—the minority group is smaller in numbers than the dominant group. Minority status is the result of a subordinate position in society, not the size of its membership.

All the racial and ethnic categories discussed in this chapter are minority groups. What are the processes that create minority status? The following section offers a response to this question.

Prejudice and Discrimination: Producing Inequality ■

"All people are created equal." As infants all human beings generally behave in accord with this principle. Yet in the course of socialization, many Americans learn to accept the belief that some groups are superior to others and, as a result, should obtain a greater share of society's political, economic, and social rewards. They accept both prejudice and discrimination.

Prejudice is a highly negative judgment toward a group, focusing on one or more negative characteristics that are supposedly uniformly shared by all group members. If a person rigidly believes that all members of a racial or ethnic group are innately lazy, stupid, stubborn, and violent, then that person is prejudiced toward the group in question. Racial, ethnic, and religious prejudice are the most prominently discussed types; in general, prejudice is not easily reversible.

Perhaps nothing so clearly demonstrates institutional racism as many public-education systems in which affluent, primarily white children generally attend better financed, more effective schools than those available for poor, primarily minority children.

The fact that prejudice is not easily reversible distinguishes it from a "misconception," in which someone supports an incorrect conclusion about a group but is willing, when confronted with facts, to change his or her opinion. The companion concept to prejudice is discrimination, which is the behavioral manifestation of prejudice. **Discrimination** is the behavior by which one group prevents or restricts another group's access to scarce resources.

Prejudice and discrimination are often a one-two punch: The behavior directly follows the judgment. The two situations do not always appear together, however. Discrimination sometimes takes place without prejudice. In the 1950s in Little Rock, Arkansas, many white ministers were not prejudiced toward black people (they wanted integrated congregations), but they continued to support discrimination against African-Americans. The ministers realized that a movement to integrate would have meant the disaffection of many affluent, white members who provided the major economic support for the churches (Campbell and Pettigrew 1959). In other situations prejudice fails to evoke discrimination. From 1930 to 1932, a white social scientist traveled throughout the United States with a Chinese couple. They received courteous treatment at hotels, motels, and restaurants, and yet 90 percent of questionnaire re-

sponses sent to the establishments visited made it clear that Chinese would be unwelcome (LaPierce 1934). The study does contain some problems—for instance, there is no assurance that the person answering the survey was the one who had served the researcher and the Chinese couple—and yet similar findings appear in later research (Kutner, Wilkins, and Yarrow 1952). Thus in some situations, prejudice and discrimination do not occur in tandem.

It is possible to analyze prejudice as an ideology. An **ideology** is a system of beliefs and principles that presents an organized explanation of the justification for a group's outlooks and behavior. **Racism** is the ideology contending that actual or alleged differences between different racial groups assert the superiority of one racial group. Racism is a rationalization for political, economic, and social discrimination. Thirty-six percent of a sample of African-Americans indicated that at some point they had been the victims of racism when seeking education, a job, a promotion, or housing (Gallup and Newport 1991).

Two types of racism are individual racism and institutional racism. Whether practiced by one person or a group, **individual racism** is an action performed by one person or a group that produces racial abuse—for example, verbal or physical mistreatment. **Institutional racism** involves

238

discriminatory racial practices built into such prominent structures as the political, economic, and education systems. The idea of institutional racism is distinctly sociological, emphasizing that social structures establish norms guiding people's behavior. By accepting the norms maintained in racist structures, individuals invariably perpetuate discriminatory conditions. Institutional racism is the prime factor maintaining racism.

For most whites and some minority-group members, institutional racism is a difficult concept to grasp because they have not consciously observed it. They do not realize that within many structures of American society, institutional racism is widespread. Consider inner-city schools with students who tend to belong to racial minorities. As in most public-school districts, a significant portion of funding comes from local tax money—a funding source which is severely diminished if the local area is poor. In such minority-dominated school districts, the feeling readily develops among various groups associated with the schools—administrators, teachers, parents, and the students themselves—that everyone is simply going through the motions of education. A writer summarizing the feelings of a mother sending her children to an inner-city school with 98 percent African-Americans students observed that the woman felt that such schools "were hardly schools at all . . . more like warehouses where kids were stored for a few years, sorted, labeled, and packed for shipment to the menial, low-paying jobs at which they would be doomed to labor the rest of their lives" (Lukas 1985, 104). Discrimination, in short, was produced by structures, not individuals' prejudices.

When the members of one group have a racist outlook toward the members of a minority group, they develop stereotypes of those individuals. A **stereotype** is an exaggerated, oversimplified image, maintained by prejudiced people, of the characteristics of the group members against whom they are prejudiced. A well-known study of stereotypes discovered that respondents considered African-Americans superstitious, lazy, happy-go-lucky, ignorant, and musical while Jews were designated shrewd, industrious, grasping, mercenary, intelligent, and ambitious (Katz and Braly 1933).

Stereotypes often prove useful to those who maintain them. Their oversimplified conclusions offer a more orderly, straightforward analysis of a minority group than a nonstereotyped evaluation would provide. Furthermore stereotypes help to either confirm that a downtrodden group should remain in its lowly position or encourage members of the dominant group to push down minority-group individuals who are starting to achieve some economic and political success (Simpson and Yinger 1985, 100–01).

One of the disturbing qualities of stereotypes is their self-fulfilling nature. A **self-fulfilling prophecy** is an incorrect definition of a situation that comes to pass because people accept the incorrect definition and act on it to make it become true. For instance, if white teachers believe that black children are lazy, happy-go-lucky, and ignorant, then they are unlikely to make a sincere effort to help them learn. The students, in turn, will recognize the teachers' disinterest or contempt and will probably exert little effort in school. The teachers see "confirmation" of what they already "know"—that their African-American students are inferior. In reality what the teachers confirm is the definition of the self-fulfilling prophecy.

With these concepts in mind, we can examine a number of explanations for prejudice, discrimination, and racism.

SOURCES

The old man nodded and smiled as she walked by, pushing the baby carriage. Her impulse was to hurry past the bench—he was unshaven, his clothes were threadbare, and the near-empty bottle leaning against his knee was no testimony to his sobriety—but she slowed down as he looked at the baby. And when he said, "Could I see her, ma'am?" she immediately pulled back the blanket. The old man's face relaxed and softened. "She's a beauty, ma'am, just a plain beauty! Look at her, laying there, peaceful and innocent. And she don't hate nobody. Black, white—it's all the same to her."

Like the old man, we make the assumption that prejudice and discrimination are learned forms of behavior. Social, economic, and psychological explanations all contribute to an understanding of the development of prejudice and discrimination. In each area it becomes apparent that the victims lose at least one significant scarce resource.

Social Explanations

Language is a significant component of culture. Without the words "black," "white," "yellow," and "red," Americans would be unable to distinguish skin-color differences. Furthermore the words associated with "black" and "white" are often highly tinged with emotion. *Roget's Thesaurus* has about 120 synonyms for "blackness," most of which are negative—for instance, blot, blight, smut, evil, wickedness, and malignance. The 134 synonyms for whiteness have primarily favorable connotations. The list includes brightness, innocence, honor, purity, fairness, and trust. Without language people would also not be able to produce such unflattering racial and ethnic designations as "frog," "honky," "kike," "kraut," "nigger," "slope," and "spic" or phrases like "lazy as a nigger" or "jew him down." Words also permit the development of stereotypes.

Countless jokes about blacks, Jews, and other minority groups elaborate these stereotypes. "What harm can a little joke be?" an observer might ask. "They're just meant to be funny, not to hurt anyone." The problem is that jokes directed at minority groups do emphasize the negative, distorted image represented by the stereotype. As a result people hearing the joke will perhaps more readily accept that members of the target group are "that way." Furthermore while members of the dominant culture might see such humor as harmless, minority-group members are likely to be infuriated and offended. Recent research has suggested that such offensive use of humor continues to be widespread (Johnson 1990).

The use of stereotypes demonstrates the existence of **social distance**: the feeling of separation between individuals or groups. In the 1920s psychologist Emory Bogardus developed a scale to measure social distance. The scale has become so widely known that social scientists simple call it "the Bogardus scale." The scale asks people to indicate their willingness to interact with various racial and ethnic groups in certain social situations, which represent seven degrees of social distance. The seven items involve an increasing social distance as one moves down the list. Respondents must indicate whether they will accept members of the particular group:

> To close kinship by marriage.
> As a regular friend.
> To the street as a neighbor.
> To employment in one's occupation.
> To citizenship in one's country.
> As a visitor only to one's country.
> Would exclude from one's country.

Over a forty-year period (from 1926 to 1966), research in the United States showed that white Americans and northern Europeans scored in the top third of the hierarchy, eastern and southern Europeans in the middle, and Asian minorities in the bottom third. The rankings stayed consistent over the forty-year period, and not just for whites. When Jewish-, Asian-, and African-Americans took the test, their results were similar to white Americans, with one exception—in each case their own group was placed at the top (Bogardus 1968).

One might consider the degrees of social distance a cluster of implicit norms. If you don't recall this concept, turn to Chapter 3. Like many norms, standards involving social distance can change over time. A case in point would be interracial marriage, which is represented in Figure 9.1. Survey data from 1991 indicated for the first time that a larger percentage of Americans approve of than disapprove of interracial marriage (Gallup and Newport 1991).

A number of social scientists have suggested that the dominant group within American society treats minority groups much as colonial nations have treated the inhabitants of their colonies, thus establishing a form of internal colonialism. These sociologists fall within the conflict-theory camp, emphasizing a power struggle for scarce resources in the political, economic, and social arenas between the dominant group and exploited minorities. While the colonial model fails in certain regards, some similarities in cultural and structural patterns between colonial contexts and race relations in American society exist. The similarities include residential segregation, cultural stereotyping of minority-group members, incorporation of minority-group individuals into the power structure to smoothe the way for control of the minority group, and the widespread exploitation of minority-group members in employment

Figure 9.1

Approval of Interracial Marriage over Time

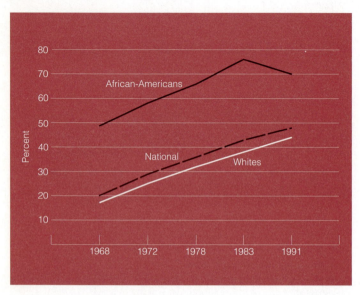

This figure shows two distinct trends: first, that over time the general trend has been greater approval of interracial marriage, and second, that African-Americans have consistently been above the national standard for approval while whites have remained below that standard.

Source: Gallup Poll Monthly. (April 1991), p. 6.

and level of material life (Feagin 1989, 37–38). Let us discuss this last point at greater length.

Economic Explanations

"Big bucks" in prejudice and discrimination? The immediate reaction might be to laugh at that idea, but a short reflection should produce a different response. In the United States and in other countries, slavery developed because it was the cheapest form of labor. A study of American history shows that a strong economic incentive for the practice existed. The northern states received little or no economic benefit from slavery, and they outlawed it soon after the Revolutionary War. Even in the South, slavery lost its popularity in the late 1700s, and many people saw it as a "necessary evil." By 1835, however, cotton had become the primary commodity of American foreign trade. At this point most white Southerners did not consider slavery a necessary evil but as a positive good that served as the foundation of a stable society and a prosperous economy (Lacy 1972).

In some cases the economic factor is present but not readily apparent. In 1942 during World War II, the American government ordered the evacuation of 110,000 Japanese from the West Coast on the pretext that they were potential collaborators with the Japanese government. A major impetus behind the relocation was an organized effort by newspaper leaders, congressmen, and wealthy farmers to convince President Roosevelt of the necessity to undertake the endeavor. For the wealthy farmers, this was an unprecedented opportunity to divert less affluent white farmers' attention from their own unpopular domination of agriculture and to redirect the small white farmers' hostilities toward the Japanese. Other economic advantages were less subtle. At the time of the relocation, Japanese had to sell homes, farms, businesses, and personal possessions at a fraction of their real value. The official government estimate is that Japanese-Americans lost more than $400 million (in 1940, pre-inflated dollars) (Berry and Tischler 1978, 370–71). To compensate these Japanese-American victims of discrimination, in 1988 Congress appropriated $1.3 billion in funds to the approximately 60,000 survivors of the relocation centers—updated in 1992 to $1.6 billion for 78,500 persons. Descendants of those who died after the legislation was passed were declared ineligible. One provision in the bill stated, "On behalf of the nation, the congress apologizes" (*Congressional Quarterly* 1992, 882; Willen 1988, 1081).

Psychological Explanations

A number of psychological perspectives exist. One approach suggests that the acquisition of prejudice and discrimination is a three-stage process that occurs to children in the course of socialization. A girl of 6 runs home to her mother and says, "Mother, what is the name of the children I am supposed to hate?" This child is at the "first stage" in learning prejudice. She has not yet associated prejudicial attributes with the culturally supported target group. In fact, a study concluded that until children reach the age of 8, they do not have a clear, stable sense of people's ethnicity. The "second stage" in learning prejudice occurs when children connect prejudice with the culturally supported target group. In a social context in which racial or ethnic prejudice exists, children in

In the course of socialization, members of different races can learn to hate and fear each other. The modern resurgence of the Ku Klux Klan, an organization with a violent, anti-black tradition, indicates how destructive this process can be.

the first and second grade often intermingle, but by the fifth grade they are usually more exclusive, choosing to stay with members of their own group. The "third stage" involves the ability to practice prejudice and discrimination subtly. In high school young people are able to express polite acceptance and tolerance toward members of other racial and ethnic groups, while often rejecting those who are not members of their own group. This approach stands in sharp contrast to 8-year-olds who have learned the prejudicial categories and speak as if they completely reject people in different racial or ethnic groups, but often behave in a nondiscriminatory manner (Aboud 1984; Allport 1954, 307–11).

An alternative psychological approach is the **scapegoat theory.** This explanation emphasizes that people blocked from achieving a goal will sometimes be unable or unwilling to take out their frustration on its source, and so they direct their aggression against an accessible individual or group. The displacement of the hostility from the real source of frustration to the scapegoat permits a release of tension called catharsis.

Three conditions make it likely that a racial or ethnic group will become a scapegoat. First, the group must be easy to identify, whether it be a skin color, a tattoo, or some insignia such as the Star of David, which the Nazis forced Jews to wear during World War II. Second, the ethnic group must be powerless enough so that it is unlikely to retaliate. Finally, in order to qualify as a scapegoat, a group must be accessible (Simpson and Yinger 1985, 73–76). The use of the concept continues in current research and analysis (Jeter 1990).

In a pre–World War II experiment that tested the scapegoat theory, all three conditions existed. The subjects were white boys attending a summer camp. The first step was to give them a pretest assessing their prejudice toward Japanese-Americans and Mexican-Americans. Then the boys received a tedious paper-and-pencil test that lasted long enough to make them miss the weekly opportunity to go to town and see a movie. Finally the subjects were given a post-test to measure prejudice toward the two minority groups. This time the rate of prejudice increased significantly (Dollard et al. 1939, 43–44). The results support the scapegoat hypothesis, which contends that people (in this case white boys) are inclined to direct their hostility toward visible, vulnerable, and accessible minority groups (here Japanese- and Mexican-Americans) when the true source of their frustration (in this situation the adults administering the test) is too powerful to attack.

The economic factor encourages prejudice and discrimination, but the factor does not act alone. A person must have personal inclinations supporting these tendencies and must also receive cultural backing. Table 9.1 summarizes explanations of prejudice and discrimination.

EFFECTS

A man named Eldridge Cleaver was in prison, and like many other prisoners put a pinup girl—from the center of E*squire* magazine—on the wall of his cell. But one evening when Cleaver returned to his cell, he was shocked and enraged to find his pinup torn into little pieces and floating in the toilet. Cleaver said that "it was like seeing a dead body floating in a lake."

The next day he asked the guard why he had done it. There were rules against pinups, the guard said. Cleaver would not accept that reply. The rule was never enforced, he pointed out. The guard smiled, immediately making Cleaver wary. He would compromise, the guard said. If Cleaver would get himself a black pinup, he would let it stay.

Cleaver was embarrassed. He called the guard two or three dirty names and walked away. But he was disturbed by what the guard had revealed. Without realizing it, he, a black man, had chosen a picture of a white woman over the available pictures of black women. Was it true? Did he really prefer white to black women? The conclusion was inescapable. He did (Cleaver 1970, 20–21).

Putting aside for the moment the serious sexism, we can link Cleaver's reaction to a widespread belief: that the members of minority groups tend to denigrate themselves and value majority-group status more highly.

Let us consider a large study that tested the issue of self-esteem with a random sample of 2,625 Baltimore school children. Sociologists Morris Rosenberg and Roberta Simmons (1971) concluded that black children do not have lower self-esteem than white children. In fact, 46 percent of the black children interviewed had high self-esteem compared with 33 percent of the whites.

The researchers uncovered certain factors that affected black children's self-esteem. Blacks who did well in school and who came from higher social-class backgrounds tended to have high self-esteem. Black children who attended integrated schools were more likely to have low self-esteem. It seemed that these black children had many opportunities to compare themselves with high-achieving white children. Apparently integrated schools can improve black students' academic achievement and provide interracial friendships, but do not raise their self-esteem.

Table 9.1   Explanations of Prejudice and Discrimination

Approach	Central idea	Illustrations
Social explanations	That different components of culture—language, values, and beliefs—contribute to the development of prejudice and discrimination	The concepts "stereotype" and "social distance"
Economic explanations	That the existence of prejudice and discrimination are economically beneficial for the dominant group	The American slavery system or the relocation of Japanese-Americans during World War II
Psychological explanations	That prejudice and discrimination derive from individuals' socialization or frustrations felt toward a strong, inaccessible group	Three-stage process of prejudice development or the scapegoat theory

Backed by other recent research, the Baltimore study makes it clear that black children do not usually hate themselves, idolize whites, and maintain low self-esteem. Further research on this topic, not only with African-Americans but also with other racial and ethnic groups, needs to consider the cautions previously indicated—in particular, the likelihood that such factors as social class, school performance, and the racial, ethnic, and class statuses of classmates have a significant effect on children's self-esteem, perhaps a more significant effect than their own race or ethnicity.

At the same time, it would be misleading to conclude that prejudice and discrimination do not produce negative effects upon people. A study using national survey data gathered between 1972 and 1985 found that when blacks and whites of similar socioeconomic background, age, and marital status were compared, blacks indicated lower life satisfaction, less trust in people, less general happiness, less marital happiness, and lower self-evaluated health (Thomas and Hughes 1986). On the last point, a recent investigation found self-reported higher blood pressure among black women who experienced incidents of either race- or sex-related discrimination in health care than among black women who did not suffer such maltreatment (Krieger 1990). It seems clear that being black in American society does adversely affect one's outlook on life.

In addition, because of the structural disadvantages they have encountered, minority groups experience major deficiencies in the eduational, occupational, and income areas. The section on American minority groups provides detailed information on these topics.

Majority and Minority Behavior Patterns

Some evidence suggests that over time Americans have become less inclined to support prejudice and discrimination. Consider the following two situations. In 1906 Mark Twain attended a banquet where a speaker received thunderous applause when he fervently told his audience of lawyers, bankers, and other middle-class professionals, "We are of the Anglo-Saxon race, and when the Anglo-Saxon wants a thing *he just takes it*," (Twain 1973, 3). These respectable American citizens showed no inclination to support the rights of anyone besides their fellow Anglo-Saxons. Yet less than sixty years later in the fall of 1963, several hundred thousand black and white Americans marched in Washington, D.C., on behalf of full civil rights for all Americans. Neither of these events was out of character with its time. Both were consistent with the dominant group's racial policies during the respective eras.

As we examine six dominant-group policies involving racial and ethnic relations, it should be kept in mind that each policy is also the product of its era. The same point emphatically applies to the various responses to minority-group status, which we also discuss.

DOMINANT-GROUP POLICIES

Dominant-group policies determine minorities' access to the highly valued resources offered by a society. The first three dominant-group patterns tend to maintain or increase social distance while the last three tend to decrease it (Simpson and Yinger 1985, 15–21).

1. **Extermination.** The most extreme pattern is the elimination of the minority group. In the nineteenth century, the British decimated the Tasmanians, and the Dutch South Africans exterminated the Hottentots. In the effort to establish a "master race," the Nazis murdered six million Jews and thousands of Romany people, known as Gypsies. People of European heritage wiped out most of the native people of Hawaii and the continental United States.

2. **Continued subjugation.** Short of destroying a people, members of the dominant group can hold them under complete control. In the United States, slavery was the outstanding example of

244

this policy. The European colonial powers in Africa and Asia successfully maintained such an intergroup pattern in some countries until after World War II. Recently in Great Britain, France, Germany, and other European countries, concern for job scarcity coupled with rising levels of nationalism and racism have supported discriminatory, sometimes brutal treatment of racial minorities. In Great Britain, for example, racism against people of African, Afro-Caribbean, and Asian descent is practiced on every social dimension, including health, housing, education, employment, and social services (Allen and Macey 1990). As the upcoming Cross-Cultural Perspective indicates, white South Africans have maintained a policy of subjugation that has only recently begun to loosen its grip.

3. **Population transfer.**   Sometimes the leaders of the dominant group decide that the more desirable solution is the movement of an ethnic group from one locale to another. In some cases leaders force the minority members to leave the country. Idi Amin, the former president of Uganda, compelled all Asians to emigrate, even though most of them were natives of the country. American authorities have also resorted to population transfers, forcing Native Americans to move to reservations. In the 1830s government officials ordered the Cherokee tribe to travel the thousand-mile "Trail of Tears" from the deep South to Oklahoma. Disease, starvation, and winter cold killed thousands along the way. A recent illustration of population transfer has occurred in Bosnia, where Serbs have been implementing a policy they call "ethnic cleansing"—establishing purely Serbian areas by forcing about 1.2 million Muslims to leave their villages and often the country (Engelberg 1992).

4. **Legal protection of minorities.**   In some instances government officials recognize that to ensure the rights of minorities, they must pass special legislation. The Civil Rights Act of 1964 has been the most significant American legislative effort to eliminate discrimination. The act covers employment practices of all businesses with more than twenty-five employees, access to all public accommodations such as hotels, motels, and restaurants, and the use of such federally supported organizations as colleges and hospitals. The Civil Rights Act of 1964 also includes voting, but other legislation focuses on this issue. The Voting Rights Act of 1965 suspended the various qualifying tests for voter registration that many southern states used, and this act has also authorized federal examiners to enter these states and register black voters. As a result of these actions, the opportunity for the registration of black voters greatly increased.

5. **Cultural pluralism.**   The policy of cultural pluralism emphasizes the existence of ethnic groups living peacefully but separately from one another. Switzerland, for example, has four separate ethnic areas, each with its own language—French, German, Italian, and Romansh. In U.S. society many Americans have retained a strong sense of ethnic identity, and successful politicians often find it necessary to acknowledge and support ethnic interests. Since the 1960s African-Americans and other minority groups have frequently emphasized their racial or ethnic affiliation in the pursuit of political or economic goals that will benefit their particular group.

6. **Assimilation.**   The use of assimilation assumes that the most productive course of action is to eliminate separate ethnic interests and develop a common identity. Assimilation can occur on a cultural level, on a racial level, or both. Brazil is a country that has been widely acclaimed for its assimilationist policies, including substantial interracial marriage; recent research, however, has been instructive about such an undocumented claim, indicating that Brazilian racial minorities encounter substantial educational and occupational discrimination (Webster and Dwyer 1988). In the United States,

assimilation among people of northern European ancestry has been extensive. In general, though, Americans marry within the same broad religious and racial categories. The early twentieth-century concept of the melting pot, in which ethnic identities would disappear through complete assimilation, has not come to pass, not even to the originally proposed extent of eliminating all ethnicities of European origin.

Thus majority groups have established a number of different policies toward minority groups. Extermination, continued subjugation, and population transfer tend to maintain or increase social distance while the legal protection of minorities, cultural pluralism, and assimilation tend to decrease it. The sociological perspective emphasizes that the policies established by majority groups are a significant social force influencing the responses of minority groups.

MINORITY RESPONSES

Starting with the southern civil-rights activities in the late 1950s, African-Americans and eventually other ethnic groups began engaging in a range of protest activities in order to combat the discrimination and limited access to valued resources faced by their respective groups. Some Americans were frightened and surprised by this particular response to prejudice and discrimination. They were familiar with avoidance, acceptance, and assimilation—the other three responses—but now there was also aggression (Vander Zanden 1972).

Avoidance

For some individuals one possible minority response is avoidance—departing from one's minority group and becoming a member of the majority group. For many people avoidance is impossible. People have skin color or other physical characteristics that make their ethnic or racial status undeniable. In other cases an accent in speech or extensive involvement in the local community would make avoidance difficult. But many others have the opportunity to engage in avoid-

ance. A study shows that during the 1920s in Washington, D.C., many light-skinned African-Americans chose to "pass." Former associates took pains not to betray the people who slipped into white society, and if those who remained were envious, they did not reveal it. In those years so many people attempted to pass that the National Theatre hired a black doorman to locate and bounce passers whom whites could not detect (Green 1967, 207–08). When Martin Luther King, Jr., was a graduate student at Boston University, he was keenly interested in the activities of an African-American student who was passing as white. Many times King and his friend watched the young black woman with her white friends, always remaining careful to keep their distance and to avoid the risk of exposing her deception (Branch 1988, 94).

Little research on passing exists, but some issues that studies could address come to mind. Does guilt often accompany the act? Certainly the possibility exists. People who deny their ethnic or racial status are cutting themselves off from family, friends, and heritage. And what about the fear of discovery—the nagging thought that a former associate would inadvertently or perhaps even purposefully reveal the passer's identity?

For people who accept their ethnic status, these problems do not develop.

Acceptance

The majority of people in a minority ethnic or racial category generally accept their status. The acceptance, however, does not mean that their self-esteem must suffer. Acceptors can take a number of productive steps to boost their self-esteem and pride. First, they can base their self-evaluations on comparisons with members of their own group, instead of the more advantageously situated majority-group members. Second, they can use traditional structures—family, neighborhood, and friends—to provide mutual support and self-enhancement. Finally those who accept their racial or ethnic status can establish special organizations, such as ethnic professional groups, study programs, or city-sponsored awareness projects, to nurture ethnic and racial pride through the use of available mass media (Bahr, Chadwick, and Stauss 1979, 329–36).

As with other racial and ethnic groups, many members of the Puerto Rican community who accept their minority status have done so with great pride and self-respect, resisting pressures to assimilate themselves completely into the dominatnt culture.

Several decades ago American cultural standards compelled African-Americans to accept "second-class citizenship." Writing in the 1930s, a researcher described a black man who had lived his entire life in the South, where blacks faced a highly restrictive lifestyle. Once the man and his wife took a trip to the North. The experience was unsettling. The man was surprised to see only one entrance to the railroad station instead of two, and he was almost dumbfounded to sit with a white family at the dinner table, to sleep in their guest room, and to drive around and meet their friends. The black man said "that it felt like 'being treated as a man'" (Dollard 1937, 266).

After a lifetime of accepting a highly restricted minority status, this man found it difficult to adjust to a social situation in which assimilation had occurred.

Assimilation into the Majority

Minority-group members are pursuing assimilation when they attempt to eliminate their minority status and become socially and culturally unified with the dominant group.

Dominant-group policies play a significant part in determining the extent to which assimilation is possible. In American society European immigrants have been able to pursue this course of action successfully. Racial minorities, most notably African-Americans, have encountered severe difficulties.

African-American executives serve as an illustration. Like all executives they experience pressures, but in addition many feel they must face a special kind of stress—the effects of American racism. After interviewing many black executives, one writer noted that while they had encountered racism growing up,

> the strains of working in a white-dominated structure and the evidence of corporate racism, cloaked by a subtly worded memo or a promotion that never comes, are new and strangely disturbing. In a recent survey by *Black Enterprise* magazine on work, nearly 75 percent of those earning more than $35,000 a year reported discrimination on their jobs. The perception of many blacks is that whites-only signs still hang on the higher rungs of the corporate ladder.

(*Campbell* 1982, 37)

Outside of work the situation can be equally stressful. In interracial social situations, blacks often feel that they are being tested, with many whites inevitably considering them representatives of their entire race and grilling them on a variety of racial issues. When faced with this situation, an individual can use different strategies. One psychiatrist suggested, "Define the situation; devise a way of getting out of it very quickly. Develop some humorous responses or brush off the question and take charge by steering the conversation in another direction" (Williams 1988, A15).

Historically situations that made African-Americans and other minority groups feel that assimilation was impossible have sometimes encouraged aggressive responses.

Aggression

What constitutes minority-group aggression varies sharply across time and space, sometimes appearing only in the distorted perception of

CROSS-CULTURAL PERSPECTIVE
South Africa and Its *Apartheid* Policy

The Republic of South Africa is a multinational state with four racial groups. In 1990 the population was 27.7 million people, with black Africans representing 71.5 percent, whites 16.2 percent, Coloreds (mixed black and white) 9.4 percent, and Indians 2.9 percent.

Since it achieved independence in 1948, South Africa has maintained a pattern of subjugation for all racial minorities. This policy poses a serious threat to the future stability of the country.

The British acquired South Africa in 1795 and controlled it until 1948, introducing Indians as sugar plantation workers and freeing blacks who had been the slaves of Dutch farmers, known as Boers. The blacks also received most political and civil rights. The Boers were unhappy with these developments, and throughout the nineteenth century, there were violent confrontations with the increasing number of British colonists. The culmination was the Boer War, which the British won with the help of the blacks. Once in power, however, the British felt that the blacks' greater numbers posed a significant threat, and so the white leadership imposed limitations—for instance, property qualifications for voting were established and blacks' geographical movement was restricted.

In 1948 South Africa received its independence, and the Nationalist Party assumed governmental control. Afrikaners, the Boers' descendants, have dominated the Nationalist Party, and under their leadership white supremacy, which existed during the colonial period, has become more and more formalized by law. Most significantly the whites established a policy of *apartheid* to ensure their domination. In Afrikaans, the Afrikaners' language, *apartheid* means "separation" or "apartness"—a policy of compulsory segregation. Historically blacks have been forced to live in rural homelands, where few opportunities for a decent living exist. The blacks and other racial minorities who find work in the cities, where opportunities for jobs are better, are forced to live in crowded townships located well outside of city limits. While in the cities, minority-group members have been compelled to use various separate facilities, including restaurants, taxis, restrooms, and staircases.

On March 17, 1992, there occurred a development that few if any observers of the country would have predicted even a year earlier. In a national referendum of whites, two-thirds of the voters supported the official end of *apartheid*. While goodwill toward minority-group members played some part, other influences included concern about three issues—revived economic sanctions imposed by the United States and European countries; a freeze on international sports participation; and continuing, even increased black rebellions.

While a vote to end *apartheid* was an important step, its significance must be carefully analyzed. In the months following the referendum, talks between top black and white leaders frequently stalled. A major point of contention was that while black leaders argued for a policy of simple majority rule, where their greater numbers would ensure political dominance, the whites wanted to hammer out a bargain guaranteeing them a certain amount of power, in spite of their small numbers.

Another issue has been the continuing violence in the country. Between February 1990 and May 1992 as the dismantling of *apartheid* proceeded rapidly, about 6,000 Africans were killed. As Israel Skosana, an African business executive, said, "Many of us will not live to see the new South Africa" (Gordon and Merkling 1992, 658). Evidence has been mounting that the police and military have played a major role in that violence, manipulating clashes between major black organizations, particularly by providing political and military training to the Inkatha Freedom Party in its struggle for power against the African National Congress. If *apartheid* is truly going to be dismantled, then the police and military must play a critical role in establishing and maintaining civil order rather than creating disorder.

248

Finally, while *apartheid* is now seriously challenged, its legacy will not readily disappear. About a decade ago, a section of the city of Durban, which had been a prime residential area located near the ocean and had been largely populated by Indians, was taken over by whites, who used the laws of *apartheid* to force the Indians out. An irate Indian leader said, "They don't need their laws anymore! They've done it! Whoever comes into power will not be able to change *this*" (Lelyveld 1985, 26-27). A. J. Christopher's recent study of racial minorities' residential location in South African cities confirmed this conclusion, indicating that racial segregation has expanded through the twentieth century, with a marked increase since the 1960s when urban segregation laws were most strongly enforced. In short, as we have seen in the United States, the impact of institutional racism will represent a basis for long-term inequity in South Africa.

Sources: A. J. Christopher. "Apartheid and Urban Segregation Levels in South Africa," Urban Studies. vol. 27 (June 1990), pp. 421–40; Diana R. Gordon and Helet Merkling. "Reform the Courts, Police: Bringing Justice to South Africa," Nation. vol. 254 (May 18, 1992), pp. 658–60; Joseph Lelyveld. Move Your Shadow: South Africa, Black and White. New York: Times Books, 1985; Richard T. Schaefer. Racial and Ethnic Groups. Boston: Little, Brown and Company, 1979; Study Commission on U.S. Policy toward Southern Africa. South Africa: Time Running Out. Berkeley and Los Angeles: University of California Press, 1981; Time. "Right of Way: A White Backlash Gathers Force," vol. 131 (March 14, 1988), p. 38; Christopher S. Wren. "South African Whites Ratify De Klerk Effort To Negotiate a Move toward Majority Rule," New York Times. (March 19, 1992), pp. A1+; Christopher S. Wren. "South African Foes Struggle to Be Partners," New York Times. (May 24, 1992), sec. 4, p. 4.

majority-group members. In the 1930s some Southerners felt that an African-American behaved aggressively if he held a prestigious job, owned a tract of land, or had a special talent. In some towns it was even considered an aggressive act for blacks to appear in public in formal attire during the week. The whites apparently wanted to see blacks in only one place: the fields (Dollard 1937).

A recent illustration of minority-group members' aggressive behavior would be the looting and rioting that occurred in the spring of 1992 in Los Angeles following the verdict releasing the policemen who had beaten Rodney King. Robin D. G. Kelley, a professor in Afro-American studies, wrote, "As I watched the . . . videotape of the black and Latino poor seizing property and destroying what many regarded as symbols of domination, I could not help but notice the joy and sense of empowerment expressed in their faces" (Kelley 1992, 796). To prevent such outbreaks in the future, government authorities need to eliminate or at least diminish what undoubtedly have been the prime sources of these rioters' frustration—namely poverty and unemployment.

At a given point in history, members of a minority group often pursue more than one response. All these four responses appear in the following discussion of American minority groups.

Before moving on to that analysis, however, we use the nearby Cross-Cultural Perspective to examine the important case of South Africa, where a majority policy of continued subjugation has been under attack by minority groups as well as by many members of the majority group.

American Minority Groups

An account of American minority groups is actually many accounts, one for each group. In this section we examine only the largest and most prominent American minority groups. Figure 9.2 indicates the size of each group and its percentage of the overall population.

AFRICAN-AMERICANS

Black slave labor existed in Virginia as early as 1619, but black slaves were more expensive than white servants in the short run, and the foreignness of their appearance, language, and general behavior offended the ethnocentric English. Almost all these early colonists preferred white laborers. In 1640 there were only 150 blacks reported in Virginia. The figure rose to 300 in 1650, 3,000 in 1680, and 10,000 by 1704. During the latter third of the seventeenth century, the plantation economy was developing, and an acute need for cheap labor arose. A new type of labor known as "chattel slavery" gradually took shape. The laws on

Figure 9.2
Prominent American Racial and Ethnic Groups[1]

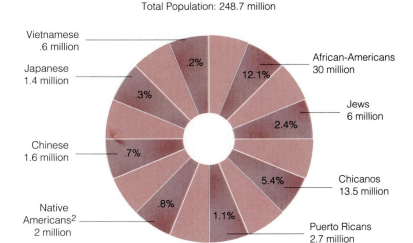

Total Population: 248.7 million

Vietnamese .6 million — .2%
Japanese 1.4 million — .3%
Chinese 1.6 million — .7%
Native Americans[2] 2 million — .8%

African-Americans 30 million — 12.1%
Jews 6 million — 2.4%
Chicanos 13.5 million — 5.4%
Puerto Ricans 2.7 million — 1.1%

[1]*Within the present figure, the representation of each group is the same size, not adjusted to its proportion to the total population.*
[2]*Includes Eskimos and Aleuts.*

This figure indicates the size of most prominent minority groups in America and the percentage each represents in the overall population.

Sources: Adapted from U.S. Bureau of the Census. Statistical Abstract of the United States: 1992, No. 16 and No. 78.

which the system was based came from English property law. Thus blacks became property that could be bought and sold. They would serve their masters for life, and children automatically became the property of their masters. The only limits upon owners' treatment of slaves was their personal discretion.

Slavery ended in 1865, but the oppression of African-Americans did not cease. In the South the so-called Jim Crow laws legalized discrimination against blacks in all institutional areas. There were also lynchings, and in many southern towns the Ku Klux Klan conducted terrorist raids. From 1880 to 1930, blacks often lived under very poor conditions. Rural southern blacks frequently had substandard diets inferior to those received under slavery, and infectious diseases spread more rapidly because of poor diet. Gonorrhea and syphilis became prevalent among blacks during this period, and many pregnancies ended in stillbirths.

In the 1920s federal legislation restricted immigration, and as a result factories lost their chief source of cheap labor. Recruiters sought

southern African-Americans, and a migration of African-Americans from the South began. This migration stopped during the Great Depression of the 1930s, but it resumed when industrialization revitalized with American involvement in World War II. The black migration to the North has continued, and by 1970 the states outside the South accounted for about half the African-American population. African-Americans migrating to the North usually experienced extensive discrimination in educational and occupational opportunities, in the availability of housing, and in the use of public facilities (bars, restaurants, grocery stores, buses, and trains, for example).

In the late 1950s and early 1960s, nonviolent demonstrations in the South protested discrimination against African-Americans. There were marches, pickets, and "sit-ins" at restaurants, on buses, and in other public facilities. During these years well-organized campaigns occurred in southern states to register black voters so that they would be able to use the political machinery to improve their living conditions.

Gradually, imperceptibly at first, the tone of

250 the protest efforts changed. Whites, who had taken a prominent role in much of the early protest activities, were told by black activists to devote themselves to eliminating racism in their own communities. In the black protest groups, a sense of African-American culture and consciousness began to appear: Afro hair styles became fashionable, dashikis (African-style shirts) were worn, and black literature was widely read. A sense of black pride developed. "Black is beautiful" became a frequent slogan. The rhetoric and style of the black protest movement lost its nonviolent character. The young African-American leaders of the 1960s began advocating and predicting massive violence against whites if discrimination against African-Americans continued. On several occasions black protesters appeared carrying guns in public. For example, a group of armed Black Panthers marched through one of the state buildings in Sacramento, California, to announce their demands, and protesters emerged from a building occupation at Cornell University carrying rifles. No documented evidence has indicated, however, that African-Americans initiated violence during major protests.

On the other hand, blacks were often the victims of violence. The two most prominent African-American protest leaders of the 1960s—Malcolm X and Martin Luther King, Jr.—were assassinated. Other prominent African-Americans were killed, including a number of the most active, outspoken leaders of the militant Black Panther Party. Large segments of the white public were terrified of blacks revolting, and so many whites were willing to accept if not condone the killings of black leaders. The only killing of an African-American leader that created widespread public sympathy among whites was the assassination of Martin Luther King, Jr., who had always advocated nonviolence in protest activity.

Situation of African-Americans Today

An assessment of the situation of African-Americans in different institutional areas shows progress has occurred, and some of this progress took place during the protest years. In the case of *Plessy v. Ferguson* (1896), the Supreme Court affirmed state court rulings that separate facilities for blacks and whites could exist as long as the facilities were equal. This segregationist standard survived largely unchallenged for nearly sixty years until *Brown v. Board of Education* (1954). At that time the Supreme Court declared that the segregation of public schools is illegal and that separate educational facilities are "inherently unequal." The same philosophy supported the Civil Rights Act of 1964, which legislated against discrimination in employment and the use of public facilities and threatened to withdraw federal funding from organizations practicing racial discrimination. In addition, during the mid-1960s, strong federal legislation assured equal rights for African-Americans and other minorities in voting and housing. Enforcement of the legislation, however, has been difficult because a limited number of government personnel have been available for the task, and their powers are often sharply restricted.

African-Americans have tended to live in segregated, crowded, low-quality housing. As whites, Hispanic-Americans, Asian-Americans, and Native Americans have attained higher income, residential restrictions have declined, but this has not been the case for African-Americans (Darden 1990; Massey and Eggers 1990; Massey and Fong 1990). Evidence indicates historical patterns of discrimination imposed on blacks. Between 1935 and 1974, for example, the Federal Housing Authority denied mortgage-loan guarantees to blacks, contending that segregation would help establish neighborhood stability and maintain housing values. In part because of this policy, vast suburban areas

Research evidence suggests that currently African-American couples sometimes encounter discrimination at various stages in the home-purchasing process, including the application for mortgages.

became all white (Judd 1991). Real-estate practice has also supported housing discrimination. Researchers studying its occurrence have used what are called "fair housing audits," in which an African-American couple and a white couple with similar incomes and credit ratings approach the same realtors. With this technique investigators have learned that African-American clients have not only received such inferior treatment as fewer home showings and less information about financing but also have been steered to residential areas that are heavily or partially integrated and away from all-white districts (Galster 1990).

In spite of these problems, African-Americans frequently seek housing in all-white areas. A black woman with whom I spoke offered this reason: "Some whites believe I want to come into an all-white neighborhood as a status move. Nothing could be farther from the truth. The fact is that a white neighborhood is the only place I can hope to find a decent place to live."

As far as jobs, income, and education are concerned, improvements for blacks have occurred, but these must be kept in perspective. A gradual increase in the percentage of African-Americans in white-collar jobs and in skilled blue-collar jobs has taken place, but blacks still dominate in the low-skill, low-paid jobs. In fact, from the middle 1970s through the 1980s, young African-American men's income and employment declined in relation to young white men's attainments, with such factors as a national decline in manufacturing, deunionization, and a sharply increasing supply of prospective workers contributing to the result. Since the middle 1960s, African-American income has remained about 60 percent of white income. It is noteworthy that the percentage gap was actually narrower before the 1954 Supreme Court decision against school desegregation, a decision supposed to be a major step in eliminating discrimination against African-Americans. The amount of education people receive influences their occupational and income opportunities. Thus it is noteworthy that on the average there is a gap of more than two years of schooling between blacks and whites. In addition, predominantly black schools are inferior to predominantly white schools in multiple respects—for example, in peer stimulation offered, in the age and condition of school buildings, and in the range and quality of facilities and supplies, such as science and language laboratories, textbooks, and libraries. Considering their more limited educational opportunities, it is hardly surprising that in 1991, 67 percent of African-Americans, age 25 and over, were high-school graduates compared to 80 percent of whites, 25 and over (Bailyn et al. 1977; Bound and Freeman 1992; U.S. Bureau of the Census, *Statistical Abstract of the United States*: 1992, No. 41; Waldrop 1990).

While poor African-Americans face many obstacles, sociologist Douglas Massey (1990) argued that the most significant problem has been racial segregation in housing. Massey pointed out that in a largely integrated area, particularly if it has diverse income groups, an increase in poverty, such as the one occurring during the economic downturn of the early 1970s, will adversely affect the area but will not alter its basic functioning: The economic strengths of the district will offset increased poverty, which will be dispersed throughout it. In contrast, if African-Americans face segregated housing, they will be forced to live in a restricted number of locales, which, given blacks' history of job discrimination, are likely to be in no better than fair economic condition in the best of times. An economic downturn will affect black residents more readily than whites since blacks' greater poverty makes them more vulnerable to the downturn. Then, given housing segregation, blacks from other locales forced to move by the downturn most likely will be funnelled into the area, contributing significantly to its economic decline. As a result most businesses will fail or be forced to leave; local opportunities for work will decline or virtually disappear; with the loss of local income, clinics and hospitals will leave the area; schooling, which is highly dependent on district funding, will sharply decline in quality; local residents will be less able to maintain their homes, landlords will be less motivated to do so, and with deterioration of residential buildings, the number of deserted buildings will increase; because of the growth of poverty, crime and violence will accelerate. Over the past two decades, this process has contributed substantially to the rapid growth of a black underclass, whose members, one expert concluded, are "walking on ice" (Waldrop 1990, 32).

HISPANIC-AMERICANS

Hispanic-Americans, who are Americans of Spanish descent, number more than 22.4 million and are classified separately from whites in the

252   census records. About 13.5 million are Mexican-American (also called Chicanos), 2.7 million are Puerto Ricans, and the remaining 6.2 million come primarily from Central America, South America, or Cuba. Although Mexican-Americans and Puerto Ricans both speak Spanish, there are marked differences in historical experience and cultural tradition.

Mexican-Americans

The first serious colonization by the Spanish occurred north of Santa Fe, New Mexico, in 1598, more than twenty years before the Plymouth settlement in Massachusetts. Large-scale Mexican immigration to the United States, however, did not start until the social upheaval accompanying the Mexican Revolution of 1909. During the next two decades, migration was steady, and by the early 1930s there were nearly 1.5 million Chicanos. Migration declined during the war years when Mexican farming was prosperous, but since the 1950s a steady flow of Mexicans into the U.S. has occurred. In the middle 1980s, worsening economic conditions in Mexico and Central America produced an increase in illegal immigration. Between 1987 and 1991, the number of illegal immigrants caught each year generally increased, with about 1 million arrested in 1991. One notable

Many of the increasing number of Mexican women who try to enter the United States illegally are caught and forced to return. This border-patrol agent is filling out a voluntary return form. First offense suspects may choose this procedure or a more complex deportation hearing.

development is that the percentage of illegal Mexican immigrants who are women rose from about 8 percent in 1987 to 15 percent in 1991. While some women are joining husbands or boyfriends, many are striking out on their own, finding that the best hope for the future is to reject a paternalistic structure that has not provided effectively for them. The combined impact of rapid immigration and a high fertility rate have made Mexican-Americans the fastest growing of all ethnic or racial groups in the United States.

Some disadvantages have helped keep many Mexican-Americans poor and badly educated. Chicano families average about $13,000 less income per year than white families, and about 56 percent have not completed high school compared to 20 percent for whites. Most Mexican-Americans are blue-collar workers, primarily in service jobs. Only about 7 percent of men and about 3 percent of women do farm work, an occupation that many Americans associate closely with Chicanos.

One of the reasons for this association is the well-publicized and remarkably successful effort of Cesar Chavez and his associates to organize migrant Mexican-American workers into the National Farm Workers' Association. This organization has sought to obtain livable wages and benefits for its members. Mexican-Americans have also become active in mainstream politics. A recent study provided two reasons why the Chicano population is increasingly likely to vote. First, Mexican-Americans' level of education has been rising, and voting studies indicate that level of education is the factor best predicting people's inclination to vote. Second, with the growth of the potential Chicano vote, both major parties have increased their efforts to mobilize support from this group, in particular offering Chicano candidates on statewide ballots (Feagin 1989; Golden 1992; Gonzalez 1988; Longoria, Wrinkle, and Polinard 1990; Moore and Pachon 1976; Pachon and Moore 1981; U.S. Bureau of the Census, *Statistical Abstract of the United States: 1992*, No. 16, No. 41, and No. 44).

Puerto Ricans

In October 1898 Puerto Rico became an American possession, permitting people to move without restriction back and forth between the island and the mainland. By 1910 about 1,500 Puerto Ricans had come to New York City, and their number rose to about 70,000 in 1940. Many of the early migrants were merchants who had lost their businesses when sugar became the dominant island crop. On the mainland, jobs were available because of restrictions in European immigration.

The major migration of Puerto Ricans started after World War II. Most of the new arrivals came in search of better-paying jobs. The majority of Puerto Ricans moving to the mainland still settle in New York City, but urban concentrations are developing in Chicago, Philadelphia, Jersey City, Newark, Los Angeles, Miami, and a number of other cities.

Economically and occupationally, Puerto Ricans have a difficult time in the United States. After Native Americans they are the poorest racial or ethnic group, with family income averaging about 49 percent of white families; about 38 percent of Puerto-Rican families fall below the official poverty line. Occupationally Puerto-Rican men are heavily represented in lower-paying blue-collar jobs and women in low-level clerical and sales positions.

Because of nonrestrictive travel and the closeness of the island to the mainland, Puerto Ricans, unlike other migrants, often return to their ethnic homeland. Trips to the island are made in order to visit relatives or sometimes, if living on the mainland proves unsatisfactory, to resettle permanently. For many members of this ethnic group, adjustment to life in New York City and other U.S. cities has been difficult. Language, color discrimination, and a different cultural perspective complicate the search for jobs, psychiatric help, or other social services.

On the other hand, Puerto Ricans choosing to return to the island encounter some distinct difficulties. In Puerto Rico the unemployment rate approaches 40 percent with over half the islanders receiving food stamps. Wage levels are lower than in the United States. The alcoholism rate, the suicide rate, and the automobile accident rate are much higher than in the United States. With such poor conditions on the island, it is not surprising that a study concluded that students who returned to Puerto Rico to live permanently had a less positive image of their teachers, schools, and themselves than a matched group of students who moved back and forth between Puerto Rico and the mainland (Fitzpatrick 1975; Fitzpatrick and Parker 1981; Guarnaccia, Good, and Kleinman 1990; Krafft 1991; Prewitt-Diaz 1984; U.S. Bureau of the Census, *Statistical Abstract of the United States*: 1992, No. 41 and No. 45).

Puerto Ricans and other Hispanic-Americans fall educationally and economically below American averages. Table 9.2 offers some comparison involving blacks, whites, and Hispanic-Americans.

Table 9.2 Some Important Statistical Facts in the Lives of Whites, Blacks, and Hispanic-Americans

Issue	Total population	White	Black	Hispanic
Median family income	$35,353	$36,915	$21,423	$23,431
Percent of persons below poverty line	13.7%	10.7%	31.9%	28.1%
Education[1]				
Four years of high school or more	78.4%	79.9%	66.7%	51.3%
Four years of college or more	21.4%	22.2%	11.5%	9.7%
Owner-occupied units	64%	67.3%	42.4%	39%

	TOTAL POPULATION	WHITE		NONWHITE	
		Male	Female	Male	Female
Life expectancy (in years)[2]	75.4	72.6	79.3	68.4	76.3

[1] All education figures are for people 25 years and older.
[2] The life expectancy figures compare whites to nonwhites.

Source: U.S. Bureau of the Census. *Statistical Abstract of the United States*: 1992, No. 41, No. 44, and No. 103.

Whites fare better than blacks and Hispanic-Americans on all these measures. Hispanic-Americans average higher income than blacks while blacks tend to be better educated.

254   AMERICAN JEWS

It is not simple to determine the criteria that make a person a Jew. Certainly Jews are not a race. Among Jews one will find a wide variety of head and nose shapes, skin types, body builds, and hair colors. Jews also do not form a religious group. They include agnostics, atheists, and also converts to many different religions. Nor are Jews a nation. Historically dispersed time and again, they come from many countries. It seems that the critical factor is "the consciousness of being a Jew." In short, Jews are people who think of themselves as Jews and are considered by others to be Jewish. Even in Israel, the reestablished homeland of Jews, uncertainly exists on this topic. Former Prime Minister Ben Gurion suggested that ". . . being a Jew is so difficult that anyone professing to be one should be believed" (Berry and Tischler 1978, 29–30). Since Jewish identity is so elusive, many Jews are concerned that high rates of intermarriage could threaten the survival of Jews as a distinct ethnic group.

The largest number of Jews reached the United States in the late nineteenth and early twentieth century from eastern Europe, where they had been poor, living in segregated villages or city ghettos. About 6 million Jews now live in the United States, forming about 2.4 percent of the American population. About three-quarters of American Jews live in large cities or their suburbs. Nearly half reside in the greater New York City area.

Jews often have been the target of hostile stereotypes and prejudices. **Anti-Semitism** is the complex of prejudicial attitudes toward Jews. The roots of this behavior lie in historical and economic conditions that go back many centuries in Asia and Europe. Anti-Semitism has also occurred in the United States. By the 1880s Jews appeared in newspaper and magazine cartoons that pictured them as "long-nosed, garishly dressed merchants speaking in broken English" or as revolutionaries trying to take over the American government. In the 1920s industrialist Henry Ford contributed to anti-Semitism, financing a crusade against Jews' rising prominence in business and professional activities. In the 1940s many Americans felt an intense hatred and fear of Jews, believing that American Jews were responsible for the outbreak of World War II. Since 1945 a gradual improvement in feelings toward Jews has occurred. Yet in 1989

the Anti-Defamation League, which keeps a record of anti-Semitic incidents, reported 1,432 episodes, the greatest number since the organization started collecting these data in 1978. The anti-Semitic incidents fall into two broad categories—vandalism; and harassment, threats, or assaults on individuals. Furthermore some stereotypic conclusions about Jews remain strong—such as a claim, which was not supported by recent research, that Jews are more inclined than Protestants or Catholics to support political candidates whose policies will help them economically.

In spite of prejudice and discrimination against them, American Jews have tended to be unusually successful in their occupational pursuits and income attainment. Success, however, often developed under trying circumstances. In the 1930s, for example, Jews were heavily represented in clothing, textiles, films, and other industries on the edge of the mainstream economy and vulnerable to unusually high risk. In social critic Carey McWilliams's phrase, Jews were "the ragpickers of American industry." In the 1950s American Jews showed a much higher proportion of men in white-collar employment than the national average. Yet from 1900 to 1950, Jews obtained few top-management positions, a fact suggesting that in this area Jews have also been the victims of discrimination.

For American Jews two significant trends have been occurring in the past twenty years. As Jews have divested themselves of their language and customs and moved into higher-status jobs, an increasing amount of intermarriage has taken place. At the same time, there has been a renewed interest in the survival of Jews as a distinct ethnic and religious group. Signs of this shift have been a revitalization of Jewish religious traditions, a greater focus of Jewish philanthropies exclusively on the needs of Jews, and a renewed emphasis on the importance of commemorating the Holocaust with courses, memorials, and museums.

American Jews have done well educationally and occupationally. Their level of education is considerably higher than the national standard, with Jews averaging nearly four more years of schooling than white Protestants. In the 1980s a majority of Jewish families had incomes above white Americans' average, with Jews more heavily represented in professional and managerial positions than white Protestants (DeParle 1990; Feagin 1989;

Judd 1990; Quigley and Glock 1979; Sigelman 1991; Sklare 1971; Waxman 1981).

ASIAN-AMERICANS

There are about 7.3 million Asian-Americans in the United States. About 1.6 million are of Chinese descent, 1.4 million are of Japanese descent, and 615,000 of Vietnamese descent. Although Asian-Americans reside in communities throughout the country, the West Coast, especially California, is where most live. In Hawaii Asian-Americans probably maintain greater economic and political prominence than in any other state. Asian-American groups not discussed in this chapter include people of Bangladeshian, Cambodian, Indian, Korean, Pakistani, Philippine, and Thai heritage.

Chinese-Americans

After 1850 Chinese immigrants arrived in the United States in substantial numbers and sought employment as laborers for mines and railroads. Within several decades the Chinese had become a source of fear to whites, who felt that they were a "yellow peril" that hated American institutions and maintained loyalty only to the homeland and their emperor. Motivated by fear, Congress passed the Chinese Exclusion Act of 1882, and the rate of immigration declined sharply.

Some Chinese-Americans have remained in ghettos (Chinatowns) and have suffered from the problems that usually accompany depressed urban living. The Chinatowns of America are located in the most deteriorated parts of cities. In New York City's Chinatown, more than a third of the tenements have rats and three-quarters have roaches. In San Francisco two-thirds of Chinatown housing is substandard compared to one-fifth substandard for the rest of the city. The Chinatowns across the country have become seriously overcrowded because of recent immigration.

Such residential areas, however, are the exception, not the rule for Chinese-Americans, who have generally been successful in basic achievement areas. They are well above the national average in high-school and college graduation rates, and they show the highest concentration of all Asian-American groups in white-collar jobs—39 percent—which is well above the national average. The median family income is nearly $3,000 over the national standard.

One reason for the success of the Chinese seems to have been their willingness to adjust to the standards of American life. For instance, immigrant parents generally do not try to restrict their children's career or marital choices. A factor contributing to Chinese-Americans' high income level has been the effective use of the "enclave" economy—family members and sometimes friends investing and working together to develop successful laundries, garment factories, and restaurants.

Success, however, has hardly eliminated all stereotypes or misconceptions of Chinese-Americans. In fact, to many Americans the view that they are quiet, passive, and nonassertive—a conclusion which research has failed to verify—helps to explain how they have attained such high levels of educational and occupational achievement. In addition, evidence indicates that Chinese-Americans have not been accepted as full-fledged members of American society. A college professor who was a third-generation American, a Korean War G.I., and a Stanford doctorate noted that it is infuriating to be frequently asked such questions as "How long have you been in the U.S.?" and "Where did you learn to speak English so well?" (Ikels 1985; Kitano 1981; Rosenthal and Feldman 1990; Sue, Sue, and Ino 1990; Wong 1987).

Japanese-Americans

Japanese began arriving in the United States in the 1880s, at the time when restriction on Chinese immigration was occurring. About 28,000 Japanese settled in the United States between 1880 and 1900 and then more than 213,000 in the next twenty years as demands for low-wage agricultural workers grew on the West Coast. By the first decade of the twentieth century, the hostile, fearful images that had developed toward the Chinese started focusing on the Japanese: "Now the Jap is a wily an' a crafty individual—more so than the Chink," warned one writer in the *Sacramento Bee* (Okimoto 1971, 15).

In spite of discrimination, the West Coast Japanese were industrious and successful as farmers, gardeners, and business people. In March of 1942, the *Los Angeles Times* reported that Japanese agricultural products brought $40 million in sales

256

annually. Japanese-Americans were growing 40 percent of the crops produced in California, specializing in those requiring intensive labor and capable of being grown profitably on small plots of marginal-quality land. As we have noted, this economic success did not protect Japanese-Americans during World War II. The American government ordered the forcible evacuation of 110,000 people of Japanese ancestry from the West Coast on the pretext that they might aid the Japanese war effort against the United States.

The forced migration was devastating to Japanese-American families. The average loss per family was about $10,000 in goods, property, income, and expenses (in 1940, pre-inflated dollars). Yet after World War II, Japanese-Americans were able to reestablish themselves in the American economy. Like the Chinese the Japanese have used education as a means of self-advancement. In recent years Japanese-Americans have had the highest college completion rate of any group in U.S. society, including majority groups, and have had an above-average placement in professional and management positions and in income. Nevertheless considering their high level of educational achievement, Japanese-Americans should be doing even better occupationally; they continue to experience subtle discrimination in management and professional positions.

Japanese-Americans have been having an increasing amount of contact with other groups. About 34 percent of all Japanese-Americans aged 18 to 64 are married to non-Japanese, and by 1985 over half of all new marriages of Japanese-Americans involved a non-Japanese spouse. Reasons for the increase include the lessening of segregation and isolation, economic mobility, and the declining control imposed by the Japanese family (Atkinson and Matsushita 1991; Feagin 1989; Fugita and O'Brien 1985; Lee and Yamanaka 1990; Leighton 1964; Taylor 1986).

Vietnamese-Americans

The arrival of the Vietnamese in the United States has produced publicity out of proportion to their numbers. Some of the approximately 260,000 refugees arriving in the United States were "boat people," who left Vietnam, Laos, and Cambodia in small, often ill-equipped craft. Some died en route, but many others were picked up at sea, brought to temporary compounds, and then distributed to various countries. Other Vietnamese reaching the United States were war orphans adopted by American families, and a few children were American servicemen's offspring who joined their fathers. Understandably many newly arrived Vietnamese felt confused and alienated. In part, such a reaction occurred because of the disruptive conditions in Southeast Asia under which they departed, but it also took place because of the significance of what was left behind: a family network in which rights and duties were clearly specified and a sense of interdependence, support, and belonging were strongly emphasized. An article suggested that the conventional strategy of encouraging recently arrived Vietnamese children to become actively involved in American life as quickly as possible should be replaced by a policy emphasizing "grief work"—establishing a new identity after a significant loss.

In what context did we previously discuss grief work? If you do not remember or did not read the material, turn to Chapter 6, "Socialization," the discussion about the death of a spouse.

Compounding these immigrants' problems has been the fact that they arrived in the United States during a difficult economic era. Frequently they have found themselves pitted against American citizens in the struggle to make a living. In Texas some people who fished for a living in the Gulf of Mexico have charged that since the arrival of the Vietnamese, certain areas have been fished out. To protest the increased competition, a local chapter of the Ku Klux Klan sponsored a fish fry during which the participants burned a fishing dinghy labeled the "U.S.S. Viet Cong." In Denver workers in a meat-packing plant were furious when they were dismissed and Vietnamese were hired at half the wage.

Because of their recent arrival, Vietnamese-Americans are well below other Asian-American groups and the American average in occupational and income level. A positive indication of future success, however, is the fact that their level of education is rising, with 62 percent high-school graduates and the average number of years of schooling scarcely below the national average (Celano and Tyler 1991; Eisenbruch 1988; Felsman et al. 1990; *New York Times* February 26, 1981; Schmidt 1981; Timberlake and Cook 1984).

NATIVE AMERICANS

The population of Native Americans (also called American Indians) numbers about 2 million at present. When Columbus arrived in San Salvador in 1492, the figure was only slightly less, probably between 700,000 and a million. Experts believe that the number declined to under 250,000 at the end of the nineteenth century, and the Indian population has increased steadily since then. Census data show an increase of about a half million Native Americans since 1980. The principal reason is that there has been a growing tendency for people with some Native American heritage to identify themselves as such on census forms.

Native Americans treated early European settlers well. For example, most of the English people who landed at Plymouth in 1620 probably would have starved without gifts of corn and information about how to fish and grow corn. As more settlers arrived, they sought increasing amounts of land. The American government signed many treaties with Indian tribes, but when new arrivals needed more land, the government agreed that they could break the treaties. If the Native Americans resisted the invasion of their lands, then the military imposed compliance.

Eventually the Indians had to leave their lands and enter reservations. This policy weakened or destroyed their traditional economies (such as the buffalo-hunting lifestyle of Plains Indians), political systems, and religious systems. In addition, the requirement that children enter white schools undermined the family structure. Control of the reservations was fairly strict, and yet some rebellions did occur.

Perhaps the best known rebellion was nonviolent. It was called the Ghost Dance, and in 1890 the practice of this dance spread quickly from tribe to tribe. The belief behind the dance was that some day all Indians, both the living and the dead, would unite on a new earth containing great herds of buffalo and wild horses and would be protected from death, disease, and misery. Those who performed the Ghost Dance would supposedly rise into the air and remain suspended until the new earth moved into place beneath them. Then they would come down onto this new earth that was without white people but did contain all their ancestors.

Government and military personnel watched the development of the Ghost Dance warily. They

In recent years Indian powwows have become increasingly popular throughout the country, providing the participants an opportunity to share their heritage with fellow Native Americans as well as other Americans.

acknowledged that it was nonviolent, but they were apprehensive about the enthusiasm for traditional customs and activities it generated. Then when it seemed that the renowned Sioux warrior Sitting Bull was joining the movement, government officials became increasingly nervous. Officials ordered the arrest of Sitting Bull, and when he resisted, he was shot and killed. Two weeks after Sitting Bull's death, a Sioux chief named Big Foot was leading his people toward Pine Rock reservation, hoping to find protection from the army. At Wounded Knee, South Dakota, the cavalry stopped the march to check the men for weapons. Fighting broke out, and about 150 men, women, and children were killed. Many were wearing the fabled ghost shirts, which were supposed to protect the wearers from any harm, including bullets. With the Wounded Knee Massacre, the belief that Indians would be elevated to a better existence ceased to exist.

In modern times Native Americans retain less than 3 percent of the land area in the United States. Officials of the Bureau of Indian Affairs estimate that Indian land ranges between critically and slightly eroded. None of it is prime land for supporting crops or animals. Native Americans are the poorest ethnic group in the United States, with an unemployment rate double the national average, severely crowded living conditions, substandard water and sanitation facilities, and high disease and infant-mortality rates. Death from liver cirrhosis, which is primarily produced by

AMERICAN CONTROVERSY
Affirimative Action for Minority Groups

Affirmative action is a government-supported directive requiring employers to develop timetables and goals for increasing the employment of women and members of minority groups. The roots of affirmative action can be traced to the Civil Rights Act of 1964, an executive order issued by President Lyndon Johnson in 1965, and a Labor Department statement produced in 1970. Affirmative-action guidelines have been applied to educational as well as occupational opportunities.

In 1991 when a national sample of adult Americans was asked whether preferences should be given to minorities in getting jobs and places in college or whether there should be reliance on test scores, 81 percent opted for test scores, and only 11 percent picked preferential treatment. Twenty-four percent of African-Americans compared to 8 percent of whites chose preferential treatment. Let us consider some of the issues involved.

The Position Backing Affirmative Action
Those supporting affirmative action can stress that such an approach is traditionally American, representing our culture's emphasis on equal opportunity by helping to remedy the historical disadvantages suffered by minorities in educational, occupational, and income areas. One team of writers noted that until the Civil Rights Act of 1964 there was "a legally sanctioned and pervasive system of discrimination" against African-Americans and other racial minorities (Wigdor and Hartigan 1990, 12). African-Americans and some other minority groups are especially disadvantaged because unlike many of the white immigrant groups arriving in the nineteenth and early twentieth century, they are seeking higher education and good jobs in a highly competitive situation against competitors whose chances for educational and occupational preparation have been better than theirs.

The intrusion of institutional racism is particularly relevant, the advocates emphasize. Employers can use such means as irrelevant educational credentials or past work history to screen out African-Americans and other members of minorities who are well qualified for jobs. It would be nice to think that subtle, polite racism does not occur in America, but it does.

A final point to be stressed by the advocates is that the goals and timetable for affirmative action are not rigid. Goals need not become quotas specifying that in a given organization a precise number of minority-group members must fill certain job slots; affirmative-action procedures are flexible guidelines but nonetheless guidelines to be taken seriously.

The Position against Affirmative Action
The opponents of affirmative action might begin by stressing that theirs is the traditionally American position because it emphasizes that the individual must succeed in a competitive setting on his or her own without governmental intervention.

The major point the opponents make is that affirmative action represents reverse discrimination, with a division of modern society into two classes—those who benefit from this doctrine and those who do not. The problem, this group emphasizes, is that such a two-part division is impractical. Why, for instance, should Chinese-Americans and Japanese-Americans, who, in spite of discrimination, have done very well occupationally and economically in this country, benefit from affirmative-action programs? On the other hand, what about poor white males? They are judged solely on the basis of their ethnicity and sex, and the fact that they are victims of the "vicious cycle of poverty" (discussed in Chapter 8, "Social Stratification") is not considered.

Furthermore, the opponents conclude, goals might not start out as quotas, but over time they inevitably harden into them, and a quota system favoring minority occupational or educational candidates epitomizes reverse discrimination.

Conclusion So these are two opposing positions on this complicated issue. Discuss your personal stances in a small group and, in particular, carefully examine the specific issues on which you disagree. Is there hope for effective compromise?

Sources: Jan H. Blits and Linda S. Gottfredson. "Equality or Lasting Inequality?" Society. vol. 27 (March/April 1990), pp. 4–11; George Gallup, Jr. and Frank Newport. "Blacks and Whites Differ on Civil Rights Progress," Gallup Poll Monthly. (August 1991), pp. 54–59; Alexandra K. Wigdor and John A. Hartigan. "The Case for Fairness," Society. vol. 27 (March/April 1990), pp. 12–16.

alcoholism, is about three-and-a-half times the national rate, and among Indian adolescents the suicide rate is up to ten times greater than the national average. On the other hand, Indian-owned businesses increased 64 percent between 1982 and 1987 while for all U.S. firms only a 14 percent rise occurred. Recently there has been a drive to develop reservation-based retail and service businesses, which would help establish sustainable local economies and counter the long-term tendency for nearly all money earned on reservations to be spent elsewhere.

Native Americans approach the future in different ways. Some believe that like all bad experiences, domination by the white majority will pass. Others have launched a legal battle to protect their rights and reclaim their lands. One significant activity has been the renewal of tribal traditions. Many tribes now emphasize teaching the younger generation tribal languages, craft skills, healing practices, tribal histories, and religious ritual and ceremonies. Since the middle 1980s, powwows, which feature traditional storytelling, dance competitions, music, and crafts, have become popular around the country, providing a connection with Indian culture for both Native Americans and other Americans. Will these revitalized cultural traditions continue to develop, or will they be submerged by the continuing efforts to mainstream Native Americans in schools and jobs? (Brown 1972; Davenport and Davenport 1987; Deloria 1981; Fost 1991; Hodge 1981; Morse, Young, and Swartz 1991; Nieves 1992; Robbins 1984; Utley 1963).

We have discussed a variety of racial and ethnic groups. All of them are affected by affirmative action, which is discussed in the nearby American Controversy.

WHITE ETHNICS

White ethnics are primarily of Irish, Italian, Polish, Slavonic, and Greek origin. Most come from south-ern and eastern Europe and often have a Catholic heritage. They are usually blue-collar workers with incomes slightly below the national average. Part of the enormous popularity of the television program "All in the Family" was that Archie Bunker expressed the furies and frustrations often attributed to white ethnics. Archie was an unabashed, devout conservative, suspicious of and hostile toward African-Americans, Puerto Ricans, and other racial minorities, contemptuous of people on welfare, and unyieldingly, unquestioningly patriotic. Others in public life have expressed the same fears and frustrations. During Richard Nixon's first term, Vice-President Spiro Agnew gained great popularity speaking out for what he called the "Silent Majority" of hard-working, non-protesting, patriotic Americans, many of whom were white ethnics.

Some evidence, however, disputes a conservative stereotype for white ethnics. A study suggested that white Catholics were more likely

Archie Bunker, the central character in the popular television series "All in the Family," was portrayed as politically conservative and racist, but some research findings have opposed such a stereotype for white ethnics.

260

than white Protestants to have opposed the Vietnam War and to have supported such liberal causes as a guaranteed annual wage, governmental assistance for the poor, medicare, and the racial integration of public facilities (Greeley 1977, Chapter 5).

Among the most recently arrived white ethnics are Irish immigrants, who have come to the United States because of deteriorating economic conditions in their homeland. At least 50,000 of them are working illegally, but their cause has been aided by Irish-American politicians, who have made certain that a substantial proportion of the immigrant visas reserved for citizens of "disadvantaged" countries—48,000 of 120,000 visas covering a three-year period—will be earmarked for them. Most white ethnics, in contrast, have effectively moved into the economic and social mainstream. Since World War II, one of the most rapidly rising white-ethnic groups has been Italian-Americans, who are heavily represented in high-paying, prestigious occupations and now have higher incomes than Irish-Americans.

For many white ethnics, especially those who move to suburban areas, the sense of ethnicity rapidly fades. Factors contributing to this loss of identity are the sharp increases in intermarriages, geographical break-up of the extended family, decreasing influence of religious organizations, and integration into the local educational, occupational, and recreational structures (*Economist* 1991; Fallows 1979; Greeley 1988; Novak 1972; Salamon 1985; Vosburgh and Juliani 1990).

Our present discussion of racial and ethnic groups has provided us a background for some consideration of where American race relations are headed.

Moving toward the Twenty-First Century   ■

During the presidential campaign of 1988, the George Bush camp widely publicized information about the case of Willie Horton, a convicted black felon who raped a white woman while out of prison on a furlough program started by Massachusetts Governor Michael Dukakis, Bush's opponent. When asked to comment on why the Bush supporters were emphasizing this incident, Lee Atwater, Bush's campaign manager, said, "The Horton case is one of those gut issues that are values issues, particularly in the South, and if we hammer at these over and over, we are going to win" (Rosenthal 1988, B5). So in politics, Atwater was saying, one should do whatever it takes to win, even if what it takes involved a major effort to inflame racial fears and hatred by suggesting that if Dukakis were elected president, white women's vulnerability to rape by black men would be increased.

Sociologist Troy Duster (1987) put this sort of issue, and race relations generally, in perspective, suggesting that while social scientists can analyze many issues involving race, a fundamental question emerges: "How and why has race been the persistent category of advantage and privilege throughout every generation of the nation's history?" (Duster 1987, 12).

Such an analysis is consistent with a conflict-theory view, indicating that racial minorities (and sometimes whites) have been submerged by dominant whites in the struggle for scarce resources. Duster's question also offers a more general sociological perspective, seeking to specify the social forces establishing dominant whites' position of superiority.

Do you agree that this is the fundamental question about American race relations? Discuss the issue in class or outside of it.

The chapter closes with the third of six research sections; this one discusses racism and racial bias in race research.

RESEARCH IN SOCIOLOGY: SECTION III

Racism and Racial Bias in Race Research

During the 1930s a pioneer in race research noted for painstakingly thorough, fair-minded, and incisive investigations, explained to his associates that while he was proud of his race studies, one point should be clear. "I'm no nigger lover," he would explain.*

Can one be confident that this man's racism was kept out of his work? Considering the impact that personal biases can have on research outcomes—a topic we examined in Chapter 2—I strongly doubt it. Let's examine some of the different ways that racism and racial bias can affect the content of race research.

Racist Interpretation of Findings and Related Issues

Perhaps the most publicized way that racism enters the research process involves the explanation of data. Since early in the twentieth century, a host of studies have interpreted racial differences in results as determined by biological or genetic factors.

For instance, in 1912, Henry Goddard, a Princeton psychologist, gave an intelligence test to a representative sample of European immigrants, concluding that 83 percent of Jews seeking to enter the country were feebleminded, along with 79 percent of Italians and 87 percent of the Russians.

In 1921 psychologist Robert M. Yerkes edited a research volume that summarized the data from intelligence tests obtained from World War I draftees. African-Americans scored lower than whites, and there were also data on draftees born in various European countries. Immigrants from England, Holland, Denmark, Scotland, Germany, and Switzerland scored quite high while those from Russia, Italy, and Poland scored low. Like Goddard, Yerkes concluded that people with lower scores simply possessed less intellectual potential than those with high scores.

In the 1960s Arthur Jensen, a psychologist, found that black children averaged about 15 points lower than white children on standard intelligence tests. Without offering any further data, he simply concluded that between one-half to three-quarters of the score differences could be attributed to genetic factors and the remainder to environmental factors and their interaction with genetic factors.

At present J. Philippe Rushton has been the leading researcher attributing racial performance differences to inborn racial factors. Rushton has argued that the three major racial groups—Mongoloids, Caucasoids, and Negroids—can be placed in that particular hierarchical order for evolutionary development. Rushton's rank ordering has been based on certain factors he designates important, such as reproductive rates and infant-mortality rates. Africans and African-Americans, for example, have large numbers of children and high infant-mortality rates, and these conditions help place Negroids at the bottom of the hierarchical order.

It appears that a consistent thread runs through the above studies, which extend across the breadth of the twentieth century. In every case the findings are attributed to inborn biological differences. The researchers fail to consider the impact of such factors as facility in English or overall educational level affecting intelligence-test

*This information comes from a person who obtained it directly from the researcher. I consider my source very reliable.

262   performance, or such influences as access to prenatal care and existence in impoverished and stressful residential areas affecting fertility and mortality rates. Thus racist
interpretations of findings have been a significant occurrence in social research.

While less explicitly racist, other explanations have followed a similar path.
Consider victim-blaming interpretations, in which the analysis focuses on individuals' inability to achieve a satisfactory level of performance and ignores the structural
conditions that have encouraged or even determined that inability. The best-known
example was a report titled *The Negro Family: The Case for National Action*, with Harvard
professor, later New York senator, Daniel Patrick Moynihan as its chief writer. The
report focused on the supposed structure of the poor, African-American family, indicating that "the tangle of pathology"—the combined impact of poverty, the absence
of fathers, and exposure to delinquency and crime—made it impossible for poor
black children, especially poor black males to perform effectively in schools and in
the work place. While representing a slight improvement from outrightly racist analyses, this report failed to look beyond the family to consider the impact of institutional
racism, which has had a major negative impact on poor African-Americans' lives.

When text writers summarize such material, the same narrow perspective is likely
to be maintained. A study of twenty-five texts on the sociology of the family indicated
that nine of the books analyzed African-American families under headings suggesting deviance or inadequate functioning. There were statements that black families
are more likely to be female-headed and to experience unemployment, illegitimacy,
and breakup than white families. Such statements are factually correct, but without
further explanation, they are misleading. Useful further discussion would indicate
how factors besides race, such as poverty and unemployment, have come into play.
Otherwise readers are likely to receive the impression "that black families are
innately problem-ridden or dysfunctional" (Bryant and Coleman 1988, 257).

Aspects of the research process itself can also influence the view of minority-
group families presented. A review of the 283 data-based articles about African-
Americans published in the *Journal of Marriage and the Family* between 1939 and 1987
indicated that since the early 1960s, there has been an increasing tendency for articles in this journal to have been quantitative studies subsidized by government
grants and conducted by researchers at large, primarily white universities. Such studies have tended to present an abstract sense of black family issues, failing to represent respondents' points of view and often, with little or no justification for claims of
their significance provided, highlighting statistical information indicating that
African-Americans are more deviant or less successful than whites. Tendencies for
this research to have been conducted at white universities and to have received government support have been consistent with this quantitative trend. White universities can best afford the mainframe computers necessary for this type of investigation,
and government sponsors have been more inclined to fund large quantitative projects than qualitative studies. In summary, one might argue that institutional racism
exists here—that historical conditions favoring white educational organizations over
black counterparts have dovetailed in support of published studies that present an
abstract, somewhat negative view of African-American families.

But important as these issues are, underlying them is an even more fundamental impact of racial bias on race-relations research.

Questions and Answers in Race Research

Recall that in the conclusion of this chapter, Troy Duster indicated that race has been
"the persistent category of advantage and privilege throughout every generation of

the nation's history" (Duster 1987, 12). In the same article, Duster went on to point out that if this conclusion is accurate, then it should have a significant impact on the content of race-relations research. Such studies should focus on the existence of the gulf among different racial groups, providing new insights on how we confront and ultimately eliminate that gulf. For instance, after World War II, a group of Jewish scholars began to consider questions about how it was possible for a modern nation to slaughter millions of Jews and hundreds of thousands of Gypsies. In particular, some of these scholars began to raise questions about an "authoritarian personality," with T. W. Adorno and his associates eventually studying the topic and publishing *The Authoritarian Personality*.

A similar perspective can apply to race research in the United States. For instance, consider two questions that might launch research. One question would ask whether blacks or whites are more likely to be living below the American poverty line. Finding that 32 percent of blacks compared to 11 percent of whites are living in poverty, one would conclude that African-Americans are about three times more likely to be poor. Armed with this information, investigators most likely would turn to studies of welfare and of its "debilitating effect" on the African-American community, where a work ethic supposedly is lacking. In short, the blaming-the-victim perspective discussed above would come into play.

In contrast, another question would inquire whether whites or blacks are more likely to earn their income by working. In this case while blacks obtain 80 percent of their income from wages and salaries, whites receive only 75 percent of their total income from this source, more often living off dividends from various sources of wealth. Following up on the answer to this second question, researchers might initiate a national study of whites, considering a widespread retreat from the nineteenth-century work ethic and the destructive impact of the scandal-ridden, get-rich-quick schemes that have involved many top financial and political leaders in recent years.

Effective analysis of modern race relations, Duster suggested, requires that both questions be raised and examined. Unfortunately, he continued, most race research has only dealt with the first type of question, tending to focus on individual minority groups and producing quantitative data in various behavioral areas that provide little or no insight about how to confront the terrible inequities that persist in our society.

Sources: *Z. Lois Bryant and Marilyn Coleman. "The Black Family as Portrayed in Introductory Marriage and Family Textbooks,"* Family Relations. *vol. 37 (July 1988), pp. 255–59; Vasilikie Demos. "Black Family Studies in the* Journal of Marriage and the Family *and the Issue of Distortion: A Trend Analysis,"* Journal of Marriage and the Family. *vol. 52 (August 1990), pp. 603–12; Troy Duster. "Purpose and Bias,"* Society. *vol. 24 (January/February 1987), pp. 8–12; Halford H. Fairchild. "Scientific Racism: The Cloak of Objectivity,"* Journal of Social Issues. *vol. 47 (1991), pp. 101–15; Arthur R. Jensen. "How Much Can We Boost IQ and Scholastic Achievement?"* Harvard Educational Review. *vol. 39 (Winter 1969), pp. 1–123; Arthur R. Jensen.* Educability and Group Differences. *New York: Methuen, 1973; Leon J. Kamin.* The Science and Politics of IQ. *New York: Wiley, 1974; Charles Leslie. "Scientific Racism: Reflections on Peer Review, Science, and Ideology,"* Social Science & Medicine. *vol. 31 (1990), pp. 891–912; Office of Planning and Research, United States Department of Labor.* The Negro Family: The Case for National Action. *Washington, DC: United States Department of Labor, 1965; J. Philippe Rushton. "Race Differences in Behaviour: A Review and Evolutionary Analysis,"* Personality and Individual Differences. *vol. 9 (1988), pp. 1009–24; J. Philippe Rushton. "Comments in Response to Leslie's 'Scientific Racism,'"* Social Science and Medicine. *vol. 31 (1990), pp. 905–9; U.S. Bureau of the Census.* Statistical Abstract of the United States: 1992, *No 722.*

STUDY GUIDE

Learning Objectives

After having studied this chapter, you should be able to:

1. Define and discuss racial group, ethnic group, and minority group.
2. Define prejudice, discrimination, ideology, racism, and institutional racism and distinguish between prejudice and discrimination, providing examples.
3. Identify and analyze the psychological, cultural, and economic explanations of prejudice and discrimination.
4. Discuss the effects of prejudice and discrimination.
5. List and describe the six dominant-group policies.
6. Examine the four minority responses to minority-group status.
7. Discuss the following large, prominent American minority groups: African-Americans, Hispanic-Americans, Jews, Asian-Americans, Native Americans, and white ethnics.
8. State and analyze what may be the fundamental question involving American race relations.

Summary

1. Although all human beings are members of the same species, they are often more inclined to emphasize their racial and ethnic differences than their shared similarities.

2. Certain concepts divide the human species into different categories. Prominent among these are racial group, ethnic group, and minority group.

3. Prejudice and discrimination are the processes producing minority groups. Prejudice is a highly negative judgment toward a group, focusing on one or more negative characteristics that are supposedly uniformly shared by all group members. Discrimination is the behavior by which one group prevents or restricts another group's access to scarce resources. Prejudice and discrimination do not always occur in tandem, but they often do. Different explanations of prejudice and discrimination exist. Social explanations emphasize the contributions of language to prejudice and discrimination, the part played by the social-distance factor, and the internal-colonialist version of conflict theory. Economic issues also encourage the development of prejudice and discrimination. Psychological perspectives include a three-stage analysis of the development of prejudice and the scapegoat theory.

Studies have examined the effects of prejudice and discrimination. While one prominent study found the self-esteem of black children higher than that of white children, negative effects of racism are numerous.

4. Dominant-group policies toward racial and ethnic groups include extermination, continued subjugation, population transfer, legal protection of minorities, cultural pluralism, and assimilation. Minority responses involve avoidance, acceptance, assimilation, and aggression.

5. The members of American racial and ethnic groups have distinctive histories. African-Americans are the largest group, with 30 million people representing 12 percent of the population. The original American blacks were slaves, and persecution of blacks has persisted since the freeing of the slaves. In the past several decades, some improvements in the economic, political, and social conditions of African-Americans' lives have occurred. However, in spite of these improvements, their current living conditions still tend to be substantially inferior to the living conditions maintained by whites.

Over 22.4 million people of Spanish descent live in the United States. About 13.5 million are Mexican-Americans, 2.7 million are Puerto Ricans, and about 6.2 million come from Central America, South America, or Cuba. They are frequently poor and badly educated, and the majority work in blue-collar jobs.

The United States has about 6 million Jews. They come from many countries and are diversified in religion and biological characteristics. In spite of having been the target of vicious stereotypes and discrimination, Jews have traditionally done well in businesses that were on the edge of the mainstream economy. In recent years Jews have attained income and educational levels that are well above the national averages.

About 7.3 million Asian-Americans live in the United States. About 1.6 million are of Chinese descent, 1.4 million of Japanese descent, and 615,000 of Vietnamese descent. Chinese immigrants began arriving about 1850 and found jobs as laborers for mines and railroads. Many have remained in ghettos and have suffered the problems of depressed living, but over all their educational and income attainments exceed the national average. Japanese-Americans began arriving in this country in the 1880s, and in spite of discrimination, they have become the most successful racial minority group, both economically and educationally. The Vietnamese have primarily arrived in the past two decades. Like earlier ethnic groups, their willingness to work hard for low pay pits them against Americans in a variety of occupations.

At present U.S. society contains about 2 million Native Americans, slightly more than when Columbus reached San Salvador in 1492. The history of the relationship of white Americans with Native Americans includes a long string of broken treaties and wars that have forced Indians to inhabit increasingly smaller amounts of inferior land. Today Native Americans are the poorest ethnic group in the United States.

White ethnics are primarily of Irish, Italian, Polish, Slavonic, and Greek origin. They generally come from southern and eastern Europe and often have a Catholic heritage. White ethnics are sometimes stereotyped as very conservative, and yet some evidence disputes such a claim.

6. The fundamental question involving American race relations appears to be how and why race has been the persistently most important basis of advantage and privilege in American society.

Key Terms

anti-Semitism the complex of prejudicial attitudes toward Jews

discrimination the behavior by which one group prevents or restricts another group's access to scarce resources

ethnic group a category of people that is set apart by itself or others because of distinct cultural or national qualities

ideology a system of beliefs and principles that presents an organized explanation of and the justification for a group's outlooks and behavior

individual racism an action performed by one person or a group that produces racial abuse

institutional racism discriminatory racial practices built into such prominent structures as the political, economic, and education systems

minority group any category of people with some recognizable trait that places it in a position of inferior status so that its members suffer limited opportunities and rewards

prejudice a highly negative judgment toward a group, focusing on one or more negative characteristics that are supposedly uniformly shared by all group members

race distinct physical characteristics, such as skin color and certain facial features, used to divide people into broad categories

racial group a number of people with the particular physical characteristics, such as skin color and certain facial features, that produce placement into a broad category

racism the ideology contending that actual or alleged differences between different racial groups assert the superiority of one racial group. Racism is a rationalization for political, economic, and social discrimination.

scapegoat theory an explanation emphasizing that people blocked from achieving a goal will sometimes be unable or unwilling to take out their frustration on its source, and so they direct their aggression against an accessible individual or group

self-fulfilling prophecy an incorrect definition

of a situation that comes to pass because people accept the incorrect definition and act on it to make it become true

social distance the feeling of separation between individuals or groups

stereotype an exaggerated, oversimplified image, maintained by prejudiced people, of the characteristics of the group members against whom they are prejudiced

Tests

True • False Test

_____ 1. Racial classification often creates a self-fulfilling prophecy.
_____ 2. Prejudice and discrimination have exactly the same meaning.
_____ 3. All modern sociologists have rejected the theory emphasizing that majority/minority relations in the United States can be analyzed as a form of internal colonialism.
_____ 4. For the first time, 1991 survey figures indicated that a larger percentage of Americans approve of than disapprove of interracial marriage.
_____ 5. Economic factors played a significant role in the relocation of Japanese-Americans during World War II.
_____ 6. As a minority response, assimilation means learning to live within the limitations of minority-group status.
_____ 7. Racial segregation in housing has contributed significantly to the growth of a black underclass.
_____ 8. From 1987 to 1991, the percentage of illegal Mexican immigrants who are female has declined.
_____ 9. Vietnamese immigrants have encountered hostility in the U.S. because they have been willing to work hard for low wages, thus competing with other workers for jobs.
_____ 10. Native Americans are the poorest ethnic group in the U.S.

Multiple-Choice Test

_____ 1. Which of the following statements about race is true?
    a. Its classifications are imprecise.
    b. There are six categories of race.
    c. Members of different races vary considerably in intelligence, creativity, and athletic ability.
    d. It never creates a self-fulfilling prophecy.

_____ 2. If a racial or ethnic group is easy to identify and weak, it may become the victim of aggression when groups are unable to direct hostility toward the real source of their frustration. This is the basic idea of:
    a. the authoritarian personality.
    b. the scapegoat theory.
    c. social distance.
    d. the stereotype.

_____ 3. *Apartheid* is:
    a. a form of extermination that was used on Native Americans.
    b. a type of assimilation.
    c. now officially ended in South Africa.
    d. a and c

_____ 4. A dominant-group policy that tends to decrease social distance is called:
    a.   continued subjugation.
    b.   legal protection of minorities.
    c.   population transfer.
    d.   extermination.

_____ 5. The decision of a light-skinned black person to "pass" into white society is an example of:
    a.   acceptance.
    b.   aggression.
    c.   assimilation.
    d.   avoidance.

_____ 6. Even with rising income, members of this (these) group(s) experience extensive residential segregation.
    a.   Native Americans
    b.   African-Americans
    c.   Asian-Americans
    d.   a, b, and c

_____ 7. Rapid immigration and a high fertility rate have made which group the fastest growing of all racial or ethnic groups in the United States?
    a.   Chinese-Americans
    b.   Puerto Ricans
    c.   Chicanos
    d.   Jews

_____ 8. Signs of a renewed interest in the survival of Jews as a distinct ethnic group include:
    a.   a revitalization of Jewish religious traditions.
    b.   a rapidly rising fertility rate.
    c.   a sharp increase in the number of American Jews emigrating to Israel.
    d.   a and c

_____ 9. Which statement best describes white ethnics?
    a.   They are likely to be Protestant.
    b.   They tend to be white-collar workers.
    c.   They live only in urban areas.
    d.   They have been stereotyped as patriotic and conservative.

_____ 10. Troy Duster's fundamental question about race relations:
    a.   uses a structural-functional perspective.
    b.   uses a conflict-theory approach.
    c.   is concerned with racism in just the past ten years.
    d.   only relates to African-Americans.

Essay Test

1. Define race and ethnicity and consider their sociological significance.
2. Define prejudice and discrimination and discuss in detail situations where both prejudice and discrimination exist as well as a situation where each exists without the other.
3. Summarize two explanations of prejudice and discrimination and analyze an event that illustrates each explanation.

268

4. What are the principal majority-group policies and minority-group responses? Discuss the relationship between the two sets of behavior, providing several examples. In other words how will a certain course of action taken by either a majority or minority group affect the other group(s) in question?

5. Summarize the history and current situation experienced by three minority groups examined in Chapter 9.

6. Summarize Troy Duster's conclusion about the significance of race, providing an illustration of the argument.

Suggested Readings

American Jewish Year Book. Philadelphia: Jewish Publication Society. The leading reference book on American Jews. This yearbook, which has been published annually since 1899, contains new articles in each edition as well as biographies, bibliographies, and statistics.

Brown, Dee. 1972. *Bury My Heart at Wounded Knee*. New York: Bantam Books. An eloquent, easily read history of the devastations suffered by Native Americans during their first 400 years of contact with whites.

Doob, Christopher Bates. 1993. *Racism: An American Cauldron*. New York: HarperCollins. A core text about contemporary American racism, using the perspective provided by internal colonialism to examine its impact on major racial minorities in such areas as politics, violence, work, education, housing, and the family.

Duster, Troy. 1987. "Purpose and Bias," *Society*. vol. 24 (January/February), pp. 8-12. A short article which raises highly provocative, disturbing issues about race relations.

Erdrich, Louise. 1984. *Love Medicine*. New York: Holt, Rinehart and Winston. A vivid, often humorous series of first-person accounts representing modern Indians' hardships and tragedies as well as their spiritual resilience.

Helmreich, William B. 1982. *The Things They Say Behind Your Back: Stereotypes and the Myths Behind Them*. Garden City, NJ: Doubleday. An informative, nicely written discussion about American ethnic and racial stereotypes.

Mowat, Farley. 1965. *Never Cry Wolf*. New York: Dell. While observing a family of wolves, a biologist develops a clearer and deeper understanding of them. Although the terms never appear, prejudice and discrimination are central issues of this nicely written, sometimes humorous, and always compelling account.

Rothenberg, Paula S. (ed.). 1992. *Race, Class, & Gender in the United States: An Integrated Study*. 2nd ed. New York: St. Martin's Press. A set of eighty-eight readings, providing diverse articles about race, class, and gender, with particularly effective material about race.

Additional Assignments

1. Read television programming for one week. Tally the number of programs based on or including people belonging to an identifiable racial or ethnic group. Then watch as many programs as possible. What can you conclude, if anything, about the way television represents minority-group members as featured characters? Are minority-group members who are secondary characters represented differently from principal characters?

2. Have minority-group attitudes and behavior changed over time? One somewhat unusual way to answer this question is to read novels that represent the lives of people from various ethnic groups in different historical periods. Form groups of six to eight students. Each group should choose one

ethnic or racial group and every member should read a novel about a different era. After reading his or her novel, each member of the group should be able to summarize the following issues:

a. The lifestyle of the minority-group members described in the novel.
b. Minority-group members' relationship with majority groups.
c. How members' minority status affects their self-images.
d. How, if at all, members of the minority group plan to change/improve their position in society.

This information should provide basic material for a group report about how minority groups' attitudes and behavior have changed over time.

Answers to Objective Test Questions

True • False Test

1. t		6. f
2. f		7. t
3. f		8. f
4. t		9. t
5. t		10. t

Multiple-Choice Test

1. a		6. b
2. b		7. c
3. c		8. a
4. b		9. d
5. d		10. b

Emerging Minorities

10

By the summer of 1992, the trend was clear: Sexual-harassment complaints to the Equal Employment Opportunity Commission had risen sharply, increasing by 50 percent in the first half of the year compared to the same period the previous year. Many employers were rushing to hire sensitivity trainers to teach men how to treat women. And many men were left wondering how they had failed to notice their female colleagues' anger.

Experts of both sexes and all political persuasions agreed that Americans' changing attitudes had occurred because of the nationally televised confirmation hearings for Judge Clarence Thomas, which, as journalist Jane Gross reported, represented a "watershed" in female-male relations. A central witness was Anita Hill, a former employee who charged Thomas with sexual harassment. Gross indicated that it was "a moment when men and women, believers and doubters, watched spellbound [Hill's] demure presentation and started to think about things differently" (Gross 1992, A1). Afterwards women felt emboldened about their rights, and both politicians and employers were uneasy about their responsibilities.

Senator Orrin Hatch, who stated that he felt Judge Thomas was innocent of all charges, nonetheless felt that "[t]he one good thing to come out of the hearing is that everybody—and I mean everybody—is more aware." Ann F. Lewis, a Democratic political consultant, agreed, saying that sexual harassment would never be a joke again. Lewis said, "Both the seriousness of sexual harassment and its force as a political issue have been established—firmly established—beyond snickers, giggles, and questions" (Gross 1992, A1).

As this material suggests, women continue to be oppressed because they are women. Women, the elderly, and disabled people qualify as minority groups, possessing respective traits—being female, old, and disabled—that place them in a position of inferior status. We begin with women and then consider the elderly and disabled people.

The Emergence of Women

For the present discussion, we need three terms as background—sex, gender, and gender role. All women or all men share the same **sex.** A variety of animal forms, including human beings, are divided into the biological categories of male and female.

Distinctions of gender, however, are not as fixed. **Gender** consists of the general behavioral standards that distinguish males and females in a given culture. In the United States, women and men have traditionally been expected to dress and to behave quite differently. Gender is a status, specifying for both women and men their culturally supported rights and obligations. In the late twentieth century, the definition of female gender has been reevaluated as the traditional expectation that women should be subordinate to men in all social activities has come under strong attack.

Gender roles are sets of specific behavioral patterns associated with either the female or male gender. As a parent of an 8-year-old girl, I would like to think that females and males are currently offered equal behavioral opportunities, but much evidence suggests that our culture gives males a more prominent position than females. For instance, undergraduates at the University of California at Los Angeles were randomly assigned to choose whether a specified woman or a specified man in a given situation would be described as a "person" or an "individual" or alternatively referred to by his or her sex. The result was that members of both sexes were much more inclined to use "individual" or "person" to refer to a male character than to a female character. This result was consistent with a general tendency in the English language—to consider males as linguistic representatives of all people but women as simply women, not permitted to represent the entire species (Hamilton 1991). Analyzing the process of gender-role development, we see extensive evidence of such bias toward women.

GENDER-ROLE DEVELOPMENT

What has been the source of women's traditional subjugation? Sigmund Freud believed that "anatomy determines destiny." While this position is not popular in modern social science, there is recognition that the biological component might affect gender-role development. Females and males have different sex-chromosome patterns, which produce different sex hormones, molding the originally undifferentiated reproductive tissues into either male or female genitals and internal reproductive systems. There also are some differences in women's and men's brains. Because men and women experience different physiological processes related to reproduction—such as the menstrual cycle in women and the erection of the penis in men—the controlling brain functions for these activities must be different. In addition, evidence has indicated that women's centers for verbal and spatial abilities are duplicated on both sides of the brain while men seem to have the speech center located on the left and the locus of spatial skills on the right side of the brain (Goleman 1978).

Focusing on the biological differences between females and males as well patterned behavioral differences between the sexes both in animal groups and human societies—such as the distinct tendency for males to wage war and for

females to care for offspring—some analysts, including the sociobiologists discussed in Chapter 6, have developed arguments concluding that the biological component is the critical one in determining men's and women's behavior and relationship with each other. But the majority of specialists have found the evidence insufficient to support such easy conclusions, suggesting that the influence on biological differences between the sexes is very complicated. As biologist R. A. Hinde wrote, "Our behavior is *caused* neither by biology nor by culture, because we are a product of both" (Hinde 1991, 604). With that thought we briefly consider cultural influences on gender-role development.

Even before a child is born, people's expectations about what is appropriate male or female behavior begin to appear. Late in pregnancy a parent might say, "The baby's kicking a lot. It must be a boy." During infancy mothers tend to look at and talk to female infants more than to males and to respond to girls more quickly when they cry. As toddlers, girls are encouraged to spend more time touching their mothers and staying close to them than are boys.

Different treatment for girls and boys intensifies at about the age of 2 when parents are able to use children's rapidly expanding language ability to mold their behavior. There are "girl" toys (dolls and dollhouses) and "boy" toys (trucks, airplanes, and rubber balls). Many 2-year-old boys who would prefer dolls are steered away from them and warned not to become "sissies." One study examined in detail the physical environment of 120 boys and girls divided into equal-sized groups of children aged five, thirteen, and twenty-five months, with each group containing equal numbers of girls and boys. Girls had more dolls, children's furniture, and other traditionally girls' toys such as handbags, doll houses, and vacuum cleaners. In contrast, boys were more likely to receive sports equipment, tools, and small and large vehicles. Color distinction was widespread. While boys wore more blue, red, and white clothing and even were likely to receive blue pacifiers, girls more often wore pink and multicolored clothes, and had pink pacifiers and jewelry. The authors suggested that sex-typed toys for infants could definitely influence later patterns of play as well as development of work-related skills and interests. They concluded

274

that the "times are changing. . . . However, the changes do not seem to to occur quickly enough to provide equal opportunities for girls and boys during their early development" (Pomerleau et al. 1990, 366).

Parental outlook also influences children's gender-role development. For instance, a study indicated that mothers of 4-year-olds are convinced that boys can perform such tasks as crossing the street, using scissors, or walking alone to a friend's house at a younger age than can girls (Lindsey 1990, 43). It is clear, however, that mothers' perceptions can differ. One study indicated that mothers who considered themselves less traditionally feminine (emphasizing accomplishment of such goals as completion of work-related tasks more than meeting people's social and emotional needs) tended to perceive their children in less stereotyped girls' or boys' roles than mothers who visualized themselves as traditionally feminine (Vogel et al. 1991).

Parents show distinctly sex-typed patterns in directing their children's activities. A large sample of children from thirty-seven states—410 respondents on a school day and 347 for a nonschool day—revealed that girls spent more time in household work and personal care and less in leisure activities than boys. In fact, 10-year-old girls were spending more time in meal preparation and cleanup than 16- to 18-year-old males. Sex-linked specialization was apparent, with girls most

While gender-role patterns have been changing in modern society, there continues to be some tendency, as this photo suggests, for children to assume traditional gender roles.

likely to be involved in meal preparation and cleanup, household cleaning, and laundry and boys in repairs, home improvement, and outdoor cleaning. Furthermore the researchers noted that children in the study spent only one-half to three-quarters of an hour per weekend day on household work. They concluded that given the sex-linked biases and modest amount of time spent on household tasks, parents were losing a chance to "develop more positive attitudes toward equitable division of household work that may carry over into adulthood" (Mauldin and Meeks 1990, 552).

While parents have the earliest impact on children's gender-role development, their peers are also influential in preparing them for gender roles. By about the age of 3, young children distinctly prefer same-sex friends, and this preference continues into late childhood and adolescence, intensifying with age and becoming particularly strong in middle childhood and early adolescence (Feiring and Lewis 1991). Boys maintain more extensive peer-group contacts, but girls have more intensive ones, more likely focusing on dyads (two-person groups) and thus providing them early training in developing intimate relationships (Lindsey 1990, 45–46).

This same-sex preference also carries into adolescent years. A study of sixty-six white middle-class adolescents indicated that the respondents felt that their friends affected their ideas about men's and women's roles. For example, one male adolescent explained, "I guess I got some of my ideas from friends in Boy Scouts. You're supposed to be rugged and live in the woods and camp out and that was supposed to be just the men" (Werrbach, Grotevant, and Cooper 1990, 358).

Besides recognizing that women and men have experienced different gender-role development, we need to consider that women have been systematically victimized in various ways.

SEXISM

Any "ism" is an ideology, a system of beliefs and principles that presents an organized explanation of and justification for a group's outlooks and behavior. **Sexism** is an ideology emphasizing that actual or alleged differences between men and women establish the superiority of men. Sexism is a rationalization for political, economic, and social discrimination against women. Let us consider how the ideology of sexism has traditionally developed in American society.

First, unless observers can distinguish one group from another, then sexism or any other discriminatory behavior is impossible. Thus women's distinct visibility makes sexism possible. Their secondary sex characteristics—breasts, absence of facial hair, fairly narrow shoulders, and relatively wide hips—and frequently distinctive manner of dress make them easily distinguishable from men. Even modern "unisex" styles of hair and dress seldom make the designation of a person's sex difficult.

Second, women have been attributed certain traits of inferiority. The sexist ideology has emphasized that women are less intelligent than men. At the emotional level, sexism claims that women are more likely to be irresponsible, inconsistent, and unstable.

Third, sexism involves rationalizations about women's status summed up by the following sentence: "Women's place is in the home." The title of Betty Friedan's well-known book, *The Feminine Mystique*, is the elusive claim that the "occupation of housewife" will provide a glamorous, fulfilling role for modern women.

Fourth, sexism appears in the behavior patterns that women have traditionally learned. These patterns are accommodations to the attributed traits and rationalizations of status just described. Traditionally, in the presence of men, women have learned to hide their intelligence or to restrict its demonstration. Women have been expected to be ever smiling, laughing, and helpless in appearance, thereby solidifying the conclusion that they are entirely content with their situation as long as men supply direction and control.

Finally discrimination is an aspect of sexism. In American society women have traditionally encountered more limitations on education than men. In the occupational area, women have suffered confinement to less prestigious jobs, with access to supervisory positions often prevented. In politics women have historically had almost no important roles. Women have also encountered multiple discriminations in everyday life, with men usually given much greater leeway in their sexual activity and general public behavior (Hacker 1951).

Not surprisingly sexism has produced various costs for women.

Costs

Three prominent costs involve psychological, career, and physical issues.

Psychological Cost Americans believe that both men and women possess positive qualities, but those attributed to women have emphatically not been those for which society offers its highest rewards. The positive traits attributed to men include their tendency to be aggressive, independent, unemotional, competitive, skilled in business, self-centered, and capable of leadership. For women the list includes the capacity to be talkative, tactful, gentle, aware of the feelings of others, and interested in their own appearance (Cox 1981; Freeman 1975).

Historically the media have supported such narrow, stereotyped images of women, with research indicating that the representation of women changed little between the late 1960s and late 1980s. In television dramatic series, women are less likely than men to be seen working outside the home; the women who do work outside the home usually are not married although often they are divorced. Female characters tend to be young and beautiful, usually averaging about ten years younger than male characters. Not only are men older but they are generally in charge, and are much more likely to combine a successful career and marriage.

Hair-care data support the valued television image of the young, beautiful woman. While hair colors are evenly distributed between sexes within racial groups in the general population, television characters' hair illustrate distinct trends. Male television characters' hair generally fits into the common brown, black, and grey categories, but female characters demonstrate a high proportion of glamorous colors—blond or red/auburn.

In many dramatic series, women are supposed to be seen but not heard. Analyzing a typical episode of the well-known dramatic series "Miami Vice," researchers found fourteen speaking parts, all taken by males. Two female characters had more than three minutes of screen time, but as ornamental girl friends of male characters, neither spoke (Davis 1990; Signorielli 1989).

Commercials show a similar trend. One of the most significant issues is voice-overs, the unseen voice of authority trying to convince consumers to

276   buy a given product. In 90 percent of commercials, men are narrators. A female reporter recalled asking a male advertising executive representing a baby-care item about this situation. "So I ask 'Is a man a mother?' The answer: 'A man just knows what he's talking about. A man just has automatic credibility on TV'" (Bretl and Cantor 1988, 607).

A study comparing gender representations in television commercials in 1988 with commercials from a decade earlier uncovered the following shifts: female voice-overs going from 7 to 9 percent; females representing domestic products shifting from 86 to 55 percent; women selling nondomestic products increasing from 22 percent to 28 percent; home settings showing women dropping from 76 to 64 percent; and out-of-home settings presenting females going from 22 to 36 percent. While the statistics show slight change over time, the author concluded that over all "[w]omen are not pictured any differently in television advertisements than they were pictured ten years ago" (Lovdal 1989, 722).

Like commercial television, commercial radio appears to support traditional gender-role socialization. An analysis of the content of nonmusic programming for two Top 40 radio stations directed to 12- to 17-year-olds indicated that males dominated as disc jockeys, newscasters, voice-overs in advertisements, sportscasters, and weathercasters. In addition, an examination of the words spoken indicated that there were nearly twice as many references to males as to females. Furthermore the content of references differed, with women most commonly described by their family affiliation and men most frequently referred to as guys (Lont 1990).

Looking beyond women's representation in the mass media, a study found that when women suffered depression, the positive attributes of both men's and women's traditional roles were absent from their lives. Their lives were without the ambition and self-confidence generally associated with men's roles; they tended to be submissive and dependent. Furthermore they lacked the sensitivity to others' needs and eagerness to soothe hurt feelings conventionally linked to women's roles (Landrine 1988). These female victims of depression, in short, did not possess the positive attributes attached to either traditional gender role.

In short, the psychological cost of sexism is that women have traditionally received negative or restricted images of themselves that tend to lock them into narrow roles offering little opportunity to achieve a high level of income, recognition, or personal satisfaction.

Career Cost   If a woman feels fulfilled concentrating on housework, then she suffers no sense of career cost. However, many women do not feel fulfilled when limited to this work role. A study of British women, whose household tasks are basically similar to those of their American counterparts, indicated that 70 percent of the women expressed an overall dissatisfaction in their assessment of housework. The monotony of the work and its loneliness were other frequent complaints. This housewife's statement sums up the most typical criticims: "It's ridiculous to pretend that anyone actually likes cleaning floors and washing dishes—how can they? Housework is awful work. It's lonely and boring. There's nothing to show for it—it's all got to be done the next day. You don't get paid for it, either" (Oakley 1974, 186).

Today many women extend themselves beyond the housewife role. Women comprise over half the population and more than 40 percent of the labor force. Yet they are much less successful than men in the occupational realm.

Socialization is one contributing factor. Traditional socialization has emphasized domestic tasks for women and breadwinning tasks for men. Many parents remain reluctant to give up the idea that boys are brighter, more talented, and better suited for valued jobs than girls. When asked about their children's ability and effort in math, parents with children of both sexes generally felt that their daughters made more effort but that their sons were more talented, even though the children's achievement-test scores and grades were about equal (Yee and Eccles 1988). We might suspect that when such a differential perception is imposed on children, it will produce the imagined result. Recall our discussion of the self-fulfilling prophecy in Chapter 9, "Racial and Ethnic Groups."

Some evidence suggests that women with successful careers have often received a socialization that has made them feel particularly secure and certain about being successful. Margaret Hennig and Anne Jardim (1977) studied female presidents and vice-presidents of nationally recognized medium-to-large business firms and compared them with a group similar in age, education, and family background whose members had never risen beyond middle management. The basis for the achievement differences apparently lay in the family dynamics. Each high-achieving executive was either an only child or the first born of an all-girl family containing no more than three siblings. Both the mother and father simultaneously valued their daughter's femaleness and achievement and saw no contradiction to the enhancement of both. The parents wanted the girl to learn early to set her own goals and standards of excellence and to gain satisfaction from effectively performing any task she approached. One other distinctive quality about the families of top women executives was that both parents had strong relationships with their daughter. As one informant said:

> From my earliest recollections my parents and I were friends . . . . I always wanted to be just like my mother and just like my father, something which I am sure gave those hearing me say it no end of amusement! Yet in spite of this I think my parents really encouraged me to think through things very carefully and to venture my own opinion, even when I was very very young. I think they really trusted me and I them.

(Hennig and Jardim 1977, 84)

Current young adults show the impact of gender-specific socialization. A study of 4,500 college students from primarily upper-middle-class families concluded that while women and men did equally well in school and asserted a similar commitment to future work roles, members of both sexes expected that women would have more prominent involvement in family activities and men greater commitment to work (Spade and Reese 1991).

It appears that more than socialization accounts for most women's relatively limited career chances. For instance, socialization does not seem to account for the fact that between 1980 and 1990, median earnings of women working full-time in relation to median earnings of men working full-time remained substantial—going from $.60 to $.71 on the dollar (U.S. Bureau of the Census, *Statistical Abstract of the United States: 1992*, No. 710). This sustained earning gap seems to be the result of a couple of causes.

In the first place, when education, training, and work experience obtained by men and women are held constant, pay differences do occur. Thus to some extent women are the victims of "unequal pay for equal work."

However, a more significant factor helps explain sex differences in pay. Occupational segregation is widespread in the American job world. Women are more heavily concentrated in low-prestige, low-paying jobs. For whites to achieve occupational balance by sex, 61 percent of either women or men would need to change jobs. While there is a greater proportion of women than men in white-collar jobs, women are generally in nursing, elementary and secondary school teaching, social work, library service, and clerical and secretarial work—jobs that are fairly low in pay and prestige (Scarpitti and Andersen 1989, 267–68).

Occupational segregation by sex is significant because it represents structural limits imposed on women's opportunities. An important implication of this point is that if we blame women's inability to reach higher occupational levels on personal shortcomings, then we are failing to evaluate the influence of important social forces. As we noted in Chapter 8, "Social Stratification," traditional values and "old boys' networks" frequently hamper women's occupational advancement. Sometimes it is difficult to obtain a clear overall picture of women's occupational prospects. A team of researchers observed that the steadily increasing percentage of women in management and professional positions over the past two decades has produced "a politics of optimism"—a widely held belief that women are successfully moving in substantial numbers to high-paying, prestigious positions. The reality, however, is illustrated by the situation encountered by women in management, who are concentrated in lower levels, with fewer opportunities for advancement and lower pay than men; from 1960 to 1980, in fact, women in management experienced a slight salary decline in relation to men (Blum and Smith 1988).

Table 10.1 offers some statistics that compare women and men on job types, income, and several other important issues.

Physical Cost A study suggested that, roughly speaking, women agree on rankings of the hurtfulness of different kinds of violence against women (Leidig 1981). At the least hurtful end of the continuum is "street hassling," which includes male verbal harassment, rude stares, and noises directed at women as they walk along the street. A

Table 10.1 Some Bread-and-Butter Issues: Men vs. Women

	Women	*Men*
EDUCATION FOR PEOPLE 25 AND OVER: 1991		
Four years of high school or more	78.3%	78.5%
One or more years of college	37.4	42.5
Four years of college or more	18.8	24.3
OCCUPATION OF PEOPLE 25 AND OVER: 1989		
White-collar positions	71.2%	48.6%
Managerial/professional	28.9	29.2
Technical/sales/clerical	42.3	19.4
Blue-collar positions	28.8	51.4
MEDIAN INCOME OF FULL-TIME WORKERS 25 AND OVER: 1990		
	$20,586	$29,172

Source: Adapted from U.S. Bureau of the Census. Statistical Abstract of the United States: 1991, No. 656; U.S. Bureau of the Census. Statistical Abstract of the United States: 1992, No. 221 and No. 710.

On bread-and-butter issues, women generally do not fare as well as men—for example, the 1990 woman's median salary was 70 percent of a man's median salary. Sometimes gender differences are deceptive at first glance. Thus women have a greater percentage of their workers in white-collar positions than do men, but about three-fifths of women's white-collar jobs are in technical/sales/clerical positions, which generally do not pay very well.

more aggressive form of "hassling" is touching or grabbing a woman without her permission, including seemingly accidental physical contact with a woman's body in subways, elevators, or other crowded areas.

A stronger form of harrassment would be sexual harassment on the job or sexual abuse by male psychotherapists and other professionals; these acts can extend from patting a woman on her knee or bottom to more extensive sexual overtures. As we noted at the beginning of the chapter, Anita Hill's testimony has brought considerable national attention to this issue.

In engaging in sexual harassment, the man does not use physical power but the power, more precisely the authority, associated with his job. Typically he either hints or indicates directly that the woman will be rewarded if she accepts his sexual advances, and that if she rejects his overtures she will be punished, perhaps losing her job (Williams 1987, 439). Sexual harassment includes sexist comments and derogatory jokes about women; offensive sexual advances made without any explicit reference to possible rewards for the targeted woman; efforts to trade sexual favors for the promise of rewards; attempts to force sexual activity by threatening punishment;

and sexual assaults (Rubin and Borgers 1990, 399).

When Professor Anita Hill claimed that she had been frequently harassed sexually by Judge Clarence Thomas while working for him, several members of the all-male Senate Judiciary Committee, before which she was testifying, asked in apparent disbelief why she hadn't left her job. Professor Hill explained that the job was very important for her career and that had she left her occupational future would have been seriously jeopardized.

Sources on sexual harassment indicate that Hill's response was quite conventional. Before quitting or complaining, a woman must assess the impact on her livelihood. She needs to consider immediate prospects for other jobs, the significance of a good recommendation compared to a poor one, and the likely response from friends, family members, and colleagues. Frequently, like Professor Hill, she calculates that the risk of leaving or protesting are simply too great—that as difficult as harassment is, she has no reasonable choice but to continue putting up with it (Schwendinger and Schwendinger 1990, 63).

Reviewing studies of sexual harassment in the academic world during the 1980s, a pair of researchers concluded that over all it appeared

This photo shows Iranian women dressed in highly traditional chador robes doing something that is distinctly untraditional for women—shooting guns. These women are spending a month in a camp near Teheran, where they are trained to become members of a women's home guard that is supposed to help defend the nation from foriegn invaders.

that about 30 percent of respondents had encountered some form of sexual harassment (Rubin and Borgers 1990, 405). Victims included not only graduate and undergraduate students but also faculty members, who can be harassed by both colleagues and students (McKinney 1990).

Pornography and prostitution also fall in this intermediate area of the continuum. Both activities designate women as an object for male exploitation, with violence often intruding in fantasy or reality.

The continuum of violence reaches the extreme with outright, unadulterated violence: rape and physical abuse. Three prominent types of rape can occur: date rape, marital rape, and stranger-to-stranger rape. Police often receive reports of the third type but not of the other two. Nonetheless it is likely that marital rape occurs more often than stranger-to-stranger rape. Many overt acts of violence against women, such as wife-abuse, often contain both a sexual and physical component. An act of violence most people regard as extremely serious is girl-child incest. A trusted family member, usually a father or stepfather, forces a girl to have sexual intercourse with him, quite possibly over a protracted period of time.

Certain trends appear among the violent acts against women. In the first place, nonreporting is a distinct pattern whether the issue is indecent exposure, battering, girl-child abuse, or rape. Reasons for nonreporting include the expectation that nothing will be done, the belief that claims will receive ridicule, and the victims' fear of repercussions if they complain. Another trend has been that violence against women was not considered a serious problem until the advent of the women's movement in the late 1960s. Historically women have listened to jokes about wife-battering and rape and heard incest described as "the game the whole family can play." A third trend that appears in the acts of violence against women is the tendency to blame them for the acts perpetuated against them. When a man is robbed or assaulted, police seldom ask if he provoked the crime, encouraged it, or dreamed about it. However, when a woman is physically or sexually assaulted,

280

she traditionally has had to endure such questions from the police, therapists, physicians, and clergy. Now many police departments demonstrate increased sensitivity in interviewing rape victims; the growing use of female officers for this task has been particularly effective.

Closely linked to the blaming-the-victim trend has been a broad belief in "female masochism." A widespread and extremely harmful contention is that women not only do not mind pain and humiliation but that they also often like it—thus the common male claim that rape victims frequently "lie back and enjoy it" (Frieze 1983). Research has shown that the victim-blaming process has produced various negative effects, including negative images of the victim and victims' expanded self-blame (McCaul et al. 1990; Williams 1987).

An idea that might prove useful in helping to understand sexual violence against women involves the perception that sex offense is like an addiction in some respects. While alcoholism tends to flourish in cultures that do not allow children to learn safe drinking practices, exploitative sex may thrive in cultures not allowing children to learn easily and safely about sex (Herman 1988).

Because of the costs of sexism, women have mobilized to combat the inequalities and brutalities imposed on them.

THE WOMEN'S MOVEMENT

Through the centuries women have become increasingly aware of their position in society. Some prehistoric cave paintings appear to be women's first representation of their social organization. Ancient Sumerian and African mothers wrote poems about being women, and speeches attributed to medieval women condemned as witches have survived to the present. In the Middle Ages, some women lived in self-sufficient monastic communities in which insights and understanding about women's role in society developed (McLaughlin 1989; Neel 1989). Inevitably women's recognition of their subordinate position has expanded during periods that stressed the importance of new ideas and influences, particularly the significance of individual rights. In the course of the eighteenth-century era called the Enlightenment, the importance of rational thought and the value of the individual man received

an increasing recognition. In 1792 Mary Wollstonecraft was simply extending the Enlightenment tradition when she published *The Vindication of the Rights of Woman*. In this book she stated:

> My own sex, I hope, will excuse me, if I treat them like rational creatures, instead of flattering their fascinating graces, and viewing them as if they were in a state of perpetual childhood, unable to stand alone. . . . I wish to persuade women to endeavor to acquire strength, both of mind and body, and to convince them that the soft phrases, susceptibility of heart, delicacy of sentiment, and refinement of taste, are almost synonymous with epithets of weakness.

(*Wollstonecraft* 1980, 459)

In the early twentieth century, a new wave of enlightenment swept across western Europe and the United States: New ideas and new ways of doing things were supported by the spread of industrialism, the occurrence of World War I, the rise of Marxism, and the rapid development of the behavioral and social sciences. The most concrete accomplishment of this movement was the 1920 passage of the Nineteenth Amendment to the U.S. Constitution, which provided women the right to vote. After the passage of the Nineteenth Amendment, women's activities became less explicitly organized and involved less public fanfare. In the 1920s, however, various important women's organizations were formed: the League of Women Voters, the National Council of Women, and the International League for Peace and Freedom. After World War I, women increasingly entered the public work place, taking an active role in the trade-union movement and also producing such professional organizations as Business and Professional Women (BPW).

Like earlier women's consciousness efforts, the modern women's movement has been a product of its time. This movement has contained two separate sections. The first, which has been more traditional, received its impetus from the President's Commission on the Status of Women established by President John Kennedy in 1961; the challenge to the status quo encouraged by Friedan's bestselling book; and the influence of a "sex" provision in the Civil Rights Act of 1964. In 1966 the National Organization for Women (NOW) was formed. Its members were primarily from the professions, labor, government, and communications and ranged in age from about 25 to 45. Its self-assigned task was to obtain equality and justice under the law, and its initial target was the executive branch, with the intention of bringing federal power to bear on behalf of women. In the intervening years, NOW's major activities have been in the economic and political spheres, most notably the narrowly defeated effort to seek passage of the Equal Rights Amendment.

The second section of the modern women's movement emerged from the 1960s civil-rights and antiwar movements, in which general human rights received extensive emphasis but women's rights commanded little attention. The idea of women's "liberation" first appeared in a memo written in 1964 by two female members of Students for a Democratic Society (SDS); the women protested the fact that in this activist student organization, women were assigned menial office tasks, were not heeded at meetings, and were generally undervalued, and, as a result, undervalued themselves (Gitlin 1989, 169). Three years later SDS women finally succeeded in passing a resolution calling for the full participation of women in SDS. Such early efforts brought no explicit result, but they did help create a "radical community" where women became increasingly aware of shared grievances and intentions. In such a context, five independent women's groups formed in 1967 and 1968 in five different cities: Chicago, Toronto, Seattle, Detroit, and Gainesville, Florida. The initial efforts to publicize a women's movement received an indifferent or hostile reaction from men (Freeman 1980).

Throughout the 1970s, however, the women's movement expanded, affecting every aspect of human existence. Its growing influence becomes apparent upon examining the results of a national sample of Americans who were asked whether they favor or oppose most of the efforts to strengthen or change women's status in society today. The percentage favoring an improvement of status increased from 42 percent in 1970 to 67 percent in 1981 (Louis Harris and Associates, *Harris Survey*, August 1981).

Continuing an examination of gender issues, the nearby Social Application analyzes one sociologist's effort to confront gender issues in the classroom.

As women of diverse backgrounds move into positions of power and prominence, girls and young women can see that such achievements, which were once impossible, are now possible. A notable case in point occurred in 1992 when Carol Moseley-Braun became the first African-American woman elected to the U.S. Senate.

THE FUTURE OF WOMEN'S RIGHTS

Two feminist writers suggested that in order to overcome traditional dependency on men, women must learn to tell their own stories—to embrace the idea that one's life can be thought of as an unfolding story about which each individual woman exercises choice. True, these writers indicated, all people are born into a certain cultural and familial context, which provides some limitations, but self-supplied direction is always possible. It is as though each person is born into a channel of water, in which she remains her entire life, but as she grows to adulthood, she has the choice of deciding to swim upstream or downstream, of staying in the middle, or perhaps switching to a side-channel that has seldom if ever been used (Rowland-Serdar and Schwartz-Shea 1991).

Currently this perspective receives widespread support, and as a result what we see today is modern women pursuing a variety of options, including militant action. In the early 1990s, new women's

SOCIAL APPLICATION
Confronting Gender Inequality in the Classroom

In fifteen years of teaching, sociologist Nancy J. Davis has frequently taught courses focusing on inequality—issues related to class, race, and gender. Professor Davis has found three basic responses, which she described as the resisting class, the paralyzed class, and the enraged class. Using examples involving gender issues, we can discuss each type of class and how she dealt with it.

The Resisting Class According to Professor Davis, students in this type of class did not accept sociological analyses about structural conditions producing gender stratification. They tended to focus on individual responsiblity, concluding that either personal failure or choice accounted for such problems as women's poverty or frequent location in low-paying clerical or secretarial jobs. The sociologist suggested that the mass media make a significant if negative contribution to these students' outlook, implying that willpower is enough to ensure modern women occupational success and that resolving demands of employment and child care is easily accomplished.

When confronted in class with the realities of gender stratification, resisting students sometimes responded defensively. In one class on the sexual division of domestic labor, a married student with children said angrily, "Well, my husband may not be very involved in day-to-day domestic life, but if there was ever . . . a real emergency—like a nuclear attack—he'd be there." Several years later Professor Davis met this woman, now a single mother, waitressing in a café. She explained, "You know, that was about the stupidest thing I ever said, but at the time, it just hit too close to home" (Davis 1992, 233).

Professor Davis agreed that sociology courses often hit too close to home for many students. In class she has used a number of techniques to help students understand how processes of inequality work. For instance, she has found simulation games useful. One game called "Star Power," which is played with eighteen to thirty-five people, focuses on trading chips and establishes a rigged system in which initial advantage or disadvantage accumulates over time. Those at the bottom feel the apathy, frustration, and withdrawal that women locked into low-paying, nonprestigious jobs often suffer. Those at the top are encouraged to abuse power and claim special privilege as dominant males, particularly those in higher-level jobs, have traditionally done. While no simulation game can produce the complex emotional and intellectual turmoil of a real stratification system, these exercises serve to introduce students to the harsh realities of gender stratification in a fairly non-threatening way.

Another approach has been to encourage students to conduct their own participant-observation studies—such as observing female and male students at a student union, fast-food restaurant, or in other group situtations. Resistance often declines when students' own work, not a teacher's lecture, focuses on stratified gender roles. Supplemental sources supplied by the teacher on topics like the devices used to silence women can prove useful.

With the paralyzed class, different challenges arise.

The Paralyzed Class The realization that our society structures unequal opportunity can produce depression, fatalism, and ultimately an inability or unwillingness to act in students. "What's the point?" some wonder. "The cards are stacked against me. So why bother trying?"

Professor Davis indicated that this suggestion is particularly potent if no alternatives to present conditions are suggested. A problem in our society is that there has been fairly weak support for collective action, and students often feel that they must face stratification systems alone, seeking without anyone else's help to overcome inequalities through hard work, networking, or some other self-help strategy. One useful course of action is to include material in stratification courses, including gender-stratification courses, that deal with social movements and suggest how mass mobilization can confront social inequalities.

Films like *The Life and Times of Rosie the Riveter, Pink Triangles,* and *Norma Rae* can make students aware of race-, class-, and sex-divided societies. Watching such films, students can become aware that positive social conditions that they take for granted, such as universal suffrage or women's opportunities to enter the general job market, simply did not exist at one time and that only collective struggle produced the changes permitting them to occur.

Empowerment, the elimination of paralysis, can be sparked by local actions. Professor Davis indicated that one of the male students in her gender course asked the manager of their campus bookstore why books on child care, gardening, and cooking were located in a section on "women's interests." As a result that section no longer exists, and books are shelved under their respective activities, with cookbooks under "cooking" and not "women." Accounts like this one are helping paralyzed students realize that conditions can be changed, sometimes easily.

The enraged class responds from a different perspective.

The Enraged Class In this instance students have often been brutalized—sexually abused, raped, or harassed—and they feel anger and often express it. Frequently their anger is not focused but directed toward the closest member or members of the advantaged group—a man or men in the case of enraged women.

Professor Davis suggested that while anger is a healthy response to injustice, it needs to be focused to become an empowering emotion. One avenue is to have students write journals to which instructors can respond with personal, constructive commentary.

Anonymous essays allow students a chance to express what they feel unable to say in class or to an instructor with signed material. Whether unsigned or signed, Professor Davis, with students' permission, has frequently read their essays to the class. This type of writing helps students focus their anger, and if their essays are read in class, they get the feeling that they are helping to educate their fellow students,

thereby engaging in a political act that will help stop what was done to them.

In the enraged class, the use of humor and satire often prove useful since they can demonstrate the injustice of stratified societies in a light, playful, but often highly incisive manner. This sociologist found that the book of feminist humor entitled *Pulling Our Own Strings,* edited by Gloria Kaufman and Mary Kay Blakely, with selections like "Menstruating Women are Unfit to Be Mothers," has always been well-received and makes its points effectively. Stories from real life and music are other, often humor-filled sources of insight about gender stratification.

Professor Davis ended her article by saying that each class is different and that in reality a given class will not fit neatly into one of her three categories. In fact, with multiple outlooks in a single class, addressing one condition might exacerbate another. So, she concluded, these "problems, common to sociology courses, require considerable sensitivity, imagination, and flexibility on the part of instructors" (Davis 1992, 238).

Source: Nancy J. Davis. "Teaching about Inequality: Student Resistance, Paralysis, and Rage," Teaching Sociology. vol. 20 (July 1992), pp. 232–38.

rights organizations spurred by anger over sexual harassment and the growing limitations on the right to obtain abortions, developed and often engaged in militant action. One of these organizations has been the Women's Action Coalition—(WAC)—which has emphasized self-empowerment and engaged in many militant actions, most notably aggressive street confrontations with anti-abortion groups. Observing WAC, Marlene

Besterman, a New York lawyer, said, "There's a heart-stopping, breathtaking energy about it. It's an incredibly exciting time to be a woman" (Manegold 1992, 25).

Women make up the majority of another emerging minority—the elderly. Whether women or men, they frequently encounter patterns of prejudice and discrimination similar to those that develop when sexism occurs.

The Emergence of the Elderly

No one doubted that Alexander Freiheit was a first-rate college teacher. In lecture his breadth of vision gracefully combined with a vast store of anecdotal information about historical figures and events. Throughout the hour Professor Freiheit would pace quickly around the room, seemingly generated by the excitement of the ideas he was expressing. But what about possible signs of senility? When asked, most faculty members readily admitted that Professor Freiheit was considerably more intelligent, alert, and witty than many colleagues half his age. The problem he confronted was bureaucratic. As a publicly funded organization, the university was under the jurisdiction of state law, which required mandatory retirement at age 70 unless the employer—in this case the uni-versity president—strongly supported continuing employment. The vice-president, speaking for his superior, refused such support, indicating that the planned "configuration" for the next two decades emphasized the decline of the history department and an increase in other subject areas where student demand was greater. "But the man is irreplaceable," one of Professor Freiheit's supporters argued. "I'm afraid that ultimately everyone is replaceable," the vice-president replied.

A group of students and faculty formed an organization to keep Professor Freiheit employed at the university. They sought and received publicity from the school paper, a faculty newsletter, and the local newspaper as well as support from several local politicians. Finally they initiated a lawsuit, but the judge ruled against the teacher. Professor Freiheit was angry and discouraged. "The President of the United States is two years older than I am, and I could have gone to school with most of the Supreme Court Justices. It looks like you need to be prominent and powerful to avoid being put out to pasture."

Obviously Professor Freiheit was feeling that the laws involving retirement were meaningless and that he was powerless to do anything about them. In spite of a recent change in this particular law, senior citizens frequently face situations where they encounter discrimination—not an insignificant fact when we consider their numbers. As Figure 10.1 indicates, the American elderly—people aged 65 and older—are now about 31.8 million in number, representing 12.6 percent of the population (U.S. Bureau of the Census, *Statistical Abstract of the United States: 1992*, No. 19) and will increase in both numbers and percentage in the United States and other industrialized nations. The elderly is the one minority group most of us can eventually expect to join.

In this section we discuss ageism and its costs, the reactions to ageism, and the future of the elderly as a minority group.

Figure 10.1

Percentage of Population 65 and More in the United States, Western Germany, and Japan over Time.

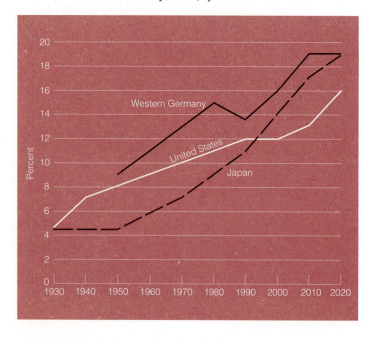

This graph illustrates that in advanced industrial nations, there is a steadily increasing percentage of people in the elderly bracket.

Source: U.S. *Bureau of the Census.* Historical Statistics of the United States: Colonial Times to 1970. *Series A, pp.* 119–134; U.S. *Bureau of the Census.* Current Population Reports: Population Estimates and Projection. *No. 74, Tables 4 and 8.*

AGEISM

Ageism is an ideology asserting the superiority of the young over the the old. Ageism is a rationalization for economic, political, and social discrimination against the elderly. Like sexism, ageism is a process that is readily apparent in daily life.

First, like sexism, ageism could not occur without high social visibility. Senior citizens do possess such visibility. Their skin is wrinkled, and some of them walk slowly or stooped over. In addition, the elderly tend to dress more blandly than more youthful people. On this point they can face a dilemma. Colorless elderly fashions mark people off as old, and yet if they wear bright, fashionable clothes, they are accused of "failing to act their age."

Second, the elderly have various negative qualities attributed to them. The prevailing stereotype of old people includes images of physical deterioration, passivity, dependency, rigidity, inefficiency, and the loss of alertness and intelligence (Nuessel 1982; Williamson, Munley, and Evans 1980). When adolescent, middle-aged, and elderly people were asked to evaluate adults in these three age groups, the elderly received the lowest overall evaluation (Luszcz and Fitzgerald 1986).

Third, there is a rationalization of old people's status—the image of the "happy disengager," the picture of smiling, fulfilled elderly people reveling in their extensive free time and nearly endless opportunities to play with grandchildren. But it is not that simple. Research shows that adjustment to retirement depends on such factors as health, financial assets, living conditions, and friends (Bowling and Browne 1991; Logue 1991; Reitzes, Mutran, and Pope 1991).

Like other minority groups, senior citizens make some accommodation to their status. This accommodation can appear as a graceful acceptance of retirement, in spite of personal reluctance, or a decision to give short, even truncated responses to an interviewer in order to avoid the slightest hint of being a rambling, senile old person.

Inevitably the elderly face discrimination, with retirement laws having been one of the most obvious illustrations. Thus it was a legislative landmark when Congress in October 1986 passed a law eliminating mandatory retirement for nearly all employed Americans. The late Claude Pepper, an 86-year-old congressman who was the chief sponsor of the bill, declared, "Abolishing age discrimination will offer new hope to older workers who are desperate to maintain their independence and dignity. . . ." (Noble 1986, E6). The new retirement law, however, has not eliminated all work-associated problems for elderly people. Until age 70 a person cannot earn more than $6,900 per year at a job without receiving a reduction in social-security benefits. Above that amount a senior citizen is required to pay $1 for every $2 earned—a 50-percent tax rate. By contrast, the relatively affluent elderly who receive capital gains or interest on savings suffer no such tax penalty (Kornblum and Julian 1989, 343–44).

The elderly's minority status also produces other costs.

Costs

In a study of 502 people aged 46 to 71, the respondents indicated that health was the principal factor contributing to life satisfaction, followed by participation in organizational or group activity, and sense of control over one's destiny (Palmore and

For many elderly people, a major cost of growing old is a state of disengagement in which isolation and loneliness dominate.

286

Luikart 1974). Let us consider some ways ageism asserts itself as a cost in each of these areas.

Health and Medical-Care Cost   Ageism appears to be a factor that influences health by affecting the quality of medical care. Several studies suggest that generally an inverse relationship exists between a person's age and the speed of emergency treatment—therefore, the older the patient, the more slowly he or she receives treatment (Simpson 1976; Sudnow 1967). Certain characteristics of senior citizens also can make them undesirable from a treatment point of view. Old people's illnesses are often chronic, tedious, uninteresting, and difficult to treat. Doctors frequently subscribe to the common sentiment that medical treatment should be immediately successful, not spoiled by situations that defy the doctor's ability to supply an instant cure. Furthermore, like the general public, physicians can be frightened by aging and death (Butler 1975) and frustrated by family members, colleagues, and hospital administrators who want to prolong life in the inevitably vain hope that somehow a miracle will restore the loved one's health (Duff and Hollingshead 1968).

The difficulties of treating the elderly are compounded if they also suffer a disability, because they are forced to deal with two service agencies, neither one of which can address all of their needs. Agencies that are concerned with blindness, for instance, do not handle elderly people's problems while organizations for the elderly cannot deal with issues related to blindness. Frequently the blind or visually impaired elderly feel caught between two agencies, neither of which can effectively respond to all their needs (Biegel et al. 1989).

Senior citizens seem to vary considerably in their ability to confront health problems, with social networks of kinship members, neighbors, and friends often playing a significant role (Stoller and Pugliesi 1991). A study found that when urban elderly were involved in these informal networks, they tended to be healthier than old people without such networks (Cohen et al. 1985).

A team of health researchers recently indicated that while the percentage of elderly Americans has been steadily increasing, surprisingly little is known about their participation in health programs. To make that participation as effective as possible, thorough research on elderly citizens' experiences in on-going programs must continue to be conducted and the suggestions emerging from the findings implemented (Carter et al. 1991).

Group-Involvement Cost   Often senior citizens feel lonely, cut off from frequent, positive interaction with others, and, as a result, depressed. With suicide higher in the elderly category than any other and depression a major contributor to it, there is widespread recognition that elderly people's isolation is not only unfortunate but can also be dangerous (Pratt et al. 1991).

Research found that elderly who were married, healthy (according to their own perception), fairly affluent, socially active, and socially fulfilled tend to be less lonely. In this study the measurement of social fulfillment was compiled from three items— a person's sense of having or not having enough friends, sufficient activities to keep busy, and a sense of being needed—and was the factor which best predicted loneliness (Creecy 1985).

With the introduction of the concept "disengagement," researchers on aging have addressed the issue of the desirability of senior citizens' group involvements. **Disengagement** is a process of mutual withdrawal involving decreasing interaction between an elderly person and others in the social system to which he or she belongs (Cumming and Henry 1961). Elaine Cumming and William Henry, who developed the concept, originally contended that disengagement was functional for society, providing a process by which power can transfer from older to younger members and also functional for individuals, initiating a less active and therefore more satisfying lifestyle. The early usage of the disengagement concept has received widespread criticism. At the very least, the original analysis was an oversimplification. A later study suggested that disengagement becomes a satisfying outcome only if the person voluntarily reduces role commitment and maintains high self-esteem in the process (Neugarten, Havighurst, and Tobin 1968).

Perhaps more significant than disengagement is continuity. Most senior citizens are willing to make adaptive changes as they age if these changes permit a sense of continuity in self-image and personally significant activities (Atchley 1989). For an elderly man, for instance, retirement might be fine so long as he can continue to have lunch twice a week with his long-time work buddies; for him the social side of the job had always been more meaningful than the job itself, and it is the social side of the job he wants to maintain. Most people seem to deal with retirement successfully. A recent study of 1,516 elderly men, 45 percent of whom were retired, suggested that retirement was not considered a major problem; from a list of thirty-one stressful events, one's own and one's spouse's retirement were rated the least stressful (Bosse et al. 1991).

The nearby Cross-Cultural Perspective describes activity that stands in bold contrast to most elderly Americans' experience.

Cost of Losing Control over One's Destiny   One of the problems senior citizens face is that they encounter many social norms that place highly limiting expectations upon them—in the sexual realm, for instance. As one elderly commentator pointed out, people do not "chide young people for being horny"; there is no such expression as a "dirty young man." The idea of "the dirty old man" is an accusation. The writer noted, "At the non-youth time of life one has no business . . . being sexual. It is unwarranted, bizarre, if not obscene" (Neubeck 1981, 314).

Relocation is another issue that can threaten old people's sense of control over their destiny. Choice and predictability are important elements in this process. Older people who relocate voluntarily are likely to adapt better than those who relocate involuntarily. In addition, new environments that are comfortable because of their similarity to the old environment are generally easier to adapt to than those that are less similar—the issue of continuity for the elderly that we discussed in the section on group-involvement cost (Bourestom and Pastalan 1981; Schultz and Brenner 1977).

Adaptation to nursing homes can be particularly difficult. A guiding principle of these organizations is that patients' social and psychological needs are less significant than the efficient performance of patient care. The rigid scheduling of meals and activities as well as movement en masse to entertainment, religious services, or therapy can be efficient practices, but they are highly disruptive activities for people who have lived a largely independent existence (Gubrium 1975).

Recent research has emphasized the significance of the quality of facilities and care provided in nursing homes. Convenient, attractive, and spacious physical features are important as well as policies which promote personal privacy, allow the choice of activity over a standard routine, and encourage residents to be more independent (Timko and Moos 1990; Timko and Moos 1991).

For many people control over their destiny is more effectively maintained without going to a nursing home. Erwin Goldstein worried about his aging father. He had trouble climbing the stairs and got tired driving. Besides it was questionable that he should drive. How does a son tell his father that he can't drive any more? Goldstein called state agencies and nursing homes but was dissatisfied with their vague, bureaucratic answers. Then he found out about Anne Sharpe, who had recently opened a geriatric consulting service. As a care manager, Sharpe found "local, reasonable" people, who could assist Goldstein's father at home. She was able to locate electric stair climbers, and she even helped Goldstein devise tactful strategies for accompanying his father on short car trips in the new car he couldn't resist buying. Sharpe's services, Goldstein explained, permitted his father to live a largely independent existence at home until he died at the age of 86. People 85 and over represent the fastest growing section of the population, and since many of them prefer not to enter nursing homes, there is a growing role for care managers (Battista 1992).

The elderly encounter ageism and other problems. What measures can they take to improve their situation?

THE ELDERLY'S FIGHT TO FEEL USEFUL AND SATISFIED

Maggie Kuhn, the founder of the Gray Panthers, an activist organization on behalf of the elderly, has said that three things please her about being old: She can speak her mind, she has succeeded in outliving most of her opposition, and she can reach out to others (Shapiro 1982, 11). Maggie Kuhn has a useful, satisfying old age. Let us consider strategies people employ to produce such results at both an individual and a group level.

Some people focus at the individual level, finding that continuing to work produces a positive

CROSS-CULTURAL PERSPECTIVE
The Elderly in Abkhasia

Do the same conditions that encourage long life also discourage disengagement? That is a difficult question to answer. It is clear, however, that in Abkhasia the living situation experienced by the elderly does promote both results.

In the then Soviet Republic of Abkhasia, an anthropologist raised a glass of wine to toast a man who looked no more than 70. "May you live as long as Moses [120 years]," she said. The man was not pleased. He was 119.

No exact figures exist for the total number of aged people in Abkhasia. However, in the village of Dzhgerda, where this researcher did her study, 15 percent of the population was 81 and over. In 1954, the last year for which figures are available, 2.58 percent of the Abkhasians were over 90. For the Soviet Union over all and the United States, the comparable figures were 0.1 and 0.4 percent respectively. Why the difference? We will see that the elderly Abkhasians experience a number of conditions very different from those encountered by their American counterparts.

First, the life of the Abkhasian elderly has a broad base of uniformity and certainty. Sexual behavior, for instance, occurs without any sense of guilt. It is a pleasurable activity to be regulated for the sake of one's health, like a good wine. The same outlook exists with work. From the beginning of life until the end, Abkhasians do the amount of work they feel capable of doing. Work, they believe, is vital to life, and the concept of retirement is unknown to them. As they become older, they gradually cut back. Observations on twenty-one men and seven women over the age of 100 showed that they averaged a four-hour workday. The men weeded and helped with the corn crop, and the women strung tobacco leaves. They worked at their own pace, moving evenly and without wasted motion, taking breaks on occasion. Both the Soviet medical doctors and the Abkhasian elderly feel that work habits have a lot to do with their long lives. The doctors suggest that the work patterns allow the vital organs to function more efficiently. The Abkhasians say, "Without rest, a man cannot work; without work, the rest does not give you any benefit."

Like other elements in Abkhasian life, the diet is stable. Investigators have found that people who are 100 years and older have eaten the same foods throughout their lives. At each of their three meals, the Abkhasians have *abista,* a cornmeal mash cooked in water without salt. Other prominent foods include cheese, buttermilk, fresh fruits, especially grapes, and fresh vegetables, particularly green onions, tomatoes, cucumbers, and cabbage. Although they are the main suppliers of tobacco for all the nations formerly belonging to the Soviet Union, few Abkhasians smoke. They drink neither coffee nor tea but do consume a local red wine of low alcohol content. At meals the food is cut into little pieces, and the people take small bites, chewing their food very slowly. As a result effective digestion usually occurs.

One more special quality about Abkhasian culture is the highly integrated nature of life coupled with the respected role of the elderly. Abkhasians bear a close, interdependent relationship with a variety of kin, and these relationships tend to enhance the strong sense of security that underlies their existence. For the elderly that sense of security is further entrenched by the deep respect they receive. The elders preside at important ceremonies, mediate disputes, and offer their experience and knowledge about farming. Quite the opposite of burdens, they serve as valued resources. As one 99-year-old Abkhasian told his doctor, "It isn't time to die yet. I am needed by my children and grandchildren, and it isn't bad in this world—except that I can't turn the earth over and it has become difficult to climb trees."

Source: Sula Benet. "Why They Live to Be 100 or Even Older, in Abkhasia," New York Times Magazine. (December 26, 1971), p. 3+.

result. In a study of 4,000 retired people who had held a variety of jobs, 73 percent of those who reported that work was a major source of satisfaction returned to work after retirement (Streib and Schneider 1971). Others found satisfaction at the individual level in entirely different ways—foster grandparenting, for instance. Before entering such a program, one woman reported that she " . . . felt like I was dead but alive. I wasn't doing much." Her husband had died years earlier, and her children had long since left home. She heard on the radio that a local hospital wanted foster grandparents for retarded children. The prospect frightened her, but she went anyway. She was brought to see a little boy. "They called him a mongoloid, but I couldn't tell. The first thing he did was hug me. He squeezed my legs so tight, I thought I'd fall over. We didn't talk much that day. We just sat and hugged. I felt warm all over" (Hultsch and Deutsch 1981, 330). This woman eventually became the foster grandparent for five children, and she convinced one of her friends to enter the program.

At the individual level, senior citizens can find different ways to feel useful and satisfied. But can they form a subculture at the community level to accomplish mutually sought goals? The answer, unequivocally, is yes. The inflationary pressures of recent years have provided a major impetus for the elderly to speak out and to act collectively on their own behalf. Like other minority groups, they have started to realize that they will be much more successful if they visualize what they had once considered individual problems as group problems. Thousands of organizations composed of elderly citizens now lobby local government officials on behalf of old people's needs. Housing, medical care, tax relief, and the construction of senior centers are some of the issues involved. Many senior citizens have become highly politicized, recognizing that their power as a voting bloc is sufficiently strong to produce a sympathetic ear from many elected politicians. On the other hand, those who try to organize the elderly often find themselves frustrated. Maggie Kuhn has suggested that many old people "want to keep their lives as bland and as pleasant and as uncontroversial as possible. You don't talk about anything disagreeable" (Shapiro 1982, 7). Certainly it is a common belief that old age should ideally be a happy time, free of significant worries, when a person can enjoy the fruits of

In Japan, as in some other cultures, older people are regarded as vital contributors to society, both in their role as family members and, for many, as part of the work force.

toil well-earned during the earlier years. Organized efforts by the elderly to protest their common grievances hardly support such an image.

Over the past two decades, Canada has developed a national, government-financed program, which has encouraged elderly citizens to initiate projects for themselves and others. Since it began in 1972, the New Horizons program has helped establish 25,000 activities. At first efforts involved the development of social and recreational centers in towns or neighborhoods that previously had provided no place for the elderly to meet and do things. Senior citizens held bake sales, raffles, teas, and lotteries to raise a lot of the necessary funds.

In 1982 program officials began to encourage senior citizens to start community-service and mutual-help projects. One education center for the elderly began in two small classrooms and now

290

enrolls more than 1,000 students. New Horizons sponsors leadership-training workshops, seniors' newspapers, and several national federations of seniors' groups. In one New Horizons report, it stated, "When they are not encumbered with society's prejudices, older people will continue to be active, creative, and productive members of their communities" (Novak 1987, 353). Would it be desirable to establish a similar program in the United States?

Concerns about meeting elderly people's needs, to be sure, go beyond the United States. On October 1, 1991, the United Nations General Assembly observed the first International Day for the Elderly. In the official statement issued that day, it stated that by the year 2025, there will be an elderly population of 1.2 billion people, six times more than the elderly worldwide in 1950. It was emphasized that elderly people should have the chance to work and to determine when to leave the work force; remain integrated in society, participating in policy formation affecting them; have access to health care allowing them an optimal level of physical, mental, and emotional well-being; and be able to develop their potential, making use of local educational, cultural, spiritual, and recreational resources (UN *Chronicle* 1992).

As we move on to the disabled minorities and their problems, we see many parallels with the situation of elderly people.

The Emergence of the Disabled ◾

On a warm day in spring, Jay D. Leventhal was walking back to his office after getting cash at a bank. While he was waiting for the traffic light to change, someone grabbed both of his upper arms from behind. Was he being mugged? No, Leventhal is blind, and this was simply the latest passerby's attempt to help him. Such incidents occur quite frequently. Leventhal explained that people yell at him, push him, pull him, grab his clothes, assuming that because he is blind, he needs help. Once when a construction crew was digging in the street, one of the workmen grabbed Leventhal's jacket with his dirty glove, saying he would walk him around the obstruction. With his cane Leventhal could have easily gone around the obstruction, but he needed assistance getting the dirt off his jacket (Leventhal 1992).

Frequently modern people believe that blind people are incompetent, invariably needing help when, in fact, most function very well on their own. In the following discussion of disabled Americans, we see that the general population has many significant stereotypes and misconceptions about disabled people.

There are about 36 million disabled Americans, and except for women they form the largest minority group (Meyerson 1988). Disability is one minority status that shows no regard for age, race, sex, or class privilege. As one observer noted, "Anyone can become disabled. A skiing accident, a highway collision, a mistaken dose of medicine—it may take seconds or it may take years" (Bowe 1978, viii).

In this section we examine the process of prejudice and discrimination encountered by the physically, mentally, and emotionally disabled. Then we look at the costs of this treatment and at the disability-rights movement.

"The disabled" is a large, diversified category of people, which has existed in all societies across time and space (Scheer and Groce 1988). The most general distinction is between those who are physically or mentally impaired, but within these two categories, there are often major differences in disability, lifestyle, and public response. With the space limitations of an introductory text, I can do little more than alert you to the complexity of the subject we are about to discuss.

PREJUDICE AND DISCRIMINATION ENCOUNTERED BY THE DISABLED

There is no "ism" to describe the process, but the same steps that occur in the sexism and ageism processes occur for the disabled. In the first place, the disabled frequently have high social visibility. For physically disabled people, the visibility can be dramatic. When a psychologist showed over a hundred students pictures of human faces lacking in noses or ears or partly caved in, they all expressed horror and disgust (Smith 1973). In other cases social visibility is just as obvious but less startling—the physically disabled in wheelchairs, for instance.

Second, the disabled encounter a range of attributed characteristics that will vary with their disability. Like other minorities the disabled are generally considered both different and inferior. The stereotypes formed about the disabled frequently lack substantiating evidence. For instance, one woman who had been in a wheelchair ever since she had been hit by a car pointed out that often people falsely assumed she could not have sex (Bowe 1978). This same assumption exists for other handicapped Americans. A frequent misperception about the disabled is that their central disability must link with others. Thus blind people often find that those addressing them will speak loudly, believing that they must also have hearing problems. Many people readily classify physically handicapped people as mentally handicapped. A team of writers warned that since rehabilitation counselors working with disabled people are members of the general culture, they must make an effort to become aware of their own "disability myths," not unconsciously conveying them to their clients (Holmes and Karst 1990).

Third, a variety of rationalizations support prejudice and discrimination against the disabled. A number of studies indicate that people generally believe that they live in a "just universe." Given this condition, then why are some individuals suffering from serious handicaps? Many people assume that one reason is that the disabled have done something wrong or that they are going to do something wrong. In short, the assumption goes, the disability represents a punishment for wrongdoing (Shaw and Skolnick 1971). Another rationalization is that disabled people's problems are always inherited and of sufficient magnitude that little or nothing can be done to help them. Toward the end of the nineteenth and the beginning of the twentieth century, it was widely believed that mental retardation was an inherited condition that was largely responsible for crime, delinquency, vagrancy, poverty, and immorality. The so-called experts felt that it would be a waste of resources to allocate funds for training schools for mentally handicapped to improve their mental and physical functioning. Instead mentally handicapped were placed in institutions, where they received no more than custodial care (Katz 1973).

Fourth, like other minorities, the disabled often accommodate to the expectations or desires of the majority. The blind, for instance, frequently recognize that they are likely to receive greater acceptance if they consider the visual dimension when dealing with sighted people. Thus they learn to face others when talking to them instead of just turning an ear to the sound of their voice. Or they will teach themselves automatic use of such phrases as "I see" or "It looks like . . ." (Bowe 1978, 51). One study of individuals with rheumatoid arthritis indicated that there was frequent "covering up," hiding the disability from others, and also "keeping up," pushing themselves to perform as if they were not suffering from the pain and swelling that interferes with normal activity (Wiener 1975).

Finally the disabled have traditionally encountered a range of discriminations: attitudinal, architectural, educational, occupational, transportational, and in housing. The Americans with Disabilities Act, which was signed into law in July 1990, guarantees equal opportunity for disabled individuals in employment, public accomodations and services, state and local government services, and telecommunications. While this sweeping legislation represents an important advancement for disabled people, it has not yet been implemented in many areas.

The prejudice and discrimination process endured by the disabled thus involves the same five steps as sexism and ageism. Table 10.2 summarizes the three processes.

Costs

The prejudice and discrimination suffered by the disabled inevitably carry some heavy costs. We consider three types of costs—the psychological, the physical, and the occupational.

Psychological Cost A labeling process often occurs with disabilities. For instance, a child not doing well in school receives a battery of diagnostic tests that educators themselves are likely to consider inadequate. If a disability is "discovered," then the officials involved can sigh with relief as they conclude, "No wonder Susie wasn't learning. She is learning disabled." With the label placed,

Table 10.2 Prejudice and Discrimination against Emerging Minorities

Components	Sexism	Ageism	Prejudice and discrimination against the disabled
High social visibility	Secondary sex characteristics and distinctive clothing	Wrinkled skin, white hair, or stooped walk	Detectable physical disabilities or deformities
Attributed traits of inferiority	Less intelligent than men; irresponsible, inconsistent, and unstable	Images of passivity, dependency, rigidity senility, and inefficiency	Unsubstantiated convictions, such as the widespread suspicion that blind people also have hearing problems
Rationalization of status	"Women's place is in the home"	Claims that the elderly are "happy disengagers"	Belief that handicaps are a punishment for wrong-doing or are so incapacitating that little or nothing can be done to help
Accommodating behavioral patterns	Hiding intelligence or acting helpless	Graceful acceptance of retirement in spite of deep-seated reluctance	Blind people's facing sighted speakers during conversations and using visually-oriented phrases
Discriminations	In education, occupation, and political activity	In health care or in control over one's destiny	In attitudes, architecture, education, housing, occupation, and transportation

Source: Adapted in part from Helen Mayer Hacker. "Women as a Minority Group," Social Forces. vol. 30 (October 1951), pp. 60-69.

the school is now off the hook for the child's inability to learn. For the child, however, the problems are just starting. Once applied, labels are difficult to remove, even when observers demonstrate they are inappropriate. There are several reasons why. First, labels are concise designations that justify an organization or activity. "He wouldn't be in this mental hospital, would he, unless he was crazy as a loon?" Another reason labels remain is that they are self-fulfilling. A child is labeled "mildly retarded" and then receives less instruction to ensure that she or he is not unduly burdened. When this child learns less than others who have been pushed harder, she or he "confirms" the original diagnosis (Bowe 1978, 139).

Perhaps the most devastating psychological effect of disability for many people is the expectation of powerlessness they encounter. Those work-

ing on behalf of the rights of the disabled stress that many, perhaps most Americans believe that handicapped people are generally powerless to do anything significant for themselves—that being disabled means that an individual invariably must be helped and continuously given social support (Fine and Asch 1988). Responding to this perspective, a rehabilitation counselor emphasized the significance of empowering disabled people. As a severely disabled person himself, he contended that to "a great extent, empowerment is a mind set"—that he needs to see himself as powerful, maintaining control over his own life. But, he also emphasized, laws and regulations must be consistent with that empowerment, making it possible for him to do all or most of the things others can do, such as assuring that he can board any airplane (Emener 1991, 8).

Powerlessness is one debilitating condition the disabled have thrust upon them. They also frequently encounter another negative situation—isolation and aloneness. Many disabled people live an existence that sharply contrasts with that of other minorities. Ethnic groups, women, and the elderly can usually find others who share their experiences and problems, but people with major deformities, injuries, or other disabilities often have nobody nearby experiencing their same fate. In fact, the disabled often seek to avoid such a sense of community. Most of them view their minority status as more distinctly abnormal and undesirable than other groups view their respective minority statuses. A little person said, "Didn't all of us, at the beginning, avoid little people because we didn't want to be identified with them? I didn't want to admit that I was little, too" (Smith 1973, 125). After reading a newspaper article based on her interview about living with rheumatoid arthritis, Bonnie Anderson said angrily, "Who would want to go to dinner, to a movie, or even to bed with someone who is afflicted. My god, she made it sound as if I have fleas!" Keen sensitivity to one's disability, the author of the article suggested, is a perception that disabled people are considered "damaged goods" (Phillips 1990, 851).

Physical Cost   Seriously disabled people, those in wheelchairs for example, frequently encounter both architectural and transportation barriers. Most buildings only can be entered after people climb steps or pass through narrow doorways. These buildings are inaccessible to people in wheelchairs.

Title II of the Americans with Disabilities Act of 1990 ensures that disabled individuals will have access to public transportation while Title III of that law involves access to public accomodations and services, such as hotels, restaurants, theaters, auditoriums, retail stores, schools, and day-care centers. Many facilities, however, currently fail to meet these standards, making physical movement arduous for disabled people. They often find it difficult or impossible to enter buildings, and barriers are a major concern when planning trips, especially for people in wheelchairs. Are there any steps at the airline terminal? And what about the hotel? The management has assured a handicapped woman that she will be able to reach her fourth-floor room, but she knows that the building

is old. So there are inevitable questions about the width of doors and accessibility to the elevator, not to mention that other ever-present problem: steps.

Some cities are becoming more receptive to the physical needs of disabled people. Atlanta is one, and Berkeley, California, is another. Two-thirds of the Berkeley intersections have either wheelchair ramps or curb cuts. In addition, the Bay Area Rapid Transit System, a modern bus and subway complex that connects Berkeley and San Francisco, is fully accessible to people in wheelchairs. In addition, all buildings constructed in the last ten years are also accessible, and even the automated tellers at local banks are built at wheelchair height. One disabled resident explained, "It's easy to forget you're in a wheelchair here. . . . But in most small towns where the disabled aren't as prevalent, it's not the same story" (Langway 1982, 84).

In a recent article, a pair of specialists indicated that by not making large sections of most modern American cities accessible to disabled people, the leadership of those cities is discriminating against them, providing "a blatant sign" that they are not welcome in that area (Gilderbloom and Rosentraub 1990).

Occupational Cost   Although the Americans with Disabilities Act of 1990 addresses the issues of architectural and transportation barriers, these

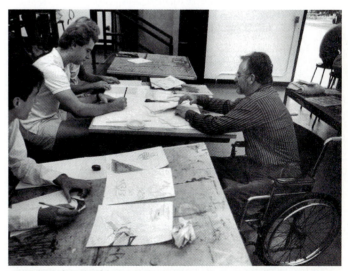

For many jobs a disability is no hindrance to effective job performance. A case in point is this professor teaching a design class at the University of California, Irvine.

294 problems currently produce an adverse effect on the work lives of many disabled people. Architectural barriers at job sites may deny entrance to the disabled. Transportation limitations may make it impossible to commute to and from work each day without paying exorbitant taxi fees. Employers' or prospective employers' attitudes can also be a problem. In a national survey, nearly half of unemployed people with disabilities said they were not working because employers did not recognize their abilities (*American Demographics* 1991). Former mental patients probably face even more difficult occupational barriers than physically disabled individuals. The 127 firms responding to a survey of the Fortune 500 corporations preferred people with physical disabilities over those with mental disabilities, and less than a quarter of the respondents said there was a corporate policy about hiring former mental patients, with firms lacking one visualizing more barriers to this form of hiring than companies with a policy (Jones et al. 1991).

For the disabled the chance to work can provide an opportunity to attain considerable personal satisfaction, daily stimulation and challenge, on-going contacts with a variety of people, and a sense of supporting oneself. By contrast, enforced idleness means the absence of all these opportunities, and it is a condition that readily stimulates self-hate and disgust (Bowe 1978; Jenkins 1991).

For some employed disabled people, the working situation can become almost intolerable once fellow workers are called upon to help them in a difficult situation involving their disability. If an epileptic has a seizure at work, other employees sometimes become overly watchful and wary in the future. One woman with this condition explained:

> You get to feel like a little baby after a while and you don't get treated the same. Every once in a while you'll see somebody coming in like to go to the bathroom on my floor when there's one on their floor. . . . In a way it makes you feel kind of bad you can't operate on your own two feet.
>
> (*Schneider* 1988, 73)

The present situation in which the disabled of America find themselves is not a particularly positive one. But analyzing the disability-rights movement, we see that there is now a tradition of working for disabled people's rights.

THE DISABILITY-RIGHTS MOVEMENT

The first two American organizations concerned with the rights of disabled people developed between the two world wars, and each was involved with a specific category of people. The Disabled American Veterans was primarily seeking to expand government benefits for disabled veterans. The National Federation of the Blind became a militant supporter for blind people's rights, lobbying for some of the early civil-rights laws guaranteeing access to different facilities regardless of disability and establishing the use of the white cane and guide dogs. In the twenty years after World War II, major organizations for disabled people included the Paralyzed Veterans of America, the National Association of the Deaf, and the American Council of the Blind.

In the 1960s several factors converged to change many disabled people's prospects. First, medical and rehabilitative advances now made it possible for many individuals, such as polio victims of the last epidemic in the 1950s, to be much more active members of society than they could have been in the past. Second, the social atmosphere was altering. Most middle-class children growing up in the 1950s and 1960s had parents who stressed self-confidence and achievement more strongly than counterparts a generation earlier, in many cases even if the children were disabled. Then came the protest years, featuring blacks' civil rights, opposition to the Vietnam War, and the assertion of women's rights. Some disabled people who were veterans of other protests began to visualize the need to respond to their disabilities in an equally militant way.

By the early 1970s, there were many local organizations seeking to improve disabled people's rights, but no coordinated effort to influence public policy existed. Then in 1974 the American Coalition of Citizens with Disabilities formed for that purpose. Increasingly the coalition and other organizations in the developing disability-rights movement became focused on the federal government.

During the 1970s the federal government helped the disability-rights movement in several ways. First, government became a major source of funding. Second, government programs helped the disability-rights movement organize itself more effectively, providing contracts for training and technical assistance and frequently seeking out disability-rights leaders for consultation, thus improving communication between the two camps and facilitating lobbying activities. Finally during the 1970s, legislation established disabled people as a class of people whose rights were protected by federal laws and whose exclusion from federally financed programs and activities became illegal.

In some respects the 1980s was a less optimistic decade than its predecessor. The Ronald Reagan administration replaced a number of officials who had worked constructively with disability-rights organizations, and the federal government became more inclined to restrict disabled people's rights and diminish their funding than to support their efforts (Scotch 1988).

But it is not simply a question of funding. Disability-rights mobilization requires more—a drive to demand respectful, potentially productive attention for disabled people. A recent assessment of the vast literature on disabilities indicated that even though disabled people have a wealth of experience living with their problems, studies have been "remarkable" for identifying with care providers and not with the recipients of their services, whose "insight into issues and problems, their manner of adaptation, their thoughts, hopes and fears" undoubtedly would contribute significantly to policy-oriented research (Groce and Scheer 1990).

STUDY GUIDE

Learning Objectives

After studying this chapter, you should be able to:

1. Summarize major conclusions about gender-role development.
2. Define sexism and summarize the five steps in the process.
3. Discuss the psychological, career, and physical costs of sexism.
4. Examine the modern women's movement and the future of women's rights.
5. Define ageism and summarize the five steps in the process.
6. Analyze the following effects of ageism—health and medical-care cost, group-involvement cost, and the cost of losing control over one's destiny.
7. Describe the strategies elderly people pursue to feel useful and satisfied.
8. Summarize the five steps in the process of prejudice and discrimination encountered by the disabled.
9. Examine the psychological, physical, and occupational costs of prejudice and discrimination suffered by the disabled.
10. Discuss the development of a disability-rights movement.

Summary

1. Women, the elderly, and the disabled are three prominent emerging minorities. A similar process of prejudice and discrimination affects all three groups.

2. The section on women begins with a discussion of gender-role development, analyzes contributions made by biological and social factors, and suggests that this process provides the groundwork for women's subjugation. Sexism is an ideology emphasizing that actual or alleged differences between men and women establish the superiority of men, and it can be analyzed as a five-step process. Sexism is a rationalization for political, economic, and social discrimination against women. In American society sexism has received extensive support. The sexist ideology has also

296 produced a variety of costs. Psychological costs include the widespread belief that women possess fewer desirable qualities than men. In addition, the media have traditionally presented a narrow, stereotyped image of women. Women have also suffered career costs. It has been widely believed that women can be fulfilled in the housewife role, and yet it is clear that this often is not the case. Women in the work force have been less successful than men. Research shows that socialization patterns are one source of women's disadvantage. Pay differences result from outright discrimination and the differing distribution of men and women into occupations. Women also encounter a variety of physical costs. Physical violence experienced by women ranges from "street hassling" to rape and physical abuse. Trends that appear among the violent acts against women include nonreporting, the failure to take the reports of violence seriously, and the tendency to blame the victim herself for the occurrence of the act.

In response to sexism, a modern women's movement has developed. Like earlier efforts by women to develop consciousness or to start a women's movement, the modern movement seems to be an outgrowth of the era in which it developed. The National Organization for Women (NOW) represents one source from which the modern women's movement originated. Another has been local women's groups that emerged from the 1960s civil-rights and antiwar movements.

Two feminist writers suggested that women must learn to tell their own stories. We discussed this issue as we considered the future of women's rights.

3. Like women, the elderly are frequently victims of modern society. Ageism is an ideology emphasizing the superiority of the young over the old. Like sexism, ageism is a process that receives extensive support in daily life. One cost of ageism is health, which is adversely affected by the medical care some senior citizens receive. Another cost for some aging Americans involves the restricted organizational activity they experience. In addition, many senior citizens feel a limited control over their destiny. This sense of powerlessness appears quite frequently when old Americans face relocation, especially relocation to a nursing home.

We can speculate about the future of the elderly in America. One significant question to ponder is whether or not a strong political movement of the elderly will develop. At present mixed indications exist.

4. The 36 million disabled Americans often face prejudice and discrimination similar to that encountered by women and the elderly. In fact, the same steps that occur in sexism and ageism also occur for the disabled. Not surprisingly the costs of prejudice and discrimination are also similar. Psychological costs include the destructive effect of labeling. Unlike women and the elderly, disabled people who would like to share experiences with others suffering the same minority status often find it more difficult to locate such people or receive less cultural support for seeking out those with a shared experience. The physical costs of being disabled include limited access to buildings and to transportation, making it difficult for wheelchair-bound people to be mobile. The occupational costs encountered by disabled Americans are the result of a variety of barriers—educational, architectural, transportational, and attitudinal.

Over the past couple of decades, a disability-rights movement has developed. At present this movement lacks the strong government support that it received in the 1970s.

Key Terms

ageism an ideology asserting the superiority of the young over the old. Ageism is a rationalization for political, economic, and social discrimination against the elderly.

disengagement a process of mutual withdrawal involving decreasing interaction between an elderly person and others in the social system to which he or she belongs

gender the general behavioral standards that distinguish males and females in a given culture

gender role a set of specific behavioral patterns

associated with either the female or male gender

sex the division of a variety of animal forms, including human beings, into the biological categories of male and female

sexism an ideology emphasizing that actual or alleged differences between men and women establish the superiority of men. Sexism is a rationalization for political, economic, and social discrimination against women.

Tests

True • False Test

_____ 1. Recent research indicated that girls no longer spend more time in household tasks and personal care than boys do.

_____ 2. In the 1990s sexism is no longer an ideology.

_____ 3. A study of nonmusic programming on commercial radio indicated that males dominated as disc jockeys, newscasters, and voice-overs in advertisements.

_____ 4. Women's recognition of their subordination expanded during periods stressing the importance of new ideas and influences, especially individual rights.

_____ 5. Like sexism, ageism could not occur without high social visibility.

_____ 6. Research has revealed that when urban elderly are involved in social networks of neighbors, friends, or kin, they tend to be less healthy than old people without such networks.

_____ 7. There are about 36 million disabled Americans.

_____ 8. One reason that labels on the disabled are hard to remove is that they are self-fulfilling.

_____ 9. A recent study indicated that large corporations are more willing to hire former mental patients than physically disabled workers.

_____ 10. During the 1970s the federal government severely restricted its earlier support of the disability-rights movement.

Multiple-Choice Tests

_____ 1. Which statement about sexism is true?
   a. Women's ability to perform, not their intelligence, has been questioned.
   b. In American society women have traditionally encountered more limitations on education than men.
   c. There are no rationalizations about women's traditional status.
   d. Women are the only minority group without social visibility.

_____ 2. A study found that when women suffered depression:
   a. they were too committed to personal success.
   b. the positive qualities of women's traditional roles were absent from their lives.
   c. they suffered from commitment to too many roles.
   d. the positive qualities of both men's and women's traditional roles were absent from their lives.

_____ 3. Margaret Hennig and Anne Jardim studied female presidents and vice-presidents of business firms and found that their achievement differences seemed to be produced by:
   a. family dynamics.
   b. work experience.
   c. training.
   d. social visibility.

_____ 4. The occurrence of sexual harassment:
  a. is rare in the academic world.
  b. has not received attention in the major commercial media in recent years.
  c. leads to victims soon quitting their jobs.
  d. does not necessarily mean that victims leave their current jobs.

_____ 5. Which statement is true of the elderly?
  a. They have low social visibility.
  b. They have negative qualities attributed to them.
  c. Disengagement no longer occurs.
  d. Most Americans will face mandatory retirement for the next couple of decades.

_____ 6. Among the elderly, suicide:
  a. has dropped sharply in recent years.
  b. occurs equally among depressed and nondepressed people.
  c. is the highest among all age categories.
  d. a and b

_____ 7. Which of the following is a situation likely to threaten the elderly's sense of controlling their destiny?
  a. arguments with one's spouse or children
  b. religious conversion
  c. relocation
  d. declining sexual activity

_____ 8. Prejudice and discrimination against the disabled are supported by the rationalization that:
  a. their disabilities represent punishment for wrongdoing.
  b. there are not enough jobs for everyone.
  c. society cannot afford the cost of all the environmental modifications they need.
  d. they are being cared for effectively enough by the welfare system.

_____ 9. When fellow workers are called upon to help disabled people in a difficult situation involving the disability:
  a. relations between the disabled person and fellow workers usually improve.
  b. other employees may become overly watchful and wary.
  c. the disabled person is likely to be fired.
  d. there is no significant impact.

_____ 10. A city which has made impressive physical adjustments to meet the needs of the physically disabled is:
  a. Rome, Italy.
  b. New York City.
  c. New Delhi, India.
  d. Berkeley, California.

Essay Test

1. Analyze gender-role development, indicating the impact of both biological and social factors in the process.
2. Define sexism and discuss the steps in the process, offering illustrations at each stage.
3. Discuss in detail three costs of sexism.
4. On what issue(s) is women's struggle for rights likely to focus in the future?
5. What is ageism? Discuss and illustrate stages in the process of ageism.
6. Describe several significant costs of ageism.

7. Examine and illustrate the steps in the process of prejudice and discrimination against the disabled.
8. Describe the principal costs encountered by disabled Americans.
9. Discuss different ways that the disabled can confront and overcome their powerlessness.

Suggested Readings

Albrecht, Gary L. 1992. *The Disability Business: Rehabilitation in America*. Newbury Park, CA: Sage. A sociological analysis of the rapid growth of disability as a commercial product in modern society.

Bowe, Frank. 1978. *Handicapping America*. New York: Harper & Row. A book for a general audience describing the state of affairs for disabled people in modern America. The author, who is deaf, is a leading authority on and advocate for disabled people.

Cruzic, Kathleen. 1982. *Disabled? Yes. Defeated? No*. Englewood Cliffs, NJ: Prentice-Hall. A nurse's detailed account of the various resources available for the disabled, their families, friends, and therapists. The book's sixteen chapters offer detailed information on such issues as shortcuts in the kitchen, pursuit of new careers, tips for traveling, and aids for recreation.

Friedan, Betty. 1963. *The Feminine Mystique*. New York: W. W. Norton. The widely read treatise that helped initiate the modern women's movement in U.S. society. As you read this book, pretend that you are a woman of three decades ago discovering suddenly that someone has articulated the feelings of confusion, uneasiness, and anger you have experienced as a housewife and mother.

Kesey, Ken. 1962. *One Flew over the Cuckoo's Nest*. New York: Signet Books. A chilling look at the alienated life of men living in the ward of a mental hospital. Kesey's novel makes it painfully clear how the process of controlling people's thoughts and actions is successfully conducted in this setting.

Lindsey, Linda L. 1990. *Gender Roles: A Sociological Perspective*. Englewood Cliffs, NJ: Prentice-Hall. A highly readable introduction to the sociological analysis of gender roles, with a restrained but resolute feminist perspective maintained throughout.

Murphy, Robert F. 1987. *The Body Silent*. New York: Henry Holt. An anthropologist's detailed, highly insightful account of an anthropological experience he was compelled to witness—the transformation produced by a tumor in the spinal column changing him from a seemingly healthy individual in 1972 to a quadriplegic in 1986.

Stahl, Sidney M. (ed.). 1990. *The Legacy of Longevity: Health and Health Care in Later Life*. Newbury Park, CA: Sage. A multidisciplinary analysis of the conceptual and practical considerations of health care for the elderly, showing how competent research can contribute to policymaking.

Additional Assignments

1. Find ten people, preferably five women and five men. Ask them to rank the following occupations from 1 (most prestigious) to 12 (least prestigious). How much agreement did you find regarding the prestige of each occupation? Did men and women rank them differently? Compare findings with other class members and relate the trends you discover to information in this chapter, indicating, in particular, how much the sex typing of occupations appeared to affect rankings. The occupations:

    1. Flight attendant
    2. Housewife
    3. Truck driver
    4. Waiter
    5. Fashion model
    6. Steward
    7. Househusband
    8. Photographer
    9. Doctor
    10. Waitress
    11. Nurse
    12. School bus driver

300

(Note: Occupations 2 and 10 are considered female occupations; occupations 4, 6, and 7 are considered male occupations. All other positions could have either male or female job holders, but we culturally identify women with occupations 1, 5, and 11 and men with 3, 8, and 9.)

2. Imagine yourself having a significant disability—being legally blind, confined to a wheelchair, or hearing-impaired. Over a two-day period, keep a record of what you discover regarding the physical facilities you use on campus, such as stairs and doors. What conclusions can you draw about your ability as a disabled person to participate in campus activities. How could your school make improvements to assist disabled students?

Answers to Objective Test Questions

True • False Test

1. f	6. f
2. f	7. t
3. t	8. t
4. t	9. f
5. t	10. f

Multiple-Choice Test

1. b	6. c
2. d	7. c
3. a	8. a
4. d	9. b
5. b	10. d

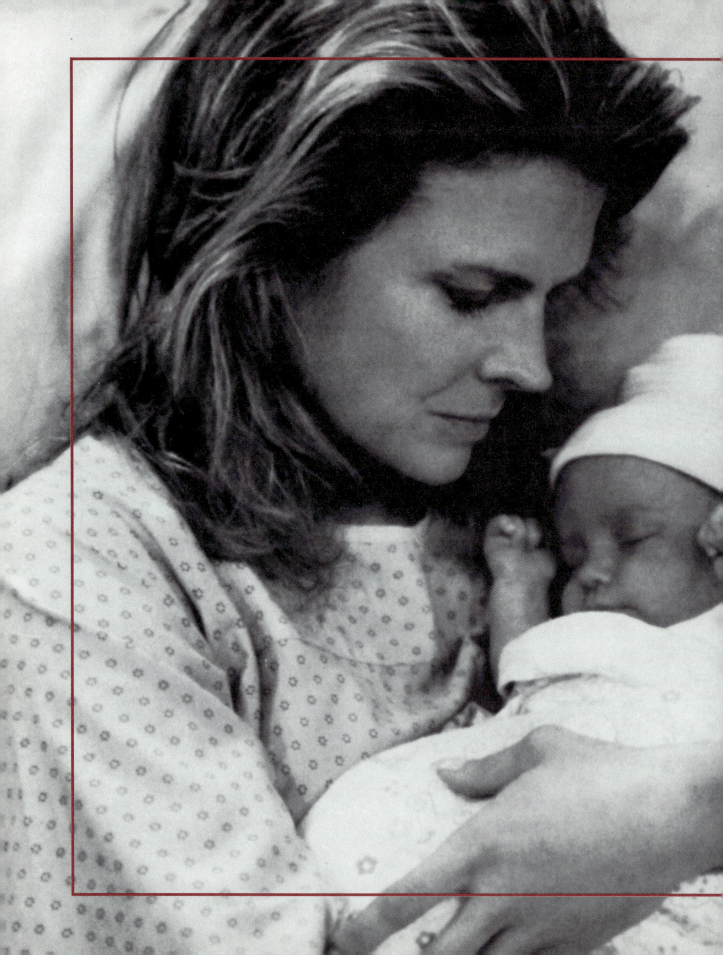

Family and Alternative Lifestyles

11

On May 21, 1992, even though Somalia and Bosnia were in turmoil, inner-city Los Angeles was in ruin, and the budget deficit was ballooning, many political leaders and ordinary citizens were preoccupied with the lifestyle of Murphy Brown, the central character in a CBS television dramatic series.

Three days earlier on the show's season finale, Brown, an unmarried woman, had given birth to a baby boy. The following day Vice-President Dan Quayle told an audience in San Francisco that our country currently suffers from a fundamental "poverty of values," with the increasing collapse of the family structure. It "doesn't help matters," Quayle added, to have Murphy Brown "mocking the importance of fathers, by bearing a child alone and calling it just another 'life style choice'" (Wines 1992, B16).

While Quayle's statement was consistent with presidential advisers' position that the decline of family values needed to be at the core of the reelection campaign, President George Bush himself seemed uncomfortable with reporters' questions about Quayle's actions. At first the president spoke in favor of stable, loving families but then threw up his hands, saying he didn't know much about the show. Once the cameras were turned off, he said to a companion in an exasperated tone, "I told you this was the issue. You thought I was kidding" (Wines 1992, B16).

Like his boss, White House spokesperson Marlin Fitzwater showed an inconsistent response. At first Fitzwater strongly endorsed Quayle's statement, but a few minutes later he felt it necessary to pacify the show's 38 million viewers, many of whom were voters, saying that Candice Bergen, who played Murphy Brown, was one of his favorite actresses and that he would meet with her any time and any place to discuss the situation.

Meanwhile Diane English, the show's creator and producer, issued a statement saying that if Quayle thought it was disgraceful for an unmarried woman to bear a child and to raise him or her without a father, then he'd better keep abortion "safe and legal"—a position that Quayle and the Republican Party opposed. An editorial in the *New Republic* indicated that Quayle's criticism of "Murphy Brown" simply represented the latest "tele-bashing" provided by the White House, which has criticized many programs, including the entire Public Broadcasting System, for promoting "bad" family values and attitudes (*New Republic* 1992).

Quayle seemed pleased with all the attention his original statement produced. Two days later, referring once again to "Murphy Brown," he told reporters, "Probably the only reason they chose to have a child rather than an abortion is because they knew the ratings would go up higher having the child" (Wines 1992, B16).

The "Murphy Brown" controversy demonstrates clearly the division of lifestyle values apparent in this country. While some Americans feel that it is fine for an unmarried woman to choose to have a child, others feel that such willingness represents a threat to the "traditional family." While many Americans favor the legalization of abortion, others are against it. Throughout this chapter we see that the modern American family is caught in the throes of change and that many issues, among them single parenthood and abortion, stir debate and controversy.

A **family** is traditionally defined as a social unit composed of two or more people who live together and are related by blood, marriage, or adoption. In the United States, the **nuclear family** has been the dominant form. This is a two-generation family that includes a father, a mother, and their children living separately from other relatives. In many other societies, however, the **extended family,** involving two or more generations of people related by blood and living together or close to each other, plays a more important role. The extended family has prevailed in rural settings. As societies have become increasingly industrialized and urbanized, the nuclear family has assumed a larger role.

The first section of this chapter discusses the functions of the family and also kinship terms.

Next we analyze the development of the modern American nuclear family. The chapter then considers changing patterns of love, courtship, and marriage and closes with a look at divorce and contemporary alternatives to marriage.

Selected Features of the Family

It will become apparent that throughout the world, families serve the same functions even though the means by which these functions are performed differ historically and cross-culturally.

SOME FUNCTIONS OF THE FAMILY

Throughout human history families have provided basic food and shelter and emotional comfort for their members. They have also supplied status placement; Americans' sense of their location in the social-class system is provided by their family membership. In addition, families are the groups that are supposed to engage in reproduction, thereby supplying new citizens for the society. Families also perform the three functions we will examine cross-culturally in this section: sexual regulation, economic activity, and socialization.

Sexual Regulation

People are likely to become nervous when contemplating the prospect of extreme sexual promiscuity. Most of us could not cope effectively with a society in which everyone was permitted to have sexual intercourse with everyone else. The universality of incest taboos demonstrates the importance that all cultures place on keeping sexual activity carefully controlled and limited.

The Incest Taboo   An **incest taboo** is a rule outlawing sexual relations between kin-group members believed to be too closely related as defined by the cultural standards of a given society. In all known societies, the incest taboo normally restricts marital relations within the nuclear family to the husband and wife. Throughout history the incest taboo has served several important functions. First, the rule eliminates the conflicts and

jealousy that would result if there were sexual rivalry among members of the nuclear family. The taboo, in short, helps maximize cooperation within the family unit. Second, the incest taboo forces people to marry outside their own nuclear families, thus reducing isolation and encouraging families to cooperate with one another. These marital alliances increase the possibility that families will share inventions and discoveries, work together in the procurement or production of food and other valued commodities, and engage in mutual protection against enemies. Third, the taboo helps keep the roles of family members clearly defined. Without the incest taboo, a single individual could be simultaneously a wife and a daughter, or a brother and a husband, and so on. If this occurred, authority within the family would become confused, and the continued existence of the nuclear family as a functioning social unit

Extended families, like this one from the Aboure tribe on the Ivory Coast, remain the norm in many societies.

would be seriously threatened (Murdock 1949, 295–97). Recent research found that families in which incest occurred demonstrated a variety of psychiatric problems, including less ability to perceive family relations clearly and objectively than families with other clinical difficulties (Madonna, Van Scoyk, and Jones 1991). Given the fundamental importance of the family within societies and the critical part that the incest taboo plays in maintaining the family, it is not surprising that the taboo exists universally.

Economic Activity

To be reputable members of a society or sometimes simply to survive, people must work. Often work has been gender-related. How often do we hear the phrase "That's women's work" or "That's a man's job"? These clichés reflect traditional gender-role definitions presently under heavy attack by many modern women and men. If we consider societies other than that of the United States, we will see that there are no tasks consistently categorized as "male" or "female" across cultures. For example, societies have existed where women were the warriors and others where men prepared the food. Societies have even existed in which men have "recovered" from childbirth while their wives went back to work. Although men's and women's family tasks often differ widely from one society to another, they all have gender-linked tasks. They also have age-linked tasks. Because of the complexity or danger associated with some important tasks, children must reach a certain level of growth before being allowed to undertake them. Hunting, warfare, and the manufacture of many intricate or important objects provide good examples.

In modern societies families generally no longer produce food, clothes, housing, and other basic subsistence items. Instead men and women work for organizations and buy with the money they earn the essential items formerly produced by the united activity of the family unit. As people become increasingly integrated into a modern industrial setting, they tend to break away from extended families, where the function of economic production is often important, and to reside in nuclear family units (Handwerker 1973). As we will see, the nuclear family is especially compatible with a modern, industrial setting.

Socialization

Social norms compel parents to provide socialization for their children, whether or not they wish to do so. However, within a given culture, socialization patterns often vary considerably (Leighton 1984).

There are many different patterns of socialization cross-culturally. For example, anthropologist Margaret Mead (1963, 40–41) noted that women in Bali hold their children in a looser and more relaxed manner than do American parents. Mead suspected that because of this manner of being held, Balinese children retain much greater physical flexibility than do American children.

Research has also suggested that personality differences can be attributed in part to variations in socialization practices. Beatrice and John Whiting and their associates (1975, 172–85) studied the typical socialization patterns in six cultures; five were non-American and agricultural and one American, specifically a New England town. The children in two of the traditional societies tended to have unsociable, aggressive, and authoritarian (rigid, conformity-oriented, and excessively obedient to authority) personalities, while the children in the New England town were relatively sociable and less aggressive. The children with aggressive, authoritarian personalities came from societies with extended families in which an adult male was the most powerful individual. With many relatives living together, often amid numerous conflicting interests, family interaction tended to be controlled by clear, sharp commands from the dominant male. By contrast, a much more casual, intimate setup is possible in the nuclear family characteristic of American towns, and this pattern was similarly reflected in the American children's personalities. The Whitings concluded that by the age of 6, children have assimilated the respective values of their cultures, and their personality structures are basically established.

Besides affecting children's personalities, family socialization also develops their abilities, with social conditions influencing the operation of the socialization process. A study of 697 3- to 6-year-old children found that the better paying a mother's job and the more substantively complex her work, the higher her child's measured verbal ability. The better pay permitted child-care arrangements that were likely to develop good verbal skills and helped the mother avoid the psychological stress that could impede effective communication with her child. Job complexity encouraged a woman to feel good about herself and to value the skills necessary for her job, making it more likely that she would be attentive and responsive to her child's development, including verbal abilities (Parcel and Menaghan 1990).

In modern times socialization has been partially usurped from the family by the government and other structures. In the former Soviet Union and the People's Republic of China, children generally spend most of the day in a collective setting. Similarly the increase in the number of working mothers within U.S. society has meant that day-care facilities for infants and young children have been rapidly expanding. In the kibbutzim (collective settlements) scattered throughout Israel, communal living is emphasized; socialization is a communal enterprise with children of the same age living together entirely apart from their parents. Although the members of one kibbutz told a researcher that they were deliberately attempting to undermine the nuclear-family structure, ties between parents and children remained strong. Families came together two hours a day and also on Saturdays and holidays. An observer wrote, "The eagerness of parents to see their children is equalled only by the eagerness of the children to see their parents" (Spiro 1970, 125).

KINSHIP TERMS

A **kinship system** is a number of people related by common descent, marriage, or adoption. Cross-culturally kinship systems have several types of marriage, customs for marriage eligibility, residential rules for newly married couples, and patterns of power within the family.

Type of Marriage

Polygamy is a marriage practice in which a person has two or more spouses of the other sex. **Polygyny** is the form of polygamy in which a man has two or more wives. **Polyandry** is the form of polygamy in which a woman has two or more husbands. **Monogamy** is a marriage practice in which there is

On this kibbutz these children have been living with their age mates since infancy.

one husband and one wife. In the United States, polygamy is illegal. About 90 percent of societies permit some form of polygamy, but it is not widely practiced because of the cost of maintaining two or more households. Polygyny is a much more common form of polygamy than polyandry. Because there is a higher death rate among male infants and men's life expectancy is shorter, there are fewer men in most societies than women. When polyandry does occur, it is because some practice creates an artificial scarcity of women; for example, the Todas of India used to drown some of their newborn infant girls.

Customs for Marriage Eligibility

Endogamy is a custom requiring a person to marry within a specific social unit, such as a kinship group, religious organization, or social class. **Exogamy** is a custom compelling someone to marry outside a specific social unit. In the United States, most marriages involve individuals similar in social-class background, religion, and race. All states have laws prohibiting marriage between members of the immediate family as well as between first cousins; some states will not permit second cousins to marry. Other societies also impose endogamous and exogamous standards.

308

In some traditional societies, endogamy helps strengthen a kinship group or community; thus people who refuse to obey this standard and marry within a particular unit are likely to suffer strong penalties.

Residential Rules for Newly Married People

Matrilocal residence involves settling with or near the wife's parents. **Patrilocal** residence requires settling with or near the husband's parents. **Neolocal** residence occurs when married people establish an independent place to live. The respective roles that men and women play in the society largely determine the residential patterns. Therefore, if men within a particular society have an especially important role in obtaining food, then a patrilocal residential pattern is likely to exist. This is even more likely if men own property that can be accumulated and if males are the heads of elaborate political systems. On the other hand, if women have the dominant role in the procurement of food and if the political organization is relatively simple, then matrilocal residence is likely to take place. Neolocal residence generally occurs in societies in which the nuclear family is economically independent. In the United States, where many people must be free to move where they can find jobs, neolocal residence predominates.

Patterns of Power within the Family

A **patriarchal** family is a family in which the husband-father is the formal head and the absolute or nearly absolute source of power. A **matriarchal** family is a family in which the wife-mother is the formal head and the absolute or nearly absolute source of power. An **egalitarian** family is a family in which the wife-mother and husband-father share power and also permit their children to participate in the family decisions. In most societies the husband-father usually had the final say in most important matters. No societies qualify as true matriarchies. American families have traditionally been patriarchal, but a gradual movement toward the egalitarian form has been encouraged by women's steadily improving educational and occupational status in the society at large.

The Modern American Nuclear Family ◼

The American nuclear family is fairly egalitarian, with neolocal residence and a monogamous marriage pattern. The dominant form is nuclear. In this section we consider how industrialization has encouraged the development of the nuclear-family type and also examine the declining functions of the American nuclear family.

INDUSTRIALIZATION AND THE NUCLEAR FAMILY

Sociologist William Goode (1963) suggested that the industrial era has encouraged people to discard the extended family and live exclusively in the nuclear family. What specific features of industrialization have prompted such a shift?

The increased need for physical movement from one specific location to another is one factor.

In an industrial setting, it is impractical to move an entire extended family in order to allow one person to take a desirable new job.

In addition, social mobility, prevalent in industrial societies, plays an important role. An emphasis on upward social mobility has supported the development of the nuclear family, which is relatively small and flexible and allows people to conform their lifestyles, dress, and speech to the standards of the successful mainstream without encountering extensive criticism from kin. Such changes frequently help people get jobs (or better jobs) in an industrial context, thereby contributing to their advancement. Recall our discussion of social mobility in Chapter 8, "Social Stratification."

Third, a member of an extended family normally has time-consuming domestic obligations toward a variety of kin. For an individual to perform effectively in an industrial setting, these obligations need to be severely limited, and the isolated nuclear family radically reduces kinship obligations.

Finally industrial society requires a family that, like the nuclear family, can afford to support children during a lengthy period of education or training provided by such social organizations as schools, corporations, and the military. In the extended family, children were expected to begin making an economic contribution to the family's upkeep soon after they started walking; for the most part, children in these families received no formal education at all.

Thus, Goode declared, industry has streamlined the family. He has also noted that the relationship between the two structures has not always been smooth and harmonious (Goode 1982, 181). Sociologist Richard Sennett (1974) has developed the last point, suggesting that the nuclear family type may be less supportive of its members' emotional and occupational growth than the extended family. He found that men living in nuclear families when they immigrated to Chicago in the late nineteenth century tended to be less occupationally successful than men who had also recently moved to the city but were still living in extended families. Sennett suspected that the latter group of men viewed their nuclear families as protection against the new and alien urban social life. These men were, in fact, quite isolated. There were no adult males with whom they could readily discuss their fears and aspirations. Such men tended to view their work defensively; they generally accepted modest positions and held on to them. Furthermore they passed the same introverted, self-protective attitudes on to their sons.

On the other hand, when male members of extended families arrived in Chicago, they tended to react to the city much less defensively because their family was more active and supportive. Work was frequently discussed with other men in the household, and sometimes friendly competition for jobs and occupational advancement would develop among them. The sons in extended families not only had a more optimistic, less tension-laden outlook on work but also tended to be more succesful than their counterparts in nuclear families.

Modern people often recognize the assets of extended families. A study conducted in a small city found that more than half the adults in a randomly selected sample indicated that among their relatives there was someone who could be considered a "kinkeeper"—usually a woman—who used telephoning, writing letters, visiting, and organizing or holding family gatherings to keep extended family members in contact with one another (Rosenthal 1985).

DECLINING FUNCTIONS OF THE NUCLEAR FAMILY

The American nuclear family has lost a number of functions since the colonial era. Because of the Industrial Revolution, the economic-productive function has been transferred from the home and family to factories, businesses, and other organizations, where one or more family members work in order to meet the family's economic needs. Therefore the family is no longer both producer and consumer, just the latter. This limited role might seem entirely natural to Americans but not to most people of the past. In fact, many preindustrial people—the Greeks and Romans, for instance—visualized production and consumption as so thoroughly fused into a single life-giving function that they even lacked a separate word for consumer.

Other functions have also been largely separated from the family. Recreation was once centered in the home or the church, but it has become increasingly specialized along age lines and is now located outside the home. Children's sport and artistic programs and facilities, motion picture theaters, and video arcades provide a few illustrations. In addition, the protective function is no longer handled by the family but rather is now the responsiblity of the police, the fire department, and other community agencies. Health care too has moved out of the home, with the dominant role played by doctors and nurses, drug stores, hospitals, and health-care agencies. Religious training, once rooted in the home, is now restricted to certain times and places outside it. Finally dramatic institutional expansion and specialization have occurred in education. Two hundred years ago, parents routinely educated their children in the home. Now, from the age of 4 or 5 onward, children are removed from the home for thirty to forty hours a week (Adams 1980, 87–88).

310   ## Consequences of the Loss of Functions

As we have noted, Richard Sennett believed that extended families were healthier places for the development of nineteenth-century American men than were nuclear families. The French historian Phillipe Ariès (1962) extended this argument to include women and children. Ariès contended that before the industrial era, women and children often encountered far fewer restrictions than they do today. The expectations that family members should constantly display mutual affection and that parents were obliged to ensure their children's maximum social and intellectual development simply did not exist. Once their household duties were completed, women and children were relatively free to do what they wanted. By contrast, Ariès described the modern nuclear family as a "prison of love."

Sociologist Arlene Skolnick (1987) made a similar point. She suggested that the nuclear family is characterized by "built-in strains." Men are freed from most obligations to the extended kinship unit, but they are compelled to support their wives and children in "the style to which they aspire to become accustomed." Skolnick has contended that women's plight is sometimes "obscured by the myth that women are the main beneficiaries of marriage." While women today have been released from their role obligations in extended family units, they now find themselves living in isolated households, often with extensive domestic duties. Skolnick pointed out that while labor-saving devices can facilitate the completion of specific tasks, they do not necessarily reduce the total number of work hours. It is possible that these devices simply raise the standards for meal preparation, house cleaning, and child care. Furthermore women now comprise nearly half of the labor force, and working wives and mothers tend to bear the burden of domestic responsibilities, even when the husband-father is vocally supportive of his wife's career and expresses a willingness to make a substantial contribution to the domestic chores.

The changes that have been occurring in people's living arrangements—most notably the relentless movement of an increasing proportion of women into the paid work force—have encouraged one sociologist to propose that the concept of nuclear family has become inaccurate, emphasizing women in traditional domestic roles and men in the work place, and should be discarded. Sociologist L. L. Cornell (1990) suggested that instead analysis should be concerned with two types of activity—productive labor focused in the marketplace and reproductive labor centered on the care and development of children—and the variety of patterns modern adults of both sexes produce to perform these two sets of tasks. It is an interesting idea worth keeping in mind in the following section.

Changing Patterns of Love, Courtship, and Marriage   ■

The modern American family is the product of an industrialized, urbanized age. That same social context has created some new developments in living arrangements. In this section we examine premarital sex, living together, choice of partners, and changing marital patterns.

PREMARITAL SEX

As a student in the 1960s, I once was present at a lecture during which the professor looked at the students half-mockingly and said, "You kids think you invented sex. Back in the 1930s and 1940s, we were doing the same things that you are, but we weren't making as much noise about it." Undoubtedly there is some truth to the statement, especially the part about not making as much noise. However, the available data, which were quite limited before the 1960s, suggest the occurrence of a sexual revolution—approval of premarital sex as well as sexual activity itself—rose sharply between the late 1960s and early 1970s. For instance, one national survey indicated that while in 1969, 69 percent of the respondents felt that premarital sex was wrong, the number plummeted to 47 percent just four years later and remained at about that level through the 1980s (Smith 1990,

422). Table 11.1 presents some data on this topic.

Two trends seem apparent for premarital sex. First, in our society, boys and girls typically hold different attitudes toward sexuality. With the implicit, if not explicit, approval of parents, teachers, and other adults, boys are frequently encouraged to experiment with sex, talk about it, and joke about it. Girls, on the other hand, are taught to avoid such easy familiarity with sexuality. They learn that sexual activity is not supposed to be an act in its own right, that it is supposed to occur for the sake of love and the creation of children.

Given this, it is not surprising that male and female sex-related behavior is often different. Male adolescents, for instance, often treat sexual contacts with females as a means of building social status in their peer groups. The emphasis is on sexual access—a highly goal-oriented approach that sometimes resembles the negotiation of a business deal more than an expression of love. Young women, by contrast, are more likely to focus on the emotional element, emphasizing the affection they feel and demonstrations of fondness or love on the male's part (Gagnon and Simon 1973). Recent research supported this trend, indicating that men continue to be more willing than women to engage in casual sex (Clark 1990).

On the other hand, there has been a trend consistent with the idea of a sexual revolution—to make sexual activity more egalitarian, with a more permissive approach applying to both women and men. One study concluded that college students' behavior has become increasingly consistent with an equal standard for sexual conduct—in short, the restriction or even elimination of a sexual double standard for males and females (Keller, Elliot, and Gunberg 1982). Supporting this trend, survey data suggest that between 1979 and 1988,

Table 11.1 Feelings about Sex before Marriage

	Wrong	Not wrong	No opinion
1991	40%	54%	6%
1985	39	52	9
1973	48	43	9
1969	68	21	11
1991 BREAKDOWNS			
Male	36%	59%	5%
Female	44	49	7
18–29 years	23	72	5
30–49 years	31	64	5
50 & older	62	30	8
White	41	53	6
Nonwhite	33	63	4
College grads	32	61	7
Some college	36	58	6
High-school grads	42	53	5
Not high-school grads	50	44	6
Religion very important	60	33	7
Fairly important	21	73	6
Not important	11	86	3

Source: *Adapted from* Gallup Poll Monthly. (*October* 1991), *p.* 69.

While over time Americans have become increasingly supportive of premarital sex, some categories of people remain more positive than others. Individuals who are male, younger, nonwhite, well-educated, and don't consider religion important are more inclined to support this activity.

Because of the sexual revolution, norms have been changing, with more egalitarian standards encouraging women to take a more active role in couple relationships than they traditionally have done.

adolescents of both sexes ranging between 15 and 19 have become increasingly inclined to engage in sexual intercourse (Zeman 1992).

LIVING TOGETHER

> I always say we never got married, because we bought our own toaster.

Danny DeVito, actor

When he made this statement, DeVito had been living with the same woman for more than ten years, and eventually they married. Recent data suggest that an increasing percentage of cohabiting couples do get married. They live together as a step toward marriage, for the economic benefits involved, or simply as an alternative to being single (Larson 1991).

Who Engages in Cohabitation?

Cohabitation has sharply increased in recent years. Among students the relaxation of college rules and increased opportunities to live off-campus have encouraged this trend. Furthermore changing sexual attitudes—a general increase in sexual permissiveness and openness—have occurred among young people. Living together has also been encouraged by some people's disenchantment with marriage and by the belief that cohabitation can help to develop interpersonal

skills that will be useful when people marry at a later date.

In the late 1960s and early 1970s, about 11 percent of adults lived together before their first marriage. By the early 1980s, that figure had risen to 44 percent and then reached nearly half by 1990. While cohabitation has been widely considered a practice engaged in by college students, it is more common among less educated people, with young people who have not completed high school most prominently represented. In addition, cohabiting occurs more frequently among children who grew up receiving welfare, living in single-parent families, or experiencing a major family disruption, such as divorce (Bumpass, Sweet, and Cherlin 1991; Larson 1991; Thorton 1991; Waldrop 1990). A recent study suggested that cohabiting individuals tend to be more aggressive than other people, in part because they generally live a more isolated existence freeing them from normal social controls (Stets 1991).

In addition, people who marry more than once are particularly likely to live together. A large study of cohabiting couples found that 60 percent of those who remarried between 1980 and 1987 lived with someone, usually the eventual spouse, beforehand (Barringer 1989).

Consequences of Living Together

In the legal realm, there are some decisive consequences of living together. Cohabiting people deny themselves some of the protections provided by the law to married couples. In some states merchants and landlords may legally refuse to sell or rent to a cohabiting couple. Children born to a cohabiting couple can be subjected to legal difficulties not imposed on a married couple's offspring.

One interesting trend revealed by research is that within ten years of the wedding, 38 percent of those who had cohabited had split up compared with 27 percent of those who married without living together. One should not simply jump to the conclusion, however, that cohabitation encourages divorce. It appears that those who cohabit often have higher expectations for the emotional and sexual rewards of marriage (Barringer 1989). In fact, people who have cohabited value the experience, arguing that it added to their personal growth and maturity, and they usually feel that they would not marry a person without first living together (Macklin 1983).

Research data on this topic require careful analysis. Drawing information from the national study of the high-school class of 1986, a pair of investigators found that if married people who had cohabited with each other before marriage were compared to couples married the same length of time who had not previously cohabited, those who had lived together before marriage showed higher rates of marital disruption (measured by the fact that the couple no longer lived at the same address). However, when the total length of the union was taken into account, the difference disappeared. Thus while former cohabitants who had been married for three years showed a higher marital disruption rate than couples who had been married for the same amount of time but had not previously cohabited, the rates were the same if couples whose combined time of cohabitation and marriage totalled three years were compared to couples who had simply been married for three years (Teachman and Polonko 1990). The results of this study illustrate a point first made in Chapter 2—that the analysis applied to data is fully as important as the data themselves.

CHOICE OF PARTNERS

Americans prize freedom of choice. It is easy to imagine someone saying, "I'll marry anyone I choose. After all, people are created equal, and so marriage should simply be a question of whom I love." Despite such attitudes, most Americans practice **homogamy,** marriage to a person having social characteristics similar to one's own. Why is this? In the first place, many of us desire mates whose values are similar to ours. Those who share our racial, religious, ethnic, and social-class statuses are especially likely to also share our values. Furthermore opportunity plays a part in promoting homogamy. Our residential areas, schools, and work places are usually somewhat segregated on the basis of race, ethnicity, and class, and so in these areas we are often going to meet people whose social characteristics are similar to ours. Another important factor promoting homogamy is informal pressure from family and friends to marry one's "own kind." We sometimes do not clearly

perceive that these forces have an impact upon our lives, but for most of us, they are definitely significant. The data on homogamy support this conclusion.

Recent research has revealed that when people marry, they tend to find partners who are similar in age, race, religion, ethnic background, intelligence, income level, educational attainment, overall physical attractiveness, and various personality characteristics (Buss 1986; Knox 1988, 150).

One of the striking conclusions drawn from research on happy marriages was that the spouses maintained many common outlooks. In a study of 351 couples married fifteen years or more, social scientists Jeanette and Robert Lauer (1989) found that 300 couples indicated that they were happily married. From a list of thirty-nine statements about marriage, the female and male spouses listed the same seven top reasons in order of frequency. They were:

1. My spouse is my best friend;
2. I like my spouse as a person;
3. Marriage is a long-term commitment;
4. Marriage is sacred;
5. We agree on aims and goals;
6. My spouse has grown more interesting;
7. I want the relationship to succeed.

In a 1990 sample, researchers found that women and men agreed on the three characteristics considered the most important—mutual attraction, dependable character, and emotional stability (Allgeier and Wiederman 1992).

Unfortunately many individuals find themselves with spouses who lack desired qualities. The nearby Cross-Cultural Perspective describes a case in point.

CHANGING MARITAL PATTERNS

Several years ago a film called *The Turning Point* portrayed two women who had made decisive choices about their lives. One had opted to become a ballerina and was successful in her career but was also lonely, with nothing in her life except her career. The other woman had married, turned away from an equally promising career, and while still satisfactorily married was always painfully aware of the choice she had made. The film raised a

CROSS-CULTURAL PERSPECTIVE
Korean Working-Class Marriages

In a study of thirty-two Korean working-class marriages, Sook-Hyun Choi and Patricia M. Keith wondered whether spouses suffered economic stress and extreme gender-role segregation as research indicated working-class American couples did. They found that these problems existed and that the main focus for complaint was emotional and communications issues.

Korean Working-class Spouses' Adjustment to Marriage Under the teachings of the Confucian philosophy, the continuity of the family was considered more important than an individual's needs. A woman would marry into a man's family, where she was expected to obey his parents and dedicate herself to their needs. In the early stages of marriage, a woman's adjustment to her parents-in-law was considered more important than to her husband. Among the respondents in this study, about half of the couples were living in an extended-family arrangement with one or both of the husband's parents.

In this investigation the respondents had no more than a high-school education. The husband worked in a blue-collar job, and about 70 percent of wives worked outside the home or helped their husbands in their stores. The average age at marriage was 24 for the wives and 27 for the husbands, and each couple had at least one child under 12. With 60 percent of the couples married through matchmakers, spouses conceded that they got married before falling in love. It was common to say that they "planted" love with their marriages and then "cultivated" their love through parenthood. For many wives marital adjustment involved learning to live with their parents-in-law, particularly the mother-in-law.

The traditional Confucian standard indicated that men's and women's roles were sharply divided, with women performing all domestic tasks. Because of this emphasis, it is not surprising that even when women were employed outside the home, they still did the lion's share of the household tasks. About 80 percent of men believed that their lives were easier than women's, but interestingly women expressed the opposite position. For instance, a 31-year-old milk delivery woman indicated that while there were many demands on her, she did not "have to worry about responsibility for making a living. That's his. I think his life is hard mentally, thus harder than mine" (Choi and Keith 1991, 299).

In the decision-making area, Korean working-class families also remained traditional, with husbands making the major decisions but usually consulting their wives in the process. Because they were consulted, most wives found the arrangement acceptable. When asked if she had complaints about her husband's decision-making power, one wife said, "I don't, because we discuss things together. If I say no, he's not the type of person who goes ahead and does something anyway" (Choi and Keith 1991, 301).

Respondents, particularly female respondents had many complaints about marital companionship. External conditions negatively affecting a close emotional relationship between spouses included long working hours, presence of children and and parents or in-laws, and financial problems. In addition, women frequently complained that their husbands would not talk about their feelings or show emotion, and the men generally accepted this charge against them. One woman said, "Particularly on special days, I want him to say nice words to me and make me feel assured that I'm cared for, but he never does that. I am disappointed" (Choi and Keith 1991, 304). And a man explained, "When I feel gloomy I sing some hymns or pop songs while I'm walking on the road. That way I can forget all the unhappy things and I can go home without them" (Choi and Keith 1991, 305).

Sexual activity hardly seemed to bring spouses together emotionally. Few respondents indicated that sex is an important dimension of a successful marriage, and most women simply suggested that sex is for men. Typically one wife explained, "I do not enjoy something like that (sex). I do it because I think it's my duty. I don't know whether I'm satisfied or not" (Choi and Keith 1991, 307).

In marriages where the communication and emotional ties were not very developed, it is hardly suprising that marital conflict, which most frequently centered on drinking and in-law problems, often went unexamined. While one quarter of the sample did work out compromises in disputes and tried to understand each other, the rest simply remained cool and and

tried to smooth things over. One man explained:

> I do not talk when I am angry. If my wife argues over conflicts with my parents, I listen to her. And then I say, "stop it, that's enough." If she goes on, I go outside and smoke a cigarette and take fresh air. That's all I can do.
>
> (*Choi and Keith*, 1991: 309)

This study arouses a number of questions. How does this description of Korean working-

class families seem similar to or different from American working-class families? To what extent do the patterns described here appear to be the result of working-class status, and to what degree do they seem to emerge from Korean culture? What changes, if any, are likely to occur in the future? In particular, what social conditions would produce more effective couple communications? In class discussion consider such issues and others of interest.

Source: Sook-Hyun Choi and Patricia M. Keith. "Are 'Worlds of Pain' Crosscultural? Korean Working Class Marriages," Journal of Comparative Family Studies. vol. 22 (Autumn 1991), pp. 293–312.

● ●

difficult question: Do women have to make a choice between career and family?

Women's increasingly common pursuit of careers is one reason the birthrate has been declining in the past three decades. Improved methods of contraception, the relentlessly increasing cost of raising children, and a growing concern about population control are others. From 1920 to 1924, there were about 3.3 children per woman. The figure rose to 3.7 children per woman in 1955–1959 and then declined, reaching 2.01 children per woman in 1989 (U.S. Bureau of the Census, *Population Profile of United States*: 1981, Table 5.1; U.S. Bureau of the Census, *Fertility of American Women*: June 1983, Table 2; U.S. Bureau of the Census, *Statistical Abstract of the United States*: 1992, No. 84).

Voluntary Childlessness

While the common belief holds that all preindustrial American couples had large families, it is not true. Between 1861 and 1865, at least 30 percent of the women in New Hampshire and Massachusetts were childless, and in nine other states, the rate was at least 20 percent (Morgan 1991). Currently about 5 percent of all couples choose childlessness, emphasizing that one's adult status can be confirmed by means other than parenthood, espe-

cially through a career. This percentage appears to be slowly rising, especially among well-educated women in higher-status occupations (Reiss and Lee 1988, 322). Voluntarily childless couples

One advantage for childless couples is that they can pursue activities like deep-sea fishing that would be too expensive or inappropriate for most couples with children.

316

emphasize that children drain away time and energy that could otherwise be devoted to one's career and other interests.

Researcher J.E. Veevers (1973) studied fifty-two voluntarily childless wives and found that many of the subjects came from unhappy homes in which the parents had supposedly stayed together for the sake of the children, thus passing on to their offspring a feeling that children generally can be a cause of strife in marriage. Some of the voluntarily childless wives were the oldest children in large families and had shouldered major responsibilities for the care of their younger brothers and sisters. These women grew up with a sharply focused awareness that motherhood can be a burdensome responsibility.

One investigation discovered that career success is often a priority for women who remain voluntarily childless (Silka and Kiesler 1977). In part because of their career emphases, childless wives often rate the importance of having children as less important than their husbands do—a reversal of the common trend (Seccombe 1991). Another study concluded that childless couples have two features that set them apart from couples with children: a tendency to value more highly women's achievement and independence and an inclination for the spouses to interact more extensively with each other in such positive ways as exchanging ideas, working together on projects, and having sexual relations (Feldman 1981).

About two-thirds of Veevers's subjects remained childless because of a series of decisions to put off childbearing until a later date. The other third had agreed not to have children as a part of an informal marriage contract (Veevers 1973). Later research has produced data related to the last point; compared with other couples who are deliberating about whether or not to have children, voluntarily childless couples are more firmly

decided against having children in the first place (Oakley 1985).

Working Mothers

Working mothers are a prominent segment of the work force. As Table 11.2 indicates, there has been a tremendous increase in the proportion of married working mothers over the past three decades.

A recent study suggested that many young women have little understanding of the demands of the combination of full-time work and motherhood. Seventy-three percent of a sample of 250 college women indicated that they wanted a career and children and that few doubted their ability to perform both of these roles successfully. The source of this conviction seemed to be the widespread contemporary thinking favoring the "do-both syndrome" (Baber and Monaghan 1988). For anyone who has actively participated in parenthood, it seems clear that these young women (and doubtless their male counterparts) are in for a shock.

Families in which women work or want to work outside the home frequently experience conflict because such behavior clashes with traditional attitudes about women's proper roles. An extreme example is provided by the husband who says, "I'm the provider. You're the homemaker. Case closed." Or perhaps the wife works, and this produces severe strains on the family. Sometimes career-oriented wives find themselves forced out of their work and back in the home. Alternative resolutions include divorce, "commuter" marriage, both spouses' lowering their career aspirations (Regan and Roland 1985), or working on different shifts. Research has found that in dual-earning households an increasing proportion of young spouses, especially wives, are working part- or full-time at

Table 11.2 Married Mothers in the Work Force

	1960	1991
With Children under 6	18.6%	59.9%
With Children 6 to 17	39	73.6

Source: U.S. Bureau of the Census. Statistical Abstract of the United States: 1992, No. 620.

In the thirty-one years between 1960 and 1991, the percentage of married women with children under 6 in the work force increased over threefold. For married women with children 6 to 17, the proportion also grew substantially, nearly doubling.

Like this 35-year-old attorney, many working mothers must find the time and energy to complete the multiple tasks required of them.

night in order to be with the children in the day and avoid the cost of day care. While such an arrangement might enhance the children's welfare, some evidence indicates that it increases family conflict (Presser 1988).

Despite some husbands' negative attitudes, many wives now work, partly because they may simply desire to do so, and partly because of the necessity for additional income. While many husbands are willing or even happy to accept this situation, the lion's share of the domestic responsibility still almost always falls on the woman's shoulders even though she may be working full time. A study of fifty-two couples over an eight-year period found that the working women were more torn between the demands of work and family than their husbands. Among the men surveyed, the majority did not share the work at home. Some refused, and others refused passively, offering a

sympathetic ear as their working wife faced the conflict both spouses considered to be hers. As a result of the multiple demands on them, the female respondents spoke more intensely about being overtired or sick. Many were fixated on sleep, discussing such issues as people they knew who needed more or less sleep or how to get back to sleep when awakened by a child. The researcher concluded that these women talked about sleep the way a starving person discusses food (Hochschild 1992).

Tension may also arise over the issue of whether or not children suffer if their mothers work. Until a few years ago, it was widely believed that some harm was inevitable or likely. However, if the mother likes her work and if effective child care is available, most studies suggest that the children will not be harmed. In fact, the daughters of working mothers are much more likely to score high on tests of independence, achievement, and positive self-image than are the daughters of non-working mothers (Hoffman and Nye 1974). Research also suggests that working women are less likely to be highly possessive of and overly ambitious for their sons largely because they are actively seeking their own fulfillment, rather than living vicariously through the children (Holmstrom 1972). Children's evaluation of their mothers' work will vary, depending on a number of circumstances. For example, one study found that children are more likely to have a positive outlook toward their mothers' work if they perceive that their mothers view it positively (Thimberger and MacLean 1982). This finding suggests that if mothers can locate jobs that please them, their children might benefit.

In spite of the demands on their time and energy, the physical, mental, and emotional well-being of employed mothers is often better than that of their nonworking counterparts. Some concern and even guilt is frequently aroused by the effort to combine the roles of mother, wife, and worker, but this is normally not a major problem, especially if they have a flexible work schedule and a supportive supervisor. Working women usually feel useful, valued, and competent, giving them higher self-esteem than nonworking mothers. Working mothers generally display greater enjoyment of their activities and relationships with their children and have more realistic expectations for their children and for themselves as mothers (Desai and Waite 1991; Ernest J. Green 1978, 171–73). All in all, if the working wife-mother is able to balance her time and energy between her family and work, she usually constitutes a healthy influence on the domestic scene.

Divorce, Remarriage, and Alternatives to Marriage

The previous section makes it clear that the norms that influence people's patterns of love, courtship, and marriage have become considerably more flexible in the past several decades. The same tendency is apparent when we examine divorce and the alternatives to marriage.

MARITAL FAILURE

While jogging on the beach in Guam, Chris Willie found a bottle containing a love note that was several years old. The writer said he was dropping the bottle into the Pacific halfway between Hawaii and Seattle. Willie followed directions in the bottle and mailed the note to the writer's wife in Seattle. The envelope was returned, however, marked "No longer at this address," and so Willie sent it to the *Seattle Times*. A newspaper official reached the woman by phone, and she asked that the note be read to her. It said:

> If, by the time this letter reaches you, I am old and gray, I know that our love will be as fresh as it is today. It may take a week, or it may take years for this note to find you. Whatever the case may be it

shall have traveled by a strange and unpredictable route—the sea. If this should never reach you, it will still be written in my heart that I will go to extreme means to prove my love to you. Your husband, Bob.

The woman laughed and laughed, the newspaper reported. "We're divorced," she said and hung up the phone (Krebs and Thomas 1981, 18).

Although surviving data are limited, research has concluded that in nineteenth-century America, there were fairly high rates of divorce, separation, and desertion (Schultz 1984). Twentieth-century data are more thorough. As Figure 11.1 indicates, divorce has increased sharply in this century. In 1910 there were just 83,000 divorces, 385,000 in 1950, and about 1.2 million in 1988. The rate rose gradually, from 0.9 divorces per thousand people in 1910 to 4.7 per thousand in 1988. In 1940 there was one divorce for every six marriages. This figure rose to one divorce for every four marriages in 1950, and then rose to nearly one divorce for every two marriages in 1988 (U.S. Bureau of the Census, *Statistical Abstract of the United States: 1992*, No. 127). It appears that the divorce rate has now peaked (Norton and Moorman 1987) and will probably

Figure 11.1

Marriage and Divorce Rates, 1910–1988

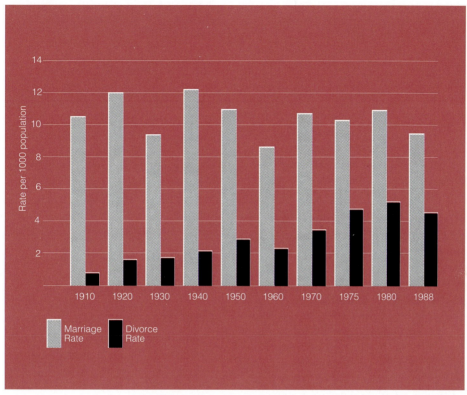

While the marriage rate has varied little over time, the divorce rate has risen steadily. In 1910 the marriage rate of 10.3 per 1,000 people was more than eleven times the divorce rate of 0.9 per 1,000. In 1988 the marriage rate of 9.7 per 1,000 people was scarcely twice the divorce rate of 4.7 per 1,000.

Source: Adapted from U.S. Bureau of the Census. Statistical Abstract of the United States: 1992, No. 127.

begin to decline. By showing the 1988 divorce rate slightly lower than the 1980 divorce rate, Figure 11.1 indicates that this trend seems to be starting.

Some Factors Influencing the Divorce Rate

Three decades ago the divorced person, especially the divorced woman, was likely to receive the brunt of the blame when she was divorced. "There must be something wrong with her," unsympathetic observers often said. "She can't hold her man." But gradually Americans have become more attuned to the sociological perspective, beginning to recognize that social forces outside the individual play a major role in the sharply increased rate of divorce over the past half-century.

Industrialization Modern industrialized nations are characterized by relatively independent courtship patterns, which permit love to become a critical criterion in mate selection. Love-based marriages tend to be especially unstable, frequently ending in divorce if the parties come to feel that love no longer endures. Consequently increasing levels of industrialization tend to mean higher divorce rates. The United States achieved a high degree of urban growth before 1930, and at that time its divorce rate was running well ahead of those typical of European societies. Between 1930 and 1965, American divorce rates increased slowly, while the rates in many European countries, which were experiencing rapid industrialization, rose sharply (Reiss and Lee 1988, 286–87).

320 ***Age of the Couple*** Age at the time of marriage is an important factor. Couples in their teens and early twenties are the least likely to have lasting marriages (Kunz and England 1988) for several reasons. First, the young are often more likely than older people to grow apart over time in their values and personal interests. Second, young people are the most inclined to turn to marriage as a means of escaping from an unhappy home environment, often failing in the process to realistically assess the chances of success. Third, young people are the most likely to decide to marry because of pregnancy, once again often without objectively assessing whether each partner is really ready to marry (Adams 1980, 375–76).

Changing Role Definitions within Marriage
None of the factors that we have discussed explain why the divorce rate shot up in the late 1960s. One significant influence was that role definitions within marriage began to change. The social protests of the 1960s, the increasing proportion of women in the work force, and then the development of the women's movement all encouraged women to seize the opportunity to be more independent and assertive than they had been in the past (Heaton 1991). Freed of traditional economic and psychological dependence on their husbands, an increasing number of wives decided that they did not need to grit their teeth and accept unhappy marriages.

Decreasing Legal and Social Constraints In 1970 California enacted the first no-fault divorce law in the United States, and forty-eight states have adopted this standard in some form. No-fault legislation simplifies divorce proceedings. One spouse no longer needs to establish grounds for divorce, testifying to the other's adultery, cruelty, or desertion and bringing in witnesses to support his or her testimony. The wife and husband are no longer forced to be adversaries. With no-fault divorce, the legal focus becomes the partners' joint endeavor to end as quickly as possible a marriage that does not work. Like the United States, Canada and Australia experienced a temporary surge in divorce rates following the passage of no-fault legislation (Weitzman and Dixon 1983; White 1990, 904). In addition, many religious groups have become less critical of divorce, no longer seeing it in moral terms. Perhaps the factor underlying both of these changes is a value issue—a strong

emphasis on freedom and happiness, with the feeling that marriage is an emotional more than a practical union and that it should be immediately discontinued if unhappy (Lamanna and Riedmann 1988, 511–12).

Consequences of Divorce

If someone's parents are divorced, he or she is said to come from a "broken home." This phrase calls to mind the image of a home in shambles, with everything—relationships, personalities, and even furniture—in disarray or even destroyed. It seems obvious that the product of a "broken home" is likely to have psychological problems, perhaps serious ones. But is this true? What, in fact, happens to spouses and children after divorce?

Consequences for the Couple Anthropologist Paul Bohannon (1970, 33) suggested that, in a sense, divorce reverses the courtship process. Instead of having been "selected" out of the whole world, the former spouse feels "de-selected." Not surprisingly research has concluded that following divorce people tend to become more depressed than they were before it occurred. The level of depression seems to be affected by the magnitude of one's economic problems, the availability of close, confiding relationships, and the extent to which one's former standard of living is maintained (Menaghan and Lieberman 1986).

Economically women tend to suffer more from divorce than men do. Recent estimates obtained from federal formulae for determining child support suggested that fathers could afford to pay more than twice the amounts presently awarded in child support (Kitson and Morgan 1990, 914).

Nonetheless there are indications that in many cases men have a more difficult time adjusting to divorce than women. While the suicide rate for divorced women has been three times that of married women, four times more divorced men than married men have killed themselves (Moffett and Scherer 1976). Furthermore evidence has indicated that men who have not remarried within six years after divorce have increased rates of car accidents, alcoholism, drug abuse, depression, and anxiety (Brody 1983). Why do women seem to adjust more effectively to divorce? Women make more practical use of kin support, relying on them more extensively and seeing this reliance in a much more optimistic light than men do. In fact, following divorce, men who seek kin support tend to suffer a high level of depression while women with such a reliance tend to be quite the opposite—more contented than most recently divorced people (Gerstel et al. 1988). Another factor operating here might be that men are more likely than women to lose custody of their children. Research concluded that some newly separated men's difficulties are compounded by their failure to accept the fact that the adaptation to their new existence will be greatly enhanced if they radically limit their interaction with their former spouse and also alter their relationship with their children (White and Bloom 1981).

Age is another social characteristic that appears to affect people's adjustment to divorce. Sociologists Morton and Bernice Hunt (1980) found that most childless people who divorce at a young age soon rejoin the never-married group, rapidly putting both the marriage and former spouse out of their minds. In contrast, people who divorce in mid life (Davis and Aron 1988) or in old age (Weingarten 1988) after many years of marriage are likely to find the experience much more difficult and adjustment a lengthier process.

Another factor coming into play is number of divorces. A study of 459 couples found that women who experienced two or more divorces demonstrated higher levels of anxiety, fear, and other forms of distress than those who had one divorce or none at all; for men the number of divorces did not affect their distress measures. The researcher suggested that since women are socialized to be more selfless and nurturant than men, they might feel more responsible for maintaining the marriage, and thus multiple divorces more likely would be considered accumulated personal failure (Kurdek 1990).

The unhappiness associated with most divorces does not mean that unhappily married people should stay married. A study indicated that individuals with unsatisfying marriages were more depressed, lonelier, and more socially isolated than were divorced people (Renne 1974).

Consequences for the Children   One day at the end of class, a student accompanied by her 12-year-old son, who was visiting the class, approached my desk. We had been discussing divorce, and our conversation continued on the same topic. After a

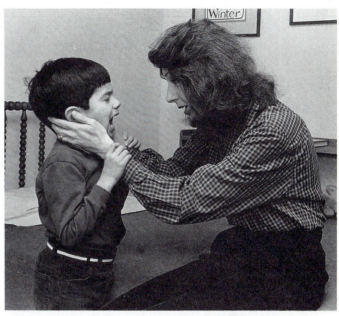

When divorce occurs, most children live all or most of the time with their mothers, who often must fulfill the diverse demands of parenthood by themselves.

few minutes, the mother said, "Ricky, tell Mr. Doob what you'd like."

Embarrassed the boy replied, "You know." The mother then explained that ever since the divorce, which occurred when he was 3, Ricky longed to be living again with both parents. The solution, he now believed, was to have his step-father marry his father's wife, and then the way would be cleared for his parents' remarriage. "He doesn't think about the others involved," the mother said sadly.

Many children suffer because of divorce. A study tracked sixty families for ten to fifteen years after the divorce, finding that five years later while half the men and two-thirds of the women said they were more content with their lives than before the divorce, about two-thirds of the children remained depressed or low-achieving in some areas. Ten years after the divorce, about 40 percent of the children were doing poorly, entering adulthood as worried, self-critical, and underachieving individuals. Adolescence, which is a stage when children's view of their ability to function in society is being established, is a particularly risky time period for the children of divorce, who frequently told the researchers that at that time they yearned for protection and clear moral guidelines for behavior. The prospect of marriage left many fearful. "I'm so afraid I'll marry someone like my dad," one young woman explained. And another respondent said, "I am in awe of people who stay together" (Wallerstein 1992, 165). Not surprisingly a study of 500 college students found that those from divorced families viewed marriage more negatively than those from intact families (Gabardi and Rosen 1991).

Following divorce the relationship between children and the nonresident parent tends to change dramatically. One study concluded that in divorce situations most children have little contact with their nonresident parent, usually the father, and what contact occurs is fairly superficial, with the nonresident parent often acting more like a pal than a parent (Furstenberg and Nord 1985).

A number of status factors seem to affect children's adjustment to divorce. Younger children seem to find the experience more difficult than older children, with children under 5 suffering the strongest emotional reactions. Boys tend to have more difficulty adjusting to divorce than girls (Greene and Leslie 1989; Lowery and Settle 1985). Probably both younger children and boys adjust more slowly because of more limited social skills. The boys' more limited social skills might result because after divorce they are less likely than girls to have role models for learning appropriate gender-related behavior (Demo and Acock 1988). Another factor affecting children's adjustment is the custodial parent's reaction to the divorce. Goode (1956, 317–21) found that the more trauma mothers experienced from their divorces, the more likely that they would describe their children as hard to handle following the split. Eighty-one percent of the mothers studied admitted that they were concerned about the impact of the divorce on their children. However, 55 percent encountered no increase in problems with their children afterwards, and only 14 percent found that their children were more difficult to deal with in the months following the divorce.

Even though divorce is painful for children, research has found that they prefer the post-divorce period to the time when the family was still intact. An 11-year-old boy indicated that while he missed his father, it was a relief to have no more fighting. He added, "The knots in my stomach were beginning to clear so things were much better" (Neugebauer 1989, 158).

REMARRIAGE

Several years ago the hostess at a party received a phone call that occupied her for nearly three-quarters of an hour. "Who was that?" she was asked when she returned.

"Poor woman!" the hostess replied. "She's desperate. Several months back her husband divorced her, and tonight she feels trapped at home, alone on a Saturday night with no place to go and no one even to talk to. The funny thing is that I don't even know her very well and really don't like her much. She's very uptight. I invited her over but she turned me down. So I just talked to her."

William Goode (1956) contended that the norms governing the behavior of divorced people are often unclear. Should they continue to socialize with their old married friends? Should they stay in the same town or move elsewhere? How should they deal with acute, even desperate loneliness such as that felt by the woman just described? One common course of action is to remarry.

As we have already noted, people tend to marry homogamously. This generalization also applies to divorced people. While over 90 percent of single men and women marry another single person, over half of divorced men and women remarry another divorced person. Among those who remarry, over 15 percent will do so within a few months of the completion of divorce proceedings and another 50 percent within three years. It takes an average of seven years for those who divorce to leave their first marriage but only three years for those who remarry to enter a second marriage (Reiss 1980, 340–42). In 1970, 31.4 percent of all marriages were remarriages; the figure rose to 43.8 percent in 1980 and then 46.1 percent in 1987 (U.S. Bureau of the Census, *Statistical Abstract of the United States*: 1991, No. 129).

How satisfactory are remarriages? A pair of sociologists claimed that divorce and remarriage are fairly effective mechanisms for replacing bad marriages with good ones—that second marriages that do not end quickly in divorce seem to be almost as successful as intact first marriages (Glenn and Weaver 1977). In another study a researcher asked his subjects to evaluate how happy their remarriages were compared with their first marriages and also how well each of their marriages compared with their acquaintances' marriages and with the level of happiness which they expected to find in marriage. The second marriages came out ahead on all these counts (Albrecht 1979). On the other hand, a study of 232 remarried and 102 first-married couples found that the remarried couples engaged in more conflict, especially over financial issues, child-rearing, and the presence of the husband's prior marriage children (Hobert 1991). Recently the Alabama Cooperative Extension Service developed an educational program to make lawyers, teachers, clinicians, and other professionals knowledgeable about and sensitive to the challenges of remarried life (Fitzpatrick, Smith, and Williamson 1992).

For children remarriages are also confusing as they are left wondering which people qualify as fellow family members. Is it the mother's family, the father's, or some combination? One study, in fact, indicated children in remarriages provided five different designations of what constituted the family unit, including the immediate household, the biological family, and the combined biological and step family (Hobart 1988; Klee, Schmidt, and Johnson 1989). Recall our discussion in Chapter 4, "Groups," that people's sense of self is shaped by primary-group or reference-group participation. Family membership qualifies in both regards. However, if one's sense of family membership is confused, then one's identity is also likely to be adversely affected.

ALTERNATIVES TO CONVENTIONAL MARRIAGE

In the past two decades, a number of factors have made people feel freer to choose various alternatives to conventional monogamous marriage. These include a sharp decrease in social pressure to have children, vast improvements in the availability of effective methods of contraception for women, increased economic self-sufficiency among many single people, and rapid improvements in the communication of new ideas (Ramey 1978, 3–5).

In the following pages we examine single-parent households, singlehood, homosexual relationships, and communes.

Single-Parent Households

The number of children under 18 living in single-parent households rose from 8.2 million in 1970 to 16.6 million in 1991, representing, as Figure 11.2 indicates, an increase from 12 to 25 percent of the

Figure 11.2

Living Arrangements of Children under 18 Years Old, 1970–1991

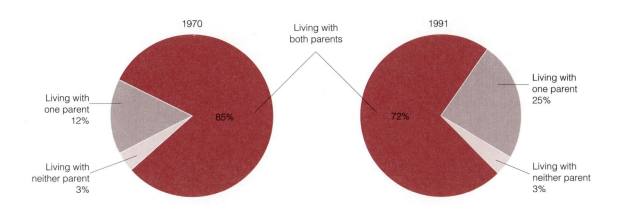

The most noteworthy finding is the decline in percentage of children living with both parents—from 85 percent in 1970 to 72 percent in 1991. The figure suggests that in the 1990s children are considerably more likely to experience parental divorce than in the 1970s.

Source: *Adapted from U.S. Bureau of the Census.* Current Population Reports, *Series P-20, Marital Status and Living Arrangements: March 1982, Table E; U.S. Bureau of the Census.* Statistical Abstract of the United States: 1992, *No. 69.*

324 total of American households containing children under 18 (U.S. Bureau of the Census, *Marital Status and Living Arrangements: March* 1982, Table E; U.S. Bureau of the Census, *Statistical Abstract of the United States*: 1992, No. 68 and No. 69). Although the distinct majority of single-parent families are headed by women, an increasing number of men are also running families by themselves—representing 12.1 percent of single parents in 1991 (U.S. Bureau of the Census, *Statistical Abstract of the United States*: 1992, No. 68). Single-parent families tend to have modest incomes, with father-child families possessing incomes that are more than twice those of mother-child families. While about 24 percent of all children are living below the poverty level, the figure is 57 percent for one-parent families (Norton and Glick 1986). However, a fair number of single parents are not poor. As they move through their thirties, some unmarried, often economically self-sufficient women, decide that if they are going to have a child, the time has arrived. As one 39-year-old woman explained, "I could imagine going through life without a man, but I couldn't imagine going through life without a child. My biological clock started sounding like a time bomb" (Smolowe 1992, 131).

Single parents face some other significant problems. Probably the most frequently expressed complaint is the overload of role commitments. Single parents must be all things to their children, not only mother but father as well, the breadwinner, the cook, and the nurse. Work schedules often conflict with parental obligations. How can the parent drive a child to day care, a Little League game, or a recital during working hours? Another difficulty is that single parents often have no one who can validate how they are treating their children. In a two-parent household, a mother or father can seek feedback for decisions from the other spouse. Single parents often have no one who can effectively provide this feedback when they are challenged by their children. As a result many begin to compromise their definition of reality, doing such things as giving in to a child whose personality development might be much more effectively nurtured if firm guidelines were established (Glenwick and Mowrey 1986; Sanik and Mauldin 1986; Turner and Smith 1983).

The single parent's sex does not seem to be a significant factor in determining his or her effectiveness. Children reared by mothers show about the same levels of self-esteem, social competencies, and severity and frequency of behavioral problems as children brought up by fathers. This finding opposes both the widely held belief that women inevitably make more effective parents than men and also the tendency of many courts to more readily award children to mothers in a custody suit (Risman and Park 1988; Schnayer and Orr 1989).

While it is widely believed that absent fathers play little or no role in single-parent families, some become quite involved with their children. A survey of adolescent female welfare recipients with children indicated that when absent fathers were employed, they were more likely to participate in the child-rearing process. Thus besides the more obvious benefits employment provides families, it appears to encourage absent fathers to assume parental obligations (Danziger and Radin 1990).

Singlehood

Being single was frowned upon during the colonial era. Women were considered old maids if they were not married by the age of 25, and bachelors were scorned, ridiculed, and sometimes even forced to pay a special tax. The Bible declares that people should be fruitful and multiply, and by not marrying and having children, single people were seen to be defying this command.

In modern times, however, a significant number of people have chosen to remain single. In 1960 about 32.8 percent of the adult population was unmarried. In 1991 about 41.5 million adults had never been married, while 13.7 million were widowed and 15.8 were divorced. This total of 71 million represented 38.7 percent, nearly two-fifths of the adult population (U.S. Bureau of the Census, *Statistical Abstract of the United States*: 1992, No. 49). It appears that the percentage of unmarried people will continue to increase; one specialist has predicted that among young people in their mid-twenties to early thirties, 12 percent of women and 10 percent of men will never marry—three times as high a proportion as in their parents' generation (Glick 1986). Singles include recent college graduates who are on their own for the first time as well as senior citizens who reside together in order to make the most of two Social Security checks. In between one finds millions of single people pursuing a diversity of lifestyles, including a host of single parents (DeWitt 1992).

Spending about half what bachelors do on entertainment, single women are more likely to use their money for pets, toys, playground equipment, and other home-centered entertainment products. Single men usually focus on entertainment fees and admissions, sporting goods, and electronic equipment (Exter 1990). Not normally perceived as homeowners, single people's share among first-time homeowners increased from one-quarter in 1987 to one-third in 1989. The average first-time single homebuyer is a 30-year-old individual who buys a $73,500 home on a $40,000 salary, with a downpayment of $9,400 and mortgage payments representing slightly more than one-fifth of monthly income (Cutler 1991).

The category of single people contains diverse outlooks and experiences. For instance, never-married people are much more likely than divorced singles to define singlehood as a permanent lifestyle, and marriage rates are higher for divorced than never-married singles (Cockrum and White 1985). People who are voluntarily single are probably most strongly committed to this status. Peter Stein (1980) studied singles and found a number of "pushes away" from marriage as well as "pulls toward" being single. "Pushes away" from married life included the possible suffocation of a one-to-one relationship, sexual frustration, and, interestingly, fear of isolation and loneliness. "Pulls toward" singlehood involved the exciting lifestyle, self-sufficiency, and the availability of sexual variety.

A significant issue affecting both single and married people is the legalization of abortion. Americans feel strongly about this topic and have deeply divided opinions. We consider those opinions in the nearby American Controversy.

Homosexual Lifestyle

Since the late 1960s, many homosexual Americans have decided that their interests will be best served if they seek to change the political, economic, and social injustices they have suffered. Gay people's public actions to produce these changes have received extensive media coverage. Yet in the diversity of current lifestyles, perhaps homosexuality remains the most mysterious and

While public discussion and debate have focused on how homosexuals are different from the general population, homosexual couples have established domestic lives that are generally similar to those maintained by heterosexual couples.

confusing. In fact, even social workers and other clinicians providing therapy to gay people generally lack a clear definition of homosexuality (Berger 1983).

Untruths about the subject abound. One is that homosexuals come from conflict-ridden families. Evidence from a study of over 320 gay men and women concluded that two-thirds perceived their relationships with their fathers as either satisfactory or extremely satisfactory and three-quarters felt that they maintained either a satisfactory or extremely satisfactory relationship with their mothers (Robinson et al. 1982). It is also widely believed that homosexuality is an indication of serious psychological disturbance. While recent research comparing hetereosexuals and homosexuals found some differences—for instance, that gay men were more expressive than hetereosexual men and lesbian women more goal-oriented than heterosexual women—findings indicated no differences in psychological adjustment (Kurdek 1987).

In addition, many people believe that homosexuality is particularly communicable to children in contact with adult gays. A preliminary study disputes this claim, suggesting that children with gay parents almost invariably prefer the toys, games, clothing, and activities typical of their own sex and as they become older report sexual fantasies or activities that are heterosexually oriented (Richard Green 1978). Finally it is often felt that

AMERICAN CONTROVERSY
Abortion: Pro-Life or Pro-Choice?

On July 3, 1989, by a five to four decision, the U.S. Supreme Court expanded the powers of the states to regulate abortions, permitting them to decide such issues as where they can be performed and how many months into a pregnancy abortion is permissible. While this decision did not overturn the earlier *Roe v. Wade* decision, which had permitted unrestricted abortion, it did represent a significant victory for the opponents of legalized abortion and a setback for its supporters. The public view was more supportive of abortion. In December 1991, 64 percent of a national sample opposed overturning *Roe v. Wade*. In January 1992, 31 percent of respondents felt that abortion should always be legal, an additional 53 percent supported its occurrence in certain circumstances, while 14 percent declared that it should always be illegal. At this time it appears that public discussion and debate about abortion will be a hot issue for years.

Pro-Life Position The opponents of abortion often label themselves "pro-life." They believe that no matter when an abortion is performed, the life of a human being is taken. To em-phasize this point, their advertisements frequently show pictures of fetuses, including fetuses in the first few weeks, to emphasize that in appearance they have the basic attributes of human beings.

How, the pro-life camp emphasizes, can one draw an arbitrary line saying that beyond one day, one month, three months, or whatever, the fetus becomes a living creature? Once conceived, a living creature exists, and that is the basic reality.

Under some circumstances it is reasonable for a person to give up her child for adoption. That, however, is no reason to kill him or her, the opponents conclude. Cherish the unborn child and then turn her or him over to the proper authorities to be placed in a good home.

Pro-Choice Position The supporters of abortion frequently refer to themselves as "pro-choice." Their emphasis is that a woman's body is her own—that she should be able to decide whether or not she wishes to have a child and that the state has no right to intervene on this issue.

If abortion becomes illegal, then women will lose this right. For all women that would be an injustice, but it would be partic-ularly discriminatory against poor women. Middle-class and upper-middle-class women would be able to do what was done several decades ago—get a family doctor or a private clinic to perform an abortion for a sizable fee. For the poor the options would be much more limited. They would either need to have an unwanted child or would seek a cheap abortion, often with tragic injury or death the result.

Finally, while it might be nice to think that all unwanted children will find good homes, that simply has never been the case and would become considerably less likely if the illegalization of abortion led to more unwanted children. At present healthy, white children are usually placed for adoption, but racial minorities and children with physical or mental difficulties often must be raised in institutional settings. This puts them at enormous psychological and intellectual disadvantage in contrast to children brought up in effectively functioning families.

Conclusion Discuss this difficult issue inside or outside of class. Is it possible to find some basis for compromise?

Source: *Larry Hugick and Lydia Saad. "Abortion: Public Support Grows for* Roe v. Wade, *But Public Seeks Middle Ground on Abortion, Supports Pennsylvania Law,"* Gallup Poll Monthly. (January 1992), pp. 5–9.

homosexuals, whether male or female, assume either an "active" or "passive" role in sexual relations. The evidence indicates, however, that gays of both sexes commonly alternate between active and passive roles (Saghir and Robins 1971).

"Straight" people's outlook on gays is often influenced by the fact that their observations of homosexuals are largely confined to the more obvious members of this group. The majority of gays lead unremarkable lives except for their sexual orientation, which often remains a well-kept secret from most people. In colleges, for example, large numbers of gay students never reveal their sexual preference to campus friends or even roommates, although a "coming out" trend has become more popular since the late 1960s.

In a study of sixty-five male and forty-seven female cohabiting gay couples, psychologist Lawrence Kurdek (1988) reached the following conclusions. First, the research showed that there were some differences between the female and male gay couples. Compared to the males, the lesbian (female homosexual) couples reported higher relationship satisfaction, greater liking of the partner, stronger motivations for being in the relationship, more trust, and more shared decision making.

Second, Kurdek found that for both male and female respondents, the length of the relationship seemed to be an important factor. Those couples who had been together six or more years tended to show greater relationship satisfaction, more liking and love of the partner, and a higher level of trust than those who had been together for a shorter period of time. Third, the couples of both sexes in this study tended to be more similar to than different from each other in such social characteristics as age, social-class background, religion, and race.

Finally Kurdek sought to isolate factors that predicted relationship quality. He found that high motivation to be in the relationship, trust in one's partner, satisfaction with the social support the relationship provided, shared decision making, and limited belief that disagreements would hurt the relationship were good predictive factors of relationship quality. As an illustration of the last point, a member of a lesbian couple referring to her partner explained, "It took her a long time to learn to get overtly angry with me. She is getting better at locating her feelings. . . . I am always

afraid that she is going to slip into this kind of apathy. And if I don't keep on top of things, we are just going to be this bored married couple" (Blumstein and Schwartz 1983, 488).

Another issue affecting many homosexual couples is that since they are not permitted to establish a legal union, their relationships do not have the legal or social support provided to straight people with an engagement and wedding. Some gay couples still have a ceremony performed. A study of ninety-two gay couples indicated that 13 percent of the couples obtained the social sanction provided by a commitment ceremony marking the beginning of the relationship and that an additional 37 percent would have liked such a ceremony had it been available (Berger 1990).

Homosexuality and Modern Society   What are the conditions that produce homosexuality? While not decisive, the biological evidence is suggestive. Two studies, one reported in 1991 and the other in 1992, concluded that there are anatomical differences in the brains of homosexual and heterosexual men, suggesting that sexual orientation has a significant biological basis (Angier 1992). In the social realm, research has not found any distinct differences between the family backgrounds of homosexuals and heterosexuals (Siegelman 1974).

There are some indications that experiencing homosexuality as a normal, pleasurable activity encourages its acceptance. A study of seventy-six preindustrial societies concluded that forty-nine of them (64 percent) accepted some form of homosexual activity as normal behavior. Among the Siwans of Africa, for instance, men who did not engage in homosexuality were considered peculiar. The Keraki of New Guinea believed that boys would not grow up healthy and well adjusted unless adult men practiced anal intercourse on them. Among the Mbundu and Nama of Africa, women were expected to perform mutual masturbation, using an artificial penis (Ford and Beach 1951).

In U.S. society experience also seems to be a determining factor. One researcher who studied lesbians concluded that in an examination of the sources of lesbianism "one factor stands out as having more . . . weight than others. This is the importance of the first sexual experience and

328   whether it is pleasurable and positive with a woman or discomforting and negative with a man" (Rosen 1974, 70). If, indeed, this finding is maintained by further research, it will be a powerful indication of how single episodes can significantly affect people's gender-role socialization.

While pleasurable experience seems to encourage people to become gay, homosexuals' lives are often difficult because of the severe economic and social sanctions they experience. In a 1991 national survey of American adults, 36 percent indicated that homosexual relations between consenting adults should be legal while 54 opposed legalization (Hugick and Leonard 1991). As gay rights organizations and spokespeople have become more outspoken, opposition to homosexuals has crystallized in many areas around the country. In 1992 the Oregon voters faced a ballot measure asking them to classify homosexuality as abnormal behavior, thereby giving the state government the right to actively discourage a homosexual lifestyle by permitting landlords the right to evict known homosexuals or employers the option to fire gay workers (Egan 1992). The voters rejected the measure, with 56 percent opposing it and 44 percent supporting it. During that same election, however, voters in Colorado passed a ballot measure overturning local anti-discrimination laws protecting homosexuals. The vote was decisive— 54 percent favoring the ban to 36 percent opposing it—and the measure overruled gay rights' ordinances previously approved in Denver, Aspen, and Boulder (Schmalz 1992).

Several days after his inauguration, President Bill Clinton sought to fulfill a campaign promise to end the ban on homosexuals in the military. Opposition was vocal and widespread—from the military, both Democrats and Republicans in Congress, and many ordinary citizens—and forced Clinton to put his executive order on hold for at least six months. A journalist concluded that the furor produced by Clinton's proposed ban on homosexuals in the military made it "clear that even middle-of-the-road Americans who said they opposed discrimination [against gays on the job] were still uncomfortable with homosexuality" (Schmalz 1993, sec. 4, p. 1).

Homosexual individuals and groups have opposed repressive measures taken against them, seeking acceptance as a minority group from a resisting public and promoting empowerment in various ways, including in the classroom. For instance, one man created an undergraduate course on lesbian and gay development, which examined personal change over the life course, the growth of close relationships, and the impact of society on homosexuals' lives (D'Augelli 1991). Another form of empowerment has been to form unarmed groups that patrol and protect neighborhoods where gays live in large numbers. With the number of anti-gay harassment incidents rising, such patrols have developed in a number of cities, including San Francisco, New York, Houston, and Chicago. Chicago's Pink Angels work closely with the police, quickly radioing in developing incidents. One member of the organization described the police as "very helpful and supportive" while, in turn, a member of the police department's civil-rights section indicated that the Pink Angels were making a valuable community contribution that other citizens should emulate (Terry 1992).

At present the greatest threat to gays comes from a nonhuman source—AIDS. Data from disease clinics surveyed by the U.S. Centers for Disease Control suggested that the rate of HIV infection, which leads to AIDS, averaged 25 percent for gay males aged 20 to 24. This was ten times the rate in the next highest risk group, which is young urban black males. As one AIDS researcher concluded, "The male gay community is at the edge of a holocaust" (Berger 1990, 46). Thus even though gay groups have made impressive efforts to educate young male homosexuals about HIV prevention, such activity needs to be continued, even accelerated (Cranston 1991).

Communes

Communes are planned, intentional communities, bringing together biologically unrelated people in order to build a large, family-like group. Many, perhaps most, communes permit couples to maintain their social and sexual exclusiveness as a couple. There are more than 1,000 communes in the United States, Canada, and several other countries. The smallest contain as few as five or six people while the largest is the Farm in Summertown, Tennessee, with more than 1,600 members (Knox 1988, 176–78). While interest in the topic is not as pronounced as it was a quarter century ago, research on the topic continues (Aidala and Zablocki 1991).

Sociologist Rosabeth Moss Kanter (1968) studied thirty nineteenth-century American communes in order to determine which qualities increased or decreased the likelihood that a commune would survive. Nine of these communes were rated as successful, defined as lasting thirty-three years or more, and twenty-one were unsuccessful, enduring less than sixteen years and averaging a life span of just four years. The successful communes tended to build strong group commitment in a number of ways. They required significant personal sacrifices (ceasing sexual activity and alcohol and tobacco use, for instance) and also major investments of time, energy, money, and property. In addition, the more successful communes also created strong in-group feelings, often demanding that members give up all primary-group contacts with the outside world. Furthermore the participants' sense of individuality was largely eliminated; their identity was shaped and controlled by community standards.

The most comprehensive study of American communes to date is based on data derived from a sample of almost 700 men and women living in sixty urban communes in Los Angeles, Houston, Atlanta, Boston, New York, and Minneapolis. Some of the communes were intensely committed to certain religious positions or other values, while others were simply places where economic sharing occurred. Some were highly structured, and others were not. In a number of cases, children were present, but such groups were in the minority. Most of the participants were single, and all the communes included both men and women. In rank order the following were the primary reasons that members cited for joining the groups:

1. Financial advantages;
2. Order and regularity;
3. Friendship and support;
4. A means of leaving home;
5. A way to break from the past;
6. A lifestyle that provided new and interesting experiences;
7. A search for like-minded people;
8. Companionship or community.

The average participant stayed for two years, with some moving on to other communes, while others returned to more traditional lifestyles. A significant proportion of the commune members in the sample led otherwise fairly normal lives as students or as workers in conventional jobs (Zablocki 1977).

Many Americans who are now living in communes do not fit 1960s stereotypes of long-haired hippies sitting around campfires in the evening singing folksongs. Often they lead quite ordinary middle-class lives, and instead of using the term "commune," they speak of "intentional communities." Such settlements have become one modern means of combatting food and heating bills, rising land prices, and high interest rates, while also serving as a way of restoring a sense of community frequently missing in modern life. In Florida, for instance, an intentional community of 100 families has permitted participants to live comfortably on less than $10,000 per year. The members have pooled their resources in order to build houses and buy land and tools. Typically houses have been built by a combination of do-it-yourself efforts, house-building parties, and outside contracting. The residents have used each other's expertise through voluntary labor exchange. Families have controlled their own land, but the community members' cooperative efforts have created a positive situation in which to live—as one observer has phrased it, "an atmosphere where things are possible" (*Futurist* 1985).

CONCLUSION

In 1980 a conference, which originally had been called the White House Conference on the Family, was renamed the White House Conference on Families. It might seem that changing one word in the title from the singular to the plural form was not significant, but it was. Sociologically speaking, the change represented an appreciation that the cultural standards shaping Americans' perception of the family have been changing—that it is now widely accepted that there is not one form of the modern American family but many (Berger and Berger 1984, 59).

Until recently most Americans expected to grow up in nuclear families and develop this type

330

of family themselves. While this option remains popular, it is just that—an option. Nowadays Americans have a variety of lifestyle choices, but they also find themselves encountering a great deal of confusion and uncertainty. In an era emphasizing individual choice and control, people, including members within families, frequently seem more on their own than in the past. Many modern parents, strong subscribers to the value position that individuals should control their own destiny, feel their obligations to their children should be distinctly limited. In *Habits of the Heart: Individualism and Commitment in American Life*, a therapist was asked if she was responsible for her children. She spoke hesitantly, "I . . . I would say I have a legal responsibility for them, but in a sense I think they in turn are responsible for their acts" (Bellah et al. 1986, 82). Do you agree with this position? Do you feel that American family members share sufficient values and activities? What differences, if any, would you like in the modern family?

STUDY GUIDE

Learning Objectives

After studying this chapter, you should be able to:

1. Define family and indicate why it is socially important.
2. Discuss with illustrations the three basic functions of the family examined in the text.
3. Identify and define kinship terms for marriage types, marriage-eligibility customs, residential rules, and family-power patterns.
4. Describe the effects of industrialization on the family and explain the nature and consequences of the nuclear family's loss of functions.
5. Discuss the sexual revolution and contemporary patterns of cohabitation.
6. Examine the topics of voluntary childlessness and working mothers.
7. Identify and discuss the factors that influence the divorce rate.
8. Describe the consequences of divorce for the couple and for children.
9. Examine prominent alternatives to conventional marriage.

Summary

1. A family is traditionally defined as a social unit composed of two or more people who live together and are related by blood, marriage, or adoption. The family provides functions that are critical for its survival and also for the maintenance of society.

2. The functions of the family include sexual regulation, economic cooperation, and socializa-

tion. In other societies these functions are often performed in ways that differ sharply from those carried out by Americans. Prominent kinship terms involve the type of marriage, customs for marriage eligibility, residential rules for newly married people, and patterns of power within the family.

3. Like other institutional structures, the modern American nuclear family has been shaped by industrialization. In the course of the industrial era, the nuclear family has lost some of its preindustrial functions, sometimes resulting in distinctly negative consequences for family members.

4. American society has experienced changing patterns of love, courtship, and marriage. In the late 1960s, the sexual revolution occurred, altering premarital sexual patterns. Living together has become widely practiced, with a number of social conditions contributing to its increased incidence. People tend to practice homogamy, marrying individuals whose social characteristics are similar to their own. Among the changing marital patterns are an increase in childlessness and in working mothers.

5. Divorce has increased sharply since the mid-1960s. Industrialization, age of the couple, changing role definitions within marriage, and decreasing social and legal constraints are factors affecting the divorce rate. There are significant, sometimes damaging effects of divorce for spouses and children. On the other hand, people's lives can become happier and more fulfilling once unhappy marriages are terminated. Frequently divorced people remarry, with second marriages often more satisfying than the first. Many Americans pursue alternatives to a conventional monogamous marriage. Among them are single-parent households, singlehood, a homosexual lifestyle, and communes.

Key Terms

commune a planned, intentional community, bringing together biologically unrelated people in order to build a large, family-like group

egalitarian a type of family in which the wife-mother and husband-father share power and also permit their children to participate in the family decisions

endogamy a custom requiring a person to marry within a specific social unit, such as a kinship group, religious organization, or social class

exogamy a custom compelling someone to marry outside a specific social unit

extended family a family involving two or more generations of people related by blood and living together or close to each other

family traditionally defined as a social unit composed of two or more people who live together and are related by blood, marriage, or adoption

homogamy marriage to a person having social characteristics similar to one's own

incest taboo a rule outlawing sexual relations between kin-group members believed to be too closely related as defined by the cultural standards of a given society

kinship system a number of people related by common descent, marriage, or adoption

matriarchal a type of family in which the wife-mother is the formal head and the absolute or nearly absolute source of power

matrilocal a type of residence that involves settling with or near the wife's parents

monogamy a marriage practice in which there is one husband and one wife

neolocal a type of residence that occurs when married people establish an independent place to live

nuclear family a two-generation family that includes a father, a mother, and their children living separately from other relatives

patriarchal a type of family in which the husband-father is the formal head and the absolute or nearly absolute source of power

patrilocal a type of residence that requires settling with or near the husband's parents

polyandry the form of polygamy in which a woman has two or more husbands

polygamy a marriage practice in which a person has two or more spouses of the other sex

polygyny the form of polygamy in which a man has two or more wives

Tests

True • False Test

_____ 1. The incest taboo exists only in Western cultures.
_____ 2. A recent analysis suggested that the concept of nuclear family has become inaccurate and
_____ should be discarded.
3. Polyandry is a much more common form of polygamy than is polygyny.
_____ 4. Richard Sennett's study of nineteenth-century Chicago families concluded that the nuclear-family type may be less supportive of male members' emotional and occupational development than the extended family.
_____ 5. The French historian Ariès suggested that in the preindustrial era, women and children encountered fewer restrictions than today.
_____ 6. The claim that a sexual revolution occurred in the late 1960s was not supported by survey data, which showed that the percentage of respondents opposing premarital sex hardly changed between the late 1960s and the early 1970s.
_____ 7. A study indicated that people who lived together before marriage were more likely to have long-lasting marriages than those who did not cohabit.
_____ 8. Research concluded that children were more likely to have a positive outlook toward their mothers' work if they perceived that their mothers viewed the work positively.
_____ 9. The divorce rate is roughly one divorce for every two marriages.
_____ 10. Recent research strongly suggested that family influences determine whether or not an individual becomes homosexual.

Multiple-Choice Test

_____ 1. Which of the following has NOT been recognized as a function of the incest taboo?
    a. elimination of conflicts and jealousies produced by sexual rivalry
    b. clear definitions of family roles
    c. encouragement of alliances between families
    d. accomplishment of age-linked tasks

_____ 2. Cohabitation is most common among:
    a. less educated people.
    b. college students.
    c. the elderly.
    d. wealthy individuals.

_____ 3. Homogamy:
    a. only involves gay couples.
    b. involves both race and religion.
    c. is not influenced by family and friends.
    d. is not apparent in a study of successful marriages.

_____ 4. The birth rate has been declining in recent years because of:
    a. involuntary childlessness.
    b. women's increasing pursuit of careers.
    c. increased fertility problems produced by environmental damage.
    d. reduced male willingness to be breadwinners.

_____ 5. Veevers's study of voluntary childlessness showed which of the following statements to be true?
   a. Women in the study tended to be youngest children and thus felt inadequate to provide child-care because of inexperience.
   b. Many of the women were neurotically dependent on others.
   c. Many of the respondents came from unhappy homes in which parents had communicated to them the feeling that children generally cause strife in marriage.
   d. Most of the research subjects had tradition-oriented husbands.

_____ 6. Which of the following statements describes a condition affecting the divorce rate?
   a. People in their teens and early twenties are more likely than older individuals to get divorced.
   b. Love-based marriages tend to be particularly stable.
   c. No-fault divorce legislation has discouraged the occurrence of divorce.
   d. Changing role definitions within marriage have made modern marriages more stable.

_____ 7. Children whose parents divorced:
   a. tend to experience more long-term suffering than their parents.
   b. view marriage more negatively than children from intact families.
   c. generally prefer the post-divorce period to the time before the divorce.
   d. a, b, and c

_____ 8. Remarriages:
   a. seldom occur less than five years after divorce.
   b. tend to be unhappier than first marriages.
   c. do not pose confusion for children of previous marriages, who can readily figure out who are their fellow family members.
   d. represent an increasing percentage of all marriages.

_____ 9. Single-parent families:
   a. tend to be less affluent than most families.
   b. declined in numbers between 1970 and 1991.
   c. declined in their proportion of all families between 1970 and 1991.
   d. b and c

_____ 10. Voluntary singlehood:
   a. can be encouraged by "pushes away" from marriage.
   b. is likely to increase in the years ahead.
   c. is more likely to be defined as a permanent lifestyle by never-married individuals than divorced people.
   d. a, b, and c

Essay Test

1. Define family. Discuss the relationship between industrialization and the nuclear family. Examine the declining functions of the nuclear family.
2. Analyze cohabitation, indicating who engages in this practice and also the consequences of living together.
3. Are modern Americans entirely free to choose their spouses? Use the concept homogamy in answering the question.
4. Examine three factors that significantly affect the divorce rate. Discuss in detail the consequences of divorce for both couples and children.
5. Describe two alternatives to conventional marriage, indicating why some people find these particular options either necessary or appealing in modern society.

334 Suggested Readings

Berger, Brigitte, and Peter L. Berger. 1984. *The War over the Family*. Garden City, NY: Anchor Books. A socio-logical analysis of both the American family and reactions to it, offering thought-provoking endorse-ment of the nuclear-family form.

Bozett, Frederick W. (ed.). 1987. *Gay and Lesbian Parents*. New York: Praeger. A collection of articles about gay families discussing such issues as types of family combinations, children's adjustment, and the impact of rearing children in a social world generally hostile to homosexuals.

Hood, Jane C. 1983. *Becoming a Two-Job Family*. New York: Praeger. A study which follows sixteen couples over six years and indicates in detail the impact of women's working on the family. Previous research and theory is effectively incorporated into the analysis throughout the book.

Phoenix, Ann, and Anne Woollett (eds.). 1991. *Motherhood: Meanings, Practices, and Ideologies*. Newbury Park, CA: Sage. A thorough introduction to the social-scientific analysis of motherhood, addressing such issues as the relationship between societal expectations of motherhood and women's self-esteem, work and motherhood, and the "right time" to have children.

Pocs, Ollie (ed.). 1992. *Marriage and Family 92/93*. 18th ed. Guilford, CT: Dushkin. An effective set of readings updated yearly, combining popular and academic sources and examining most of the issues dis-cussed in this chapter.

Scanzoni, Letha Dawson, and John Scanzoni. 1988. *Men, Women, and Change*. 3rd ed. New York: McGraw-Hill. A nicely written, comprehensive, visually effective undergraduate text on marriage and the family.

Skolnick, Arlene S., and Jerome H. Skolnick (eds.). 1989. *Family in Transition*. 6th ed. Boston: Little, Brown. Forty-three articles divided into eleven chapters on a variety of topics involving marriage, the family, and related issues. The book includes a good general introduction and effective part openers.

Stacey, Judith. 1990. *New Families: Stories of Domestic Upheaval in Late Twentieth Century America*. New York: Basic Books. A richly detailed sociologist's account of two families headed by white, working-class women, revealing a great deal about the relationship among gender, economic, and family issues.

Additional Assignments

1. Write a set of marriage vows which you believe acknowledges the important matters to be covered in a marriage relationship. If you are involved in a serious relationship, you might want to seek input from your partner. Compare the wording of your vows with the content of typical vows, containing such phrases as "to have and to hold," "to love and to cherish (or obey)," "in sickness and in health," and "until death does us part." Is the marriage your vows describe traditional or nontradtional? Compare your vows with classmates' efforts.

2. Using the text's list of alternatives to conventional marriage and also the option of cohabitation, ask at least ten people to rate the different choices on desirability—"1" would be a very low desirability and "10" would be the highest. For your respondents seek a balance of males and females and also younger and older people. What explanations can you supply for your results? Discuss findings with other classmates.

Answers to Objective Test Questions

True • False Test

1.	f	6.	f
2.	t	7.	f
3.	f	8.	t
4.	t	9.	t
5.	t	10.	f

Multiple-Choice Test

1.	d	6.	a
2.	a	7.	d
3.	b	8.	d
4.	b	9.	a
5.	c	10.	d

Religion and Education

12

In recent years many parents who are among the 80 million Americans considering themselves evangelical or born-again Christians have sent their children to private, Christian schools, where Biblical perspectives are related to all subject matter and strong preference exists for conservative positions on such issues as premarital sex, homosexuality, and political policy. At present 2,778 schools belong to the Association of Christian Schools International, and about 1,200 schools are members of the American Association of Christian Schools International. The number of students in non-Catholic Christian schools increased sharply during a seven-year period, rising from about a million in 1980–1981 to more than 1.7 million in 1987–1988.

Janet Nason, the principal of Charlotte Christian School in Charlotte, North Carolina, explained that at her school at least one parent needed "to share our philosophy and faith commitment." She indicated that Christian schools "see themselves as an extension of the church or as an extension of the family" (Sullivan 1991, 46).

Sociologists are likely to agree that religion and education are related, with both serving as forms of socialization, whose participants are concerned about the values and beliefs passed on to children. When the risk develops that these cultural elements will not be passed along, people become agitated, and we will see that this is often the case with both religion and education. The two topics arouse strong feelings. In the case of Christian schools, the supporters applaud having Christian values permeating the entire curriculum, feeling that these are the best values to which children can be exposed and are an appropriate part of the learning process. Opponents find this a disturbing reality, saying that a religious point of view offers a perceptual bias that is not fundamental to learning and should be kept out of the classroom. Let us consider the meanings of religion and education.

In sociology an analysis of religion is likely to begin with the concept of "the sacred." The **sacred** is anything that is superior in power, is set apart from the ordinary and practical, and creates a sense of awe. Something sacred is so special that it cannot be questioned. Members of a group or society accept sacred items or activities as representations of the fundamental meaning of life. That acceptance creates a sense of unity and common purpose among those people and serves as the basis for the formation of their religion. Thus what makes an item or idea sacred in a sociologi-

cal sense is the way people regard it and the unifying effect it produces, not any quality inherent within it. The same wafers and wine that many Christians consider to be sacred, representing the body and blood of Christ, would be regarded as ordinary food and drink by non-Christians. In contrast to the sacred, those things that people consider ordinary and closely linked to practical demands are termed **profane.** Profane items do not create unity and a sense of common purpose the way sacred things do.

A **religion** may be defined as a unified system of beliefs and practices that focuses on sacred things and serves to create a community of worshippers (Durkheim 1975, 123). Among other things religions may be analyzed as efforts to develop philosophical and spiritual insights that can be used in facing the stresses, confusions, and complexities of human existence. In the first half of this chapter, we consider functions of religion and prominent trends in religion today.

Like religion, education is a type of socialization. **Education** is the transmission of knowledge, skills, and values by either formal or informal means. This transmission is critical for the survival of a culture. In modern societies the education process is, in general, highly formalized. In the second half of the chapter, we examine theoretical perspectives on education, and reform in American education, as well as education and equality.

Functions of Religion

Just as children must undergo socialization in order to become members of society, people must be socialized before they become members of a religious organization. Once socialized, people find that their religious organizations perform a number of functions. In this section we examine four functions of religion, three of which are associated with prominent sociological theories. We also discuss functional equivalents of religion.

PROVIDING SOCIAL COHESION

Émile Durkheim (1961; 1964) emphasized that as people in traditional societies performed religious rituals, they were focused on what was special and awe-inspiring—the sacred. Durkheim claimed that collective concentration on selected sacred ideas and activities helped create a sense of common purpose and unity.

The sense of common purpose and unity that religion provided assured preindustrial people's commitment to it, in part because of the demands it made upon them. Durkheim indicated that religion places

> constraint upon the individual. It forces him into practices which subject him to small or large sacrifices which are painful to him. He must take from his goods the offerings that he is compelled to present to the divinity; he must take time from his work or play in which to observe rites; he must impose upon himself every sort of privation which is demanded of him, even to renounce life if the gods ordain.
>
> (*Durkheim* 1964, 92)

The deep commitment that preindustrial religion required of all worshippers strengthened their sense of involvement within the local community or society.

In preindustrial societies, then, religion generally served a cohesive function. But with the advent of industrialism, secularization occurred. **Secularization** is the process by which religion

Religious organizations often promote social cohesion along with rejection of outsiders, but sometimes at a great price. After barricading themselves inside their compound near Waco, Texas, for fifty-one days, at least eighty-one members of the Mount Carmel Branch Davidians died in a fire started from inside.

loses influence within groups and societies. Secularization involves the replacement of religious faith with belief in scientific principles, and, in addition, it leads to an increasing separation between the religious and nonreligious areas of life. Activities such as work, war, government, commerce, and learning and science become increasingly divorced from religion (Johnstone 1975, 296; O'Dea 1966, 81–86). An analysis of paintings in the Metropolitan Museum of Art in New York ranging from the fourteenth to the twentieth centuries indicated that over time the presence of religious themes declined (Silverman 1989). Yet a recent analysis suggested that even in modern secularized societies, religious organizations can still promote social cohesion. While Margaret Thatcher was prime minister of Great Britain, many prominent church leaders criticized her government's actions in Durkheimian terms. They emphasized the need for the government to shift its support away from secularized individual acts undertaken purely for economic gain toward activities promoting collective benefit and focusing, with the help of religious officials' direction, on shared sacred elements (Thompson 1991).

340

SUPPORTING AND MAINTAINING SOCIAL CONTROL

Many church congregations include prominent, wealthy, and powerful members of the community. The clergy of such churches are likely to feel that they must support dominant standards of social control, no matter how their personal feelings differ, in order to retain these members' economic and social support. For instance, in the 1950s, white ministers in Little Rock, Arkansas, in spite of their personal inclinations, often publicly opposed the integration of their congregations because they feared that integration would drive out the wealthy and powerful white members (Campbell and Pettigrew 1959).

Mark Twain, a strong opponent of organized religion, emphasized that churches backed dominant practices of social control with a vengeance. On the issue of slavery, Twain suggested, religious leaders originally focused on Biblical texts that supported the practice. In time, however, public opposition to slavery became widespread. "There was no place in the land where the seeker could not find some small budding sign of pity for the slave. No place in the land but one—the pulpit." Finally, Twain continued, organized religion eventually started opposing slavery. "It . . . did what it always does, joined the procession—at the tail end" (Twain 1973, 109).

Karl Marx (1970, 131–32) also suggested that the primary function of religion is to support the status quo. Marx's analysis was centrally concerned with the class distinction between the exploited workers and the wealthy capitalists, who own the factories and farms where the workers labor. According to Marx, religion provides "illusory happiness" for workers, promising that the righteous will receive their just reward in heaven. In an often quoted Marxist phrase, religion is "the opium of the people." Thus Marx believed that religion has advanced the interests of the dominant capitalist class, providing a means by which capitalists could distract workers from their own immediate, pressing interests. Marx believed that in order for workers to perceive correctly the exploitation that they suffer, they must abandon religion. Once freed, they could start organizing to change their economic and political situation.

A review of Marx's writings suggested that were Marx to return to earth more than a century after his death, he would still find plenty of evidence supporting his conviction about the destructive effect of religion on workers (Gurley 1984). Research using Marx's perspective on religion continues (Flynn and Kunkel 1987; Katz 1992).

PROMOTING SOCIAL CHANGE

In the course of a major study of world religions, Max Weber suggested that religion has promoted social change by supporting the development of capitalism. Unlike Marx, who considered religion little more than a reflection of the economic system, Weber suggested that this institution has played an important role in the development of the economy. Weber conceded that capitalism has also influenced religion, but he basically reversed Marx's cause-and-effect relationship. That is, religion became the cause, and the economic system (capitalism) became the effect.

Weber (1958) developed his argument in *The Protestant Ethic and the Spirit of Capitalism*. He suggested that Calvinism is the theology that has had the strongest influence on the development of capitalism. In this Protestant denomination, God was originally thought of as an aloof, inscrutable being maintaining total control over the universe. Human beings existed solely for the glorification of God and were expected never to question God's decisions; they were supposed to accept them on faith. One critical article of faith involved the doctrine of predestination. This doctrine suggested that people were destined for either salvation or damnation before birth. While nothing could be done to earn salvation, God did provide certain signs that indicated whether or not particular individuals were likely to be among the elect, the minority who would be saved. In particular, if people dedicated themselves to their occupations and achieved wealth, then it was likely that they were destined for salvation.

Devout Calvinists, Weber contended, were thus given "a positive incentive to asceticism." They were driven to work hard, to save, and to invest what they had saved in order to become wealthy. Wealth itself had no spiritual value, but accumulated wealth gave evidence that people were fulfilling their calling, glorifying God. Furthermore they were proving both to themselves and to others that they were bound for salvation.

Weber argued that precapitalist merchants were stimulated in their quest for material success by the competitive challenge—what we might call the joy of the hunt. By contrast, early Calvinist capitalists were under the influence of a religious standard for the conduct of life.

According to Weber, this drive to obtain wealth through thrift and hard work—in short the spirit of capitalism—has endured despite the decline of Calvinism. As a case in point, Weber quoted Benjamin Franklin, who wrote in the eighteenth century. "Remember, that money is of the prolific, generating nature. Money can beget money, and its offspring can beget more, and so on. Five shillings turned is six, turned again it is seven and threepence, and so on, till it becomes a hundred pounds" (Weber 1958, 49). Saving, investing, and building wealth might no longer be seen as providing proof of salvation in the next world, but Franklin's words suggest that these activities can become the key to the achievement of success in the present life. Thus the spirit of capitalism remains strong in the industrial era, even though its link to Calvinism was severed long ago.

It has been difficult to test Weber's conclusions in the United States. Numerous studies seeking to determine whether or not Protestant religion has influenced the development of capitalism have often been sharply criticized. One significant drawback to such research has been that comparisons of occupational success between Protestants and Catholics are probably invalidated by the fact that Catholics have tended to experience more discrimination, placing them at a distinct occupational disadvantage to Protestants. Work using Weber's perspective continues, with a recent analysis suggesting that sociologists involved in graduate programs view a selected segment of graduate students as among the elect, who are predestined for success, possessing the qualities that would make them capable of providing significant contributions to sociological knowledge. For students entering graduate school in sociology, the major criteria used appear to be scores on standardized tests and letters of recommendation. Within this system there is a highly uneven distribution of rewards, with those who supposedly "have it" receiving the lion's share. The writer suggested that there is little reason to believe that this system effectively assesses sociological talent, and thus it should be revised, with

For the original settlers of the Plymouth colony pictured here, life was focused on the glorification of God, and thus public worship was very serious business.

fellowships, assistantships, and other prized commodities distributed among students based on need and not on a questionable evaluation of merit (Plutzer 1991). A scholar suggested that Weber's thesis will continue to provoke analysis and controversy (MacKinnon 1988a; MacKinnon 1988b).

MAKING THE WORLD COMPREHENSIBLE

The biblical explanation of human creation is straightforward, concise, and complete. Like Christianity, many other religions also provide answers to such cosmic questions about how humanity originated and why people were created. Some religions, such as the Unitarian-Universalist Association, either deemphasize or deny belief in God and salvation, but they still believe that the pursuit of good works, such as continuing service to humanity, can make the world more comprehensible.

In 1990, 63 percent of the people interviewed in a national survey said that religion can provide answers for contemporary problems, while 18 percent said that religion is largely old-fashioned and out-of-date. In 1957, 81 percent of the public expressed faith in religion's ability to provide answers to contemporary problems, and only 7 percent considered it old-fashioned in this regard (Gallup and Newport 1990). The declining popular support for religion's function of making the world

342 comprehensible is not surprising in a society that has been becoming increasingly secularized. It seems that Americans nowadays more frequently turn to a number of nonreligious specialists, including natural scientists, social scientists, and psychiatrists, for answers to contemporary problems.

Nonetheless religion continues to supply profound meaning for many individuals, especially in crises. Following devastating floods, ministers found that their greatest contribution was the use of rituals, readings, and sermons "to address the ultimate need of survivors to find meaning in their suffering" (Bradfield and Wylie 1989, 404).

Table 12.1 summarizes the four functions of religion that we have discussed.

FUNCTIONAL EQUIVALENTS OF RELIGION

Sometimes the functions normally provided by a particular structure are supplied by a different source. A **functional equivalent** is an organization or activity that provides service or assistance to an individual or group more commonly received from some other organization or activity. A number of organizations may be considered functional equivalents of religion. For example, Transcendental Meditation (TM) is a group that teaches meditation techniques claimed to promote physical, social, and spiritual well-being. Erhard Seminars Training (est) is a commercial program providing group workshops for the pursuit of increased self-

understanding. Socialism is a political philosophy that many national governments have endorsed, beginning with the Soviet Union in 1917. In each case the leaders and members of these groups and movements deny that they are involved in religious activity. In a formal sense, they are correct. Their concerns focus on the immediate, empirical world, not on the supernatural level of existence. Like religions, however, each of these functional equivalents has a founding prophet, follows certain sacred or quasi-sacred texts, provides a world view that precludes or at least subordinates most other world views, and seeks to convert outsiders.

Furthermore functional equivalents can serve the same functions as religions. Soviet socialism supported social change. A French visitor to the Soviet Union in the 1930s was impressed by the changes that the leaders promised. He wrote, "Like many other visitors, I saw model factories, clubs, pleasure grounds, at which I marveled. I asked for nothing better than to be carried away with admiration and to convert others as well" (Crossman 1952, 160). In that same era, Soviet socialism also fostered strong social cohesion; people were unified by the hope that they were building a better, more just world. The same French traveler observed "a feeling of humanity, an immediate upsurge of brotherly love." Children were "well-fed, well-cared-for, cherished and happy. Their eyes were clear and full of confidence and hope" (Crossman 1952, 159).

In the United States, functional equivalents of religion also exist. A prominent example is American civil religion. A **civil religion** is a shared,

Table 12.1 Some Functions of Religion

The function	Illustration
1. Providing social cohesion	1. Durkheim's contention that religion can support a common sense of purpose
2. Supporting and maintaining social control	2. Marx's conviction that religion is "the opium of the people"
3. Promoting social change	3. Weber's conclusion that Calvinism has served as an incentive for capitalist expansion
4. Making the world comprehensible	4. The belief, which is shared by the majority of Americans, that religion can provide answers to contemporary problems

The respective theoretical contributions of Durkheim, Marx, and Weber on religion can be visualized as illustrations of three separate functions of religion.

public faith in the nation, a faith linked to people's everyday life through a set of beliefs, symbols, and rituals that contain religious elements and overtones that are not formally affiliated with any particular religion. Common beliefs include statements made by American presidents ranging across time from Washington and Jefferson to Kennedy and Reagan and contending that the United States is on a divinely supported mission to fulfill God's will for humanity. Sacred symbols of the American civil religion include the flag, a Judeo-Christian god, the Declaration of Independence, the Bill of Rights, the eagle, and a host of buildings and structures such as the Capitol, the White House, the Washington Monument, the Lincoln and Jefferson Memorials, and many more. Major rituals of the American civil religion include Memorial Day, Veterans Day, Thanksgiving, and the Fourth of July (Bellah 1967). A recent analysis indicated that public schools play a major role in transmitting civil religion—in daily rituals such as the pledge of allegiance, in holiday observances in which classroom assignments and activities emphasize their significance, and in the social studies curriculum that often glorifies American history, symbols, and accomplishments. In addition, the emphasis on American civil religion in school tends to make children intimately involved in other religious traditions feel marginal (Gamoran 1990).

During his presidency Ronald Reagan was a skilled spokesman for civil religion. An analysis of

Like these kindergarten students, most American children begin the school day by performing the pledge of allegiance, a prominent ritual of the American civil religion.

his speeches revealed that Reagan implicitly described a "genesis story" of American society in which a "golden age," where private initiative was prominent, existed before "the fall"—Franklin Roosevelt's New Deal in which the federal government involved itself extensively in people's lives by initiating social-welfare programs that supposedly destroyed private initiative. Reagan preached "a revival," which he felt would occur when the role of government in people's lives was reduced and as a result harmony between the individual and social good restored (Adams 1987).

Prominent Trends in Religion Today ■

Many Americans have been socialized to make attendance at religious services a consistent practice. In 1939, 41 percent of a national sample had attended services at a church or synagogue in the past seven days. The figure rose to 49 percent in 1955 and 1958 and then dropped back to 40 percent in 1990 (Gallup and Newport 1990).

In this section we examine religion from an organizational perspective. It is clear that membership is an important factor determining whether or not religious organizations survive. Modern religious groups have developed a number of ways of building membership. Of the mod-

ern religious movements, fundamentalism has had the greatest success in the area of membership growth.

Figure 12.1 presents the percentages of the adult American population affiliated with major religious groups.

THE DECLINING INFLUENCE OF MAJOR RELIGIONS

Religion has sometimes been referred to as "a war for souls." If we think of religious activity in this

Figure 12.1
Americans' Religious Preferences

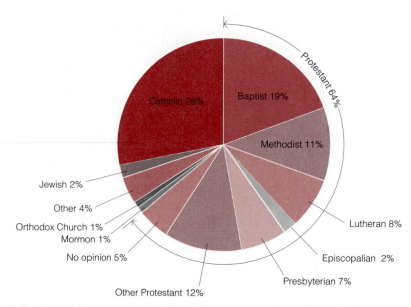

This pie graph shows percentages of the adult American population affiliated with major religious groups.

Source: Adapted from Frank Newport and Lydia Saad. Gallup Poll Monthly. (April 1992).

way, then it seems as if the battleground has broadened in recent years. Many people display bumper stickers urging the unsaved to convert. Religious organizations purchase advertisements on radio and television. Various cults seek out young and confused people, offering them kindness and understanding and eventually imploring them to join their organizations.

Americans' feelings about the influence of religion have varied over time. In 1957, 69 percent of all Americans believed that the influence of religion was increasing, and only 14 percent felt that its power was decreasing. During the 1960s the percentage of the public that believed the influence of religion was increasing fell sharply, and then the figure gradually rose during the early 1970s until it reached 44 percent in 1976. After that it dropped again, registering 35 percent in 1980 and 33 percent in 1990 (Gallup and Newport 1990).

In the mid-1950s, popular ministers like Billy Graham and Norman Vincent Peale led a religious revival. The rapid increase in the size of the middle class and this group's widely held belief that attending church was "the thing to do" were also contributing factors to the growth of religion dur-

ing this era. The 1960s were characterized by widespread disillusionment regarding social institutions, especially among young people. The present era has represented a mild religious revival.

Fighting Back: Selling Organized Religion

The decline in interest in religion is a life-and-death matter for religious organizations. Consider some of the more dramatic shifts in membership. Since the mid-1960s, the leading Christian fundamentalist denominations—Southern Baptists, the Assembly of God, and the Seventh-Day Adventists—have increased their membership by at least 30 percent, while the leading established "main-line" Christian denominations—the United Methodists, the Episcopalians, the Lutheran Church in America, and Presbyterian Church (U.S.A.)—have all lost membership (U.S. Bureau of the Census, *Statistical Abstract of the United States: 1966,* No. 45; U.S. Bureau of the Census, *Statistical Abstract of the United States: 1992,* No. 77). Many religious leaders have actively worked to reverse their organizations' declining influence. Three ways of maintaining and building religious membership deserve special attention.

1. ***Adjusting organizational practices to meet members' changing requirements.*** Since World War II, many American Jews have been deeply concerned with Jewish survival. This preoccupation has supported such trends as the restoration of Hebrew to religious services and the establishment of many new religious schools (Cohen and Fein 1985). In spite of many complaints with the Catholic Church, some of its parishes show considerable vitality, largely because of voluntary organizations that have met members' social and psychological needs by providing marriage preparation programs, conferences for married couples, and support groups for divorced Catholics (Ebaugh 1991). In Canada Buddhist temples with Japanese congregations have been finding it necessary to change some practices to accommodate their younger, Westernized members (Mullins 1988).

2. ***Using modern public-relations techniques.*** A number of years ago, Catholic leaders in Michigan decided to conduct an intensive campaign to defeat a state referendum liberalizing abortion statutes. These leaders realized that one benefit of winning such a campaign would be a renewal of their followers' faith that the Catholic Church remains a vigorous organization that can still defeat opponents' misguided efforts. The organizers hired an advertising and public-relations firm, and members of the Church carefully coordinated the campaign, regularly providing up-to-date details to local personnel throughout the state. In addition, the Church bought a great deal of television and radio time. Partly as a result, the antiabortion forces won on election day despite being considerably behind (according to independent polls) less than a month earlier (Hinsberg 1974).

3. ***Developing entrepreneurial skills.*** Some clergy have become proficient salespeople in order to gain converts. This is not a new development. In December 1734

Jonathan Edwards initiated the first American revival, a recruiting drive to counteract poor attendance at church services. This campaign was known as the "Great Awakening." With "terrible vividness and earnestness," Edwards urged his listeners to flee the wrath of God and seek refuge in religion (Sweet 1950, 130). One of the most celebrated modern salesmen of religion is the Reverend Robert Schuller, the founder of the first (and still the wealthiest) drive-in church in the world, located in southern California. His "Hour of Power" TV show is carried by eighty-eight stations, and he claims an audience of about thirty million people a week. According to Schuller, if a person continues to strive while putting his or her faith in God, success (material or otherwise) is inevitable. Schuller's supporters say that he provides hope and that he makes them feel good about their lives in a world where many people feel uprooted from traditional ties (Allman 1976). Analyzing the founders of two modern religious movements, a sociologist concluded that they "are like entrepreneurs with novel products and bold visions who turn out also to be accomplished chief executive officers of an expanding firm" (Johnson 1992, S8).

FUNDAMENTALISM

While the influence of many religious organizations has declined in the United States, Christian fundamentalism has recently been very successful. In his well-known novel *Elmer Gantry*, Sinclair Lewis wrote about a fictional fundamentalist minister and how he achieved popularity. For his first sermon in the town of Zenith, Gantry chose the topic "Can Strangers Find Haunts of Vice in Zenith?" He was gratified to see 400 people turn out when his predecessor had had to settle for 100. In his sermon Gantry told how he had gone to a local beach and found—What a shock!—"mixed bathing." The minister titillated the men in the audience by describing the ladies' legs. Then he mentioned the two women who had tried to pick

346

him up, the waiter who had offered to sell him liquor despite Prohibition, the illegal, all-night poker game he had discovered, and more. As he spoke Gantry became increasingly emotional, chastising his congregation for tolerating such rampant vice: "We're lazy. We're not burning with a fever of righteousness. On your knees, you slothful, and pray God to forgive you and to aid you and me to form a brotherhood of helpful, joyous, fiercely righteous followers of every commandment of the Lord our God" (Lewis 1970, 305). Gantry had let several newspaper reporters know that something special would be taking place in church that Sunday morning, and the papers reprinted almost the entire sermon. The next week 700 people turned out, and Gantry was solidly established as a local favorite.

It was during the period covered in *Elmer Gantry*—the post-World War I era—that the third of five Christian fundamentantalist revivals in the United States took place. The first revival occurred during the 1730s; the fifth is taking place today. The five revivals have displayed six common themes:

1. **Individualism.** Fundamentalism focuses on personal woes and personal salvation, with supporters urged to examine their own private spirituality and to commit themselves to a personal relationship with Jesus Christ.

2. **Emotionalism.** Fundamentalism is a religion of the heart, not the head. Conversion is a highly emotional experience that remains almost unchanged since the early eighteenth-century revivals.

3. **Moralism.** Fundamentalism emphasizes living a Christian life. The path to salvation requires a recognition of one's own sinfulness and a determination to live righteously, resisting all temptations.

4. **Conservatism.** People who embrace fundamentalism are generally suspicious of most social change.

5. **Nondenominationalism.** Fundamentalists maintain that no one church has a monopoly on the attainment of salvation. While revivalists do not dismiss established religious organizations, their primary focus is on a moral crusade against evil, a crusade that rests on a nondenominational basis.

6. **Evangelism.** Revivalism depends on evangelistic ministers, who use oratory and personal magnetism to generate enthusiasm in revival campaigns. Evangelists are more likely to be prophets than messiahs, more interested in listeners than followers. Billy Graham, for instance, has characterized himself as "the Western Union Messenger of God" (Wilson 1978, 67–68).

Beyond sharing these six themes, fundamentalists differ in some regards. For instance, followers of Pat Robertson emphasize speaking in tongues and faith healing and are fairly moderate politically. In contrast, Jerry Falwell's followers are more conservative politically and believe in biblical infallibility (a literal acceptance of biblical statements) (Guth and Green 1988). While most fundmentalists condemn homosexuality, there is a Christian organization called Good News, with a membership that is both fundamentalist and gay (Thumma 1991).

Fundamentalism seems to have become so popular in recent years because once individuals choose Christ as their personal savior, they are not only comforted but also spared the necessity of needing to personally struggle with interpretations of such complex modern issues as the possibility of nuclear war and the apparent end of economic growth (Hammond 1985).

Some fundamentalists have been active politically. In 1980 Jerry Falwell and members of his Moral Majority launched a successful $1 million political campaign called "Target 80," during which television and radio spots and mailings of campaign literature strongly suggested that the primary intention was to give reasons why five prominent liberal Democratic senators should be defeated rather than why their opponents should be elected. More recently active fundamentalist organizations have sought to limit the power of government to legitimize such activities as abortion, homosexuality, and sex education in public schools (Fields 1991).

Until the 1980s fundamentalists were fairly inactive politically. If future efforts to mobilize them are even moderately effective, the outcomes of many elections might be affected (Fields 1991).

AMERICAN CONTROVERSY
Religion in the Public Arena

Should religious leaders be permitted to participate extensively in public life? We will consider positions favoring and opposing this possibility.

The Position Favoring Religious Leaders' Involvement in Public Life Initially it should be emphasized that the first amendment to the Constitution indicates not only that people have the freedoms of speech, press, and assembly but also that they have the freedom to establish and practice religion, without fear of intervention. Thus the Constitution supports religious leaders' right to involve themselves in public life.

But it is more than a question of legality. When religious spokespeople comment on public issues or even political candidates, Americans receive information and opinions from people who are unusually moral, people who are struggling to understand the meaning of life and the significance of our existence on earth. Who could possibly be a better choice to make a thoughtful, worthwhile commentary on such issues as prayer in the schools, creationism in the curriculum, and the moral character and godliness of different political candidates?

A final point for this position: In modern times people who criticize the right of religious officials to be involved in public life are, in reality, simply liberals who oppose conservative religious leaders' political philosophy. Such people would be happy enough if conservative clergy—in particular, Jerry Falwell and Pat Robertson—were banned from political participation. However, they favor liberals' activities—for instance, Catholic bishops' calls for a reduction in nuclear weaponry and for a much more extensive governmental commitment to eliminating poverty in the United States.

The Position Favoring Restriction of Religious Leaders' Involvement in Public Life How much restriction should be imposed on religious leaders? Some, perhaps many, critics of clergy's involvement in politics would say that there is quite a difference between a Jerry Falwell, who attempts to assess the religious quality of specific candidates, and people and groups that issue general pronouncements about social and political issues. The first activity means direct involvement in a political contest, while the second is usually no more than a general declaration of political and social opinions provided in sermons.

But there is a topic of even greater concern. In its indisputable wisdom, the United States has preserved a separation of church and state. There is no official American religion. Were there a national religion, we would run the danger of a few unscrupulous people using the enormous influence that religion can generate to create a mass allegiance. The prospect of the United States becoming like Iran, which was controlled by a religious dictator and his team of Islamic officials until his death in 1989, might seem far-fetched to us. However, the analogy is thought-provoking. Consider the influence exercised by Reverend Moon of the Unification Church over thousands of young people or the power exercised by the deranged cult leader Jim Jones, who led a mass suicide of more than 900 Americans in 1978. No, the supporters of this position assert, it is safer and saner to have religious leaders removed from public issues.

Conclusion So what do you think? Do you agree wholly with one position or the other? If you end up somewhere between the two positions, indicate precisely which points you support and oppose. Discuss these issues informally in small groups or examine them in class.

348

The nearby American Controversy discusses issues related to the role of religion in public life.

Our focus now shifts from religion to education. We have seen that religion involves socialization—that participants in it concern themselves about the transmission of beliefs and values. As we have already noted, education also involves transmission—in this case transmission of knowledge, skills, and values by either formal or informal means.

The relationship between religion and education has shown itself throughout American history. In fact, the earliest American schools were run by churches. For instance, the Society of Friends (Quakers) opened a school in Philadelphia in 1689, and for the next century-and-a-quarter the only schools in Pennsylvania were run by churches (Binzen 1970, 38). In 1636 Harvard College was created because the Puritans dreaded "to leave an illiterate ministry to the churches when our present ministers shall lie in the dust" (Bailyn et al. 1977, 159). In recent years there has been a revival of religious schools, increasing from several hundred in the 1960s to 13,000 in 1985. What is parents' primary motive for sending their children to such schools? Apparently they are seeking a Christian education for their children, an education which they feel has been denied in tax-supported schools since the Supreme Court's ban on school prayer in 1962. As one British observer noted, "They want the moral and religious instruction that publicly-financed schools cannot now provide without bumping up against the constitution" (*Economist* 1985, 25). These parents, in short, want to control the kind of education their children receive. In both religion and education, control over the content of socialization is often a major concern for people involved.

Theories of Education

Among sociologists there exist different perspectives about the impact of education upon people. Does it provide socialization that permits people to fit smoothly into modern society? The structural-functional theory would answer in the affirmative while conflict theory would respond negatively.

THE STRUCTURAL-FUNCTIONAL THEORY

The structural-functional theory of education emphasizes that education reduces conflict in modern society and contributes significantly to its stability. Even though structural-functional theorists are likely to suggest that individuals can use education to become socially mobile, they emphasize that the education system basically helps maintain the existing distribution of wealth and power.

We examine six functions of education.

Cultural Transmission

For a society to survive, culture must be handed from one generation to the next. Once children in modern societies reach 4 or 5, the schools begin to assume the burden of this task. American children must study such academic subjects as English, mathematics, geography, and history and also learn about such nonacademic topics as patriotism, culturally acceptable behavior, and morality.

The United States has been more inclined to stress patriotism in its schools than has England, perhaps because of the necessity of integrating a continuous flow of immigrants. High-school civics textbooks, for instance, have traditionally avoided virtually all unpleasant and controversial aspects of American life. A study concluded that American schools did a more effective job of molding loyal and obedient citizens than did those in the Soviet Union (Banks 1976). Many critics feel that there has been too much emphasis on obtaining obedience and not enough on helping students to grasp the meaning of fundamental cultural content. One educator indicated that key features of Western civilization are not sufficiently emphasized in schools—that students need to obtain a detailed understanding of how constitutional government, the rule of law, and the primacy of individual rights are central cultural elements in the United States and other Western nations (Stotsky 1992).

Social Control

The final straw for Bob Pike occurred when his son told him that he had received a piece of candy from the principal for opening the door for a teacher whose arms were filled with books. The child was confused, considering that he had performed a simple courtesy and did not need to be rewarded. Pike removed his son from the school, concluding that he was being exposed to a compliance-oriented system with standards "so low as to be positively immoral" (Pike 1992, 564).

Although Bob Pike did not use the term, his article made it clear that his child was in a school system dominated by the **hidden curriculum**: a set of school rules that emphasizes blind obedience and that is seldom made explicit but is recognized as important by students. Pupils have traditionally been expected to sit only in assigned seats, to answer questions when called on to do so, to take tests when told to take tests, and the rest of the time keep quiet. Many American teachers emphasize "repetition, redundancy, and ritualistic action" above all else (Jackson 1968, 6). One article argued that part of the hidden curriculum in academically ambitious schools is the idea that cheating may be necessary because success is critical; moral sensibilities are numbed by the premium on getting good grades (Power and Kohlberg 1987).

Exposure to the hidden curriculum begins in kindergarten. Children are expected to take part in a number of carefully supervised activities. Those who submit to the imposed discipline and eventually learn the habit of unthinking obedience tend to be evaluated by the school as good students. Those who accept the routines of the school but do not personally identify with them will probably find themselves in the category of adequate students. Finally children who refuse to accept the rules of the school will often receive the label of "problem children" or "bad students." In modern times schools frequently engage clinical psychologists or other therapists to help teachers deal with such children (Gracey 1977).

Transmission of Knowledge and Academic Skills

Schools pass on critical knowledge and skills that make it possible for people to participate in the

At *school, children literally learn to play by the rules.*

central activities of their society. Without the ability to read, write, and compute, Americans find themselves highly limited in the job market and are also unable to participate in a host of other activities that occur in daily life; they cannot calculate their own income tax, understand a street map, or keep a checkbook accurately. The current development of basic skills in American schools is not very effective. For example, a survey of American fourth and eighth graders found that while the children were creative in their choice of topics, their writing was usually disorganized and poorly developed (De Witt 1992).

Educators often find it difficult to justify studying the liberal arts beyond certain basic topics to students who insist that they are unwilling to devote attention to any topic that will not contribute directly to their future economic success. People who are concerned only about the immediate advantages of education will not appreciate the broader benefits that students can obtain from studying literature, social science, a language, or calculus.

Sorting

Another critical function that the schools perform is the sorting of people into different occupational roles. Research strongly suggests that a person's occupational placement is determined largely before he or she completes elementary school. Teachers and principals evaluate students' elementary school records and then use this

350

evaluation as the primary basis for recommending whether or not particular students should be placed in a high track, which will qualify them for a college preparatory program, or a low track, which will direct them toward vocational courses or some other program that is not college-bound. Sometimes the recommendation will change as a result of performance in junior-high school, but such changes are uncommon. Those who successfully complete college-preparatory programs then proceed to college and perhaps post-graduate study and eventually gain the more prestigious and higher-paying jobs. The occupational prospects of even 10-year-olds, in short, are often quite determined (Parsons 1968).

Development of Social Skills

"Sally, I don't know how you did it!"

"It was easy, Hank. Really!"

While having fun whispering to each other, these two little boys also are developing communications skills.

"But you presented the boss exactly the same proposal that I did. Nothing more and nothing less."

Sally smiles. "It's not what I said that was important, Hank. It's how I said it."

Sally is clearly aware of the importance of social skills. Tactfully (perhaps too tactfully for Hank to understand), she implies that his social skills could use some improvement. One of the functions of education is to help develop these abilities. Children who are evaluated as good students because they have learned to accept the rules that teachers emphasize also tend to develop the social skills that will help them behave appropriately in middle-class occupational spheres. Minority students with distinctly different cultural backgrounds often lack some of the social skills emphasized in the dominant culture, but experimental programs have shown that these initial performance disadvantages sharply declined if early instruction took their cultural traditions into account, easing the transition into the mainstream system. For example, an instructional program with native Hawaiian children emphasized small-group work and used peer teaching, which is a traditional cultural practice (Taylor 1991).

Research on successful management personnel has concluded that a high level of intelligence has been judged neither necessary nor desirable, and specialized or technical skills are of minor significance. The importance of managers' social skills is apparent when one realizes that corporate advancement often occurs when a manager becomes a member of a team or clique that provides assistance to a sponsoring higher executive. Failure in business can be largely explained by lack of social skills. A survey of seventy-six large corporations concluded that 90 percent of the managers fired from their jobs were believed to lack desirable personality traits (Collins 1979, 32).

Advancement of Knowledge

The role expectations for faculty in colleges and universities vary considerably. In the elite schools, the basic principle is "publish or perish." Either faculty members produce a substantial quantity of high-quality publications (books, articles, or both), or they will be dismissed. Less elite colleges and universities favor publications and may require them for promotion or other forms of public recognition but do not consider them absolutely mandatory in order to keep a job.

There is no doubt that contributions to the advancement of knowledge are highly prized throughout the academic world. One's colleagues may respect first-rate teaching, but the only way to receive meaningful recognition, especially beyond the confines of one's own school, is to make a contribution to knowledge in one's field, normally in written form.

The process of advancing knowledge can bring new members into a discipline. When graduate students or undergraduate majors participate in a faculty-research project, they start to obtain the knowledge and skills that can make them productive members of that field and eventually contributors to its further advancement. Many academic departments provide courses that introduce students to the process of knowledge advancement in their field; the methods course in sociology is an example.

THE CONFLICT THEORY

While structural-functional theory emphasizes that education contributes to the stability and conflict-free condition of society, conflict theory argues that education perpetuates existing inequalities among people. Conflict theorists will not accept the structural-functionalists' claim that social control in schools simply promotes an orderly society. The advocates of conflict theory emphasize that the current education system tends to produce unquestioning obedience to authority, like the frightening blind obedience Stanley Milgram created in the experiment reported in Chapter 2, "Doing Research in Sociology."

A Reexamination of Several Functions of Education

Conflict theory considers the functions we have just examined in a different light. While structural-functional theory emphasizes that education provides students information that encouages them to interact intelligently in modern society, the con-flict approach is less optimistic; it claims that schools are simply trying to prepare students to become dull, conforming members of modern society by developing unthinking patriotism, good work habits, and good manners. Since American public education started, the schools have tended to stress the transmission of conservative values. As early as the 1840s, textbooks and teachers propagandized for the positive qualities of the American way of life, especially the capitalist economic system. In school immigrant children were told that if they simply worked hard and lived virtuously, they would eventually become successful, honored, and even wealthy. Educators emphasized this theme constantly, even including it in the arithmetic lessons. The following example illustrates how one test simultaneously taught subtraction and sermonized about drunkenness: "There were 7 farmers, 3 of whom drank rum and whiskey and became miserable. The rest drank water and were healthy and happy. How many drank water?" (Quoted in Binzen 1970, 43).

Like conflict theorists, some observers of South Africa have been deeply concerned about possible harmful effects of the current education system on black children. The nearby Cross-Cultural Perspective addresses this issue.

Structural-functional and conflict theory agree on only one point about the issue of sorting: that it does take place. The structural-functional perspective claims that students are placed in tracks according to their abilities. Conflict theory, on the other hand, focuses on the fact that there is a distinct relationship between income and race, and students' tracks. Specifically, those who come from affluent families and are white are more likely to be in college-preparatory tracks than those who are not from affluent famiiies and belong to racial minorities. A recent analysis indicated that the idea of sorting or tracking is deeply rooted in American culture, concluding that norms supporting the legitimacy of sorting and claiming that certain groups are more intelligent than others have become entrenched in our school systems. The most effective way to eliminate that system is to develop a set of counternorms—"a culture of detracking"—that emphasizes both the importance and the practicality of dismantling this system (Oakes and Lipton 1992).

Structural-functional theory indicates that schooling will provide practical knowledge and

CROSS-CULTURAL PERSPECTIVE
Education for Black South Africans after *Apartheid*

As we noted in Chapter 9, "Ethnic and Racial Minorities," in 1992 the South African *apartheid* system, which mandated separate facilities and living arrangements for whites and racial minorities, was officially overturned. But as important as this development was, it hardly eliminated major hardships for South Africa's racial minorities. Education for black citizens is a case in point. Looking toward the future, we consider reasons for pessimism and reasons for optimism about blacks' schooling in South Africa.

Reasons for Pessimism A significant problem is money. As one observer phrased it, South Africa is a country of "grinding poverty and massive wealth," with most blacks, and certainly most black school districts, suffering grinding poverty. In a country where racial inequality has been the order of the day, the per-capita expenditure for pupil education in 1991 was about four times greater for white children than black children. Observing several black schools, a visitor heard repeated complaints about the absence of chalk, paper, textbooks, and desks for children as well as grumblings about double sessions and shortages of teachers. While some movement toward an equalization of racial expenditure is likely to occur, actual equalization is very unlikely since bringing all minority student expenditures

to the level of white students would absorb half of all government costs.

Another difficulty for black students is that to graduate from high school, they face a tough system that requires passage of a battery of difficult, European-oriented exams administered outside of their schools. Increasingly black citizens have complained about the system. One black administrator explained that most of the information blacks obtained in high school was irrelevant to them and that they also learned "how inferior they are because of studying battles where whites beat blacks. What they learn in school can only be applied in the white man's world" (Murphy 1992, 369).

Within such a restrictive system, it is hardly surprising that most black teachers have few formal qualifications. In 1991 about half of the teachers in black primary schools lacked even high-school diplomas. Furthermore the educational tradition dominating black schools has been highly authoritarian, with memorization and recall the order of the day and independent, critical thinking deemphasized. Teachers continue to teach as they were taught, and thus the education system does little to help black children learn to think for themselves.

Another difficulty involves deficiencies in the bureaucratic structure for black schooling. The central government controls an education system that

has separate departments for each of the country's four racial groups, with unequal distribution of government funding to the different groups as well as extensive bureaucratic wastefulness and corruption.

Reacting to the ongoing problems of minority education, many black students have used the schools as staging areas for disruption, and in response to their boycotts and school takeovers, the police have responded with arrests, detentions, and killings. There has been a mixed reaction to black students' involvement in liberation movements. While many observers have praised their willingness to put their lives on the line, others have criticized them for lacking discipline, using the system as an excuse for not working hard, and showing no respect for and willingness to obey their teachers.

Black school teachers have found themselves subjected to extensive criticism—by government officials for not carrying out education policy and keeping order in schools and classrooms; by many parents because they have been unable to control and teach their children; by militant individuals for not joining the recent liberation movements. The breaking point for thousands of black teachers came in 1990. They organized protest marches, delivering lists of grievances to regional offices of the Department of Education and Training. Increasingly in a strong rejection of the current corrupt, racist education system, militant teachers have begun refusing to prepare lessons or to be evaluated.

Summarizing the negative aspects of the present education system for blacks, educator Jerome T. Murphy wrote:

> Whatever the jumble of causes and motivations, black schooling is in utter disarray. Nobody is in charge of an inferior and illegitimate system, designed by whites and despised by blacks, teetering on the edge of collapse.

(Murphy 1992, 371)

But with further examination we see that the news is not all bad.

Reasons for Optimism One reason for optimism is that in spite of its problems, South Africa's economy is the wealthiest in Africa and its political system has been very stable. Quite possibly this combination of economic prosperity and political stability could make it possible to reduce the combined conditions of unemployment, poverty, and inequality and, in the process, address blacks' educational deficiencies.

A second encouraging condition is that there are signs of real change among whites in South Africa. Many white leaders have accepted the idea that power must be shared with blacks—that otherwise the country will remain in "a violent equilibrium" with blacks and other minorities lacking the clout to overthrow the system but constantly protesting and clashing with the police and disrupting ordinary activity, including schooling. The word *apartheid* means separate, and, indeed, blacks and whites have lived separate lives in South Africa and today remain ignorant about and frightened of each other. One white taxi driver, who, as he explained, had been "raised a racist," said that his perceptions of blacks changed dramatically after four months of transporting black passengers and, in the process, talking with them. Quite possibly integrated schooling could produce the same positive impact for black and white students.

The final basis for optimism is the remarkable record of largely unpublicized protests in which ordinary black citizens have engaged—a fifteen-year record of disobedience to *apartheid* laws "forged in theatres and hotels and restaurants, on trains, on beaches and sportsfields, in universities and private schools, in shops and offices, in mines and factories" (Kane-Berman 1990, 7). Parents, students, and teachers are certain to continue this relentless effort to improve blacks' lives. This "silent revolution" has been apparent when thousands of undereducated black teachers have returned to school in the late afternoons to upgrade their qualifications.

The future of blacks' education in South Africa will be forged by the country's political leaders, but, in addition, the efforts of ordinary teachers, parents, and students will play a prominent role.

Sources: John Kane-Berman. South Africa's Silent Revolution. *Johannesburg: South Africa Institute of Race Relations*, 1990; *Jerome T. Murphy. "Apartheid's Legacy to Black Children,"* Phi Delta Kappan. vol. 73 (January 1992), pp. 367–74.

skills that make it possible for people to participate in the central activities of the society. On the other hand, the conflict perspective, which focuses on the inequities existing in modern society, stresses that the knowledge that students obtain in school can make them aware of how and why injustices have developed in U.S. society. While structural-functionalists find it difficult to demonstrate the practical significance of a liberal education, the advocates of a conflict approach emphasize that students who have received an effective liberal education will be able to think clearly and independently, thereby equipping themselves to resist any tyrannies the elite might contemplate (Lichtenstein 1985; Oestereicher 1982).

Credentials and Social Skills

It has been widely recognized that a steadily increasing proportion of Americans are overeducated for their particular jobs (Clogg and Shockey 1984). Conflict theorists have sharply criticized this situation, claiming that beyond the development of mass literacy, education is generally irrelevant to on-the-job productivity and sometimes even has a negative impact on it. Concrete vocational skills seem to be learned much more commonly

354

through work experience than in school. Furthermore the findings of a series of studies indicate that there is little or no relationship between school grades and success in the occupational world (Collins 1979). If in reality the educational system provides few skills relevant to effective job performance, then why is there such a widespread emphasis on academic credentials among employers?

Conflict theorists offer an answer. They claim that most occupations in modern society require a loyal and obedient work force that will perform work tasks that entail limited responsibility and minimal independent decision making. The advocates of the conflict approach contend that certificates of graduation from most high schools or colleges clearly indicate to employers that the young people in question have received training in school that has prepared them to serve effectively in the work world. As one study indicated, these certificates "get you in the door" (Bills 1988). Elite high schools and colleges might place more emphasis on responsibility and self-direction, but, according to conflict theorists, the differences are only superficial. The graduates of elite schools are socialized to be just as unquestioningly loyal and obedient on the job as individuals who receive their credentials from nonelite schools (Bowles and Gintis 1976; Collins 1979).

Prospects for Change

Conflict theorists contend that the current system of education will not change in any significant respects in the foreseeable future because the elite members of American society believe that their interests would suffer with any changes. According to the supporters of the conflict approach, the wealthy and powerful will usually tolerate and even encourage such innovations as open classrooms or newly developed teaching styles because they give the false impression that significant change is occurring, which might tone down some critics' protests. Conflict theorists argue that the educational reforms that the elite will find threatening are those that will develop less readily obedient workers or open up elite status to large numbers of people in the nonelite classes. The impact of leaders' indifference to public education is particularly damaging in devastated inner-city areas, where all who could afford to do so have left and those remaining "are the ones with broken wings" (Kozol 1992, 34). Such schools usually have large classes, poor facilities, high dropout rates, and very little effective learning.

Supporters of both theories are likely to agree that significant measures of educational reform need to be initiated in our society.

Educational Reform ■

On the football field, Dexter Manley was recognized as big and bad—a towering, menacing defensive end for the Washington Redskins—but it was another story when Manley appeared before a Senate panel. Manley began to read a prepared statement; the sweat rolled down his cheeks and tears filled his eyes. There was a long pause, and then Wally (Famous) Amos, the cookie magnate and spokesman for Literacy Volunteers, approached the witness table, put his arm around Manley, and spoke to him. After Amos had returned to his seat, Paul Simon, chairman of the Senate Education Committee, turned to Manley

and said, "Don't worry about that prepared statement. This takes more courage than anything you've done on the football field" (New York Times 1989, B17). So Manley went on to explain how he had failed in school, or, more accurately, how the schools had failed him. Three years earlier, concerned about his future after football, he had started taking night classes and vastly improved his second-grade reading level.

Dexter Manley is hardly a unique case. Since 1983 when the National Commission on Excellence on Education issued a report entitled A Nation at Risk, there has been extensive national attention paid to the problems of American public education. The findings of this report indicated that about 23 million Americans were functionally illiterate, thus unable to read and write well enough to meet such demands of modern life as reading road signs or filling out an application for a home-insurance policy. In addition, the report indicated that about 13 percent of American adolescents (and 40 percent of minority teenagers) were functionally illiterate (Goldberg and Harvey 1983).

A *Nation at Risk*, however, created some misconceptions about rampant educational decline when it suggested that between 1963 and 1980, there had been a steady decline in students' Scholastic Aptitude Test (SAT) scores. In writing about what he called "the big lie," educator Gerald W. Bracey (1991) indicated that while SAT scores did drop between the early 1960s and early 1970s, they started rising in the middle 1970s and had reached an all-time high by 1986. Furthermore Bracey suggested that modern observers of public education need to recognize that unlike much of the publicity emphasized since the early 1980s, the high-school dropout rate has not been sharply increasing. In fact, the national high-school graduate level went from 10 percent in 1910 to about 75 percent in 1965, and in 1989 about 83 percent of all high-school students received a diploma twelve years after starting school.

Now accompanying this information, there needs to be a note of caution. American education does have serious problems, and the dropout rate, while not rising overall, remains high, especially for poor minority students.

Educational reform could be beneficial in many areas, with the following suggestions representing no more than a brief sampling. First, a productive step is community involvement in schools. Recently a new principal was listening to the complaints of a number of parents, and she realized that perhaps more important than what they said was what they were not saying—that they wanted to have their children taken care of and all educational problems solved without taking any responsibility themselves. A better system, this principal found, has been to foster parental involvement, and in an article she indicated how teams of parents, students, and teachers could work together to ensure safety at school bus stops. Such team efforts, she concluded, can promote the growth of

Recognizing the importance of parents' involvement in their children's education, many educators, like this second-grade teacher, strongly encourage conferences where the teacher, the student, and a parent or parents can discuss the child's schooling.

all parties' involvement and cooperation and limit friction and hostility (Meadows 1992).

A central element in educational reform is the curriculum. One educator suggested that if students are going to find school rewarding, the material must be interesting and stimulating, with deemphasis of memorization and a focus on the creative application of ideas and information. It is particularly useful for students to obtain the sense that what they are learning in school will prove helpful in later life, and so effective teachers will relentlessly demonstrate this connection (Glasser 1992). Such an approach will prove helpful, even inspiring to the large number of teachers who have long felt that the modern emphasis on standardized tests stands in the way of getting a good education (Stake 1992).

Finally a conflict perspective emphasizes an important point—the role of wealthy and powerful citizens. Are they willing to support significant education reform? Or, should reform efforts simply continue without trying to involve them?

Education and Equality

Frederick Douglass (1968), a well-known nine-teenth-century black leader, published a book about his childhood experiences as a slave. He indicated that plantation owners were determined that their slaves should not learn how to read. The owners realized that literate slaves could obtain more extensive knowledge, and such knowledge could lead to discontentment with their situation and ultimately even encourage revolt. Douglass himself learned to read only by trading bread to poor white boys for "the more valuable bread of knowledge."

More recently black activists have consistently emphasized the importance of education. In the late 1930s and early 1940s, the National Association for the Advancement of Colored People (NAACP) and its allies began a concerted attack on segregated education, emphasizing that without equal educational opportunity, black people would forever be seriously handicapped in a highly competitive society. In the May 17, 1954, decision of *Brown v. the Topeka, Kansas, Board of Education*, the United States Supreme Court ruled that segregated schools were inherently unequal. The years that followed saw widespread efforts to integrate America's public schools. The Coleman Report played a significant part in stimulating these efforts.

THE COLEMAN REPORT AND BUSING

As part of the Civil Rights Act of 1964, Congress ordered the federal commissioner of education to conduct a study of the availability of educational opportunities for Americans of different races, religions, and national origins. The project was massive. About 600,000 children in more than 4,000 schools across the country were tested. Some 60,000 teachers, several thousand principals, and several hundred school superintendents were also interviewed.

More than halfway though the research, sociologist James Coleman, who had been named to direct the project, predicted that the study's findings on the differing quality of the education available to the average white child and to the typical black child were "going to be striking" (Hodgson 1973, 37). They were not. To Coleman's surprise the results of the study indicated that the physical facilities and the formal curriculula in segregated schools attended by blacks and whites were roughly similar and that the test scores of black and white students were only marginally affected by physical facilities, formal curricula, and other measurable characteristics of schools.

Nevertheless about 85 percent of the black students scored below the white students' average on the standardized tests administered by the researchers. The reason for this seemed to involve a combination of nonschool factors operating among blacks: in particular, poverty, nonsupportive community attitudes toward education, and the low education level achieved by most black parents. Coleman and his associates found that black children and other poor, primarily minority children generally possess less effective educational skills at the time that they enter school and that the schools have been largely unable to overcome this disadvantage (Coleman et al. 1966).

While the Coleman Report has received criticism, many educators and social scientists have accepted its basic findings. One particular finding has had an especially significant effect on social policy: that students from poverty areas were frequently able to improve their academic performance substantially when they attended schools with students living in affluent areas. This conclusion led directly to the practice of busing.

BUSING AND EQUALITY

Why has busing been used to promote school integration? To begin, recall that school districts normally serve only their immediate residential areas. Most of these areas are racially segregated, and in such situations the only way to bring affluent white children and poor black children into contact in the same schools is by physically moving them by means of busing. Busing in order to promote racial balance in the schools has provoked considerable controversy and even violence. Most white parents have not cited integrated classrooms as their reason for opposition. Instead they have claimed to be concerned about the supposed inferiority of inner-city schools, their unfamiliarity with the facilities, the lengthy days resulting from long-distance busing, the danger their children face by entering high-crime areas, and the destruction to community spirit produced by the loss of neighborhood schools (Armor 1989, 26). One study concluded that nonracial factors such as those just cited were at least as important as the racial composition of schools in predicting white students' refusal to be bused to inner-city schools (Rossell 1988).

Sixteen years after the Coleman Report was published, James Coleman wrote about busing, acknowledging "the general unpopularity of this policy, greatest among whites, but also true for Hispanics and blacks. . . " (Coleman et al. 1982, 197). Coleman suggested that new ways of promoting equal opportunities in education need to be devised.

Specialists in the area of equality in education currently acknowledge that busing and others efforts to integrate schools have produced modest academic improvements for blacks and other racial minorities (Jaynes and Williams 1989, 373–74). It is also appreciated that other issues are at stake. In particular, an analysis of about a dozen major studies demonstrated that minorities who attend desegregated primary and secondary schools tend to continue integration in college and their work lives. Thus desegregating schools is more than a question of teaching children to improve their reading or writing skills. More significantly it is a question of opening the gateway to mainstream opportunities (Braddock, Crain, and McPartland 1984).

EQUAL EDUCATIONAL OPPORTUNITIES IN DEVELOPMENT

During the 1970s there was extensive emphasis on equalization of educational opportunity. Several court rulings addressed the concern that heavy reliance on property taxes, which are levied by cities and towns as a prominent means of financing public education within their locale, tends to create sharp differences in the quality of education provided to children, with the richer districts characterized by better facilities and more highly qualified personnel. In 1968 Demetrio Rodgriguez and other parents in a poor, almost exclusively minority section of San Antonio, Texas, filed a suit demanding that there be an equalization of educational expenditure for children in their district with funding for children in other areas. In the

Edgewood area, the Rodriguez family's district, payment, including state aid, was $231 per child, while in Alamo Heights, the wealthiest area, it was $543 per child, including state aid. The case was brought to the Supreme Court, which concluded that the issue should not focus on different property values in living areas but on educational equality and that as a result of lower student expenditure in the poorer area, their quality of education would suffer. Yet, the court contended, the focus of its concern needed to be on the traditional standard for expenditure—the guarantee *only* of a "minimum" basic education, not the assurance that all children would receive the same quality of education. The result of that focus was that in 1991 in Texas, educational expenditure still varied greatly between wealthy and poor districts, with per-capita spending $2,000 in the poorest and $19,000 in the wealthiest. Then early in 1993, a new spending plan mandating some redistribution of funding was presented to the state legislature. At this writing, however, the Supreme Court's decision in the Rodriguez case remains in force, permitting in Jonathan Kozol's (1991) phrase "savage inequalities" to continue for poor minority students.

Another minority group in schools has been disabled people, for whom significant legislation was passed during the 1970s. By the middle of the decade, about twenty state legislatures had passed bills mandating equal educational opportunities for handicapped people. Educators struggled to comply, complaining of a lack of special teachers, instructional materials, and funds. In response Congress passed the Education for All Handicapped Children Act in 1975. This was a massive effort, designed to provide individualized schooling for five to seventeen million physically, mentally, and emotionally handicapped children (Brodinsky 1979). While efforts to weaken this legislation have been prevented, many school districts have failed to comply fully with the law (Kuipers 1992; Scotch 1988). A pair of educators suggested that the integration of severely handicapped children in public schools might benefit all students, making it possible for both handicapped and nonhandicapped children to learn from each other (Hanline and Murray 1984).

Besides legislative remedies many steps can be taken to equalize educational opportunity. Educators have focused on such issues as the representation in history courses of the dramatic

This photo illustrates an increasingly popular, modern educational policy which emphasizes that all students will benefit if those with disabilities are integrated into school activities to the fullest extent possible.

struggles of oppressed people around the globe as a means of encouraging minority students (Education for Democracy Project 1987); the replacement of school texts that either deny or deemphasize the significance of multicultural traditions in the United States (Epstein and Ellis 1992); and the need to improve the likelihood that children of all economic and racial backgrounds can possess and nurture dreams (Eitzen 1992).

Commentary ■

In this chapter we have examined two types of socialization. When people initiate religious activity, they are transmitting values and beliefs. When people administer education, they are transmitting knowledge, skills, and values. Both institutional areas arouse strong feelings in many people because they appreciate the processes that are unfolding: Members of society, especially children, can be significantly influenced by both religion and education, and the nature of the content and its extent of influence obviously is determined by those in control.

We have seen a significant difference between the types of socialization represented in this chapter and family-centered socialization discussed in Chapter 6. The activity in these two institutions is much more public, thereby inspiring continual public discussion, debate, controversy, and evaluation.

This chapter closes with the fourth of six research boxes.

RESEARCH IN SOCIOLOGY: SECTION IV

The Tricky Business of Studying Cults

Since the early 1980s, sociologists have conducted a large number of studies on religious cults, which are religious groups based on a substantially new insight or revelation, usually provided by a person believed to possess special knowledge. These studies have been interesting and provocative, often helping to break down the stereotype of cult members as "crackpots, psychological basket cases, or brainwashed robots" (Ayella 1990, 562). The research, however, has often run into significant problems.

Throughout this discussion it will be clear that researchers and cult members have different, often clashing goals. Sociologists' priority is conducting research, requiring some detachment and independence from the group studied. Cult members have a very different goal—to spread their message and gain converts. That aim leads members to try to involve researchers, either seeking to convert them or to convince them to present the group in a favorable light in their reports. Such cult efforts tend to endanger the investigator's detachment and independence, threatening the effectiveness of the study. Consider research on cults as a three-step process.

Gaining Access

For some researchers this initial step has been hard to accomplish. Roy Wallis wanted to study Scientology, a cult dedicated to mental and physical healing and requiring members to maintain complete conformity to its doctrines. Wallis decided that the data he received would be more interesting if he presented himself as a person coming off the street, not as a sociologist. So he signed up at an introductory "Communications Course" in Scientology, staying at a Scientology boarding house during the course. After two days, however, Wallis felt compelled to leave, saying that the indoctrination process required converts constantly to reaffirm their commitment to Scientology's doctrines and that since he did not share that commitment, it proved awkward to remain.

Eileen Barker, who studied the Unification Church, had a much more favorable access. After two years of negotiation, Barker obtained a list of all Church members, making it possible for her to draw a random sample for interviews. Unlike Wallis, Barker was approached by officials of the cult she wanted to study. They came to her because they considered her a reputable specialist in the sociology of religion, who was sufficiently fair-minded to listen to what they had to say. It was important, Unification Church officials felt, to have some balanced public information about their organization since the only reporting by individuals outside of the Unification Church had been both scanty and negative.

Barker's research suggests the sensitive nature of obtaining access to a cult. Researchers are well advised to keep in mind that such a group is going to try to use them for its own purposes, and so ticklish situations can be created. What if a researcher has severe doubts about a particular cult's activities and then discovers that his or her study might contribute to that organization's vitality? There are other problematic issues. Since cult members often hope that a research report will contribute favorably to their organization's image, then it is likely that some effort will be made to control what the investigator learns about the cult, possibly denying him or her full access to organizational activities or information members believe the sociologist might view negatively.

Such complications continue once the study is established.

Maintaining Access

Like initiating access to cults, maintaining it can be difficult for sociologists. Cult members tend to be highly motivated, goal-oriented individuals, and if they do not see a researcher's activity contributing to their group's effort, then they are likely to terminate or disrupt the research.

In his well-known study of an early Unification Church group, John Lofland felt that he and the group leader shared the understanding that "I was personally sympathetic to, and accepting of, them and desired to understand their endeavors, but I was not likely to be a convert" (Lofland 1966, 274). But while the leader never was explicit on the topic, Lofland eventually realized that she maintained hopes of converting him. When the research project was nearly a year old, she told Lofland "that she was tired of playing the 'studying the movement' game" (Lofland 1966, 274). So he was forced to leave.

In a later study of the Unification Church, Marybeth Ayella had a similar experience. Like Lofland she declared that her sole purpose was to conduct research, but throughout her three-week stay, she was treated more as a potential convert than as a researcher. This perception seriously disrupted her study. For instance, when attempting to obtain background information on members, she was repeatedly interrupted and asked to do something else. Then one evening when she indicated that she would prefer not to attend a lecture, instead spending the time rereading her notes, Ayella was barraged with requests to attend until she decided that if she chose not to do so, the badgering would continue indefinitely.

Studying the Hare Krishna cult in Los Angeles, E.B. Rochford had similar difficulties. Like Lofland, Rochford presented himself as a sympathetic, even devoted outsider, but as in Ayella's study, members constantly pressured him to participate in their activities, making if difficult for him to perform his research. Nonetheless for several years, he was able to maintain his status as a fringe devotee. Having established this relationship with one Krishna group, Rochford was permitted to extend his research into Krishna communities in other cities. Interestingly he received a higher rate of questionnaire completion from the Krishna groups in the other cities than from the Los Angeles community, where members' lengthy opportunity to observe his status as a fringe devotee left many dissatisfied and uncooperative.

Like the other two stages in the study of cults, leaving the group presents its own problems.

Leaving the Group

The longer sociologists study cults, the more confident they become that they have penetrated the public front, grasping the full range of the group's activities and building trust with the members. But when is the appropriate time to leave? Because cults tend to be unstable and unpredictable, a researcher has little basis for knowing what will happen to the group. Is it about to fold? Will it persist in its present form for an indefinite period of time? Possibly it is about to burst into much greater, even national prominence? John Lofland, whose graduate students continued to study the Unification Church group after he was forced to leave, might have tried to extend his research indefinitely if he had an inkling that the small, obscure cult he was observing would eventually become a large, powerful, and wealthy religious organization.

Sociologists who have completed studies of cults can face the risk of legal problems if cult leaders feel that the research done on their group represents it negatively. Unification Church officials tried to stop the publication of two investigations of their organization, and Synanon, a cult dedicated to drug treatment, responded to an unfavorable book with a libel suit.

Conclusion

Throughout the process of studying cults, researchers face the distinct possibility of their activities clashing with that of their research subjects. To do effective studies of cults, sociologists need detachment, the opportunity to examine cult activities as fairly objective, unconverted observers. But cult members' interests are very different. They have come to believe that all individuals who spend extensive time in their vicinity should contribute to the group's advancement, and researchers are seldom considered an exception. This orientation means that they try to break down the sociologist's role as detached observer, and often the struggle is unrelenting.

To conduct studies on cults, sociologists must become sufficiently involved in group activities to satisfy cult members and yet remain detached enough to meet the demands of the research role. Eileen Barker explained:

> It seems to be difficult for those who have not been engaged in first hand research of this kind, to understand how one can be involved in one sense, and yet remain uninvolved in another sense. I have used. . . the analogy of the actor to try to convey something of this rather schizoid position.

(*Barker* 1983, 203)

Another constant challenge faced by sociolologists studying cults is that the group they are examining is often much more unstable than most examined by researchers. In short order the cult can grow, alter its course, or disappear, and the researcher must adjust accordingly. Ultimately those studying cults accept this type of challenge, realizing that the interesting, even fascinating data that can be obtained justifies putting up with a difficult, unstable situation.

Sources: *Marybeth Ayella. "They Must Be Crazy: Some of the Difficulties in Researching 'Cults,'" American Behavioral Scientist. vol. 33 (May/June 1990), pp. 562–77; Eileen Barker. "Supping with the Devil: How Long a Spoon Does the Sociologist Need?" Sociological Analysis. vol. 44 (Fall 1983), pp. 197–206; Raymond M. Lee and Claire M. Renzetti. "The Problems of Researching Sensitive Topics," American Behavioral Scientist. vol. 33 (May/June 1990), pp. 510–28; John Lofland. Doomsday Cult. Englewood Cliffs, NJ: Prentice-Hall, 1966; E. B. Rochford. Hare Krishna in America. New Brunswick, NJ: Rutgers University Press, 1985; Roy Wallis. The Road to Total Freedom. New York: Columbia University Press, 1977.*

STUDY GUIDE

Learning Objectives

After studying this chapter, you should be able to:

1. Define religion and education and explain their significance in modern societies.
2. Identify and describe four major functions of religion.
3. Examine two prominent trends in religion today: the declining influence of major religious organizations and the prominence of fundamentalism.
4. Discuss the structural-functional and conflict theories of education.
5. Analyze recent developments in educational reform.

6. Examine education and equality, describing the Coleman Report, busing, and recent activities in this area.
7. Indicate why both religion and education are personal types of socialization.

Summary

1. A religion is a unified system of beliefs and practices that focuses on sacred things and serves to create a community of worshippers. The sacred is anything that is superior in power and dignity, set apart from the mundane and practical, and creates a sense of awe.

Education is the transmission of knowledge, skills, and values by either formal or informal means. Like religion, education is a type of personal socialization.

2. Religions serve a variety of functions, including providing social cohesion, supporting and maintaining social control, promoting social change, and making the world comprehensible. There are also functional equivalents of religion.

3. One trend in modern religion is the declining influence of major religions. In the past several decades, religious membership and attendance have also been declining. Nonetheless established religious organizations have fought back with a number of strategies for selling religion. Fundamentalism is a strong modern religious movement. Its basic themes are individualism, emotionalism, moralism, conservatism, nondenominationalism, and evangelism.

4. The structural-funtional theory of education is a prominent theoretical perspective on that subject. Cultural transmission, social control, transmission of knowledge and academic skills, sorting, development of social skills, and advancement of knowledge are six important functions of education.

The conflict theory of education focuses on the part that education plays in the perpetuation of inequalities among people. This theory provides a reexamination of the functions analyzed by structural-functional theory and also offers its own conclusions about credentials and social skills as well as the prospects for change.

5. Educational reform requires a systematic approach. Although one can outline such an approach, it is questionable whether powerful and wealthy individuals will support significant improvements in the educational system.

Attacks on inequality in American schools started in the 1930s. The Coleman Report concluded that the fact that black students on the average scored below whites on standardized tests was primarily because of nonschool factors. Findings in the Coleman Report supported the initiation of busing. During the 1970s extensive emphasis on equalization of educational opportunity occurred.

Key Terms

civil religion a shared, public faith in the nation, a faith linked to people's everyday life through a set of beliefs, symbols, and rituals that contain religious elements and overtones that are not formally affiliated with any particular religion

education the transmission of knowledge, skills, and values by either formal or informal means

functional equivalent an organization or activity that provides service or assistance to an individual or group more commonly received from some other organization or activity

hidden curriculum a set of school rules that emphasizes blind obedience and that is seldom made explicit but is recognized as important by students

profane anything that people consider ordinary and closely linked to practical demands

religion a unified system of beliefs and practices that focuses on sacred things and serves to create a community of worshippers

sacred anything that is superior in power, is set apart from the ordinary and practical, and creates a sense of awe

secularization the process by which religion loses influence within groups and societies

Tests

True • False Test

_____ 1. Profane items do not create unity and a sense of common purpose the way sacred things do.
_____ 2. Both Weber and Marx regarded religion as no more than an effect of the economic system.
_____ 3. In modern secularized societies, religious organizations cannot promote social cohesion.
_____ 4. The text suggests that all major religious organizations have declined in membership in recent years.
_____ 5. Some modern fundamentalist groups have become involved in politics.
_____ 6. The structural-functional theory of education suggests that the principal function of education is the pursuit of upward social mobility.
_____ 7. Research evidence has strongly suggested that people's occupational placement is largely determined before they complete elementary school.
_____ 8. Advocates of the conflict theory emphasize that the current educational system tends to encourage unquestioning obedience to authority.
_____ 9. Because of the official elimination of *apartheid* in South Africa, education for blacks will be equal in quality to education for whites within a decade.
_____ 10. The Supreme Court verdict in the Rodriguez case indicated that children living in a poor school district should not expect to receive the same quality of education as children living in a wealthy district.

Multiple-Choice Test

_____ 1. According to Durkheim, secularization:
   a. is more prominent in preindustrial societies than in industrial societies.
   b. is more prominent in industrial societies than in preindustrial societies.
   c. declines as the influence of science increases.
   d. tends to promote cohesion in societies.

_____ 2. Marx's notion of "illusory happiness" relates to his view of religion as:
   a. the opium of the people.
   b. a support for slavery.
   c. a source of alienation for the wealthy and powerful.
   d. a Protestant ethic.

_____ 3. Weber believed that the reason Calvinism encouraged the development of capitalism was because it:
   a. created a common purpose and unity in communities.
   b. raised morale by indicating that everyone would eventually enter heaven.
   c. condemned the ruling class.
   d. encouraged people to work hard, to save, and to invest their savings.

_____ 4. Prominent functions of religion discussed in the text include:
   a. making the world comprehensible.
   b. limiting social control.
   c. lessening social cohesion.
   d. slowing down social change.

_____ 5. Which of the following is true of civil religion?
   a. It has declined sharply in importance since the Civil War.
   b. It is simply another term for religious fundamentalism.

_____ c.   It was represented by socialism in the former Soviet Union.
         d.   a and b

_____ 6. Religion and education:
         a.   are types of socialization.
         b.   have not changed in any significant ways in recent years.
         c.   are topics of rapidly declining interest to most Americans.
         d.   a and c

_____ 7. The hidden curriculum in schools emphasizes:
         a.   sorting.
         b.   blind obedience to rules.
         c.   a prohibition against students' cheating on tests.
         d.   advancement of knowledge.

_____ 8. The structural-functional theory of education supports the idea that:
         a.   cultural transmission should not occur in schools.
         b.   schools pass on critical knowledge and skills that permit people to participate in the central activities of their society.
         c.   knowledge helps students understand how and why social injustices have developed in U.S. society.
         d.   education is irrelevant to on-the-job productivity.

_____ 9. Conflict theorists believe that:
         a.   the wealthy oppose the open classroom concept.
         b.   loyalty and obedience should be central values in the classroom.
         c.   the elite will support innovations which create a false impression of significant change in education.
         d.   elite high schools and colleges encourage considerably more thought and action than nonelite schools.

_____ 10. Educational reform should include:
         a.   the issue of the overall decline in SAT scores.
         b.   the need to improve children's ability to memorize.
         c.   parents' involvement in their children's schools.
         d.   b and c

Essay Test

1. Define religion and distinguish between the sacred and the profane.
2. Discuss three functions of religion, giving illustrations of how they are performed in modern American society.
3. Define the functional equivalent of religion and provide examples from two countries.
4. Why are major religions declining in the United States? What are three techniques for selling established religions? Which of these techniques do you think would be the most effective and why?
5. Define education. Indicate why it is important in American society.
6. Evaluate the contributions that both the structural-functional and conflict theories make to understanding the role of education in modern America.
7. Discuss the steps that might be taken to initiate significant educational reform.
8. Summarize the relationship between education and equality, evaluating the busing program in the course of the analysis.

Suggested Readings

Bruce, Steve. 1990. *Pray TV: Televangelism in America*. London: Routledge. An effective factual introduction to the modern phenomenon of televangelism, with the writer adopting the thesis that the impact of this activity is quite limited.

Durkheim, Émile. 1961. *The Elementary Forms of the Religious Life*. Trans. Joseph Ward Swain. New York: Collier Books. A classic work in the sociology of religion, indicating how religion contributes to social cohesion in technologically simple societies.

Farber, Jerry. 1970. *The Student as Nigger*. New York: Pocket Books. A series of sharp, humorous essays demonstrating the repressive character of American higher education.

Kozol, Jonathan. 1991. *Savage Inequalities: Children in America's Schools*. New York: Crown. The latest book written by one of the country's most hard-hitting critics of inequality in education, relating with effective case-study material the impact of low-quality schooling on poor children.

Phi Delta Kappan. A leading educational journal featuring historical essays, surveys, and evaluative studies. It is worth thumbing through if only to obtain a sense of the primary issues being analyzed and debated by American educators.

Sociological Analysis. A current sociological journal specializing in studies and essays on religious topics.

Sociology of Education. A contemporary sociological journal focusing on sociological studies and essays addressing a range of educational topics.

Teaching Sociology. A current sociological journal containing articles about teaching sociology as well as reviews of books and films that can be used in sociology courses.

Weber, Max. 1958. *The Protestant Ethic and the Spirit of Capitalism*. Trans. Talcott Parsons. New York: Charles Scribner's Sons. Original Parsons translation in 1930. Weber's best-known work in the sociology of religion. This challenging essay examines the relationship between the Calvinist ethic and the development of capitalism.

Additional Assignments

1. In your school library, go to the periodicals file. Select two periodicals from different religious organizations. Look through at least five recent issues of each periodical. List the topics covered in each issue. Do the interests reflected in the two periodicals seem similar or different? What conclusions can you draw about the two organizations' efforts to "sell" their religion? What about their respective interests in social issues/problems?

2. Talk to at least five people about their memories of the teacher they liked most and the teacher they liked least. What characteristics seem to have been most significant in shaping their good/bad opinions of teachers? Has the information you received suggested support or criticism for either the structural-functional theory or conflict theory? What insights, if any, have your discussions provided about teacher training and educational reform?

Answers to Objective Test Questions

True • False Test

1. t	6. f
2. f	7. t
3. f	8. t
4. f	9. f
5. t	10. t

Multiple-Choice Test

1. b	6. a
2. a	7. b
3. d	8. b
4. a	9. c
5. c	10. c

The Political and Economic Institutions

13

On March 5, 1946, Winston Churchill stood at a podium at Westminster College in Fulton, Missouri, and declared, "From Stettin in the Baltic to Trieste in the Adriatic an iron curtain has descended across the Continent" (Clines 1992, A14). In his famous "Iron Curtain" speech, Churchill was alerting Western nations to the peril represented by communism, particularly Soviet communism. The speech helped mark the beginning of the so-called "cold war" between Western nations and the Soviet Union—a mutual antagonism lasting nearly a half-century in which both sides developed huge nuclear arsenals, and fear and suspicion of each other were ever-present realities.

Forty-six years later, Mikhail Gorbachev stood at that same podium and declared that the confrontation between Western powers and the Soviet Union had ended. He spoke regretfully of the cold war, indicating that its existence had been an enormous, costly waste. Gorbachev said:

> If the United States and the Soviet Union had been capable of comprehending their responsibility and sensibly correlating their national interests and strivings with the rights and interests of other states and peoples, the planet today would be a much more suitable and favorable place for human life.

> (*Gorbachev* 1992, A14)

While extensive political changes had occurred in relations between the two great superpowers, Gorbachev clearly was pushing for even more change. He advocated that the United Nations, particularly the Security Council, needed to create new structures that would protect human rights, imposing sanctions on countries violating peoples' rights, especially the rights of minority groups.

Besides advocating political change, Gorbachev was also a victim of it. The previous August a group of military leaders initiated a coup to wrest political leadership from Gorbachev. While they proved unsuccessful, Gorbachev was forced to resign as president of the Soviet Union, and one of the results of the coup was that the Soviet Union itself, threatened for several years by independence movements in many of its fifteen republics, ceased to exist (Hosking 1992).

The political changes also affected economic realities. Writing enthusiastically about Russia's president Boris Yeltsin, former U.S. president Richard Nixon noted that Yeltsin had made "unequivocal commitment to free elections, free markets, and free people" (Nixon 1992). To support Russia's move toward political democracy, Nixon advocated that a proposed $24 billion in American aid should be provided only if Yeltsin's democracy-oriented political reforms passed in the Russian parliament. Nixon suggested that U.S. assistance to Russia needed to include technical assistance to guide the newly independent nation in creating property and commercial law that would help support the growth of a free market along with loans to small businesses that would hire unemployed workers and also start the accumulation of domestic capital.

There is an intimate relationship between the political and economic realms. Participants in both institutions are concerned with power. **Power** is the ability of an individual or group to implement wishes or policies, with or without the cooperation of others. And why study power? Power, it seems, is an integral element of social relationships. All of us live with it, and to some extent, exercise it. A child demonstrates power when he or she makes choices about what clothes to wear, breakfast food to eat, or film to attend. The president of the United States exhibits power when exerting influence on behalf of a federal tax cut, or increased military expenditure, or in vetoing a congressional bill. Extensive power is often "heady stuff," the opportunity of having many others executing one's wishes. Great power is sufficiently seductive that it often overshadows any associated distastefulness. Americans do not usually support organized crime and yet display widespread interest, even fascination, in the Mafia leader who can literally order an enemy's death with the flick of his fingers.

Authority is power that people generally recognize as rightfully maintained by those who use it. If a person with a gun forces a driver over to the side of the road, then that person has simply demonstrated power. On the other hand, if a police officer flags down a motorist, the officer is employing his or her authority.

Power, authority, and politics are closely related. The **political institution** is the system of norms and roles that concerns the use and distribution of authority within a given society. Participants in the political process maintain

social order and enact changes in the legal structure. The American political system is a democracy. A **democracy** is a government in which those in power are acting with the consent of the governed.

The **economic institution** is the system of norms and roles developed for the production, distribution, and consumption of goods and services. The economic institution meets the basic material needs and demands of the citizens within a society.

In the following sections, we examine two prominent theories about the distribution of authority and the three systems by which leaders obtain and exercise authority. Then the discussion shifts to American politics and its corruption. The second principal part of the chapter examines modern economic systems, with the dominant role played by capitalism in our society and an analyis of work in modern times the main topics addressed.

Theories on the Concentration of Authority

The following discussion demonstrates that social scientists have developed varied conceptions about the role of authority in American society. The two theories discussed in this section provide such different perspectives that one might even begin to lose sight of the fact that their proponents are describing the same political system.

PLURALISM

Pluralism is a theory that emphasizes that a dispersion of authority exists in American government. The supporters of this theory point out the existence of elected officials at the local, state, and national levels, all of whom are held accountable to constituents who in turn exercise authority with their votes. Proponents of pluralism believe that if authority is dispersed, then:

1. Authority will be controlled and limited to decent purposes because different centers will counterbalance each other. The evil, coercive use of power will remain at a minimum.

2. Minorities, who will have the authority to veto policies they strongly oppose, will be partners in the exercise of authority and therefore be more cooperative in the long run.

3. Constant negotiations among different centers of authority will be necessary to reach resolutions on political issues. The process of negotiation will provide those engaged in politics with opportunities for learning how to reach peaceful decisions beneficial to all parties in contention (Dahl 1967).

Recent research on pluralism has examined its relationship to the development of minor political parties (Kim and Ohn 1991), the education of American leaders (Lee 1991), and the growth of democracy in Far Eastern nations (Tiglao 1991).

Some leading proponents of pluralism have acknowledged that American democracy has been plagued with serious problems—in particular, the abuse of authority by political leaders during the Vietnam War and the Watergate and Iran-*contra*

370

scandals as well as a failure to achieve the resolution to such social problems as the maldistribution of income and wealth, racial inequality, inadequate health care, and unemployment (Dahl 1982; Lindblom 1982). Although some leading pluralists have acknowledged various limitations to American democracy, they tend to be supporters of the political status quo. With this fact in mind, one critic has recently questioned whether pluralists are willing to advocate sufficient change in the political system to eliminate or even curtail the problems they now acknowledge (Manley 1983).

POWER-ELITE PERSPECTIVE

This theory, popularized in the work of C. Wright Mills (1959), opposes the pluralist approach. The **power-elite perspective** is a theory emphasizing that in American society a group of high-status people—well educated, often wealthy, and placed in high occupational positions—control the political process, including political authorities. The members of the power elite see themselves as an exalted group set apart from the other members of society. They "accept one another, understand one another, marry one another, tend to work and to think if not together at least alike" (Mills 1959, 11). According to Mills, the power elite controls basic political, economic, and military policy. Mills visualized three levels of society in America. At the top is the power elite. Then there is a middle class of white-collar employees. The members of this class are "in no political way united or coherent." They are dominated by the corporations and the government agencies for which they work. They have, in short, little or no control over their own lives. At the bottom there is a mass society of people, whose lives lack purposeful direction and whose access to channels of authority and influence is entirely cut off (Mills 1959).

Sociologist G. William Domhoff (1983; 1990) provided evidence supporting the power-elite the-

ory in the United States. He studied the upper class composed of about 0.5 percent of the population and measured by membership in the Social Register (restricted to families that consider themselves an economic and social elite—"high society"), attendance at elite private schools, membership in exclusive clubs, and wealth. He found that members of this class have disproportional representation in high positions in business, politics, and the military. Extensive evidence also indicated that the American government has aggressively acted on behalf of powerful business interests, both nationally and internationally. Sometimes the government has even backed violent intervention in support of wealthy commercial interests. A number of years ago, a notable case in point was the participation of the Central Intelligence Agency (CIA) and International Telephone and Telegraph (ITT) in the unsuccessful effort to prevent the election of Salvador Allende to the presidency of Chile and then later their involvement in the successful effort to overthrow his socialist regime (Wise 1976; Wolfe 1973). Domhoff concluded that the only possible way to adopt a pluralistic perspective would be to ignore the privileged backgrounds, wealth, and diversified and interrelated activities and interests of people in the upper class.

A study of 243 corporations donating large sums of money to congressional candidates found considerable support for this theory's emphasis on a shared conservative ideology among power-elite members (Neustadtl and Clawson 1988). Furthermore other studies have analyzed the relationship between a power elite and unemployment (Korpi 1991), the savings-and-loan scandal (Thomas 1991), and interest-group development (Walker 1991).

We have examined two opposing theories involving the dispersion of authority. The upcoming section also focuses on authority, offering a theoretical analysis of three authority patterns.

Types of Authority ∎

Max Weber (1947), the German sociologist, described three systems of authority that exist in political systems throughout the world. These sys-

tems of authority are ideal types, and as we saw in the discussion of bureaucracies in Chapter 4, "Groups," ideal types are simplifications of reality made to improve understanding. Actual political systems usually contain elements of two or even all three of Weber's authority systems. The United States is such a society, with the traditional, legal-rational, and the charismatic types all represented in the political structure.

TRADITIONAL SYSTEM

A **traditional system of authority** is an authority system in which the standard of political leadership passes down from one generation to another. Weber said that within the traditional system inherited authority is believed "to have always existed." In this political context, the leaders' authority ranges widely because followers must fulfill almost unlimited obligations (Weber 1947, 341–42). Yet within such a system, people's loyalty focuses on the position and not the incumbent, as the following declaration indicates: "The King is dead! Long live the King!"

Throughout American history citizens have demonstrated mixed reactions toward a traditional system of authority. During the first session of the Senate, Vice-President John Adams and others sought to make "His Highness" the title by which citizens would address the president. Adams and his associates lost out to the simpler title "Mr. President." Some of the most prominent leaders, including George Washington, James Madison, Alexander Hamilton, and John Adams, saw themselves as a natural aristocracy, "a gentlemanly elite to whom ordinary people, if they were only left alone, would naturally defer" (Bailyn et al. 1977, 359). In his farewell address, Washington contended that political parties were a mistake. Parties would readily become factions and thus sources of conflict.

Thomas Jefferson shared Washington's dislike of political parties, but he believed that they were necessary. Jefferson was disturbed by the extent to which early government leaders had consolidated authority. He also believed that these leaders were detached from ordinary citizens' interests. Jefferson led the movement to form the Democratic Republican Party (which later became the Democratic Party) in order to defeat the aristocratic interests of Washington, Adams, and other prominent leaders.

The American curiosity about the British royal family, especially about Charles and Diana's troubled marriage, demonstrates that while the United States has no traditional system of authority, its citizens are intrigued by the principal players in such a system.

Although the American government has had some traditional tendencies, it more distinctly resembles Weber's second authority type.

LEGAL-RATIONAL SYSTEM

The **legal-rational system of authority** is an authority system based on laws enacted to produce rational behavior and the achievement of formally designated goals. The system depends on participants' competent performance. These people are "servants of the state" (nation), who work within government departments and agencies at the national, state, county, and local levels. Like bureaucrats generally, government officials must follow rationally determined rules and meet the formal qualifications of education and experience that will ensure competent performance in their specific positions (Gerth and Mills 1946, 79, 196–98).

Many Americans are generally critical of the legal-rational element in the government. People frequently claim that the federal government is too large and too encumbered with "red tape." For over half-a-century politicians have spoken about curtailing the size of the federal government, with a particular emphasis on the elimination of overlapping functions performed by different agencies. In the past three decades, most presidents have stressed that the best way to restrict the size of the federal government is to transfer increasing responsibility in education, transportation, community development, and social services to the states.

Recently Ralph Hummel (1990), an expert on management practices, asserted that unlike many of its trade competitors, the United States does not possess a coherent bureaucratic policy to structure productive activity in either the private or public sector. As a result when changes are enacted in bureaucratic structures, the absence of policy encourages disorganization, even chaos. For instance, when American dominance of mass production began slipping in the 1970s, industrial leaders desperately started introducing Japanese production methods into their factories, accepting the Japanese bureaucratic directive that hands-on workers possessed a distinct type of knowledge that contributed to quality production. However, in their frantic rush to incorporate this new approach, most company officials had little sense of how this knowledge was obtained or how it could be communicated to management. Thus the benefits provided by this superficial adaptation of the Japanese system were at best modest (Hummel 1990).

Both the traditional and legal-rational systems tend to entrench themselves in societies, often persisting generation after generation no matter what individuals fill the leadership roles. As we will see, the charismatic system is different in this respect.

CHARISMATIC SYSTEM

The **charismatic system of authority** is an authority system in which leadership develops because of the personal magnetism of an individual, whose followers believe that he or she possesses superhuman qualities. In Weber's phrase the charismatic leader maintains authority "by proving his strength in life." If followers decide to reject a charismatic leader's sense of mission, then the leadership collapses. Few things are ordinary or regularized about a charismatic leader: no career

pattern, no formal training, and the rejection of conventional institutions and behavioral standards.

Charismatic leaders often arise when deep-seated problems exist within a society, and their mission usually involves an effort to change society and eliminate social problems, thereby producing a better life for their followers. The behavior of charismatic leaders is often disruptive, opposing established policies and practices (Gerth and Mills 1946, 245–50; Seligman 1991).

A number of prominent American politicians have been considered to possess charismatic qualities. One would be the late Senator Robert Kennedy. He was killed on the evening of his victory in the California presidential primary, when the road to the White House seemed unblockable. To Americans of wide-ranging political views, Robert Kennedy seemed to be the presidential candidate who could best move toward the resolution of the various social problems which helped create the dissensions and conflicts of the late 1960s. In this respect he was charismatic. In one Weberian respect, however, he did not qualify as a charismatic leader—he operated within the established political system.

Charismatic leaders are likely to appeal to the discontented, deprived members of society. By Weber's standard John Brown, Sitting Bull, Malcolm X, and Charles Manson qualify as charismatic. Outside the United States, Mao Zedong, Fidel Castro, Adolf Hitler, Joan of Arc, and Napoleon would qualify. Manson and Hitler were charismatic individuals who clearly illustrate the fact that the possession of charisma is not an attribute restricted to people most of us would consider "humanitarian" or "good." It is simply a question of whether a person performs the function of the charismatic leadership role, and someone who does qualifies as charismatic. (This chapter concludes with a research section about charismatic leadership.)

Thus the American political system has contained elements of Weber's three authority types. Table 13.1 summarizes the previous discussion.

Now move beyond theory and consider the actual workings of the political system.

Table 13.1 Weber's Three Authority Systems

Authority system	Basis of authority	Possessors of authority	Controversial appearance in American society
Traditional	Standard of political leadership passed from one generation to another	Royalty or chieftains	Political orientation of the early leaders' "gentlemanly elite"
Legal-rational	Laws enacted to produce rational behavior and the achievement of formally designated goals	Government bureaucrats	Presidents' and other politicans' half-century effort to trim the size of the federal government
Charismatic	Followers' belief that a leader possesses special, even supernatural qualities	Individuals who appear at crisis times and promise to establish a better life for their followers	Political activities of leaders like Robert Kennedy and Malcolm X, whose sense of mission primarily represented the dispossessed and conflicted with many Americans' economic and political priorities

Source: Adapted from Hans Gerth and C. Wright Mills (eds.). From Max Weber. New York: Oxford University Press, 1946.

American Politics and Its Corruption

In the 1830s a young Frenchman named Alexis de Tocqueville (1966) visited America and wrote about American society. Some of his observations about the American political process remain accurate today. A pair of his insights summarize central themes of this section: the widespread desire of people to participate in the democratic process and the tendency of influential citizens to corrupt the process.

On the first point, de Tocqueville felt that a large amount of political activity occurred in America, with a wide range of groups mobilizing political action on behalf of their own interests. The Frenchman concluded that nothing was more important to Americans than discussion about their political involvement. According to de Tocqueville, Americans often became so involved in politics that they tended to speak as if addressing a meeting. In fact, Americans could become so excited with the subject that they would sometimes address an audience of one as "Gentlemen."

De Tocqueville claimed that many wealthy people appeared to support democracy. They tended to dress simply and to maintain a modest manner. If an affluent man met his shoemaker in the street, he would stop to talk with him, and most likely they would discuss politics. When they parted, they would inevitably shake hands as equals. If democracy were ever in peril, however, this same affluent man would be happy to help bring about its demise if his interests would benefit. Hence, while de Tocqueville saw authority widely dispersed in American society, he recognized the dangerous potential for the concentration of power in the hands of a few.

Corruption, de Tocqueville seemed to recognize, was an ever-present possibility in American politics. In this section we see the impact of corruption in discussions of interest-group activity, and patronage and the political machine. First, though, we examine the American system of politics.

This display represents the leaders of France's major political parties and suggests that they should have a one-round free-for-all to decide which party dominates. An equivalent American display would present only two figures.

THE TWO-PARTY SYSTEM

At the American Constitutional Convention of 1787, the delegates opposed "factions" because they feared that political parties would destroy the newly formed nation. Early advocates of political parties like Thomas Jefferson and James Madison believed that opposing, lasting differences of opinion, which political parties represent, are necessary in a free country, even if clashing party ambitions will sometimes endanger the existence of the country. Jefferson, Madison, and others felt that it would be impossible to support the basic freedoms of speech, press, and assembly and simultaneously oppose the development of political parties. The convention's decision to hold peri-

odic elections among the people also favored the development of political parties (Dahl 1976, 275–77).

Political parties provide a number of functions. First, they make the transfer of authority from one administration to another peaceful and smooth. When presidents, governors, or mayors leave office, the newly elected officials move in, bringing with them a slate of the party faithful who can fill government posts, judicial openings, or office staff positions. Thus for such transfers parties can act as large personnel agencies. Second, parties are a major source of recruitment for government leaders. People who run for local, state, and federal offices have usually been active in party politics, where they display potential leadership qualities. Third, parties simplify voters' choices by providing party labels as a guideline. The majority of American citizens have limited knowledge about the wide array of candidates for whom they are entitled to vote, and so without the party labels to assist them, they would often be completely lost. Fourth, American parties supply a series of platforms and policies. These directives may be somewhat vague and are not always clearly differentiated between the two major parties, but they do broadly support the interests of different voter groups—more distinctly with some issues than others (Grant 1979, 196–97).

Certainly the American political parties do not always meet their members' needs and interests. Yet the two parties have been successful enough to have dominated most of U.S. political history. Two parties have prevailed for several reasons. In the first place, in the United States, a broad consensus on political issues shared by both political parties exists. Whether Democrats or Republicans, Americans generally express a commitment to democracy, the Constitution, the free-enterprise economic system, universal free public education, and religious and racial tolerance. In contrast, in some other democratic countries, sharp disagreement on specific issues can be the basis for lasting political factions—for instance, Catholic parties in Italy and the Netherlands, farmers' parties in the Scandinavian countries, and working-class parties throughout Europe. Second, the electoral process also encourages a two-party system. In the United States, a winner-take-all process prevails. For instance, in the Congressional elections each state is divided into districts, and within each district the person receiving the highest vote total obtains the seat. In a number of other democratic countries, on the other hand, there is a system of proportional representation, where each party receives the percentage of seats that corresponds with its total vote. Such a system encourages minority parties, which will receive little or no representation under the U.S. political system. Finally another factor supporting the two-party system is the force of habit and tradition. For over a century, the current two parties have dominated politics. Many Americans receive their party loyalties and political positions from their parents and in turn transmit similar loyalties and positions to their own children (Dahl 1976, 287–91).

In recent years the two-party system has worked more effectively for some Americans than for others. The Republican administration's tax and spending policies have benefitted most Republicans and also affluent Democrats. On the other hand, low-income Democrats have either seen their tax burdens increase or have received the proportionally smallest tax reductions (Edsall 1986). In many other political systems, there would be one or more political parties to represent this group's specific interests.

For over two centuries, the United States has maintained a stable political democracy. We are not directly aware of the problems a country must face as it moves from dictatorship to political democracy. Spain accomplished this shift in the late 1970s, as the nearby Cross-Cultural Perspective indicates.

INTEREST GROUPS

Some efforts to influence politicians are illegal, but there is nothing inherently illegal about trying to influence politicians. In fact, interest groups are widespread in American society. An **interest group** is a group whose members seek to influence elected politicians or government bureaucrats to initiate the legislation or policies they want. In the American political system, there are thousands of organizations "representing or claiming to represent trade unionists, veterans, business people, industrialists, taxpayers, bankers, oil companies, copper importers, doctors, women's clubs, nature lovers, stream pollutionists, conservationists, foreign policy groups, old people" (Dahl 1976, 482).

Some citizens' interest groups write letters to politicians, organize petition drives, or advertise in the media. Large, wealthy interest groups might advertise and write to politicians, but they are more likely than citizens' groups to engage extensively in lobbying activities. **Lobbying** is a face-to-face effort to persuade legislators and other government personnel to support the proposals of an interest group. Those proposals might involve the provision of tax loopholes that benefit various businesses, or lobbying might help produce legislation that protects the needs of organizations as diverse as the American Medical Association, the Associated Milk Producers, Inc., and United Aircraft. On the other hand, interest groups or their representatives might act to postpone legislation; the lobbying efforts of the National Rifle Association have prevented the passage of any effective gun-control legislation. Studies indicate that at the federal level, the amount of interest-group activity has sharply increased in recent years. In particular, political-action committees (PACs) started by large corporations have been making major contributions to conservative presidential and congressional candidates.

A recent study of PACs found that it was possible to predict quite accurately what companies would have them. Among the most likely corporations were those that are large—thus have the financial ability to make large investments to increase their massive profit potentials—and those that are likely to be subjected to extensive governmental regulation, particularly in the areas of environmental pollution and occupational safety—thus those that are in a situation to benefit extensively from politicians' intervention with government officials on their behalf (Humphries 1991). Table 13.2 summarizes PAC contributions to candidates during the 1989–1990 congressional campaigns.

Why are interest groups so prevalent in U.S. society? A prominent reason is that the political system rests on the simple idea that government exists in order to protect people's rights. A well-known phrase states the condition widely believed by Americans to effectively protect these rights: The government governs best that governs least. John Locke expressed this political philosophy in his *Second Treatise on Civil Government*, and when Thomas Jefferson wrote the Declaration of Independence, he received much of his inspiration

CROSS-CULTURAL PERSPECTIVE
From Dictatorship to Democracy: The Spanish Case

The transition from dictatorship to democracy is a complex and ticklish process. Because of a combination of skillful national leadership and cooperative efforts from the major political parties involved, Spain successfully completed the transition in 1977.

On November 20, 1975, Francisco Franco, the dictator of Spain for thirty-six years, died. The new head of state was King Juan Carlos, who had been appointed by Franco as the individual most likely to perpetuate the standards and the structures of the Franco dictatorship. For a six-year period before Franco's death, Juan Carlos expressed public loyalty to the regime, but only his most intimate friends knew that he had strong sympathies for a democratic form of government.

Nonetheless Juan Carlos's first appointments were a disappointment to supporters of democratic rule. In particular, legal restrictions made it impossible to choose a democratically oriented prime minister, and he picked Arias Novarro, a strong backer of Francoist policies. Arias held office for about six months. His refusal to support significant political and economic reforms provoked strikes and major street demonstrations. Toward the end he even lost the support of his fellow Francoists when he agreed to make the most modest reforms to existing policies.

Arias resigned, and in his place King Juan Carlos appointed Adolfo Suarez. By all reasonable criteria, Suarez seemed to be the finest choice as prime minister for the difficult period of transition to democracy. He was experienced politically, having held diverse posts in the Franco regime. He clearly saw that the remaining Franco supporters lacked the backing to maintain their system but that no opposition parties had the public support or the organizational unity and strength to assume the leadership. Suarez realized it was up to him to lead his nation gradually but relentlessly toward democratic rule. Besides knowledge and perceptiveness, Suarez had the right personal qualities for the task. He was flexible, self-disciplined, emotionally controlled, energetic at public relations, and above all, forceful.

During the late 1970s, Suarez maneuvered skillfully around the obstacles that opposed a transition to democratic rule. He worked carefully with his closest allies—King Juan Carlos and a number of other influential, progressively oriented individuals. He also managed to maintain effective relations with the army, enlisting senior officers' support for his reformist program. A prominent reason these individuals and groups were willing to back Suarez was his determination to act entirely within the guidelines of the legal processes set down in the Francoist Constitution.

While the prime minister was courting the support of established individuals and groups, he was also determined to obtain backing from the developing political parties. The moderate opposition to Francoism—the Liberals, Christian Democrats, and the Social Democrats—readily approved his program. Even the rapidly growing Spanish Socialist Workers' Party recognized that Suarez's program for restoring democracy was in the best interest of the nation—that at times, as one leader said, "it's most revolutionary to be moderate."

Finally negotiations with the Communists were the only obstacle. Suarez was reluctant to cooperate with the Communists, whose support for his program seemed doubtful. Other moderates agreed that it would be better to keep the Communists out of the upcoming elections. The Communists were unhappy with this prospect, and one of their most prominent leaders appeared openly in Madrid—a public challenge to Suarez's government since his party was still illegal. To maintain his authority, Suarez had no choice but to arrest this Communist leader. That action, in turn, endangered Suarez's entire program. Most of the moderates had no use for the Communists, but the arrest of their leader undermined the democratic credentials of Suarez and his administration. Suarez had no other option. He released the Communist leader and enlisted the help of King

Juan Carlos and Vice-President Gutierrez Mellado to convince the military leaders, the staunchest opponents of Communism, that it was essential to permit the Communists to become a legal political party. Army leaders publicly expressed their dissatisfaction with this decision but said that out of patriotism they would cooperate. No military coup occurred. The Communist leaders, in turn, also made a number of significant concessions.

In this context of cooperation and compromise, a national vote on the government's political reform was held on December 15, 1976. Over 77 percent of the electorate went to the polls, and 94.2 percent of those voters supported the government's political reform, which featured elections in June 1977.

The elections were a triumph for an expanding democratic program. The Suarez coalition received 34.3 percent of the popular vote, and the Spanish Socialist Workers Party was

a highly respectable runner-up, with 28.5 percent. Both the remnants of Francoism and the Communists received modest support. In 1982 the Socialist party won majority control in the national elections. Thus, within less than a decade, a modern European nation had used a democratic political process to move across the political spectrum: from a repressive, highly conservative dictatorship to an elected socialist government.

Sources: Raymond Carr and Juan Pablo Fusi Aizpurua. Spain: Dictatorship to Democracy. 2nd ed. London: George Allen and Unwin, 1981, pp. 207–58; Meir Serfaty. "Spanish Democracy: The End of the Transition," Current History. vol. 80 (May 1981), pp. 213–17+.

from Locke's book. In the more than two hundred years since the signing of the Declaration, Americans have generally accepted this political philosophy. As a result there has been much less government regulation in the lives of the American citizenry than in many other societies. Wealthy and powerful interests have been prominent beneficiaries of this clear absence of regulation (Roelofs 1967, Chapter 6). When these groups have chosen to further their own interests at the expense of

ordinary citizens, they have encountered few if any limits or penalties. Through the late 1970s and into the early 1980s, the rapid rise in oil prices accompanied by a large increase in company profits was a case in point.

A recent analysis indicated that in the late 1960s and early 1970s, new anti-pollution and occupational safety legislation promoted a massive mobilization of interest groups dedicated to convincing politicians to intervene with officials

Table 13.2 PAC Contributions to Congressional Campaigns: 1989–90[1]

	Corporations	HOUSE OF REPRESENTATIVES Trade associations[2]	Labor
Democrats	18.7	19.3	25.8
Republicans	16.7	13.3	1.8

	Corporations	SENATE Trade associations	Labor
Democrats	6.1	4.2	5.6
Republicans	11.9	5.8	.4

[1] In millions of dollars
[2] A variety of occupationally affiliated organizations

Source: U.S. Bureau of the Census. Statistical Abstract of the United States: 1992, No. 447.

Political-action committees (PACs) raise money to support the candidates of their choice. This table shows that Republican congressional candidates receive a slightly larger share of corporate contributions, while their Democratic opponents receive much greater support from labor.

378   on behalf of corporate clients' needs for relaxing regulations to which they were subjected. In 1971 less than 200 companies had registered lobbyists in the capital; a decade later the number had increased tenfold, to over 2,000 corporations with hired political representation (Greider 1992).

One of Dan Quayle's duties as vice-president was the chairmanship of what started as an obscure committee called the President's Council on Competitiveness. Privately Quayle was able to use that post to weaken or disregard regulations considered unfriendly by corporations that had made large donations to Republican candidates, with air pollution serving as the most prominent target. Following requests from a number of large corporations to relax new federal standards for air pollution applying to the 34,000 chemical plants, oil refineries, factories, and power plants owned by large corporations, Quayle's staff issued a list of "suggested changes" that permitted these companies to rewrite their own air-regulation permits providing almost unlimited rights to release toxic pollutants. Corporate leaders were only required to notify their state environmental agencies of the revisions they sought, and if they heard nothing in seven days—a virtual certainty with normal bureaucratic inefficiency—they were cleared to proceed (Sibbison 1991).

While interest groups and lobbying are legal, pay-offs to politicians obviously are not. The problem is where to draw the line. One could argue that even when lobbyists take politicians to dinner, they are actually offering them a low-level bribe: spending money on them in order to encourage action on behalf of their own interests. Evidence from the past fifteen years demonstrates that many prominent politicians have taken much more substantial bribes from lobbyists. On the list have been a president (Richard Nixon), a vice-president (Spiro Agnew), a Supreme Court justice who had been nominated for chief justice (Abe Fortas), and a long list of governors, congressmen, and mayors. In the 1980 Abscam scandal, a senator and a half-dozen congressmen accepted bribes from undercover FBI agents pretending to act on behalf of Arab oil men seeking political favors. A team of historians claimed that these various scandals represent "the fall of the great men." Each new scandal "was more shocking than the last, and each set an historic precedent" (Bailyn et al. 1977,

In April 1992 Charles Keating, Jr., former head of Lincoln Savings and Loan and the most publicized participant in the savings and loan scandal, was in obvious distress as he awaited sentencing for seventeen counts of securities fraud. For the American taxpayers the distress comes in the form of a $500 billion price tag.

1262). The most massive scandal has been an enormous scheme of fraud and mismanagement that has undermined the savings and loan industry, implicated hundreds of politicians, and could cost the American taxpayers as much as $500 billion over forty years (Stevenson 1992). In one writer's phrase, it was "the greatest ever bank robbery" (Thomas 1991).

Not surprisingly Americans do not believe that politicians lead exemplary lives. When in October 1991 a national sample of adult Americans was asked about confidence in various structures, only 18 percent indicated a great deal or quite a lot of confidence in Congress. This figure was the lowest since the question was first asked in 1973 when the reply to the same question was 42 percent. In 1991 other structures were much better regarded than Congress—with 69 percent of respondents opting for a great deal or quite a lot of confidence in the military and 56 percent making the same choices for organized religion (Gallup and Newport 1991).

PATRONAGE AND THE POLITICAL MACHINE

George Washington Plunkitt, a prominent, corrupt nineteenth-century politician, once said: "Men ain't in politics for nothin, they want something out of it" (Riordan 1963, 21).

Candidates for political office would agree. If elected they will reward those who worked for their election. The distribution of favors to political supporters is called **patronage.** Sometimes patronage simply means giving jobs, which can be done in a legal manner, but it can also involve illegal activities: provision of construction contracts, defense contracts, banking and insurance funds, and specialized treatment by government agencies (Tolchin and Tolchin 1972, 6). Favors such as these will establish the loyalty of one's supporters and thus help secure a politician in power.

In the United States, civil-service systems require that applicants for many government jobs be chosen under a merit, not a patronage system (Ranney 1966, 468). However, the most powerful nonelected government jobs remain appointments, which are subject to the patronage system. Evidence suggests, for example, that patronage is a prominent factor influencing presidents' selection of their cabinet members (Burstein 1977).

Political machines also use a patronage system. A **political machine** is an organization established to control a city, county, or state government. At the head is a political boss, who seeks to dominate political activity within the machine's jurisdiction. In exchange for political control and perhaps pay-offs, too, bosses and their associates provide certain advantages for different groups.

Robert Merton's (1968) well-known analysis of urban political machines in American cities argued that these arrangements emerged to satisfy a variety of local citizens' needs left unfulfilled by local city governments. Recently, however, a careful historical examination of the development of urban political machines revealed a critical factor about their emergence—that these structures only developed when the executive authority within a city was officially consolidated in the hands of one individual—the strong-mayor system—or in the hands of a few people—the commission form of government. Then, this argument went, that individual or group had the authority to control political patronage and with that control the means to establish and entrench the political machine (Digaetano 1988).

Throughout the discussion of the political institution, we have seen that in both its legitimate and illegitimate use, power is the politician's everyday companion. For business people, particularly big business people, we will see that power is also a tool quickly grasped.

From the earliest days of American history, a relationship between the political and economic institutions has existed. In 1629 John Winthrop, the first governor of Massachusetts, was a prosperous business man. Throughout American history the two institutions have shared an ideology emphasizing people's right to pursue an unrestricted existence: There is the Jeffersonian ideal that the politician who governs best governs least and Adam Smith's free-enterprise standard of the self-regulating market. At the same time, both politicians and business people are power brokers, affecting or controlling the destinies of thousands, and in some cases, millions of people.

The Corporate State

In his study of American society, Alexis de Tocqueville observed not only the American political process but successful American business enterprises as well. De Tocqueville claimed that the superiority of American businesses over their European counterparts was based on one factor: the ability to ship their goods more cheaply. But

why? American ships cost as much as the European vessels, and the sailors received higher wages than their European counterparts. The reason, de Tocqueville concluded, was that the American sailors were willing to take more chances. Admittedly they were shipwrecked more frequently, but no one else crossed the ocean so

380

quickly, and this timesaving saved money. For example, a captain would leave Boston and go to China to buy tea. He would arrive at Canton, stay a few days, and come back. In less than two years, he had gone around the world, and he had seen land only once. During an eight- to ten-month voyage, he had drunk brackish water and eaten only salted meat. The captain had fought the sea, disease, and boredom, but on his return he could sell tea a few pennies cheaper than his English competition. And that in a nutshell was what he was trying to do (de Tocqueville 1966, 368–69).

In writing about what he called "the commercial greatness of the United States," de Tocqueville emphasized the daring of American sailors. But a number of other factors encouraged the explosive development of the economic system—in particular, a range of rich natural resources, a large adult labor force arriving from Europe and Africa, isolation from the disruptive European wars, and, in particular, Adam Smith's revolutionary ideas about economic development.

The rest of this chapter examines the economic institution—the system of norms and roles developed for the production, distribution, and consumption of goods and services. Throughout the material on the political institution, we have frequently seen its relationship with the economic institution—in particular, in discussions indicating that many business people attempt to influence politicians to establish policies or pass laws which they want. The relationship between the two institutions remains apparent in the upcoming sections, especially in the analysis of how corporations exert influence in the political sphere.

ECONOMIC IDEOLOGIES: CAPITALISM VERSUS SOCIALISM

Perhaps we in the United States are more concerned than are the people of other nations with the threat of opposing values, beliefs, and activities. After all, we have a word for it: "un-American." The British or the French do not have a comparable word. Even our most recent powerful political rivals—the Soviets—did not classify any people's values, beliefs, and activities as "un-Soviet." We in this country are unique in this respect. In fact, at one time a congressional committee existed—the House Un-American Activities Committee—to investigate such matters. Such a classification pre-

sents a problem: It tends to preclude thoughtful analysis. Consider, for instance, the two economic systems we are about to examine. To many Americans capitalism is American/good, and socialism is un-American/bad. To some people there is no need to look further. We will.

Capitalism and socialism are economic systems, and therefore both concern themselves with the production and distribution of goods and services. The American system is capitalist. **Capital** is money, goods, or other forms of wealth invested to produce more wealth. **Capitalism** is an economic system where capital is controlled by private citizens who own the means of production and distribution of goods and services. **Socialism** is an economic system with collective ownership of the means of production and distribution of goods and services. Socialist measures range from limited steps advocating the public ownership of a few businesses to extensive control over economic planning and its implementation.

The Development of Capitalism

To Americans 1776 is renowned as the year when the Declaration of Independence was written and signed and the nation officially began. To the rest of the Western world, however, 1776 has received more recognition as the year the Scottish philosopher Adam Smith (1723–1790) published *The Wealth of Nations*, in which he presented the first complete theory of economic behavior (Smith 1930).

Smith began with the central idea that the great motivator of economic activity is all participants' powerful desire to better their own condition—in short, self-interest. Self-interest, Smith argued, produces the miracle of the capitalist system: the self-regulating market. If consumers are free to spend their money as they wish and if business people can compete equally for their patronage, then capital and labor certainly will be used where they are most needed. Thus if consumers want more shoes than are currently produced, they will pay high prices for shoes, and shoemakers will make a good profit. Those profits, in turn, will draw new investors into the shoe market. If more shoes are produced than consumers want, the price will fall, and investors will turn to other products—socks perhaps. In addition, competition wipes out the inefficient businesses, rewarding those who turn out the best products at the lowest prices and forcing even the successful people to invest in new products and procedures if they want to stay ahead of their competitors. Smith explained that this process keeps production rising, pulling up wages at the same time. The overall result is that while business people are seeking only their own profit, they become part of a market process that promotes the common good.

In Adam Smith's view, however, business people are likely to attempt to undermine the common good by trying to fix prices and keep down wages, efforts Smith believed could succeed only if government actively helps business. For this reason Smith strongly advocated that the economic system be "laissez-faire" (literally, let do), meaning that it should be allowed to function without government intervention.

By the early nineteenth century, many people had read *The Wealth of Nations*, and most Western governments accepted Smith's basic ideas. Open competition in the marketplace became the standard of the day, and the power of Adam Smith's theory seemed indisputable to many. Businessmen accumulated and reinvested capital in awesomely large amounts compared to the amounts of precapitalist times. For instance, the world production of pig iron (iron in an unrefined state) rose from 10 million tons in 1867 to 357 million tons a century later. As recently as 1850, human muscle and animal power produced 94 percent of the energy used in American industry, whereas today these sources supply less than 1 percent.

Although capitalism created industrial expansion, it was also a disruptive force. The Industrial Revolution wiped out the rural cottage industries and forced workers to enter the new factory towns, where living conditions were crowded and squalid. Wages were low, and to help support their families, children as young as 8 would work up to fourteen hours a day in factories and mines. At the same time, Andrew Carnegie, John D. Rockefeller, and other capitalists accumulated vast fortunes. In addition, there were depressions, which caused economic analysts to question whether the market could be self-regulating.

The Great Depression of the 1930s inspired the economic theory of John Maynard Keynes. Keynes, a British economist, argued that a government can generate an economic upsurge by using tax cuts, extensive government spending, and the outright creation of more money. Since World War II, capitalist governments have adoped Keynesian measures, and none of them would ever consider leaving a depression to right itself. Consequently widespread agreement now exists that a modern capitalist system cannot be entirely self-regulating; at least some government intervention appears periodically necessary (Greenberg 1974; Samuelson 1980).

Adam Smith provided the theory on which capitalism was based. For socialism Karl Marx supplied the basic perspective.

The Development of Socialism

In 1848, in *The Communist Manifesto*, Karl Marx described the conditions he believed would produce socialism from capitalism. Marx contended that within capitalism the interests of the capitalists and their workers are irreconcilably opposed. The capitalists' dominant interest is in increasing their profits. The workers' primary concern is increasing wages and improving job conditions. But since the owners are more powerful, their drive for profits will dominate. As a result certain developments will occur—in particular, the growing concentration of wealth in the hands of a few large businesses that absorb the small ones; the increasing use of machinery; the displacement of more and more workers, thereby creating widespread unemployment; and the recurrence of periodic, increasingly acute breakdowns in the economy.

At some point the workers will recognize that the economic system is the source of their problems and that these problems are shared by all workers. The workers will also see that since they represent the majority of the citizenry, they are potentially stronger that the owners. Eventually they will organize themselves into an army and will rise up and overthrow the owners. At this point the means of production and distribution will be in the hands of the people—in short, socialism (Marx 1932).

Socialist Philosophy   Marx devoted his energy to the criticism of capitalism. He wrote little about the content of socialism and did not live to see the existence of a socialist nation.

A few elements distinctly characterize modern socialist philosophy. They include:

1. ***Government ownership of productive resources.*** Key industries such as railroads, coal, and steel are nationalized in the effort to downplay the role of private property.

2. ***Planning.*** Coordinated, centralized planning replaces the free play of the profit motive in a laissez-faire economy. There is an emphasis on "production for use rather than profit." Citizens are encouraged to develop craftsmanship and social services and to downplay the materialistic tendencies so strong in the Western "acquisitive societies."

3. ***Redistribution of income.*** Government taxing power sharply reduces inherited wealth. Social-security benefits and cradle-to-grave assistance programs will insure the well-being of previously poor people (Samuelson, 1980, 816–17).

The former Soviet Union, the People's Republic of China, and Cuba have practiced socialism, and Chile, Sweden, Great Britain, Norway, Australia, and France have had governments with socialist platforms.

Americans have traditionally opposed socialism. In a 1942 survey, 25 percent of the respondents indicated that some form of socialism would be a good thing for the country, and 40 percent felt it would be a bad thing (Roper Organization, *Fortune Survey* 1942). Thirty-four years later, only 10 percent of the respondents said they would support the introduction of socialism in the United States, whereas 62 percent opposed its introduction (*Cambridge Reports* March 1976). These are not surprising findings when we consider the dominance of capitalist activities in U.S. society.

It should be emphasized that like all ideologies both capitalism and socialism seldom exist in absolutely pure form. Capitalist societies often contain some socialist elements—a range of governmental assistance programs in health care and income subsidy, for instance—and socialist nations have permitted foreign capitalist involvement.

Two scholars, one from Russia and the other from the United States, argued that the recent collapse of socialist governments in the former Soviet Union and in eastern Europe suggested to many observers that around the world, socialism was dead and capitalism would triumph. These writers disagreed, suggesting that former socialist nations are likely to develop a synthesis of socialism and capitalism—that while capitalism will make further advances into these countries, evidence indicates that their citizens fear the risks and inequalities of capitalism and that therefore they are likely to develop market systems that foster the public welfare rather than private gain (Halal and Nikitin 1990).

CAPITALIST ACTIVITY

Mark Twain once wrote that the leading capitalists live by the following gospel: "Get money. Get it quickly. Get it in abundance. Get it in prodigious abundance. Get it dishonestly if you can, honestly if you must" (Twain 1973, 224). In Twain's day, especially at the end of the nineteenth century, the opponents of big business grew rapidly in number. Monopolies, which involve exclusive control by one or several corporations over the production of a commodity, were widely denounced as a conspiracy, evidence of greed, and a misallocation and underuse of resources (Bailyn et al. 1977, 843). But the critics had little effect upon the increasing concentration of corporate power and wealth.

Corporate Power and Wealth

A **corporation** is a legally designated organization that has powers and responsibilities separate from its workers and owners. For instance, in an unincorporated business, the owner may be forced to sell his or her home and possessions to settle business debts. Investors in corporations, however, have limited liability. No investor is responsible for more than the initial investment, and this limited liability attracts backers and serves as a primary basis for extensive capital accumulation and massive growth in the size of some corporations.

In a given year, the 500 largest corporations account for over half—about 55 percent—of the Gross National Product, the sum total of the value of the goods and services produced in the United States in a year. The top hundred corporations have assets of over $1 billion each and yearly sales of more than $2.5 billion each. Corporations with over $250 million in assets account for nearly 75 percent of all corporate income.

The major corporations exert impressive political and social power through a number of sources. They include:

Their wealth. Because of their market domination, the business giants have enormous sums of money that their owners and managers can use the way they choose. They use these sums for continued market domination, especially for increased political and social power. For instance, vast expenditures on advertising support not only the sale of the particular products but also the company image and the legitimate use of the corporate system in general. With profits in mind, American corporations give about $3 billion to charity each year; these contributions frequently serve as an effective form of advertising when the contribution is publicized.

Their accumulation of skilled and talented people. No other modern organization has such a range of talented members, with the possible exception of the federal government. At a moment's notice, a giant corporation can mobilize scientists, social scientists, engineers, lawyers, accountants, management experts, and systems analysts to work together on a problem designated important by management, no matter what it may be— new product development, basic research, public relations, or overseas expansion.

The linkage between citizen and corporate well-being. Large corporations are massive organizations that employ hundreds of thousands of people, and each major corporation has numerous large companies to which it subcontracts its work. In the early 1970s, General Motors employed over 700,000 people, and in a single week in 1980 this largest American corporation laid off 155,000 workers, the population of a small city. In his campaign for a major government loan to stave off bankruptcy, Chrysler President Lee Iaccoca frequently emphasized that if his company went bankrupt, hundreds of thousands of citizens would be forced out of work and into the already long unemployment lines.

Commitment of all public officials to the existing economic and social system. Liberals and conservatives or Republicans and Democrats might have somewhat different outlooks on the economic and social order, but they agree on one fundamental point: The basic principles of the current economic system should not be challenged. With rare exceptions public officials do not make such radical proposals as massive income distribution, restraints on corporate autonomy, or the establishment of public control over the production process. In fact, the relationship between government personnel and corporate leadership is frequently intimate, especially in the realm of national defense and foreign policy. From 1940 to 1967, 77 percent of the individuals who directed the principal foreign policy departments (secretaries and undersecretaries of state and defense, the military service secretaries, the chairmen of the Atomic Energy Commission, and directors of the CIA) came from big business and high finance (Almond 1991; Dugger 1988; Gilpin 1975; Greenberg 1974; Navarro 1988).

The power and influence of U.S. corporations extends well beyond the boundaries of our society. In the twenty-year period following World War II, the United States was dominant in productivity and in its ability to influence the world economy. Currently its economic dominance has slackened as Japan and Germany have surpassed the United States in the rate of economic development.

Recently twenty-five well-known business scholars published a report emphasizing that compared to Japanese and German corporations, U.S. companies invest heavily in short-term profits, thereby restricting growth and failing to provide the long-term benefits to shareholders, workers, companies, and the economy produced in the other two countries (Lohr 1992).

Multinationals

As American corporations helped establish their economic dominance by investing directly in the economies of other countries, multinationals have developed. A **multinational** is a large corporation with production plants and distribution centers in many countries. It draws its natural resources and labor supply and sells its products—as varied as

384   autos, clothes, computers, and oil—around the world. About 200 American corporations are multinational. In 1992 the five largest multinationals were General Motors, Royal Dutch/Shell, Exxon, Ford, and IBM, with all but Royal Dutch/Shell centered in the United States. It is an understatement to say that multinationals are large. Of the 100 largest economic structures in the world, about half are multinationals. The total sales revenue for General Motors in 1992 were greater than the sum of the Gross National Products for Algeria, Egypt, Cuba, and Ethiopia. Figure 13.1 matches the yearly sales revenues of various multinationals with the Gross National Products of different countries.

Figure 13.1

Gross National Products Compared to Corporate Sales: Some Matchings[1]

Sales (billions of dollars)	Gross National Product (billions of dollars)
General Motors (1)[2] $123.8	Denmark $125.7
Royal Dutch/Shell Group (2) $103.8	Austria $103.2
Exxon (3) $103.2	Iran $97.6
Ford (4) $89	Indonesia $80
IBM (5) $65.4	Hungary $64.6
Daimler-Benz (10) $57.3	Algeria $54.1
Unilever (20) $41.3	Egypt $38.3
United Technologies (50) $21.3	Cuba $20.9
Ruhrkohle (100) $14.9	Cameroon $12.9
Noranda (200) $7.2	Ethiopia $6.6
Kia Motors (350) $3.9	Albania $3.8
Pennzoil (500) $2.7	Afghanistan $3

[1]*The Gross National Product is the financial value of yearly goods and services in a national economy. In an economic sense, the GNP is comparable to corporate sales. Both represent the financial value of the products their respective units produce.*
[2]*The numbers in parentheses represent the world corporate rank in sales for 1992.*

This figure demonstrates the enormous wealth and associated power of some major world corporations by comparing their corporate sales in 1992 with the gross national products of foreign countries in 1992.

Sources: Fortune. *vol.* 126 (July 27, 1992); The 1992 Information Please Almanac. 45th ed. New York: Houghton Mifflin, 1991.

Massive corporations invest their capital in a number of ways. Some investments bring raw products to the United States for use domestically: for example, shipment of oil for refinement and use. Other investments involve the sale of American goods abroad. In some cases, such as the automobile industry, a corporation will open a factory abroad to manufacture products for local sale. In addition, the products manufactured abroad are often sold in the United States.

What conditions have encouraged the development of multinationals? In the first place, in many countries tariffs restrict the importation and sale of American products. Any locally manufactured goods, including those produced by multinationals, escape that restriction. Second, foreign labor is likely to be considerably cheaper than in the United States. Third, the shift of operations abroad allows multinationals to avoid some payments of taxes; thus a corporate division in a country with high taxes can avoid these taxes by transferring products to a division in a country with low taxes. Fourth, a multinational strategy seems consistent with a basic capitalist belief— the conviction that continuous growth is a desirable condition—and foreign markets obviously represent a massive growth opportunity. Finally, since World War II, presidential administrations have encouraged large-scale foreign investment as a means of establishing American preeminence internationally (Gilpin 1975; Greenberg 1974; Salomon and Bernstein 1982).

According to economist Immanuel Wallerstein (1974), the formation of multinationals represents the fourth and most recent stage of an international economy, which began to develop in the sixteenth century and was never limited by national boundaries. Following worldwide expansion of industrial activity during the century that ended in 1917, the leading capitalists began to consolidate enormous wealth, with multinationals establishing global political and economic control.

Multinationals' ability to cross national

As American multinationals spread around the world, they must cooperate with local governments. In Beijing this McDonald's restaurant, which opened in April 1992, is a 50-50 joint venture with the Beijing General Corporation of Agriculture and is expected to serve 15,000 customers daily.

boundaries sometimes occurs in opposition to national policies if profits seem promising. In 1938 ITT, using a German subsidiary, bought a company that produced military aircraft for the Nazis during World War II. After the war ITT sought and received government compensation for the damage American bombers did to its German plants. During an Arab boycott of the United States in the early 1970s, Exxon gained favor with the Arabs by refusing to sell to a U.S. Navy base in the Philippines (Horton, Leslie, and Larson 1991, 70).

The nearby American Controversy considers in greater detail some of the issues of modern capitalism that we have already examined.

Material in this section has suggested that within our economic system, a small number of corporations have accumulated a lion's share of wealth and power and that their dominant concern is extension of their wealth and power. But what about workers' needs? This issue will be considered in the upcoming discussion.

Work in Modern Times

A staff member for a major management consultant firm posed a question to American white-collar workers. "Do you really need an office as

such at all?" He went on to suggest that by the beginning of the twenty-first century, two-way communication will be sufficiently advanced to

AMERICAN CONTROVERSY
Capitalism in America: Desirable or Undesirable?

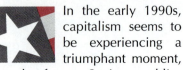 In the early 1990s, capitalism seems to be experiencing a triumphant moment, as the former Soviet republics and other socialist nations have become increasingly receptive to it. Nonetheless the strengths and weaknesses of capitalism in this society are likely to be discussed and debated in the years ahead.

The Pro-Capitalist Position
Supporters of capitalism are likely to claim that theirs is the economic philosophy consistent with a democratic society, because it exists in a free market. Consumers are protected from maltreatment by sellers, because they can always turn to other sellers; employees are shielded from the tyranny of bosses since they can always seek other jobs; and sellers are protected from consumers' exploitation, because they can hold out until less exploitative consumers appear. Thus economic activities are regulated by supply and demand. Basically no outside intervention is necessary; as Adam Smith indicated, the invisible hand of the marketplace acts for the common good.

Admittedly in complex modern economies, governments sometimes have had to play a role—to clarify the rules by which the economic game is played, such as preventing monopolies, and to serve as an umpire between disputing parties. Government's role, however, has and should remain minimal. What capitalist nations want to avoid is the situation that has developed in socialist countries, where government largely controls the economy and the options for both business people and consumers are highly limited. In the former Soviet republics and in other socialist nations, this deficiency has been appreciated, and an increasing number of capitalist ventures are developing.

The Anti-Capitalist Position
In theory capitalist philosophy is appealing and consistent with the American emphasis on freedom and individualism. If the open-marketplace approach actually worked, many current opponents of capitalism would say their opposition would decline or disappear. The problem is that it does not.

Instead of acting neutrally, government generally serves as an ally of big business. Consider, for instance, the relationship between the U.S. government and the major petroleum companies. Seeking to ensure an independent supply of American oil, the federal government encouraged American companies' investment in the Middle East during World War II. Since then the government has used such measures as nearly eliminating corporate taxes to make certain that these organizations continuously received enormous profits. In addition, few restrictions were placed upon them. Occasionally, to be sure, even government officials were disturbed by the oil companies' practices. In 1973 the Federal Trade Commission charged the eight largest petroleum companies with monopolizing oil production—working together to inflate profits on crude oil and to drive independent companies out of business. But the regulatory effort failed. In fact, later that same year, the oil companies retaliated, claiming that because of a boycott by oil-producing Arab nations, oil and gasoline were suddenly very scarce. Actually the United States had been importing only about 3 percent of its petroleum from Arab countries, and domestic supplies were greater than they had been a year earlier. Nonetheless the majority of the public accepted the false claim that the long lines at the gasoline pumps, the accelerated price for petroleum products, and the massive inflationary effect on the economy should be blamed on the Arabs.

The major point, the opponents of capitalism conclude, is that in modern times the invisible hand of the marketplace is not only invisible but nonexistent. Inevitably those who are wealthy use their wealth and associated power to unscrupulously promote their own economic interests, and all other interests, including those of needy people, are subordinated.

Conclusion
What do you believe? Review the specific points covered here and consider what would be the economic characteristics of your ideal society.

encourage widespread working at home. At present many office workers perform tasks—entering data, typing, retrieving, and totaling columns of figures—that require few, if any face-to-face communications. In addition, many of the tasks performed by engineers, draftsmen, and other white-collar employees could be done more readily or as readily at home as at the office with often nothing more required than a computer terminal. Such a change would provide a greater work flexibility, an opportunity for more extensive family and community involvement, and a decisively lessened cost for transportation. Writer Alvin Toffler has called this pattern of people increasingly working at home "the electronic cottage," a modern version of the preindustrial cottage industries where workers performed their labors in their own homes (Toffler 1981, Chapter 16).

Whether or not Toffler is correct, the scheme he proposed is consistent with the historical trend by which significant social eras create major changes in people's work patterns. The industrial age brought people into central places—factories and offices. Perhaps, as Toffler suggested, the postindustrial age will allow many people to do their work, or most of their work, in their homes. In this section we examine changing outlooks on work over time and the modern perception of work.

CHANGING OUTLOOKS ON WORK

People have attached as great a variety of meanings to work as they have to sex and to play. To the ancient Greeks, who had a slave-based economy, work was a curse. Homer claimed that the gods hated humanity and therefore condemned people to work. Greek thinkers did consider the possibility that agriculture allowed independence and thus might be tolerable but that the mechanical arts were brutalizing to the mind. In general, the Greeks felt that work possessed two distinct attributes: It was humiliating and necessary.

The Hebrews shared the Greek outlook on work, and they believed that people had to engage in it as a punishment for Adam and Eve's fall from divine grace. By working, people could regain some of their lost dignity. In fact, early Jewish scholars emphasized that working, no matter how lowly the labor one faced, was never as repugnant as idleness.

Like the Greeks and the Hebrews, the early Christians gave little respect to work, but they also despised idleness. The early Christians believed that the most honorable labor in which people could engage was the contemplation of heavenly existence and that any other work served as a diversion from this noble task. From the eleventh to the fourteenth century, the Catholic Church became more involved in community activities, and religious leaders started to give more consideration to work. St. Thomas Aquinas took a position that closely resembles the current Catholic view: Work is a natural right and duty providing the foundation for property and profit, but it is always just a means to a higher spiritual goal.

In the sixteenth and seventeenth centuries, a sharply different outlook on work developed: The only effective way to serve God was through good work. During this period scientific and technological innovations provided the basis for the development of capitalism, and Protestant theology supported the emphasis on work, as we noted in Chapter 12, "Religion and Education." The Protestant-ethic focus on the importance, even sanctity, of work was consistent with a number of positions that both preceded and followed it. Examples are the early Christians' disgust for idleness as well as the outlook on work, thrift, and success maintained by such prominent American capitalists as Carnegie, Rockefeller, and Ford (Wilensky 1966, 119–23).

The modern American conception of work also has some distinct attributes.

MODERN PERCEPTION OF WORK

Americans' feelings about work seem to be linked to four cultural values:

1. ***The good provider conception.*** Traditionally men have been the breadwinners, and a "real" man is one who can take care of his family.
2. ***The ability to maintain independence.*** A paying job is the way to establish freedom and independence. Most adult Americans are uncomfortable if they are financially dependent on others.
3. ***The emphasis on material success.*** The

higher people's wages or salaries, the more capable they will be to purchase the expensive homes, cars, clothes, and other material items that they enjoy and that are indicators to others of their occupational achievement.

4. **The importance of performing a good job.** For Americans, work is a source of self-respect, and so the people who do their job well have higher self-esteem than those who do not (Yankelovich 1974).

Unemployed people are unable to attain any of these cultural standards. Therefore it is not surprising that the effects of unemployment on individuals can be serious. One long-term study has indicated that when the rate of national unemployment rises 1 percentage point, suicide increases 4.1 percent, homicide 5.7 percent, and stress-related disorders such as heart disease 1.9 percent (Riegle 1982). While other factors besides the increase in unemployment might contribute to the rise in these problems, that increase has probably played a dominant role. Table 13.3 indicates how large a problem unemployment represents in modern times.

Job Satisfaction Today

In a study of Americans at work, journalist Studs Terkel offered the following commentary about the significance of people's jobs.

> During my three years of prospecting, I may have, on more occasions than I imagined, struck gold. I was constantly astonished by the extraordinary dreams of ordinary people. No matter how bewildering the times, no matter how dissembling the official language, those we call ordinary are aware of a sense of personal worth—or more often a lack of it—in the work they do.
>
> (Terkel 1974, xxiv)

Sociological studies have uncovered the following causes of job satisfaction or dissatisfaction:

1. **Monetary compensation.** Satisfied workers believe that they are paid well for their efforts. Besides wages or salary, such fringe benefits as medical care, retirement, and paid vacation time are important considerations.
2. **Control.** People generally are happier in jobs that give them some chance for con-

Table 13.3 American Unemployment, Past and Present

	UNEMPLOYMENT OVER TIME		RECENT FIGURES (June 1992)	
	Number (in millions)	*Percent of labor force*		*Percent of labor force*
1950	3.3	5.2	Total (all civilian workers)	7.5
1955	2.9	4.3	Men, 20 years and over	7.3
1960	3.9	5.4	Women, 20 years and over	6.1
1965	3.4	4.4	Both sexes, 16–19	20.0
1970	4.1	4.8	White	6.5
1975	7.9	8.3	Black	14.7
1980	7.6	7.0	Hispanic	11.3
1985	8.3	7.1	Married men, spouse present	5.1
1988	6.7	5.4	Married women, spouse present	4.9
1991	8.4	6.6	Women who maintain families	10.0

Sources: *Adapted from U.S. Department of Labor.* Employment and Earnings. *(May 1992), Table A-1 and Table A-39.*

This two-part table demonstrates two general conclusions: first, that American unemployment has tended to remain between 5 and 7 percent in the past four decades and second, that individuals with certain social characteristics are more likely to suffer unemployment. Such categories of people, by the way, are inclined to be in low-paying jobs that do not require extensive education or training.

trol, especially over their own schedules. Recent research, in fact, has suggested that for many people this is the factor most strongly affecting job satisfaction.

3. **Location issues.** Workers are more satisfied in a place which is pleasant in a physical sense—not too hot or cold, too dirty, too noisy, or too crowded—and that, in particular, is not dangerous. For many individuals it is useful to be able to personalize their work space, thereby helping them to cope with the emotional demands of their jobs.

4. **Organizational amenities.** Desirable facilities include cafeterias, lounges, and gyms and such features as training programs or promotion-from-within policies.

5. **Prevailing economic, political, and social conditions.** If prosperity exists within a society, then workers' outlook on their jobs will tend to be optimistic.

6. **Psychological satisfaction.** Employees are pleased when they have a chance to learn on the job, when the work relates to their particular abilities and preferences, and when it occurs in a nonconflictful atmosphere (Appelberg et al. 1991; Leigh 1991; Morton 1977; Rice, Gentile, and McFarlin 1991; Scheiberg 1990; Spector, Dwyer, and Jex 1988; Worchel and Shackelford 1991).

Whether it is miniature dinosaurs and photos or some other meaningful items, people often go to some pains to personalize their work space.

Work Alienation Karl Marx noted that with the technological innovations of capitalism, the nature of work began to change. People's jobs were in factories, where the individual worker "becomes an appendage of the machine, and it is only the most simple, most monotonous and most easily acquired knack that is required of him" (Marx 1932, 328).

Since Karl Marx's era, many studies have focused on the absence of job satisfaction. An analysis of Marx's writings reveals two prominent sources of work alienation:

1. **Control over the product.** Workers are unhappy because they produce commodities whose sale falls under the direction of the company owner.

2. **Control over the process of one's labors.** As the quotation from Marx indicates, the nature of work itself can be dissatisfying to workers.

Sociologist Melvin Kohn (1976) interviewed 3,101 men in a wide range of civilian occupations, and he learned that these respondents were much more concerned about the work process than about control over the product. In assessing the literature on work alienation, Kohn concluded that three factors were intimately linked with satisfaction on the job: closeness of supervision, routinization, and substantive complexity. With Kohn's conclusions in mind, one might propose the following definition. **Work alienation** is loss of control over the process of one's labor, with the resulting dissatisfaction primarily caused by overly close supervision, highly routine tasks, and an overall simplicity to one's job.

In recent years a number of occupational groups have become increasingly alienated on the job. In particular:

1. During the protest years of the 1960s, African-Americans and other minorities started to reject dead-beat jobs and demanded more work respectability, which training and higher education could produce.

2. Some teachers, government employees, social workers, and counselors have been demonstrating a growing discontent with their organizations' extensive bureaucratic regulations and limited job autonomy, conditions that often prevent advancement and the development of more refined job skills. Rapid unionization among these workers seems to have been one indication of their discontent.

3. A steadily increasing number of women have been rejecting the tradition that women's work is in the home, doing housework and caring for children. In 1960, 30.5 percent of married women were in the labor force. In 1991, 58.5 percent of married women were working (U.S. Bureau of the Census, *Statistical Abstract of the United States*: 1992, No. 619).

4. Since the 1970s many factory workers have been openly responding in a negative way to their work. In 1972 at the General Motors plant in Lordstown, Ohio, factory workers went on strike, not for higher wages but in opposition to the alienating conditions of assembly-line work. The heart of the 1973 contract settlement between the Big 3 auto manufacturers and the United Auto Workers involved a reduction in work demands. Central issues were a restriction on compulsory overtime and the establishment of a full retirement plan for those with thirty years seniority. In recent years difficult economic conditions have reestablished the priority of financial factors, but such a shift, of course, does not eliminate the underlying discontent.

5. The American Management Association has indicated that some managers have expressed dissatisfaction with their work,

that they feel "robbed by computers" of decision-making duties. In the last couple of decades, professionals, managers, and executives in their forties and fifties have frequently changed their careers (Gartner and Riessman 1974).

Thus work alienation cuts across occupational types and class lines. In *Working* journalist Studs Terkel interviewed more than 130 people about a wide range of different jobs. An awareness of work alienation usually permeated the interviews. Many of the blue-collar workers made statements similar to this one expressed by a steelworker.

> After forty years of workin' at the steel mill, I am just a number. I think I've been a pretty good worker. That job was just right for me. I had a minimum amount of education and a job using a micrometer and just a steel tape and your eyes—that's a job that was just made for me. . . . Bob [his son] worked in the mill a few months during a school vacation. He said, "I don't know how you done it all these years. I could never do it." I said, "I been tellin' you all your life never get into that mill." (Laughs.)

> (*Terkel* 1974, 557–58)

As new technologies make the workplace more automated, people are likely to feel less actively involved in the work process and become more alienated. Information obtained from telephone workers indicated that since 1980 increasing automation on the job has made them feel that their work is less autonomous and challenging (Vallas 1988).

White-collar employees also indicate work alienation. For example, Terkel interviewed an audit-department head at a bank who described his job in the following way:

> The job is boring. It's a real repetitious thing. . . . It's always the same. Nothing exciting ever happens.

> It's just the constant supervision of people. It's more or less like you have a factory full of robots working the machinery. You're there checking and making sure the machinery is constantly working. . . . If they break down, replace them. You're just like a man who sits and watches computers all day. Same thing. . . .

> A man should be treated as a human, not as a million-dollar piece of machinery. People aren't

treated as good as an IBM machine is. Big corporations turn me off. I didn't know it until I became a supervisor and I realized the games you have to play.

(*Terkel* 1974, 400)

What can be said about job satisfaction in the years ahead? One point seems fairly obvious: As the structure of work changes, values will change, including people's sense of what is satisfying or dissatisfying work.

Computers have been becoming increasingly prominent in many jobs, and some observers believe that by the beginning of the twenty-first century, their prevalence in the work world will have a profound effect upon a variety of job holders. It has been suggested that working with computers supports an emphasis on personal freedom and self-expression on the job. One observer noted that the work force in the year 2000 might feature "young workers wearing sunglasses and having their ears plugged in to their own private music. The personal freedom they choose is having their inner consciousness free to roam" (Deutsch 1985, 11).

Certainly this image will not represent the entire work force at the beginning of the next century. But if a significant component of Americans have computer-based jobs, several problems might develop. First, one might wonder whether there will be enough creative, computer-related work for all who are interested. If there is not—and certainly that seems to be a strong possibility—then those who have trained for it will be disappointed and easily become alienated if compelled to pursue what they perceive to be lower-quality jobs. Second, because of the autonomous, even solitary nature of many computer-based activities, it will be important and interesting to observe whether the holders of such jobs will be able to work smoothly with others in organizations. In the past people have been trained to function effectively in organizational settings, but perhaps the nature of computer-based work will undermine that capacity.

Conclusion

This chapter has examined both the political and economic institutions. The relationship between the two institutions has been apparent throughout. Both politicians and business people are prominent power brokers, whose decisions and activities can affect many people's lives. There are also numerous interrelationships between the two institutions. For instance, politicians often find that business people are a major source of financial support. Business people, in turn, can use either legal or illegal means to influence politicians. In particular, the great wealth of modern corporations permits them to exert enormous power.

Use the sociological pespective to consider the combined impact that these two institutions have on our daily lives. Imagine what it would be like not to live in a political democracy or in a capitalist economy. Would these two sets of changes significantly affect your life? If so, how?

The chapter concludes with the fifth of six Research in Sociology sections. This one involves studies about charisma.

RESEARCH IN SOCIOLOGY: SECTION V

The Case of Charisma: Research on an Elusive Concept

What is charisma? What is charismatic leadership? These words conjure up romantic notions, images of heroic, magnetic individuals arriving at crucial moments to lead their followers to victory or security. The charismatic individual makes the difference; it is the stuff of successful novels or films. Research analyzing the concept is fairly extensive. Sociologists have examined the resignation of a charismatic leader, the development of charisma in a mayoral election, and the relationship between personal charisma and both nonverbal skills and initial attraction felt by others.

But in spite of this growing body of research, there has been a significant problem with investigations of the topic. Recall a point raised in the chapter—that charisma is a condition that is unusual, even rare in the real world. The rarity of true Weberian charisma has meant that individuals conducting studies of it have been compelled to follow one of two strategies: Either they revised Weber's definition or carefully chose research sites where something approximating Weber's definition could be claimed to exist. In the first instance, the definition had to be broadened to include modern leaders who did not actually meet the requirements of Weber's definition. In the second situation, investigators chose contexts that were either preindustrial or small, thus avoiding conventional modern political situations where Weber's conception of charismatic leadership could not legitimately be claimed to exist.

The material in this section is about the definition of a research concept and related matters. To some observer, this might seem at first to be fairly insignificant stuff. It is not! As we saw in Chapter 2, "Doing Research in Sociology," good research builds on a series of distinct stages. How could we effectively study charismatic leadership without having a distinct sense of what charisma is? Actually it makes no more sense than sending a person out to buy bread or coffee when the person does not know what bread or coffee is. Fundamental issues such as this one should be addressed by researchers. The first reason to do so is that the investigation is made more rigorous and thus improved. Furthermore if researchers do not effectively evaluate such concerns, it is likely that their critics will, sometimes to investigators' embarrassment, in a book review or written comment in a professional journal on an article published earlier within that journal. As we noted in Chapter 2, people doing sociological studies sometimes move too rapidly through the early steps of the research process; the thrust of this analysis is that this is a fundamental error.

After discussions about broadening the definition of charisma and researching charisma in contexts where Weber's definition was preserved, we briefly consider the future of research on the concept.

Broadening Weber's Definition of Charismatic Leadership

Politicians, sports celebrities, actors and actresses, and many others appear to possess charisma. Is charisma actually widespread in our society? No, not according to Max Weber's definition. Sociologists Joseph Bensman and Michael Givant have indicated that when Weber wrote of charisma, he was emphasizing three conditions: a personal relationship between leaders and followers, a radical or revolutionary

Mohandas Gandhi, shown here with Jawaharlal Nehru (right), was one of the most influential, charismatic leaders of the twentieth century. Using the strategy of passive resistance, he helped hasten India's independence from British control.

situation, and irrationality (seeking followers not by an appeal to reason but by the magnetism of his or her personality).

Bensman and Givant have contended that most if not all modern uses of the term involve situations in which these conditions are absent. In politics the very size and impersonality of modern mass societies have prevented the personal appeals of Weber's kind of charismatic leaders; furthermore current politicians' communications are highly rational, often carefully planned by media experts to produce the most potent impact upon the public. Bensman and Givant have concluded that instead of using the term charisma, it makes more sense to speak of "pseudo-charisma," the use of the appearance and imagery of charismatic leadership as a rational device to obtain or maintain power.

Arthur Schweitzer's *The Age of Charisma* is an example of a study of charisma that, in reality, examines pseudocharisma. Unlike Weber, Schweitzer claimed that charismatic leaders are not truly radical or revolutionary but are adaptable, seeking to ally themselves with established political parties, ideologies, armies, and even state bureaucracies. Schweitzer examined fifty-five examples of twentieth-century charismatic leadership, including Churchill, de Gaulle, Hitler, John Kennedy, and Martin Luther King, Jr. Weber would not have considered any of these leaders charismatic, but then, as Bensman and Givant emphasized, Weber's definition of charismatic leadership is virtually nonapplicable to industrial societies.

Preserving Weber's Definition of Charisma

Since charisma as Weber defined it is so difficult to find in industrial societies, those interested in the concept can either broaden the definition as Schweitzer did, or they

394 can keep Weber's definition and search out charisma in contexts where it conceivably can be found.

Richard Emerson, a sociologist, chose this second course of action, studying charismatic leadership in a preindustrial state. Emerson examined the formation of the state of Baltistan, a republic of Tibetan-speaking Islamic people in South Asia. His research included an analysis of the contribution of charismatic leadership, and his evidence came from somewhat unusual secondary sources. In Chapter 2 we learned that secondary sources are data banks produced by other individuals and organizations. Emerson's secondary sources were considerably more artistic than most—dances, songs, and other types of folklore. For instance, Emerson analyzed a long epic poem about King Kesar of the kingdom of Ling that has been passed on orally for over four centuries. King Kesar

> is a mythical charismatic warrior-king whose exploits and magical fighting powers are recounted in the saga at great length. But despite the supernatural powers of this warrior-ruler-deity, the vulnerability of his kingdom (Ling) is a major theme in the saga, symbolized by the frequent abduction of his wife, the queen Lomo Brugmo.

> (Emerson 1983, 429)

Emerson concluded that this and other examples from Baltistan folklore reveal an important point about charismatic leadership and vulnerability. He suggested that unless people consider themselves vulnerable, they will not follow a charismatic leader. For instance, no matter how appealing and magnetic a personality, the leader of a powerful army facing modest opposition will not inspire the fervent loyalty charismatic leaders normally receive; in this situation people do not feel vulnerable and thus the loyalty gladly given to a protecting leader is not inspired.

Emerson, in short, was suggesting that followers' perception of their own vulnerability will significantly affect whether or not they will perceive an individual as their charismatic savior. Is Emerson correct? Perhaps his conclusion is best viewed as an hypothesis, which needs further testing.

Emerson's insights about charismatic leadership were based on information contained in ancient folklore. In contrast, Phyllis Day, a social researcher at Purdue University, obtained insights about charisma from investigating Roseland, a contemporary home for troubled girls. An unusual feature of Day's project was the fact that it was a study of charisma at an organizational level. Like Emerson, Day was not studying charisma in a modern, political context. Therefore, again like Emerson, she could approximate the characteristics of charismatic leadership emphasized by Weber. Remember what those characteristics are: a personal relationship between leaders and followers, a radical or revolutionary situation, and an appeal based on the magnetism of the leaders' personality.

Roseland possessed a leader with these three qualities. This woman, who was the director of an agency containing twenty-two residents and a staff of nine, had a powerful personal relationship with her followers and a magnetic impact on them. A staff members' statement suggested the existence of both conditions.

> She's always with us, and she always has time for the kids, too, even if it's only five minutes. Her door is never closed. She tunes in with the kids. She's involved in everything and involves us—I'm learning as much here as in any grad school.

> (Day 1980, 56)

In addition, the leader's goal was widely considered controversial, even radical—namely the decision to shift the emphasis in the program from caring for pregnant girls to helping girls who were poor, emotionally disturbed, and frequently delinquent. After this shift in goal, Roseland was no longer a "nice" middle-class agency, and its support by the United Way and other established organizations was endangered.

Commentary on Future Research of Charismatic Leadership

We have learned that researchers who have studied charismatic leadership have been compelled to follow one of two options. Either they have needed to broaden Weber's definition of charisma to acknowledge political conditions in industrial societies or they have had to seek either preindustrial or organizational contexts that approximated the conditions described in Weber's definition of the concept.

But what about the future? Let us consider two possibilities. One option is to suspend all research on charismatic leadership, recognizing, as Bensman and Givant wrote, that industrial society de-emphasizes conditions that promote charisma as defined by Weber. Another seemingly more interesting approach would be to pursue studies seeking to determine whether or not industrial and postindustrial societies can produce leadership which, though not always charismatic in the literal Weberian sense, contains interesting, provocative elements found in his description of charisma.

One of the productive ideas in Weber's discussion of charisma is its suggestion that followers are willing to follow such leaders without question. The director at Roseland possessed such an appeal, and I did a year-long study of a federally funded agency in which the director maintained a similar control over staff members. It is an impressive, yet frightening phenomenon to behold. In a recent paper on charisma, a psychiatrist indicated that in our society some charismatic, or perhaps we should say pseudocharismatic, people can be dangerous.

> They offer *the* Answer, and promise purpose, meaning, and freedom from choice. It is the kind of intense charisma that especially needs to be explored.

(*Newman 1983, 204*)

What are your ideas about interesting directions for future research on charisma?

Sources: Joseph Bensman and Michael Givant. "Charisma and Modernity: The Use and Abuse of a Concept," Social Research. vol. 42 (Autumn 1975), pp. 570–614; Phyllis J. Day. "Charismatic Leadership in the Small Organization," Human Organization. vol. 39 (Spring 1980), pp. 50–58; Christopher Bates Doob. How the War Was Lost. Unpublished manuscript, 1970; Richard M. Emerson. "Charismatic Kingship: A Study of State-Formation and Authority in Baltistan," Politics and Society. vol. 12 (1983), pp. 413–44; Hans Gerth and C. Wright Mills (eds.). From Max Weber. New York: Oxford University Press, 1946; Robert J. House, William D. Spangler, and James Woycke. "Personality and Charisma in the U.S. Presidency: A Psychological Theory of Leader Effectiveness," Administrative Science Quarterly. vol. 36 (September 1991), pp. 364–96; Richard Ling. "The Production of Synthetic Charisma," Journal of Political and Military Charisma. vol. 15 (Fall 1987), pp. 157–70; Ruth G. Newman. "Thoughts on Superstars of Charisma: Pipers in Our Midst," American Journal of Orthopsychiatry. vol. 53 (April 1983), pp. 201-08; Susan J. Palmer. "Charisma and Abdication: A Study of the Leadership of Bhagwan Shree Rajneesh," Sociological Analysis. vol. 49 (Summer 1988), pp. 119–35; Arthur Schweitzer. The Age of Charisma. Chicago: Nelson-Hall, 1984; Adam B. Seligman. "Charisma and the Transformation of Grace in the Early Modern Era," Social Research. vol. 58 (Fall 1991), pp. 591–620.

STUDY GUIDE

Learning Objectives

After studying this chapter, you should be able to:

1. Define power, political institution, and economic institution and indicate the general functions performed by the two institutions.

396

2. Compare and contrast the pluralist and power-elite theories of authority.
3. Define authority and define and describe Weber's three types of authority—the traditional, legal-rational, and charismatic.
4. Discuss the American two-party political system and explain its dominance in the American political process.
5. Examine the influence of interest groups and lobbying in American politics, indicating the impact of corruption.
6. Define patronage and political machine and briefly analyze both issues.
7. Define capitalism and socialism and discuss their respective economic ideologies.
8. Describe the political and social power of large American corporations and the conditions encouraging the development of multinationals.
9. Indicate how outlooks on work have changed over time.
10. Identify and discuss the cultural values associated with Americans' feelings about work.
11. List and examine the factors associated with workers' satisfaction or dissatisfaction on the job.
12. Define work alienation and discuss groups that have become increasingly alienated on the job in recent years.
13. Examine the relationship between the political and economic institutions.

Summary

1. Power is the ability of an individual or group to implement wishes or policies, with or without the cooperation of others. Authority is power that people generally recognize as rightfully maintained by those who use it. The political institution is the system of norms and roles that concerns the use and distribution of authority within a given society.

The economic institution is the system of norms and roles developed for the production, distribution, and consumption of goods and services.

2. The two leading theories on the concentration of authority are the pluralist and the power-elite perspectives. Pluralism focuses on the dispersion of authority in government, and the power-elite thesis claims that a privileged few control the political process. On a given issue, one finds that the two theories will focus on different facts, thus providing divergent insights into the political process.

3. Max Weber has designated three systems of authority—the traditional, the legal-rational, and the charismatic—and elements of each system appear in the American political process.

4. One of the prominent features of the American political process is the two-party system. In U.S. society this system dominates for a number of reasons, including the existence of a broad consensus on political issues, the winner-take-all quality of the American electoral process, and the force of habit and tradition. Another feature of the American political process is the existence of interest groups. While these structures are legal, many of the wealthier interest groups lobby illegally. Traditionally corruption has been widespread in American politics, with urban political machines playing a significant part.

5. In the United States, capitalism is the dominant economic system. It is an economic system where capital is controlled by private citizens who own the means of production and distribution of goods and services. In *The Wealth of Nations*, Adam Smith first described the theoretical workings of a capitalist system. He explained that self-interest would produce a self-regulating economy. In modern capitalist states, however, governments have found some regulation necessary. Socialism is an economic system in which collective ownership of the production and distribution of goods exists. Key elements in a socialist economy include government ownership of productive resources, coordinated, centralized planning, and a redistribution of income.

In the United States, the 500 largest corporations control about half of the Gross National Product in a given year. The major corporations exert political and social power through their wealth, their accumulation of skilled and talented people, the general support for business in the United States, citizens' link to corporate well-being, and the commitment of all public officials to the existing economic and social system. Multinationals, large corporations with production plants and distributions centers in many countries, are a major source of American corporate dominance.

6. Over time societal outlooks on work have been changing. The ancient Greeks and Hebrews shared a negative outlook on work, and whereas early Christians recognized that it might help insure the health of the body and soul, they too showed little respect for work. By the sixteenth and seventeenth century, a distinctly positive attitude toward work had developed: The only way to serve God effectively was through good work.

Americans' feelings about work appear to be linked to four cultural values: the good provider conception, the ability to maintain independence, the emphasis on material success, and the importance of performing a good job. Satisfaction or dissatisfaction in one's occupation is the product of a number of causes. They include monetary compensation, control, location issues, organizational amenities, prevailing economic, political, and social conditions, and psychological satisfaction. Following the lead of Karl Marx, sociologists have studied work alienation, the loss of control over the process of one's labor. In recent years a number of conditions have encouraged work alienation. They include the protest tradition of the 1960s, white-collar workers' growing unhappiness with organizational bureaucracy and limited job autonomy, an increasing tendency for women to reject the traditional woman's role, factory workers' negative response to their work, and managers' dissatisfaction with their jobs.

Key Terms

authority   power that people generally recognize as rightfully maintained by those who use it

capital   money, goods, or other forms of wealth invested to produce more wealth

capitalism   an economic system where capital is controlled by private citizens who own the means of production and distribution of goods and services

charismatic system of authority   according to Max Weber, an authority system in which leadership develops because of the personal magnetism of an individual, whose followers believe that he or she possesses supernatural qualities

corporation   a legally designated organization that has power and responsibilities separate from its workers and owners

democracy   a government in which those in power are acting with the consent of the governed

economic institution   the system of norms and roles developed for the production, distribution, and consumption of goods and services

interest group   a group whose members seek to influence elected politicians or government bureaucrats to initiate the legislation or policies they want

legal-rational system of authority   according to Weber, a system of authority based on laws enacted to produce rational behavior and the achievement of formally designated goals

lobbying   a face-to-face effort to persuade legislators and other government personnel to support the proposals of an interest group

multinational   a large corporation with production plants and distribution centers in many countries

patronage   distribution of favors to political supporters

pluralism   a theory that emphasizes that a dispersion of authority exists in American government

political institution   the system of norms and roles that concerns the use and distribution of authority within a given society

political machine   an organization established to control a city, county, or state government

power   the ability of an individual or group to implement wishes or policies, with or without the cooperation of others

power-elite perspective   a theory emphasizing that in American society a group of high-status people—well educated, often wealthy, and placed in high occupational positions—control the political process, including political authorities

398

socialism   an economic system with collective ownership of the means for the production and distribution of goods and services

traditional system of authority   according to Weber, an authority system in which the standard of political leadership passes down from one generation to another

work alienation   the loss of control over the process of one's labor, with the resulting dissatisfaction primarily caused by overly close supervision, highly routine tasks, and an overall simplicity to one's job

Tests

True • False Test

_____   1. A policeman who flags down a motorist is using power and not authority.

_____   2. As long as elections take place in a society, it can be considered a democracy.

_____   3. Charismatic leaders are likely to appeal to the discontented, deprived members of society.

_____   4. A two-party system has dominated political activity in all Western nations.

_____   5. Corporations which are subjected to extensive regulation are more likely to develop PACs than those not exposed to extensive regulation.

_____   6. Adam Smith suggested that as business people pursue self-interest in a capitalist system, they are promoting the common good.

_____   7. Keynesian economic measures support the maintenance of a laissez-faire economy.

_____   8. A major source of political and social power in corporations is the accumulation of skilled and talented people these organizations can mobilize.

_____   9. Work alienation occurs when people lose control over the process of their labor.

_____ 10. The political and economic institutions are completely independent of each other.

Multiple-Choice Test

_____   1. Pluralism emphasizes that:
     a. the evil, coercive use of power will be frequent.
     b. elected officials tend not to be accountable to voters.
     c. minorities will be without authority.
     d. constant negotiations among centers of authority will occur.

_____   2. C. Wright Mills concluded that:
     a. a power elite no longer exists in the U.S.
     b. white-collar employees are dominated by the corporations and government agencies for which they work.
     c. pluralism is a more accurate theory in the 1980s than in the 1960s.
     d. a and c

_____   3. Recently Ralph Hummel asserted that the United States:
     a. does not possess a coherent policy to structure productive activity in either the private or public spheres.
     b. has successfully incorporated Japanese production methods into their factory systems.
     c. has rejected Japanese production methods in favor of German techniques, which have proved successful throughout Europe.
     d. a and c

_____ 4. The American political system contains elements of:
   a.   the legal-rational system of authority.
   b.   the charismatic system of authority.
   c.   the traditional system of authority.
   d.   a, b, and c

_____ 5. Factors encouraging a two-party system in the U.S. include:
   a.   the force of habit and tradition.
   b.   the electoral process.
   c.   a broad consensus on political issues.
   d.   a, b, and c

_____ 6. As chairman of the President's Council on Competitiveness, Dan Quayle:
   a.   acted to make certain that small to medium-sized companies were able to establish themselves in a highly competitive business climate.
   b.   served to publicize how American sport develops the traits and skills essential to success in modern society.
   c.   used the position to weaken or disregard regulations considered unfriendly by large corporations that made donations to Republican candidates.
   d.   a and b

_____ 7. Adam Smith's theory of economics emphasizes the importance of:
   a.   group interest rather than self-interest.
   b.   government intervention to prevent depressions.
   c.   socialism.
   d.   self-interest.

_____ 8. A recent report by twenty-five well-known business scholars concluded that:
   a.   U.S. companies invest too heavily in short-term profits.
   b.   Japanese and German corporations have become too competitive with each other.
   c.   the most productive capitalist nations will soon be the former socialist countries.
   d.   a and c

_____ 9. A source of corporate political and social power is:
   a.   job enrichment.
   b.   wealth.
   c.   socialist philosophy.
   d.   union labor.

_____ 10. Research on charisma:
   a.   has always used Weber's definition of the concept.
   b.   has sometimes used Weber's definition of the concept and sometimes has not.
   c.   has been discontinued because charismatic leadership is so difficult to find.
   d.   has demonstrated that charisma cannot be found in organizations.

Essay Test

1. Define power, authority, political institution, and democracy and give examples of each.
2. Summarize the pluralist and power-elite theories and apply them to the American political process.
3. Define Weber's three systems of authority. Describe an episode or event in American history illustrating each type.
4. Would American democracy be significantly different without a two-party system or would it be essentially the same? Consider the alternatives of a single-party and a multiparty system.

5. What are interest groups? Evaluate their functions and dysfunctions in the American political process.
6. Why does corruption exist in the American political system? Discuss the development of political machines.
7. Define the economic institution. What are the similarities and differences between the capitalist and socialist economic systems?
8. How do major American corporations exert power and influence? Discuss various functions and dysfunctions of corporate activities.
9. What is a multinational? What conditions have encouraged their development?
10. Discuss the changing conceptions of work societies have maintained through different historical periods.
11. What are five prominent factors that determine people's satisfactions and dissatisfactions toward their jobs? Indicate five occupational groups that have become more alienated from their work in recent years. Why have they become more alienated?

Suggested Readings

Breslin, Jimmy. 1976. *How the Good Guys Finally Won*. New York: Ballantine Books. A beautifully written, entertaining, sometimes humorous, always informative account of the congressional impeachment proceedings against Richard Nixon. In the course of the book, the reader learns a great deal about the workings of Washington politics.

Domhoff, G. William. 1983. *Who Rules America Now? A View for the Eighties*. Englewood Cliffs, NJ: Prentice-Hall. An updated version of Domhoff's analysis of modern American politics, offering a wealth of documented support for the power-elite theory.

Hampsher-Monk, Iain. 1992. A *History of Modern Political Thought: Major Political Thinkers from Hobbes to Marx*. Cambridge, MA: Blackwell. A clearly written introduction to important political theorists' works, effectively placing individual thinkers in the context of their time.

Lerner, Max (ed.). 1948. *The Portable Veblen*. New York: Viking. The sharpest and most powerful writings of a well-known critic of American capitalism. Veblen lived and wrote at the end of the nineteenth and the early twentieth century, the era when the great corporate monopolies were establishing themselves.

Robertson, Roland. 1992. *Globalization*. Newbury Park, CA: Sage. A sociological analysis of the development and significance of the modern global society, attempting to eliminate the confusion often associated with the concept and indicating the narrowness of many current studies of the topic.

Skolnick, Jerome H., and Elliott Currie (eds.). 1991. *Crisis in American Institutions*. 8th ed. New York: HarperCollins. An excellent reader about major American social problems, with particularly strong sections on corporate power, economic crisis, the workplace, and national security.

Terkel, Studs. 1974. *Working*. New York: Pantheon Books. A set of over 130 interviews showing how Americans in a wide range of occupations feel about their work. Terkel, a sensitive, perceptive writer, presents these detailed, insightful interviews as monologues—a form that increases the emotional power of people's commentary about their jobs.

Warren, Robert Penn. 1946. *All the King's Men*. New York: Harcourt, Brace & World. A fictionalized version of Huey Long's life, describing Governor Willie Stark's drive for power and privilege during the depression years.

Wilensky, Harold. 1966. "Work as a Social Problem," In Howard S. Becker (ed.), *Social Problems: A Modern Approach*. New York: John Wiley and Sons, pp. 117–66. A sociologist's particularly effective analysis of work. The essay includes a historical examination of work as well as a detailed, penetrating study of work alienation.

Additional Assignments

1. Talk to at least six Americans who are old enough to have voted in two presidential elections. (If you can find three Democrats and three Republicans, that will be useful for sensitizing you to some party differences in perception.) Ask them the following questions:
   a. What were the main issues in the presidential election of ———? (Fill in year of most recent election.)
   b. What were the differences in Democratic and Republican presidential candidates' views on each of these issues?
   c. Who were the vice-presidential candidates for each party? What did they say about the issues?
   d. What factor(s) made you choose a particular candidate?
   e. How did the issues in this presidential campaign differ from the campaign four years earlier?
   On the basis of your findings, can you conclude that our two-party system does or does not encourage politicians' taking significantly different positions on issues? As you think about what your interviewees said, would you be optimistic or pessimistic about using the political process to produce changes you might advocate? Does the information you gathered stimulate any ideas about changing the American political process?
2. Without consulting the text, daydream for a few minutes about the occupation you are considering. Then make two lists—the positive and negative features you feel are associated with this occupation. Now consult the text material examining sources of job satisfaction/dissatisfaction. Are the factors listed there consistent with your perception of what is satisfying or dissatisfying about the job you are considering? How does your occupational choice rate using these criteria?

Answers to Objective Test Questions

True • False Test

1. f	6. t
2. f	7. f
3. t	8. t
4. f	9. t
5. t	10. f

Multiple-Choice Test

1. d	6. c
2. b	7. d
3. a	8. a
4. d	9. b
5. d	10. b

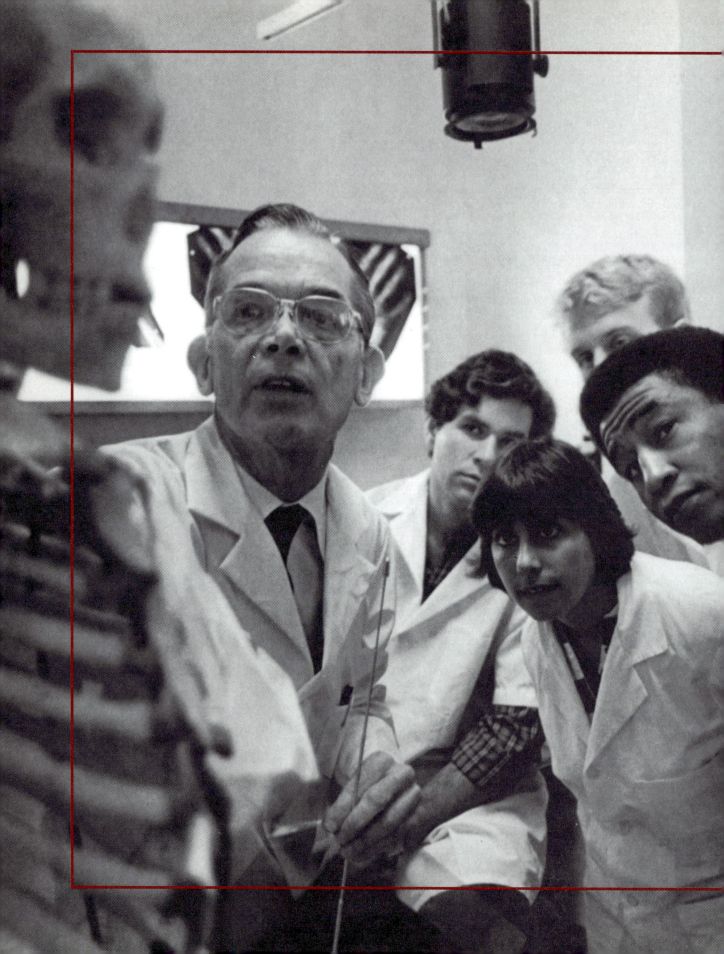

Science, Medicine, and Health Care

14

In the summer of 1988 at the Fourth International Conference on AIDS in Stockholm, Robert Gallo was in his glory. Usually described as the codiscoverer of the AIDS virus or as the leading AIDS researcher in the United States, Gallo had already received every major award in biomedicine, except for the Nobel Prize. Furthermore with his name appearing on over 900 scientific papers, Gallo was one of the most prolific researchers alive.

At the Stockholm conference, thousands of reporters were in attendance, and Gallo was the object of great interest. Mobbed like a rock star wherever he went, the always flamboyant Dr. Gallo seemed to thrive on the attention. All reporters received interviews, but in most cases these were restricted to three minutes. For the largest American papers and networks, however, a special setting was supplied.

One at a time, these privileged reporters were ushered into a private room by one of Washington's most expensive public-relations specialists. There, in essence, they were introduced to the king and his court—Dr. Gallo along with the vaccine specialists Dani P. Bolognesi of Duke University and Maurice Hilleman of the Merck, Sharp & Dohme pharmaceutical company reclining in plush leather chairs with crystal decanters, brandy snifters, and espresso cups arrayed on a nearby counter.

While Dr. Gallo has had such triumphs, he has also been controversial. In April 1984 the U.S. secretary of Health and Human Services announced that Gallo had found the virus that causes AIDS. The French virologist, Luc Montagnier, who months earlier had claimed the discovery, challenged the announcement, saying that Gallo had either purposely or accidently used a viral strain that he (Montagnier) had supplied, and later filed a suit against the United States and Gallo for the patent on the first AIDS antibody blood test. In 1987 the French prime minister and the U.S. president signed an agreement stating that Gallo and Montagnier would share credit for the discovery of the AIDS virus and the organizations with which they were associated would split the proceeds from the patents.

Seven years after the quarrel started, Dr. Gallo admitted that accidently he had used Montagnier's virus, and the controversy started once again, with Montagnier saying that years earlier Gallo had lied about what happened. Then in 1991 Gallo wrote a book in which he provided great detail about the events surrounding his claim to be the sole discoverer of the AIDS virus (Specter 1991).

Like other people whose lives are centered around scientific and medical issues, Robert Gallo is trying both to make a significant contribution and achieve personal goals. Because considerable mystique surrounds both science and medicine, we delve into a variety of sources that attempt to demystify those fields by analyzing their everyday workings.

Science is a systematic effort to develop general principles about a particular subject matter based on actual observations and stated in a form that can be tested by any competent person. The body of knowledge that comprises a science represents the efforts of a scientific community, not simply the results of individual experience. In modern times scientific investigation has become the most widely accepted activity for accumulating knowledge, and it has taken over the role that religious specialists, astrologers, and philosophers usually had in preindustrial societies.

Science seldom existed in preindustrial societies. As we noted in Chapter 12, "Religion and Education," secularization occurred as societies industrialized: The belief in scientific principles replaced religious faith, and a new institution developed. In modern times theory and research based on the scientific method are located at the core of many different disciplines; the results of scientific endeavors diffuse through modern life, affecting such diverse subjects as prenatal care, childrearing techniques, nutrition and dieting, building and bridge construction, the refinement of clean-energy forms, the development of weapons systems, and health care. In the first half of this chapter, we discuss the development of science and also scientists and scientific work.

Medicine is the scientifically based practice concerned with the prevention and treatment of disease and the treatment of injury. Doctors and other medical personnel ideally use the most recent scientifically tested knowledge to treat illness and injury. Prevention has received more emphasis in the public-health movement than in traditional medical practice.

The second half of this chapter is concerned with **medical sociology**—the study of the social settings in which health, sickness, and health care occur. This field, which has existed since the middle of the twentieth century, examines all subject matter involving health and health care but emphasizes disease and the medical professions. We discuss disease and death in the United States. After that we look briefly at American health care and the medical professions, and the chapter closes with an analysis of patient-doctor relations.

In both institutional areas, science and medicine, we will see that over time knowledge has increased and technical skill has improved. We will also learn that in spite of such advancements and often because of such advancements, problems and controversy often develop in both areas.

The Development of Science

During most of human history, science and the scientist have had a negligible role in people's lives. Their potential to be important was always there, as science can be a major source of technological advances. For a number of reasons, however, science made very modest contributions to societies until modern times. The reasons include:

Limited range of practical tasks for science. In the realm of astronomy, for instance, ancient societies made certain practical advances through crude scientific investigation—in particular, the formation of a calendar, the establishment of dates for seasonal festivals, and the prediction of eclipses. But after the early societies in Babylon, Egypt, Greece, India, and Mexico had mastered the technology necessary to complete these tasks, they visualized no practical reasons for further innovation. This was because innovation was motivated entirely by practical considerations and not by the modern scientific tradition emphasizing continuing research and development.

Little incentive to incorporate scientific analysis in most areas where technological development was occurring. In some preindustrial societies, technological advance was an ongoing process, but progress was possible without contributions from science. Architecture and construction engineering are good cases in point. Ancient architects and engineers learned from working directly with their materials. They transmitted little knowledge in writing, and any drawings they used were simple and free of abstraction. Early buildings, bridges, and other structures were much more precise than they would have been if their developers had relied on contemporary scientific formulations.

Opposition to scientific inquiry. In some cases the use of science would have threatened a traditional system of belief. For example, if an ancient priest or priestess used religious ritual to determine when to hold a seasonal festival, he or she probably would have opposed the adoption of a scientifically derived calendar that would have eliminated a ritual that he or she both enjoyed performing and believed represented a significant religious activity.

In one ancient society—Greece—science did play a significant part. For about two hundred years (from the fourth to the second century B.C.), a flowering of pure science occurred in mathematics and physics, which both maintained a formal linkage with philosophy. However, the significance

The spectacular advances of modern science could not have occurred without the contributions made by scientists in the past.

of these scientific disciplines declined when science and philosophy separated. With the separation many people turned to philosophy for answers to moral-religious and political problems. Science, widely considered little more than excess baggage, became the endeavor of a few learned men living an isolated existence in Alexandria. The most practical sciences—medicine and astronomy—continued to flourish until the second century A.D.

It was not until the seventeenth century in England that science received widespread acceptance. Two factors seem to have contributed to that development. In the first place, science gradually obtained a central part in the emerging conception of progress. Scientists and business people began to establish close relationships, with the production of better navigation techniques and instruments a particular concern. In England the mathematicians Robert Recorde and John Dee served as consultants to large trading companies. Henry Biggs, the first professor of mathematics at Gresham College in London, belonged to the London (later the Virginia) Company, which was the first commercial group to sail to the New World. Besides their common involvement in navigation, English scientists and business people showed mutual interest in machines, mining, lens

grinding, and the construction of watches and other instruments.

A second factor that supported the rise of science to prominence in the seventeenth century was the contribution of Protestantism, which was much more inclined to permit individual believers to develop their own interpretations of the Bible than either Catholicism or Judaism. It was possible for Protestants to believe in good conscience that God's will and scientific progress were in harmony. Not all Protestants, to be sure, supported the development of science. In some small, self-contained Protestant communities in Switzerland, Scotland, and Germany, the citizens regarded science with less tolerance than the people of Catholic countries. But in England such religious control was not imposed, and the rise of science received early acceptance. It was similarly supported in America, where the Puritan settlers emphasized a regularized, patterned quality to all activity and readily accepted the conclusion that scientific investigation could provide human beings with extensive practical knowledge about the universe.

THE RISE OF SCIENCE IN THE UNITED STATES

At the beginning of the twentieth century, the leaders of American industry began to recognize the potential contributions that a full-time professionalized scientific staff could make to the manufacture of new and more effective products. These industrial leaders encouraged the development of graduate programs where students could receive a Ph.D. in a variety of scientific fields. Within the U.S. system of professional education, degree recipients were expected to keep abreast of scientific advances, to initiate research, and to contribute generally to the advancement of science. One of the outgrowths of this research emphasis has been the extensive development of professional-scientific associations, which often sponsor journals as well as regional and national conventions. In addition, the belief in the significance of the professional researcher has meant a stronger support for increasingly complex and sophisticated types of organized research than in Europe, where research has traditionally been less professionalized.

At present large research units exist at universities and also in governmental and industrial settings. After World War II, a major impetus to government-sponsored research has been the interest of the national government in nuclear weapons and atomic energy. Scientists have become advocates and consumers of federal expenditure for research and also advisers and decision makers in important areas of public policy. Figures indicate a steadily increasing federal governmental support for research. The federal expenditure for research and development activities rose (in current dollars) from $5.2 billion in 1953, to $26.1 billion in 1970, and about $145.5 billion in 1990. Within universities, government, and private industry, more than a half-million scientists and engineers are engaged in full-time research. Almost 100,000 scientific journals currently exist, and they publish more than 2 million scientific papers each year. A major argument supporting continued heavy funding for science is that its endeavors have led to technological progress, which in turn has created wealth and prosperity for society (Ben-David 1971; *Economist* 1991; Merton 1973, 228–54; U.S. Bureau of the Census, *Statistical Abstract of the United States*: 1984, No. 1016; U.S. Bureau of the Census, *Statistical Abstract of the United States*: 1992, No. 956; Williams 1970, 570–75; Wyngaarden 1984). Figure 14.1 illustrates one result of the strong American scientific emphasis.

One of the most impressive developments in the history of science was Isaac Newton's *Principia* in which he described the universe as guided by laws of motion harmonizing the forces of nature. Inspired by Newton's analysis, John Locke, Adam Smith, and James Madison supposedly discovered laws guiding and harmonizing human behavior. With scientific insight as a guide, it seemed that America would be able to move steadily in the direction of increased rationality, greater wealth, a more pleasant, civilized lifestyle—in short, unending progress.

In recent years, however, there has been a growing skepticism about such broad, scientifically linked claims, with increasing attention paid to the dangerous or destructive consequences of scientific developments—the immense destruction that could be created by nuclear weaponry, environmental pollution resulting from diverse by-products of the industrial world, death and injury caused by automobiles and other modern forms of technology, and the exploitation of poor countries by wealthy nations seeking resources and markets for their greater enrichment (Cleveland 1988). The dangers of modern life and the growing public sense that science does not provide easy solutions is suggested by the following anonymous couplet.

> Strange that man should make up lists of living things in danger.
> Why he fails to list himself is really even stranger.

408

Figure 14.1

Twentieth-Century Nobel Prize Laureates in the Sciences:[1] Selected Countries

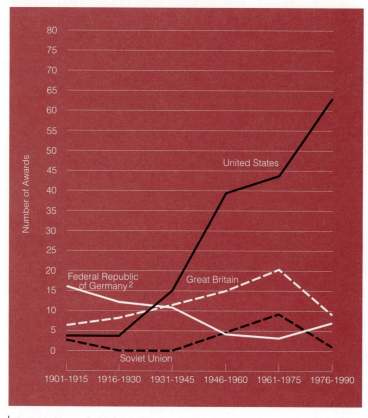

[1]*Chemistry, physics, and physiology/medicine.*
[2]*Includes East Germany before 1946.*

Winning a Nobel prize in science is an individual achievement, but as this graph suggests, some countries provide better contexts for encouraging this kind of scientific achievement than others do. In the United States, the professionalization of science, which has received the combined support of industry, higher education, and government, has helped produce a record of unparalleled success in this area of scientific achievement.

Source: Adapted from U.S. Bureau of the Census. Statistical Abstract of the United States: 1992, No. 977.

Scientists and Scientific Work ▪

In one national survey, 93 percent of Americans favored scientific endeavor, with 74 percent indicating that it is very important and 19 percent concluding that it is fairly important that the United States be a leader in scientific growth and development (Roper Organization, *Roper Reports*, May 1979).

The public support for scientific endeavors is undoubtedly one factor that has provided scientists the freedom to conduct research without much concern for citizens' needs and interests. In this section the topics are the practice of scientific norms and two controversial areas of research.

Table 14.1 presents some significant characteristics of American scientists and engineers.

Table 14.1 Characteristics of American Scientists and Engineers: 1989[1]

	Percent
SEX	
Male	82.8
Female	17.2
RACE	
White	88.5
Asian-American	9.2
African-American	1.6
Other or not reported	0.7
SCIENTIFIC SPECIALTY	
Life science	25.8
Engineering	16.7
Physical science	15.7
Psychology	13.5
All social science except economics	11.5
Computer science	4.4
Environmental science	4.4
Economics	4.1
Mathematics	3.9

[1]*All scientists and engineers included in this table have doctorates.*

Source: *Adapted from* U.S. Bureau of the Census. Statistical Abstract of the United States: 1992, No. 973.

THE PRACTICE OF SCIENTIFIC NORMS

Are scientists morally superior beings who lead exemplary professional lives? Some evidence disputes such a claim, indicating that scientists have their fair share of such uninspiring traits as driving personal ambition (Specter 1991), loss of productivity (Levin and Stephan 1991), and indifference to scientific advancement in their fields (Moravcsik 1985). Robert Merton (1973, 268-78), in contrast, described four scientific norms which he suggested promote a high moral standard of scientific behavior:

1. ***Universalism.*** **Universalism** is a norm stating that all scientific claims of truth need to be evaluated by impersonal criteria consistent with existing knowledge in that field. Scientists will disregard such considerations as class, race, and national membership when they assess colleagues' work.

2. ***Communism.*** As a basic scientific norm, **communism** signifies that the substantive findings of science represent a common heritage, not the exclusive property of individual discoverers and their heirs. Thus Newton's famous remark—"If I have seen farther it is by standing on the shoulders of giants"—both expresses indebtedness to the common heritage and acknowledges the expectation that all scientists will contribute to that heritage.

3. ***Organized skepticism.*** In scientific pursuits **organized skepticism** is the conclusion that no scientist's contribution to knowledge is acceptable without careful scrutiny. Sometimes this norm brings scientists into conflict with the members of other institutions—clergymen and politicians, for instance. A prominent controversy is the question of how humanity originated. Scientists' support for organized skepticism has simply made it impossible for them to accept the biblical story of creation when archaeological evidence suggests the occurrence of an evolutionary process.

4. ***Disinterestedness.*** The fourth norm of **disinterestedness** is a requirement that scientists avoid the pursuit of work that is self-serving and self-interested. It is possible that science draws people with higher ideals than other occupations, but no evidence supports this position. More likely the emphasis on disinterestedness is the result of the public nature of scientists' work, which tends to encounter more rigorous policing than the work in many other professions.

A study of forty-two scientists associated with the Apollo lunar missions offered some evidence opposing Merton's four scientific norms. One scientist spoke against the claim of organized skepticism, saying, "It takes commitment to be a scientist. One thing that spurs a scientist on is competition, warding off attacks against what you've published" (Mitroff 1974, 588).

All the scientists rejected the idea of the objective, emotionally disinterested scientist as naive. One scientist noted, "The [emotionally]

410 disinterested scientist is a myth. Even if there were such a being, he probably wouldn't be worth much as a scientist. I still think you can be objective in spite of having strong interests and biases" (Mitroff 1974, 588).

A basic conclusion emerging from this research was that scientists were more likely to use the norms designated by Merton in situations where the problems were well-defined and clearly structured. On the other hand, the less clear and less settled a problem, the more frequently the scientists were inclined to develop intensely personal hypotheses and interpretations. Under these circumstances they often rejected the norms described by Merton for a set of "counter-norms," which the quotations above illustrate. Table 14.2 summarizes both Merton's scientific norms and the counter-norms.

In addition, we might consider that another norm affecting many scientists' lives is the requirement to find funding—an activity that can take up to a quarter of scientists' time and that has become more difficult in the past decade as government sources have been cut back. An analysis of professionals' job satisfaction concluded that the pressure to obtain funding was probably the major reason, according to survey data, that scientists were less satisfied with their work than computer specialists, lawyers, medical doctors, clergy, college teachers, and professionals in the arts (Trankina 1991).

IN THE THROES OF CONTROVERSY: DNA AND NUCLEAR-WEAPONS RESEARCH

Two richly funded areas of contemporary scientific research are the studies of DNA and of nuclear weapons. A discussion of these topics raises interesting and troubling questions about the conduct of scientific research. We turn now to a summary of the positions for and against each type of research and then consider the social conditions that permit these activities to continue unabated when they are so controversial.

DNA Research

The basis for these investigations is the relatively recent discovery that the combination of genetic material from one organism with genetic material from another can produce a new organism with entirely new properties.

Some supporters of this new technology claim that it will revolutionize health care by introducing new means of curing various diseases created by genetic deficiencies. Other advocates contend that DNA studies will help solve world food problems by producing huge crops of corn and wheat capable of supplying their own nitrogen fertilizer or that new organisms can be invented to perform critical tasks like cleaning up oil spills, producing valuable hormones such as insulin, or possibly even curing cancer.

Table 14.2 Scientific Norms and Counter-Norms

Merton's scientific norms	*Counter-norms*
Universalism: that scientists use impersonal criteria to evaluate all claims to truth	Particularism: that scientists accept or reject claims primarily on the basis of colleagues' personal characteristics
Communism: that the substantive findings of science represent a common heritage	Solitariness or "miserism": that scientists consider the disposition of their discoveries within the realm of property rights
Organized skepticism: that no scientists' contribution to knowledge is acceptable without careful scrutiny	Organized dogmatism: that scientists must have complete conviction about their own findings while doubting the worth of others' findings
Disinterestedness: that scientists avoid the pursuit of work that is self-serving and self-interested	Interestedness: that scientists achieve self-satisfaction in work by serving special-interest communities such as their own research units

Source: Adapted from Ian I. Mitroff. "Norms and Counter-Norms in a Select Group of the Apollo Moon Scientists: A Case Study of the Ambivalence of Scientists," American Sociological Review. *vol. 39 (August 1974), pp. 579–95.*

On the other hand, the opponents of DNA research point out that this modern technology contains unknown, perhaps devastating potential for human destruction and that the possible costs considerably outweigh the possible gains. One of the critics' greatest fears is that the E. *coli* bacteria used in most DNA experiments might accidentally escape a laboratory and produce disastrous results. For instance, a lab technician might breathe or swallow a few particles containing E. *coli*. These organisms might then combine with the E. *coli* that exists in the intestines of all human beings, and the result could be a particularly virulent virus that might eventually endanger or even destroy all humanity.

Nuclear-Weapons Research

Two laboratories at the University of California are entirely responsible for the conception, design, and testing of every nuclear warhead the United States has ever developed—from the first bomb dropped on Hiroshima to the most recent nuclear weaponry. The University of California has operated the labs from their beginning—Los Alamos since 1943 and Livermore since 1952. The Department of Energy has provided about $3.8 million yearly to fund Los Alamos and Livermore.

The proponents of nuclear-weapons research contend that the only way to survive in the modern world is to maintain a superior military presence and that nuclear weaponry represents the most crucial component of that strength. Without a massive stockpile of nuclear weapons, the proponents state, the United States will be vulnerable to attack from powerful foreign enemies and that even with the end of the cold war, a powerful nuclear capability remains necessary. Nuclear weaponry, in short, represents a deterrent to World War III.

The opponents of nuclear-weapons research contend that the idea of nuclear-weapons superiority is a fantasy—that both sides would be destroyed in a nuclear war and that there would be only losers, not winners. Nuclear-weapons research, the opponents contend, should cease. Instead of bolstering the nuclear arsenals, there should be an immediate curtailment of nuclear weaponry.

Both the scientific community and the American public are divided on these two research issues.

The Conduct of Controversial Research

The following conditions help to sustain the research on DNA and nuclear weaponry in spite of their controversial nature:

1. ***Scientists' strong support for the research goals.*** Scientists need to believe sufficiently strongly in what they are doing so that they can block out or at least significantly surbordinate the issues raised by opponents.

   It seems likely that most if not all scientists involved in controversial studies must personally support the value positions underlying their research. For nuclear-weapons research, a commitment to the proponents' position on nuclear weaponry seems necessary. A team of writers noted:

   > Only by increasing the quantity and sophistication of our weapons, the proponents argue—improving their range, accuracy and maneuverability as well as total number of warheads—can we be sure they will not be used in warfare. Indeed, if this proposition is not true, in the context of today, there can be no point to weapons research: if it increases the chance of war, it is impossible to justify. As one Livermore Lab employee has stated, "In order to work here, you have to believe in nuclear deterrence."

   > (*University of California Nuclear Weapons Conversion Project* 1980, 96)

2. ***Enthusiastic governmental sponsorship.*** In order to conduct controversial research effectively, scientists need federal funding, governmental assistance in establishing favorable regulations, or both. In the case of DNA research, a number of the committee members who created the federal guidelines have had ties to the precise companies they have supposedly regulated. This situation has represented a blatant conflict of interest

(Rifkin 1980). In nuclear-weapons research, the process has been similar. For the Strategic Arms Limitation Talks (SALT) with the Soviet Union, a number of directors and former directors of both the Livermore and Los Alamos laboratories served as technical experts and participants. Recently, however, conditions promoting nuclear-weapons research have changed. With the demise of the Soviet Union, the fear of a nuclear confrontation has diminished sharply. A report from the National Academy of Sciences suggested that perhaps the supply of nuclear warheads could be cut by 90 percent. While this estimate might be high, it is indicative of the fact that government sponsorship of nuclear-weapons research is becoming less enthusiastic (*Economist* 1991a). Still, ever anxious to keep themselves employed, nuclear scientists persist, with Los Alamos designers trying to convince Navy and Air Force leaders to adopt a new line of small nuclear weapons—the 10-ton "micronuke," the 100-ton "mininuke," and the 1000-ton "tinynuke" that they claim would produce "reduced fallout" and prove useful in wars in developing nations (Arkin 1992).

3. **Policy of secrecy.** People conducting controversial research often conclude that an effective way to avoid controversy is to keep their research hidden, thereby preventing the public from learning about the dangers that might be developing. Several years ago an interviewer asked the Attorney General of New Jersey, who was in charge of investigating DNA research in his state, whether he knew of any firms planning to do P-4 (maximum-risk) DNA studies in New Jersey. The Attorney General replied that he did not. The interviewer then explained that the Hoffman-LaRoche Company was constructing a P-4 facility in Nutley, New Jersey (Rifkin 1980, 151).

Secrecy also prevails in the nuclear-research area, as Senator Stuart Symington learned during an inspection trip. Symington, who was a member of the Joint Committee on Atomic Energy and a former secretary of the Air Force, was relatively well informed on nuclear matters. Yet he explained:

> Not until I became a member of the Joint Committee and travelled to Europe with Sen. Pastore . . . in 1971, did I realize the military strength of the U.S. and become acquainted with the vast lethal power of our nuclear arsenal. I actually learned more about the true strength of the U.S. forces in Europe in those six days than I had in some 18 years on the Armed Services Committee. One cannot help but consider the implication to our defense and foreign policies if these facts were known by the appropriate committees of Congress, as well as . . . by the American people.

(*University of California Weapons Conversion Project* 1980, 101–02)

4. **An in-group for scientists.** Both kinds of controversial research are possible because of the primacy of the research goal, governmental support, and a context of secrecy. But another factor also seems to contribute. In the course of their work, individuals often need support and encouragement from others to perform effectively. Recall the concept "in-group" from Chapter 4, "Groups." An "in-group" is any group whose membership maintains a strong sense of

This Rockwell B-1 bomber can carry either nuclear or conventional weaponry.

identification and loyalty and a feeling of exclusiveness toward nonmembers.

In both DNA and nuclear-weapons research, scientists and technicians encourage each other's efforts, emphasizing the tremendous importance of what they are doing and dismissing outsiders' criticisms of their work as the ignorant chatter of the lay public.

Thus controversial scientific research, like all social activity, is fostered by certain social conditions. Our analysis of four conditions related to two types of controversial research reveals that these activities are strongly supported by a number of groups and practices.

Looking at the dangers posed by such scientific innovations as those we have been discussing, two prominent Hungarian engineers suggested that the citizens of modern countries desperately need to use modern technology for worldwide communication to develop a common set of ethical standards benefiting all humanity and subordinating the selfish goals of a privileged few (Bendzsel and Kiss 1987). The idea has a distinctly conflict-theoretical flavor to it. How could it be implemented? An American specialist in public administration with a similar, if less global outlook proposed that that those who oversee the application of scientific innovations learn about them thoroughly, understand the implications of their use, and consult carefully with a wide range of experts in different fields before making decisions about their use (Cleveland 1988). One of many challenges is to figure out some way to make certain that the bureaucracies that regulate scientific and technological innovations carry out their mandate fully and competently. For the past half-century, American regulatory agencies have not had a good track record in this regard.

The nearby American Controversy addresses a difficult, well-publicized issue involving the use of modern technology.

We have just seen that science often involves itself with controversial subject matter; certainly medical activity often stirs controversy as well. This tendency is hardly surprising because medicine, even more than science, is concerned with life-and-death issues. The fundamental relationship between the two institutions is emphasized by the fact that our definition of medicine contains a reference to science: Medicine is the scientifically based practice concerned with the prevention and treatment of disease and the treatment of injury.

Over the past three-and-a-half centuries, scientific advances have been the source of medicine's rapid advancement. For instance, in 1628 William Harvey provided the first description of the circulation of blood; in 1673 Anton Leewenhoek invented the microscope; in 1797 Edward Jenner discovered smallpox vaccine; in 1846 William Morton perfected ether as an anesthetic; in 1866 Joseph Lister first used antiseptic methods in surgery; in the 1880s Robert Koch discovered the causes of anthrax, cholera, and tuberculosis; in 1954 Jonas Salk discovered polio vaccine; in 1970 John Charnley made the first hip joint socket replacement (Coe, 1978, 188). In modern times many people simply take these advancements for granted. But what would life be like without them? Consider, for instance, a society periodically ravaged by smallpox, cholera, and tuberculosis, or having an operation without an anesthetic!

Disease and Death in the United States ◼

Medicine is concerned with the treatment of **disease,** which is a condition of biological nonhealth. Microorganisms, which are either bacteria or viruses, invade human beings and other organisms and produce specific diseases. In this section we examine disease and the ultimate conqueror of all medical practice—death.

DISEASE

The United States Public Health Service (USPHS) has long recognized that an effective attack on disease requires knowledge of the number of people who have contracted various diseases and the extent to which different categories of individuals

AMERICAN CONTROVERSY
Do We Want Nuclear Energy?

 On April 1986 the worst nuclear accident in history occurred at the Chernobyl nuclear plant in Pripyat, a town in the then Soviet Union. This serious accident revitalized the debate about whether or not the use of nuclear power should be continued.

One might consider such an issue within a structural-functional framework: One side emphasizes the dysfunctions of nuclear energy and the other its functions. Actually it is even more specific than that: One side emphasizes the *latent* dysfunctions of nuclear energy and the other its *manifest* functions. (If this distinction is unclear, check the meanings of these concepts in Chapter 1, "Sociology: The Key to Understanding the Social World.")

Opponents of nuclear energy reading this chapter might be struck by the conclusions about controversial research discussed in the previous section. In particular, they might emphasize that those employed in producing a particular type of technology are unlikely to assess the risks carefully because their own livelihood is dependent on that technology.

Opponents will also stress the problem of assessing the long-term impact of nuclear contamination. While nuclear proponents might say that the fallout from the Three Mile Island accident or the nuclear fire at Brown's Ferry, the routine emissions occurring at all plants, and leaks from stored nuclear wastes have not proved harmful, optimism is premature. The impact of strontium 90, which can cause leukemia, is not detectable for up to five years, and some tumor malignancies can take twenty or even thirty years to appear. A particularly serious problem is the magnified effects of nuclear fallout in the food chain; some fish concentrate the impact of radiation up to 100,000 times its occurrence in the environment. Furthermore our water-treatment systems are not equipped to remove radioactive particles, and health departments cannot monitor all our food.

No, we are better off harnessing the wind, the sun, and the tides, the opponents conclude. We can burn municipal garbage, obtain methane from existing landfills, and mine coal safely and burn it cleanly as Australia does.

The proponents of nuclear power will say that opponents are exaggerating. They will point out that a large part of the cost of nuclear-power plants goes for insurance in the form of layer after layer of physical protection: fuel traps for radioactive gases, steel casings for uranium, and enormously strong concrete and steel containment buildings. Unfortunately the Soviets did not take the same precautions as we have; the differences are tragically apparent when one compares the minimal impact produced by the Three Mile Island accident with the much more extensive damage created in the Chernobyl situation.

Nuclear power now lights about one out of every six bulbs in the United States. In France, which uses plants based on our designs, it is about three out of every four bulbs. It seems important to continue to develop this cheap, safe form of power as a means of ensuring our energy independence from foreign energy sources.

What do you think? Certainly a problem in debating this issue is that more specialized information enters here than with most subjects analyzed in these American Controversies. For that reason perhaps it is tempting simply to let political leaders, with the advice of experts, resolve the issue. But can we trust them to make wise, balanced decisions that are truly in the American people's interest?

In discussing and debating the issue of nuclear energy, you might consider the reasons why people will take one side or the other on this issue. Evaluate not only experts but average citizens on this point.

Sources: Jeremy M. Hellman. "U.S. Plants Are Safe; Go Full Speed Ahead," USA TODAY. (April 30, 1986), p. 12A; Jeanne Honicker. "To Save Ourselves, Stop Nuclear Pollution," USA TODAY. (April 30, 1986), p. 12A.

are vulnerable to particular diseases. In the late 1950s and early 1960s, USPHS started three monthly surveys that collected a wealth of data on health and health care throughout the country.

The results of these surveys make it clear that some distinct trends in vulnerability to disease exist—in particular, in the likelihood that various groups will catch acute or chronic disorders. Acute diseases such as influenza, dysentery, and measles are likely to be intense, even incapacitating, but short-term, whereas chronic diseases such as heart conditions and arthritis can usually be controlled but not cured.

One pattern is that the older people become, the more likely they are to develop chronic ailments and the less likely they are to catch acute diseases. From a biological point of view, one would expect to find a higher rate of chronic disease among older people because such ailments are primarily the result of the degeneration of bodily tissue and the increasing ineffectiveness of various organs. On the other hand, younger people are less likely to have developed immunities through exposure to acute diseases than their elders have.

Women tend to have more acute and less chronic disease than do men. Once children pass the age of 10, females have a higher rate of acute disorders for the rest of their lives than males, and after the age of 17, males maintain a greater likelihood of developing chronic ailments than females. Several factors may account for men's greater susceptibility to chronic disease. It is possible that women are stronger physically than men—they do live longer—and therefore their bodies are more resistant to chronic disorders in old age. On the other hand, social conditions might play a significant part. Traditionally men have been more involved in the work world than women; perhaps work-related exposure to stress has made men more vulnerable to such chronic ailments as heart disease and ulcers.

There is also a relationship between income and disease. In general, the higher the income group, the lower the rate of disease. A number of factors are relevant. People in higher income groups generally live in cleaner and more sanitary situations; they also tend to have better nutrition, more effective medical services, and greater knowl-edge about disease and illness (Coe 1978, 61–64; Twaddle and Hessler 1977, 59–62).

Most data-gathering systems on disease statistics depend on information coming from health-care providers, with underreporting and reporting bias being frequent limitations. To overcome these difficulties, statisticians have been seeking alternative data sources, and one of the most promising appears to be medical centers' computerized data bases which include laboratory, inpatient, and outpatient information (Watkins, Lapham, and Hoy 1991).

DEATH

Just as certain categories of people are more vulnerable to disease, some status groups are more susceptible to death.

Age is one important factor. During the first year of life, there is a high death rate; the likelihood of death then remains low until about the age of 40 when physical deterioration and vulnerability to a number of serious chronic diseases cause the death rate to increase sharply.

At most ages males have a higher death rate than females. Working conditions, such as risk of injury and the likelihood of stress, are significant factors. As we have noted, it also seems possible that women are physically stronger than men, possessing in particular the capacity to resist more effectively a variety of diseases.

Married people tend to live longer than those who are not. Widowed individuals have higher death rates than married people, and the rates are the highest among those who have never been married. Perhaps part of the explanation for the relationship between marriage and long life is that married people are more likely to have an orderly existence and a range of relationships that will lessen the impact of stress.

Finally the higher an individual's social class position, the lower the death rate. Some high-risk factors faced by individuals with low socioeconomic status include physically dangerous occupations, inadequate housing, poor nutrition, limited access to medical facilities, crowded living conditions, and exposure to a relatively high level of violence (Larsen 1990; Twaddle and Hessler

416 1977, 78–84). In the United States, whites, whose social-class position tends to be considerably higher than blacks', average about six to seven years longer life expectancy (Keith and Smith 1988).

A recent article concluded that since virtually all nations base cause-of-death statistics on information supplied on death certificates, it would be useful to researchers to know something about the quality of this information, particularly whether some systematic biases occur in this area of reporting (Sirken et al. 1987). Table 14.3 lists the diseases that have been the leading causes of death over time.

No disease in modern times has created the attention and fear that AIDS has produced. The nearby Social Application uses historical information to reach some tentative conclusions about AIDS.

Table 14.3 Death Rates for Different Diseases: 1990

	Deaths per 100,000 Americans
Heart diseases	289
Cancer	201.7
Respiratory system	57.3
Digestive system	48.4
Genital organs	23.1
Breast	18
Leukemia	7.4
Cerebrovascular diseases[1]	57.9
Pneumonia and influenza	31.3
Diabetes	19.5
Chronic liver disease and cirrhosis	10.2

[1] *For instance, strokes.*

Source: *Adapted from U.S. Bureau of the Census. Statistical Abstract of the United States: 1992, No. 114.*

Health Care in the United States   ■

By seeking to avoid disease and death, people make these subjects significant issues in their lives. The significance is implied by the following statement: "Well, at least I've got my health." How many times have you heard people make such a statement? Fairly often, I suspect. Since people do not like to be unhealthy, they usually take measures to restore their health. **Health care** is the variety of public and private organizations that support an individual's effective physical, mental, and social adaptation to his or her environment. Modern American health care has some significant problems, which we will review.

SICKNESS IN THE SYSTEM

One prominent difficulty with modern health care is its cost. There has been a steady increase in the total expenditure, the per capita expenditure, and the percent of the Gross National Product. For instance, between 1970 and 1990, the total expenditure rose from $74.4 billion to $666.2 billion, increasing from $346 to $2,566 per capita and from 7.3 to 12.2 percent of the Gross National Product (U.S. Bureau of the Census, *Statistical Abstract of the United States: 1992*, No. 135).

Physicians' increasing fees have contributed to the rising cost of health care. Before World War II, medical doctors averaged about two-and-a-half times the income of all full-time workers. Now they average more than five times the national average, making them the highest paid occupational group in the country. The cost of specialization helps account for rising fees; six of seven practicing physicians are now specialists compared with about half in the early 1960s. Hospital costs, however, have made a more significant contribution to soaring health costs than doctors' fees. The increasing number of hospital workers as well as their rising wages or salaries have been contributing factors. A more significant influence on increasing costs has been the recent intensification of hospital care—the growing use of laboratory tests, X-rays, and such new and expensive advances as CAT scanners and heart-bypass surgery.

Admittedly most people do not pay for most of their health care. About 83 percent of health care is paid by "third parties"—private health-insurance companies, company health plans, and government programs, especially Medicare and Medicaid. With the expansion of these third

SOCIAL APPLICATION
What Does the History of Sexually Transmitted Diseases Reveal about AIDS?

By early 1992 at least 12.9 million people had contracted the human immunodeficiency virus (HIV), the virus that causes AIDS. A team of forty experts and researchers from around the world concluded that by the year 2000, between 40 and 110 million people will be infected. Obviously AIDS is a huge international problem.

In developing policies to combat the disease, one valuable source is historical information. In the past half century, American health-care officials have had little experience dealing with infectious, epidemic diseases, but in the 1930s they did, with the venereal (sexually transmitted) diseases of syphilis and gonorrhea causing debilitating symptoms and death and creating widespread fear. While we must be careful generalizing from the impact of those diseases to that produced by AIDS, there are some parallels, which can provide us with lessons.

Fear of the Disease Will Be Exaggerated and Influence Health-Care Policy Early in the twentieth century, the general public tended to believe that syphilis could be transmitted by touching or using an infected person's pen, pencil, toothbrush, towel, or bed. During World War I, the U.S. Navy removed doorknobs from its battleships, fearing that they could prove a source of infection. How could concern with

To combat AIDS *effectively, ads should not simply try to create fear. Instead they also should emphasize that sex with condoms can be pleasurable.*

casual transmission be so strong, especially with increasingly conclusive medical evidence that syphilis could only be transmitted sexually? It appears that at the root of the fears was the Victorian moral order, which emphasized a rigidly disciplined lifestyle and the postponement of sex until marriage. Venereal disease represented a blatant threat to that order, at a time when the Victorian code was being more subtlely attacked by the growth of cities and their sophisticated lifestyle; the influx of large immigrant groups, whom many Victorians considered immoral; and the increasingly weakened family structure.

With AIDS there is also widespread, misplaced fear that

the disease can be contracted by casual means. Many Americans fear exposure by using public toilet seats, drinking glasses, or water fountains. Once again there is a concrete pattern to the sense of threat; this time it seems to be centered on the two categories of people most frequently stricken by the disease and widely considered deviants—male homosexuals and intravenous drug users. Homosexuals, in particular, have experienced increased hostility and provoked exaggerated fears. For instance, during a major protest by gays in 1989, New York City police at the site wore surgical gloves. In addition, some medical personnel have refused to treat AIDS patients.

418

Education Will Have Limited Impact Controlling the Disease

Early in the twentieth century, many physicians, public-health officials, and social reformers attacked the Victorian code which declared that all discussion of sexuality and disease was unseemly. Only when the public understood the sources of venereal disease, these people argued, could it be fought effectively. While this idea was sensible, most of the campaigns promoted fear, with pamphlets and films describing and showing the most drastic cases of disfigured, blind, or insane victims. To avoid such a horrible outcome, young people were told to abstain from sexual activity. One prominent sex educator declared that fear is "the protective genius of the human body." But it turned out not to be true: The fear campaigns did not reduce the infection. Finally during World War II, a different approach was used: Soldiers were urged to use condoms. As one medical official indicated, "It is difficult to make the sex act unpopular."

A similar approach appears necessary with AIDS. There is a growing recognition that the most effective advertisements advocating condom use are not the ones trying to frighten people but those emphasizing the pleasurable quality of sex with a condom.

Compulsory Health Measures Will Not Control the Disease

In 1906 the Wassermann test was developed, permitting the detection of syphilis by a simple blood analysis. As a result it became possible to test a large number of people quickly and easily, and by the end of World War II, virtually all states required a Wassermann test for individuals getting married. This effort, however, has produced modest evidence of syphilis—in 1978, for example, turning up scarcely 1 percent of the cases of the disease detected that year. The problem was that premarital screening tests examined a low-risk group. Such testing, in fact, could prove counterproductive, driving high-risk individuals away from testing and treatment. In recent years some people have called for a similar program of AIDS testing, screening job applicants or even the entire population. Such widespread testing would be highly inefficient, with the distinct possibility that in a one-shot test individuals would not have developed sufficient antibodies to demonstrate that they had contracted the disease. In addition, a single test would not provide any assurance against people getting the virus in the future. Furthermore, as in the case of syphilis, high-risk individuals might feel pressured to avoid testing and treatment.

The AIDS Epidemic Will Not Quickly End with the Development of a Vaccine

In 1943 Dr. John S. Mahoney's penicillin injections of syphilis-infected rabbits were successful in eliminating the disease. After repeating his experiment with human subjects, the massive production of penicillin began. Incidence of syphilis fell from 72 cases per 100,000 population in 1943 to 4 per 100,000 in 1956, and gonorrhea was almost eliminated. But in later years, as educational efforts and searching out affected individuals have been reduced, the rate of syphilis has risen, reaching over 13 per 100,000 population by the late 1980s. Thus it is not simply a question of developing a vaccine for AIDS; it also must be delivered effectively.

Conclusion

This analysis has not been particularly optimistic, but there is no implication that the situation is hopeless. What the historical lessons teach is that there are certain obvious pitfalls to be avoided. Education, testing, and research are sources of hope for combatting this dread disease: They simply must be used under the most effective conditions.

Sources: Lawrence K. Altman. "Researchers Report Much Grimmer AIDS Outlook," New York Times. (June 4, 1992), pp. A1+; Allan M. Brandt. "AIDS in Historical Perspective: Four Lessons from the History of Sexually Transmitted Diseases," American Journal of Public Health. vol. 78 (April 1988), pp. 367–71; Jonathan M. Mann. "AIDS: a Global Strategy for a Global Challenge," Impact of Science on Society. vol. 38 (1988), pp. 159–67; Lawrence Shulman and Joanne E. Mantell. "The AIDS Crisis: A United States Health Care Perspective." Social Science and Medicine. vol. 26 (1988), pp. 979–88.

•••

parties in the 1960s, a "fees for service" system was devised: the more services provided, the greater the payment. It is widely agreed that this system is the major culprit in spiraling health-care costs (Kornblum and Julian 1989, 35).

Another major symptom of deficiency in American health care involves limited access to competent medical care. This difficulty is summed up by the sentence: "I can't find a doctor." The situation has two aspects. First, some people are unable to locate a physician qualified to treat their particular medical complaint. This is because throughout the country there are not enough doctors in certain medical areas—emergency care, home care, and care outside of regular working hours, in particular. Second, certain groups within the society face particular access problems. The poor, ethnic and racial minorities, and rural people are often deprived of effective medical care. The principal reason is that many members of these groups lack adequate incomes and insurance to pay for standard medical treatment. An additional factor operating here is that most physicians prefer to locate their offices in middle- or upper-income areas, and so poorer people's access problem is also geographical (Wolinsky 1980, 416–19).

Sickness in the American health-care system is apparent when one compares Americans' life-expectancy and infant-mortality rates with other major industrialized nations. In spite of the fact that Americans spend more per capita on health care than people in other countries, American life expectancy in 1991 was lower than that of people in eighteen other nations. On infant mortality (death in the first year), twenty-one countries had a lower rate than the United States in 1991 (U.S. Bureau of the Census, *Statistical Abstract of the United States*: 1992, No. 1361).

How could American health care be improved? This country desperately needs a national health-care program that operates within a prescribed budget and makes comprehensive benefits universally available. A number of states are developing programs that meet these standards. For instance, Minnesota has enacted legislation that would provide health insurance to uninsured people by taxing doctors, hospitals, and other health-care businesses. Oregon has been seeking federal approval to insure all poor families under its Medicaid program. In Vermont there will be uni-

While this physician's efforts to provide medical care for homeless people is commendable, such individual efforts do not compensate substantially for the nation's failure to establish a national health-care program covering all citizens.

versal health care by 1995, with a state health-care agency having what the governor called "enormous leverage" to gain effective coverage at low rates and a new set of taxes subsidizing the system (Butterfield 1992).

European nations supply all or most of citizens' medical coverage. Why, one might wonder, does the United States, which is wealthier than most of these nations, fail to provide comparable coverage? Certainly one significant factor is cultural—the American emphasis on autonomy and individualism. Each individual or family is widely felt responsible for meeting personal needs. Inability to do so represents a significant failure, and many Americans feel that the government should not step in and bail out that person or family. In contrast, the sociological perspective emphasizes the social forces producing the vicious cycle of poverty (discussed in Chapter 8, "Social Statification"), putting poor people at a tremendous disadvantage to other Americans.

The focus now shifts from the health-care system to the central figures in that system—physicians and nurses.

Medical Careers

When Americans evaluate professions, medicine will be at or near the top of the list. But what is it that separates a profession from other occupational groups? Within their specialty area, the members of a profession have the exclusive right

to "determine what the problem is, how the problem is to be dealt with, and what price is to be paid for dealing with it" (Freidson 1970, 368–69).

The members of a profession, in short, have autonomy in their work, and they receive both

420

cultural and legal backing in this regard. Physicians are the only people permitted to diagnose and treat disease and injury, and they also set the fees for their work. No outsiders may interfere; the policing of any irregularities is done by the members of the profession.

PHYSICIANS AND THEIR PROFESSIONAL ACTIVITIES

What status characteristics do you associate with physicians? If "male" and "white" come to mind, then you are considering two prominent characteristics of most modern doctors. At present women and racial minorities are still underrepresented in medical schools. In addition, medical students tend to come from professional backgrounds and from families with above-average incomes. We see, in short, that a distinct selection exists for students entering medical school.

Socialization of Doctors

For the first two years, medical students' education is concentrated in the basic sciences associated with medicine: anatomy, biochemistry, biophysics, cellular biology, genetics, microbiology, pathology, pharmacology, and physiology. During those two years, students are expected to absorb a great deal of knowledge from these different specialties.

Medical students find themselves in an

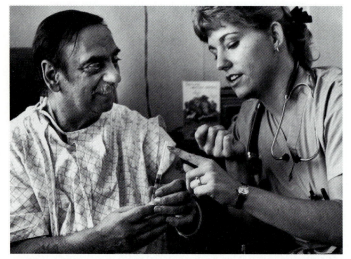

With more emphasis on teaching medical students interpersonal skills, doctors are increasingly likely to develop the ability shown here to communicate effectively with their patients.

instructional environment that is generally much less structured than in college. At one medical school, a directive to beginning students reads in part:

> We do not use the comfortable method of spoon-feeding. . . . Limits are not fixed. Each field will be opened up somewhat sketchily. . . . You will begin to paint a picture on a vast canvas but only the center of the picture will be worked in any detail. The periphery will gradually blur into the hazy background. And the more you work out the peripheral pattern, the more you will realize the vastness of that which stretches an unknown distance beyond.

> (*Fox* 1978, 190)

During their first two years, medical students begin to distinguish three kinds of "vastness" stretching in front of them. The first type involves their imperfect mastery of current knowledge. The second type concerns the limitation to current knowledge; physicians presently do not possess answers to innumerable questions. A third type of "vastness" results from the inability to distinguish between the first two types. In the course of their schooling, medical students must be able to grasp the third uncertainty—to appreciate that grave consequences can result if they are unable to do so.

But doctors' socialization involves more than simply compiling specialized knowledge. In recognition of many patients' complaints that their doctors lack interpersonal skills, some medical schools are trying to teach their students how to establish effective patient-doctor relations. At Mt. Sinai Hospital in Manhattan, medical students have been required to confront actors who play patients, and these encounters have been videotaped, with the students receiving copies for their analysis along with written evaluations from their "patients." Dr. Daniel J. Klass, a member of the National Board of Medical Examiners, is developing a section on doctor-patient relations to be added to the licensing exam as early as 1995. Dr. Klass indicated that new physicians "should have skills that allow them to relate to patients well, to listen properly, to hear what's said, so the patient leaves the encounter thinking, 'Hey, I just saw a real doctor'" (Belkin 1992a, B5).

Doctors' Relations with Colleagues

"Harry, I'm worried." Dr. Finchlow stares straight

ahead, lost in thought. "I've called you in for this consultation because Mary Perkins doesn't seem to be responding to treatment. I wanted to talk to you because you're our top person in neuro-surgery. I'll give you a detailed rundown on her condition and treatment to date, and then you tell me what you think." Such scenes appear frequently in soap operas, but they do not seem to be a prominent part of medical activity.

Sociologist Elliot Freidson (1978) has pointed out that many people believe that the mere exis-tence of group practice will encourage a higher level of medical performance than if each doctor works alone. However, for group practice to have such an effect, doctors must be able to exercise some social control over each other's behavior, and such control is possible only with systematic and extensive exchange of information about patients by their physicians. Studying the subject, Freidson found that this process did not generally occur.

Doctors would frequently make referrals to other doctors in their group practice, but the infor-mation contained in the referral was often brief and superficial, thus providing the physician receiving the referral little information about the colleague's competence. In addition, within the group practice, no effort existed to make informa-tion available to all others about each physician's performance. For instance, pediatricians and internists worked at parallel services, seldom if ever referring to each other and so having little opportunity to learn about the competence of each other's work.

An important issue involved mistakes. Doctors were willing to discuss their own and colleagues' mistakes if they were relatively minor, not reflect-ing on their basic competence. With a clear blun-der, however, they tended to be protective. Freidson interviewed a surgeon who had recently examined a young girl. The girl had a cancerous thyroid, that, according to her chart, had only "blossomed" in the last few weeks. The surgeon spoke with the physician who had made the refer-ral. This man admitted that the family doctor who had been treating the case for years had made a mistake, and the referring physician told the sur-geon, "Look, the less said about it the better. The man who sent her to me feels horrible about it. He realizes now he missed something and he said, 'Forget it. Don't say anything about it.' He really feels badly about it, you see." The surgeon agreed

with his colleague's comments about the family doctor. The surgeon said, "All right, he knows. What more can you do? After a man knows and he realizes, you are not going to go in and twist a knife in his back" (Freidson 1978, 237).

Freidson concluded that while group practice does provide a fine opportunity to collect and share information and to evaluate colleagues' per-formances, such tasks are generally not pursued. In fact, it has been his observation that the bene-fits of group practice are no more than negligible.

Recently, in fact, doctors have been much less concerned about colleagues' evaluations than federal governmental regulation. In 1992 the Medicare program developed new rules to help control costs, the Occupational Safety and Health Administration (OSHA) imposed standards to pro-tect medical personnel from exposure to hepatitis and AIDS, and the Department of Health and Human Services produced new laboratory regula-tions to ensure accurate test results.

Commenting on the situation, the chairman of the board of the American Medical Association acknowledged that the "goals are laudable, com-mendable and designed to protect the public" but that physicians had never been compelled to face "this type of regulatory overload occurring simulta-neously" (Belkin 1992b, 33).

Doctors are not pleased, with some feeling overwhelmed. Faced with the new Medicare rules, an internist began looking into computer systems that might simplify the process. Finding that his best course of action was to hire an office manager at $75,000, the physician decided to start phasing out his practice and retire at the end of the year. A pediatrician and his nurse used to wash their white lab coats at home but new OSHA regulations require that coats exposed to blood or other bod-ily fluids be washed on the premises, and so the doctor removed a large tropical-fish tank in his waiting room and installed a combination washer-dryer. An OSHA official acknowledged that many physicians had complained but said that most of these were overreacting, falsely expecting to be subjected to surprise inspections and heavy fines for anything but complete compliance with the new regulations. Instead, the official explained, OSHA simply would respond to employee com-plaints about exposure. "The last thing we need to do," she said, "is spend a good deal of our time going to places where a high likelihood of danger doesn't exist" (Belkin 1992b, 37).

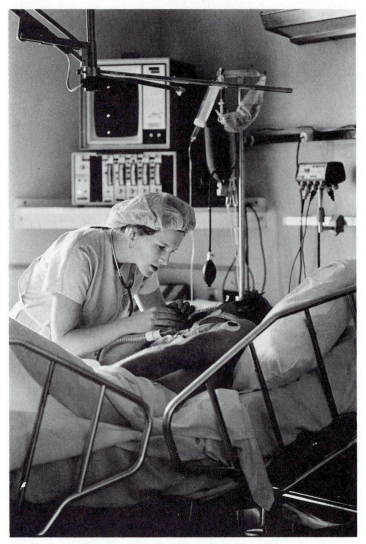

Nurses, particularly those working in intensive-care units and other special areas, are highly trained and skilled professionals. However, the relatively low status and limited advancement opportunities compel many nurses to change careers.

NURSES AND THEIR PROFESSIONAL DEVELOPMENT

In the latter half of the nineteenth century, the women who provided nursing care were either patients themselves, residents of nearby prisons, or women hired off the street. Physical strength, particularly a strong back, and a pleasing disposition were the major job requirements. Hiring was often a casual process. In one case the matron of a Boston Hospital wanted a nurse, but none of the applicants met her qualifications. So she had a recuperating patient become the laundress, and the laundress was promoted to nurse (Reverby 1981, 221).

Certainly nursing has changed a great deal in the past century. The first three accredited nursing schools in the United States were founded in 1873. Hospitals were willing to finance the early training of nurses in exchange for their services in the hospital. The first nursing schools were sufficiently successful to encourage the formation of a number of new schools during the late 1800s and early 1900s. At present three distinct types of nursing education have emerged. In the hospital diploma programs, the student receives three years of practical training, with a strong emphasis on the nurse's readiness to follow doctor's orders without questioning them. The second type of nursing education is the baccalaureate program. There are now more than 430 baccalaureate programs in the United States, producing over a fifth of the new nurses each year. This training is less practical and more theoretical than the instruction received in the diploma program. The third type of nursing education—the associate degree program—is a "fence straddler." The students receive a more theoretically oriented program than their colleagues at diploma schools—two years at a community college—but a less extensive professional emphasis than the baccalaureate candidates.

Once on the job, nurses' performance continues to be evaluated. A survey conducted with directors of nursing in the northeastern states indicated that nurses received an annual assessment, with the system most frequently revised in the past one to three years and appraisal most often supplied by a single rater. Some nurses appeal their evaluations, and one recent study suggested that it might prove useful to incorporate self-appraisal into the evaluation process (Cardy and Korodi 1991; Somers and Birnbaum 1991).

While evaluation can be taxing, the work itself can be particularly stressful. Nurses must not only do their best to help patients get well, but they are also supposed to fill an emotional role, creating whenever possible a "therapeutic environment" (Jamal and Baba 1991; Mallett et al. 1991). Nurses interviewed in one study reported that they often felt badly equipped to do this, especially with critically ill patients (Gray-Toft and Anderson 1981). An investigation of student nurses found that other major sources of stress include conflicts with other nurses and insecurity about professional skills (Parkes 1985).

It is not surprising that student nurses feel this insecurity, because members of the profession face a number of status problems. First, there is resistance to this field receiving the social prestige, monetary rewards, and deference normally associated with the major professions. The American public tends to view nursing with the limited respect accorded social work and elementary school teaching. One reason is that many people believe that nurses are no more than assistants to physicians. In addition, as a "female" occupation, nursing receives the brunt of many people's antifeminist bias.

A second status problem encountered by nurses involves the multiple demands they must satisfy. In particular, hospital nurses must face the dual pressure of serving in administrative capacities and also performing nursing services for patients. Both are difficult tasks that together can make overwhelming demands on a nurse's time and energy.

Finally a significant conflict often exists between the ideology of nursing and the realities of status advancement. Within the nursing profession, the conviction continues that the central activity should be the direct care of patients. However, in modern times the greatest tangible rewards—increased salary and promotions—come from administrative work (Coe 1978, 246–48).

According to a prominent nursing administrator, nurses, like medical personnel generally, are likely to find themselves confronting increasingly sophisticated corporate, organizational, and individual purchasers, who will carefully and hardheadedly evaluate the contributions nurses make. To succeed when subjected to such analyses, nurses must make certain that the participation they specify in a given program is making a contribution that could not be made just as effectively by less trained, lower-cost personnel, or in some cases they will find their services will be cut. On the other hand, when they clearly make effective contributions within current health-care systems, they should be duly rewarded. At present many hospitals have incentive plans for executives, but few of these plans include nurse administrators (McNerney 1988; Navarre 1988).

Patient-Doctor Relations

Portions of the two previous sections serve as effective background for the present one. Patient-doctor relations involve the problems of disease and death, and those relations are significantly affected by physicians' professional status.

424 CONCEPTUAL PERSPECTIVES

Sociologist Talcott Parsons (1951) analyzed the sick role. Like any other role, this one has a distinct set of behaviors associated with it. First, if someone has a disease or injury, it is legitimate to consider oneself ill, to remain bedridden if necessary, and to be freed from one's normal obligations. Second, the sick person is expected to recognize that his or her disease or injury is undesirable and that it should be cured as quickly as possible. Third, sick people and the members of their families are aware that physicians supply the most effective treatment of disease and injury, and so they seek doctors when they become sick.

Parsons's conception of the sick role has been extensively criticized. It has been pointed out, in particular, that going to the doctor may be the end, not the beginning of a complex system of help-seeking behavior, which starts with informal consultations with family members and friends. In addition, Parsons's scheme implies standard treatment for all patients, failing to consider the likelihood that higher-income patients will receive longer, more thorough consultations. Furthermore Parsons's analysis does not address the issue of control—since patients are seeking advice and assistance based on doctors' education and experience, physicians ultimately must maintain control in order to dispense their contributions most effectively (Phillips and Jones 1991; Turner 1987, 45–48). Finally the Parsons scheme does not consider that patients can play a part in their own treatment. In spite of limits to Parsons's perception of the sick role, however, the concept has been used extensively by sociologists studying health, disease, and sickness in modern American society (Wolinsky and Wolinsky 1981).

Unlike Parsons, psychiatrists Thomas Szasz and Marc Hollender (1956) acknowledged that patients play a significant role in the treatment process. They produced a classification of the kinds of relationships likely to develop between doctors and patients. Hollender and Szasz suggested that the nature of a disease or injury will strongly influence or determine the relationship between doctor and patient. Three types of relationships are proposed:

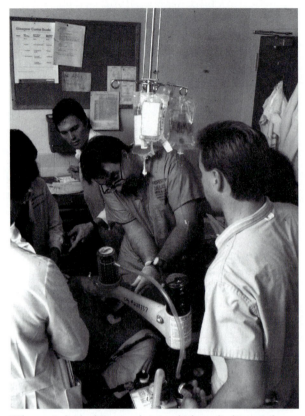

When an individual is seriously injured, the medical team takes an active role, while the patient is only capable of a passive response.

1. **Activity-passivity.** This type of relationship exists in medical emergencies when severe injury, delirium, coma, or blood loss makes the patient helpless. Treatment occurs whether or not the patient makes a contribution.

2. **Guidance-cooperation.** Such a relationship develops in less dangerous circumstances than those just described. When patients have acute, especially infectious disorders, they are likely to be very ill, but they are able to follow physicians' orders, respecting their doctors as experts who know the best way to produce a cure.

3. **Mutual participation.** This approach is often useful for the management of such chronic diseases as diabetes and hypertension, where the patient performs most of the treatment and only consults the physician occasionally. In this relationship doctors help patients to help themselves. The instructions that patients receive are often complex. This relationship is so unlike the other two kinds of

doctor-patient relationships that children and mentally retarded or profoundly immature individuals will often be unable to participate. In his well-known *Love, Medicine & Miracles*, physician Bernie Siegel (1988) indicated that the most effective way to treat cancer patients is to establish "a healing partnership" between doctor and patient, with the emphasis on sharing and caring and a disregard or toning down of the doctor's expert status.

SPECIAL FEATURES OF PATIENT-DOCTOR RELATIONS

Hank Johnson calls up the garage. "Charlie, I can't get the Ford started again. Do you think you could send a man over before noon?" Hank Johnson has just purchased a service. When most of us encounter doctors, we too are purchasing a service, a service that, to be sure, has some noteworthy features. In the first place, those who perform the service—doctors—are held in very high regard. As Table 14.4 indicates, 54 percent of a national sample assessed doctors as ranking very high or high in honesty and ethical standards. Only druggists and pharmicists at 60 percent and clergy at 57 percent scored better in the survey (Hugick and Hueber 1991).

Another particular quality about medical service is that doctors will sometimes provide a less-than-complete summary of the patient's condition. One reason physicians withhold information is their belief that patients generally lack the expertise to assimilate the information they receive. Another reason is the nature of certain cases—cases of terminal illness, in particular. Doctors and nurses often find such situations emotionally trying, and so they may frequently have as little as possible to do with such patients. A study indicated that physicians provided more information about treatment when patients asked questions and expressed concern. One notable factor influencing patients' communication with their doctors was physicians' own efforts to share information by soliciting patients' questions, concerns, and opinions (Armstrong 1987; Freidson 1981, 189-90; Quint 1978, 94; Street 1991; Trinkaus 1991).

Another important aspect of medical service is

Table 14.4 The Medical Profession in Comparative Perspective

VERY HIGH OR HIGH STANDARDS OF HONESTY AND ETHICAL STANDARDS	
Druggists/pharmacists	60%
Clergy	57
Medical doctors	54
Dentists	50
College teachers	45
Engineers	45
Policemen	43
Funeral directors	35
Bankers	30
TV reporters	29
Lawyers	22
Business executives	21
U.S. senators	19
Insurance salesmen	14
Car salesmen	8

Source: Larry Hugick and Graham Hueber. Gallup Poll Monthly. (May 1991).

The results of this survey demonstrate that doctors are well regarded compared to a variety of other occupational groups.

the fact that physicians' examinations of illness involve a variety of risks and costs in situations that can literally determine life and death. For instance, in trying to decide whether or not to continue an exploration of an illness without a clear diagnosis, a physician must weigh the following factors: the time and financial cost, the possible risks of medical tests, and the psychological distress for patients of continued investigation (Mechanic 1978, 422–23). If they make mistakes, doctors face the distinct possibility of malpractice suits. Patients who initiate suits tend to seek extensive input from various relatives and friends, including friends who are lawyers; to question their doctor's competence; and to feel that they have experienced a serious injury (May and Stengel 1990)

A fourth noteworthy feature of medical services is that low-status people receive inferior medical care. One study, which involved research conducted in both Michigan and Australia, found that doctors in both places had particularly negative stereotypes of certain categories of patients who possessed characteristics negatively valued in their societies and/or were especially difficult to

426 treat—in particular, patients who were alcoholic, unhygienic, angry, addicted to drugs, obese, or mentally disturbed (Najman, Klein, and Munro 1982; Pope 1990).

Millions of American are too poor to have health insurance or have limited and intermittent coverage, and as a result they receive inferior medical care (Bayer et al. 1988). Compared with middle-class citizens, the poor usually have greater difficulty gaining hospital admittance, receive less effectively coordinated treatment, and are much more likely to obtain the burden of care from "beginners"—medical students, interns, and residents. In addition, poor patients receive much more public care than their middle-class counterparts. One observer commented on the public treatment of the poor person: "Several staff members will congregate to examine him, and talk about him, callously and contemptuously ignoring him, talking over him, not to him" (Ryan 1976, 168).

Old people are another category of low-status people who often receive inferior medical treatment. Sociologist Elizabeth Markson (1971) examined the records of 174 elderly people admitted to Fairview State Hospital, a publicly funded mental hospital in New York City. Markson found evidence backing the frequent claim that elderly people are often sent to low-status institutions, especially mental hospitals, to die. She learned that the patients admitted to this hospital had a multiplicity of serious physical illnesses, especially heart and circulatory diseases. In fact, a full quarter of the sample died within a month of admission, especially those arriving incapacitated. This sociologist concluded that little effort was made to separate people with symptoms indicating serious physical disorder from those suffering old-age mental disabilities. The staff doctors apparently supported the idea that the Fairview geriatrics patients should be provided little more than "a hiding place to die."

We have just seen that medical practice is often controversial, and this trend was also apparent when we discussed science, another topic that involves life-and-death matters. Besides both being controversial, we have also seen that the two institutional areas have changed rapidly over time, with progress a priority for each of them.

STUDY GUIDE

Learning Objectives

After studying this chapter, you should be able to:

1. Define science and medicine and discuss their social importance.
2. Examine the development of science in ancient societies, seventeenth-century England, and in the United States since the beginning of this century.
3. Identify and discuss the norms and counter-norms of scientific practice.
4. List and explain the factors that help sustain controversial scientific research.
5. Define disease and examine the trends on vulnerability to disease and death.
6. Analyze sickness in the American health-care system.
7. Briefly discuss the socialization of doctors and their relations with colleagues.
8. Describe the development of nursing in the United States and examine nurses' status problems.
9. Summarize Parsons's analysis of the sick role and Szasz and Hollender's classification of doctor-patient relationships and indicate differences between the two approaches.
10. Discuss the factors influencing patient-doctor relations.
11. Describe the relationship between the two institutions examined in this chapter—science and medicine.

Summary

1. A science is a systematic effort to develop general principles about a particular subject matter based on actual observations and stated in a form that can be tested by any competent individual. Medicine is the scientifically based practice concerned with the prevention and treatment of disease and the treatment of injury.

2. Until modern times science made modest contributions to societies. Reasons included limited breadth of practical tasks for science, little incentive to incorporate scientific analysis into technological development, and opposition to scientific inquiry. In ancient Greece science did play a fairly significant role for about 200 years. Science began to receive widespread acceptance in seventeenth-century England. Factors contributing to this acceptance included the growing recognition of the part science played in the emerging conception of progress and the contribution of Protestantism, which permitted supporters to believe that God's will and scientific activity were harmonious. In twentieth-century America, science received a boost when graduate schools started to develop professionally qualified research workers. Since World War II, the American government has provided massive support for a wide range of scientific research. In recent years there has been a growing recognition of the problems associated with scientific innovations.

3. In examining scientists and scientific work, we have considered the practice of scientific norms. Robert Merton has suggested that four norms dominate scientific practice: universalism, communism, organized skepticism, and disinterestedness. A study of forty-two scientists associated with the Apollo lunar missions provided some evidence opposing Merton's set of norms. A set of "counter-norms" seems to exist.

Certain conditions help to sustain such controversial research projects as studies on DNA and nuclear weaponry. These conditions include the scientists' strong support of the research goals, effective governmental sponsorship, a policy of secrecy, and an active in-group for scientists.

4. Disease is a condition of biological non-health. Some distinct trends in vulnerability to disease exist. People's age, sex, and income are status characteristics that provide an indication of their likelihood of catching acute or chronic diseases. Just as certain categories of individuals are more vulnerable to disease, some status groups are more susceptible to death.

5. There is sickness in the American health-care system, including rapidly rising costs and, for many Americans, limited access to competent medical personnel. In some significant respects, health care in a number of other industrialized nations appears to be more effective.

6. There are certain particularly significant elements in doctors' careers. Inevitably doctors' training involves a standardized socialization—attendance at medical school and postgraduate studies. During their schooling they must learn to work effectively in a context where they face three different kinds of "vastness." Most modern doctors tend to exchange a fairly limited amount of information about their respective practices. In general, peer review is not an effective mechanism.

Nurses represent the largest category of health-care personnel. Three different kinds of nursing programs are available. Nurses encounter a number of severe status problems, including the difficulty of establishing nursing as a widely recognized profession, the necessity of satisfying multiple demands on the job, and the conflict between the ideology of nursing and the realities of advancement.

7. Parsons's analysis of the sick role focuses on three distinct behavioral patterns. Szasz and Hollender produced a three-part classification of the kinds of relationships likely to develop between doctors and patients.

Four factors have a significant influence on doctors' relations with patients: the public's high regard for physicians, doctors' tendency to provide a less-than-complete summary of the patient's condition, life-and-death risks and costs involved in medical practice, and the provision of inferior medical treatment for low-status patients.

Key Terms

communism a requirement that the substantive findings of science represent a common heritage, not the exclusive property of individual discoverers and their heirs

disease a condition of biological nonhealth

disinterestedness a standard that scientists avoid the pursuit of work that is self-serving and self-interested

health care the variety of public and private organizations that support an individual's effective physical, mental, and social adaptation to his or her environment

medical sociology the study of the social setting in which health, sickness, and health care occur

medicine the scientifically based practice concerned with the prevention and treatment of disease and the treatment of injury

organized skepticism the conclusion that no scientist's contribution to knowledge can be accepted without careful scrutiny

science a systematic effort to develop general principles about a particular subject matter based on actual observations and stated in a form that can be tested by any competent person

universalism a norm stating that all scientific claims of truth need to be evaluated by impersonal criteria consistent with existing knowledge in that field

Tests

True • False Test

_____ 1. In some preindustrial societies, technological advance could occur without contributions from science.

_____ 2. Figures indicate steadily increasing federal governmental support for research.

_____ 3. In recent years there has been growing evidence that scientific innovations exclusively produce positive results.

_____ 4. Robert Merton's set of four scientific norms is based on information obtained from a study of scientists associated with the Apollo lunar missions.

_____ 5. Recent survey data indicated that scientists were more satisfied with their work than computer specialists, lawyers, medical doctors, and college teachers.

_____ 6. The existence of their own in-groups encourages scientists to pursue controversial research.

_____ 7. In recent years some medical schools have concluded that doctors' ability to relate effectively to patients is an innate skill that cannot be taught.

_____ 8. There is little or no evidence indicating that group practice produces effective evaluation of colleagues' performances.

_____ 9. At one time the practice of nursing was so casual that patients, prison inmates, and women hired off the street were allowed to serve as nurses.

_____ 10. Parsons's analysis of the sick role has focused on the contribution patients make to the treatment process.

Multiple-Choice Test

_____ 1. Which of the following statements is true about the relationship between science and Protestantism in the seventeenth century?
   a. Protestants violently opposed science.
   b. English Protestants supported science but American Protestants did not.
   c. All early Protestants endorsed the development of science.
   d. In both England and America, Protestants backed science.

_____ 2. After World War II, a major impetus to government-sponsored research was the national government's interest in:
   a. nuclear weapons and nuclear energy.
   b. soil conservation.
   c. the development of synthetic chemicals.
   d. a greater range of cheap, high-quality consumer products.

_____ 3. Scientists' reluctance to accept creationism in the face of archeological evidence supporting the occurrence of evolution in human beings and other animals illustrates which scientific norm?
   a. universalism
   b. communism
   c. organized skepticism
   d. disinterestedness

_____ 4. Which condition does NOT support controversial research?
   a. primacy of the research goal
   b. disinterestedness
   c. governmental support
   d. a policy of secrecy

_____ 5. Which statement is true?
   a. Younger people are more likely than the old to have developed immunities to illness.
   b. During the first year of life, there is a low death rate.
   c. Acute illnesses occur primarily because of the degeneration of bodily tissues.
   d. The higher the income level, the lower the rate of disease.

_____ 6. Historical lessons relating to AIDS suggest that:
   a. education will have limited impact controlling the disease.
   b. fear will not affect health-care policy.
   c. compulsory health measures will not control the disease.
   d. a and c

_____ 7. Comprehensive health care for all citizens:
   a. does not exist in any country.
   b. is not possible in a capitalist democracy.
   c. is now developing in several states.
   d. a and c

_____ 8. One of the most significant recent developments affecting doctors' professional activity is:
   a. the development of new federal safety standards.
   b. the decline in group practice.
   c. the recent passage of a congressional bill providing comprehensive medical coverage for all citizens.
   d. a and b

_____ 9. Which statement is true of nurses?
   a. Their career enjoys high status.
   b. Three distinct types of nursing programs exist.
   c. Increased salary and promotions are most readily received by nurses working directly with patients.
   d. Currently nurses' work performance is much less frequently evaluated than in the past.

_____ 10. The doctor-patient relationship analyzed by Szasz and Hollender that is best for the management of chronic diseases like diabetes and hypertension is:

    a. mutual participation.

    b. guidance-cooperation.

    c. activity-passivity.

    d. Parsons's perception of the sick role.

Essay Test

1. Define science. Discuss the conditions that encouraged the development of science in seventeenth-century England.
2. Why has the United States had such enormous growth in the scientific area during the twentieth century?
3. List and define Merton's four scientific norms. Summarize Mitroff's criticism of Merton's scheme.
4. What conditions encourage the continuance of controversial research? Use DNA and nuclear-weapons research to illustrate the different points made.
5. Define disease and summarize males' and females' disease and death patterns.
6. Evaluate American health care, focusing on major problems in the system.
7. Discuss doctors' socialization and their relations with colleagues, indicating the problems they face evaluating each other's work.
8. List and analyze three status problems nurses must face.
9. Summarize the three types of doctor-patient relationships analyzed by Szasz and Hollender. Then discuss in detail two special features of the patient-doctor relationship.

Suggested Readings

Arditti, Rita, Pat Brennan, and Steve Cavrak (eds.). 1980. *Science and Liberation*. Boston: South End Press. A set of twenty-five articles analyzing significant problems that science and scientists help create and discussing areas in which a more liberated, humane science can develop.

Coe, Rodney M. 1978. *Sociology of Medicine*. 2nd ed. New York: McGraw-Hill. A nicely written comprehensive text on the sociology of medicine. Though covering a large, often complicated subject, the book is interesting and easy to read. The author has a flair for clear, thought-provoking sociological conceptualization.

Harding, Sandra. 1991. *Whose Science? Whose Knowledge? Thinking from Women's Lives*. Ithaca, NY: Cornell University Press. An analysis of the relationship between science and feminism, considering the gendered character of science and the variety of challenges feminism presents for science as well as those science provides for feminism.

Merton, Robert K. 1973. *The Sociology of Science*. Chicago: University of Chicago Press. A series of twenty-two scholarly essays by the most prominent investigator of the sociology of science. The papers are divided into five sections that address the sociology of knowledge, the sociology of scientific knowledge, the normative structure of science, the reward system of science, and the processes of evaluation of science.

Murcott, Anne. 1993. *Health, Disease, and Medicine: An Introduction*. Cambridge, MA: Blackwell. A coverage of the basic topics in medical sociology, examining in detail all the subjects addressed in this chapter's health and medicine sections, along with such issues as health, gender, and ethnicity; health and social class; and dying and the social construction of death.

Nelkin, Dorothy, David P. Willis, and Scott V. Parris (eds.). 1991. *A Disease of Society: Cultural and Institutional Responses to AIDS*. Cambridge, England: Cambridge University Press. An unusual book containing essays demonstrating the widespread impact of a disease, namely AIDS, on such prominent structures or activities as the mass media, medical practice, the arts, voluntary associations, the family, prisons, and government regulation of drugs.

Siegel, Bernie S. 1988. *Love, Medicine & Miracles*. New York: Harper & Row. A surgeon's moving account of how cancer patients and doctors' cooperative efforts, using a wide range of approaches, including spiritual techniques, can prolong life or produce unexpected cures.

Starr, Paul. 1982. *The Social Transformation of American Medicine*. New York: Basic Books. A Pulitizer prize-winning sociological analysis of how American medical practice has become increasingly subjected to corporate control over time.

Additional Assignments

1. We now have scientifically based technologies for both saving lives and artificially prolonging life. We can also alter the production of life through sperm banks, artificial transplants, and embryo transplants. Join with several other members of the class in a "braininstorming" session to develop a list of life-death technologies. Then produce for each technology a set of moral questions which the members of our society must face in evaluating these technologies and ultimately deciding whether to accept them or reject them.

2. For a week watch a soap opera which at least in part takes place in a medical setting. Keep notes on the interaction patterns of doctors-doctors, doctors-nurses, nurses-nurses, doctors-patients, and nurses-patients. Do the patterns you observed seem consistent with conclusions about these different interaction patterns presented in this chapter? If not, what are the primary inconsistencies?

Answers to Objective Test Questions

True • False Test

1. t	6. t
2. t	7. f
3. f	8. t
4. f	9. t
5. f	10. f

Multiple-Choice Test

1. d	6. d
2. a	7. c
3. c	8. a
4. b	9. b
5. d	10. a

Urbanization, Population Growth, and Environmental Issues

URBANIZATION
The Development of Cities
American Cities: Problems and Prospects

POPULATION GROWTH
Basic Demographic Concepts and Theories
An Overview of World Population Problems

ENVIRONMENTAL ISSUES
Resource Depletion
Environmental Pollution
Restoration of a Healthy Environment

STUDY GUIDE

15

The critical date was May 27, 1992. On that day Olympia & York Developments Ltd., the largest development corporation in the world, sought British court protection for Canary Wharf, the half-finished office project that was the largest in Europe. The immediate condition that had made the Canadian corporation file for bankruptcy was that the majority of the eleven banks from five countries that had invested in the project indicated that they were against providing further financing. Canary Wharf had fallen victim to the longest recession to hit Britain since the 1930s—an economic downturn that had caused vacancy rates to skyrocket and office rents to plunge (Prokesch 1992). Olympia & York was so huge that, according to a prominent Canadian economist, uncertainty over the corporation's fate "adds to the economic malaise and sense of gloom,... [encouraging] consumers [to] keep their wallets zipped and could delay the recovery substantially" (Farnsworth 1992, D1).

Gerald D. Hines, the largest developer of office buildings in the United States, accepted the fact that the 1990s has represented a decade of industrial retrenchment during which the need for new office space has declined sharply. One option, according to Hines, has been abundant development opportunities in southeastern Asia, eastern Europe, and the former Soviet Union (Stuart 1992).

Whether the economic times are bad or good, the major players in urban development have become fewer and larger since the early 1980s, with the trend likely to continue into the future (Feagin and Parker 1990). Furthermore as we have seen, these development corporations operate on an international stage, moving like Olympia & York or Gerald Hines where the possibilities for profit seem most distinct.

Increasingly some sociologists are recognizing that various issues, including the topics covered in this chapter— cities, population, and the environment—are subjected to policies set by top economic and political leaders and that these policies are played out on local, national, and international levels. On the local level, for instance, the educational, job, and housing needs of poor and middle-income residents might be subordinated to large corporate interests' drive to maximize their profits. On the international dimension, developing nations can find themselves victimized, with their raw materials and labor bought cheaply, thereby maximizing profits for developed nations' corporate leaders (Feagin and Parker 1990; Lyman 1992; Portes and Walton 1981; Robertson 1992; Walton 1985). Throughout this chapter, especially in the areas of population growth and environmental issues, it becomes apparent that international economic exploitation plays a significant role.

This chapter examines three interrelated issues. The first section considers the development of cities. Then the focus shifts to the problem of population growth and finally to the topic of environmental destruction.

Urbanization

Let us start with a pair of definitions. A **city** is a large, densely settled concentration of people permanently located within a relatively confined geographical area where nonagricultural occupations are pursued. **Urbanization** is the process by which a city forms and develops.

The earliest cities appeared about 5,500 years ago, first along rivers in Mesopotamia (modern-day Iraq) and later in the Nile, Indus, and Yellow River Valleys. The growth of cities was slow until the Industrial Revolution got underway. By 1850 only 2 percent of the world population lived in cities of 100,000 people or more. Currently about 25 percent of people live in such cities, and by the year 2000 about 40 percent of the population will reside in cities of that size. Consequently, from a world perspective, we must recognize that cities are becoming the homes of an increasing percentage of the population.

In this section we examine the development of cities, with special attention to the growth of cities in the United States. Then we consider some of the problems and prospects of urban living.

THE DEVELOPMENT OF CITIES

To begin, it can be argued that human beings' adjustment to urban living has been remarkable. For over fifteen million years, the hominids, who were ancestors of human beings, and human beings themselves were "nomadic, small-group, wide-open-spaces creatures." With this lengthy history, it is not surprising that people have trouble getting along in cities; what is notable is that they can do it at all, living "in the same place year round, enclosed in sharp-cornered and brightly-lit rectagular spaces, among noises, most of which are made by machines, within shouting distances of hundreds of other people" (Pfeiffer 1989, 6). Keep in mind too that many Americans have much more living space than most people in other countries.

Considering that during most of human existence there was nothing resembling cities, one might wonder how they developed. Did a Mesopotamian leader awake one morning propelled by a vision that he wanted to transform into reality? More than a mere vision was necessary for the building of the first city.

Early cities developed because three conditions were simultaneously favorable. First, there had to be an environment encouraging a large concentration of people—in particular, a climate and soil supporting an abundant growth of crops, an adequate supply of fresh water, and a location along a trade route, such as a river or a road, favoring contact between people of different cultures. Second, advances in technology were essential: the development and refinement of animal husbandry, irrigation works, metallurgy, the wheel, and especially the domestication of grains. These innovations freed a few members of the populace from the everyday tasks of producing food, clothes, and shelter and permitted them to govern the

cities. Finally a well-developed social organization was essential. Techniques for the distribution of goods had to be produced, and an integration and coordination of the different occupational groups was necessary. An elite group developed to direct these tasks.

Once preindustrial cities evolved, they generally had certain characteristics. Populations of these cities were small, with most containing no more than 5,000 or 10,000 people. In contrast with modern cities, these early settlements lacked the transportation and storage capacities necessary for maintaining large concentrations of people. Another quality of these cities was that the city center served as the focus of government and religious activity as well as the location for elite housing, with lower-status residents pushed toward the outskirts. Thus the privileged people managed to avoid difficult and time-consuming commuting, which had to be accomplished on foot, by boat, on horseback, or in a carriage. In addition, preindustrial cities had a highly restrictive social-class system in which a small privileged group controlled power, wealth, religion, and education, basing their claims to authority on appeal to tradition and religious absolutes. Furthermore, within these early cities, economic growth was slow because of the ruling group's conservative commercial policies, the exclusiveness of the guilds (an early form of unions), the lack of standardized prices, currency, and measures, and few opportunities for credit and capital development.

In spite of their modest accomplishments, these early cities served a couple of important functions. First, they were founded at key locations along trade routes and so were able to control the most important commerce of their societies. In addition, preindustrial cities were important because they were the places where the elite lived and worked. The elite chose the cities because they could more readily protect themselves in urban areas, which tended to be walled enclosures, than in the open countryside. Another reason members of the elite resided in cities was that, concentrated in the central districts, they could efficiently work together to establish political, economic, and religious policies (Schwab 1982, 108–09; Sjoberg 1960, 27–31, 323–28.)

When people took up residence in cities, their outlook and behavior started to change. In 1887 Ferdinand Tönnies wrote a book in which he

Like other ancient cities, Pompeii had its political and religious leadership living and working in the center of the city.

discussed how urbanized, industrialized living altered people's lifestyle. Tönnies suggested that in small, homogeneous, preindustrial communities people generally spend their lives in the same locale. The social structure tends to be simple but rigid. People's position at birth determines where they belong, and few, if any, challenge the situation. Citizens strongly support the moral code and local conventions. In such simple communities, the basic social unit is the family, and an individual's life assumes meaning only in the context of family activity. The community itself, in fact, resembles a large family. Social relationships are personal and supportive. Privacy and individualism are minimal.

In modern urban society, Tönnies contended, self-interest prevails, with the accumulation of property becoming more important than personalities. The use of a legal device—the contract—becomes the chief means to ensure that both parties will fulfill an agreement. The family and the church gradually lose their influence. Individuals are freer to think and act as they please, but the danger exists that they will become isolated and alienated, feeling that life is meaningless and that they are powerless to do anything about it (Tönnies 1957).

Tönnies's ideas certainly apply to American society. As the United States has urbanized, people's outlooks and social relationships have changed.

The Growth of American Cities

It seems useful to divide the history of American cities into four eras: the colonial period, the period of westward expansion, the period of metropolitan growth, and the modern period (Spates and Macionis 1982, Chapter 7). Figure 15.1 shows that over time the United States has become increasingly urbanized.

Colonial Period During the colonial era, most American cities were small both in physical size and in population. None of the North American urban settlements had as many as 10,000 inhabitants until the eighteenth century, and at the time of the Revolutionary War, Philadelphia, the largest American city, had only 40,000 people. These cities were not only small, but they also had little ethnic and religious diversity; the residents were primarily of northern European ancestry and Protestant. People shared a common lifestyle and outlook on life, with extensive contacts among neighbors and regular church attendance representing widely accepted patterns of behavior.

In spite of the fact that colonial cities seemed to be nothing more than small, intimate villages, they were important trading centers, whose residents sought profit and supported growth. As time passed, American merchants began to resent British directives that they (the merchants) serve

Figure 15.1

190 Years of American Urban Growth

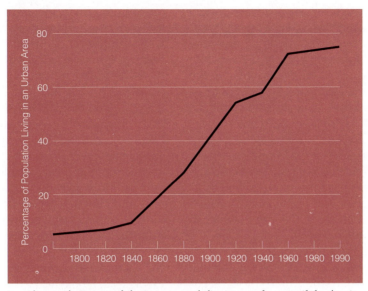

According to the Bureau of the Census, people live in an urban area if the place is incorporated and contains 2,500 residents or more. By this definition the urban population, which rose steadily until 1960, has started to level off.

Source: U.S. *Bureau of the Census.* Current Population Reports, Population Characteristics, P–20, No. 374, *Table 2–4;* U.S. *Bureau of the Census.* Statistical Abstract of the United States: 1992, No. 29.

as export centers for American raw products to be shipped to the mother country. These colonial businessmen began to compete with the British, establishing their own trade agreements with the West Indies and even with European countries.

Period of Western Expansion   Between 1800 and 1880, American cities grew at a faster rate than at any time before or since. It is worth noting that among the fifty largest cities in the United States, only seven were incorporated before 1816. Thirty-nine were incorporated between 1816 and 1876, and only four have been incorporated since then. At the beginning of the nineteenth century, business leaders began to recognize the tremendous economic potential of the rich westward lands, and they started to develop plans to link these new territories with eastern cities. Roads, canals, and later railroads provided the connections. By 1830 New York, Philadelphia, and Baltimore were the most prominent coastal cities, primarily because of their control over commercial relations with the Ohio Valley.

In the course of the nineteenth century, indus-trialization was also expanding. By the 1830s in the vicinity of Boston, for example, a proliferation of factory towns contained textile mills, paper mills, shoe factories, and iron foundries.

Period of Metropolitan Growth   Between 1880 and 1940, U.S. cities reached the third phase: the period of metropolitan growth. A **metropolis** is a territorial unit composed of a large central city and the surrounding cities and towns.

During this era cities grew in size—explosively. Two factors appear to have been largely responsible for the accelerated population increase. First, a movement of people from rural areas into the cities occurred. Between 1880 and 1890, almost 40 percent of the country's more than 25,000 townships actually lost population. Remarkably thousands of farms were simply abandoned as machinery made handpowered labor obsolete and encouraged people to seek more lucrative jobs in the cities. Second, immigration was also an important factor in urban growth. By 1890 New York City possessed half as many Italians as Naples, as many Germans as Hamburg,

440 twice as many Irish as Dublin, and two-and-a-half the number of Jews as Warsaw. Between just 1901 and 1910, more than 9 million immigrants came to the United States. The recent arrivals were packed into slums and offered the lowest-paying, most menial jobs. At the turn of the century, influential native-born Americans, primarily WASPS (white Anglo-Saxon Protestants), tended to blame the immigrants, many of whom were Catholics or Jews, for the sins of the city—slum housing, inferior health conditions, and crime, in particular. It was time, most of these powerful citizens agreed, to cut off immigration. Therefore in 1924 Congress established a quota system that severely restricted the number of immigrants from the southern and eastern European countries that had made the heaviest numerical contributions in the late nineteenth and early twentieth centuries.

But this curtailment caused new problems. At that time industrial concerns needed a reliable source of cheap labor, which until then recent immigrants had supplied. Now industrialists started to recruit from within the country, and American cities received a new stream of immigrants, many of them southern blacks. Between 1920 and 1929, more than 600,000 blacks migrated to northern cities from the South, and the groundwork for the racial tension that has characterized many American cities in recent years was established. As early as 1925, the rapid influx of blacks created an acute housing shortage and such strong tensions that in Detroit riots broke out.

Toward the end of this period in the history of American cities, another important event occurred. The stock market crash of 1929 threw the country into financial chaos, and most cities were forced to face difficult economic times. In 1932 large numbers of urban residents voted for Franklin Roosevelt in the hope that he could help their cities. The following year the mayors of fifty cities met in Washington, D.C., and founded the U.S. Conference of Mayors, and the members of this organization then started to lobby the Roosevelt administration on behalf of the cities. They were very successful. The National Industrial Recovery Act appropriated $3.3 billion for important public works and housing operations, and later bills supplied billions more in federal funding for housing, highway construction, and other projects that aided the cities. This policy, whereby cities depend on the federal government for extensive financial assistance, continued until the early 1980s when federal aid to cities was sharply cut.

The Modern Period From 1940 to the present, two broad trends have dominated U.S. cities: decentralization and the growth of urban centers in the Sunbelt. Decentralization means moving out of cities, often into suburbs. A **suburb** is a politically independent municipality that develops next to or in the vicinity of a central city.

Why has the suburban movement occurred? Three reasons stand out. First, by about 1950, an increasing number of businesses, especially

Street trolleys were an early response to the need for mass transit in increasingly populated cities.

manufacturing concerns, were moving away from central-city areas. Some assembly-line procedures needed more space than was readily available in the old central business districts. Growing crime rates, high taxes, and traffic congestion were other factors promoting a proliferation of "industrial parks" on the fringe of cities. As factories moved to the suburbs, workers often followed.

Second, technology has played an important part in the growth of suburbs. During the twentieth century, the use of electric power became widespread. Unlike its predecessor, steam power, electricity can be transmitted for long distances, thereby making it possible for both industries and residences to disperse throughout a large area. Automobiles and trucks have had a similar effect, permitting far greater flexibility in movement and location than rail transportation, which had a dominant position during the latter half of the nineteenth and early twentieth century.

A third reason for suburban growth is that some people found city living distasteful. For example, at the end of World War II, millions of servicemen returned home to discover various conditions in their residential neighborhoods that they did not like—in particular, extensive physical deterioration because of neglected urban-repair projects during the war years and in some cases (for whites) the proximity of black and other minority-group families. Many veterans took advantage of low-interest loans supplied by the Federal Housing Authority and bought homes outside the center of the city or in the suburbs.

Looking back, we can easily see how this government policy contributed to urban deterioration. The policy encouraged white, middle-class people to leave cities, and their departure produced a substantial loss of tax revenue. This loss of revenue, in turn, meant the decline of local facilities and services. As police and fire protection, schools, and other facilities and services became more impoverished, people who could afford to leave cities often hastened to do so, further eroding the tax base.

In recent years American suburbs have changed. During the decade from 1970 to 1980, a prominent trend was the movement of urban black residents outward, often replacing suburban white inhabitants. While this pattern occurred in both the South and the North, blacks and whites in the South were more likely to share the same suburban locale (Stahura 1988). Figure 15.2 shows Americans' distribution in cities, suburbs, and rural areas.

In recent years a dramatic urban change has been the growth of the Sunbelt cities. During the late 1970s and early 1980s, a shift of population and affluence from the industrial heartland of the Northeast to the fast-growing cities in southern districts has occurred. The population of the fifteen Sunbelt states has grown from 61 million in 1970 (about a third of the nation's population) to 85 million in 1976 (nearly 40 percent of the total) and will expand to a projected 112 million inhabitants, representing 43 percent of the population, in the year 2000. We might readily wonder why.

Figure 15.2
Where Americans Live: 1990

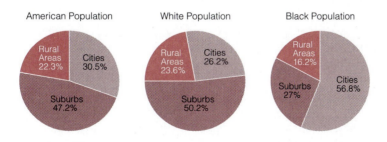

These figures demonstrate that Americans of various ethnic heritages tend to live in certain areas. Whites are overrepresented in the suburbs, while blacks, as well as other less affluent ethnic groups, are disproportionately located in cities.

Source: U.S. *Bureau of the Census.* The Black Population in the United States: March 1990 and 1989, *Table* 3.

442

The Sunbelt cities have had a series of distinct advantages over the historically prominent northern cities. In many cases these southern and southwestern urban centers have industrialized only in recent years, and so they have been able to build modern, efficient plants. In addition, the recent development of the Sunbelt cities has meant that their superhighways most efficiently promote access to industrial parks. Furthermore, because their affluence has meant that they have not been pressed for cash, these new cities have been able to offer significant tax incentives to businesses that might want to relocate. Other advantages of the Sunbelt cities have included modern services, low energy costs, and limited unionization, which means lower labor costs. The prominent northeastern cities have not fared well in comparison. They contain aging, outmoded plants, superhighways providing limited access to industrial areas, few incentives to entice new business, deteriorating services, high energy costs, and extensive unionization. All in all, it is hardly surprising that businesses have been leaving the North by the thousands and heading for the cities of the South and the Southwest.

On the other hand, a cloudy side to life in the Sunbelt has developed. Rapid expansion has led to a massive, disorganized urban pattern, rising air pollution, and an overuse of the water and sewage systems. The influx of more than 10 million illegal aliens from Mexico and a number of other Latin American countries has heightened the problems. In many cases the immigrants are uneducated and unable to speak English, and those who have been able to find employment have taken the lowest-paying, most menial jobs. In a number of southwestern cities, the immigrants' residential areas have begun to resemble the poverty-stricken slums of Third World countries (Palen 1981, Chapter 3; Spates and Macionis 1982, Chapter 7). In the middle 1980s, the loss of affluence in the oil industry had a distinctly negative impact on many Sunbelt cities, which started to suffer the economic woes long experienced in other parts of the country.

We have now briefly examined the history of American urban development, and in the course of this review, we have seen that a number of problems exist. In the following discussion, we focus on some of these problems and on possible solutions to them.

AMERICAN CITIES: PROBLEMS AND PROSPECTS

Daniel Boone, the frontiersman, apparently felt that the neighborhood was getting crowded when he could see the smoke from the nearest cabin. Mr. Boone would have had serious difficulty adjusting to modern, urbanized existence.

The massive movement of population and manufacturing from central cities to fringe areas has created "urban sprawl," where one metropolitan area frequently merges with the next. A **megalopolis** is a string of closely bound metropolitan areas (Gottman 1961). The largest American megalopolis runs from southern New Hampshire to Prince William County, Virginia. It contains part or all of ten states and the cities of Boston, New York, Philadelphia, Baltimore, and Washington, D.C. The population of "Bos Wash" exceeds 44 million people, representing about one-fifth of the American population. Megalopolitan growth is presently most rapid in the Sunbelt areas: the Southwest, Florida, and southern California.

As metropolitan areas expand and eventually form a megalopolis, serious urban problems often develop.

Urban Deterioration

The influence of powerful economic and political interests, governmental proliferation, and financial limitations contribute significantly to the urban crisis.

Powerful Political and Economic Interests Lewis Mumford (1971), a well-known city planner, has claimed that throughout human history technological advances have generally been under the control of powerful economic and political groups whose primary goal has been to expand their own wealth and power. Therefore in modern cities, Mumford contended, business people and politicians have cooperated to increase the number of highway miles, automobiles, and retail stores within their communities. As a result their own interests benefit, but the quality of city living for average inhabitants steadily deteriorates.

Modern conflict theorists agree with Mumford. The so-called "new urban sociology" emphasizes that in cities a conflictive struggle for scarce resources occurs, with local wealth encouraging organized efforts to control both urban land and its major profit-making enterprises.

According to this perspective, the major players in modern cities are land developers, large landowners, real-estate companies, commercial corporations (in particular, those engaged in retail trade), industrial companies, and banks and insurance companies. Individuals and groups with wealth and power tend to delegate the day-to-day implementation of policies to management personnel, who faithfully carry out their employers' directives. The majority of people working in cities are salaried personnel; whether filling white- or blue-collar jobs, they are not involved in the decisions determining the way land in the city is used.

In particular, conflict theorists studying modern American cities have emphasized the prominence of **growth coalitions**—a number of developers, bankers, and industrialists working together to produce economic expansion (Feagin and Parker 1990, 16–18). Participants in growth coalitions seek to maximize profits, with the overall benefit of their activities to the general urban citizenry usually considered unimportant. The impact can be destructive for cities. For instance, even when developers could no longer fill new office buildings constructed in the early 1980s, they kept putting them up, concluding that what had once been a profitable enterprise would become so once again if the new skyscrapers were filled (Feagin and Parker 1990, 102–06). They were not, and in many cities increasingly large sections of downtown land became underutilized. A similar approach often failed with downtown malls. They appeared to be a major source of profit both to developers and to retail store owners, but an analysis of pedestrian malls in six American cities indicated that in the drive for profits, prospective customers' needs and interests were poorly assessed. As a result these enterprises did not intensively use downtown land, threatening to turn it into giant wastelands (Robertson 1990).

Governmental Proliferation At present there are about 80,000 governmental units in the United States, averaging nearly 1,600 per state. This proliferation of governments makes it extraordinarily difficult to plan rationally. For instance, greater St. Louis is a typically "government-crowded" metropolis, where the participants are the federal government, two states, seven counties, 194 munici-

palities, and 615 special districts (concerned with such issues as water and sewage). Given such a massive number of organizations, it should be clear that coordinated policies will be difficult to achieve (Odom 1991; Schwab 1982).

Financial Limitations American cities have been caught in a powerful financial squeeze, with affluent citizens' and businesses' outmigration, weak local economies, and inflationary pressures the major sources of the problem, according to an analysis of 234 American cities (Pagano 1988). In the early 1980s, the federal government eliminated a range of social and public-works programs that benefitted cities. At the same time, strict, local tax-cut measures were legislated in many states and cities. In 1982 in Massachusetts, for example, only 0.5 percent of the state budget was allotted for maintenance and repair—a policy that one expert on the state's budget called "pennywise and pothole foolish" (Beck 1982, 12).

The **urban infrastructure** involves a city's basic physical and technical features such as roads, bridges, and water, sewer, and transit systems. For the city to function, its infrastructure must be in working order.

The American investment in the general infrastructure has steadily declined, failing to keep pace with the GNP. For instance, in 1960, total public spending on infrastructure was 3.6 percent of GNP while in 1985 it dropped to 2.6 percent. Over time federal investment declined, and state and local governments picked up some of the

While the deterioration of the nation's urban infrastructure generally receives little attention, there are spectacular exceptions, such as the collapse of the Mianis River Bridge on the Connecticut Turnpike, killing serveral people.

444

slack. However, the pattern among different states has been uneven—not a surprising outcome when one considers that rational investment strategies and policies have not been pursued.

Because of the connection extending from one infrastructure system to another, this lack of planning exacerbates problems. For instance, the unwillingness of one city to improve its water quality or modernize its sewage system will affect those facilities in other cities.

Throughout the country, infrastructure problems are significant; in cities, particularly in the central areas of the oldest American cities, these facilities are in the greatest disarray. The chief reason is that in those areas the water, sewer, and transportation systems are older than elsewhere and thus as one urban analyst said "have outlived their life cycle" (Kaplan 1990, 372–73).

Unfortunately infrastructure expenditures are not appealing to politicians, who do not want to be responsible for public costs that do not produce visible public structures or services. As one HUD official stated, "Have you ever seen a politician presiding over a ribbon-cutting for an old sewer system that was repaired?" (Beck 1982, 13).

Yet, a prominent business expert observed recently, infrastructure development is vital economically. He noted that the world's most competitive economies, notably Japan and Germany, invest heavily in airports, roads, and bridges, recognizing that productive business activity cannot occur without such facilities in top condition (Rohatyn 1991, 8). Clearly in the United States, this message has not been received.

In the previous pages, it has been apparent that the problems of modern cities often have a profound, intimate impact on urban dwellers' lives. Let us continue to consider that idea.

The Urban Existence: Is Revitalization Possible?

During the late evening on April 19, 1989, an investment banker jogging through Central Park in New York City was brutally beaten and raped by an adolescent gang. Perhaps because the victim was white and the rapists were black, there were extensive angry outbursts. What was generally unrecognized by the public was that during the same week twenty-eight other women, primarily African-Americans and Hispanics, reported being raped in New York City. Evidence of the brutality of modern urban living frequently surfaces. For many years sociologists have been analyzing the sources of such problems.

Georg Simmel (1950) examined the effect of city living on people's personalities. He observed that each individual encounters a great many people and experiences every day. Cities provide so much stimulation that serious mental disturbance can result. To protect themselves from overstimulation, urban residents must remain psychologically distant from most people. Otherwise they will be unable to cope with the pressures of daily living. Simmel wrote, "As a result of this reserve we frequently do not even know by sight those who have been our neighbors for years. And it is this reserve which in the eyes of the small-town people makes us appear to be cold and heartless" (Simmel 1950, 415).

Louis Wirth (1938) shared Simmel's outlook on the city. Wirth believed that three factors—the size of cities, their densely populated neighborhoods, and continuous contact with strangers—produce deteriorating interpersonal relations in cities. The social significance of the family declines, neighborhood interaction disappears, and specialized outside agencies, such as the police, health agencies, and welfare organizations, assume tasks once handled by the family or community.

Sociologists like Simmel and Wirth have recognized that the quality of urban life is often low. What are measures that might offer improvement?

Emphasis on an Active Neighborhood Life   Recent research has concluded that metropolitan residents have distinct preferences about their neighborhoods: They tend to prefer them small rather than large and away from the inner-city instead of close to it (Dahmann 1985).

Other factors also affect the quality of neighborhood life. Jane Jacobs, a well-known city planner, has contended that the best way to ensure neighborhood vitality is to combine a variety of land-use patterns in a given area. If neighborhoods contain a mixture of residences, small stores, schools, restaurants, bars, theaters, and parks, then there will be people on the streets from early morning until fairly late at night. Jacobs argued that a busy street life helps create a stimulating neighborhood and also makes it a relatively safe place, as the following account suggests.

One day Jane Jacobs was watching an incident from her second-floor window. A struggle was going on between a little girl of 8 or 9 years and a man. The man was alternately trying to coax the girl to come with him and then ignoring her. The girl had made herself rigid against the wall of a building. She was determined not to move.

As Jacobs watched from her window and tried to decide whether or not to intervene, she saw that intervention would not be necessary. From the butcher shop, the owner came out with her arms folded and a determined look on her face. The man who ran the delicatessen across the street also emerged. Two men from the bar next to the butcher shop moved to the doorway and waited. On her own side of the street, Jane Jacobs saw that the locksmith, the fruitman, and the laundry owner had all come out of their shops and were standing on the street. Other heads had appeared at windows. The man and the little girl were surrounded. Jacobs wrote, "Nobody was going to allow a little girl to be dragged off, even if nobody knew who she was. I am sorry—sorry purely for dramatic purposes—to have to report that the little girl turned out to be the man's daughter" (Jacobs 1961, 39).

The protection offered by this city community turned out to be unnecessary. Nonetheless, the incident offered evidence that a vital city neighborhood will help protect people, even strangers.

Neighborhood organizations are a proven means of helping to build strong neighborhoods. The nearby Social Application examines this topic.

Experiments Advancing Low-Income Citizens' Interests Traditionally advocates of poor, inner-city residents have received little or no response from political leaders, but sometimes circumstances alter that outcome. Consider a couple of instances.

Prompted by their constituencies, government leaders can help promote low-income people's interests, with recent events in Boston a notable case in point. Two factors have encouraged a major urban mobilization on behalf of less affluent citizens. First, to be elected mayor, Ray Flynn needed strong support from Boston's working-class whites, whose members had never been significant beneficiaries of the city's wealth. On their behalf Flynn became a proponent of **linkage**—a municipal procedure requiring developers engaged in large commercial projects to provide a substantial fee earmarked for low-cost housing. By October 1989, less than six years after Flynn had become mayor, developers had committed over $76 million in linkage funds. Second, since linkage fees normally represent less than one percent of the value of development ventures, linkage only generates significant capital in a city with extensive development. In 1989 Boston's program was one of the strongest in the nation (Dreier and Keating 1990).

Pressured by local citizens' groups and anti-discrimination laws, banks across the country have begun providing mortgages to inner-city residents. The rules for providing loans have started to change. In Philadelphia, for instance, where $60 million has been lent in a widely watched program, most participants have low income and some have irregular job patterns or even are on welfare. Traditionally such people could never have received mortgages from banks. However, if after studying individuals' history of bill payments and providing financial counseling, bank officials are convinced that they represent reasonable risks, then the loans are made. For bankers such innovative programs represent a new market. Cathy Bessant, a senior vice-president of Nationsbank said, "There's a lot of good business to be had. About 60 percent of American households have an annual income of less than $25,000. It's a huge market that is absolutely underbanked and there are not many underbanked markets out there" (Wayne 1992, 1).

Efforts to Bring Middle-Class People Back into Cities This trend has become so widespread in recent years that a concept has developed to describe it. **Gentrification** is the move of middle- and upper-middle-class people to formerly deteriorated, inner-city neighborhoods. A recent study concluded that characteristics of cities encouraging gentrification include the existence of a substantial segment of affluent, young adults not interested in having children but wanting to be "where the action is," the presence of corporate wealth that can subsidize redevelopment projects, and real-estate groups that can execute such projects (London et al. 1986). Extensive conversion of apartments to condominiums has already happened in many American cities. Middle-class people who purchase condominiums have the advantage of owning property that increases steadily in value as well as the tax breaks that go with that ownership. Gentrification has helped transform the deteriorating centers of many

SOCIAL APPLICATION
Neighborhood Organizations: What Factors Can Make These Structures Strong?

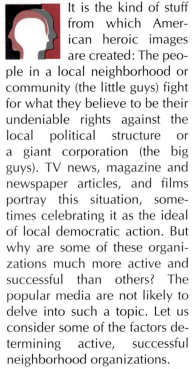

It is the kind of stuff from which American heroic images are created: The people in a local neighborhood or community (the little guys) fight for what they believe to be their undeniable rights against the local political structure or a giant corporation (the big guys). TV news, magazine and newspaper articles, and films portray this situation, sometimes celebrating it as the ideal of local democratic action. But why are some of these organizations much more active and successful than others? The popular media are not likely to delve into such a topic. Let us consider some of the factors determining active, successful neighborhood organizations.

In a study of the Waverly-Belmont neighborhood in Nashville, Tennessee, psychologist Abraham Wandersman and his associates concluded that individuals' sense of community—their shared interests and concerns about the area in which they lived—was an important factor determining their involvement in local neighborhood organizations. People with a strong sense of community tended to examine their neighborhoods carefully, recognizing local problems and the need to mobilize citizens to change the conditions producing these problems. In addition, such individuals tended to interact extensively with their neighbors, thus providing a setting for neighborhood mobilization. They also maintained a feeling of control

and empowerment, believing that group actions could be taken to alleviate negative conditions.

Sociologist Pamela Oliver examined neighborhood organizations in Detroit and found that active members were better educated and, curiously, more pessimistic about their neighbors' willingness to make an active contribution than inactive members. On the last point, Oliver suggested that active participants are people who are convinced that if they do not join and participate actively in these structures, then nobody will; pessimism, in short, seems to encourage involvement.

Like active and inactive individuals, active and inactive neighborhood organizations differ in characteristics. Compared to inactive neighborhood organizations, those which are active tend to have leaders who are more experienced in organizational activity, are more likely to involve their members in the decision-making process, and are more capable of establishing high levels of cohesion and stability within the group. I spent over two years studying the development of neighborhood organizations. It was not difficult to separate those with leaders who had effective organizational skills from those without such leaders. Some relevant questions that will help draw the distinction: Does the leader enter meetings with a well-organized agenda? Does he or she have

sufficient respect from members to hold their attention and generate enthusiasm? Do members come to the meetings regularly? What, if any, organizational business is completed between meetings?

I also learned that active neighborhood organizations are more effective at pursuing tactics designed to produce physical and social improvements in the neighborhood area. In what often appears as a David versus Goliath contest, the members of local neighborhood groups can obtain a tremendous morale boost—and with it increased longevity for their organization—if the members can win a battle against the local power structure. Consider the following example.

In an upstate New York city, I was present the day after the leaders of city government agreed to the demands made by three local black-power leaders to tear down some old buildings that were considered dangerous temptations to children playing in the area. Local people spoke admiringly of the way the neighborhood organization leaders had handled themselves.

MRS. ALBRIGHT: I think those guys handled themselves perfectly.

MRS. ROCHESTER: Right!

MRS. ALBRIGHT: The politicians won't do anything, because you who are reasonable go down to City Hall and request something. When the three guys from the neighborhood group went down to the mayor's office, they made it clear that if they didn't get what they wanted, they were going to torch those buildings.

MRS. RICHETTE: At City Hall they must have freaked out!

MRS. ALBRIGHT: The threat was there. Certainly appearances helped get their point across. Those politicians took a look at Leroy's Afro, Carl's dashiki [African-style shirt] and beads, and . . .

MRS. ROCHESTER: and Marcus's scar-covered face . . .

MRS. ALBRIGHT: That's right! And then they started thinking of Detroit.

(The worst riots of the 1960s occurred there in 1967.)

(Doob 1970, 93–94)

Finally active neighborhood organizations are more capable of accomplishing their goals, particularly their initial ones, than inactive groups. Saul Alinsky, a prominent organizer of community groups, believed that the way to build such organizations is much like training a prize fighter—that like the fighter, the neighborhood organization must be brought along slowly with progressively tougher opponents. Alinsky felt that in the beginning it is often helpful if those in charge set up what he called "a cinch fight," where the accomplishment of the goal is a certainty and thus assures that members' morale can be boosted for future, more difficult tasks. As an example Alinsky described a situation where he organized a demoralized neighborhood in Chicago to obtain infant welfare services. He knew that the services would be supplied the moment they were sought, but he did not tell the members. He wanted their apparent victory to serve as momentum for pursuing more difficult goals. Some people might say that Alinsky was deceptive, even dishonest. Most likely his reply would have been that in the harsh reality of city politics, one must often use harsh methods to accomplish neighborhood organizations' goals.

Sources: Saul D. Alinsky. Rules for Radicals. New York: Vintage Books, 1971; David M. Chavis and Abraham Wandersman. "Sense of Community in the Urban Environment: A Catalyst for Participation and Community Development," American Journal of Community Psychology. vol. 18 (February 1990), pp. 55–81; Ram A. Cnaan. "Neighborhood-Representing Organizations: How Democratic Are They?" Social Service Review. vol. 65 (December 1991), pp. 614–34; Christopher Bates Doob. How the War Was Lost. Unpublished manuscript, 1970; Pamela Oliver. "'If You Don't Do It, Nobody Else Will': Active and Token Contributors to Local Collective Action," American Sociological Review. vol. 49 (October 1984), pp. 601–10.

American cities but usually at a significant cost: When old buildings are torn down and replaced or simply renovated, the former tenants are dispossessed. For many of them, this means hardship, but for the poor, who were barely surviving with modest rent rates, the result is often homelessness (Hopkins 1989).

Increased Federal and State Assistance   As we have noted, since the 1930s, the federal government has provided major financial help to cities. Many financially troubled cities could benefit significantly from federal and state grants.

The recovery plan used in New York City can serve as a useful model. The gist of such a plan is to offer aid in exchange for financial reorganization. In 1975 the nation's largest city faced the threat of bankruptcy. City officials initiated tight management, local investment, and sharp controls on municipal workers' salaries in exchange for federal and state financial assistance. In the middle of 1983, New York City had a substantial budget surplus, one of the few large American cities able to make such a claim. The New York City plan has been far from ideal—fiscal stability has been accompanied by a drastic cutback in local services—and yet this situation shows that if realistic financial reorganization accompanies federal and state aid, some fiscal improvement is possible (Alpern 1981).

Observers of American cities have some reason for optimism. Over all, though, the prospects are not positive. One specialist on urban affairs noted that

the poor in cities have increased dramatically, the feminization of poverty has accelerated, the dropout rate in high schools for blacks and hispanics is about 75%, unemployment for black youth is over 50%, teen-age births have reached new highs, infant mortality has increased, and deindustrialization has reduced the number of jobs in large cities.

(Gittell 1985, 19)

In May 1992, *seeking a restoration of cutbacks in federal spending for the nation's cities, about 35,000 American citizens marched in Washington, D.C.*

bread, exercise their right peacably to assemble, and to petition the government for a redress of grievances.

(*Elliott* 1991, 2)

While organizers had predicted over 100,000 participants, only about 35,000 took part (Krauss, 1992a). But in spite of limited public arousal about the condition of American cities, some political mobilization did occur. About a month later, Congress, no longer willing to wait for White House support, passed a bill allotting $2 billion for emergency aid to cities to create summer jobs for inner-city youths, expand preschool programs for urban children, and rebuild businesses destroyed in the Los Angeles riots of spring 1992. Edward Kennedy, one of the sponsors of the bill, said that the legislation could "make a clear and present difference to cities across America this summer." In contrast, Thad Cochran, a Mississippi senator, expressed a common sentiment among lawmakers from rural states when he indicated that the big cities should not be permitted to appropriate federal money while rural areas' needs were often neglected. He added that the violence in Los Angeles "shouldn't be rewarded with a lot of new assistance programs for many cities" (Krauss 1992b, 7). In a tight economy, such disputes over the distribution of federal expenditures seem inevitable.

In recognition of such conditions, a former editor-in-chief of *Newsweek* magazine, Osborn Elliott, and the U.S. Conference of Mayors under the leadership of Raymond L. Flynn of Boston organized a national march on Washington. Anticipating the march, Elliott indicated that "brutal cutbacks" in federal spending for schools, housing, food stamps, mass transit, and social services had "taken a terrible toll" on American cities. He wrote:

> It's high time that urban Americans, as well as suburbanites who depend on the cities for their daily

Population Growth ◼

The crowded, deteriorated sections of American cities illustrate that overpopulation exists in some places within U.S. society. The devastating population growth that many developing nations in Africa, Asia, and Latin America currently face, however, is a considerably more serious situation.

In the pages ahead, we consider the principal factors that affect population size. A **population** is all the people who live within a specified geographic area such as a nation, a region, or a city. **Demography** is the study of human populations. Demographers examine birth, death, and migration rates to understand population changes. This section introduces the basic concepts and theories in demography and then examines the overpopulation issue in the developing and developed nations.

BASIC DEMOGRAPHIC CONCEPTS AND THEORIES

Rapid population growth is a new and distinctly frightening phenomenon. About 1750 the world population started to grow rapidly, and it has continued to do so. It took from the beginning of the Christian era to 1650 for the population to double, but, with the current growth rate, it will take only thirty-five years for the world's population to double to about 10 billion people. Why has this dramatic growth occurred? The central concept has been the death rate.

Before 1750 the primary reason for the low rate of population growth was the high death rate common in almost all societies. The most significant contributor to this high death rate was a high infant-mortality rate. In a given year, as many as one-half of all infants would die before the age of one. For both adults and children, disease and famine were the major causes of the high death rate. The single most devastating disease in human history has been the bubonic plague, also known as the Black Death. A conservative estimate is that during the fourteenth century, 40 percent of all Europeans died of the disease. While the bubonic plague was the most devastating disease, others were also very destructive during the same period. Typhus, malaria, tuberculosis, and small-pox were at the top of the list. Famine has also helped limit population growth. Through history Asian famines have been more serious than the European ones, primarily because of the less pre-dictable climate and rainfall of that continent. For example, a severe famine occurred in China in 1877-1878. In the course of the devastation, between 9 and 13 million people died of hunger, violence, and disease. Death was so prevalent that bodies were put in mass graves, which sometimes contained as many as 10,000 corpses (Petersen 1975).

In the nineteenth century, the death rate started to drop in industrial nations, and the popu-lation began to rise, first in Western and later in non-Western countries. If we start by understand-ing a number of demographic concepts, then we can examine theories and problems of population growth.

The Factors in Population Growth

Demographers focus their attention on birth, death, migration, and growth rates as they attempt to predict population trends around the world.

Birth Rate   The **crude birth rate** is the number of births per 1,000 persons in a society in a given year. This statistical measure is called "crude" because it does not provide specific information about the births. The crude birth rate, for instance, does not indicate the percentages of children born within different ethnic, racial, or class categories. The American crude birth rate of about 14 per 1,000 per year is scarcely a third of the rate in such develop-ing nations as Bangladesh, Biafra, or Zaire.

A crude birth rate gives an indication of the fertility of women in a given society. The **fertility**

rate is the number of actual births per 1,000 women between the ages of 15 and 44. That thirty-year span is the approximate length of time during which women are capable of giving birth. One must distinguish fertility from fecundity, the bio-logical potential for reproduction. No society has ever approached its reproductive potential.

Death Rate   The **crude death rate** is the number of deaths per 1,000 persons in a society in a given year. Once again, the designation "crude" means that the statistical measure provides no specific information, in this instance about death. It does not indicate, for instance, that in the United States the mortality rate (death rate for children during the first year) is 18 per 1,000 black infants per year, more than double the figure of 8 per 1,000 white infants per year (U.S. Bureau of the Census, *Statistical Abstract of the United States: 1992*, No. 109).

Migration Rate   **Migration** is the flow of people in and out of a particular territory (city, region, or country). The **in-migration rate** is the number of people per 1,000 members of the population mov-ing into an area, and the **out-migration rate** is the number of people per 1,000 members of the popu-lation moving out of an area. The **net migration rate** is the difference between the in-migration rate and the out-migration rate.

For several reasons data on migration are less effective than data on birth and death rates. In the first place, an individual's birth and death are more easily measured, occurring only once, while migra-tion can and often does take place many times dur-ing a lifetime. In addition, demographers started to study migration rates much more recently than birth and death rates. Thus less extensive data are available on migration.

Migration can have a significant influence on a nation's population. The United States is certainly a case in point. Between 1919 and 1955, over forty million people immigrated to this country, with the peak years early in the twentieth century. In six of the eleven years from 1905 to 1915, more than a million immigrants per year reached American shores. Although restrictive legislation sharply limited the number of people who could arrive legally after 1920, significant numbers of immi-grants have kept coming to the United States, and in recent years estimates indicate that as many illegal as legal immigrants have entered the United States.

450 ***Growth Rate*** Immigration can significantly affect population growth, but birth and death tend to be the major influences. The **growth rate** is the crude birth rate minus the crude death rate. Colombia, for instance, has a crude birth rate of about 31 per 1,000 people and a crude death rate of about 9 per 1,000. Thus the crude growth rate is 22 per 1,000 or 2.2 percent growth per year. The American growth rate is much lower, about 0.7 percent per year (United Nations, *Demographic Yearbook*, 1985 1985, Table 7).

A growth rate of 2.2 percent might seem relatively small at first glance, but the long-term result will be an enormous population increase. Consider, for instance, a nation of 10 million that increases 2.2 percent per year. After a year the population will be 10,220,000, and the following year it will total 10,444,840. Each year the population increases by an additional 2.2 percent, and as the population grows, that 2.2 percent represents a larger figure each year. In about thirty-two years that population of 10 million will double.

Doubling time is the time span necessary for a population to double in size. A growth rate of 1 percent produces doubling in seventy years, a growth rate of 2 percent means twice the population in thirty-five years, and a 3.5 percent rate leads to doubling in only twenty years.

The frightening fact is that the developing nations of Africa, Asia, and Latin America currently have a growth rate of about 2.1 percent, which means an average doubling time of only thirty-three years. Starvation and malnutrition are already widespread in many of these countries, and such rapid population growth will only expand these tragic problems.

Two Significant Demographic Theories

The following two theories consider the disastrous effect that overpopulation can produce.

Malthusian Theory In 1798 Thomas Robert Malthus published the *First Essay on Population*. In this essay the author, a minister, emphasized that humanity was guilty of original sin and, as a result, was destined to suffer. According to Malthus, God had established two conditions that would operate simultaneously to make continuous suffering inevitable: first, an unquenchable passion between the sexes ensuring rapid reproduction and second, a limited capacity to produce food. Malthus contended that population growth occurs at a geometric rate (2, 4, 8, 16, . . .), whereas the food supply expands at a mere arithmetic rate (2, 3, 4, 5, . . .). Malthus wrote, "A slight acquaintance with numbers will shew [show] the immensity of the first power in comparison to the second" (Malthus 1798, 14).

He believed that over time the scarcity of food would become increasingly alarming. While conceding that war, famine, and disease would hold population partially in check, Malthus thought that the future for most of the world population was bleak: bare subsistence at a very low level of material existence.

Malthus's first essay was an attack on the contemporary belief that large families among the poor are a blessing to be encouraged. The essay received extensive criticism, and five years later Malthus wrote a revision in which he emphasized that late marriage and fewer children could prevent a population disaster. Malthus advocated financial incentives as a means to restrict the number of children. He rejected birth control and abortion on religious grounds. The second essay was more popular in Malthus's day, but in modern times he is much better known for the earlier work.

Certainly Malthus's first essay has shortcomings. In the first place, he did not anticipate significant improvements in agriculture that have made it possible to increase food production much more quickly than he had expected. Second, the industrial societies have not shared Malthus's distaste for birth-control methods. By using a variety of techniques, a number of nations have been able to limit population much more effectively than the pious minister anticipated.

Yet, in spite of these criticisms, Malthusian theory has turned out to be prophetic. As we see in the pages ahead, the population has outstripped the food supply in most developing countries. In addition, Malthus's theory applies to advanced industrial societies. In the West other resources besides food are rapidly running out—in particular, clean air, clean water, and energy sources. Several years ago a report to the House Committee on Agriculture included the following question: "Will Americans discover too late that Thomas Malthus is a 200-year-old alarmist whose time has finally arrived?" (Committee on Agriculture 1976, 253)

Figure 15.3
Demographic-Transition Theory

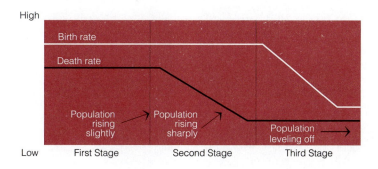

High

Birth rate

Death rate

Population rising slightly → Population rising sharply ↗ Population leveling off →

Low   First Stage   Second Stage   Third Stage

While the United States and other developed nations are attaining the population stability of the third stage, many developing nations are experiencing the rapid population expansion of the second stage.

Demographic-Transition Theory As Figure 15.3 indicates, the demographic-transition theory provides a three-stage analysis of population growth. The first involves high mortality and high fertility. This stage could occur in preindustrial societies where there is an absence of effective health care. It can also occur in modern societies which are highly stratified and which have privileges, particularly health care and education, restricted to a small elite. In both types of societies, most people suffer a high death rate, while continuing to have large numbers of children since the family remains the basic unit on which survival depends.

The second stage involves falling mortality and high fertility, and it applies to most developing nations. With independence from colonial rule, the new leadership generally promises basic social reforms but offers quite a mixed bag. While such basic health measures as immunization are established, most education and health care remain focused on the elite. As a result the death rate starts to fall, but, especially in rural areas, poor people continue to depend on the family unit for survival, especially in their old age, and thus they still have large families.

The third stage features low mortality and low fertility, and it occurs when countries establish wide-ranging reforms involving land and income redistribution, educational reform, and primary health care. Now average citizens find that the government and other structures provide security and employment, and so they no longer find it neces-

sary to have large numbers of children (Hartmann 1987). In short, this theory argues that when people realize that they do not need large families to survive, then they start restricting their number of children. We should keep that idea in mind as we move ahead in this section.

We examine the effects of population problems in both developing nations and in the United States and also consider efforts to reduce overpopulation.

AN OVERVIEW OF WORLD POPULATION PROBLEMS

What are some of the results of massive population growth? In the first place, crowding occurs. While people's perception of whether or not a situation is crowded varies according to their cultural standards, it seems safe to conclude that the more people, the more probable individuals will perceive a living situation as crowded. Some studies do suggest that as the number of people in a space increases, they are more inclined to experience nervous disorders and to engage in child abuse, incest, and suicide. Certainly the prospect of extreme crowding confronts us when we look at how rapid the population expansion in developing nations has been. In 1840 the earth's population was about 1 billion. Currently it increases by about 95 million a year, and if present projections hold, the figure will reach about 6 billion by 1998—

This rural Mexican family, with five children, is living in the second stage of the demographic-transition theory. In contrast, the American family, with two children, is in the third stage.

nearly a sixfold increase in 160 years (Ehrlich and Ehrlich 1991).

Shortage of food is another serious problem produced by rapid population growth. In the past many famines were **distribution famines**—food shortages existed in certain provinces or regions of a country, not throughout the nation. Distribution famines usually result from inadequate transportation or the unwillingness of leaders in one region to help starving people in another. In contrast, **deficit famines** are situations in which no food supplies exist elsewhere in a nation sufficient to compensate for local inadequacies. In many developing nations, rapid population growth coupled with limited food supplies makes the occurrence of deficit famines increasingly likely in the future (Sullivan et al. 1980, 111–17).

The future for many developing nations appears frightening. Figure 15.4 shows that a developing nation, such as India, generally has a disproportionately large young population, and therefore its prospect for continuing rapid growth

seems excellent. A recent report issued by the National Academy of Sciences has concluded that perhaps the greatest danger of excessive population growth is environmental destruction, particularly the pollution of air, water, and soil and the elimination of forests and various species of plants and animals (Silk 1986). Developed nations like the United States and Sweden have a much smaller proportion of young people, and so they are unlikely to have rapid growth in the years ahead.

The American Population Picture

Like other Western societies, the United States has passed through a phase of rapid population growth. Because of a steady flood of immigrants, the national population increased by about 30 percent each decade during the second half of the nineteenth century. Then in the 1920s, restrictions on immigration along with a declining birth rate slowed the rate of population growth. After World War II, the "baby boom" occurred, and in 1955 the birth rate reached its highest postwar figure. From that time the rate dropped steadily until 1975 before increasing slightly. The so-called "baby bust" of the past two decades has resulted because young people are having or plan to have fewer children than adults had in the past.

To obtain **zero population growth**—a situation in which the population size stabilizes—

Figure 15.4

Three Basic Population Pyramids—India, United States, and Sweden: ca. 1980

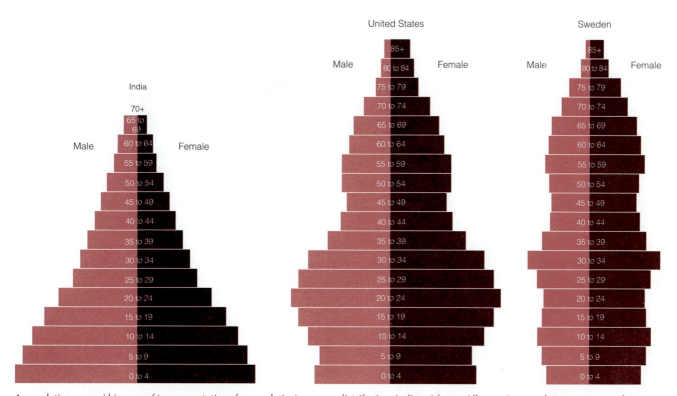

A population pyramid is a graphic representation of a population's age-sex distribution. India, with a rapidly growing population, presents a bottom-heavy pyramid typical of developing nations. A century ago the American population pyramid had a similar shape. At present our age-sex distribution is gradually moving toward the Swedish pattern.

Sources: U.S. *Bureau of the Census.* Current Population Reports, Population Characteristics, P-20, No. 374, *Table* 3-1; *United Nations Publishing Service.* Demographic Yearbook, 1985, *Table* 7.

American couples need to average about 2.1 children, slightly more than enough children to replace themselves in order to compensate for offspring who die and people who remain childless. In 1990 lifetime births expected for women aged 18 to 34 was 2.116 children, just about the figure needed for population stabilization (U.S. Bureau of the Census, *Statistical Abstract of the United States:* 1992, No. 97). It is apparent that unless the birth rate shoots up, the American prospects for zero population growth are good.

Yet the current American population situation contains some serious problems. First, while the overall fertility rate has been dropping, the proportion of births to unmarried mothers has been increasing. In 1989, 27.1 percent of all births were out of wedlock, about five times the percentage in 1960. Many of these children face distinct economic and social disadvantages in the years ahead (U.S. Bureau of the Census, *Statistical Abstract of the United States:* 1989, No. 89; U.S. Bureau of the Census, *Statistical Abstract of the United States:* 1992, No. 90). Second, certain economic strains have developed. Insufficient jobs and housing currently exist to meet the needs of Americans. One of the reasons the crime rate is particularly high among young people seems to be that they are especially prone to unemployment. Third, a number of valuable resources are in increasingly short supply. A shortage of water already exists in the Southwest,

454

and this problem will spread north and east in the years ahead. Food production could become an issue in American society, particularly if there is strict enforcement of the laws regulating the use of pesticides and various chemical fertilizers. With the average American using 450 pounds of wood and wood products each year, there will be continuing deterioration of the nation's lumber supply. Fourth, an increase in the population size will inevitably produce more pollution. In a highly developed country like the United States, the amount of water, air, and soil pollution is considerably greater per capita than in developing countries like India, Zaire, and Peru.

The American population problem seems to be quite effectively under control, but in developing nations, overpopulation is an increasingly serious threat. What can be done to overcome this threat?

In *highlighting the importance of cutting the nation's birthrate, the Indian government provides this billboard giving an on-going computerized estimate of the country's population.*

Attempts to Set Limits

How can we visualize the enormous number of people on this planet? In Robert Graves's (1962) historical novel, *Claudius, the God*, the Roman Emperor Claudius ordered a census taken of his kingdom, and the total number of Roman citizens was 5,984,072. On a page, Claudius admitted, the figure was not very impressive, but it was impressive if one considered it in human terms. Claudius explained, "If the whole Roman citizenry were to file past me at a brisk walk, toe to heel, it would be two whole years before the last one came in sight" (Graves 1962, 479). Claudius ruled nearly 6 million people. The current population of the earth is about 5.3 billion people, about 898 times the population of Claudius's Rome, and growing by about 95 million a year. At the current growth rate, the planet will contain about 14 billion in another century. On the other hand, if some form of effective birth control is used by 75 percent of the world's couples, restricting their number of children to two or fewer, the population will stabilize at about 9 billion by 2050 (Exter 1991). That, however, is a tall order.

It is easy to feel overwhelmed by the numbers and simply to believe that they are so large that nothing can be done to control overpopulation. Yet some practical measures do exist.

Contraception Many experts feel that the key to lowering the fertility rate and thus reducing population growth resides in technology: specifically, easy-to-use and effective means of contraception. Certainly the widespread use of contraceptives would curtail the population expansion. Some devices are more effective than others. Sterilization, oral contraceptives, and intrauterine devices (IUDs) are the most effective methods. They are followed by the condom, diaphragm and spermicide, withdrawal, spermicide alone, rhythm, and douche in order of declining effectiveness.

Sterilization is the most popular form of contraception, with 150 million people sterilized worldwide by 1987. Of the more than 400 million people using some form of birth control, 35 percent have been sterilized, 19 percent use IUDs, 18 percent use such "traditional" methods as rhythm, withdrawal, and abstinence, 15 percent use birth-control pills, and 10 percent use condoms. In developing nations, where since the early 1960s there has been a sixfold increase in the use of contraception, the average woman who once bore at least six children now produces fewer than four (Cutler 1991). Evidence clearly indicates that in poor developing nations like Kenya, educated women are more receptive to contraceptive use (Njogu 1991).

Family Planning **Family planning** is a program that encourages people to decide how many children they want, when they want them, and what contraceptives, if any, they wish to use to achieve their goals. Family-planning programs have helped to reduce the birth rate in such countries as Taiwan, Singapore, South Korea, and Hong Kong. In Africa, Zimbabwe has a family-planning program run by local people and not outsiders, as are many birth-control efforts in developing nations; the program builds on widely accepted cultural values and stresses a message of well-being for both mother and child. Familes are encouraged to allow more time between children and to avoid pregnancy if they are in the "high-risk" years— under 18 and over 35 (Mathews 1991).

Family planning alone, however, has not been able to halt population growth in any country. One difficulty is that many programs are poorly financed, thus permitting only a small number of people to use their services. The major problem, though, is that the family size a couple wants and the size that will be suitable for the needs of a nation are often not the same. In many cases people turn to family planning after they have had large families, not before. Therefore a major challenge involves incentive: motivating people to accept small families.

Incentives The most obvious incentives are financial, and several countries have experimented with paying cash for sterilization or the use of IUDs. Another possibility is to permit tax deductions for only the first two children or to impose a "child tax" on parents with more than a certain number of children. The chief problem with such proposals is that under them large, poor families would only encounter increased suffering. Some incentive plans are more far-ranging, emphasizing the development of social and economic policies that would weaken social norms encouraging large families. Whereas couples would be free to decide the number of children, they would encounter pressure from family, friends, and government officials to keep that number low.

Coercion If family planning and incentives fail to lower the birth rate, some countries may be forced to impose limits on the number of children people are permitted to have. Such a policy, naturally, would create an uproar in a country like the United States where there has been a strong emphasis on the rights of individuals to conduct their private lives without government interference as long as they do not hurt anyone else. Of course, therein lies the problem. In many developing nations, if citizens continue to have large families, the current inadequacies of food and other resources will only worsen, and all, or at least many will suffer.

By what measures could a government administer a policy of coercive population control? One approach would be to issue a license to every woman of childbearing age permitting her to have the number of children that would be most suitable for that society's welfare. Another proposal would be to provide a chemical inhibitor for the entire population: some agent that would reduce fertility but not entirely eliminate childbirth. The goal of such an approach would be to regulate the chemical dosage so that the desired number of children would be produced each year. To Americans as well as to citizens of many other countries, such measures seem intolerable. And yet in the future, the governments of nations faced with explosive population growth might decide that no other approach will work.

Modern Success Stories While countries like the People's Republic of China have launched massive and successful population-control programs, impressive population control has sometimes occurred without such efforts. Between 1965 and 1980, Cuba's birth rate dropped by nearly half. In this poor country, that has a per capita income of roughly a tenth of that in the United States, economic and social reforms provided a greatly improved standard of life. This permitted citizens to appreciate an important reality raised in the discussion of demographic-transition theory: They no longer needed to have many children because the state now had assumed responsibility for their survival. In Sri Lanka such sweeping social policies as free supplementary rice rations, job and old-age security provisions, and free education and health care have helped people reach a similar conclusion, and in spite of modest economic development, the fertility rate dropped sharply, with Sri Lanka now possessing one of the lowest birth rates among developing nations. In the cases of Cuba and Sri Lanka, progressive economic and social

456 policies convinced citizens that they no longer needed to produce the large families required for survival under earlier oppressive regimes (Hartmann 1987, 277–80).

As the population of a nation grows, its environmental problems are likely to increase. The American case demonstrates, however, that other factors make a more prominent contribution.

Environmental Issues

A riddle taught to French children asks the following question. If the number of lilies in a pond doubles each day and if the pond is entirely filled with lilies on the thirtieth day, when will the pond be half filled? The answer: on the twenty-ninth day (Brown 1978). If the lilies represent the human population and the pond stands for the environment, is it reasonable to suspect that humanity is now in the twenty-ninth day?

The subject of this section is the **natural environment,** the combination of land, climate, water, air, mineral resources, and plant and animal life that together compose the physical world where people live. Ecologists point to the existence of a "web-of-life": an intimate, delicate relationship of plants and animals to each other and to the environment. With the development of mechanical sources of power, we human beings have assumed a dominant role in this community of interdependent living organisms and perhaps have brought ourselves to the eve of "the twenty-ninth day." Ecologists emphasize that many valuable resources are dangerously scarce and that environmental pollution has become increasingly serious.

RESOURCE DEPLETION

Food supplies and natural resources are two major areas of resource depletion. Both pose significant difficulties that will become even more significant in the years ahead.

Food Supplies

At least three-quarters of a billion, primarily rural people living in developing nations in Africa, Asia, and Latin America do not have sufficient food to sustain productive, healthy lives. Some live on roots, coarse grains, wild fruits, and vegetables while others engage in a subsistence activity, just barely surviving. In many rural areas, the growing population forces the people to overuse the land for both crops and grazing animals and to deforest large areas to obtain wood for fuel, practices which contribute to soil-mineral depletion and erosion, mortgaging the future simply to stay alive in the present.

A major issue contributing to world hunger is that countries where people are starving do not produce enough food or the kind of food they need. At least fifteen such nations grow more acres of food for export than acres of staples such as wheat, corn, rice, vegetables, and fruits that could sustain their own people. As a result they must import these staples, but seldom can they import enough to prevent famine (Mellor 1991).

Inadequate food supply is the primary problem in developing countries. In developed nations the greatest challenge involves natural resources.

Natural Resources

The most publicized concern in this area is energy. Western nations depend on oil for almost half of their energy needs, and at present the world consumption level is awesome: almost 30,000 gallons of oil every second. Estimates suggest that the available supplies of both oil and natural gas will run out within fifty to seventy-five years.

Water is another important, exhaustible resource. American society has required an ever increasing amount of water. In 1900 Americans used 40 billion gallons of water a year. By 1970 the figure had risen to 350 billion gallons. At the end of the century, estimates indicate that consumption will be between 700 and 1,000 billion gallons. Certain sections of the country are most vulnerable to running dry, especially arid agricultural areas that depend on large amounts of irrigation water. For instance, the Ogallala aquifer, which supplies irrigation water to Texas, Oklahoma, Kansas, Nebraska, Wyoming, Colorado, and New Mexico, is in serious trouble, with rainfall running about a trillion gallons of water a year short of keeping up with use.

Americans also employ a large proportion of various raw materials that are fast running out. We use over 60 percent of the planet's natural gas, more than 40 percent of the aluminum and coal, over 33 percent of the nickel, petroleum, platinum, and copper, and about 25 percent of the iron, gold, mercury, silver, tin, lead, zinc, and tungsten.

Technological advances now permit increased extraction of minerals from low-grade ore, but the associated activities—more mining, crushing, treating with chemicals, heating, cooling, and dumping—will greatly expand environmental pollution (Adler 1991; Barnet 1980; Meadows et al. 1972; Ridker and Watson 1980).

ENVIRONMENTAL POLLUTION

As we have noted, ecologists indicate that we human beings are a component in the "web of life." The pollution we create also enters this process. Barry Commoner (1972), an ecologist, described several principles of environmental pollution. First, he suggested that within the environment all the parts are interrelated and that a change in one part of the system causes changes in other parts. Second, nothing just disappears. Pollution will simply move from one place to another, or perhaps it will be transformed. Third, nature is enormously complicated. Commoner suggested that the environment is like a watch. If you closed your eyes and poked a pencil into the works, the watch might run better, but the chances are it will be seriously damaged. The odds that "poking around" in the environment has been and will continue to be harmful are overwhelming. Commoner concluded that people have ignored these principles and violated the environment for such a long period of time that the current pollution problems literally threaten the survival of humanity.

Americans are becoming increasingly aware of environmental problems. Table 15.1, which contains data from a nationally conducted survey, indicates the extent of public concern with major environmental problems as well as some mea-sures respondents have taken to improve the environment. We will examine some major types of pollution in U.S. society.

The nearby Cross-Cultural Perspective looks outside the United States, examining the efforts of environmental activists in other countries to establish their own political parties.

Increasingly citizens recognize that environmental pollution does not acknowledge national boundaries—that the problems readily blow, flow, or spill from one country to another. Certainly air pollution is a case in point.

Air Pollution

When asked early in 1991 to express their concern about air pollution, 59 percent of a national sample said they were extremely concerned ("6" on a six-point scale ranging from 6 to 1) and another 27 percent opted for very concerned ("5" on the scale) (Hueber 1991).

There are four major sources of air pollution: transportation, power generation, industry, and waste incineration. Auto emissions represent the most serious contributor to air pollution. In the United States, 90 million cars release millions of tons of carbon monoxide, sulfur dioxide, hydrocarbons, and nitrogen oxides per year.

While air pollution is a serious problem in many parts of the United States, it is often worse elsewhere. In Santiago, Chile, where air quality is among the worst of all Latin American cities, the major culprit is the city's fleet of 11,000 buses, which are old and burn fuel inefficiently.

Table 15.1 Outlook toward Environmental Issues

EXTENT RESPONDENT WORRIES ABOUT SERIOUSNESS OF ENVIRONMENTAL PROBLEMS		
	Great deal	*Fair amount*
Contamination of soil and water by radioactive waste	62%	21%
Ocean and beach pollution	53	26
Loss of habitat for wildlife	53	27
Damage to the earth's ozone layer	49	24
Loss of tropical rain forest	42	25
Greenhouse effect or global warming	35	27
Acid rain	34	30

STEPS TAKEN BY RESPONDENT OR HOUSEHOLD MEMBER TO IMPROVE THE ENVIRONMENT	
Voluntary recycling of newspapers, glass, aluminum, motor oil, or other items	86%
Cutting household use of energy by improving insulation or changing the heating or air-conditioning system	73
Cutting household's use of water	68
Avoiding buying or using aerosol sprays	68
Replacing a "gas guzzling" automobile with one that is more fuel efficient	67
Contributing money to an environmental, conservation, or wildlife preservation group	51
Avoiding use of a product because it is not recyclable	49
Cutting down on the use of a car by carpooling or taking public transportation	46
Boycotting a company's product because of its record on the environment	28
Working as a volunteer for an environmental, conservation, or wildlife preservation group	18

Source: Graham Hueber. Gallup Poll Monthly. (April 1991).

Recent survey data suggest that many Americans are concerned about major environmental problems and have taken modest steps to improve the environment.

In recent years air pollution has been receiving extensive attention for two reasons. First, there has been growing international concern about destruction of the ozone layer, which protects the earth from ultraviolet radiation that can produce skin cancer, cataracts, and destruction to the immune system in human beings and also cause damage to other animals and plants. The major source of ozone destruction has been chlorofluorocarbons (CFCs), which are versatile, low-cost chemicals used as coolants in refrigerators and air conditioners, as propellants in aerosol spray cans, as solvents, and in foam insulation.

In 1987 over fifty nations signed the Montreal Protocol, which mandated substantial cuts in use of CFCs and other chemicals that can damage the ozone layer. This agreement required signatory nations to halve their use of five CFCs by 1998 and to freeze their use of three halons used in firefighting and containing ozone-destroying bromine. In 1990 the Montreal Protocol was revised, adding to the list of problem chemicals and specifying bans instead of cutbacks on most CFCs and halons. While it appears that CFC replacement will be considerably less expensive than thought in 1987, a current drawback for ozone protection is that some developing nations seeking to expand their industrial goals, as well as heavy chemical producers like the United States and Japan, have expressed reservations about later restrictions (Hoke 1991; Makhijani, Bickel, and Makhijani 1991; Miller 1991).

The other significant recent concern related to air pollution has involved the impact of the "greenhouse effect," which is a chemical process that begins when the sun's rays penetrate the earth's

CROSS-CULTURAL PERSPECTIVE
Guarding the Commons: Green Political Parties

For many centuries throughout Europe, herders let their animals run free on common land, allowing them to overgraze the areas and eventually to strip them of all vegetation, thus exposing the land to erosion. Ecologist Garrett Hardin suggested that had it occurred to individual herders to conserve the grazing land, they would have realized such actions would prove impractical when others most likely would have ignored their well-intentioned lead. In modern society, Hardin suggested, we can no longer afford to disregard this lesson.

Green political parties have taken the lesson to heart. At least at the local level, such parties have developed in Canada, western Europe, Japan, the United States, Mexico, Costa Rica, Chile, Argentina, and Brazil. Green-party members serve in the parliaments of eight European countries—Austria, Belgium, Finland, Germany, Italy, Luxembourg, Sweden, and Switzerland.

In western Europe, where green politics has been strongest, activists usually share similar social backgrounds and political and social values. They tend to be young, urban, and well-educated and to be students, teachers, academicians, or professional civil servants. In many cases green-party members have been previously involved in some special issue such as the promotion of peace, women's rights, or the eco-

nomic development of Third World citizens.

Green-party platforms generally display certain distinct characteristics. Foremost is the belief that participants' nations are in the midst of a world-threatening ecological crisis produced by the drive for uncontrolled economic and technological growth. The only way to counter the threat, they believe, is to establish and enforce immediate strict environmental regulations. In addition to this most basic position, green parties usually favor a significant redistribution of basic goods and services both within their own countries and between developed and developing nations. Furthermore in the political process, these individuals strongly support egalitarian and democratic principles and practices.

Besides the similarities among European green parties, differences also occur, particularly in the means to accomplish common goals. Moderates tend to accept piecemeal reforms, emphasizing the importance of maintaining a respectable, law-abiding posture. In contrast, the more radical green-party members believe the current economic system should be challenged frontally and are often willing and sometimes eager to encourage violent confrontations with authorities. In Great Britain, Sweden, and Finland, the moderates prevail, while radicals are well represented in the green parties of Italy, Germany,

and Luxembourg.

Whether moderate or radical, green-party activists must consider their future political approach. To survive these parties need to develop a stable electorate that identifies with their cause and can be depended upon to vote consistently for their candidates. But to obtain such a following, the parties require stable structures that can consistently perform the activities and services provided by established political parties. Often environmental activists are reluctant to support hierarchical structures, preferring to maintain "grassroots" democracy with the absence of elites. Thus a dilemma unfolds. Green-party activists want consistent voter support, but they find it difficult or impossible to obtain it without a traditional political hierarchy, and they find such a structure ideologically distasteful.

A similar problem could carry beyond green-party organizational structure into dealings with established political parties. To accomplish their political goals, will environmental activists be willing to enter into political coalitions with these parties? Such dealings might force idealistic individuals to compromise their goals, and yet failure to do so might lose green-party support among constituents who are committed to fairly rapid environmental improvements.

These issues must be examined very carefully. Sara Parkin, an official in Great Britain's

460

Green Party, indicated that green activists have been "very naive about power and its dynamics," failing to evaluate how subversive most of their goals are to people committed to the status quo and how fiercely such individuals will fight their programs. "Ignoring power does not make it go away—it simply allows it to fall into the hands of others" (Kelly et al. 1991, 19).

Petra Kelly, a co-founder of the West German Green Party, agreed. Speaking directly to American environmental activists, Kelly said not to "shy away from taking power." She added:

> There is a desperate need to expose the long-term societal failures of Democrats and Republicans alike in the USA. They have brought us to the brink of [environmental] disaster. Greens must offer a clear and credible alternative to American voters.
>
> (*Kelly et al.* 1991, 20)

Sources: Hilary F. French. "Strengthening Global Environmental Governance," In Lester R. Brown et al. (eds.), State of the World 1992. New York: W. W. Norton, 1992, pp. 155–73; Sheldon Kamienicki. "Political Mobilization, Agenda Building and International Environmental Policy," Journal of International Affairs. vol. 44 (Winter 1991), pp. 339–58; Petra Kelly et al. "Why Not Here? Prospects for Green Politics in America," Greenpeace. (July/August 1991), pp. 18-20; Bruce Piasecki and Peter Asmus. In Search of Environmental Excellence. New York: Simon & Schuster, 1990; Wolfgang Rudig. "Green Party Politics Around the World," Environment. vol. 33 (October 1991), pp. 6–9.

---

atmosphere and reach its surface, where land and water absorb them. The surface, in turn, radiates infrared energy back into the atmosphere, where under pollution-free conditions, most of it escapes back into outer space. However, some of that infrared energy is absorbed in the atmosphere, raising the planet's surface temperature. The amount of absorbed infrared energy has been growing because of rising atmospheric pollution involving the so-called "greenhouse gases"—carbon dioxide, methane, and CFCs—which have been blocking increasing amounts of infrared energy from returning to outer space. As a result temperatures on the planet have been rising steadily. The seven hottest years in a century of American weather statistics occurred from 1980 to 1990, and 1990 represented the warmest year on record. While reputable environmental scientists have been unable to declare with absolute certainty that this trend is the product of the greenhouse effect, they feel the probability is great (K. Schneider 1991; S. Schneider 1991).

At the Earth Summit held in Rio de Janeiro in June 1992, most of the 178 nations participating signed a treaty pledging to stabilize the auto and factory emissions producing greenhouse gases, but, at President Bush's insistence, no precise targets or timetables were specified (Stevens 1992).

Water Pollution

In the famous 1960s film, Dr. *Strangelove*, General Jack D. Ripper never drank water straight from the tap. He believed that only superdistilled H_2O would protect his "precious bodily fluids" from a "Communist plot" to fluoridate U.S. water. While General Ripper's fear of fluoridation was unrealistic, people today are indeed anxious to protect themselves from the pollutants in the American water supply. In 1991, 67 percent of a national sample expressed a great deal of concern about the pollution of drinking water, and an additional 19 percent indicated a fair amount of concern (Hueber 1991).

Several sources of water pollution exist. One prominent contributor is sewage. As towns and cities have grown, their sewage treatment facilities have often failed to expand accordingly. Even when sewage is properly treated, it still contains considerable pollution, including biological wastes and nutrients. A greater problem is that some sewage dumped into coastal waters has received only superficial treatment, removing just the grossest contaminants. Then in areas combining household and storm sewers, the systems can overflow with heavy rains, carrying large amounts of raw sewage into areas used for fishing and swimming. Sometimes septic tanks discharge their refuse into the same underground water supply that people use for drinking. In a public restroom along the upper Mississippi River, a statement scribbled on the wall read, "Flush the toilet. They need the water in St. Louis." This sarcastic bit of humor might contain more truth than St. Louis's citizenry would like to acknowledge. Another significant source of water pollution is industrial waste. Since the beginning of industrialization, American factories have been located near waterways, and manufacturers have long recognized that nothing works as well as a river to make one's own waste problems belong to someone else. Hundreds of millions of pounds of toxic pollutants enter American water each year, in spite of a National Resources Defense Council lawsuit forcing the Environmental Protection Agency (EPA) to regulate over 125 toxic pollutants released by the nation's largest industries. Furthermore poison runoff from such sources as fertilizer and pesticides, oil and other pollutants collecting on pavements, and soil erosion caused by timber harvesting close to waterways accounts for at least half the nation's water pollution (Adler 1991; MacLeish 1992).

While such publicized episodes as the 1989 *Exxon Valdez* oil spill are damaging, the destructive impact of many unheralded, systematic dumping activities is greater. A case in point involved the pharmaceutical company Ciba-Geigy, which ran a ten-mile pipeline from its dye and resin plants and dumped more than four million gallons per day of waste containing lead, chromium, and such extreme carcinogenic (cancer-producing) chemicals as PCBs and nitrogen-bearing compounds into the ocean off New Jersey. The governor, both senators, other state politicians, and the EPA were aware of the dumping, but no significant action to prevent it was taken (Cockburn 1988).

Pesticide Residues

In 1981 the Mediterranean fruit fly damaged the fruit and vegetable crops in several sections of California. In order to prevent the further spread of the fruit fly, the governor reluctantly authorized the widespread spraying of insecticides. Shortly afterwards a survey firm asked a national sample of Americans whether they thought spraying the insecticides was the right or wrong thing to do. Seventy-two percent indicated it was the right thing, 8 percent felt it was wrong, and 20 percent had mixed feelings or did not know. However, after the fruit fly problem started, 41 percent of the respondents—more than two in five—changed their attitudes or behavior about buying California fruits and vegetables or noted that the stores in their area had made a change (Roper Organization,

Roper Reports, November 1981). These survey items suggest that many Americans have a two-part attitude toward pesticides. Such people feel they are necessary but want to have as little personal contact with them as possible.

Certainly recognition of the significance of the problem exists, with the EPA in 1986 declaring pesticide pollution the most urgent environmental problem facing the United States. In twenty-six states pesticides have been found in the underground water, which supplies half the nation's drinking water. Insecticides kill beneficial as well as harmful insects, with, for instance, an annual $135 million agricultural loss because the destruction of bees means reduced crop pollination. Each year there are an estimated 300,000 Americans poisoned by pesticides; only about one-third (194 of 600) of the active ingredients found in pesticides have been fully reviewed to determine their impact on human beings. At present thousands of pesticide products that might produce cancer, birth defects, sterility, and chromosome damage are being marketed and purchased, and little or no information about their damage-causing potential is being given to consumers (Hagood 1991).

The pesticide issue is a difficult one. Farmers and consumers want to produce food as cheaply as possible, and pesticides help do this. In recent years, however, many consumers have become increasingly concerned that the food they buy is infected by carcinogenic pesticides. Florida and the South, which are particularly vulnerable to plant diseases and insects, would be hardest hit if pesticides were restricted or banned. A soil scientist said, "What we're seeing is a very real conflict in values out there. Some people say the only acceptable use of pesticides is no use. But the only way we can get high quality vegetables in Florida at the volumes we need and prices we expect is with pesticides" (Schneider 1989, A14).

Radioactivity Effects

Soon after the Three Mile Island accident, a vice-president of the Metropolitan Edison Company, which operated the nuclear-power plant, said, "We didn't injure anybody, we didn't seriously contaminate anybody and we certainly didn't kill anybody" (Mathews 1979, 25).

It is still much too soon, however, to make

462

such a definite statement. Increasing evidence suggests that soldiers and civilians exposed to nuclear testing in the 1950s took many years, sometimes decades, to show symptoms of cancer or leukemia.

Nuclear-power plants pose several significant dangers. The fallout from a major accident could be the equivalent of that released by hundreds of Hiroshima-sized atomic bombs. Following the accident at the Chernobyl nuclear plant in the Soviet Union, heavy doses of radioactivity were detected in many European countries. Almost every plant in the United States has been shut down at some time because of an operating problem that could create a hazardous accident.

Another important problem produced by nuclear-power plants is their waste. Tiny quantities of this waste can cause cancer or birth defects. Large doses can kill people quickly. The major problem with radioactive waste concerns storage. Unfortunately much of the waste remains radioactive for hundreds, even thousands of years—in some instances as long as 300,000 years. Yet storage tanks are often not sufficiently sturdy to contain the waste for such long periods. The most troubling case in point involves the most lethal wastes: the strontium 90 and plutonium buried underground in concrete tanks, primarily in Richmond, Washington. This concentrated radioactive waste, which will remain deadly for thousands of years, has leaked at least sixteen times since 1968, releasing 115,000 gallons of radioactive liquid in 1974. The Nuclear Regulatory Commission is still seeking effective ways to dispose of nuclear wastes. The difficulties are as much political as technical. As one energy department official indicated, the problem is "deciding in which congressional district to put them."

The Chernobyl disaster reinforced antinuclear fears everywhere. In 1988 and 1989, controversy erupted over the safety of nuclear-weapons facilities supervised by the U.S. Department of Energy. In addition, antinuclear sentiments forced the shutdown of the Savannah River plutonium facility; promoted opposition to the start-up of nuclear reactors on Long Island, New York, and in Seabrook, New Hampshire; encouraged resistance to Department of Energy plans for nuclear-waste dumps in Nevada and New Mexico; and prompted governors in Colorado and Idaho to block transport or deposit of nuclear wastes (Caldwell 1990).

With the economical working lives of power plants about thirty to forty years in duration (less if their steam generators or other highly vulnerable parts start deteriorating), there is the eventual problem of dismantling such units. Unlike other kinds of discarded plants, nuclear facilities cannot just be leveled with a wrecking ball; contaminated parts and equipment must be isolated, sometimes for as long as thousands of years. Around the world more than twenty plants are already shut down; sixty-three more will probably be closed by the turn of the century and another 162 between 2000 and 2010 (Pollock 1986; Robertson 1980).

Ten years after the Three Mile Island accident, there were 111 nuclear-power plants in the United States, supplying nearly 20 percent of electrical needs. At that time there had been no new orders for plants since 1978, and more than 110 plants ordered after 1973 had been cancelled. In the future nuclear plants will face stiff competition from efficient use of fossil fuels and from other technologies, like solar power (Wald 1989).

It seem reasonable to wonder why the Nuclear Regulatory Commission has continued a program that involves such extreme risks. The answer is that a variety of interests, including recent presidential administrations, major corporations, and many American citizens, believe that the United States must meet its growing energy requirements while decreasing reliance on foreign suppliers, regardless of the environmental impact.

What will happen in the future? Will we be able to survive the environmental challenge we currently face? Let us consider some measures that could help reduce the current environmental problems.

RESTORATION OF A HEALTHY ENVIRONMENT

The issue of the damaged ozone layer suggests the well-known image of "spaceship earth"—a delicate vehicle hurtling through space. Political boundaries mean little; a hole in the ozone layer in Antarctica affects all of us. Throughout the text we have seen that modern Americans often are isolated, with little sense of anything significant shared. But whether people like it or not, the factors producing environmental pollution have made everyone share this major problem.

Certainly such a conclusion is consistent with the global perspective discussed at several points in this chapter. The problem, as one expert noted, is that Americans "have always been good at reacting and rather poor at long-range planning" (Comp 1991, 12). Yet such long-range or comprehensive planning now appears necessary, and ideally it should be international in scope, with all major environmental issues addressed simultaneously. Environmentalists have found that when they dealt with one problem at a time, pollution-control efforts either have been unsuccessful or have compounded other problems. Comprehensive environmental planning is a huge task that can only be broadly considered here.

Two major barriers exist. First, there are practical political difficulties. Comprehensive environmental planning is expensive—hardly a selling point in an economically troubled era. In addition, the emphasis on comprehensiveness runs counter to the modern nature of expertise, where narrow, specialized training prepares professionals to focus in distinct niches and not to analyze and confront problems that straddle a number of disciplines. Even environmentalists, though accepting the idea of comprehensiveness in the abstract, will often opt for short-term, narrow improvements, feeling that broader efforts should be avoided until some vague future date when the political climate seems more receptive.

Second, a large body of scholarly research has suggested that comprehensive environmental planning is too idealistic and impractical for individuals, organizations, and nations (Bartlett 1990). Yet increasingly, modern environmental problems such as ozone depletion and the greenhouse effect make it painfully clear that solutions to major sources of environmental destruction can only occur with "people thinking big" and protecting themselves against "the tyranny of small decisions" (Bartlett 1990, 244).

In the years ahead, a more comprehensive approach seems likely, if not inevitable, with some technological advances proving helpful. For instance, satellites are now equipped with a variety of sensors responsive to different portions of the electromagnetic spectrum. From infrared reflections they record data on greenness, amount of vegetation, and temperature and thus contribute significant global information on the state of the planet (Magnuson and Drury 1992).

It seems inevitable that in the future an emphasis on restoring the environment will affect people's daily lives. We might need to keep our homes and offices less warm in the winter and less cool in the summer. We might need to pay more for electricity, fruit, and vegetables. But isn't it better to make small sacrifices than the ultimate one—the death of the planet and its inhabitants?

STUDY GUIDE

Learning Objectives

After studying this chapter, you should be able to:

1. Define urbanization and describe the conditions encouraging the development of preindustrial cities.
2. List and discuss the four eras in the growth of American cities.
3. Analyze the primary causes of urban deterioration.
4. Discuss measures that could revitalize urban existence.
5. Define demography and discuss factors in population growth: birth rate, death rate, migration rate, and growth rate.
6. Examine in detail the Malthusian theory and the demographic-transition theory.

464

7. Identify and explain the population problems of the United States and the world.
8. List and discuss the different measures for limiting population.
9. Discuss major resource-depletion problems.
10. Examine the major types of environmental pollution.

Summary

1. The three issues in this chapter—cities, population growth, and environmental problems—are interdependent, with top economic and political leaders contributing to policy formation in all three areas.

2. A city is a large, densely settled concentration of people permanently located within a relatively confined geographical area where nonagricultural occupations are pursued. Urbanization is the process by which a city forms and develops.

Preindustrial cities generally had certain characteristics: small populations, limited transportation and storage facilities, a center serving as the focus of governmental and religious activity as well as elite housing, and a highly restrictive social-class system. We can distinguish four eras in the development of American cities: the colonial period, the period of westward expansion, the period of metropolitan growth, and the modern period. In the course of their development, American cities have undergone many changes, and in recent years the deterioration of urban facilities and services as well as a steadily eroding tax base have posed serious difficulties.

Central problems of modern cities are powerful political and economic interests, governmental proliferation, and financial limitations. Measures to revitalize American cities include an emphasis on an active neighborhood life, experiments advancing low-income citizens' interests, efforts to bring middle-class people back into cities, and increased federal and state assistance.

3. A population is all the people who live within a specified geographic area such as a nation, a region, or a city. Demography is the statistical study of human populations. To determine population changes, demographers analyze birth, death, and migration rates. Prominent demographic theories include the Malthusian theory and the demographic-transition theory. In the developing nations, population growth now occurs at a rapid rate, and millions of people currently starve to death each year. In the United States, population growth has slowed down. Nonetheless with the current population size, problems do exist—in particular, insufficient jobs and housing, a strain on the supply of natural resources, and significant levels of pollution. Attempts to set population limits throughout the world involve the use of contraception, family planning, incentives, coercion, and a combination of different techniques.

4. The natural environment is the complex of land, climate, water, air, mineral resources, and plant and animal life that together compose the physical world where people live. Resource depletion is a serious environmental problem. In developing nations the inadequacy of food supplies is the dominant issue related to this topic. In developed nations the chief difficulty is the declining supplies of major natural resources. In recent years Americans have become increasingly concerned about environmental pollution. Serious problems involve air pollution, water pollution, pesticide residues, and radioactivity effects. Currently there are signs that many Americans are willing to commit themselves to the restoration of a healthy environment.

Key Terms

city a large, densely settled concentration of people permanently located within a relatively confined geographical area where nonagricultural occupations are pursued

crude birth rate   the number of births per 1,000 persons in a society in a given year

crude death rate   the number of deaths per 1,000 persons in a society in a given year

deficit famine   situation in which no food supplies exist elsewhere in a nation sufficient to compensate for local inadequacies

demography   the study of human populations

distribution famine   a food shortage existing in certain provinces or regions of a country, not throughout an entire country

doubling time   the time span necessary for a population to double in size

family planning   a program that encourages people to decide how many children they want, when they want them, and what contraceptives, if any, they wish to use to achieve their goals

fertility rate   the number of actual births per 1,000 women between the ages of 15 and 44

gentrification   the move of middle- and upper-middle-class people to formerly deteriorated inner-city neighborhoods

growth coalition   a number of developers, bankers, and industrialists working together to produce economic expansion

growth rate   the crude birth rate minus the crude death rate

in-migration rate   the number of people per 1,000 members of the population moving into an area in a given year

linkage   a municipal procedure requiring developers engaged in large commercial projects to provide a substantial fee earmarked for low-cost housing

megalopolis   a string of closely bound metropolitan areas

metropolis   a territorial unit composed of a large central city and the surrounding cities and towns

migration   the flow of people in and out of a particular territory (city, region, or country)

natural environment   the combination of land, climate, water, air, mineral resources, and plant and animal life that together compose the physical world where people live

net migration rate   the difference between the in-migration rate and the out-migration rate

out-migration rate   the number of people per 1,000 members of the population moving out of an area in a given year

population   all the people who live within a specified geographic area such as a nation, a region, or a city

suburb   a politically independent municipality that develops next to or in the vicinity of a central city

urban infrastructure   a city's basic physical and technical features such as roads, bridges, and water, sewer, and transit systems

urbanization   the process by which a city forms and develops

zero population growth   a situation in which the population size stabilizes

Tests

True • False Test

_____ 1. In preindustrial cities the city center contained governmental and religious activities and also elite housing.

_____ 2. Ferdinand Tönnies believed that when people took up residence in cities, their outlooks and behavior started to change.

_____ 3. A metropolis is a preindustrial version of a megalopolis.

_____ 4. Members of growth coalitions seek to maximize profits, with the benefit to the overall citizenry considered unimportant.

_____ 5. Gentrification is the move of elderly people to inner-city areas.

_____ 6. Fertility refers to the biological potential for reproduction.

_____ 7. In most countries migration is the principal factor affecting population growth.

_____ 8. Sterilization is the most popular form of contraception.

_____ 9. At least fifteen nations where hunger and starvation are significant problems grow more acres of food for export than acres of staples that could support their people.

_____ 10. A variety of powerful interests, including presidential administrations and major corporations, have opposed the development of nuclear-power plants.

Multiple-Choice Test

_____ 1. Which of the following qualities was characteristic of preindustrial cities?
   a. an open social-class system
   b. efficient transportation
   c. rapid economic growth
   d. elites' authority based on appeals to tradition and religious absolutes

_____ 2. Which of these factors did NOT contribute significantly to suburban development?
   a. widespread use of electric power
   b. movement of factories out of central cities
   c. unionization of workers in factories
   d. FHA loans to subsidize suburban housing

_____ 3. Jane Jacobs's ideas on improving the quality of urban life by combining land-use patterns in a given area illustrates which measure for improving urban life?
   a. experiments with metropolitan solutions
   b. emphasis on an active neighborhood life
   c. efforts to bring middle-class people back into cities
   d. increased federal and state assistance

_____ 4. The crude death rate:
   a. is determined by a combination of the fertility rate and the migration rate.
   b. provides no specific information about the characteristics of those who die.
   c. determines the growth rate.
   d. is the same as the infant-mortality rate.

_____ 5. A limitation of Malthusian population theory is that Malthus did not anticipate:
   a. people's distaste for birth-control methods.
   b. financial incentives as a means to restrict the number of children.
   c. significant improvements in agriculture that have increased the food supply.
   d. that a century after his death people would marry at a later age.

_____ 6. The third stage of the demographic-transition theory occurs when:
   a. people believe that they need large families to survive.
   b. countries cut back on wide-ranging reforms involving income, education, and health.
   c. individuals start restricting their number of children.
   d. a, b, and c

_____ 7. Where no food supplies exist elsewhere in a nation sufficient to compensate for local inadequacies, there is a:
   a. Malthusian famine.
   b. distribution famine.
   c. chronic famine.
   d. deficit famine.

_____ 8. Commoner suggested that all but one of the following statements about the environment is true. Which position was NOT asserted:
   a. The more things change, the more they stay the same.
   b. All parts of of an environment are interrelated, with a change in one part affecting other parts.
   c. Nothing just disappears.
   d. Nature is enormously complicated.

_____ 9. Major air-pollution problems in recent years have included:
   a. the outhouse effect.
   b. the destruction of the ozone layer.
   c. the uncontrollable growth of the ozone layer.
   d. a and c

_____ 10. Serious problems with nuclear plants include:
   a. the disposal of nuclear wastes.
   b. nuclear fallout.
   c. dismantling of plants at the end of their working lives.
   d. a, b, and c

Essay Test

1. Discuss major trends of modern urban living, using studies and issues cited in the text to illustrate your conclusions.
2. Will American cities be significantly different in twenty years? What bits of evidence support your conclusion?
3. Discuss the Malthusian theory of population and the demographic-transition theory. What are their similarities and their differences?
4. Do you think rapidly growing developing nations can limit their population increase in the near future? What means will be most productive? Discuss.
5. Summarize the most serious U.S. environmental problems.
6. If you were president of the United States, what steps, if any, would you take to combat resource depletion? What about environmental pollution?

Suggested Readings

Brown, Lester R., et al. 1992. *State of the World: 1992*. New York: W. W. Norton. A yearly, internationally oriented volume, with the 1992 edition featuring eleven prominent environmentalists analyzing either major environmental problems or progressive actions.

Donaldson, Peter J. 1990. *The United States and the World Population Crisis: 1965–1980*. Chapel Hill, NC: University of North Carolina Press. An informative account of the American government's creditable effort to reduce world population growth, revealing the complex challenges embodied in this difficult issue.

Feagin, Joe R., and Robert Parker. 1990. *Building American Cities: The Urban Real Estate Game*. 2nd ed. Englewood Cliffs, NJ: Prentice-Hall. An unrelenting analysis and critique of how urban growth coalitions dominate the development and deterioration of modern American cities.

468   Fuller, R. Buckminster. 1970. *Operating Manual for Spaceship Earth*. New York: Pocket Books. A brief book filled with powerful ideas and expressing this well-known inventor's concern about environmental deterioration and his belief that a careful, imaginative use of technology can preserve our "spaceship earth."

Heer, David M. 1975. *Society and Population*. 2nd ed. Englewood Cliffs, NJ: Prentice-Hall. A brief introduction to the field of demography that succinctly discusses the basic concepts, theories, and the problem of overpopulation.

Humphrey, Craig R., and Frederick R. Buttell. 1982. *Environment, Energy, and Society*. Belmont, CA: Wadsworth. A textbook that effectively examines issues of environment, energy, and population and includes "radical," "liberal," and "conservative" perspectives on most of the topics.

Jacobs, Jane. 1961. *The Death and Life of Great American Cities*. New York: Vintage Books. An analysis of the different factors that cause cities to be either healthy or unhealthy places to live. Jacobs's writing has been controversial, but whether or not you agree with her, you should find her thinking original and provocative.

Sennett, Richard. 1974. *Families against the City*. New York: Vintage Books. A sociologist's analysis of how middle-class families adjusted to life in industrial Chicago in the late nineteenth century. Using census data, historical sources, and some sharp thinking, Sennett presents an interesting set of hypotheses.

Wirth, Louis, 1938. "Urbanism as a Way of Life," *American Journal of Sociology*. vol. 44 (July), pp. 3–24. In spite of its age, this widely read sociological article provides a useful introductory analysis of the dominant characteristics of urban life.

Additional Assignments

1. Using material from the text and library sources, outline two sets of population proposals, one for the United States and the other for the world. Include a discussion of the following issues:
   a. The dilemma of governmental intervention in family decision making: a limitation on personal freedom versus the need to control population growth.
   b. The most effective/desirable forms of birth control.
   c. The prospects for limiting population growth that your programs will produce.
2. Urban areas are centers of high population density. It is a common theme for "disaster" literature and films to contemplate possible harm to large numbers of people. Pick a pollution problem and provide an account describing both the effects on people's lives produced by sudden drastic levels of pollution and the local resources needed to cope with the problem. Think about your own living area. Does it have the service organizations to handle your pollution "disaster"?

Answers to Test Objective Questions

True • False Test

1. t 6. f
2. t 7. f
3. f 8. t
4. t 9. t
5. f 10. f

Multiple-Choice Test

1. d 6. c
2. c 7. d
3. b 8. a
4. b 9. b
5. c 10. d

Collective Behavior, Social Movements, and Social Change

16

On August 24, 1992, the 40 miles from Miami south to Florida City were transformed from a comfortable suburban district to a devastated area containing wrecked houses, downed trees and power lines, destroyed vehicles, and bands of looters.

When the full force of the hurricane hit at about 4 A.M., the Mullins family watched in horror as the concrete walls of their building, which was both their home and a fish store, started to shake and take in water. Meanwhile with shingles torn off the roof, water also started pouring in through the ceiling. "We were pretty sure that the rear wall was going to just come on down," said Mrs. Mullins the next day. "We moved into the fish locker. Now we all smell like fish, but we are all alive" (Manegold 1992, A1).

Still shaken by the events of the previous night, three women down the street spoke all at once to the reporter. Brenda Hill explained that the roof had fallen in on them. She added, "We stayed there and just put mattresses over ourselves and hoped that we would live" (Mangeold 1992, B7).

Farther south in Cutler Ridge, Jim Bossick and a friend were guarding a shop to prevent looting. After sending his wife to a shelter, he had hidden in a closet. Next time, he explained, he would go to a shelter, too. "I'm telling you, I'm never living through one of those things again. I was just scared to death, scared to death, scared to death" (Manegold 1992, B7). Meanwhile throughout the area, looting was occurring.

Collective behavior is social activity that occurs under conditions that are temporarily unstructured and unstable because of the absence of clearly defined norms. People's responses to situations in which collective behavior occur can be normal, or they can be highly emotional or unpredictable. The key factor is that collective behavior involves situations occurring outside the confines of ordinary social activity. A disaster like Hurricane Andrew is an illustration of collective behavior, creating destruction and havoc and forcing people to adjust to physical and social conditions that are abruptly different from those in which they normally interact.

All of us occasionally enter collective behavior situations—in particular, when we mingle in crowds. Do crowds stimulate any special feeling? Have you ever considered how you would act if you were in a crowded movie theater and fire broke out? Let us consider another type of collective behavior—rumors. What is your response to rumors that you encounter? Do you willingly believe them and pass them on to others? Or are you careful to confirm information you receive before you transmit it to others? As we discuss the different forms of collective behavior, perhaps you will develop a clearer sense of how you would

behave in each case. The difficulty in making such a prediction is that collective-behavior activities take us out of ordinary social situations and put us in relatively unusual, unstructured situations, where much of what happens, including our own behavior, is likely to be quite unpredictable.

Besides collective behavior we will examine two other topics—social movements and social change. **Social movements** are organized, collective activities undertaken by people to promote or resist social change. Social movements—the women's or civil-rights movements, for instance—involve activities similar to collective behavior in the respect that to some extent they occur outside existing normative guidelines. However, social movements often are more stable and longer lasting than forms of collective behavior, and they can eventually become organizations, where the normative standards and members' behavior are quite conventional.

Social movements and collective behavior often occur in situations where social change is taking place and, in turn, they frequently encourage its occurrence. **Social change** involves any modifications in culture, social organization, and social behavior. Generally the topic does not include changes that occur within a small group or an organization. The focus of social change is alterations that take place within institutions or societies.

In the following section, we examine the best-known theory of collective behavior and social movements. Next the focus shifts to crowds; the discussion includes an examination of theories of crowd behavior and the analysis of several different kinds of crowd situations. The third topic, rumors, is followed by a look at social movements, and the chapter concludes with an analysis of different sources of social change.

Smelser's General Theory

A section of George Orwell's *Animal Farm* can serve as an illustration of Neil Smelser's (1963) general theory of collective behavior and social movements.

One day the message filtered among the animals of Manor Farm that Old Major, a prize boar, had a strange dream the previous night and wanted to communicate it to the other animals. They regarded Old Major with such high regard that as soon as Mr. Jones had stumbled off to bed, drunk as usual, the animals all gathered in the barn to hear what the ancient boar had to say.

With the animals before him, Old Major cleared his throat and started to speak. He indicated that, indeed, he had had a strange dream the previous night, but before he discussed the dream, he needed to speak about something else: the abuse the animals experienced. Old Major spoke about how hard they worked and how little they were fed. He indicated that when each had reached the point where he or she was no longer useful, Mr. Jones would simply put an end to that animal's miserable life. All their problems, Old Major emphasized, were the result of human tyranny. It was clear that the only course of action was to get rid of their human overlords.

Then the old boar described his dream. It involved a time well into the future when humanity would have vanished from the earth. A dominant feature of the dream was a stirring song called "Beasts of England." The song described the glorious future when all animals would be free of human control and would be able to share earth's edible bounty among themselves. Old Major began singing the song, and almost before he had finished the animals joined in.

Three nights after his speech, Old Major died peacefully in his sleep. That was early in March. During the next three months, there was considerable secret activity. Old Major's speech provided the more intelligent animals with an entirely different outlook on life. They did not know when the rebellion would happen—perhaps it would not even take place in their lifetimes—but they all felt that it was their duty to prepare for it. Teaching and organizing were the principal preparatory activities. As the most intelligent animals on the farm, the pigs took a dominant leadership role. Two boars—Snowball and Napoleon—elaborated Major's teachings into a complete system of thought, which they called Animalism. Several nights a week after Mr. Jones had gone to sleep, they held meetings where they discussed principles of Animalism and convinced most of the animals that rebellion was in their interest.

It turned out that the rebellion occurred much sooner than anyone had expected. One Saturday in June, Mr. Jones went into town and got so drunk that he did not return until Sunday afternoon when he immediately went to sleep on the drawing-room sofa with a newspaper over his face. The farm hands had milked the cows on Sunday morning, but with their boss absent, they went out rabbit hunting, not even bothering to feed the animals. Evening arrived and the animals still had not been fed. Finally they could stand it no longer. One of the cows broke down the shed door with her horns, and all the animals started to help themselves from the bins.

At that point Mr. Jones awoke, and a few moments later he and the farm hands were in the shed with whips in their hands, lashing out wildly at the animals. That was more than the animals could endure. They attacked Jones and his men, butting and kicking them from all sides. The men were shocked. They had never seen animals behaving in this manner before, and this sudden uprising frightened them out of their wits. After no more

When George Orwell's novel Animal Farm *was published, Joseph V. Stalin (second from right) was the top political leader in the Soviet Union. In 1939, just before this photograph was taken, Stalin signed a nonaggression treaty with Nazi German leaders.* Animal Farm *is a thinly disguised indictment of the political corruption that occurred after the Communist Party took control of Russia.*

than a moment of trying to defend themselves, they took to their heels with the animals in hot pursuit. The animals chased the men out of the barn and off the farm, slamming the five-barred gate behind them (Orwell 1946, 17–22).

Let us suppose that the fleeing men ran into town, and someone asked one of them what had happened. The man might have replied, "It's that new grain we've been feeding the livestock. I told Jones it would bring him nothing but trouble."

People frequently offer one-factor explanations for the occurrence of collective-behavior episodes and social movements. In contrast, Smelser's theory outlines six elements necessary for the development of these activities. These elements develop in sequence, and as each one occurs, the likelihood of some alternate activity decreases. By the time the fifth element appears, collective action is inevitable.

1. **Structural conduciveness.** The first point involves basic conditions that permit or allow collective behavior or a social movement to emerge. The animals' abil-

ity to speak English, to assemble, and to organize themselves for an expected rebellion were conditions of structural conduciveness. Real farm animals, of course, lack the capacities just mentioned, and so they are unable to rebel.

2. **Structural strain.** Various immediate conditions such as prejudice and discrimination, economic exploitation, and poor communication between groups or nations can create a significant amount of tension or pressure for people. Structural strain can lessen people's willingness to stay within normal behavioral limits. Insufficient food, too much work, and death the moment they proved no longer useful were severe structural strains the animals experienced.

3. **Growth and spread of a generalized belief.** As collective behavior or a social movement develops, an interpretation of the situation and how to respond to it will begin to emerge. The generalized belief supports a break with conventional

behavior, emphasizing the current social strain and the rewards collective activity will produce. At the beginning of the account of *Animal Farm*, it is clear that the animals might have simply accepted harsh treatment for the rest of their lives—they could not imagine any other way of living. But then Old Major called them together and explained in painful detail how exploited they were and pointed out that, through rebellion, they could obtain another, much more desirable form of life. The song that he sang them and that they all readily learned summarized these ideas of freedom and equality in a powerful way. After Old Major's death, several pigs developed the doctrine of Animalism, producing an entire system of thought from Old Major's ideas.

4. ***Precipitating factor.*** Some incident or set of incidents must initiate collective behavior or a social movement. The first three elements of Smelser's theory create a situation that resembles a bone-dry forest vulnerable to devastation by fire. That destruction will not occur, however, unless a match falls unheeded on the forest floor. The precipitating factor is that match. In *Animal Farm* the precipitating factor was the fact that one day the animals were not fed.

5. ***Mobilization for action.*** At this point all that remains is the occurrence of col-

lective activity. At such a time, people typically find that the rewards and punishments promoting ordinary, everyday behavior are no longer present. The doctrine of Animalism had prepared the animals to understand and want to overthrow the unjust system under which they had been forced to live, and not being fed that Sunday was the outrage that finally produced rebellion against Jones's control.

6. ***Social control.*** Smelser's final stage concerns the various ways that people in authority act to encourage or discourage a particular incident of collective behavior. After the rebellion, no authorities besides the animals remained. They chased Mr. Jones and his men off the farm, and then they slammed the gate, thereby locking out the men and ending the confrontation between beasts and human beings.

A significant limitation of Smelser's theory is that like other strain theories, it pays little attention to significant resources necessary to produce some forms of collective behavior and social movements, in particular. As we see in the section on social movements, money, power, social networks, and other resources are often essential elements in their development.

Smelser's theory can analyze social movements and all types of collective behavior, including crowds, the topic of the following section.

Crowds

A **crowd** is a temporary gathering of individuals who share a common concern or interest and find themselves in close physical contact with one another. "Common concern or interest" and "close physical contact" suggest some similarities between crowds and groups. We will see, however, that crowd activity is not as responsive to established norms as group behavior. This section examines crowd characteristics, crowd theories, violent crowds, and frightened crowds.

CHARACTERISTICS

Certainly crowds vary in their qualities and behavior. Some, such as ordinary street crowds, are composed of people sharing little or no common purpose; others, including the people gathered to hear a popular political candidate, possess a common interest. In many instances crowds are orderly (those attending an opera or a concert of classical music), and in other situations they are not (the participants in a mob or riot). In general, the members of crowds behave in distinct ways.

1. **Suggestibility.** People in crowds do not have the distinct guidelines for behavior that are normally available. They turn to their fellow crowd members for direction, literally "going along with the crowd."

2. **Anonymity and spontaneity.** Individuals in a crowd recognize that they are in a wilderness of strangers—that they are "lost in a crowd." The sense of anonymity permits them to act more openly and freely than they normally would. They are likely to lose a sense of responsibility for any misdeeds. "Don't blame me," an individual might say after a riot. "Everyone was breaking things and stealing."

3. **Impersonality.** Since people in crowds are detached from their everyday normative guidelines, they often treat others in a more impersonal, harsh manner than they normally would. When fans at a baseball game yell "Kill the umpire," they are not stopping to consider that the object of their wrath is a human being. For many participants violent crowd activity would be difficult to perform without this element of impersonality.

THEORIES

Perhaps the brief discussion of crowd characteristics seems disturbing. You might have the impression that people in crowds can behave in much the same fashion as a herd of stampeding cattle. One of the perspectives we will consider makes such a claim. The other approach is more sophisticated.

Contagion Theory

At the end of the nineteenth century, Gustave Le Bon (1952), a writer, developed the contagion theory. That era was a time of major upheaval characterized by the erosion of traditional religious, political, and social beliefs and their replacement by modern scientific and industrial standards. Le Bon suspected that disorder, even chaos, lay ahead, and crowds would become an increasingly destructive force.

Contagion theory contends that the presence of a crowd encourages or compels people to think and act in a uniform manner.

Le Bon claimed that, when in a crowd, an individual inevitably becomes less civilized: "Isolated, he may be a cultivated individual; in a crowd, he is a barbarian—that is, a creature acting by instinct. He possesses the spontaneity, the violence, the ferocity, and also the enthusiasm and heroism of primitive beings" (Le Bon 1952, 32).

Le Bon's work gives the impression that when people enter crowds, something both magical and terrible happens. Herbert Blumer's (1975) analysis of contagion is more systematic. Blumer has considered contagion a process where crowd members become increasingly preoccupied with each other's behavior, and outlooks and events that would normally concern them become insignificant. Eventually each crowd member becomes so focused on the others' activities that he or she loses self-consciousness, which usually is a "means of barricading oneself against the influence of others." At this point each individual will simply follow the crowd.

It is likely that anonymity also promotes contagion. A study of twenty-one cases in which crowds were present when people threatened to jump off a building, bridge, or tower suggested that certain conditions of anonymity would prompt members of the crowd to encourage individuals to jump: specifically membership in a large crowd, the protection of nighttime, and a considerable physical distance between the crowd and victim (Mann 1981).

Another context in which contagion might operate is suicide. When presented with accounts of adolescents who committed suicide, high-school respondents tended to believe that students under stress might follow the lead if the public was generally sympathetic to individuals who killed themselves (Gibson and Range 1991; McDonald and Range 1990).

Emergent-Norm Theory

"As the fire spread, people were panicking all around us," the 12-year-old boy explained. "My mom just stood there in the middle of the circus tent and gripped my hand tighter than ever before and looked around. Then after what seemed a century, she said, 'Over that way there's an exit.'" Hundreds were swept up in the contagion of panic, got trapped at the main entrance, and died in Hartford's tragic circus fire. But in spite of the rapidly spreading panic, this mother managed to avoid that response and to maintain a calm, searching approach that permitted her to bring her son and herself to safety. In accord with this true incident, the proponents of emergent-norm theory reject the idea that all the members of a crowd think and behave in the same way.

Emergent-norm theory analyzes the process by which a new social standard develops within a crowd—a standard that in reality receives a more enthusiastic acceptance from some crowd members than others, in spite of the fact that both crowd members and observers tend to perceive nearly unanimous support for it.

According to the emergent-norm theory, people in crowds often find themselves in a normative void—no clear standard of behavior exists. At this point some active people are inclined to take the initiative and present a new standard: an emergent norm, which could advocate such diverse activities as starting to throw rocks and bottles at the police or standing and clapping in appreciation at a graduation ceremony when the name of an especially beloved individual has been read off a list of retiring faculty members. Once the norm develops, the more assertive individuals in the crowd are likely to support behavior consistent with it and to oppose behavior against the norm. This helps to develop the impression that the crowd acts in unanimity.

There are important differences between contagion theory and emergent-norm theory. As we have noted, the emergent-norm perspective rejects the idea that crowd members possess a uniform mental state. Accounts of Nazi crowds attacking Jewish merchants often distorted the actual situation in which a few storm troopers harassed and beat the victims while a disapproving crowd afraid to express dissent watched silently.

Another difference is that emergent-norm theory applies to a wider range of emotional situations. Contagion theory cannot effectively analyze crowds in a subdued state, but emergent-norm theory can. For example, there have been situations where late arrivals reaching the site of an automobile accident or airplane crash loudly exclaimed, "What happened?" Disapproving looks and gestures from people in the crowd immediately prevented any further loud commentary. In this case the emergent norm required onlookers to speak quietly out of respect for the crash victims.

Finally, unlike contagion theory, the emergent-norm perspective does not attempt to analyze crowd behavior as separate from the rest of social behavior. In its use of the concept "norm," emergent-norm theory makes a more concerted effort to extend conventional sociological thinking to an unconventional context—collective behavior (Brown and Goldin 1973; Turner 1964; Turner and Killian 1972; Vander Zanden 1981).

As you read the nearby Cross-Cultural Perspective, try to determine how the different theories we have discussed apply.

VIOLENT CROWDS

A typical scene from a cowboy film illustrates a contagion perspective on riots. Standing in front of the seething crowd, the grief-stricken ranch hand shouts, "Hal Smith was a good man who'd give a stranger the shirt off his back. Now he's lyin' dead in his coffin and them stinkin' townspeople are responsible. They ain't gettin' away with it. Let's tear up the town!" And a moment later they mount their horses and gallop down the main street, destroying everything in their path.

Mobs and riots are related phenomena, but we can draw a distinction between them. A **mob** is a crowd whose members engage in destructive and aggressive behavior in the pursuit of a short-term but valued goal. A mob, for instance, might want to catch a certain person and hang him or her or

Besides the obvious physical damage done by riots, they also produce a strong impact on observers, notably children. In May 1992 this third grader, who lived in the area where the Los Angeles riots occurred, did sketches representing his memories of the previous week's destruction.

478

During the spring of 1989, hundreds of thousands of Chinese students demonstated in favor of more democracy in the People's Republic of China. The demonstrations started in Beijing, spread to other major Chinese cities, and then to Taiwan, Hong Kong, Australia, and the United States. In some respects the protests were similar to the idealistic, light-hearted demonstrations launched by American students in the 1960s. Calling for universal freedom, Chinese students in Beijing's Tiananmen Square constructed a styrofoam goddess of liberty. They also popularized a mocking song calling for the resignation of China's top three leaders. In sharp contrast to China's much larger protests two decades earlier, the student demonstrations were largely nonviolent.

The government, however, did not respond nonviolently. After warnings against public demonstrations, troops moved into Tiananmen Square, where they opened fire on unarmed protesters killing hundreds, perhaps even thousands, and arrested hundreds; a few of those arrested were executed while many of the others received long prison terms.

Like all social activity, collective behavior does not occur in a vacuum. So why did the demonstrations occur? At the root of the students' discontent seemed to be the economic-reform program initiated about a decade ago by Deng Xiaoping,

the country's top leader, who wanted to replace central planning with market-oriented, capitalist incentives. This program produced a number of confusing, frustrating difficulties:

1. **Leaders' failure to acknowledge citizens' rights and interests.** Deng Xiaoping recognized that economic reform was impossible without some relaxation of political controls. This relaxation encouraged students and intellectuals to express their grievances, but they were frustrated, because in China's nondemocratic setting, their statements and analyses went largely unreported in the mass media and thus were without impact. None of China's top leaders had any semblance of Mikhail Gorbechev's understanding that citizens' support for the government would be increased if they felt its leaders were responsive to their rights and interests.

2. **The corruption of socialist ideals.** The political leadership undermined the country's forty-year socialist tradition, replacing the once-honored ideal of "serve the people" with the position "to get

rich is glorious." In a country where the passage of wealth and power from parents to children had been condemned, this corruption became a widespread practice among the Communist Party's elite.

3. **The ineffectiveness of economic reforms.** A two-year freeze on price reform was declared, significant cuts in capital investment were made, and inflation, especially in rural areas, was a serious problem. By the beginning of 1989, three out of four million workers in the private construction industry were out of jobs, and 20 million workers in unprofitable rural industries were at risk of losing theirs.

These were factors precipitating the student demonstrations—demonstrations which were largely orderly and peaceful even when troops were sent in to suppress them.

A significant problem, however, is that peaceful demonstrations, like any social activity, can be perceived in various ways by different sets of eyes. Undoubtedly the most important set of eyes observing the protests belonged to Deng Xiaoping. Deng had been a victim of the Red Guard demonstrations two decades earlier during what was known as the Cultural Revolution, when young people had humiliated, beaten, and, in about a half-million cases, killed government officials or other established professionals whom they believed were involved in corrupt practices. Deng was treated quite leniently, being denounced in public and exiled to a menial job in south China, but one of his sons was thrown out of a window and crippled for life.

Even though the 1989 protests were peaceful, neither Deng nor his close advisor Yang Shangkun, who was also dismissed from an important post during the Red Guard era, saw a significant difference from the earlier demonstrations. In a country where Deng almost completely controlled basic policy, this represented a significant perception. In late April as the demonstrations developed, Deng told colleagues, "What they are doing now is altogether the same stuff as what the rebels did during the Cultural Revolution. All they want is to create chaos under heaven" (MacFarquhar 1989, 8).

So the demonstrations were repressively ended, and the students' demands for democratic participation were silenced. What will happen in the future? One development is certain.

Because of the fact that most of the senior leaders are old—Deng was 87 at this writing—they will soon be replaced. It seems almost as likely that without significant policy changes, students' grievances, as well as those maintained by other major groups, will not simply disappear. Will a new, more progressive leadership attuned to citizens' major needs and interests arise or will the 1989 Tiananmen Square massacre prove to be the forerunner of further bloody confrontations between the Chinese government and its people?

Sources: Fox Butterfield. "Deng Reappears with a Chilling Lesson about Power in China," New York Times. (June 11, 1989), sec. 4, p. 1; Roderick MacFarquhar. "The End of the Chinese Revolution," New York Review of Books. vol. 36 (July 20, 1989), pp. 8–10; Sheryl Wu Dunn. "Spies Learn Students Can Be Stern Teachers," New York Times. (May 29, 1989), p. A7.

destroy a particular piece of property. A **riot** is aggressive crowd behavior that is less focused or unified than mob activity. A crowd of angry, frustrated people might run through city streets indiscriminately looting and burning buildings.

Between 1966 and 1968 in Los Angeles, Newark, Detroit, Washington, D.C., Cleveland, and a host of other American cities, extensive rioting occurred. Table 16.1 lists some of the costs involved. The bloodiest riot of that era happened in Detroit from July 23 to July 28, 1967. Forty-three people were killed and over a thousand injured. The rioters destroyed more than 1,300 buildings and sacked more than 700 businesses (Brown and Goldin 1973).

But the single most destructive riot of the

Table 16.1 Ghetto Riots and Interracial Clashes

	Number of events identified[1]	Estimated number of participants[2]	Reported deaths	Reported injuries	Reported arrests
Period I (June 1963–December 1965)	48	100,000	56	1,800	12,500
Period II (January 1966–June 1968)	200	150,000	140	6,156	37,362
Period III (July 1968–December 1970)	256	100,000	42	1,050	4,632

[1]*The statistics reported here are based on a tally of newspaper accounts.*
[2]*Only private citizens are counted, not the police, National Guardsmen, and other officials involved in riot suppression.*

Source: Adapted from Ted Robert Gurr. "Political Protest and Rebellion In the 1960s," pp. 49–76 In Hugh Davis Graham and Ted Robert Gurr (eds.). Violence in America: Historical Perspectives. Beverly Hills, CA: Sage, 1979, p. 54.

More riots occurred in Period III than in Period II, but participation, casualties, and arrests were much more extensive in the second period.

480

twentieth century occurred in Los Angeles in the spring of 1992. Fifty-eight people were killed, nearly 1,800 were injured, about 6,400 people were arrested, and property damage was in the hundreds of millions of dollars, with 3,767 fires occurring in the city (Reinhold 1992).

Smelser's theory can help analyze the development of the Los Angeles riots. First, there were certain structurally conducive conditions. For instance, in a city like Los Angeles, especially in poor neighborhoods, people live in crowded conditions, which permit them to communicate quickly their feelings and emotions. In a rural area, such communication would be more arduous. In addition, mass-media coverage of the riots and related events was extensive, permitting participants to be influenced by the information and emotion they picked up from their television sets.

Structural strain was also apparent. Most participants in the riots were poor—Hispanics, blacks, and whites. Among Hispanic-American immigrants, who represented over half the first 5,000 people arrested, unemployment rates had tripled in the previous two years. There was widespread disillusionment, and out of frustration with their economic plight, some joined in the burning and looting. The week before the riots was unseasonably hot, contributing to the strain and to people's frustration (Davis 1992).

On the topic of generalized belief, one might argue that American society has always shown a tolerance, even an acceptance of violence. Our television programs and films have often presented violent individuals as glamorous or heroic, and as we saw in Chapter 3, "Culture," such images are widely admired both at home and abroad. There is little reason to suspect that given this cultural trend, people who are poor and feeling frustrated would be exempt from it.

In the Los Angeles riot, the precipitating factor was the verdict in the trial of four white policemen who had been videotaped beating black motorist Rodney King. What was particularly infuriating to many people was that the videotape made it clear that the officers had systematically beaten King for two minutes, and yet it took an all-white jury less than a day to acquit the defendants. Mayor Tom Bradley, usually very controlled, spoke in uncharacteristically passionate terms, saying, "The jury's verdict will never blind us to what we saw on that videotape" (Stevenson 1992a, D22). With the out-

break of riots the next day, other Los Angeles citizens responded violently.

Mobilization for action occurred because angry people frustrated by limited prospects were not motivated to abide by conventional norms. Riots offered them a chance to strike out against the system and, more particularly, the groups and individuals that they believed were oppressing them. In Los Angeles the sources of these grievances were complex. While the verdict in the Rodney King beating trial set off the riots, many young blacks, including black gang members, mobilized to loot and burn almost 2,000 stores belonging to Koreans, with whom blacks had been feuding since the previous year when 15-year-old Latasha Harlins had been killed by a Korean grocer in a dispute over a bottle of orange juice (Davis 1992).

Police and National Guardsmen eventually occupied the riot areas, imposing some social control. In Los Angeles there was widespread criticism of the slowness with which the police acted; for instance, they made no effort to save Koreans' stores. A full week after the riots, one writer described the largest Hispanic district as being in a state of siege. Elite police units would sweep through searching for stolen goods while border patrolmen from as far away as Texas prowled the streets, looking for illegal aliens. Meanwhile thousands of looters faced with absurdly high bails—one man captured with a packet of sunflower seeds and two cartons of milk was held on $15,000—were stuck in prison (Davis 1992; Stevenson 1992b).

The emergent-norm perspective also proves useful in analyzing the Los Angeles riots. In most past riots, a single racial group engaged in the activity, but in this instance, the participants established a multiracial participatory standard, with Hispanic-Americans, African-Americans, and whites all taking part. One writer suggested that looters focused on stores where they had resented spending their money—groceries, liquor stores, discount clothing and shoe retailers, gas stations, and 7-Elevens (Nessel 1992).

It is noteworthy that while many riots have occurred in the United States, other countries had much more extensive rioting. Table 16.2 provides data that addresses this issue.

The research section at the end of the chapter examines the topic of prison riots.

Table 16.2 Rebellion[1] in Selected Countries, 1961–1970[2]

	Person days of rebellion per 100,000 citizens	Conflict deaths per 10 million citizens
LARGEST WESTERN DEMOCRACIES (1970 POPULATION 50 MILLION+)		
United States	250	18.3
West Germany	0	0.3
Britain	20	0.5
Italy	1,300	8.0
France	15,000	17.1
SOME SMALL WESTERN DEMOCRACIES		
Canada	700	1.5
Australia	0.1	0
Sweden	0	0
Israel	70	11.8
Republic of Ireland	70	0
Northern Ireland	40,000	129.3
OTHER MAJOR NATIONS OF THE WORLD		
Europe: USSR	0.3	18
Poland	0	118
Spain	1,900	13
Middle East: Turkey	50	14
Egypt	40	9
Iran	10	76
Asia: India	4,700	42
Indonesia	100,000+	30,000+
Japan	0.5	0.1
Africa: Nigeria	150,000+	250,000+
South Africa	200	16
Latin America: Brazil	150	7
Mexico	9,000	26
Argentina	35,000	31

[1]An outbreak against those in authority.
[2]Within each group countries are listed by descending population rank. The data are rounded to reflect their imprecision. Estimates of death are more accurate than estimates of person days. Estimates for Western countries are more accurate than those for Communist and third-world countries.

Source: Adapted from Ted Robert Gurr. "Political Protest and Rebellion in the 1960s," pp. 49–76 In Hugh Davis Graham and Ted Robert Gurr (eds.). Violence in America: Historical Perspectives. Beverly Hills, CA: Sage, 1979, p. 60.

During the 1960s a number of nations suffered a considerably higher proportion of death produced by rebellion and conflict than the United States did. Nigeria and Indonesia, which had devastating internal wars, were at the extreme.

FRIGHTENED CROWDS

In panics and mass hysteria, the emotional level is high, just as in riots. Members of frightened crowds, however, seek to escape the source of shared concern.

Panics

A **panic** is a collective flight to safety. Panic occurs under specific circumstances. It takes place only if people believe that escape routes are available but limited or closing. It will not occur if people are

482

convinced that there is no way to escape; under this condition they might experience terror or start behaving like children, but they usually do not panic (Smelser 1963). Panic can be dangerous, with research evidence concluding that panic attacks can increase the likelihood of heart attack or stroke (Weissman et al. 1991).

One observer of a fire that started in a crowded theater in Chicago in 1903 and killed 602 people offered some evidence for contagion theory when he indicated that heel prints were apparent on many dead faces. The marks testified "to the cruel fact that human animals stricken by terror are as mad and ruthless as stampeding cattle" (Foy and Harlow, in Turner and Killian 1957, 96–97).

Experimental studies involving panic suggest that its occurrence depends primarily on the availability of information about the amount of danger involved, people's perception of the availability of opportunities to escape, and their sense of whether or not those present will help each other (Brown and Goldin 1973). On the last point, the quality of leadership can make a significant difference. In the course of experiments with 144 college-aged males, Andrew Klein (1976) offered his subjects financial rewards if they could escape from handcuffs and threatened an electric shock if they could not. Klein found that effective leadership could reduce the likelihood of panic by countering the lack of coordination that "can make a minor crisis a major tragedy." S.L.A. Marshall (1947, 130) indicated that if an army unit is under attack and the leader says, "Let's get out of here!" then panic is quite possible. However, if the leader simply tells his troops to follow him to a nearby destination, then the chances of panic sharply decrease. Both studies suggest that the effectiveness of an emergent norm established by leaders in an anxiety-laden situation will significantly influence the likelihood of panic.

Mass Hysteria

Mass hysteria is a type of panic that occurs when people are scattered over a wide geographical area. Often the mass media play a significant role in promoting these incidents. More than 180 reports have been published describing incidents where many individuals were suddenly inflicted with an ailment for which no medical source could

be located. A recent case involved the sudden physical illness—headache, dizziness, abdominal pain, and nausea—of 247 middle- and high-school performers during a concert in Santa Monica, California. Although some parents suspected that fumes or toxic material were responsible, no evidence was found, and researchers were convinced that it was a clear illustration of mass hysteria (Small et al. 1991).

A celebrated example of mass hysteria occurred the day before Halloween, October 30, 1938. Millions of Americans found themselves listening to a broadcast on CBS radio. It was entitled "The War of the Worlds," an adaptation of H.G. Wells's novel of the same title. At the beginning of the radio play, Orson Welles, the narrator, explained that what followed was, in fact, fiction, but many who tuned in late never heard the statement, and some who listened from the beginning were swept along by the drama and simply forgot what Welles had said.

The play told how Martians had invaded the United States. They landed in New Jersey, then headed north toward New York City, killing hundreds of troops sent to stop them as well as large numbers of civilians. Hadley Cantril (1940), who studied this incident of mass hysteria, wrote:

> Long before the broadcast had ended, people all over the United States were praying, crying, fleeing frantically to escape death from Martians. Some ran to rescue loved ones. Others telephoned farewells or warnings, hurried to inform neighbors, sought information from newspapers or radio stations, summoned ambulances and police cars. At least six million people heard the broadcast. At least a million of them were frightened or disturbed.
>
> (*Cantril* 1940, 47)

Cantril conducted 130 detailed interviews soon after the event. He found some people who thought that the invasion had been no more than a story, whereas others were convinced it was true. Several different characteristics, Cantril found, made some people more inclined to believe that an invasion had been occurring. In particular, the idea of an invasion fitted better with some people's preconceptions than with those of others. Some respondents had been expecting a foreign invasion from the Germans or Japanese, and for these people the threat of a Martian attack was a concrete illustration of their war-related dread. Apparently invaders were simply invaders, whether from across the ocean or from outer space. Other people questioned whether they were sufficiently competent to pit their judgment against that of the announcers, scientists, and government authorities supposedly being presented on the program. Uneducated people, in particular, lost confidence in their own judgment (Cantril 1940).

As this incident suggests, mass hysteria may happen when people suddenly believe that they face serious, rapidly approaching danger. The conventional guidelines no longer seem fully applicable, and terror-stricken people grapple for some way to save themselves. In contrast, if they have an opportunity to prepare for the approaching danger, the conventional norms are likely to remain intact, and mass hysteria is much less likely to occur.

A case in point happened at Halloween time, forty-four years after the original broadcast of the "War of the Worlds." In October 1982 widespread concern developed about the poisoning of Halloween candy following seven nationally publicized deaths involving cyanide-contaminated Extra Strength Tylenol capsules. As the mayor of Vineland, a New Jersey city of 53,000 residents, explained, "I got scared thinking what an opportunity this was for some nut to do something" (Barron 1982, 81).

That mayor banned trick-or-treating. In other towns and cities, officials employed a variety of

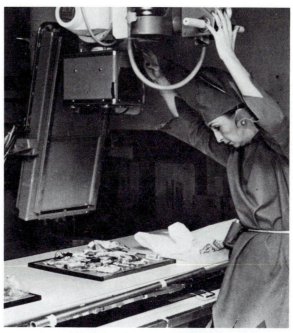

In the wake of the Tylenol killings of October 1982, steps taken to prevent possible injury to children eating Halloween candy included the use of x-rays to scan candy for razor blades or other metal objects.

measures. Police chiefs urged parents to limit their children's Halloween visits, school officials promised prizes to children who stayed home, and hospitals offered to scan candy with the same sort of x-ray devices used on luggage at airports. There were no serious injuries that Halloween, nor any panic or mass hysteria.

Rumors

As part of the breakdown in normative guidelines that occurs in crowd situations, established channels of communication are either out of order or are unable to supply explicit, thorough, and up-to-date information. Rumors are likely to develop.

A **rumor** is a report transmitted informally (often by word of mouth) and concerned with subject matter difficult to verify. Rumors involve information that is important to people, and in this respect they differ from gossip. Frequently rumors provide false information, but that is not necessarily the case.

A recent analysis suggested that four conditions predict the likelihood of rumor development and transmission. They are more likely to develop and spread when:

1. The topic is important to people—for instance, the rumor involves a life-threatening situation to loved ones and thus encourages the individual to determine the rumor's accuracy, an activity making it more widely known.
2. There is general uncertainty suggested by the rumor. Under this condition one is likely to look for information about the rumor, thereby helping to publicize it.
3. The rumor produces a high level of

484

personal anxiety. The more concerned people are about a rumored subject, the more likely they will present it to others, seeking comfort, support, or some other gratification and, once again, help to make others aware of the rumor.

4. One's belief in the rumor is strong. The more firmly people believe a rumor, the more inclined they are to discuss it with others as a means of sharing and perhaps lessening their discomfort (Rosnow 1988; 1991).

THE DEVELOPMENT OF RUMORS

The content of a rumor is likely to change over time, with the amount of change strongly affected by the emotional reaction the rumor creates. The greater the capacity to excite emotion, the more extensive the changes in content are likely to be. Those who transmit the rumor tend to eliminate some details and, in turn, to emphasize others. The changes in detail generally reflect the fears, prejudices, hopes, and other prominent feelings of the people who pass on the rumor.

The transmission of a rumor is a collective process in which individuals can play a number of roles. Some people are messengers, relaying the information. Others act as skeptics, expressing doubt about what they hear. Individuals can also be interpreters, trying to figure out what is happening. Finally there are likely to be decision makers, who initiate action in response to the news the rumor brings (Shibutani 1966).

The "shortage" of bathroom tissues was an incident that illustrates how rumors can develop. On December 11, 1973, Harold V. Froehlich, a Wisconsin congressman, issued a statement after many complaints from people in his district about what they perceived as a rapidly developing paper shortage. Mr. Froehlich said, "The United States may face a serious shortage of toilet paper within a few months. . . . I hope we don't have to ration toilet tissue. . . . A toilet paper shortage is no laughing matter. It is a problem that will touch every American" (Malcolm 1980, 497).

Froehlich and his staff were amazed at how much attention the news release received. This was an era when members of the mass media and the public were becoming increasingly aware of

and concerned about shortages. A shortage of toilet tissue seemed no more unlikely than short supplies of gasoline, heating oil, coffee, sugar, and a number of other commodities. As the rumor spread, the message became clear and decisive in line with people's expectations and fears. Qualifying words like "potential" disappeared.

Certain individuals played important roles in the transmission of this rumor. One celebrity became a messenger. "You know, we've got all sorts of shortages these days," Johnny Carson told his late-night television audience. "But have you heard the latest? I'm not kidding. I saw it in the paper. There's a shortage of toilet paper" (Malcolm 1980, 497). The day after these comments, a toilet-paper-buying binge began nationally. Some shoppers—we can consider them "decision makers"—went to local stores and bought huge supplies of toilet tissue. Other people remained skeptics, proving correct in their analysis that the rumor of a shortage was false.

Like Carson with the bathroom-tissue rumor, other celebrities sometimes underestimate their impact as messengers. During the "Stupid Pet Tricks" segment of his late-night show, David Letterman presented a poodle which walked upright on its hind legs while balancing a glass of water on an upside-down Frisbee. As the dazzled audience watched, Letterman said, "The only thing that kind of detracts from that [the animal act] is I know that the woman has performed intricate spinal surgery on the dog and that's illegal and she'll end up doing time. But as far as the trick goes it's a 10" (*New Haven Register* July 26, 1986, 14). Letterman only meant to be humorous. However, there were some immediate negative effects when that segment of his show was rebroadcast at an early evening hour to an audience unused to his off-beat humor. The owner's pet-grooming business rapidly lost customers, and the dog's budding show-business career—modeling, performances at birthday parties, and even some commercials—was seriously damaged. The owner sued Letterman for $1 million.

EFFORTS TO STOP RUMORS

Rumors can be troublesome and persistent. Can individuals or organizations take steps to terminate them?

A number of years ago the rumor started that McDonald's was selling hamburgers with worms in them. In some areas sales dropped 30 percent, in spite of the company's advertisements emphasizing that McDonald's sold only "100 percent pure beef" or suggesting that at $5 to $8 a pound for worms, it would be crazy to put them in hamburgers.

Soon after the incident, market researchers at Northwestern University conducted a study. The subjects were sixty-four graduate students, divided into four- to six-member groups. The researchers told the students that they would participate in an experiment evaluating their reaction to violence. Each group watched a typical evening television show containing three commercials for McDonald's. After the third commercial, a young man who, unknown to the students, was working for the researchers casually indicated that the commercials reminded him that McDonald's had worm meat in their hamburgers.

When the television show was over, the investigators treated various groups in different ways. A couple of groups received no additional information from the research team. In several other groups, a researcher repeated a statement similar to McDonald's own advertisements—that a Food and Drug Administration study had concluded that the company's beef was 100 percent pure and that, besides, worms were simply too expensive to be used in hamburgers. In other groups the researcher asked the students about their own experiences with McDonald's—where and how often they went and whether the franchises they visited had indoor seating. The object of these questions was to stimulate neutral or positive thoughts that would counter the rumors. In a third collection of groups, one of the researchers tried to create a positive attitude toward worms in the students' minds. He told these groups of students that he had taken his mother-in-law to Chez Paul, an expensive Chicago restaurant, where they had eaten a very tasty sauce made out of worms.

At the end of the experiment, the students rated the quality of McDonald's food as well as their likelihood of eating there. The results:

1. The least favorable ratings came from those who simply heard the worm rumor and had no follow-up experience. This outcome occurred in spite of the fact that in a separate test, most of these students indicated that they did not believe the worm story.
2. The ratings from those who heard the worm rumor and the same denials that McDonald's had presented in their own advertisements were almost as low as those of the first group of students.
3. The students who had the opportunity to discuss their own experiences with McDonald's gave significantly higher ratings. Their ratings, in fact, were as high as those from people who had not heard any rumors.
4. The students who heard about the worm sauce at Chez Paul gave equally high ratings (Rice 1981).

The rumor of worms in McDonald's hamburgers created structural strain for the students. The most effective means to combat the strain was to shift the students' attention to conventional social situations, where structural strain was absent: either their memories of worm-free meals at McDonald's or the situation at Chez Paul, where a worm sauce was considered a delicacy.

More recently a study of rumors about AIDS supported one of the conditions previously described about rumor transmission—that the greater the anxiety a rumor produced, the more likely it would be transmitted. The most intense concern involved the belief that there was a high risk of getting AIDS from a blood transfusion, and more rumors generated from this idea than any other on the topic of AIDS. The researchers suggested that while education about AIDS is crucial, it is essential not to promote high levels of anxiety because rumors transmitting false information will be encouraged (Kimmel and Keefer 1991).

The nearby Social Application examines another situation in which collective behavior occurs.

Both collective behavior and social movements involve behavior that occurs to some extent outside existing normative guidelines. Social movements, however, are somewhat more conventionally structured, with the distinct possibility that they will eventually become part of established society. Table 16.3 provides some comparisons among violent crowds, social movements, and organizations.

Table 16.3 Some General Comparisons among Violent Crowds, Social Movements, and Organizations

	Violent crowd	Social movement	Organization
Leadership	Informal	Increasingly formalized over time	Formal
Duration	Minutes or hours	From a few months to to many years, depending on the movement	Many years frequently
Normative guidelines	Informal and emergent	Increasingly formalized over time	Formal
Structural strain on members	Excessive	Considerable when individuals join but generally declining as the movement ages	Variable, depending on the nature of people's tasks

With the passage of time, the characteristics of social movements become increasingly like those of organizations.

Social Movements

As we have noted, a social movement is an organized, collective activity undertaken by people to promote or resist social change. The members of a social movement share:

1. An ideology justifying their actions;
2. A sense of unity;
3. A set of norms prescribing followers' behavior;
4. Some division of labor between leaders and followers and among the different categories of followers (Killian 1964).

Neil Smelser (1963) outlined a distinction between norm-oriented and value-oriented social movements. The goal of a norm-oriented social movement is to create new norms or occasionally to restore old ones. Examples would be a reform movement agitating for a local park or for more police protection, a group of workers seeking to establish their own independent union, or groups mobilizing at the state or national level for tax reform, nuclear disarmament, or lower gasoline prices. The goal of a value-oriented social movement is to change a society's values, which are the basic principles upon which social behavior is based. Value-oriented social movements often involve efforts to make revolutionary change. They tend to be more demanding of members' time, energy, and emotional commitment than are norm-oriented social movements. Political revolutionaries, religious "cult" members, and people in utopian communities may be considered members of social movements advocating new values.

In the upcoming discussion, we examine two theoretical approaches to social movements.

THEORIES OF SOCIAL MOVEMENTS

Strain theories dominated the analysis of social movements until the early 1970s. Since then resource-mobilization theory has assumed a more prominent role (Hannigan 1985; Kerbo and Shaffer 1986; Klandermans 1984; Nielsen 1985).

Strain Theory

As we noted in the discussion of the second stage of Smelser's theory, a number of social conditions

SOCIAL APPLICATION
The Impact of Hurricane Andrew in South Florida

 A disaster is an irregular or abnormal event compelling significant response and adjustment because the existing social order is disrupted or destroyed. Sociologists interested in collective behavior have studied a variety of disasters, including explosions, fires, floods, tornadoes, earthquakes, and hurricanes. Perhaps you can see why disasters qualify as contexts in which collective behavior occurs. Like other activities we have been examining in this chapter, disasters disrupt everyday conditions and norms, disorienting and frightening people and abruptly altering their lives.

When Hurricane Andrew slammed into south Florida on April 25, 1992, it immediately qualified as a disaster. In Florida and in Louisiana, where Andrew hit the next day, thirty-three people were killed, often crushed in their homes, 63,000 homes were destroyed, $30 billion in damages occurred, and 300,000 people were left homeless. Like a huge tornado, Andrew cut a twenty- to thirty-five-mile swath through suburban neighborhoods south of Miami, levelling everything in its path and summoning among its victims "a kind of terror the country had not felt since the 1906 San Francisco earthquake" (Matthews et al. 1992, 22). Andrew was a Force 5 hurricane, which generally occurs only about once or twice a century.

Victims' Responses Being caught in such a storm was a horrifying experience. Chris Heagan survived the hurricane crouched in a closet with his wife and their two young children as chunks of metal whizzed by them. Later he told a reporter, "You haven't lived through anything until you find a trailer flying into your house." He added, "There are no words to describe the fear" (Matthews et al. 1992, 23).

In another Miami suburb, Jo and Bruce Powers, her sister Karen Brocato, the two Powers children, and several neighbors protected themselves in a pair of small bathrooms. For two hours bracing his foot against the sink, Powers pressed his 200-lb. frame against the door to stop the winds from ripping it open. Meanwhile water poured in, the tub became dislodged from the wall, and outside the door glass kept shattering and thudding into the walls. "I've never been so scared in my life," Karen Brocato explained. "I hope I die if I'm ever that afraid again. We all dirtied our pants" (*Time* 1992, 15)

While the storm itself represented the most terrible experience, the aftermath was also very difficult.

Recovery In Andrew's aftermath individuals and families faced different situations. Some, the comparatively lucky, made it through with their houses not completely destroyed. Still they faced many problems. Troy Di-

nardo, who had been sleeping in his car with his wife and baby because damage to their roof had made it too wet to sleep inside, said, "There is just enough left to make us want to stay, but where do you begin putting it back together?" (French 1992, A10). Those who had started that process found that at each step they were competing with thousands of others for the attention of insurance claims processors, roofers, carpenters, and other highly sought specialists.

Meanwhile those forced into homelessness were often unhappy with arrangements made to house them. A week after the hurricane when a tent city was erected in Homestead, Florida, many prospective residents expressed displeasure at the prospect of living there, saying that they feared having the few remaining possessions in their damaged homes stolen or that they had managed to get to know their fellow residents in shelters and did not wish to go through the arduous process again.

It appears that poorer individuals were given the least and slowest relief. In a destroyed labor camp in Florida City, migrant workers found themselves ignored and isolated for a week. Occasionally a squad car or ambulance would stop, with its occupants quickly checking for life-threatening problems and then moving on. Five days after Andrew, several hundred, desperately hungry workers and

488

their children started cooking rancid food on a makeshift barbeque, producing nine cases of food poisoning to add to the other difficulties. Domingo Torres, who has lived at the camp since it opened in 1973, was stunned at the isolation following the storm. "A lot of people left because they can't handle this," he said. "I can't handle this. But I don't have a car, so I can't leave" (Manegold 1992, A12).

Future Prospects Hurricane Andrew's economic devastation has been impressive in south Florida. The area's agricultural base, which has been the nation's principal source of lime groves, avocados, and ornamental plants, is in ruins. A week after the storm, a twenty-mile stretch of U.S. 1 was decimated, with about one store in fifty open and the majority heavily damaged or destroyed. When the stores reopened, customers were in short supply since many residents of south Florida had little disposable income.

Looking ahead, planners and politicians can learn from what happened in south Florida. As one reporter tersely phrased it, Andrew hit an area where "population outstripped social infrastructure" (Matthews et al. 1992, 24). The number of new homes had mushroomed, with poor construction widespread and building codes geared to much weaker storms.

Another lesson comes from the relief effort, which overall was not well handled. At the center was the Federal Emergency Management Agency (FEMA), which has had a history of scandal and inefficiency and, at least on the latter point, generally maintained its reputation following Hurricane Andrew, underestimating the damage and responding slowly. More efficient were the Public Health Service, the Army Corps of Engineers, and the Department of Agriculture, which acted quickly and sent such essentials as medical supplies, water, and food.

For the future more effective relief seems imperative, especially when we consider that some experts suspect that one possible effect of global warming is the likelihood that Force 5 hurricanes will become more common.

Sources: Sharon Begley. "Was Andrew a Freak—Or a Preview of Things to Come?" Newsweek. vol. 120 (September 7, 1992), p. 30; Howard W. French. "Lucky Homeowners Facing Long Limbo before Repairs," New York Times. (September 4, 1992), p. A10; Peter T. Kilborn. "Soothing Calm of Normal Life Is Years Away in Storm Area," New York Times. (September 3, 1992), pp. A1+; Catherine S. Manegold. "In a Migrant Labor Camp, Relief Is Slow and Chaotic," New York Times. (September 1, 1992), p. A12; Tom Matthews et al. "What Went Wrong," Newsweek. vol. 120 (September 7, 1992), pp. 22–24+; Joseph B. Perry, Jr., and M. D. Pugh. Collective Behavior: Response to Social Stress. St. Paul, MN: West, 1978; Neil J. Smelser. Theory of Collective Behavior. New York: Free Press, 1962; Time. "Mother Nature's Angriest Child," vol. 140 (September 7, 1992), pp. 14–17; Joseph B. Treaster. "Questions Arise as Tents Go Up in Stricken City," New York Times. (September 2, 1992), p. A15.

Sometimes the efforts of social movements can help produce surprisingly positive results. The massive mobilization to reform South Africa's racial inequality encouraged a two-thirds majority of the country's whites to end the dreaded apartheid system and, for the first time, to permit blacks to vote.

can create structural strain, which is a significant amount of tension or pressure for people, and this strain lessens their willingness to stay within normal behavioral limits. Recently strain theory has been applied to religious fundamentalism (Fields 1991) and democratization in Mexico (Monsivais 1990).

James Davies (1962) developed a strain theory of social movements. He studied historical accounts of the French and Russian revolutions, gathering evidence that revolutions occur when social conditions improve. Davies concluded that during such periods people's expectations inevitably rise, outstripping their capacity to achieve expectations. As long as the gap between expectations and the capacity to achieve expectations remains fairly small, strain will be minimal, and no revolution will occur. The strain, however, becomes great if people's actual capacity to

Figure 16.1
The J-Curve: Strain and Revolution

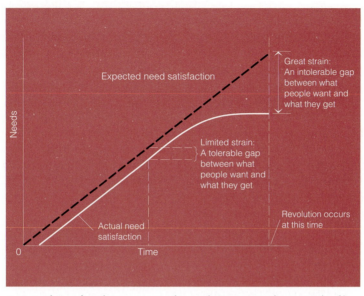

Davies's theory of revolution suggests that revolutions occur when an intolerable gap develops between people's actual need satisfaction and their expected need satisfaction.

Source: *Adapted from James C. Davies "Toward a Theory of Revolution,"* American Sociological Review. *vol. 27 (February 1962), p. 6.*

achieve need satisfaction levels off (somewhat like the partially inverted curve of the letter "j" as represented in Figure 16.1), while the expected need satisfaction continues to rise. As Figure 16.1 suggests, an intolerable gap then exists between what people want and what they can get. This gap sets the stage for revolution.

Consider the application of strain theory to the modern women's movement, which we discussed briefly in Chapter 10, "Emerging Minorities." In 1963 Betty Friedan published *The Feminine Mystique*, which attempted to analyze the plight of modern women. Friedan was referring to strain when she summarized women's situation as something seldom discussed or understood—"the problem that has no name." In 1966 Friedan and others founded the National Organization for Women (NOW) when the federal government did not take any action to improve women's second-class status. Only a few years later, another large group of women became interested in women's rights. These women, who were generally younger than the members of NOW, had participated in civil-rights and antiwar activities and had begun to

feel that they faced the contradiction (a specific type of strain) of working in freedom movements and finding themselves restricted to traditional women's roles that permitted almost no use of creative skills and leadership capacities.

Strain appears to have been a factor in the development of the modern women's movement, and one might argue that it plays a role in the development of most social movements. In recent years, however, many social scientists have become increasingly convinced that the explanatory capacity of strain theories is quite limited and that the resource-mobilization perspective makes a more valuable contribution to understanding how social movements have developed (Gurney and Tierney 1982; Kerbo 1982).

Resource-Mobilization Theory

Resource-mobilization theory focuses on the process by which the members of social movements acquire and use certain resources necessary to accomplish their collective goals. The supporters of this theory agree that strain can encourage

490 people to join social movements but that social movements will not develop until the members have access to such necessary resources as money, goods, power, members' commitment of time and energy, votes, or communication techniques (Gamson 1975; Tilly 1978). Resource-mobilization theory continues to be widely used, with recent published papers employing it for analyzing the Nicaraguan revolution (Cuzan 1990; 1991); assessing its contribution to the sociology of religion (Hannigan 1991); and examining the unemployed workers' movement in the 1930s (Valocchi 1990).

Successful social movements do not simply seek to recruit large numbers of people. Their priority is the recruitment of politically experienced and well-adjusted groups and individuals (Oberschall 1973).

Resource-mobilization theory helps explain the development of the modern women's movement. For instance, one resource that encouraged the creation of NOW was a citizen's advisory council on women's issues established in the early 1960s. This organization provided a communications network through which women could discuss their common grievances and decide what actions to take. Once NOW existed, it broadened and deepened those channels of communication.

The younger segment of the women's movement acquired its own, informal communications resource: the discussion group. These groups engaged in a process known as "consciousness-raising." Women came together in groups of five to fifteen members and discussed their feelings, experiences, problems, and concerns. The participants soon realized that what they had considered personal problems were usually the result of limited opportunities imposed on all of them since birth. They started to understand that the women's movement represented a very effective vehicle for reaching a solution. Sociologist Jo Freeman concluded:

> Once women have gone through such a resocialization, their views of themselves and the world are never the same again even if they stop participating actively in the movement. Those who do drop out rarely do so without spreading feminist ideas among their own friends and colleagues. All who undergo consciousness-raising feel compelled themselves to seek out other women with whom to share the experience.
>
> (*Freeman* 1979, 562)

Sources of Social Change ▪

Social change and social movements often have a reciprocal relationship. While social change may set the stage for social movements, the members of social movements often strive to produce social change. In fact, in the following discussion of the sources of social change, social movements is one of the four factors examined. The others are cultural innovation, population, and environment.

CULTURAL INNOVATION

A **cultural innovation** is the recognition or development of new material or nonmaterial elements in a culture. There are three prominent means by which cultural innovation occurs: discovery, invention, and diffusion.

Discovery

Discovery is the perception of something that already exists but that had not been previously recognized. A discovery can be a material item (another continent or a new "wonder" drug) or a nonmaterial item (the principle of gravity).

A discovery often takes place because of chance. Random strikes of lightning undoubtedly played an important part in the process by which people first learned about fire. It is likely that it took many chance encounters before early humanity began to appreciate the potential contribution that fire could make for cooking food and providing warmth, and it is also probable that efforts to control fire began only after these potentials were recognized and appreciated.

Something that is discovered does not have an effect on social change until it is used widely. In ancient Alexandria, Greece, the residents discovered how to use steam power, and they even employed steam power as a means of hauling firewood to the top of the lighthouse on the nearby island of Pharos. However, it was not until about 1,700 years later that the use of steam to power boats and trains revolutionized transportation and produced significant social and economic change in Western societies (Linton 1973).

Scientific research tends to be highly routinized, with its systematic pursuit producing the discovery of new drugs for treating various diseases.

Invention

An **invention** is a combination of existing knowledge to produce something new. The invention of the airplane involved the combination of such elements as the wings of a glider, an internal-combustion engine from an automobile, and the adaptation of a ship's propeller. Though less well known, nonmaterial inventions are also common. The city-manager plan, for instance, represents the transfer of business-management techniques to city government (Murdock 1956).

It is important to recognize that, like any other cultural element, an invention is a piece in a cultural puzzle, not a disconnected event. Because of this interrelation, the development of an innovation is likely to generate pressure for change in other parts of social life. Thus the invention and production of the automobile, for instance, has stimulated the formation of an entire new body of law. Television led to further innovations in dozens of areas, including advertising, regulatory law, political campaign styles, family life, and even diet (for example, TV dinners).

All inventions do not produce an equally strong impetus for change. A new method of painting, for instance, might have no apparent effect beyond a small circle of artists and critics. A new religious doctrine might arouse interest and support only among a highly select group of followers. An invention that affects the way people obtain the material necessities of life, however, will produce extensive changes in a society. The spear, which permitted early hunters to kill animals for food at a much greater distance than had previously been possible, and the automobile, which allowed people to travel distances much more quickly and easily than they could before its introduction, are cases (Lenski and Lenski 1982). Without very much thought, you can probably figure out how the existence of the automobile has affected all five major institutional structures.

It is widely recognized that the most potent discoveries and inventions are produced by mavericks often working outside the research mainstream, where orthodox thinking prevails and creative, irreverent approaches are criticized and disregarded. Physicist Lord Kelvin said that had scientific funding existed in the stone age, humanity would now have magnificent stone machines and no metal. Thus to get optimal results from science, government and industry should fund free-thinking, unorthodox mavericks, but since funding emerges from the scientific mainstream, that is not nor is it likely to be the case (*Economist* 1991).

Diffusion

Diffusion is the process by which cultural traits move either from one culture to another or from one part of a culture to another. Some scholars

492

believe that about 90 percent of all cultural development results from diffusion. To illustrate this point, anthropologist Ralph Linton wrote a well-known essay, which with tongue-in-cheek he entitled "One Hundred Percent American." He began, "There can be no question about the average American's Americanism or his desire to preserve this precious heritage at all costs" (Linton 1982, 58). Then Linton indicated that unfortunately some "insidious foreign ideas" have managed to enter American civilization. He went on to reveal that virtually all material objects average Americans encounter in their homes—their pajamas, clocks, toothbrushes, razors, coffee, waffles, newspapers, and so on—are innovations that originated in other cultures.

The diffusion process displays certain distinctive characteristics. First, some cultural elements diffuse more readily than others. Material objects and technology generally spread more easily than do belief systems and forms of social organization. The members of different academic disciplines, for example, are often highly resistant to new theories or concepts.

Second, innovations that diffuse are often adapted in modified form by the receiving culture. For example, the Africans who were brought to Brazil as slaves carried their religion with them. While their descendants became Catholics, they retained certain modified elements of their tribal religion. These descendants linked particular African gods with different saints, and they developed some interesting mixed beliefs: For example, a hollow-log drum must receive spiritual control through baptism, or it will fail to call the appropriate deities to a religious ceremony.

A third significant point about diffusion is that it is often a two-way process. Films, novels, history books, and also sociology texts have strongly emphasized the diffusion of culture traits from whites to Native Americans: horses, guns, alcohol, clothing, religion, schooling, and eventually all major elements of the modern American lifestyle. Much less attention has focused on the cultural contributions that Native Americans have given to white Americans and also to the members of other countries. A few of the better-known American-Indian plants include corn, beans, squash, sweet potatoes, and the so-called "Irish" potatoes. Prominent modern drugs well known among Native-American cultures include coca (the source of cocaine and novocaine), curare (an anesthetic), cinchowa bark that produces quinine, and cascara used in laxatives. Furthermore Native-American music has had a significant impact on a number of American composers, who borrowed melodies and themes from Indians (Lauer 1977; Zupan 1991).

Finally, within a single culture, conditions can produce the diffusion of a particular cultural trait more readily to certain areas or groups than to others. For example, in the United States, automobiles and telephones were most quickly adopted in urban areas with extensive commercial activity and in more affluent rural areas (Fischer and Carroll 1988). Table 16.4 lists products that have diffused to American culture.

POPULATION

At the extremes population size can have a profound effect on a society. If the population becomes small enough, a society will cease to exist. Disease, famine, and annihilation can produce such a result. The Native-American population was probably between about 700,000 and one million when Columbus reached the New World. It dropped to about 250,000 at the end of the nineteenth century, and a substantial number of tribes simply disappeared. Most historians agree that more Indians died of white people's diseases than died in warfare. Unlike the whites the Indians had not developed any immunities to smallpox, typhoid, yellow fever, and the other diseases brought over from Europe, and in some areas the effects were devastating, killing 90 percent of the indigenous population (Farley 1982, 111–12).

On the other hand, rapid population growth can also lead to destructive social change. As the population expands in many rural areas in Africa, Asia, and Latin America, more food must be grown in soil too poor in nutrients to sustain the present annual plantings. To survive the present, however, subsistence farmers have no alternative but to keep planting land that steadily declines in crop production (Mellor 1991).

A change in the size of particular segments of the population can also promote social change. For instance, the American baby boom of 1946–1965 led to a period of growth for schools and colleges until the early 1970s. However, the past two decades, during which the youthful

Table 16.4   A Variety of Products That Diffused to Modern American Culture

Food and drink	*Place of origin*[1]
Alcoholic beverages	Near East (Syria, Lebanon, and Israel)
Bananas	South Asia
Beans	Eastern United States (Indians)
Butter	Near East
Chocolate	Mexico
Coffee	Abyssinia (Ethiopia)
Corn	Eastern United States (Indians)
Eggs	Southern Asia
Grains	Near East
Milk	Asia Minor (Turkey)
Squash	Eastern United States (Indians)
Sugar	India
Sweet potatoes	Eastern United States (Indians)
Tea	China

Other material products for everyday use	*Place of origin*
Bathtub	Rome (Italy)
Bed	Persia (Iran) or Asia Minor (Turkey)
Checks	Persia (Iran)
Cigar	Brazil
Cigarette	Mexico (A.D. 400 to 1400)
Clock	Medieval Europe
Coins	Lydia (Turkey)
Cotton	India
Fork	Italy
Glass	Egypt
Linen	Near East
Paper	China
Paper money	China
Printing	China
Shoes	Greece
Soap	Gaul (France)
Spoon	Rome (Italy)
Toilet	Rome (Italy)

Important nonmaterial products	*Place of origin*
Alphabet	Phoenicia (Syria and Lebanon)
Banking (credits, loans, discounts, and mortgages)	Babylonia (Iraq) and later influences of Italy and England
Family organization	Medieval Europe
Language	England
Numerical system	India[2]
System of real-property ownership[3]	Medieval Europe

[1]*If the product first appeared in a country with an ancient name, the modern name appears in parentheses.*
[2]*The numerical system originated in India, diffused to the Middle East, and then eventually reached Europe.*
[3]*Ownership of such fixed, immovable things as land and buildings.*

Sources: *Ruth Benedict. "The Growth of Culture," pp. 182–95 In Harry L. Shapiro (ed.). Man, Culture, and Society. New York: Oxford University Press, 1956; Ralph Linton. "One Hundred Percent American," American Mercury. vol. 40 (April 1937), pp. 427–30; George Peter Murdock. "How Culture Changes," pp. 247–60 In Harry L. Shapiro (ed.). Man, Culture, and Society. New York: Oxford University Press, 1956.*

494

population has declined, has featured teacher layoffs and also the elimination of some schools in many districts. In addition, the baby boom has contributed to intensified job competition and to unemployment in many job areas.

More generally it appears that if prospective parents are part of a large generation, then they will probably find themselves caught in a highly competitive job situation. They will take a fairly long time to establish themselves occupationally, and they will therefore be likely to start having children relatively late in life and to produce a small number of offspring. On the other hand, as members of a small generation, these children will find it somewhat easier to establish themselves occupationally. Thus they will be able to start having children at a younger age and will therefore be likely to produce more of them. Census data indicate that these two patterns have alternated with each other since the 1890s (Ryder 1980).

THE ENVIRONMENT

At present Americans find themselves confronting two contradictory priorities—one emphasizing environmental protection and the other stressing economic growth. In April 1991 a national sample of Americans was read two statements, with one emphasizing environmental protection at the risk of curbing economic growth and with the other reversing the two priorities. Seventy-one percent opted for environmental protection and only 20 percent for economic growth. A decade earlier the respective percentages were 61 and 28 (Hueber 1991).

In spite of growing public support for environmental protection, controlling and reducing environmental pollution is difficult. Air pollution is a case in point. What represents a reasonable goal in this area? Is it enough to remove all pollutants detectable by the human senses, or should we be concerned with impurities identifiable only by scientific instruments? In the late 1940s in Pittsburgh, industrial leaders, politicians, and the public agreed that air pollution was a serious problem, but the different groups could never accept a single comprehensive plan for air-pollution control. The restrictions eventually placed on

air pollution were limited, concerned only with solving the immediate, observable problem (Stiefel 1982).

SOCIAL MOVEMENTS

As we noted earlier in the chapter, two broad types of social movements exist. Norm-oriented social movements maintain a narrow focus, seeking to change a specific law or practice. Value-oriented social movements, which attempt to alter or replace existing values, are much more ambitious. Effective value-oriented movements can significantly change people's values, beliefs, and behavior.

Four conditions seem to play an especially important role in the development of effective social movements. First, a sense of strain must exist among a large number of people—a clearly shared awareness of the disparity between existing conditions and the ideal state of affairs. Second, developing social movements require close interaction and communication among members. Without such contacts people's perceptions of the strains that they are encountering are apt to be less clear, and they are considerably less likely to develop coherent ideologies. Third, social movements are more likely to grow if the members share prominent statuses—for instance, are women, students, blacks, or the elderly—and thus possess common outlooks, experiences, and grievances. Fourth, the existence of previous social-movement activity is usually important. Unless the members see actual evidence indicating that large-scale social change is possible, then they are unlikely to believe that their own movement will succeed (Morrison 1973). The more developed these factors, the more successful the social movement is likely to be, at least initially, and successful social movements have the ability to produce significant social change.

When these conditions occur simultaneously, a social movement can develop quickly. A case in point would be women's studies programs in American colleges and universities. Starting in 1969 at Cornell University and San Diego State University, women's studies initially involved individual courses. In the early 1970s, degree programs followed. Women's studies centers then developed at Stanford and Wellesley and now number more than fifty.

Once women's studies programs were established, their impact on the general curriculum became a major concern. A survey conducted at Princeton University in 1976 indicated that in spite of the growth of women's studies, it was having little effect on that university's general curriculum. So at Princeton and at many other colleges and universities, the goal became curriculum integration for women's studies, with many schools diversifying general course offerings required of all students to include extensive material on women, ethnic and racial minorities, and people of other cultures (Chamberlain 1990).

The chapter concludes with the sixth of six Research in Sociology sections. This one involves prison riots.

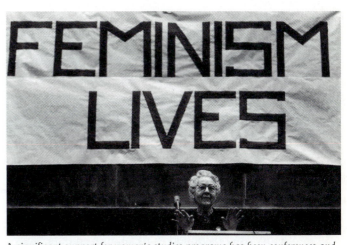

A significant support for women's studies programs has been conferences and speeches about women's rights, which, like this rally in Cambridge, Massachusetts, are either on or conveniently close to college and university campuses.

RESEARCH IN SOCIOLOGY: SECTION VI

Prison Riots: Which Theory Can Explain Them?

If a sociological theory contains clear, thought-provoking statements, has it managed to establish the accuracy of its claims? The answer is a resounding "NO." As we noted in the first two chapters, scientists' work must encounter colleagues' critical review. A sociological theory can be subjected to such a review by determining whether or not it can explain relevant data.

In Chapter 16 we saw that both the strain theory and the resource-mobilization theory can be applied to social movements. They also can be used to analyze prison riots. Does one theory succeed in explaining why prison riots occur while the other one fails? That does not seem to be the case. It appears that in the late 1960s and early 1970s, the causes of prison riots were consistent with resource-mobilization theory, while in the 1980s the factors encouraging riots have fitted better with the strain theory. To illustrate this shift, we will examine a study of the Attica riot, the most devastating prison rebellion of the 1970s, and analyze research involving the New Mexico riot of 1980. Then we will be able to understand more thoroughly the relationship between theory and research.

The Attica Riots

Between September 9 and September 13, 1971, forty-three citizens of New York state were killed in the correctional facility at Attica, New York. Thirty-nine of the deaths occurred during the fifteen minutes it took the state police to recapture the prison, which had been controlled by inmates.

Shortly after the Attica riot, the governor of New York asked the five justices of the state's Appellate Division to appoint a citizens' committee—the New York State Special Commission on Attica—to lead an investigation that would try to explain what happened, and why, and also make recommendations to prevent such violence in the future. This nine-person commission hired a staff which then conducted the investigation. These people interviewed most of the inmates who had been at Attica during the riot—about 1,600 men—as well as the majority of the corrections officers and state police who were present during the conflict. It would be helpful to know just what questions were asked or if the researchers had a standard interview for each category of people examined. Unfortunately this information was not made public.

While it is possible to have reservations about how the data for the report were gathered, its presentation is straightforward and clear and its findings consistent with those produced by other investigators of the Attica riot. And what are those findings? Most basically the investigators found that the Attica rioters were products of their social era, a time when protest against inequality and oppression was popular.

Could one argue that conditions in the prison were poor and deteriorating, thus creating strain for inmates? No, the commission concluded. Prison conditions, in fact, were improving under the new state commissioner of corrections. The root of the problem was the tone of the times. According to the report, those who participated actively in the riot were part of a new breed of younger, more aware inmates, largely black, who came to prison full of deep feelings of alienation and hostility against the established institutions of law and government, enhanced self-esteem, racial pride, and political awareness, and an unwilling-ness to accept the petty humiliations and racism that characterize prison life.

(*New York State Special Commission on Attica* 1972, 105)

Using the resource-mobilization perspective, one can consider these angry young men a potential resource encouraging the development of a riot. "Potential" is an important word here. As we saw in the section on riots, anger and pride are not enough to generate a riot; there must be mobilization. Thus the resource must be developed to contribute to collective action—in this case a riot. The Attica report indicated that, indeed, this did happen. About a month before the riot occurred, the three major militant organizations among the inmates—the Black Panthers, the Young Lords, and the Black Muslims—reached an accord where they were in suffi-cient agreement to override their differences and recognize their common grievances against the power structure of the prison. In addition, these common grievances were solidified by the death of George Jackson, a prominent black radical, in a California prison under conditions that made the inmates believe the guards had either coop-erated in his death or actually killed the man themselves.

The Attica report concluded that the riot was unplanned, that it began following a confrontation between guards and inmates. Because a central gate failed to func-tion and the communications system within the prison was outmoded, the inmates were able to take over large sections of the prison quickly.

It seems that a resource-mobilization perspective can also be applied to the time period after the takeover. Supporters of this theory would point out that while the inmates lacked the resource of a full-fledged organization at the time of the take over, they had a fairly united group of like-minded participants whose common grievances allowed them to be welded into a fairly cohesive unit once the outbreak took place. About an hour after the riot occurred, one of the "inmate lawyers"—a man who, though lacking formal training, was sufficiently knowledgable of the law to help fel-low inmates prepare legal petitions—took a bullhorn and spoke. This man was greatly respected, and when he said that they needed to organize themselves effec-tively, the others listened. A definite tone was set. The report stated:

Now, inmate after inmate jumped up on the table and took the bullhorn, extolling brother-hood among inmates and calling for the presentation of demands for reform. The speakers were principally those men to whom other inmates naturally turn for guidance and advice: outstanding athletes, leaders of political groups, and, of course, the "inmate lawyers."

(*New York State Special Commission on Attica* 1972, *p.* 297)

Because of the resource of angry, united inmates, the mobilization of a fairly well-organized group was easily accomplished.

The New Mexico Riot

The New Mexico riot of 1980 was a different situation. The political outlook and rhetoric of the 1960s and early 1970s had lessened or disappeared. Within the prison itself, conditions were not improving as at Attica; they were becoming worse. In this era and particularly within this prison, the strain theory seems to offer a more effec-tive explanation than the resource-mobilization perspective.

From this photo, which was taken during the New Mexico prison riot, it would appear that an actual war was raging.

The data on the New Mexico riot come from two articles based, in turn, on two sources—the official investigation conducted by the attorney general's office shortly after the riot and sociologist Bert Useem's interviews in 1985 with the remaining thirty-six inmates who had been present during the riot.

When interviewed, inmates mentioned problems that are compatible with strain theory. Perhaps most significantly they often indicated that the turning point toward worse prison conditions occurred in 1975, when the deputy warden was fired and the warden, named Felix Rodriguez, was transferred. One inmate explained that the new warden

> came in like a real maniac. People can say what they want about Rodriguez, and maybe he did have his finger in the pie, but all I know, man, all I know empirically, when he was warden here, you didn't have guys stabbing each other in wholesale numbers, you didn't have guys breaking out and running up the fence 15 or 20 at a time because it was too heavy for them to do time here. . . . It was a mellow, laid-back place under Rodriguez."

> (Useem 1985, 683)

According to Useem's data analysis, inmates compared the conditions under different wardens 181 times; 160 of those comparisons favored the Rodriguez administration.

The change in administrations created strain throughout the entire prison system. Inmates related to each other differently after Rodriguez left; robbery and violence were more widespread and trust rarer. Perhaps the new administration's most decisive means of producing strain was its establishment of a system of inmate informants. "Snitching" became the order of day, and most of the inmates despised the snitches.

When the New Mexico riot occurred, it did not closely resemble the one at Attica. While this outbreak was also unplanned, the inmates behaved differently, reflecting the dissimilar factors behind the violence. The New Mexico riot lacked the resource of inmates capable of being rapidly organized to make demands for reform. Instead these men were wild and uncontrollable, undone by the destructive prison system that had been imposed on them; strain, in short, appears to have been the primary factor igniting this riot. And victims of that strain—the rioters—took out their fury and frustration on those they considered responsible. The twelve guards held as hostages were repeatedly beaten, sodomized, and threatened with death, though none were actually killed. Most of the thirty-three inmates killed were informers, and they were killed with incredible brutality: beaten, raped, mutilated, and tortured to death with acetylene torches.

Perhaps no point indicates the difference between the two riots as sharply as the respective role played by blacks. At Attica aroused young blacks were the largest group in the prison and at the focus of the riot. In contrast, in New Mexico, black inmates represented only 9 percent of the prison population, and the uprising occurred during a politically more apathetic era. These men formed a group for their mutual protection and stayed away from the violence. Thus they mobilized themselves for inaction, quite the opposite of what was done by many black inmates at Attica.

Comment on the Relationship of Theory and Research

As we learned in Chapter 2, "Doing Research in Sociology," theory and research need to go hand-in-hand, supporting each other. Effective theory must fit the facts studies provide.

What theoretical contributions will occur in the next few years? While this section strongly implies that it would be difficult to produce a general theory of prison riots, such a theory would be a formidable contribution as current analyses of recent riots either suggest or imply. Can a theory be developed which more effectively predicts prison outbreaks than intelligent officials or inmates who are on the scene? That would be quite an accomplishment. We never know what's ahead. Perhaps at this very moment, some sociologist is preparing to publish a paper or a book that will significantly improve this body of theory. With prison riots a frequent reality, practical insights offered by such a theory would be useful.

Sources: Linda R. Acorn. "Camp Hill Riots Lead to Pennsylvania DOC Overhaul," Corrections Today. *vol.* 53 (July 1991), *pp.* 72–74; Burton M. Atkins and Henry R. Glick (eds.). Prisons, Protests and Politics. Englewood Cliffs, NJ: Prentice-Hall, 1972; Mark Colvin. "The 1980 New Mexico Prison Riot," Social Problems. *vol.* 29 (June 1982), *pp.* 449–63; Rod Morgan and Helen Jones. "Prison Discipline: The Case for Implementing Woolf," British Journal of Criminology. *vol.* 31 (Summer 1991), *pp.* 280–91; New York State Special Commission on Attica. Attica: The Official Report of the New York State Special Commission on Attica. New York: Bantam Books, 1972; John Pallas and Bob Barker. "From Riot to Revolution," Issues in Criminology. *vol.* 7 (1972), *pp.* 1–19; Richard Phillips. "Crisis in Talladega," Corrections Today. *vol.* 53 (December 1991), *pp.* 122+; Bert Useem. "Disorganization and the New Mexico Prison Riot," American Sociological Review. *vol.* 50 (October 1985), *pp.* 677–88.

STUDY GUIDE

Learning Objectives

After studying this chapter, you should be able to:

1. Define collective behavior and social movements and discuss their occurrence in daily life.
2. Discuss and illustrate Smelser's general theory of collective behavior and social movements.
3. Define crowds and discuss their characteristics.
4. Examine the contagion and emergent-norm theories of crowds, defining and illustrating them.
5. Define mobs and riots and use the two different crowd theories discussed to analyze riots.
6. Discuss panics and mass hysteria, defining and illustrating them.
7. Define rumors, examine their development, and describe efforts to stop them.
8. Summarize the major conclusions of strain theory and resource-mobilization theory.
9. Discuss prominent sources of social change.

Summary

1. Collective behavior is social activity that occurs under conditions that are temporarily unstructured.

2. Smelser's general theory of collective behavior and social movements contains six stages—structural conduciveness, structural strain, growth and spread of a generalized belief, the precipitating factor, mobilization for action, and social control.

3. A crowd is a temporary gathering of individuals who share a common concern or interest and find themselves in close physical contact with each other. Crowd characteristics include suggestibility, anonymity and spontaneity, and impersonality. Crowd theories include contagion theory and emergent-norm theory.

Mobs and riots occur in violent crowds. A mob is a crowd whose members engage in destructive and aggressive behavior in the pursuit of a short-term but valued goal. A riot is aggressive crowd behavior that is less focused or unified than mob activity. Costly riots occurred between 1966 and 1968, but the single most destructive riot of the twentieth century took place in the spring of 1992 in Los Angeles. Smelser's theory and the emergent-norm perspective are useful in analyzing riots.

Panics and mass hysteria involve frightened crowds. A panic is a collective flight to safety. Mass hysteria is a type of panic that occurs when people are scattered over a wide geographical area. As "The War of the Worlds" situation demonstrated, some people are more prone to mass hysteria than others. Some measures can be taken to reduce the likelihood of mass hysteria.

4. A rumor is a report transmitted informally (often by word of mouth) and concerns subject matter difficult to verify. The content of a rumor is likely to change over time, with the elimination of some details and the emphasis of others. The transmission of a rumor is a collective process in which individuals can play a number of roles. A study of a rumor claiming that McDonald's hamburgers had worms in them examined different ways to limit the impact of rumors.

5. A social movement is an organized, collective activity undertaken by people to promote or resist social change. Smelser outlined a distinction between norm-oriented and value-oriented social movements.

One theory has indicated that the tension and pressure of structural strain are the chief reasons social movements develop. On the other hand, resource-mobilization theory focuses on the process by which the members of a social movement acquire and use certain resources necessary to accomplish their collective goals.

6. Prominent sources of social change include cultural innovation, population, the environment, and social movements. Discovery, invention, and diffusion are three means by which cultural innovation occurs. Some scholars believe that about 90 percent of all cultural development results from diffusion.

A massive increase in population can produce a number of negative changes in societies. In the United States, the size of different age groups will help determine their effect on society.

For Americans two contradictory priorities face them on environmental issues. One places a priority on a clean environment, and the other emphasizes economic development. Even where support for the first priority is strong, it is difficult to accomplish substantial social change.

Social movements are another source of social change. Once the conditions producing a social movement occur, social change can rapidly follow.

Key Terms

collective behavior social activity that occurs under conditions that are temporarily unstructured and unstable because of the absence of clearly defined norms

contagion theory a perspective emphasizing that the presence of a crowd encourages or compels people to think and act in a uniform manner

crowd a temporary gathering of individuals who share a common concern or interest and find themselves in close physical contact with one another

cultural innovation the recognition or development of new material or nonmaterial elements in a culture

diffusion the process by which cultural traits move either from one culture to another or from one part of a culture to another

discovery the perception of something that already exists but that had not been previously recognized

emergent-norm theory a perspective analyzing the process by which a new social standard develops within a crowd—a standard that in reality receives a more enthusiastic acceptance from some crowd members than others

invention a combination of existing knowledge to produce something new

mass hysteria a type of panic that occurs when people are scattered over a wide geographical area

mob a crowd whose members engage in destructive and aggressive behavior in the pursuit of a short-term but valued goal

panic a collective flight to safety

resource-mobilization theory a perspective that focuses on the process by which the members of social movements acquire and use certain resources necessary to accomplish their collective goals

riot aggressive, destructive crowd behavior that is less focused or unified than mob activity

rumor a report transmitted informally (often by word of mouth) and concerned with subject matter difficult to verify

social change modifications in culture, social organization, and social behavior

social movement an organized, collective activity undertaken by people to promote or resist social change

---

Tests

True • False Test

_____ 1. Collective behavior is rare in modern societies.

_____ 2. Smelser's general theory can be used to analyze collective-behavior activities but not social movements.

_____ 3. Recent research with high-school students suggested that contagion might contribute to suicide.

_____ 4. The emergent-norm theory rejects the idea that crowd members contain a united mental state.

_____ 5. While panics are frightening, there is no evidence suggesting that they can adversely affect people's health.

_____ 6. Mass hysteria is a type of panic that occurs when people are scattered over a wide geographical area.

_____ 7. A recent study indicated that the greater the anxiety rumors produced, the less likely they would be transmitted.

_____ 8. Resource-mobilization theorists would suggest that the consciousness-raising group was an important resource in the development of the modern women's movement.

_____ 9. Discoveries always involve material, not nonmaterial items.

_____ 10. The current funding process for scientific research fails to effectively encourage important discoveries and inventions.

502   **Multiple-Choice Test**

_____ 1. In Smelser's general theory, basic conditions that permit or allow collective behavior or a social movement to emerge are termed:
   a.   structural conduciveness.
   b.   structural strain.
   c.   growth and spread of a generalized belief.
   d.   a precipitating factor.

_____ 2. Blumer suggested that contagion occurs in crowds when:
   a.   anonymity decreases.
   b.   crowd members lose awareness of each other's activities.
   c.   key crowd members establish norms for each other.
   d.   crowd members become increasingly preoccupied with each other's activities.

_____ 3. Which of the following statements about crowd theories is true?
   a.   Contagion theory is useful for analyzing crowds in subdued states.
   b.   Emergent-norm theory applies to a wider range of crowd types than contagion theory.
   c.   Emergent-norm theory analyzes collective behavior as separate from the rest of social behavior.
   d.   Emergent-norm theory supports the idea that all crowds are destructive forces.

_____ 4. People who oppose the policies of a certain organization overturn a bus belonging to that organization and smash its windows and then disperse. These people have been participating in:
   a.   a mob.
   b.   a riot.
   c.   mass hysteria.
   d.   panic.

_____ 5. The reaction to the radio broadcast of H.G. Wells's "The War of the Worlds" was an example of:
   a.   a riot.
   b.   panic.
   c.   a rumor.
   d.   mass hysteria.

_____ 6. Rumors are more likely to spread when:
   a.   the topic produces a high level of personal anxiety.
   b.   the issue is unimportant to people.
   c.   one's belief in the rumor is strong.
   d.   a and c

_____ 7. Compared to violent crowds, social movements:
   a.   last longer.
   b.   have a more informal leadership.
   c.   have more informal normative guidelines.
   d.   a, b, and c

_____ 8. Strain theory:
   a.   makes the analysis of resource mobilization a priority.
   b.   was used by James Davies to analyze the French and Russian revolutions.
   c.   cannot analyze such modern social movements as the women's movement.
   d.   only examines norm-oriented social movements.

_____ 9. Cultural innovation occurs through all of the following means EXCEPT:
   a.   discovery.
   b.   invention.
   c.   diffusion.
   d.   displacement.

_____ 10. Which of the following situations occurs during diffusion?
   a.   Belief systems change more rapidly than material elements.
   b.   Innovations that diffuse are often adopted in a modified form.
   c.   Diffusion is usually a one-way process.
   d.   A new cultural trait gains equal acceptance from all groups within the receiving culture.

Essay Test

1.   Define collective behavior and indicate how it differs from other social behavior.
2.   Apply the six-stage Smelser theory to a collective-behavior situation that you choose.
3.   Evaluate the effectiveness of the contagion and emergent-norm theories for analyzing crowd behavior, providing examples whenever possible.
4.   Use one of the crowd theories to analyze the occurrence of a riot.
5.   Define panic and mass hysteria and discuss the conditions encouraging these activities of frightened crowds.
6.   Recall a rumor you heard recently or make up a rumor. Then examine the development of the rumor and also possible efforts to stop the rumor.
7.   What is a social movement? Choose a prominent modern social movement (not the women's movement) and use both strain theory and resource-mobilization theory to analyze its development.
8.   What are four prominent sources of social change? Give an example of each.

Suggested Readings

Branch, Taylor. 1988. *Parting the Waters: America in the King Years 1954–63.* New York: Simon & Schuster. A highly detailed, beautifully written account of the development of civil-rights protests, with Martin Luther King Jr.'s activities central to the presentation.

Dalton, Russell J., and Manfred Kuechler (eds.). 1990. *Challenging the Political Order: New Social and Political Movements in Western Democracies.* New York: Oxford University Press. A book of readings examining the so-called "new social movements" in Europe, that focus on such issues as feminism, environmentalism, and the pursuit of peace.

Erikson, Kai. 1976. *Everything in Its Path: Destruction of Community in the Buffalo Creek Flood.* New York: Simon & Schuster. Along with the death and physical damage they bring, disasters also destroy social networks, leaving little worthwhile in people's lives. This well-written book provides a painfully detailed account of how a flood devastated a mining community in West Virginia.

Gamson, William. 1975. *The Strategy of Social Protest.* Homewood, IL: Dorsey Press. A study of several hundred protest groups that challenged the American political structure between 1800 and 1945.

Levine, Adeline Gordon. 1982. *Love Canal: Science, Politics, and People.* Lexington, MA: Lexington Books. A study of one of the nation's most publicized environmental crises, showing how local people eventually were able to organize a social movement that forced concessions from the federal government and a major chemical company.

Orwell, George. 1946. *Animal Farm.* New York: Harcourt, Brace & World. A short, simply written novel that describes the life of a social movement as it progressed from a pure beginning to complete corruption.

504

Perry, Joseph B., Jr., and M. D. Pugh. 1978. *Collective Behavior*. St. Paul, MN: West. A clearly written, short overview of collective-behavior theory, disaster research, crowd violence, and social movements. This book has done a particularly good job of blending theoretical analyses with modern and historical illustrations.

Robertson, Roland. 1992. *Globalization: Social Theory and Global Culture*. London: Sage. A well-written discussion of the concept of globalization, providing an informative introduction to this process which is transforming modern citizens' lives.

Schneider, Louis. 1976. *Classical Theories of Social Change*. Morristown, NJ: General Learning Press. A short summary and analysis of fourteen major theoretical contributions to the topic of social change. With no more than a couple of hours of fairly easy reading, a student can develop a basic understanding of these classical theories of social change.

Additional Assignments

1. Play the following well-known children's game with about a half-dozen classmates. The first person whispers a fairly elaborate story to the next person, who then whispers it to the next in line, and so on. At the end of the game, the last person will tell the story to everyone. What changes in content occurred along the way? With everyone's help try to reconstruct where information was lost or altered. What insights have you obtained about the transmission of rumors? How would a high-stress situation affect the ability to transmit information accurately?

2. Get back issues of newspapers, newsmagazines (such as *Time* or *Newsweek*), or watch the evening network news for a week and list items covered which would be considered either (a) collective behavior or (b) social movements. Do some activities get more or different coverage than others? Is coverage of some activities more dramatic than others? What reactions to or commentaries about the different topics are found in the media? From your observations what collective activity is "news"? How might an awareness of what serves as "news" affect how people behave collectively to gain their objectives?

Answers to Objective Test Questions

True • False Test

1. f	6. t
2. f	7. f
3. t	8. t
4. t	9. f
5. f	10. t

Multiple-Choice Test

1. a	6. d
2. d	7. a
3. b	8. b
4. a	9. d
5. d	10. b

GLOSSARY

A

absolute wealth the cash value of an individual's economic assets

ageism an ideology asserting the superiority of the young over the old. Ageism is a rationalization for political, economic, and social discrimination against the elderly.

aggregate two or more people who share physical space but lack the interaction maintained by group members

anomie the confusing situation produced when norms are either absent or conflicting

anticipatory socialization the acceptance of a group's standards preparatory to becoming a member of the group

anti-Semitism the complex of prejudicial attitudes toward Jews

authoritarian leader a leader who controls all aspects of group activity yet stays somewhat aloof from the group

authority power that people generally recognize as rightfully maintained by those who use it

B

backstage the physical area or region where people construct the illusions and impressions they will use in a performance

belief a statement about reality that people accept as true

bourgeoisie the class of modern capitalists who own the means of economic production and employ wage labor

bureaucracy the administrative section of a formal organization that has the task of controlling its operation

bureaucratic personality a type of personality that emphasizes rules and procedures and tends to lose track of organizational goals

C

capital money, goods, or other forms of wealth invested to produce more wealth

capitalism an economic system where capital is controlled by private citizens who own the means of production and distribution of goods and services

causation a situation in which one variable can produce the occurrence of another

charismatic system of authority according to Max Weber, an authority system in which leadership develops because of the personal magnetism of an individual, whose followers believe that he or she possesses supernatural qualities

city a large, densely settled concentration of people permanently located within a relatively confined geographical area where nonagricultural occupations are pursued

civil religion a shared, public faith in the nation, a faith linked to people's everyday life through a set of beliefs, symbols, and rituals that contain religious elements and overtones that are not formally affiliated with any particular religion

class consciousness recognition by the members of a class of the role they play in the production process

cognitive ability the capacity to use perception, thought, memory, and other mental processes to acquire knowledge

collective behavior social activity that occurs under conditions that are temporarily unstructured and unstable because of the absence of clearly defined norms

commune a planned, intentional community, bringing together biologically unrelated people in order to build a large, family-like group

communism a requirement that the substantive findings of science represent a common heritage, not the exclusive property of individual discoverers and their heirs

community a settlement of people living in a specific geographical area and maintaining a system of interrelationships that satisfies many of the people's physical and social needs

conflict theory a theory contending that the struggle for power and wealth in society should be the central concern of sociology

conformity (from Chapter 5) behavior that supports the norms of a certain group

conformity (from Chapter 7) a nondeviant adaptation, where individuals pursue legitimate goals and the culturally accepted means to achieve them, even though it is likely they will not attain those goals

contagion theory a perspective emphasizing that the presence of a crowd encourages or compels people to think and act in a uniform manner

corporation a legally designated organization that has power and responsibilities separate from its workers and owners

correlation a statistical description of the relationship between variables

counterculture a subculture whose members consciously and often proudly reject some of the most important cultural standards of the mainstream society

crime an act that violates criminal law

crowd a temporary gathering of individuals who share a common concern or interest and find themselves in close physical contact with one another

crude birth rate the number of births per 1,000 persons in a society in a given year

crude death rate the number of deaths per 1,000 persons in a society in a given year

cultural innovation the recognition or development of new material or nonmaterial elements in a culture

cultural relativism the recognition that a culture should be evaluated by its own standards and not by those of any other culture

cultural universals traits believed to exist in all cultures

culture all the human-made products associated with a society

culture shock the psychological and social maladjustment many people suffer when they visit or live in another culture

D

deficit famine situation in which no food supplies exist elsewhere in a nation sufficient to compensate for local inadequacies

democracy a government in which those in power are acting with the consent of the governed

democratic leader a leader who permits group members to determine many policies and take an active role in discussion

demography the study of human populations

dependent variable a variable that is the consequence of some cause

deviance behavior that violates social norms considered sufficiently significant that the majority of a group or society responds negatively to their violation

diffusion the process by which cultural traits move either from one culture to another or from one part of a culture to another

discovery the perception of something that already exists but that had not been previously recognized

discrimination the behavior by which one group prevents or restricts another group's access to scarce resources

disease a condition of biological nonhealth

disengagement a process of mutual withdrawal involving decreasing interaction between an elderly person and others in the social system to which he or she belongs

disinterestedness a standard that scientists avoid the pursuit of work that is self-serving and self-interested

distribution famine a food shortage existing in certain provinces or regions of a country, not throughout an entire country

doubling time the time span necessary for a population to double in size

dramaturgic sociology a theoretical approach that analyzes social interaction as if the participants were actors in a play

dysfunction a disruptive or destabilizing consequence produced by an item, individual, or group and affecting a particular group or society

E

economic institution the system of norms and roles developed for the production, distribution, and consumption of goods and services

education the transmission of knowledge, skills, and values by either formal or informal means

egalitarian a type of family in which the wife-mother and husband-father share power and also permit their children to participate in the family decisions

ego Sigmund Freud's conception of the self that must cope with pressures from three often contradictory forces

emergent-norm theory a perspective analyzing the process by which a new social standard develops within a crowd—a standard that in reality receives a more enthusiastic acceptance from some crowd members than others

endogamy a custom requiring a person to marry within a specific social unit, such as a kinship group, religious organization, or social class

ethnic group a category of people that is set apart by

itself or others because of distinct cultural or national qualities

ethnocentrism the automatic tendency to evaluate other cultures by the standards of one's own, ultimately finding them inferior

ethnomethodology the study of the sometimes recognized, often unrecognized social order, the set of underlying shared norms and expectations that promote harmony in most everyday social interactions

exogamy a custom compelling someone to marry outside a specific social unit

experiment a research technique in which the investigator manipulates conditions so that the effects produced by one independent variable can be isolated and observed

explicit norm a standard that is out in the open

expressive concerned with emotional or social issues

extended family a family involving two or more generations of people related by blood and living together or close to each other

F

family traditionally defined as a social unit composed of two or more people who live together and are related by blood, marriage, or adoption

family planning a program that encourages people to decide how many children they want, when they want them, and what contraceptives, if any, they wish to use to achieve their goals

fertility rate the number of actual births per 1,000 women between the ages of 15 and 44

folkway a norm that specifies the way things are customarily done. Folkways are concerned with standards of behavior that are socially approved but not considered morally significant.

formal organization a group characterized by formally stated rules, clearly defined members' roles, and distinct objectives

formal social control official pressure intended to convince potential deviants to conform to social norms

frontstage the physical area or region where people present a performance

function an adjustive or stabilizing consequence produced by an item, individual, or group and affecting a particular group or society

functional equivalent an organization or activity that provides an individual or group service or assistance more commonly received from some other organization or activity

G

game according to George Herbert Mead, a group activity in which each participant's role requires interaction with two or more individuals

gender the general behavioral standards that distinguish males from females in a given culture

gender role a set of specific behavioral patterns associated with either the female or male gender

generalized other an image of the role expectations for all the game participants with whom a person must interact

gentrification the move of middle- and upper-middle-class people to formerly deteriorated inner-city neighborhoods

grief work the process by which people attempt to establish a new identity after the death of a loved one

group two or more interacting people who share certain expectations and goals

growth coalition a number of developers, bankers, and industrialists working together to produce economic expansion

growth rate the crude birth rate minus the crude death rate

H

health care the variety of public and private organizations that support an individual's effective physical, mental, and social adaptation to his or her environment

hidden curriculum a set of school rules that emphasizes blind obedience and that is seldom made explicit but is recognized as important by students

homogamy marriage to a person having social characteristics similar to one's own

human ecology the study of human beings' relationship with the environment

hypothesis a scientifically researchable suggestion about the relationship between two or more variables

I

id according to Sigmund Freud, the part of the personality that is unconscious and primitive

ideal norm a standard requiring strict obedience to the guidelines provided

ideal type a simplified description of some phenomenon based on an analysis of concrete examples, emphasizing those characteristics that best help us to understand its essential nature

ideology a system of beliefs and principles that presents an organized explanation of and the justification for a group's outlooks and behavior

implicit norm a standard that normally is not discussed and is not easily stated

impression management the attempt to control others' evaluations by presenting oneself in the most favorable light

incest taboo a rule outlawing sexual relations between kin-group members believed to be too closely related as defined by the cultural standards of a given society

income people's earnings obtained through wages, salaries, business profits, stock dividends, and other means

independent variable a variable that influences another variable—the dependent variable

informal social control unofficial pressure intended to convince potential deviants to conform to social norms

in-group any group characterized by a strong sense of identification and loyalty and a feeling of exclusiveness toward nonmembers

in-migration rate the number of people per 1,000 members of the population moving into an area in a given year

innovation a deviant adaptation that develops when a person seeks legitimate goals but is blocked from effectively using culturally accepted means to achieve them

instincts unalterable behavior complexes that parents transmit genetically to their children

institution a system of statuses, roles, groups, and behavioral patterns that satisfies a basic human need and is necessary for the survival of a society

institutional racism discriminatory racial practices built into such prominent structures as the political, economic, and educational systems

instrumental intended to promote the pursuit of group goals

interest group a group whose members seek to influence elected politicians or government bureaucrats to initiate the legislation or policies they want

intergenerational mobility a comparison of a parent's and a child's social-class positions

internalized through socialization, social expectations have become part of the personality structure

interview a type of survey composed of questions that are delivered face-to-face or over the telephone

intragenerational mobility an analysis of an individual's occupational changes in the course of a lifetime

invention a combination of existing knowledge to produce something new

K

kinship system a number of people related by common descent, marriage, or adoption

L

laissez-faire leader a leader who does not take an active role in group discussions, leaving group members free to reach individual or group decisions

language a system of symbolic communication that uses words, which are sound patterns that have standardized meanings

latent function a function that is not intended and often unrecognized by members of the group producing it

law a norm that is recorded by political authorities and supported by police or other enforcement officials

leadership the exercise of influence or authority within a group by one or more members

legal-rational system of authority according to Max Weber, a system of authority based on laws enacted to produce rational behavior and the achievement of formally designated goals

linguistic-relativity hypothesis the contention that the unique grammatical forms and vocabulary of a language actually shape the thoughts and perceptions of its users

linkage a municipal procedure requiring developers engaged in large commercial projects to provide a substantial fee earmarked for low-cost housing

lobbying a face-to-face effort to persuade legislators and other government personnel to support the proposals of an interest group

looking-glass self according to Charles Cooley, our understanding of what sort of person we are is based on how we imagine we appear to other people

M

macro-order the large-scale structures and activities that exist within societies and even between one society and another

manifest function   a function that is intended and openly recognized by members of the group producing it

mass hysteria   a type of panic that occurs when people are scattered over a wide geographical area

mass media   the instruments of communication that reach a large audience without any personal contact between the senders and the receivers

matriarchal   a type of family in which the wife-mother is the formal head and the absolute or nearly absolute source of power

matrilocal   a type of residence that involves settling with or near the wife's parents

medical sociology   the study of the social setting in which health, sickness, and health care occur

medicine   the scientifically based practice concerned with the prevention and treatment of disease and the treatment of injury

megalopolis   a string of closely bound metropolitan areas

membership group   a group to which an individual belongs

methodology   the set of principles and procedures that guides sociological research

metropolis   a territorial unit composed of a large central city and the surrounding cities and towns

micro-order   the structure and activity of small groups

migration   the flow of people in and out of a particular territory (city, region, or country)

minority group   any category of people with some recognizable trait that places it in a position of inferior status so that its members suffer limited opportunities and rewards

mob   a crowd whose members engage in destructive and aggressive behavior in the pursuit of a short-term but valued goal

monogamy   a marriage practice in which there is one husband and one wife

mores   norms people consider vital

mortification process   a series of degradations and humiliations of inhabitants systematically carried out by staff members of total institutions

multinational   a large corporation with production plants and distribution centers in many countries

N

natural environment   the combination of land, climate, water, air, mineral resources, and plant and animal life that together compose the physical world where people live

natural sciences   older sciences such as astronomy, biology, chemistry, and physics that study the physical world

nature   inborn biological characteristics or heredity

neolocal   a type of residence that occurs when married people establish an independent place to live

net migration rate   the difference between the in-migration rate and the out-migration rate

nonparticipant observation   a method of observation in which an investigator examines a group process without taking part in the group activities

norm   a standard of desirable behavior. Norms are the rules people are expected to follow in their relations with each other.

nuclear family   a two-generation family that includes a father, a mother, and their children living separately from other relatives

nurture   socialization

O

objective definition of social class   a measuring technique that uses certain quantifiable factors—income, occupational prestige rank, or level of education, for example—as the basis for determining an individual's social-class position

objectivity   the ability to evaluate reality without using personal opinions and biases

object permanence   according to Jean Piaget, the childhood recognition that specific objects still exist after they are removed from one's line of vision

organized skepticism   the conclusion that no scientist's contribution to knowledge can be accepted without careful scrutiny

out-group   people who do not belong to an in-group, outsiders who are viewed with hostility and even contempt by the in-group members

out-migration rate   the number of people per 1,000 members of the population moving out of an area in a given year

P

panic   a collective flight to safety

participant observation   a method of observation in which an investigator becomes involved in the activities of the group being studied

patriarchal   a type of family in which the husband-father is the formal head and the absolute or nearly absolute source of power

patrilocal   a type of residence that requires settling with or near the husband's parents

patronage   distribution of favors to political supporters

play   according to George Herbert Mead, the process of taking the role of specific individuals and thereby starting to learn the rights and obligations their particular roles entail

pluralism   a theory that emphasizes that a dispersion of authority exists in American government

political institution   the system of norms and roles that concerns the use and distribution of authority within a given society

political machine   an organization established to control a city, county, or state government

polyandry   the form of polygamy in which a woman has two or more husbands

polygamy   a marriage practice in which a person has two or more spouses of the other sex

polygyny   the form of polygamy in which a man has two or more wives

population   (for research) the entire category of people possessing the characteristics that interest a researcher undertaking a particular study

population   (about people) all the people who live within a specified geographic area such as a nation, a region, or a city

power   the ability of an individual or group to implement wishes or policies, with or without the cooperation of others

power-elite perspective   a theory emphasizing that in American society a group of high-status people—well educated, often wealthy, and placed in high occupational positions—controls the political process, including political authorities

prejudice   a highly negative judgment toward a group, focusing on one or more negative characteristics that are supposedly uniformly shared by all group members

prestige   possession of attributes that elicit recognition, respect, and some degree of deference

primary deviance   violation of a social rule but the individuals in question are not labeled and so do not see themselves as deviant

primary group   a group in which relationships are usually stable over long periods of time, members are able to expose many facets of their personality, and a strong sense of affection and identity develops

principle of *verstehen*   Max Weber's concept that involves an effort to grasp the relationship between individuals' feelings and thoughts, and their actions

privilege system   a framework for inmates' resocialization

profane   anything that people consider ordinary and closely linked to practical demands

proletariat   the class of modern wage laborers who possess no means of production and thus must sell their own labor in order to survive

Q

questionnaire   a type of survey in which a respondent writes the answers to a list of questions

R

race   distinct physical characteristics, such as skin color and certain facial features, used to divide people into broad categories

racial group   a number of people with the particular physical characteristics, such as skin color and certain facial features, that produce placement into a broad category

racism   the ideology contending that actual or alleged differences between different racial groups assert the superiority of one racial group. Racism is a rationalization for political, economic, and social discrimination.

random sample   a sample drawn from a population by a process that assures that every individual in that population has an equal probability of being included

real norm   adjustment of a standard to the practical conditions of living

rebellion   a deviant adaptation displayed when a person decides that the existing society imposes barriers preventing the achievement of success goals. Therefore that individual strikes out against the society, seeking to change its goals and also the existing means for achieving goals.

reference group   a group whose standards a person uses to help shape his or her own values, beliefs, and behavior

relative wealth   the value of an individual's economic assets compared to the assets possessed by other citizens in that society

reliability   consistency in measurement

religion   a unified system of beliefs and practices that focuses on sacred things and serves to create a community of worshippers

replication a repetition or near repetition of an earlier study to determine the accuracy of its findings

reputational definition of social class a measuring technique in which researchers use batteries of resident experts from the community to assess their neighbors' social-class position

resocialization a systematic effort to provide an individual new cultural content, permitting him or her to become a smoothly functioning member of a group or society

resource-mobilization theory a perspective that focuses on the process by which the members of social movements acquire and use certain resources necessary to accomplish their collective goals

retreatism a deviant adaptation in which an individual pursues neither the culturally prescribed goal of success nor the means for achieving this goal because of limited opportunities or a sense of personal inadequacy

riot aggressive, destructive crowd behavior that is less focused or unified than mob activity

ritualism a behavioral pattern that occurs when culturally prescribed success goals are no longer actively sought, but the legitimate means for achieving those goals are conscientiously pursued

role a set of expected behaviors associated with a particular status

role conflict an incompatibility between two or more roles associated with different statuses

role strain an incompatibility between two or more roles associated with the same status

rumor a report transmitted informally (often by word of mouth) and concerned with subject matter difficult to verify

S

sacred anything that is superior in power, is set apart from the ordinary and practical, and creates a sense of awe

sample a limited number of individuals chosen from a population for the purpose of conducting research

scapegoat theory an explanation emphasizing that people blocked from achieving a goal will sometimes be unable or unwilling to take out their frustration on its source, and so they direct their aggression against an accessible individual or group

science a systematic effort to develop general principles about a particular subject matter, based on actual observations and stated in a form that can be tested by any competent person

secondary analysis a study using data banks available to researchers but produced by other individuals and organizations for their own purposes

secondary deviance authorities label individuals deviants and the individuals accept that status

secondary group a group of people who cooperate with each other for specific, practical reasons and maintain few, if any, strong emotional ties within the group

secularization the process by which religion loses influence within groups and societies

self one's perception of his or her own person, formed as a result of other people's response in the course of socialization

self-fulfilling prophecy an incorrect definition of a situation that comes to pass because people accept the incorrect definition and act on it to make it become true

sex the division of a variety of animals forms, including human beings, into the biological categories of male and female

sexism an ideology emphasizing that actual or alleged differences between men and women establish the superiority of men. Sexism is a rationalization for political, economic, and social discrimination against women.

sign an object or event that stands for something else

social category a number of people who have one or more social characteristics in common

social change modifications in culture, social organization, and social behavior

social class a large category of people who are similar in income level, educational attainment, and occupational prestige-ranking

social control the application of systematic behavioral restraints intended to motivate people to obey social expectations

social distance the feeling of separation between individuals or groups

social interaction the basic process through which two or more people use language and gestures to affect each other's thoughts, expectations, and behavior

socialism an economic system with collective ownership of the means for the production and distribution of goods and services

socialization the process by which a person becomes

a social being, learning the necessary cultural content and behavior to become a member of a group or society

social mobility   the movement of a person from one social class or status level to another

social movement   an organized, collective activity undertaken by people to promote or resist social change

social sciences   the sciences that focus on various aspects of human behavior

social stratification   structured inequality of access to rewards, resources, and privileges that are scarce and desirable within a society

society   the interacting people who share a culture

sociobiology   a field in which the proponents contend that through the evolutionary process, human beings have acquired tendencies that determine much of their behavior

sociological theory   a combination of observations and insights that offers a systematic explanation about social life

sociology   the scientific study of human behavior in groups and of the social forces that influence that behavior

status   a position that indicates where a person fits into a group or society and how that person should relate to others in the structure

stereotype   an exaggerated, oversimplified image, maintained by prejudiced people, of the characteristics of the group members against whom they are prejudiced

structural-functional theory   a theory suggesting that groups in interaction tend to influence and adjust to one another in a fairly stable, conflict-free pattern

subculture   the culture of a specific segment of people within a society, differing from the dominant culture in some significant respects

subjective definition of social class   a measuring technique that requires people to indicate the social class to which they belong

suburb   a politically independent municipality that develops next to or in the vicinity of a central city

superego   according to Sigmund Freud, the part of the personality that has internalized standards of right and wrong, a conscience

survey   a research technique that uses carefully constructed questions to obtain a variety of facts about people's thoughts and behavior

symbol   a sign with a meaning fixed not by the nature of the item to which it is attached but by the agreement of the people who use it to communicate

symbolic interaction   a theory that emphasizes the dominant part played by symbolic communication—gestures and above all language—in the development of the individual, group, and society

T

technology   any repeated operation people use to manipulate the environment to achieve some practical goals

total institution   a place of residence where inhabitants experience nearly complete restriction of their physical freedom in an attempt to effectively resocialize them into a radically new identity and behavioral pattern

traditional system of authority   according to Max Weber, an authority system in which the standard of political leadership passes down from one generation to another

U

universalism   a norm stating that all scientific claims of truth need to be evaluated by impersonal criteria consistent with existing knowledge in that field

urban infrastructure   a city's basic physical and technical features such as roads, bridges, and water, sewer, and transit systems

urbanization   the process by which a city forms and develops

V

validity   the condition in which a research item accurately measures what it claims to measure

value   a general conviction about what is good or bad, right or wrong, appropriate or inappropriate

variable   a factor that has two or more categories or measurable conditions

vicious cycle of poverty   a pattern in which the parents' minimal income significantly limits the educational and occupational pursuits of the children, thereby keeping them locked into the same economic status

victimless crime   the willing (hence "victimless") exchange among adults of strongly desired but illegal goods or services

W

wealth people's economic assets—their cars, homes, stocks, bonds, and real estate—which can be converted into cash

white-collar crime crime committed by people of higher socioeconomic status in the course of their business activities

work alienation the loss of control over the process of one's labor, with the resulting dissatisfaction primarily caused by overly close supervision, highly routine tasks, and an overall simplicity to one's job

Z

zero population growth a situation in which the population size stabilizes

REFERENCES

Chapter 1

Babbie, Earl. 1992. "Sociology: An Idea Whose Time Has Come," *Footnotes*. 20 (May), p. 3.

Blumer, Herbert. 1969. *Symbolic Interactionism: Perspective and Method*. Englewood Cliffs, NJ: Prentice-Hall.

Coleman, James S. 1990. *Foundations of Social Theory*. Cambridge, MA: Harvard University Press.

Dahrendorf, Ralf. 1959. *Class and Class Conflict in Industrial Society*. Stanford, CA: Stanford University Press.

D'Antonio, William V. 1992. "Sociology's Lonely Crowd—Indeed!" *Footnotes*. 20 (May), p. 3.

Davis, Mike. 1992. "In L.A., Burning All Illusions," *Nation*. 254 (June 1), pp. 743–46.

Domhoff, G. William. 1990. *The Power Elite and the State: How Policy Is Made in America*. New York: Aldine de Gruyter.

Egan, Timothy. 1992. "Los Angeles Riots Spurring Big Rise in Sales of Guns," *New York Times*. (May 14), pp. A1+.

Hirsch, Eric L. 1990. "Sacrifice for the Cause: Group Processes, Recruitment, and Commitment in a Student Social Movement," *American Sociological Review*. 55 (April), pp. 243–54.

Levine, Felice J. 1992. "Testimony of the American Sociological Association," *Footnotes*. 20 (February), p. 2.

Lyman, Stanford M. 1988. "Symbolic Interactionism and Macrosociology," *Sociological Forum*. 3 (Spring), pp. 295–301.

Mattox, William R., Jr. 1992. "America's Family Time Famine," In Ollie Pocs (ed.), *Marriage and Family 92/93*. 18th ed. Guilford, CT: Dushkin, pp. 59–63.

Merton, Robert K. 1968. *Social Theory and Social Structure*. 3rd ed. New York: Free Press.

Mills, C. Wright. 1956. *The Power Elite*. New York: Oxford University Press.

Mydans, Seth, and Michel Marriott. 1992. "Riots Ruin a Business, and a Neighborhood Suffers," *New York Times*. (May 18), pp. A1+.

Rutten, Tim. 1992. "A New Kind of Riot," *New York Review of Books*. 39 (June 11), pp. 52–54.

Terry, Don. 1992. "Hope and Fear in Los Angeles as Deadly Gangs Call Truce," *New York Times*. (May 12), pp. A1+.

Toner, Robin. 1992. "Los Angeles Riots Are a Warning, Americans Fear," *New York Times*. (May 11), pp. A1+.

Whyte, William Foote. 1955. *Street Corner Society*. Revised ed. Chicago: University of Chicago Press.

Wilkerson, Isabel. 1992. "Searing Lesson for Children: How Hate Can Undo a World," *New York Times*. (May 5), pp. A1+.

Chapter 2

Bandura, Albert, et al. 1963. "Imitation of Film-Mediated Aggressive Models," *Journal of Abnormal and Social Psychology*. 66, pp. 3–11.

Baumrind, Diana. 1964. "Some Thoughts on Ethics of Research: After Reading Milgram's 'Behavioral Study of Obedience,'" *American Psychologist*. 19 (June), pp. 421–23.

Bonney, Charles. 1989. "Correlation and Causality," In Earl Babbie (ed.), *The Practice of Social Research*. 5th ed. Belmont, CA: Wadsworth, pp. 66–67.

Buenos Aires Herald. 1992. "Latin American News." (July 3), p. 3.

Card, Josefina J. 1989. "Facilitating Data Sharing," *Footnotes*. 17 (January), p. 8.

Cole, Stephen. 1980. *The Sociological Method*. 3rd ed. Chicago: Rand McNally.

Doob, Christopher Bates. 1970. "Family Background and Peer Group Development in a Puerto Rican District," *Sociological Quarterly*. 11 (Fall), pp. 523–32.

Footnotes. 1992. "Revising the ASA Code of Ethics." 20 (February), p. 5.

Gallup, George. 1972. *The Sophisticated Poll Watcher's Guide*. Princeton, NJ: Princeton Opinion Press.

Hallowell, Lyle. 1985. "The Outcome of the Brajuha Case: Legal Implications for Sociologists," *Footnotes*. 13 (December), pp. 1+.

Milgram, Stanley. 1963. "Behavioral Study of Obedience," *Journal of Abnormal and Social Psychology*. 67, pp. 371–78.

————. 1974. *Obedience to Authority*. New York: Harper & Row.

Moore, Marvin L. 1992. "The Family as Portrayed on Prime-Time Television, 1947–1990: Structure and Characteristics," *Sex Roles*. 26 (January), pp. 41–61.

Rank, Mark R. 1989. "Fertility among Women on Welfare: Incidence and Determinants," *American Sociological Review*. 54 (April), pp. 296–304.

Robinson, Ian. 1991. "Confidentiality for Whom?" *Social Science & Medicine*. 32, pp. 279–86.

Sieber, Joan E., and Barbara Stanley. 1988. "Ethical and Professional Dimensions of Socially Sensitive Research," *American Psychologist*. 43 (January), pp. 49–55.

Steelman, Lala Carr, and Brian Powell. 1991. "Sponsoring the Next Generation: Parental Willingness to Pay for Higher Education," *American Journal of Sociology*. 96 (May), pp. 1505–29.

Summers, Russel J. 1991. "Determinants of Judgments of and Responses to a Complaint of Sexual Harassment," *Sex Roles*. 25 (October), pp. 379–92.

Weinberg, Elizabeth A. 1992. "Perestroika and Soviet Sociology," *British Journal of Sociology*. 43 (March), pp. 1–10.

Whyte, William Foote. 1955. *Street Corner Society*. Revised ed. Chicago: University of Chicago Press.

Chapter 3

Block, Jeanne Humphrey. 1973. "Conceptions of Sex Role: Some Cross-Cultural and Longitudinal Perspectives," *American Psychologist*. 28 (June), pp. 512–26.

Bohannon, Laura. 1975. "Hamlet and the Tiv," *Psychology Today*. 9 (July), pp. 62–66.

Bovasso, Gregory, John Jacobs, and Salomon Rettig. 1991. "Changes in Moral Values over Three Decades, 1958-1988," *Youth & Society*. 22 (June), pp. 468–81.

Cahow, Eric. 1992. "International Students Adapt to American Way," *Southern News*. 23 (March 12), pp. 1+.

Chagnon, Napoleon A. 1977. *Yanamamö: The Fierce People*. 2nd ed. New York: Holt, Rinehart and Winston.

Corcoran, Elizabeth. 1992. "Robots for the Operating Room," *New York Times*. (July 19), sec. 3, p. 9.

Feder, Barnaby F. 1992. "Robotics Comes Back to Reality," *New York Times*. (April 29), pp. D1+.

Gallup, Alec, and Frank Newport. 1991. "Death Penalty Support Remains Strong," *Gallup Poll Monthly*. (June), pp. 40–45.

Gallup, George, Jr., and Larry Hugick. 1990. "Racial Tolerance Grows, Progress on Racial Equality Less Evident," *Gallup Poll Monthly*. (June), pp. 23–32.

Gallup, George, Jr., and Frank Newport. 1991. "Almost Half of Americans Believe Biblical View of Creation," *Gallup Poll Monthly*. (November), pp. 30–34.

Giovannini, Maureen. 1992. "Female Anthropologist and Male Informant: Gender Conflict in a Sicilian Town," In John J. Macionis and Nijole V. Benokraitis (eds.), *Seeing Ourselves*. 2nd ed. Englewood Cliffs, NJ: Prentice-Hall, pp. 27–32.

Gitlin, Todd. 1992. "World Leaders: Mickey, et al.," *New York Times*. (May 3), sec. 2, pp. 1+.

Gitlin, Todd, and Ruth Rosen. 1987. "Give the 60's Generation a Break," *New York Times*. (November 14), p. 27.

Harris, Marvin. 1974. *Cows, Pigs, Wars and Witches*. New York: Random House.

Hoffman, Curt, Ivy Lau, and David Randy Johnson. 1986. "The Linguistic Relativity of Person Cognition: An English-Chinese Comparison," *Journal of Personality and Social Psychology*. 51 (December), pp. 1097–1105.

Hueber, Graham. 1991. "Americans Report High Levels of Environmental Concern, Activity," *Gallup Poll Monthly*. (April), pp. 6–12.

Hugick, Larry, and Jennifer Leonard. 1991. "Sex in America," *Gallup Poll Monthly*. (October), pp. 60–73.

Jacobson, Jodi L. 1992. "Improving Women's Reproductive Health," In Lester R. Brown et al. (eds.), *State of the World*: 1992. New York: W. W. Norton, pp. 83-89.

Konner, Melvin. 1990. "Mutilated in the Name of Tradition," *New York Times Book Review*. (April 15), pp. 5–6.

Molotch, Harvey, and Serena Vicari. 1988. "Three Ways to Build the Development Process in the United States, Japan, and Italy," *Urban Affairs Quarterly*. 24 (December), pp. 188–214.

Murdock, George P. 1965. *Culture and Society*. Pittsburgh: University of Pittsburgh Press.

Ryan, William. 1976. *Blaming the Victim*. Revised ed. New York: Vintage Books.

Sack, Allen L. 1991. "The Underground Economy of College Football," *Sociology of Sport Journal*. 8 (March), pp. 1–15.

Sapir, Edward. 1921. *Language: An Introduction to the Study of Speech*. New York: Harcourt, Brace & World.
———. 1929. "The Status of Linguistics as a Science," *Language*. 5, pp. 207–14.

Shannon, William V. 1966. *The American Irish*. Revised ed. New York: Macmillan.

Slomczynski, Kazimierz, et al. 1981. "Stratification, Work, and Values: A Polish-American Comparison," *American Sociological Review*. 46 (December), pp. 720–44.

U.S. Department of State. 1990. *Americans Abroad: What You Should Know before You Go!* Washington, DC: U.S. Government Printing Office.

Vig, Norman J. 1990. "Presidential Leadership: From the Reagan to the Bush Administration," In Norman J. Vig and Michael E. Kraft (eds.), *Environmental Policy in the 1990s: Toward a New Agenda*. Washington, DC: Congressional Quarterly Press, pp. 33–58.

Whorf, Benjamin L. 1956. *Language, Thought, and Reality*. New York: John Wiley and Sons.

Williams, Robin M., Jr. 1970. *American Society*. 3rd ed. New York: Alfred A. Knopf.

Chapter 4

Agyeman-Duah, Baffour, and Olatunde B. J. Ojo. 1991. "Interstate Conflicts in West Africa," *Comparative Political Studies*. 24 (October), pp. 299–318.

Albert, Edward. 1991. "Riding a Line: Competition and Cooperation in the Sport of Bicycle Racing," *Sociology of Sport Journal*. 8 (December), pp. 341–61.

Applebaum, Herbert A. 1982. "Traditional versus Bureaucratic Methods," *Anthropological Quarterly*. 55 (October), pp. 224–34.

Barrett, Mark E., D. Dwayne Simpson, and Wayne E.K. Lehman. 1988. "Behavioral Changes of Adolescents in Drug Abuse Intervention Programs," *Journal of Clinical Psychology*. 44 (May), pp. 461–73.

Baum, Howell S. 1991. "Creating a Family in the Workplace," *Human Relations*. 44 (November), pp. 1137–59.

Bellah, Robert, et al. 1986. *Habits of the Heart: Individualism and Commitment in American Life*. New York: Harper & Row.

Blau, Peter M., and W. Richard Scott. 1963. *Formal Organizations*. London: Routledge & Kegan Paul.

Colinvaux, Paul A., and Mark B. Bush. 1991. "The Rain-Forest Ecosystem as a Resource for Hunting and Gathering," *American Anthropologist*. 93 (March), pp. 153–60.

Cooley, Charles Horton. 1962. *Social Organization*. New York: Schocken Books. (Originally published in New York: Charles Scribner's Sons, 1909.)

Durkheim, Émile. 1946. *The Division of Labor in Society*. Trans. George Simpson. Glencoe, IL: Free Press.

Dyer, Gwynne. 1985. *War*. New York: Crown.

Gallup, George, Jr., and Frank Newport. 1991. "Large Majorities Continue to Back AIDS Testing," *Gallup Poll Monthly*. (May), pp. 25–28.

Gallup Poll Monthly. 1991. "Americans Say Police Brutality Frequent." (March), pp. 53–57.

Gerth, Hans, and C. Wright Mills (eds.). 1946. From

Max Weber: Essays in Sociology. New York: Oxford University Press.

Halloran, Richard. 1988. "Skipper Defended," *New York Times*. (July 4), pp. A1+.

Hugick, Larry. 1992. "Public Sees Crime Up Nationally," *Gallup Poll Monthly*. (March), pp. 51–53.

Jacobs, Struan. 1990. "Popper, Weber and the Rationalist Approach to Social Explanation," *British Journal of Sociology*. 41 (December), pp. 559–70.

Janis, Irving L. 1972. *Victims of Groupthink*. Boston: Houghton Mifflin.

Kay, Robert E. 1991. "Let's Stop Teaching and Let Our Children Learn," *Social Policy*. 22 (Summer), pp. 8–12.

Kohn, Melvin L. 1971. "Bureaucratic Man: A Portrait and an Interpretation," *American Sociological Review*. 36 (June), pp. 461–74.

Leonard, Wilbert Marcellus. 1980. *A Sociological Perspective of Sport*. Minneapolis: Burgess.

Liddell, Christine, S. Peter Henzi, and Merrill Drew. 1987. "Mothers, Fathers, and Children in an Urban Park Playground: A Comparison of Dyads and Triads," *Developmental Psychology*. 23 (March), pp. 262–66.

McCracken, Paul W. 1992. "Will the Third Great Wave Continue?" In LeRoy W. Barnes (ed.), *Social Problems 92/93*. Guilford, CT: Dushkin, pp. 167–70.

Mann, Thomas. 1955. *Confessions of Felix Krull, Confidence Man*. New York: Alfred A. Knopf.

Merton, Robert K. 1968. *Social Theory and Social Structure*. 3rd ed. New York: Free Press.

Michener, James A. 1976. *Sports in America*. New York: Random House.

Miller, Arthur H., Christopher Wlezien, and Anne Hildreth. 1991. "A Reference Group Theory of Partisan Coalitions," *Journal of Politics*. 53 (November), pp. 1134–49.

Mowat, Farley. 1965. *Never Cry Wolf*. New York: Dell.

Naisbitt, John. 1982. "The New Economic and Political Order of the 1980s," In Leonard Cargan and Jeanne R. Ballantine (eds.), *Sociological Footprints*. Belmont, CA: Wadsworth, pp. 168–79.

Naples, Nancy A. 1991. "Contradictions in the Gender Subtext of the War on Poverty: The Community Work and Resistance of Women from Low Income Communities," *Social Problems*. 38 (August), pp. 316–32.

Nasar, Sylvia. 1992. "However You Slice the Data the Richest Did Get Richer," *New York Times*. (May 11), pp. D1+.

Newcomb, Theodore M., et al. 1967. *Persistence and*

Change: Bennington College and Its Students after 25 Years. New York: Wiley.

Peter, Lawrence J., and Raymond Hull. 1969. *The Peter Principle*. New York: William Morrow.

Redfield, Robert. 1941. *The Folk Culture of Yucatan*. Chicago: University of Chicago Press.

Redner, Harry. 1990. "Beyond Marx-Weber: A Diversified and International Approach to the State," *Political Studies*. 38 (December), pp. 638–53.

Roethlisberger, Fritz J., and William J. Dickson. 1939. *Management and the Worker*. Cambridge, MA: Harvard University Press.

Scott, William A., and Ruth Scott. 1981. "Intercorrelations among Structural Properties of Primary Groups," *Journal of Personality and Social Psychology*. 41 (April), pp. 279–92.

Sherif, Muzafer, and Carolyn W. Sherif. 1956. *An Outline of Social Psychology*. Revised ed. New York: Harper & Brothers.

Slater, Philip. 1976. *The Pursuit of Loneliness*. Revised ed. Boston: Beacon Press.

Stouffer, Samuel A., et al. 1949. *The American Soldier: Combat and Its Aftermath*. vol. 2. Princeton, NJ: Princeton University Press.

Summer, William Graham. 1906. *Folkways*. Boston: Ginn.

Tabor, Mary B. W. 1991. "State Worker's Fiscal Coup: Windfall for Massachusetts," *New York Times*. (June 8), pp. 1+.

Tönnies, Ferdinand. 1957. *Community and Society*. New York: Harper.

Warren, Mark. 1988. "Max Weber's Liberalism for a Nietzschean World," *American Political Science Review*. 82 (March), pp. 31–50.

Wilder, David A. 1990. "Some Determinants of the Persuasive Power of In-Groups and Out-Groups: Organization of Information and Attribution of Independence," *Journal of Personality and Social Psychology*. 59 (December), pp. 1202-13.

Wilder, David A., and P. N. Shapiro. 1991. "Facilitation of Outgroup Stereotypes by Enhanced Ingroup Identity," *Journal of Experimental Social Psychology*. 27 (September), pp. 431–52.

Wood, B. Dan. 1988. "Principals, Bureaucrats, and Responsiveness in Clean Air Enforcements," *American Political Science Review*. 82 (March), pp. 213–34.

Wright, Sara E., and Paul C. Rosenblatt. 1987. "Isolation and Farm Loss: Why Neighbors May Not Be Supportive," *Family Relations*. 36 (October), pp. 391–95.

Chapter 5

American Broadcasting Company. 1988. "Remembering Marilyn," May 8 (a television program).

Asch, Solomon E. 1963. "Effects of Group Pressure upon the Modification and Distortion of Judgments," In Harold Geutzkow (ed.), *Group, Leadership and Men*. New York: Russell and Russell, pp. 177–90.

Bales, Robert F. 1953. "The Equilibrium Problem in Small Groups," In Talcott Parsons, Robert Bales, and Edward A. Shils (eds.), *Working Papers in the Theory of Action*. Glencoe, IL: Free Press, pp. 111–61.

Bales, Robert F., and Philip E. Slater. 1955. "Role Differentiation in Small Decision-Making Groups," In Talcott Parsons, Robert F. Bales, et al. (eds.), *Family, Socialization and Interaction Process*. Glencoe, IL: Free Press, pp. 259–306.

Bales, Robert F., and Fred L. Strodtbeck. 1968. "Phases in Group Problem-Solving," In Dorwin Cartwright and Alvin Zander (eds.), *Group Dynamics*. New York: Harper & Row, pp. 389–98.

Belknap, Penny, and Wilbert M. Leonard II. 1991. "A Conceptual Replication and Extension of Erving Goffman's Study of Gender Advertisements," *Sex Roles*. 25 (August), pp. 103–18.

Berkowitz, Leonard. 1980. *A Survey of Social Psychology*. 2nd ed. New York: Holt, Rinehart and Winston.

Blumer, Herbert. 1969. *Symbolic Interactionism: Perspective and Method*. Englewood Cliffs, NJ: Prentice-Hall.

Boden, Deidre. 1990. "The World as It Happens: Ethnomethodology and Conversation Analysis," In George Ritzer (ed.), *Frontiers of Social Theory*. New York: Columbia University Press, pp. 185–213.

Brosius, J. Peter. 1988. "Significance and Social Being in Ifugao Agricultural Production," *Ethnology*. 27 (January), pp. 97–110.

Brown, Clifton. 1989. "Changing Team Chemistry Adds Risk to Equation," *New York Times*. (March 5), sec. 8, pp. 1+.

Burley, Kim A. 1991. "Family-Work Spillover in Dual-Career Cycles: A Comparison of Two Time Perspectives," *Psychological Reports*. 68 (April), pp. 471–80.

Cooper, Andrew Fenton, Richard A. Higgott, and Kim Richard Nossal. 1991. "Bound to Follow? Leadership and Followership in the Gulf Conflict," *Political Science Quarterly*. 106 (Fall), pp. 391–410.

Curtis, Craig, et al. 1991. "Improving Legal Compliance by Noncoercive Means: Coproducing Order

518

in Washington State," *Social Science Quarterly*. 72 (December), pp. 645–60.

Duxbury, Linda Elizabeth, and Christopher Alan Higgins. 1991. "Gender Differences in Work-Family Conflict," *Journal of Applied Psychology*. 76 (February), pp. 60–74.

Flaherty, Michael G. 1990. "Two Conceptions of the Social Situation: Some Implications of Humor," *Sociological Quarterly*. 31 (Spring), pp. 93–106.

Fort, Karen Orendurff. 1989. "Bringing Up Father," In Kurt Finsterbusch (ed.), *Sociology 89/90*. Guilford, CT: Dushkin, pp. 79–82.

Garfinkel, Harold. 1967. *Studies in Ethnomethodology*. Englewood Cliffs, NJ: Prentice-Hall.

———. 1988. "Evidence for Locally Produced, Naturally Accountable Phenomena of Order, Logic, Reason, Meaning, Method, etc., in and as of the Essential Quiddity of Immortal Ordinary Society (I of IV): An Announcement of Studies," *Sociological Theory*. 6 (Spring), pp. 103–09.

Goffman, Erving. 1959. *The Presentation of Self in Everyday Life*. New York: Doubleday.

———. 1961. *Encounters*. Indianapolis: Bobbs-Merrill.

Hilbert, Richard A. 1990. "Ethnomethodology and the Micro-Macro Order," *American Sociological Review*. 55 (December), pp. 794–808.

Hock, Ellen, and Debra K. DeMeis. 1990. "Depression in Mothers of Infants: The Role of Maternal Employment," *Developmental Psychology*. 26 (March), pp. 285–91.

Jacobs, Gerald A., Randal P. Quevillon, and Matt Stricherz. 1990. "Lessons from the Aftermath of Flight 232: Practical Considerations for the Mental Health Profession's Response to Air Disasters," *American Psychologist*. 45 (December), pp. 1329–35.

Jennings, Luther B., and Stephen G. George. 1984. "Group-Induced Distortion of Visually Perceived Linear Extent: The Asch Effect Revisited," *Psychological Record*. 34 (Winter), pp. 133–48.

King, Vance R. 1991. "Redefining Ourselves to Leadership and Ethics in Law Enforcement," FBI *Law Enforcement Bulletin*. 60 (January), pp. 24–26.

Krantz, James. 1990. "Lessons from the Field: An Essay on the Crisis of Leadership in Contemporary Organizations," *Journal of Applied Behavioral Science*. 26, pp. 49–64.

Kruglanski, Arie W., and Donna M. Webster. 1991. "Group Members' Reactions to Opinion Deviates and Conformists at Varying Degrees of Proximity to Decision Deadline and Environmental Noise,"

Journal of Personality and Social Psychology. 61 (August), pp. 212–25.

McAllister, Hunter A. 1990. "Effects of Eyewitness Evidence on Plea-Bargain Decisions by Prosecutors and Defense Attorneys," *Journal of Applied Social Psychology*. 20 (October), pp. 1461–73.

MacEwen, Karyl E., and Julian Barling. 1991. "Effects of Maternal Employment Experiences on Children's Behavior via Mood, Cognitive Differences, and Parenting Behavior," *Journal of Marriage and the Family*. 53 (August), pp. 635–44.

McGlashan, Charles Fayette. 1879. *History of the Donner Party*. Truckee, CA: Crowley and McGlashan.

May, Brett A. 1991. "The Interaction between Ratings of Self, Peers' Perceptions, and Reflexive Self-Ratings," *Journal of Social Psychology*. 131 (August), pp. 483–93.

Orwell, George. 1959. *Down and Out in London and Paris*. New York: Berkley Medallion. (Originally published in 1933.)

Powlick, Philip J. 1991. "The Attitudinal Bases for Responsiveness to Public Opinion among Foreign Policy Officials," *Journal of Conflict Resolution*. 35 (December), pp. 611–41.

Reifman, Alan, et al. 1991. "Stress, Social Support, and Health in Married Professional Women with Small Children," *Psychology of Women Quarterly*. 15 (September), pp. 431–45.

Schachter, Stanley. 1959. *The Psychology of Affiliation*. Stanford, CA: Stanford University Press.

Scheff, Thomas J. 1988. "Shame and Conformity: The Difference-Emotion System," *American Sociological Review*. 53 (June), pp. 395–406.

Schellenberg, James A. 1990. "William James and Symbolic Interactionism," *Personality and Social Psychological Bulletin*. 16 (December), pp. 769–73.

Siminoff, L.A., and J.H. Fetting. 1991. "Factors Affecting Treatment Decisions for a Life-Threatening Illness: The Case of Medical Treatment of Breast Cancer," *Social Science and Medicine*. 32, pp. 813–18.

Siverson, Randolph M., and Juliann Emmons. 1991. "Birds of a Feather: Democratic Political Systems and Alliance Choices in the Twentieth Century," *Journal of Conflict Resolution*. 35 (June), pp. 285–306.

Sooklal, Lessey. 1991. "The Leader as a Broker of Dreams," *Human Relations*. 44 (August), pp. 833–56.

Stoner, J.A.F. 1961. A Comparison of Individual and Group Decisions Involving Risk. Master's thesis, Massachusetts Institute of Technology.

Weimann, Gabriel. 1991. "The Influentials: Back to the

Concept of Opinion Leaders," *Public Opinion Quarterly*. 55 (Summer), pp. 267–79.

Wiersma, Uco J., and Peter van den Berg. 1991. "Work-Home Role Conflict, Family Climate, and Domestic Responsibilities among Men and Women in Dual-Earner Families," *Journal of Applied Social Psychology*. 21 (August 1-15), pp. 1207–17.

Chapter 6

Ariès, Phillipe. 1962. *Centuries of Childhood: A Social History of Family Life*. Trans. Robert Baldick. New York: Vintage Books.

Baron, James N., and Peter C. Reiss. 1985. "Mass Media and Violent Behavior," *American Sociological Review*. 50 (June), pp. 347–63.

Barringer, Felicity. 1992. "Laid-Off Bosses Scramble in a Changing World," *New York Times*. (July 12), sec. 4, p. 6.

Bohannon, Paul (ed.). 1970. *Divorce and After*. Garden City, NY: Doubleday.

Booth, Alan, and Paul Amato. 1991. "Divorce and Psychological Stress," *Journal of Health and Social Behavior*. 32 (December), pp. 396–407.

Brand, Handre J., and Rosylyn C. Pullen. 1991. "Work-Related Self-Concept and Family Relations in Unemployed Married Men," *Psychological Reports*. 68 (June), pp. 1091–96.

Bronfenbrenner, Urie. 1970. *Two Worlds of Childhood*. New York: Russell Sage Foundation.

Caporael, Linnda R., and Marilynn B. Brewer. 1991. "Reviving Evolutionary Psychology: Biology Meets Society," *Journal of Social Issues*. 47, pp. 187–95.

Carnegie Quarterly. 1990. "Adolescence: Path to a Productive Life or a Diminished Future?" 25 (Winter/Spring), pp. 1–13.

Cherlin, Andrew. 1983. "Remarriage as an Incomplete Institution," In Arlene Skolnick and Jerome H. Skolnick (eds.), *Family in Transition*. 4th ed. Boston: Little, Brown, pp. 388-402.

Clarke-Stewart, K. Alison. 1991. "A Home Is Not a School: The Effects of Child Care on Children's Development," *Journal of Social Issues*. 47, pp. 105–23.

Coleman, James. 1961. *The Adolescent Society*. New York: Doubleday.

Coleman, John R. 1992. "Homeless on the Streets of New York," In John J. Macionis and Nijole V. Benokraitis (eds.), *Seeing Ourselves: Classic, Contemporary, and Cross-Cultural Readings in Sociology*. Englewood Cliffs, NJ: Prentice-Hall, pp. 81–91.

Collins, Clare. 1992. "Adults Reaching Out to Troubled Teen-Agers," *New York Times*. (May 3), sec. 13, pp. 8–9.

Cooley, Charles Horton. 1964. *Human Nature and the Social Order*. New York: Schocken Books. (Originally published in 1902.)

Counts, Robert M., and Anita Sacks. 1985. "The Need for Crisis Intervention during Marital Separation," *Social Work*. 30 (March/April), pp. 151–58.

Davis, Kingsley. 1948. *Human Society*. New York: Macmillan.

Davison, Peter, and Jane Davison. 1979. "Coming of Age in America," In Phillip Whitten (ed.), *Readings in Sociology*. New York: Harper & Row, pp. 52–55.

Dishion, T. J., et al. 1991. "Family, School, and Behavioral Antecedents to Early Adolescent Involvement with Antisocial Peers," *Developmental Psychology*. 27 (January), pp. 172–80.

Dunaway, R. Gregory, and Francis T. Cullen. 1991. "Explaining Crime Ideology: An Exploration of the Parental Socialization Perspective," *Crime and Delinquency*. 37 (October), pp. 536–54.

Ellis, Lee. 1991. "A Synthesized (Biosocial) Theory of Rape," *Journal of Consulting and Clinical Psychology*. 59 (October), pp. 631–42.

Ellis, Margaret McMahon, and William N. Ellis. 1989. "Cultures in Transition: What the West Can Learn from Developing Countries," *Futurist*. 23 (March/April), pp. 22–25.

Farrington, Keith. 1992. "The Modern Prison as Total Institution? Public Perception versus Objective Reality," *Crime & Delinquency*. 38 (January), pp. 6–26.

Freud, Sigmund. 1952. *A General Introduction to Psychoanalysis*. Trans. Joan Riviere. New York: Washington Square Press. (Originally published in 1920.)

Frost, Taggart F., and Dennis E. Clayson. 1991. "The Measurement of Self-Esteem, Stress-Related Life Events, and Locus of Control among Unemployed and Employed Blue-Collar Workers," *Journal of Applied Social Psychology*. 21 (September 1–15), pp. 1402–17.

Gallup Poll Monthly. 1991. "Signs Encouraging for an Upsurge in Reading in America." (February), pp. 43–53.

Goffman, Erving. 1961. *Asylums*. Garden City, NY: Anchor Books.

Gracey, Harry L. 1977. "Learning the Student Role:

Kindergarten as Academic Boot Camp," In Dennis H. Wrong and Harry L. Gracey (eds.), *Readings in Introductory Sociology*. 3rd ed. New York: Macmillan, pp. 215–26.

Guttman, Herta A. 1991. "Parental Death as a Precipitant of Marital Conflict in Middle Age," *Journal of Marital and Family Therapy*. 17 (January), pp. 81–87.

Harlow, Harry F., and Margaret K. Harlow. 1962. "Social Deprivation in Monkeys," *Scientific American*. 207 (November), pp. 137–47.

Harlow, Harry F., and R. R. Zimmerman. 1959. "Affectional Responses in the Infant Monkey," *Science*. 130, pp. 421–23.

Henslin, James M. 1990. "When Life Seems Hopeless: Suicide in American Society," In James M. Henslin (ed.), *Social Problems Today: Coping with the Challenges of a Changing Society*. Englewood Cliffs, NJ: Prentice-Hall, pp. 99–107.

Hiebert, Ray Eldon, Donald F. Ungurait, and Thomas W. Bohn. 1974. *Mass Media*. New York: David McKay.

Hiltz, Starr Roxanne. 1980. "Widowhood: A Roleless Role," In Arlene Skolnick and Jerome H. Skolnick (eds.), *Family in Transition*. 3rd ed. Boston: Little, Brown, pp. 237–53.

Hobart, Charles. 1991. "Conflict in Remarriages," *Journal of Divorce & Remarriage*. 15, pp. 69–86.

Hofferth, Sandra L., and Deborah A. Phillips. 1991. "Child Care Policy Research," *Journal of Social Issues*. 47, pp. 1–13.

Hoffman, William S., et al., 1991. "Initial Impact of Plant Closings on Automobile Workers and Their Families," *Families in Society*. 72 (February), pp. 103–07.

Hultsch, David F., and Francine Deutsch. 1981. *Adult Development and Aging*. New York: McGraw-Hill.

Jones, Diane Carlson, and Renate Houts. 1992. "Parental Drinking, Parent-Child Communication, and Social Skills in Young Adults," *Journal of Studies on Alcohol*. 53 (January), pp. 48–56.

Kagan, Jerome. 1983. "The Psychological Requirements for Human Development," In Arlene Skolnick and Jerome H. Skolnick (eds.), *Family in Transition*. 4th ed. Boston: Little, Brown, pp. 409–20.

Kamerman, Sheila B. 1991. "Child Care Policies and Programs: An International Overview," *Journal of Social Issues*. 47, pp. 179–96.

Kessler, Ronald C., J. Blake Turner, and James S. House. 1988. "Effects of Unemployment on Health

in a Community Survey: Main, Modifying, and Mediating Effects," *Journal of Social Issues*. 44, pp. 69–85.

King, Roy D., and Kathleen McDermott. 1990. "'My Geranium Is Subversive': Some Notes on the Management of Trouble in Prisons," *British Journal of Sociology*. 41 (December), pp. 445–71.

Kirkendall, Lester. 1968. "Understanding the Problems of the Male Virgin," In Isadore Rubin and Lester Kirkendall (eds.), *Sex in the Adolescent Years*. New York: Association, pp. 123–29.

Liebert, Robert, and Rita W. Poulos. 1972. "TV for Kiddies — Truth, Goodness, Beauty, and a Little Bit of Brainwash," *Psychology Today*. 6 (November), pp. 122–24.

Loether, Herman J. 1975. *Problems of Aging*. 2nd ed. Encino, CA: Dickenson.

Lopata, Helena Znaniecka. 1988. "Support Systems of American Urban Widowhood," *Journal of Social Issues*. 44, pp. 113–28.

Lueck, Thomas J. 1992. "Sharing Horrors of Childhood Sexual Abuse, 3 Join Legal Debate," *New York Times*. (May 5), pp. B1+.

Lund, Dale A., et al. 1990. "Stability of Social Support Networks after Later-Life Spousal Bereavement," *Death Studies*. 14, pp. 53–73.

McCrae, Robert R., and Paul T. Costa, Jr. 1988. "Psychological Resilience among Widowed Men and Women: A 10-Year Follow-up of a National Sample," *Journal of Social Issues*. 44, pp. 129–42.

Main, Mary, and Carol George. 1985. Responses of Abused and Disadvantaged Toddlers to Distress in Agemates: A Study in the Day Care Setting," *Developmental Psychology*. 21 (May), pp. 407–12.

Mead, George Herbert. 1930. "Cooley's Contribution to American Social Thought," *American Journal of Sociology*. 35 (March), pp. 693–706.

———. 1934. *Mind, Self and Society*. Chicago: University of Chicago Press.

Mills, Marlene Christine. 1983. "Adolescents' Self-Disclosure in Individual and Group Theme-Centered Modeling, Reflecting, and Probing Interviews," *Psychological Reports*. 53 (December), pp. 691–701.

Mitic, Wayne. 1990. "Parental versus Peer Influence on Adolescents' Alcohol Consumption," *Psychological Reports*. 67 (December), pp. 1273–74.

National Commission on the Causes and Prevention of Violence. 1969. *Violence in America: Historical and Comparative Perspectives*. Washington, DC: U.S. Government Printing Office.

O'Bryant, Shirley L., and Leslie A. Morgan. 1990. "Recent Widows' Kin Support and Orientations to Self-Sufficiency," *Gerontologist*. 30 (June), pp. 391–98.

Oyama, Susan. 1991. "Bodies and Minds: Dualism in Evolutionary Theory," *Journal of Social Issues*. 47, pp. 27–42.

Patten, Sylvia B., et al. 1989. "Posttraumatic Stress Disorder and the Treatment of Sexual Abuse," *Social Work*. 34 (May), 197–203.

Phillips, John L., Jr. 1969. *The Origins of Intellect*. San Francisco: W. H. Freeman.

Piaget, Jean. 1970. "Piaget's Theory," In Paul H. Mussen (ed.), *Carmichael's Manual of Child Psychology*. 3rd ed. New York: John Wiley and Sons, pp. 707–32. (Translation of the Piaget article by Guy Gellerier.)

Powell, Douglas H., and Paul F. Driscoll. 1979. "Middle-class Professionals Face Unemployment," In Peter I. Rose (ed.), *Socialization and the Life Cycle*. New York: St. Martin's Press, pp. 309–19.

Prior, Lindsay. 1991. "Community versus Hospital Care: The Crisis in Psychiatric Provision," *Social Science and Medicine*. 32, pp. 483–89.

Raywid, Mary Anne. 1992. "Why do These Kids Love School?" *Phi Delta Kappan*. (April), pp. 631–33.

Reynolds, Shirley, and Paul Gilbert. 1991. "Psychological Impact of Unemployment: Interactive Effects of Vulnerability and Protective Factors on Depression," *Journal of Counseling Psychology*. 38 (January), pp. 76–84.

Rothstein, Mervyn. 1992. "Isaac Asimov, Whose Thoughts and Books Traveled the Universe, Is Dead at 72," *New York Times*. (April 7), p. B7.

Rushton, J. Philippe, and Ian R. Nicholson. 1988. "Genetic Similarity Theory, Intelligence, and Human Mate Choice," *Ethnology and Sociobiology*. 9 (January), pp. 45–58.

Shapiro, Joan, and Lee Kroeger. 1991. "Is Life Just a Romantic Novel? The Relationship between Attitudes about Intimate Relationships and the Popular Media," *American Journal of Family Therapy*. 19 (Fall), pp. 226–36.

Simmons, Roberta G., Florence Rosenberg, and Morris Rosenberg. 1973. "Disturbance in the Self-Image at Adolescence," *American Sociological Review*. 38 (October), pp. 553–68.

Skinner, B. F. 1972. *Beyond Freedom and Dignity*. New York: Alfred A. Knopf.

Slater, Philip E. 1976. *The Pursuit of Loneliness*. Revised ed. Boston: Beacon Press.

Spitz, René. 1945. "Hospitalism," *The Psychoanalytic Study of the Child*. 1, pp. 53–72.

Straits, Bruce C. 1991. "Bringing Strong Ties Back In: Interpersonal Gateways to Political Information and Influence," *Public Opinion Quarterly*. 55 (Fall), pp. 432–48.

Stroebe, Wolfgang, Margaret S. Stroebe, and Gunther Domittner. 1988. "Individual and Situational Differences in Recovery from Bereavement: A Risk Group Identified," *Journal of Social Issues*. 44, pp. 143–58.

Sutton, John R. 1991. "The Political Economy of Madness: The Expansion of the Asylum in Progressive America," *American Sociological Review*. 56 (October), pp. 665–78.

Thomas, L. Eugene, Robert C. DiGiulio, and Nancy W. Sheehan. 1988. "Identity Loss and Psychological Crisis in Widowhood: A Re-evaluation," *International Journal of Aging and Human Development*. 26, pp. 225–39.

Thompson, Larry W., et al. 1984. "Effects of Bereavement on Self-Perceptions of Physical Health in Elderly Widows and Widowers," *Journal of Gerontology*. 39 (May), pp. 309–14.

Vachon, Mary L.S., and Stanley K. Stylianos. 1988. "The Role of Social Support in Bereavement," *Journal of Social Issues*. 44, pp. 175–90.

Warr, Mark, and Mark Stafford. 1991. "The Influence of Delinquent Peers: What They Think or What They Do?" *Criminology*. 29 (November), pp. 851–64.

Watson, John B. 1924. *Behavior*. New York: W. W. Norton.

Whitbeck, Les B., et al. 1991. "Family Economic Hardship, Parental Support, and Adolescent Self-Esteem," *Social Psychological Quarterly*. 54 (December), 353–63.

Williamson, Jeffrey M., Charles M. Borduin, and Barbara A. Howe. 1991. "The Ecology of Adolescent Maltreatment: A Multilevel Examination of Adolescent Physical Abuse, Sexual Abuse, and Neglect," *Journal of Consulting and Clinical Psychology*. 59 (June), pp. 449–57.

Wilson, Edward O. 1978. *On Human Nature*. Cambridge, MA: Harvard University Press.

Zaslow, Martha J. 1991. "Variation in Child Care Quality and Its Implications for Children," *Journal of Social Issues*. 47, pp. 125–38.

Zisook, Sidney, and Stephen R. Shuchter. 1991. "Depression through the First Year after the Death of a Spouse," *American Journal of Psychiatry*. 148 (October), pp. 1346–52.

Chapter 7

Agnew, Robert. 1985. "A Revised Strain Theory of Delinquency," *Social Forces*. 64 (September), pp. 151–67.

Bacon, Donald C. 1979. "Ripoffs: New American Way of Life," In Leonard Cargan and Jeanne Ballantine (eds.), *Sociological Footprints*. Boston: Houghton Mifflin, pp. 283–90.

Bayles, Michael D. 1991. "A Note on the Death Penalty as the Best Bet," *Criminal Justice Ethics*. 10 (Winter/Spring), pp. 7–10.

Bell, Daniel. 1962. *The End of Ideology*. New York: Free Press.

Benson, Michael L. 1984. "The Fall from Grace," *Criminology*. 22 (November), pp. 573–93.

Box, Steven, and Chris Hale. 1984. "Liberation/Emancipation, Economic Marginalization, or Less Chivalry," *Criminology*. 22 (November), pp. 473–97.

Broad, William J. 1983. "Rising Use of Computer Networks Raises Issues of Security and Law," *New York Times*. (August 26), pp. 1+.

Chambliss, William J. 1969. *Crime and the Legal Process*. New York: McGraw-Hill.

———. 1973. "The Saints and the Roughnecks," *Society*. 11 (December), pp. 24–31.

Chambliss, William J., and Robert B. Seidman. 1971. *Law, Order, and Power*. Reading, MA: Addison-Wesley.

Cheatwood, Derral. 1988. "Is There a Season for Homicide?" *Criminology*. 26 (May), pp. 287–306.

Chin, Ko-Lin. 1993. "Social Sources of Chinese Gang Delinquency," In Joel M. Charon (ed.), *The Meaning of Sociology: A Reader*. 4th ed. Englewood Cliffs: Prentice-Hall, pp. 286–92.

Clayton, Obie, Jr. 1987. "An Empirical Assessment of the Effects of Prison Crowding upon Recidivism Utilizing Aggregate Level Data," *Journal of Criminal Justice*. 15, pp. 201–10.

Clinard, Marshall B. 1974. *Sociology of Deviant Behavior*. 4th ed. New York: Holt, Rinehart and Winston.

Clinard, Marshall B., and Richard Quinney. 1973. *Criminal Behavior Systems: A Typology*. 2nd ed. New York: Holt, Rinehart and Winston.

Cloward, Richard A., and Lloyd E. Ohlin. 1960. *Delinquency and Opportunity: A Theory of Delinquent Gangs*. New York: Free Press.

Cohen, Albert K. 1966. *Deviance and Control*. Englewood Cliffs, NJ: Prentice-Hall.

Cohen, Albert K., and James F. Short, Jr. 1976. "Crime and Juvenile Delinquency," In Robert K. Merton and Robert Nisbet (eds.), *Contemporary Social Problems*. 4th ed. New York: Harcourt Brace Jovanovich, pp. 47–100.

Dombrink, John, James W. Meeker, and Julie Paik. 1988. "Fighting for Fees—Drug Trafficking and the Forfeiture of Attorney's Fees," *Journal of Drug Issues*. 18 (Summer), pp. 421–36.

Dotter, Daniel L., and Julian B. Roebuck. 1988. "The Labeling Approach Reexamined: Interactionism and the Components of Deviance," *Deviant Behavior*. 9, pp. 19–32.

Draper, Theodore. 1989. "The Oliver North Library," *New York Review of Books*. 35 (January 19), pp. 38–45.

Dworkin, Andrea. 1989. *Letters from the War Zone: Writings 1976–1989*. New York: E. P. Dutton.

Economist. 1991. "AIDS Has Strengthened the Case for Legalizing Brothels." 320 (May 7), pp. 28–29.

Fijnaut, Cyrille. 1990. "Organized Crime: A Comparison between the United States of America and Western Europe," *British Journal of Criminology*. 30 (Summer), pp. 321–40.

Foote, C. 1954. "Compelling Appearances in Court-Administration of Bail in Philadelphia," *University of Pennsylvania Law Review*. 102, pp. 1031–79.

Fox, Vernon. 1985. *Introduction to Criminology*. 2nd ed. Englewood Cliffs, NJ: Prentice-Hall.

Gallup, Alec, and Frank Newport. 1991. "Death Penalty Support Remains Strong," *Gallup Poll Monthly*. (June), pp. 40–45.

Gove, Walter R., et al. 1985. "Are Uniform Crime Reports a Valid Indicator of the Index Crimes? An Affirmative Answer with Minor Qualifications," *Criminology*. 23 (August), pp. 451–91.

Grasmick, Harold G., Robert J. Bursik, Jr., and John K. Cochran. 1991. "'Render unto Caesar What Is Caesar's': Religiosity and Taxpayers' Inclinations to Cheat," *Sociological Quarterly*. 32 (May), pp. 251–66.

Green, Mark J., Beverly C. Moore, and Bruce Wasserstein. 1979. "Criminal Law and Corporate Disorder," In Jerome H. Skolnick and Elliot Currie (eds.), *Crisis in American Institutions*. 4th ed. Boston: Little, Brown, pp. 527–47.

Hilts, Philip J. 1991. "Hero in Exposing Science Hoax Paid Dearly," *New York Times*. (March 22), pp. A1+.

Hollinger, Richard C., and John P. Clark. 1982. "Formal and Informal Social Controls of Employee Deviance," *Sociological Quarterly*. 23 (Summer), pp. 333–43.

Hollinger, Richard C., and Lonn Lanza-Kaduce. 1988. "The Process of Criminalization: The Case of

Computer Crime Laws," *Criminology*. 26 (February), pp. 101–26.

Huang, Chien Ju, and James G. Anderson. 1991. Anomie and Deviancy: Reassessing Racial and Social Status. Unpublished paper.

Hunt, Morton M. 1961. "How Does It Come to Be So?" *New Yorker*. 36 (January 28), pp. 39–40+.

Ianni, Francis A. J. 1973. *Ethnic Succession in Organized Crime*. Washington, DC: U.S. Government Printing Office.

Jackson, Patrick G. 1988. "Assessing the Validity of Official Data on Arson," *Criminology*. 26 (February), pp. 181–95.

James, George. 1992. "In Every Category, Crime Reports Fell Last Year in New York City," *New York Times*. (March 25), pp. A1+.

Jensen, Michael C. 1975. "Watergate Donors Still Riding High," *New York Times*. (August 24), sec. 3, pp. 1+.

Johnston, David. 1992. "Survey Shows Number of Rapes Far Higher than Official Figures," *New York Times*. (May 24), p. A14.

Kaplan, Howard B., and Robert J. Johnson. 1991. "Negative Social Sanctions and Juvenile Delinquency: Effects of Labeling in a Model of Deviant Behavior," *Social Science Quarterly*. 72 (March), pp. 98–122.

Klofas, John M., Stan Stojkovic, and David A. Kalinich. 1992. "The Meaning of Correctional Crowding: Steps toward an Index of Severity," *Crime & Delinquency*. 38 (April), pp. 171–88.

Leger, Robert G. 1988. "Perception of Crowding, Racial Antagonism, and Aggression in a Custodial Prison," *Journal of Criminal Justice*. 16, pp. 167–81.

Lein, Laura, et al. 1992. "The Attitudes of Criminal Justice Practitioners toward Sentencing Issues," *Crime & Delinquency*. 38 (April), pp. 189–203.

Lemert, Edwin M. 1951. *Social Pathology*. New York: McGraw-Hill.

Lester, David. 1991. "The Climate of Urban Areas in the United States and Their Rates of Personal Violence (Suicide and Homicide)," *Death Studies*. 15, pp. 611–16.

Lindsey, Linda L. 1990. *Gender Roles: A Sociological Perspective*. Englewood Cliffs, NJ: Prentice-Hall.

Linz, Daniel, Barbara J. Wilson, and Edward Donnerstein. 1992. "Sexual Violence in the Mass Media: Legal Solutions, Warnings, and Mitigation through Education," *Journal of Social Issues*. 48, pp. 145–71.

Manegold, Catherine S. 1992. "A Grim Wasteland," *New York Times*. (June 14), pp. 41+.

Margolin, Leslie. 1992. "Deviance on Record: Techniques for Labeling Child Abusers in Official Documents," *Social Problems*. 39 (February), pp. 58–70.

Massing, Michael. 1989. "Dealing with the Drug Horror," *New York Review of Books*. 36 (March 30), pp. 22–26.

Merton, Robert K. 1968. *Social Theory and Social Structure*. 3rd ed. New York: Free Press.

———. 1976. "Introduction: The Sociology of Social Problems," In Robert K. Merton and Robert Nisbet (eds.), *Contemporary Social Problems*. 4th ed. New York: Harcourt Brace Jovanovich, pp. 3–43.

Messner, Steven F. 1988. "Merton's 'Social Structure and Anomie': The Road Not Taken," *Deviant Behavior*. 9, pp. 33–53.

Messner, Steven F., and Kenneth Tardiff. 1985. "The Social Ecology of Urban Homicide: An Application of the 'Routine Activities' Approach," *Criminology*. 23 (May), pp. 241–67.

Miethe, Terance D., and Charles A. Moore. 1985. "Socioeconomic Disparities under Determinate Sentencing Systems: A Comparison of Preguideline and Postguideline Practices in Minnesota," *Criminology*. 23 (May), pp. 337–63.

Nader, Ralph. 1985. "America's Crime without Criminals," *New York Times*. (May 19), sec. 3, p. 3.

Newfield, Jack, and Paul Dubrul. 1979. "The Political Economy of Organized Crime," In Jerome H. Skolnick and Elliot Currie (eds.), *Crisis in American Institutions*. 4th ed. Boston: Little, Brown, pp. 414–27.

Parmerlee, Marcia A., Janet P. Near, and Tamila C. Jensen. 1982. "Correlates of Whistle-blowers' Perception of Organizational Retaliation," *Administrative Science Quarterly*. 27, pp. 17–34.

Peterson, Ruth D., and William C. Bailey. 1991. "Felony Murder and Capital Punishment: An Examination of the Deterrence Question," *Criminology*. 29 (August), pp. 367–95.

Pittman, David J., and C. Wayne Gordon. 1968. *Revolving Door*. New York: Free Press.

Proctor, Robert N. 1988. *Medicine under the Nazis*. Cambridge, MA: Harvard University Press.

Quinney, Richard. 1974. *Critique of Legal Order: Crime Control in Capitalist Society*. Boston: Little, Brown.

———. 1975. *Criminology*. Boston: Little, Brown.

Reid, Sue Titus. 1982. *Crime and Criminology*. 3rd ed. New York: Holt, Rinehart and Winston.

———. 1985. *Crime and Criminology*. 4th ed. New York: Holt, Rinehart and Winston.

Reiman, Jeffrey H. 1979. *The Rich Get Rich and the Poor Get Prison*. New York: John Wiley and Sons.

Rosecrance, John. 1988. "Whistleblowing in Probation Departments," *Journal of Criminal Justice*. 16, pp. 99–109.

St. Lawrence, Janet, and Doris J. Joyner. 1991. "The Effects of Sexually Violent Rock Music on Males' Acceptance of Violence against Women," *Psychology of Women Quarterly*. 15 (March), pp. 49–63.

Sessions, William S. 1991. "Computer Crimes: An Escalating Crime Trend," FBI *Law Enforcement Bulletin*. 60 (February), pp. 12–15.

Shaw, Clifford R., and Henry D. McKay. 1942. *Juvenile Delinquency and Urban Areas*. Chicago: University of Chicago Press.

Simon, Rita James. 1975. *Women and Crime*. Lexington, MA: D.C. Heath.

Smith, M. Dwayne. 1987. "Patterns of Discrimination in Assessments of the Death Penalty: The Case of Louisiana," *Journal of Criminal Justice*. 15, pp. 279–86.

Stevenson, Robert J. 1990. "The Officer-Enlisted Distinction and Patterns of Organizational Reaction to Social Deviance in the U.S. Military," *Social Forces*. 68 (June), pp. 1191–1209.

Sutherland, Edwin H., and Donald R. Cressey. 1978. *Criminology*. 10th ed. Philadelphia: J. B. Lippincott.

Taylor, Ian, Paul Walton, and Jock Young. 1973. *The New Criminology*. London: Routledge & Kegan Paul.

Thio, Alex. 1978. *Deviant Behavior*. Boston: Houghton Mifflin.

Thornberry, Terence P. 1973. "Race, Socioeconomic Status and Sentencing in the Juvenile Justice System," *Journal of Criminal Law and Criminology*. 64, pp. 90–98.

Thrasher, Frederic M. 1926. *The Gang*. Chicago: University of Chicago Press.

Tittle, Charles R. 1988. "Two Empirical Regulations (Maybe) in Search of an Explanation: Commentary on the Age/Crime Debate," *Criminology*. 26 (February), pp. 75–85.

U.S. Bureau of the Census. 1992. *Statistical Abstract of the United States: 1992*. 112th ed. Washington, DC: U.S. Government Printing Office.

Warr, Mark, and Mark Stafford. 1991. "The Influence of Delinquent Peers: What They Think or What They Do?" *Criminology*. 29 (November), pp. 851–64.

Whyte, William H. 1956. *The Organization Man*. New York: Simon & Schuster.

Wolfgang, Marvin E. 1967. "A Sociological Analysis of Criminal Homicide," In Marvin E. Wolfgang (ed.), *Studies in Homicide*. New York: Harper & Row, pp. 15–28.

Zeisel, Hans. 1973. "FBI Statistics: A Detective Story," *American Bar Association Journal*. 59 (May), p. 510.

Chapter 8

Beeghley, Leonard. 1978. *Social Stratification in America: A Critical Analysis of Theory and Research*. Santa Monica, CA: Goodyear.

Bellah, Robert, et al. 1986. *Habits of the Heart: Individualism and Commitment in American Life*. New York: Harper & Row.

Berelson, Bernard, and Gary A. Steiner. 1964. *Human Behavior*. New York: Harcourt, Brace & World.

Blau, Peter M., and Otis Dudley Duncan. 1967. *The American Occupational Structure*. New York: John Wiley and Sons.

Braddock, Jomills Henry II, and James N. McPartland. 1987. "How Minorities Continue to Be Excluded from Equal Employment Opportunities: Research on Labor Market and Institutional Barriers," *Journal of Social Issues*. 43, pp. 5–39.

Breed, Warren. 1963. "Occupational Mobility and Suicide among White Males," *American Sociological Review*. 28 (April), pp. 179-88.

Bridges, William P., and Wayne J. Villemez. 1991. "Employment Relations and the Labor Market: Integrating Institutional and Market Perspectives," *American Sociological Review*. 56 (December), pp. 748–64.

Coleman, Richard P., and Lee Rainwater, with Kent A. McClelland. 1978. *Social Standing in America: New Dimensions of Class*. New York: Basic Books.

Dahl, Robert A. 1967. *Pluralist Democracy in the United States*. Chicago: Rand McNally.

Davis, Fred. 1959. "The Cabdriver and His Fare: Facets of a Fleeting Relationship," *American Journal of Sociology*. 65 (September), pp. 158–65.

Davis, Kingsley, and William E. Moore. 1945. "Some Principles of Stratification," *American Sociological Review*. 10 (April), pp. 242–49.

Demo, David H., and Ritch C. Savin-Williams. 1983. "Early Adolescent Self-Esteem as a Function of Social Class: Rosenberg and Pearlin Revisited," *American Journal of Sociology*. 88 (January), pp. 763–74.

DiPrete, Thomas A., and David B. Grusky. 1990. "Structure and Trend in the Process of Stratification for American Men and Women," *American Journal of Sociology*. 96 (July), pp. 107–43.

Domhoff, G. William. 1990. *The Power Elite and the State: How Policy Is Made*. New York: Aldine de Gruyter.

Duberman, Lucille. 1976. *Social Inequality: Class and Caste in America*. Philadelphia: J.B. Lippincott.

Economist. 1986. "America's Underclass." (March 15), pp. 29–32.

Economist. 1992. "Wooing Mr. Average." (March 7), pp. 18–19.

Egan, Jack. 1986. "Changing Course," U.S. *News and World Report*. 101 (October 6), pp. 46–47.

Ellis, Robert A., and W. Clayton Lane. 1967. "Social Mobility and Social Isolation," *American Sociological Review*. 32 (April), pp. 237–53.

Faris, Robert E. L., and H. Warren Dunham. 1939. *Mental Disorders in Urban Areas*. Chicago: University of Chicago Press.

Farr, Kathryn Ann. 1988. "Dominance Bonding through the Good Old Boys' Sociability Group," *Sex Roles*. 18 (March), pp. 259–77.

Featherman, David L., and Robert M. Hauser. 1978. *Opportunity and Change*. New York: Academic Press.

Gallup, George, Jr. 1988. "The Sources of Poverty in America," *Gallup Poll Monthly*. (September), pp. 48–51.

Gecas, Viktor, and Monica A. Seff. 1990. "Social Class and Self-Esteem: Psychological Centrality, Compensation, and the Relative Effects of Work and Home," *Social Psychology Quarterly*. 53 (June), pp. 165–73.

Gerth, H. H., and C. Wright Mills (eds.). 1946. *From Max Weber: Essays in Sociology*. New York: Oxford University Press.

Gilbert, Dennis, and Joseph A. Kahl. 1982. *The American Class Structure*. Revised ed. Homewood, IL: Dorsey Press.

Gold, Ray. 1952. "Janitors versus Tenants: A Status-Income Dilemma," *American Journal of Sociology*. 57 (March), pp. 486–93.

Grusky, David B., and Robert H. Hauser. 1984. "Comparative Social Mobility Revisited: Models of Convergence and Divergence in 16 Countries," *American Sociological Review*. 49 (February), pp. 19–38.

Gurley, John G. 1984. "Marx's Contributions and Their Relevance Today," *American Economic Review*. 74 (May), pp. 110–15.

Hagan, John. 1990. "The Gender Stratification of Income Inequality among Lawyers," *Social Forces*. 68 (March), pp. 835–55.

Hall, Wayne. 1986. "Social Class and Survival on the S.S. Titanic," *Social Science and Medicine*. 22, pp. 687–90.

Haller, Max, et al. 1985. "Patterns of Career Mobility and Structural Positions in Advanced Capitalist Societies: A Comparison of Men in Austria, France, and the United States," *American Sociological Review*. 50 (October), pp. 579–603.

Hodge, Robert W., Paul M. Siegel, and Peter H. Rossi. 1966. "Occupational Prestige in the United States: 1925–1963," In Reinhard Bendix and Seymour Martin Lipset (eds.), *Class, Status, and Power*. New York: Free Press, pp. 322-34.

Hodges, Harold M. 1964. *Social Stratification*. Cambridge, MA: Schenkman.

Howell, Joseph T. 1973. *Hard Living on Clay Street*. Garden City, NY: Doubleday.

Illsley, Raymond. 1990. "Comparative Review of Sources, Methodology and Knowledge," *Social Science & Medicine*. 31, pp. 229–36.

Ishida, Hiroshi, John H. Goldthorpe, and Robert Erikson. 1991. "Intergenerational Class Mobility in Postwar Japan," *American Journal of Sociology*. 96 (January), pp. 954–92.

Kahl, Joseph A. 1957. *The American Class Structure*. New York: Rinehart Press.

Katz, Claudio J. 1992. "Marx on the Peasantry: Class in Itself or Class in Struggle?" *Review of Politics*. 54 (Winter), pp. 50–71.

Kessin, Kenneth. 1971. "Social and Psychological Consequences of Intergenerational Occupational Mobility," *American Journal of Sociology*. 77 (July), pp. 1–18.

Kessler, Ronald C., and Paul D. Cleary. 1980. "Social Class and Psychological Distress," *American Sociological Review*. 45 (June), pp. 463–78.

Koepp, Stephen. 1986. "Playing the New Tax Game," *Time*. 128 (October 13), pp. 66–67.

Kohn, Melvin L., 1976. "Interaction of Social Class and Other Factors in the Etiology of Schizophrenia," *American Journal of Psychiatry*. 133, pp. 179–80.

Kohn, Melvin L., et al. 1990. "Position in the Class Structure and Psychological Functioning in the United States, Japan, and Poland," *American Journal of Sociology*. 95 (January), pp. 964–1008.

Lahelma, Eero, and Tapani Valkonen. 1990. "Health and Social Inequities in Finland and Elsewhere," *Social Science & Medicine*. 31, pp. 257–65.

Lamb, H. Richard. 1990. "Will We Save the Homeless Mentally Ill?" *American Journal of Psychiatry*. 147 (May), pp. 649–51.

526

Landale, Nancy C., and Avery M. Guest. 1990. "Generation, Ethnicity, and Occupational Opportunity in Late 19th Century America," *American Sociological Review*. 55 (April), pp. 280–96.

Landrine, Hope. 1987. "On the Politics of Madness: A Preliminary Analysis of the Relationships between Social Roles and Psychotherapy," *Genetic, Social, & General Psychology Monographs*. 113 (August), pp. 341–406.

Laumann, Edward O. 1966. *Prestige and Association in an Urban Community*. Indianapolis: Bobbs-Merrill.

Lenski, Gerhard E. 1966. *Power and Privilege*. New York: McGraw-Hill.

Lenski, Gerhard E., and Jean Lenski. 1982. *Human Societies*. 4th ed. New York: McGraw-Hill.

Lerner, Michael A. 1982. "The Elite Meet in Retreat," *Newsweek*. 100 (August 2), pp. 21–22.

Logan, John R., and O. Andrew Collver. 1983. "Residents' Perceptions of Suburban Community Differences," *American Sociological Review*. 48 (June), pp. 428–33.

McAdoo, Harriette P. 1982. "Stress Absorbing Systems in Black Families," *Family Relations*. 31 (October), pp. 479–88.

Maloney, Lawrence. 1981. "America's New Middle Class," *U.S. News and World Report*. 90 (March 30), pp. 39-41+.

Marx, Karl, and Friedrich Engels. 1959. "Manifesto of the Communist Party," In Lewis S. Feuer (ed.), *Marx and Engels: Basic Writings on Politics and Philosophy*. Trans. N. I. Stone. Garden City, NY: Anchor Books, pp. 6–41.

Mergenhagen, Paula. 1991. "Doing the Career Shuffle," *American Demographics*. 13 (November), pp. 42-44+.

Mills, C. Wright. 1956. *The Power Elite*. New York: Oxford University Press.

Morrison, Ann M., and Mary Ann Von Glinow. 1990. "Women and Minorities in Management," *American Psychologist*. 45 (February), pp. 200–08.

Moskos, Charles C. 1969. "Why Men Fight," *Transaction*. 7 (November), pp. 13–23.

Nasar, Sylvia. 1992a. "Fed Gives New Evidence of 80's Gains by Richest," *New York Times*. (April 21), pp. A1+.

———. 1992b. "Those Born Wealthy or Poor Usually Stay So, Studies Say," *New York Times*. (May 18), pp. A1+.

Newport, Frank. 1990. "Tax Reform Fails to Achieve Its Goals," *Gallup Poll Monthly*. (March), pp. 6–10.

Petersen, Carol Dawn. 1992. "Can JOBS Help the Underclass Break the Cycle of Poverty?" *Journal of Economic Issues*. 26 (March), pp. 243–54.

Pomeroy, Wardell B. 1972. *Dr. Kinsey and the Institute for Sex Research*. New York: Harper & Row.

Rainwater, Lee. 1964. "Marital Sexuality in Four Cultures of Poverty," *Journal of Marriage and the Family*. 26 (November), pp. 457–66.

Reiss, Ira L. 1980. *Family Systems in America*. 3rd ed. New York: Holt, Rinehart and Winston.

Reiss, Ira L., and Gary R. Lee. 1988. *Family Systems in America*. 4th ed. New York: Holt, Rinehart and Winston.

Rossides, Daniel W. 1976. *The American Class System*. Boston: Houghton Mifflin.

Rubin, Lillian Breslow. 1983. "Blue-Collar Marriage and the Sexual Revolution," In Arlene Skolnick and Jerome H. Skolnick (eds.), *Family in Transition*. 4th ed. Boston: Little, Brown, pp. 234–50.

Runciman, W. G. 1990. "How Many Classes Are There in Contemporary British Society?" *Sociology*. 24 (August), pp. 377–96.

Schatzman, Leonard, and Anselm Strauss. 1972. "Social Class and Modes of Communication," In Saul D. Feldman and Gerald W. Thielbar (eds.), *Life Styles: Diversity in American Society*. Boston: Little, Brown. pp. 48–60.

Schneider, Jane, and Peter Schneider. 1991. "Sex and Respectability in an Age of Fertility Decline: A Sicilian Case Study," *Social Science & Medicine*. 33, pp. 885–95.

Seligman, Martin E.P. 1988. "Boomer Blues," *Psychology Today*. 22 (October), pp. 50–55.

Sennett, Richard, and Jonathan Cobb. 1973. *The Hidden Injuries of Class*. New York: Vintage Books.

Shiller, Bradley R. 1970. "Stratified Opportunities: The Essence of 'The Vicious Circle,'" *American Journal of Sociology*. 76 (November), pp. 426–41.

Simon, William, and John Gagnon. 1972. "Sex, Marriage, and Social Class," In Saul D. Feldman and Gerald W. Thielbar (eds.), *Life Styles: Diversity in American Society*. Boston: Little, Brown, pp. 86–88.

Simpson, Ida Harper, David Stark, and Robert A. Jackson. 1988. "Class Identification Processes of Married, Working Men and Women," *American Sociological Review*. 53 (April), pp. 284–93.

Snarey, John R., and George E. Vaillant. 1985. "How Lower- and Working-Class Youth Become Middle-Class Adults: The Association between Ego Defense Mechanisms and Upward Social Mobility," *Child Development*. 56 (August), pp. 899–910.

Solon, Gary R. 1992. "Intergenerational Mobility in

the United States," *American Economic Review*. 82 (June), pp. 393–408.

Sorokin, Pitrim A. 1927. *Social Mobility*. New York: Harper & Brothers.

Srole, Leo, Thomas S. Langner, Stanley T. Michael, Marvin K. Opler, and Thomas A. C. Rennie. 1962. *Mental Health in the Metropolis*. New York: McGraw-Hill.

Steinmetz, George, and Erik Olin Wright. 1990. "Reply to Lindner and Houghton," *American Journal of Sociology*. 96 (November), pp. 736–40.

Surrey, Stanley A. 1973. *Pathways to Tax Reform*. Cambridge, MA: Harvard University Press.

Syme, S. Leonard, and Lisa F. Berkman. 1981. "Social Class, Susceptibility, and Sickness," In Peter Conrad and Rochelle Kern (eds.), *The Sociology of Health and Illness*. New York: St. Martin's Press, pp. 35–44.

Townsend, John Marshall, and Gary D. Levy. 1990. "Effects of Potential Partners' Physical Attractiveness and Socioeconomic Status on Sexuality and Partner Selection," *Archives of Sexual Behavior*. 19 (April), pp. 149–64.

Treiman, Donald J. 1977. *Occupational Prestige in Comparative Perspective*. New York: Academic Press.

Tumin, Melvin M. 1953. "Some Principles of Stratification: A Critical Analysis," *American Sociological Review*. 18 (August), pp. 387–94.

———. 1957. "Some Unapplauded Consequences of Social Mobility in a Mass Society," *Social Forces*. 36 (October), pp. 32–36.

———. 1967. *Social Stratification*. Englewood Cliffs, NJ: Prentice-Hall.

Turner, Jonathan H., and Charles E. Starnes. 1976. *Inequality: Privilege and Poverty in America*. Pacific Palisades, CA: Goodyear.

U.S. Bureau of the Census. 1986. *Household Wealth and Asset Ownership: 1984, Current Population Reports*. Series P-70, Washington, DC: U.S. Government Printing Office.

U.S. Bureau of the Census. 1992. *Statistical Abstract of the United States: 1992*. 112th ed. Washington, DC: U.S. Government Printing Office.

Warner, W. Lloyd, and Paul S. Lunt. 1941. *The Social Life of a Modern Community*. New Haven, CT: Yale University Press.

Whitener, Leslie A. 1985. "The Migrant Farm Work Force: Differences in Attachment to Farmwork," *Rural Sociology*. 50 (Summer), pp. 163–80.

Wing, Steve. 1988. "Social Inequalities in the Decline of Coronary Mortality," *American Journal of Public Health*. 78 (November), pp. 1415–16.

Wong, Raymond Sin-Kwok. 1990. "Understanding Cross-national Variation in Occupational Mobility," *American Sociological Review*. 55 (August), pp. 560–73.

Wright, Erik Olin. 1985. *Classes*. London: Verso.

Wright, Erik Olin, and Donmoon Cho. 1992. "The Relative Permeability of Class Boundaries to Cross-Class Friendships: A Comparative Study of the United States, Canada, Sweden, and Norway," *American Sociological Review*. 57 (February), pp. 85–102.

Wright, Erik Olin, and Bill Martin. 1987. "The Transformation of the American Class Structure, 1960–1980," *American Journal of Sociology*. 93 (July), pp. 1–29.

Zimmerman, L. J. 1965. *Poor Lands, Rich Lands: The Widening Gap*. New York: Random House.

Chapter 9

Aboud, Frances E. 1984. "Social and Cognitive Bases of Ethnic Identity Constancy," *Journal of Genetic Psychology*. 145 (December), pp. 217–30.

Allen, Sheila, and Marie Macey. 1990. "Race and Ethnicity in the European Context," *British Journal of Sociology*. 41 (September), pp. 375–93.

Allport, Gordon W. 1954. *The Nature of Prejudice*. Cambridge, MA: Addison-Wesley.

Atkinson, Donald R., and Yoshiko J. Matsushita. 1991. "Japanese-American Acculturation, Counseling Style, Counselor Ethnicity, and Perceived Counselor Credibility," *Journal of Counseling Psychology*. 38 (October), pp. 473–78.

Bahr, Howard M., Bruce A. Chadwick, and Joseph H. Stauss. 1979. *American Ethnicity*. Lexington, MA: D.C. Heath.

Bailyn, Bernard, et al. 1977. *The Great Republic*. Lexington, MA: D.C. Heath.

Berry, Brewton, and Henry L. Tischler. 1978. *Race and Ethnic Relations*. 4th ed. Boston: Houghton Mifflin.

Bogardus, Emory. 1968. "Comparing Racial Distance in Ethiopia, South Africa, and the United States," *Sociology and Social Research*. 52 (January), pp. 149–56.

Bound, John, and Richard B. Freeman. 1992. "What Went Wrong? The Erosion of Relative Earnings and Employment among Young Black Men in the 1980s," *Quarterly Journal of Economics*. 107 (February), pp. 201–32.

528

Branch, Taylor. 1988. *Parting the Waters: America in the King Years*, 1954–63. New York: Simon & Schuster.

Brown, Dee. 1972. *Bury My Heart at Wounded Knee*. New York: Bantam Books.

Campbell, Babe Moore. 1982. "Black Executives and Corporate Stress," *New York Times Magazine*. (December 12), pp. 36–39+.

Campbell, Ernest Q., and Thomas Pettigrew. 1959. *Christians in Racial Crisis*. Washington, DC: Public Affairs Press.

Celano, Mariane P., and Forrest B. Tyler. 1991. "Behavioral Acculturation among Vietnamese Refugees in the United States," *Journal of Social Psychology*. 131 (June), pp. 373–85.

Cleaver, Eldridge. 1970. *Soul on Ice*. New York: Dell.

Congressional Quarterly. 1992. "Panel Ups Funds for Internees." 50 (April 4), p. 882.

Darden, Joe T. 1990. "Differential Access to Housing in the Suburbs," *Journal of Black Studies*. 21 (September), pp. 15–22.

Davenport, Judith A., and Joseph Davenport III. 1987. "Native American Suicide: A Durkheimian Analysis," *Social Casework*. 68 (November), pp. 533–39.

Deloria, Vine, Jr. 1981. "Native Americans: The American Indian Today," *Annals of the American Academy of Political and Social Science*. 454 (March), pp. 139–49.

DeParle, Jason. 1990. "1989 Surge in Anti-Semitic Acts Is Reported by B'nai B'rith," *New York Times*. (January 20), p. 10.

Dollard, John. 1937. *Caste and Class in a Southern Town*. New Haven, CT: Yale University Press.

Dollard, John, Leonard Doob, Neal E. Miller, O.H. Mowrer, and R. R. Sears. 1939. *Frustration and Aggression*. New Haven, CT: Yale University Press.

Duster, Troy. 1987. "Purpose and Bias," *Society*. 24 (January/February), pp. 8–12.

Economist. 1991. "Irish-Americans: The Second Coming." 320 (July 27), pp. 26–27.

Eisenbruch, Maurice. 1988. "The Mental Health of Refugee Children and Their Cultural Development," *International Migration Review*. 22 (Summer), pp. 282–300.

Engelberg, Stephen. 1992. "Muslims Tell of Serbs' 'Ethnic Cleansing,'" *New York Times*. (July 31), p. A3.

Fallows, Marjorie R. 1979. *Irish Americans: Identity and Assimilation*. Englewood Cliffs, NJ: Prentice-Hall.

Feagin, Joe R. 1989. *Racial & Ethnic Relations*. 3rd ed. Englewood Cliffs, NJ: Prentice-Hall.

Felsman, J. Kirk, et al. 1990. "Estimates of Psychological Distress among Vietnamese Refugees: Adoles-

cents, Unaccompanied Minors and Young Adults," *Social Science and Medicine*. 31, pp. 1251–56.

Fitzpatrick, Joseph P. 1975. "Puerto Ricans in Perspective: The Meaning of Migration to the Mainland," In Norman R. Yetman and C. Hoy Steele (eds.), *Majority and Minority*. 2nd ed. Boston: Allyn & Bacon, pp. 297–304.

Fitzpatrick, Joseph P., and Lourdes Travieso Parker. 1981. "Hispanic-Americans in the Eastern United States," *Annals of the American Academy of Political and Social Science*. 454 (March), pp. 98–110.

Fost, Dan. 1991. "American Indians in the 1990s," *American Demographics*. 13 (December), pp. 26–29+.

Fugita, Stephen S., and David J. O'Brien. 1985. "Structural Assimilation, Ethnic Group Membership, and Political Participation among Japanese Americans: A Research Note," *Social Forces*. 63 (June), pp. 986–95.

Gallup, George, Jr., and Frank Newport. 1991. "Blacks and Whites Differ on Civil Rights Progress," *Gallup Poll Monthly*. (August), pp. 54–58.

Galster, George C. 1990. "Racial Steering in Urban Housing Markets: A Review of the Audit Evidence," *Review of Black Political Economy*. 18 (Winter), pp. 105–29.

Golden, Tim. 1992. "Mexican Women, Doffing Old Ways, Join Exodus," *New York Times*. (June 7), pp. 1+.

Gonzalez, Judith Teresa. 1988. "Dilemmas of the High-Achieving Chicana: The Double-Bind Factor in Male/Female Relationships," *Sex Roles*. 18 (April), pp. 367–80.

Greeley, Andrew. 1977. *The American Catholic*. New York: Basic Books.

————. 1988. "The Success and Assimilation of Irish Protestants and Irish Catholics in the United States," *Sociology and Social Research*. 72 (July), pp. 229–36.

Green, Constance McLaughlin. 1967. *The Secret City: A History of Race Relations in the Nation's Capital*. Princeton, NJ: Princeton University Press.

Guarnaccia, Peter J., Byron J. Good, and Arthur Kleinman. 1990. "A Critical Review of Epidemiological Studies of Puerto Rican Mental Health," *American Journal of Psychiatry*. 147 (November), pp. 1449–56.

Hodge, William. 1981. *The First Americans: Then and Now*. New York: Holt, Rinehart and Winston.

Ikels, Charlotte. 1985. "Parental Perspectives on the Significance of Marriage," *Journal of Marriage and the Family*. 47 (May), pp. 253–64.

Jeter, Kris. 1990. "Kings and Scapegoats in Twentieth

Century Families and Corporations," *Marriage and Family Review*. 15, pp. 225–42.

Johnson, A. Michael. 1990. "The 'Only Joking' Defense: Attribution Bias or Impression Management?" *Psychological Reports*. 67, pp. 1051–56.

Judd, Dennis R. 1991. "Segregation Forever?" *Nation*. 253 (December 9), pp. 740+.

Judd, Eleanore Parelman. 1990. "Intermarriage and the Maintenance of Religio-Ethnic Identity: The Denver Jewish Community," *Journal of Comparative Family Studies*. 21 (Summer), pp. 251–68.

Katz, David, and Kenneth Braly. 1933. "Racial Stereotypes of One Hundred College Students," *Journal of Abnormal and Social Psychology*. 28 (October), pp. 280–90.

Kelley, Robin D. G. 1992. "Straight from Underground," *Nation*. 254 (June 8), pp. 793–96.

Kitano, Harry H. L. 1981. "Asian-Americans: The Chinese, Japanese, Koreans, Philippinos, and Southeast Asians," *Annals of the American Academy of Political and Social Science*. 454 (March), pp. 125–38.

Kluegel, James R. 1990. "Trends in Whites' Explanations of the Black-White Gap in Socioeconomic Status, 1977–1989," *American Sociological Review*. 55 (August), pp. 512-25.

Krafft, Susan. 1991. "New York Puerto Ricans: Living in Two Worlds," *American Demographics*. 13 (April), p. 49.

Krieger, Nancy. 1990. "Racial and Gender Discrimination: Risk Factors for High Blood Pressure?" *Social Science and Medicine*. 30, pp. 1273–81.

Kutner, Bernard, Carol Wilkins, and P.R. Yarrow. 1952. "Verbal Attitudes and Overt Behavior Involving Racial Prejudice," *Journal of Abnormal and Social Psychology*. 47 (July), pp. 649–52.

Lacy, Dan. 1972. *The White Use of Blacks in America*. New York: McGraw-Hill.

LaPierce, Richard T. 1934. "Attitudes vs. Actions," *Social Forces*. 13 (October), pp. 230–37.

Lee, Sharon M., and Keiko Yamanaka. 1990. "Patterns of Asian American Intermarriage and Marital Assimilation," *Journal of Comparative Family Studies*. 21 (Summer), pp. 287–305.

Leighton, Alexander H. 1964. *The Governing of Men*. New York: Octagon Books. (Originally published in Princeton, NJ: Princeton University Press, 1945.)

Longoria, Thomas, Jr., Robert D. Wrinkle, and J. L. Polinard. 1990. "Mexican American Voter Registration," *Social Science Quarterly*. 71 (June), pp. 356–71.

Lukas, J. Anthony. 1985. *Common Ground*. New York:

Alfred A. Knopf.

Massey, Douglas S. 1990. "American *Apartheid*: Segregation and the Making of the Underclass," *American Journal of Sociology*. 96 (September), pp. 329–57.

Massey, Douglas S., and Mitchell L. Eggers. 1990. "The Ecology of Inequality: Minorities and the Concentration of Poverty, 1970–1980," *American Journal of Sociology*. 95 (March), pp. 1153–88.

Massey, Douglas S., and Eric Fong. 1990. "Segregation and Neighborhood Quality: Blacks, Hispanics, and Asians in the San Francisco Metropolitan Area," *Social Forces*. 69 (September), pp. 15–32.

Moore, John W., and Harry Pachon. 1976. *Mexican Americans*. 2nd ed. Englewood Cliffs, NJ: Prentice-Hall.

Morse, Janice M., David E. Young, and Lise Swartz. 1991. "Cree Indian Healing Practices and Western Health Care: A Comparative Analysis," *Social Science & Medicine*. 32, pp. 1361–66.

New York Times. 1981. "750 Attend Klan Rally for Fishermen in Texas." (February 26), p. 36.

Nieves, Evelyn. 1992. "Powwows: Path of New Traditions," *New York Times*. (July 23), p. B4.

Novak, Michael. 1972. *The Rise of the Unmeltable Ethnics*. New York: Macmillan.

Okimoto, Daniel I. 1971. *American in Disguise*. New York: John Weatherhill.

Pachon, Harry P., and John W. Moore. 1981. "Mexican Americans," *Annals of the American Academy of Political and Social Science*. 454 (March), pp. 111–24.

Prewitt-Diaz, Joseph O. 1984. "Migrant Students' Perceptions of Teachers, School and Self," *Perceptual and Motor Skills*. 58 (April), pp. 391-94.

Quigley, Harold E., and Charles Y. Glock. 1979. *Anti-Semitism in America*. New York: Free Press.

Robbins, Susan P. 1984. "Anglo Concepts and Indian Reality: A Study of Juvenile Delinquency," *Social Casework*. 65 (April), pp. 235–41.

Rosenberg, Morris, and Roberta G. Simmons. 1971. *Black and White Self-Esteem: The Urban School Child*. Washington, DC: American Sociological Association.

Rosenthal, Andrew. 1988. "Foes Accuse Bush Campaign of Inflaming Racial Tension," *New York Times*. (October 24), pp. A1+.

Rosenthal, Doreen A., and S. Shirley Feldman. 1990. "The Acculturation of Chinese Immigrants: Perceived Effects on Family Functioning of Length of Residence in Two Cultural Contexts," *Journal of Genetic Psychology*. 151 (December), pp. 495–514.

Salamon, Sonya. 1985. "Ethnic Communities and the

Structure of Agriculture," *Rural Sociology.* 50 (Fall), pp. 323-40.

Schmidt, William E. 1981. "Dismissed Workers Call Meat Plant Sale a 'Shame,'" *New York Times.* (November 7), p. 7.

Sigelman, Lee. 1991. "If You Prick Us, Do We Not Bleed? If You Tickle Us, Do We Not Laugh? Jews and Pocketbook Voting," *Journal of Politics.* 53 (November), pp. 977–92.

Simpson, George Eaton, and J. Milton Yinger. 1985. *Racial and Cultural Minorities: An Analysis of Prejudice and Discrimination.* 5th ed. New York: Plenum Press.

Sklare, Marshall. 1971. *America's Jews.* New York: Random House.

Sue, David, Diane M. Sue, and Steve Ino. 1990. "Assertiveness and Social Anxiety in Chinese-American Women," *Journal of Psychology.* 124 (March), pp. 155–63.

Taylor, Stuart, Jr. 1986. "Justices to Hear Plea on Internment of Japanese-Americans," *New York Times.* (November 18), p. A26.

Thomas, Melvin E., and Michael Hughes. 1986. "The Continuing Significance of Race: A Study of Race, Class, and Quality of Life in America, 1972–1985," *American Sociological Review.* 51 (December), pp. 830–41.

Timberlake, Elizabeth M., and Kim Oanh Cook. 1984. "Social Work and the Vietnamese Refugee," *Social Work.* 29 (March/April), pp. 108–13.

Twain, Mark. 1973. *Mark Twain and the Three R's.* Maxwell Geismar (ed.). Indianapolis: Bobbs-Merrill.

U.S. Bureau of the Census. 1992. *Statistical Abstract of the United States: 1992.* 112th ed. Washington, DC: U.S. Government Printing Office.

Utley, Robert M. 1963. *The Last Days of the Sioux Nation.* New Haven, CT: Yale University Press.

Vander Zanden, James W. 1972. *American Minority Relations.* 2nd ed. New York: Ronald Press.

Vosburgh, Miriam G., and Richard N. Juliani. 1990. "Contrasts in Ethnic Family Patterns: The Irish and the Italians," *Journal of Comparative Family Studies.* 21 (Summer), pp. 269–86.

Waldrop, Judith. 1990. "Shades of Black," *American Demographics.* 12 (September), pp. 30–34.

Waxman, Chaim I. 1981. "The Fourth Generation Grows Up: The Contemporary American Jewish Community," *Annals of American Political and Social Science.* 454 (March), pp. 70–85.

Webster, Peggy Lovell, and Jeffrey W. Dwyer. 1988. "The Cost of Being Nonwhite in Brazil," *Sociology and Social Research.* 72 (January), pp. 136–38.

Willen, Mark. 1988. "World War II Internees to Get Cash, Apology," *Congressional Quarterly.* 46 (April 23), p. 1081.

Williams, Lena. 1988. "Uneasy Mingling: When Small Talk at Parties Tackles Large Racial Issues," *New York Times.* (October 21), p. A15.

Wong, Bernard. 1987. "The Role of Ethnicity in Enclave Enterprises: A Study of the Chinese Garment Factories in New York City," *Human Organization.* 46 (Summer), pp. 120–30.

Chapter 10

American Demographics. 1991. "The Cost of Hiring the Disabled." 13 (March), p. 12.

Atchley, Robert C. 1989. "A Continuity Theory of Normal Aging," *Gerontology.* 29 (April), pp. 183–90.

Battista, Carolyn. 1992. "Professionals Stand by to Plan Care for Elderly," *New York Times.* (May 3), sec. 13, p. 4.

Biegel, David E., et al. 1989. "Unmet Needs and Barriers to Service Delivery for the Blind and Visually Impaired Elderly," *Gerontologist.* 29 (February), pp. 86–91.

Blum, Linda, and Vicki Smith. 1988. "Women's Mobility in the Corporation: A Critique of the Politics of Optimism," *Signs.* 13 (Spring), pp. 528–45.

Bosse, Raymond, et al. 1991. "How Stressful Is Retirement?: Findings from the Normative Aging Study," *Journal of Gerontology.* 46, pp. 9–14.

Bourestom, Norman, and Leon Pastalan. 1981. "The Effects of Relocation on the Elderly," *Gerontologist.* 21 (February), pp. 4–7.

Bowe, Frank. 1978. *Handicapping America.* New York: Harper & Row.

Bowling, Ann, and Peter D. Browne. 1991. "Social Networks, Health, and Emotional Well-being among the Oldest Old in London," *Journal of Gerontology.* 46, pp. S20–S32.

Bretl, Daniel J., and Joanne Cantor. 1988. "The Portrayal of Men and Women in U.S. Television Commercials: A Recent Content Analysis and Trends over 15 Years," *Sex Roles.* 18 (May), pp. 595–609.

Butler, Robert N. 1975. *Why Survive? Being Old in America.* New York: Harper & Row.

Carter, William B., et al. 1991. "Participation of Older Adults in Health Programs and Research: A Critical Review of the Literature," *Gerontologist.* 31 (October), pp. 584–92.

Cohen, Carl I., et al. 1985. "Social Networks, Stress, and Physical Health: A Longitudinal Study of an Inner-City Elderly Population," *Journal of Gerontology*. 40 (July), pp. 478–86.

Cox, Sue. 1981. *Female Psychology*. 2nd ed. New York: St. Martin's Press.

Creecy, Robert F. 1985. "Loneliness among the Elderly: A Causal Approach," *Journal of Gerontology*. 40 (July), pp. 487–93.

Cumming, Elaine, and William Henry. 1961. *Growing Old: The Process of Disengagement*. New York: Basic Books.

Davis, Donald M. 1990. "Portrayals of Women in Prime-Time Network Television: Some Demographic Characteristics," *Sex Roles*. 22 (September), pp. 325–32.

Duff, Raymond S., and August B. Hollingshead. 1968. *Sickness and Society*. New York: Harper & Row.

Emener, William G. 1991. "Empowerment in Rehabilitation: An Empowerment Philosophy for Rehabilitation in the 20th Century," *Journal of Rehabilitation*. 57 (October/November/December), pp. 7–12.

Feiring, Candice, and Michael Lewis. 1991. "The Transition from Middle Childhood to Early Adolescence: Sex Differences in the Social Network and Perceived Self-Competence," *Sex Roles*. 24 (April), pp. 489–509.

Fine, Michelle, and Adrienne Asch. 1988. "Disability beyond Stigma: Social Interaction, Discrimination, and Activism," *Journal of Social Issues*. 44, pp. 3–21.

Freeman, Jo. 1975. *The Politics of Women's Liberation*. New York: David McKay.

———. 1980. "The Roots of Revolt," In Sheila Ruth (ed.), *Issues in Feminism*. Boston: Houghton Mifflin, pp. 511–24.

Friedan, Betty. 1963. *The Feminine Mystique*. New York: W. W. Norton.

Frieze, Irene Hanson. 1983. "Investigating the Causes and Consequences of Marital Rape," *Signs*. 8 (Spring), pp. 532–53.

Gilderbloom, John I., and Mark S. Rosentraub. 1990. "Creating the Accessible City: Proposals for Providing Housing and Transportation for Low Income, Elderly and Disabled People," *American Journal of Economics and Sociology*. 49 (July), pp. 271–82.

Gitlin, Todd. 1989. *The Sixties: Years of Hope, Days of Rage*. New York: Bantam Books.

Groce, Nora, and Jessica Scheer. 1990. "Introduction to Cross-Cultural Perspectives on Disability," *Social Science & Medicine*. 30, pp. v–vi.

Gross, Jane. 1992. "Suffering in Silence No More: Fighting Sexual Harassment," *New York Times*. (July 13), pp. A1+.

Gubrium, Jaber F. 1975. *Living and Dying at Murray Manor*. New York: St. Martin's Press.

Hacker, Helen Mayer. 1951. "Women as a Minority Group," *Social Forces*. 30 (October), pp. 60–69.

Hamilton, Mykol C. 1991. "Masculine Bias in the Attribution of Parenthood," *Psychology of Women Quarterly*. 15 (September), pp. 393-402.

Hennig, Margaret, and Anne Jardim. 1977. *The Managerial Woman*. Garden City, NY: Anchor Press.

Herman, Judith Lewis. 1988. "Considering Sex Offenders: A Model of Addiction," *Signs*. 13 (Summer), pp. 695–724.

Hinde, R. A. 1991. "A Biologist Looks at Anthropology," *Man*. 26 (December), pp. 583–608.

Holmes, Gary E., and Ronald H. Karst. 1990. "The Institutionalization of Disability Myths: Impact on Vocational Rehabilitation Services," *Journal of Rehabilitation*. 56 (January/February/March), pp. 20–27.

Hultsch, David F., and Francine Deutsch. 1981. *Adult Development and Aging*. New York: McGraw-Hill.

Jenkins, Richard. 1991. "Disability and Social Stratification," *British Journal of Sociology*. 42 (December), pp. 557–80.

Jones, Brian J., et al. 1991. "A Survey of Fortune 500 Corporate Policies Concerning the Psychiatrically Handicapped," *Journal of Rehabilitation*. 57 (October/November/December), pp. 31–35.

Katz, Elias. 1973. "The Mentally Retarded," In Don Spiegel and Patricia Keith-Spiegel (eds.), *Outsiders USA*. San Francisco: Rinehart Press, pp. 132–53.

Kornblum, William, and Joseph Julian. 1989. *Social Problems*. 6th ed. Englewood Cliffs, NJ: Prentice-Hall.

Landrine, Hope. 1988. "Depression and Stereotypes of Women: Preliminary Analyses of the Gender-Role Hypothesis," *Sex Roles*. 19 (October), pp. 527–41.

Langway, Lynn. 1982. "A Bad Year for the Disabled," *Newsweek*. 99 (February 8), pp. 82+.

Leidig, Margorie Whittaker. 1981. "Violence against Women: A Feminist-Psychological Analysis," In Sue Cox (ed.), *Female Psychology*. 2nd ed. New York: St. Martin's Press, pp. 190–205.

Leventhal, Jay D. 1992. "Blind, Not Incompetent," *New York Times*. (August 13), p. A19.

Lindsey, Linda L. 1990. *Gender Roles: A Sociological Perspective*. Englewood Cliffs, NJ: Prentice-Hall.

532

Logue, Barbara J. 1991. "Women at Risk: Predictors of Financial Stress for Retired Women Workers," *Gerontologist*. 31 (October), pp. 657–65.

Lont, Cynthia M. 1990. "The Roles Assigned to Females and Males in Non-Music Radio Programming," *Sex Roles*. 22 (June), pp. 661–68.

Lovdal, Lynn T. 1989. "Sex Role Messages in Television Commercials: An Update," *Sex Roles*. 21 (December), pp. 715–34.

Luszcz, Mary A., and Karen M. Fitzgerald. 1986. "Understanding Cohort Differences in Cross-Generational, Self, and Peer Perceptions," *Journal of Gerontology*. 41 (March), pp. 234–40.

McCaul, Kevin D., et al. 1990. "Understanding Attributions of Victim Blame for Rape: Sex, Violence, and Foreseeability," *Journal of Applied Social Psychology*. 20 (January), pp. 1–26.

McKinney, Kathleen. 1990. "Sexual Harassment of University Faculty by Colleagues and Students," *Sex Roles*. 23 (October), pp. 421–38.

McLaughlin, Mary Martin. 1989. "Creating and Recreating Communities of Women: The Case of Corpus Domini, Ferrara, 1406–1452," *Signs*. 14 (Winter), pp. 293–320.

Manegold, Catherine S. 1992. "No More Nice Girls," *New York Times*. (July 12), p. 25.

Mauldin, Teresa, and Carol B. Meeks. 1990. "Sex Differences in Children's Time Use," *Sex Roles*. 22 (May), pp. 537–54.

Meyerson, Lee. 1988. "The Social Psychology of Physical Disability: 1948 and 1988," *Journal of Social Issues*. 44, pp. 173–88.

Neel, Carol. 1989. "The Origins of the Beguines," *Signs*. 14 (Winter), pp. 321–41.

Neubeck, G. 1981. "Getting Older in My Family: A Personal Reflection," In David F. Hultsch and Francine Deutsch (eds.), *Adult Development and Aging*. New York: McGraw-Hill, pp. 313–15.

Neugarten, Bernice L., Robert J. Havighurst, and Sheldon S. Tobin. 1968. "Personality and Patterns of Aging," In Bernice L. Neugarten (ed.), *Middle Age and Aging: A Reader in Social Psychology*. Chicago: University of Chicago Press, pp. 173–77.

Noble, Kenneth B. 1986. "End of Forced Retirement Means a Lot to a Few," *New York Times*. (October 26), p. E5.

Novak, Mark. 1987. "The Canadian New Horizons Program," *Gerontologist*. 27 (June), pp. 353–55.

Nuessel, Frank H. 1982. "The Language of Ageism," *Gerontologist*. 22 (June), pp. 273–76.

Oakley, Ann. 1974. *The Sociology of Housework*. London: Martin Robertson.

Palmore, Erdman, and C. Luikart. 1974. "Health and Social Factors Related to Life Satisfaction," In Erdman Palmore (ed.), *Normal Aging II: Reports from the Duke Longitudinal Studies 1970-1973*. Durham, NC: Duke University Press.

Phillips, Marilynn J. 1990. "Damaged Goods: Oral Narratives of the Experience of Disability in American Culture," *Social Science & Medicine*. 30, pp. 849–57.

Pomerleau, Andree, et al. 1990. "Pink or Blue: Environmental Gender Stereotypes in the First Two Years of Life," *Sex Roles*. 22 (March), pp. 359–67.

Pratt, Clara C., et al. 1991. "A Model Community Education Program on Depression and Suicide in Later Life," *Gerontologist*. 31 (October), pp. 692–95.

Reitzes, Donald C., Elizabeth Mutran, and Hallowell Pope. 1991. "Location and Well-Being among Retired Men," *Journal of Gerontology*. 46, pp. S195–S203.

Rowland-Serdar, Barbara, and Peregrine Schwartz-Shea. 1991. "Empowering Women: Self, Autonomy, and Responsibility," *Western Political Quarterly*. 44 (September), pp. 605–24.

Rubin, Linda J., and Sherry B. Borgers. 1990. "Sexual Harassment in Universities during the 1980s," *Sex Roles*. 23 (October), pp. 397–411.

Scarpitti, Frank R., and Margaret L. Andersen. 1989. *Social Problems*. New York: Harper & Row.

Scheer, Jessica, and Nora Groce. 1988. "Impairment as a Human Constant: Cross-Cultural and Historical Perspectives on Variation," *Journal of Social Issues*. 44, pp. 23–37.

Schneider, Joseph W. 1988. "Disability as Moral Experience: Epilepsy and Self in Routine Relationships," *Journal of Social Issues*. 44, pp. 63–78.

Schultz, Richard, and G. Brenner. 1977. "Relocation of the Aged: A Review and Theoretical Analysis," *Journal of Gerontology*. 32, pp. 323–33.

Schwendinger, Julia R., and Herman Schwendinger. 1990. "Sexual Extortion," In James M. Henslin (ed.), *Social Problems Today*. Englewood Cliffs, NJ: Prentice-Hall, pp. 63–64.

Scotch, Richard K. 1988. "Disability as the Basis for a Social Movement: Advocacy and the Politics of Definition," *Journal of Social Issues*. 44, pp. 159–72.

Shapiro, Bruce. 1982. "Wrinkled Radical," *New Haven Advocate*. (July 28), pp. 6–7+.

Shaw, J. I., and P. Skolnick. 1971. "Attribution of Responsibility for a Happy Accident," *Journal of Personality and Social Psychology*. 18, pp. 380–83.

Signorielli, Nancy. 1989. "Television and Conceptions

about Sex Roles: Maintaining Conventionality and the Status Quo," *Sex Roles*. 22 (September), pp. 341–60.

Simpson, Michael A. 1976. "Brought in Dead," *Omega*. 7, pp. 243–48.

Smith, Richard W. 1973. "The Physically Deviant," In Don Spiegel and Patricia Keith-Spiegel (eds.), *Outsiders* USA. San Francisco: Rinehart Press, pp. 99–115.

Spade, Joan Z., and Carole A. Reese. 1991. "We've Come a Long Way, Maybe: College Students' Plans for Work and Family," *Sex Roles*. 24 (March), pp. 309–21.

Stoller, Eleanor Palo, and Karen L. Pugliesi. 1991. "Size and Effectiveness of Informal Helping Networks: A Panel Study of Older People in the Community," *Journal of Health and Social Behavior*. 32 (June), pp. 180–91.

Streib, Gordon F., and C. J. Schneider. 1971. *Retirement in American Society: Impact and Process*. Ithaca, NY: Cornell University Press.

Sudnow, David. 1967. *Passing On: The Social Organization of Dying*. Englewood Cliffs, NJ: Prentice-Hall.

Timko, Christine, and Rudolf H. Moos. 1990. "Determinants of Interpersonal Support and Self-Direction in Group Residential Facilities," *Journal of Gerontology*. 45, pp. S184–S192.

———. 1991. "A Typology of Social Climates in Group Residential Facilities for Older People," *Journal of Gerontology*. 46, pp. S160–S169.

UN *Chronicle*. 1992. "New Principles on Ageing Adopted by Assembly." 29 (March), p. 86.

U.S. Bureau of the Census. 1992. *Statistical Abstract of the United States: 1992*. 112th ed. Washington, DC: U.S. Government Printing Office.

Vogel, Dena Ann, et al. 1991. "Children's and Adults' Sex-Stereotyped Perceptions of Infants," *Sex Roles*. 24 (May), pp. 605–16.

Werrbach, Gail B., Harold D. Grotevant, and Catherine R. Cooper. 1990. "Gender Differences in Adolescents' Identity Development in the Domain of Sex Role Concepts," *Sex Roles*. 23 (October), pp. 349–62.

Wiener, C. 1975. "The Burden of Rheumatoid Arthritis: Tolerating the Uncertainty," *Social Science and Medicine*. 9, pp. 97–104.

Williams, Juanita H. 1987. *Psychology of Women: Behavior in a Biosocial Context*. 3rd ed. New York: W. W. Norton.

Williamson, John B., Anne Munley, and Linda Evans. 1980. *Aging and Society*. New York: Holt, Rinehart and Winston.

Wollstonecraft, Mary. 1980. "A Vindication of the Rights of Women," In Sheila Ruth (ed.), *Issues in Feminism*. Boston: Houghton Mifflin, pp. 457–63.

Yee, Doris K., and Jacquelynne S. Eccles. 1988. "Parent Perceptions and Attributions for Children's Math Achievement," *Sex Roles*. 19 (September), pp. 317–33.

Chapter 11

Adams, Bert N. 1980. *The American Family*. 3rd ed. Chicago: Rand McNally.

Aidala, A. A., and B. D. Zablocki. 1991. "The Communes of the 1970s: Who Joined and Why," *Marriage and Family Review*. 17, pp. 87–116.

Albrecht, Stan L. 1979. "Correlates of Marital Happiness among the Remarried," *Journal of Marriage and the Family*. 41, pp. 857–67.

Allgeier, Elizabeth Rice, and Michael W. Wiederman. 1992. "Love and Mate Selection in the 1990s," In Ollie Pocs (ed.), *Marriage and Family 92/93*. 18th ed. Guilford, CT: Dushkin, pp. 39–41.

Angier, Natalie. 1992. "Scientists, Finding Second Idiosyncrasy in Homosexuals' Brains, Suggest Orientation Is Physiological," *New York Times*. (August 1), p. 7.

Ariès, Phillipe. 1962. *Centuries of Childhood*. New York: Vintage Books.

Baber, Kristine M., and Patricia Monaghan. 1988. "College Women's Career and Motherhood Expectations: New Options, Old Dilemmas," *Sex Roles*. 19 (August), pp. 189–203.

Barringer, Felicity. 1989. "Doubt on 'Trial Marriage' Raised by Divorce Rates," *New York Times*. (June 9), pp. A1+.

Bellah, Robert N., et al. 1986. *Habits of the Heart: Individualism and Commitment in American Life*. New York: Harper & Row.

Berger, Brigitte, and Peter L. Berger. 1984. *The War over the Family*. Garden City, NY: Anchor Books.

Berger, Raymond M. 1983. "What Is a Homosexual? A Definitional Model," *Social Work*. 28 (March/April), pp. 132–35.

———. 1990. "Men Together: Understanding the Gay Couple," *Journal of Homosexuality*. 19, pp. 31–49.

Blumstein, Philip, and Pepper Schwartz. 1983. *American Couples*. New York: William Morrow.

Bohannon, Paul (ed.). 1970. *Divorce and After*. Garden City, NY: Doubleday.

Brody, Jane E. 1983. "Divorce's Stress Exacts Long-Term Health Toll," *New York Times.* (December 13), pp. C1+.

Bumpass, Larry L., James A. Sweet, and Andrew Cherlin. 1991. "The Role of Cohabitation in Declining Rates of Marriage," *Journal of Marriage and the Family.* 53 (November), pp. 913–27.

Buss, David M. 1986. "Human Mate Selection," In Ollie Pocs (ed.), *Marriage and Family, 86/87.* 12th ed. Guilford, CT: Dushkin, pp. 60–65.

Clark, Russell D. III. 1990. "The Impact of AIDS on Gender Differences in Willingness to Engage in Casual Sex," *Journal of Applied Social Psychology.* 20 (May), pp. 771–82.

Cockrum, Janet, and Priscilla White. 1985. "Influences on the Life Satisfaction of Never-Married Men and Women," *Family Relations.* 34 (October), pp. 551–56.

Cornell, L.L. 1990. "Constructing a Theory of the Family: From Malinowski through the Modern Nuclear Family to Production and Reproduction," *International Journal of Comparative Sociology.* 31 (January-April), pp. 67–78.

Cranston, Kevin. 1991. "HIV Education for Gay, Lesbian, and Bisexual Youth: Personal Risk, Personal Power, and the Community of Conscience," *Journal of Homosexuality.* 22, pp. 247–59.

Cutler, Blayne. 1991. "Single and Settled," *American Demographics.* 13 (May), p. 10.

Danziger, Sandra K., and Norma Radin. 1990. "Absent Does Not Equal Uninvolved: Predictors of Fathering in Teen Mother Families," *Journal of Marriage and the Family.* 52 (August), pp. 636–42.

D'Augelli, Anthony R. 1991. "Teaching Lesbian/Gay Development: From Oppression to Exceptionality," *Journal of Homosexuality.* 22, pp. 213–27.

Davis, Bea, and Arthur Aron. 1988. "Perceived Causes of Divorce and Postdivorce Adjustment among Recently Divorced Midlife Women," *Journal of Divorce.* 12, pp. 41–55.

Demo, David H., and Alan C. Acock. 1988. "The Impact of Divorce on Children," *Journal of Marriage and the Family.* 50 (August), pp. 619–48.

Desai, Sonalde, and Linda J. Waite. 1991. "Women's Employment during Pregnancy and after the First Birth: Occupational Characteristics and Work Commitment," *American Sociological Review.* 56 (August), pp. 551–66.

DeWitt, Paula Mergenhagen. 1992. "All the Lonely People," *American Demographics.* 14 (April), pp. 44–46.

Egan, Timothy. 1992. "Oregon Measure Asks State to Repress Homosexuality," *New York Times.* (August 16), pp. 1+.

Exter, Thomas. 1990. "Entertaining Singles," *American Demographics.* 12 (August), pp. 6–7.

Feldman, Harold. 1981. "A Comparison of Intentional Parents and Intentionally Childless Couples," *Journal of Marriage and the Family.* 43 (August), pp. 593–600.

Fitzpatrick, Jacki A., Thomas A. Smith, and Sally A. Williamson. 1992. "Educating Extension Agents: An Evaluation of Method and Development of a Remarried Family Educational Program," *Family Relations.* 41 (January), pp. 70–73.

Ford, Clellan S., and Frank A. Beach. 1951. *Patterns of Sexual Behavior.* New York: Harper & Row.

Furstenberg, Frank F., Jr., and Christine Winquist Nord. 1985. "Parenting Apart: Patterns of Childrearing after Marital Disruption," *Journal of Marriage and the Family.* 47 (November), pp. 893–904.

Futurist. 1985. "Land Co-op." 19 (April), pp. 62+.

Gabardi, Lisa, and Lee A. Rosen. 1991. "Differences between College Students from Divorced and Intact Families," *Journal of Divorce and Remarriage.* 15, pp. 175–91.

Gagnon, John H., and William Simon. 1973. *Sexual Conduct.* Chicago: Aldine.

Gerstel, Naomi. 1988. "Divorce and Kin Ties: The Importance of Gender," *Journal of Marriage and the Family.* 50 (February), pp. 209–19.

Glenn, Norval D., and Charles Weaver. 1977. "The Marital Happiness of Remarried Divorced Persons," *Journal of Marriage and the Family.* 39 (May), pp. 331–37.

Glenwick, David S., and Joel D. Mowrey. 1986. "When Parent Becomes Peer: Loss of Intergenerational Boundaries in Single Parent Families," *Family Relations.* 35 (January), pp. 57–62.

Glick, Paul C. 1986. "How American Families Are Changing," In Ollie Pocs (ed.), *Marriage and Family 86/87.* 12th ed. Guilford, CT: Dushkin, pp. 23–26.

Goode, William J. 1956. *After Divorce.* New York: Free Press.

———. 1963. *World Revolution and Family Patterns.* New York: Free Press.

———. 1982. *The Family.* 2nd ed. Englewood Cliffs, NJ: Prentice-Hall.

Green, Ernest J. 1978. *Personal Relationships.* New York: McGraw-Hill.

Green, Richard. 1978. "Sexual Identity of 37 Children

Raised by Homosexual or Transsexual Parents," *American Journal of Psychiatry.* 135 (June), pp. 692–97.

Greene, Robert M., and Leigh A. Leslie. 1989. "Mothers' Behavior and Sons' Adjustment Following Divorce," *Journal of Divorce.* 12, pp. 235–51.

Handwerker, W. Penn. 1973. "Technology and Household Configuration in Urban Africa: The Bassa of Monrovia," *American Sociological Review.* 38 (April), pp. 182–97.

Heaton, Tim B. 1991. "Time-Related Determinants of Marital Dissolution," *Journal of Marriage and the Family.* 53 (May), pp. 285–95.

Hobart, Charles. 1988. "The Family System in Remarriage: An Exploratory Study," *Journal of Marriage and the Family.* 50 (August), pp. 649–61.

———. 1991. "Conflict in Remarriages," *Journal of Divorce and Remarriage.* 15, pp. 69-86.

Hochschild, Arlie. 1992. "The Second Shift: Employed Women Are Putting in Another Day of Work," In Ollie Pocs (ed.), *Marriage and Family: 92/93.* 18th ed. Guilford, CT: Dushkin, pp. 64–66.

Hoffman, Lois Wladis, and F. Ivan Nye. 1974. *Working Mothers.* San Francisco: Jossey-Bass.

Holmstrom, Lynda Lytle. 1972. *The Two-Career Family.* Cambridge, MA: Schenkman.

Hugick, Larry, and Jennifer Leonard. 1991. "Sex in America," *Gallup Poll Monthly.* (October), pp. 60–73.

Hunt, Morton, and Bernice Hunt. 1980. "Another World, Another Life," In Arlene Skolnick and Jerome H. Skolnick (eds.), *Family in Transition.* 3rd ed. Boston: Little, Brown, pp. 340–54.

Kanter, Rosabeth M. 1968. "Commitment and Social Organization: A Study of Commitment Mechanisms in Utopian Communities," *American Sociological Review.* 33 (August), pp. 499–517.

Keller, James F., Stephen S. Elliott, and Edwin Gunberg. 1982. "Premarital Sexual Intercourse among Single College Students: A Discriminant Analysis," *Sex Roles.* 8 (January), pp. 21–32.

Kitson, Gay C., and Leslie A. Morgan. 1990. "The Multiple Consequences of Divorce: A Decade Review," *Journal of Marriage and the Family.* 52 (November), pp. 913–24.

Klee, Linnea, Catherine Schmidt, and Colleen Johnson. 1989. "Children's Definitions of Family Following Divorce of Their Parents," *Journal of Divorce.* 12, pp. 109–27.

Knox, David. 1988. *Choices in Relationships.* 2nd ed. St. Paul, MN: West.

Krebs, Albin, and Robert M. Thomas, Jr. 1981. "A Message of Love Travels in High Seas," *New York Times.* (August 28), p. 18.

Kunz, Phillip R., and J. Lynn England. 1988. "Age-Specific Divorce Rates," *Journal of Divorce.* 12, pp. 113–26.

Kurdek, Lawrence A. 1988. "Relationship Quality of Gay and Lesbian Cohabiting Couples," *Journal of Homosexuality.* 15, pp. 93–118.

Kurdek, Lawrence A. 1990. "Divorce History and Self-reported Psychological Distress in Husbands and Wives," *Journal of Marriage and the Family.* 52 (August), pp. 701–08.

Lamanna, Mary Ann, and Agnes Riedmann. 1988. *Marriages & Families.* 3rd ed. Belmont, CA: Wadsworth.

Larson, Jan. 1991. "Cohabitation Is a Premarital Step," *American Demographics.* 13 (November), pp. 20–21.

Lauer, Jeanette, and Robert Lauer. 1989. "Marriages Made to Last," In Ollie Pocs (ed.), *Marriage and Family 89/90.* 15th ed. Guilford, CT: Dushkin, pp. 85–88.

Leighton, Alexander H. 1984. "Then and Now: Some Notes on the Interaction of Person and Social Environment," *Human Organization.* 43 (Fall), pp. 189–97.

Lowery, Carol S., and Shirley A. Settle. 1985. "Effects of Divorce on Children: Differential Impact of Custody and Visitation Patterns," *Family Relations.* 34 (October), pp. 455–63.

Macklin, Eleanor. 1983. "Nonmarital Heterosexual Cohabitation," In Arlene Skolnick and Jerome H. Skolnick (eds.), *Family in Transition.* 4th ed. Boston: Little, Brown, pp. 264–85.

Madonna, Philip G., Susan Van Scoyk, and David P. H. Jones. 1991. "Family Interaction within Incest and Nonincest Families," *American Journal of Psychiatry.* 148 (January), pp. 46–49.

Mead, Margaret. 1963. "Children and Ritual in Bali," In Margaret Mead and Martha Wolfenstein (eds.), *Childhood in Contemporary Cultures.* Chicago: Phoenix Books, pp. 40–51. (Originally published in Chicago: University of Chicago Press, 1955.)

Menaghan, Elizabeth G., and Morton A. Lieberman. 1986. "Changes in Depression Following Divorce: A Panel Study," *Journal of Marriage and the Family.* 48 (May), pp. 319–28.

Moffett, Robert K., and Jack F. Scherer. 1976. *Dealing with Divorce.* Boston: Little, Brown.

Morgan, S. Philip. 1991. "Late Nineteenth- and Early Twentieth-Century Childlessness," *American Journal of Sociology.* 97 (November), pp. 779–807.

Murdock, George Peter. 1949. *Social Structure.* New York: Macmillan.

Neugebauer, R. 1989. "Divorce, Custody, and Visitation: The Child's Point of View," *Journal of Divorce.* 12, pp. 153–68.

New Republic. 1992. "Father Knew Best." 254 (June 8), p. 772.

Norton, Arthur J., and Paul C. Glick. 1986. "One Parent Families: A Social and Economic Profile," *Family Relations.* 35 (January), pp. 9–17.

Norton, Arthur J., and Jeanne E. Moorman. 1987. "Current Trends in Marriage and Divorce among American Women," *Journal of Marriage and the Family.* 49 (February), pp. 3–14.

Oakley, Deborah. 1985. "Premarital Childbearing Decision-Making," *Family Relations.* 34 (October), pp. 561–63.

Parcel, Toby L., and Elizabeth G. Menaghan. 1990. "Maternal Working Conditions and Children's Verbal Facility: Studying the Intergenerational Transmission of Inequality from Mother to Young Children," *Social Psychology Quarterly.* 53 (June), pp. 132–47.

Presser, Harriet B. 1988. "Shift Work and Child Care among Young Dual-Earner American Parents," *Journal of Marriage and the Family.* 50 (February), pp. 133–48.

Ramey, James. 1978. "Experimental Family Forms—the Family of the Future," *Marriage and Family Review.* 1 (January/February), pp. 1–9.

Regan, Mary C., and Helen E. Roland. 1985. "Rearranging Family and Career Priorities: Professional Women and Men of the Eighties," *Journal of Marriage and the Family.* 47 (November), pp. 985–92.

Reiss, Ira L. 1980. *Family Systems in America.* 3rd ed. New York: Holt, Rinehart and Winston.

Reiss, Ira L., and Gary R. Lee. 1988. *Family Systems in America.* 4th ed. New York: Holt, Rinehart and Winston.

Renne, Karen S. 1974. "Correlates of Dissatisfaction in Marriage," In Robert Winch and Graham Spanier (eds.), *Selected Studies in the Family.* 4th ed. New York: Holt, Rinehart and Winston.

Risman, Barbara J., and Kyung Park. 1988. "Just the Two of Us: Parent-Child Relationships in Single-Parent Homes," *Journal of Marriage and the Family.* 50 (November), pp. 1049–62.

Robinson, Bryan E., et al. 1982. "Gay Men's and Women's Perceptions of Early Family Life and Their Relationships with Parents," *Family Relations.*

31 (January), pp. 79–83.

Rosen, David H. 1974. *Lesbianism.* Springfield, IL: Charles C. Thomas.

Rosenthal, Carolyn J. 1985. "Kinkeeping in the Familial Division of Labor," *Journal of Marriage and the Family.* 47 (November), pp. 965–74.

Saghir, M.R., and E. Robins. 1971. "Male and Female Homosexuality: Natural History," *Comparative Psychiatry.* 12, pp. 503–10.

Sanik, Margaret M., and Teresa Mauldin. 1986. "Single versus Two Parent Families: A Comparison of Mothers' Time," *Family Relations.* 35 (January), pp. 53–56.

Schmalz, Jeffrey. 1992. "Gay Areas Are Jubilant over Clinton," *New York Times.* (November 5), p. B8.

———. 1993. "Homosexuals Wake to See a Referendum: It's on Them," *New York Times.* (January 31), sec. 4, pp. 1+.

Schnayer, Reuben, and R. Robert Orr. 1989. "A Comparison of Children Living in Single-Mother and Single-Father Families," *Journal of Divorce.* 12, pp. 171–84.

Schultz, Martin. 1984. "Divorce in Early America: Origins and Patterns in Three North Central States," *Sociological Quarterly.* 25 (Autumn), pp. 511–26.

Seccombe, Karen. 1991. "Assessing the Costs and Benefits of Children: Gender Comparisons among Childfree Husbands and Wives," *Journal of Marriage and the Family.* 53 (February), pp. 191–202.

Sennett, Richard. 1974. *Families against the City.* New York: Vintage Books. (Originally published in 1970.)

Siegelman, M. 1974. "Parental Background of Male Homosexuals and Heterosexuals," *Archives of Sexual Behavior.* 3, pp. 3–18.

Silka, Linda, and Sara Kiesler. 1977. "Couples Who Choose to Remain Childless," *Family Planning Perspectives.* 9 (January/February), pp. 16–25.

Skolnick, Arlene. 1987. *Intimate Environment.* 4th ed. Glenview, IL: Scott, Foresman.

Smith, Tom W. 1990. "The Polls—a Report: The Sexual Revolution?" *Public Opinion Quarterly.* 54 (Fall), pp. 415–35.

Smolowe, Jill. 1992. "Last Call for Motherhood," In Ollie Pocs (ed.), *Marriage and Family 92/93.* 18th ed. Guilford, CT: Dushkin, p. 131.

Spiro, Melford E. 1970. *Kibbutz.* 2nd ed. New York: Schocken Books.

Stein, Peter J. 1980. "Singlehood: An Alternative to Marriage," In Arlene Skolnick and Jerome H. Skolnick (eds.), *Family in Transition.* 3rd ed. Boston: Little, Brown, pp. 517–36.

Stets, Jan E. 1991. "Cohabiting and Marital Aggression: The Role of Social Isolation," *Journal of Marriage and the Family*. 53 (August), pp. 669–80.

Teachman, Jay D., and Karen A. Polonko. 1990. "Cohabitation and Marital Stability in the United States," *Social Forces*. 69 (September), pp. 207–20.

Terry, Don. 1992. "'Pink Angels' Battle Anti-gay Crime," *New York Times*. (April 7), p. A18.

Thimberger, Rosemary, and Michael J. MacLean. 1982. "Maternal Employment: The Child's Perspective," *Journal of Marriage and the Family*. 44 (May), pp. 469–75.

Thornton, Arland. 1991. "Influence of the Marital History of Parents on the Marital and Cohabitational Experiences of Children," *American Journal of Sociology*. 96 (January), pp. 864–94.

Turner, Pauline H., and Richard M. Smith. 1983. "Single Parents and Day Care," *Family Relations*. 32 (April), pp. 215–26.

U.S. Bureau of the Census. 1983. *Marital Status and Living Arrangements: March 1982, Current Population Reports*. Series P-20, Washington, DC: U.S. Government Printing Office.

U.S. Bureau of the Census. 1984. *Population Characteristics. Current Population Reports*. Series P-20, Washington, DC: U.S. Government Printing Office.

U.S. Bureau of the Census. 1991. *Statistical Abstract of the United States: 1991*. 111th ed. Washington, DC: U.S. Government Printing Office.

U.S. Bureau of the Census. 1992. *Statistical Abstract of the United States: 1992*. 112th ed. Washington, DC: U.S. Government Printing Office.

Veevers, J. E. 1973. "Voluntarily Childless Wives: An Exploratory Study," *Sociology and Social Research*. 57 (April), pp. 356–66.

Waldrop, Judith. 1990. "Living in Sin," *American Demographics*. 12 (April), pp. 12–13.

Wallerstein, Judith S. 1992. "Children after Divorce: Wounds That Don't Heal," In Ollie Pocs (ed.), *Marriage and Family 92/93*. 18th ed. Guilford, CT: Dushkin, pp. 163–68.

Weingarten, Helen R. 1988. "The Impact of Late Life Divorce: A Conceptual and Empirical Study," *Journal of Divorce*. 12, pp. 21–39.

Weitzman, Lenore J., and Ruth B. Dixon. 1983. "The Transformation of Legal Marriage through No-Fault Divorce," In Arlene Skolnick and Jerome H. Skolnick (eds.), *Family in Transition*. 4th ed. Boston: Little, Brown, pp. 353–66.

White, Lynn K. 1990. "Determinants of Divorce: A Review of Research in the Eighties," *Journal of Marriage and the Family*. 52 (November), pp. 904–12.

White, Stephen W., and Bernard L. Bloom. 1981. "Factors Related to the Adjustment of Divorcing Men," *Family Relations*. 30 (July), pp. 349–60.

Whiting, Beatrice, and John W. M. Whiting. 1975. *Children of Six Cultures: A Psycho-Cultural Analysis*. Cambridge, MA: Harvard University Press.

Wines, Michael. 1992. "Appeal of 'Murphy Brown' Now Clear at White House," *New York Times*. (May 21), pp. A1+.

Zablocki, Ben. 1977. *Alienation and Investment in the Urban Commune*. New York: Center for Policy Research.

Zeman, Ned. 1992. "The New Rules of Courtship," In Ollie Pocs (ed.), *Marriage and Family: 92/93*. 18th ed. Guilford, CT: Dushkin, pp. 42–43.

Chapter 12

Adams, David S. 1987. "Ronald Reagan's 'Revival': Voluntarism as a Theme in Reagan's Civil Religion," *Sociological Analysis*. 48 (Spring), pp. 17–29.

Allman, T. D. 1976. "Jesus in Tomorrowland," *New Republic*. 177 (November 27), pp. 6–9.

Armor, David J. 1989. "After Busing: Education and Choice," *Public Interest*. 23 (Spring), pp. 24–37.

Bailyn, Bernard, et al. 1977. *The Great Republic*. Lexington, MA: D.C. Heath.

Banks, Olive. 1976. *The Sociology of Education*. Revised ed. New York: Schocken Books.

Bellah, Robert N. 1967. "Civil Religion in America," *Daedalus*. 96 (Winter), pp. 1–21.

Bills, David B. 1988. "Educational Credentials and Promotions: Does Schooling Do More than Get You in the Door?" *Sociology of Education*. 61 (January), pp. 52–60.

Binzen, Peter. 1970. *Whitetown, USA*. New York: Random House.

Bowles, Samuel, and Herbert Gintis. 1976. *Schooling in Capitalist America: Educational Reform and the Contradictions of Economic Life*. New York: Basic Books.

Bracey, Gerald W. 1991. "Why Can't They Be Like We Were?" *Phi Delta Kappan*. 73 (October), pp. 104–17.

Braddock, Jomills Henry II, Robert L. Crain, and James S. McPartland. 1984. "A Long-Term View of School Desegregation: Some Recent Studies of Graduates as Adults," *Phi Delta Kappan*. 66 (December), pp. 259–64.

Bradfield, Cecil, and Mary Lou Wylie. 1989. "After the Flood: The Response of Ministers to a Natural Disaster," *Sociological Analysis*. 49 (Winter), pp. 397–407.

Brodinsky, Ben. 1979. "Something Happened: Education in the Seventies," *Phi Delta Kappan*. 61 (December), pp. 238–41.

Campbell, Ernest Q., and Thomas Pettigrew. 1959. *Christians in Racial Crisis*. Washington, DC: Public Affairs Press.

Clogg, Clifford C., and James W. Shockey. 1984. "Mismatch between Occupation and Schooling: A Prevalence Measure, Recent Trends and Demographic Analysis," *Demography*. 21 (May), pp. 235–57.

Cohen, Steven M., and Leonard J. Fein. 1985. "From Integration to Survival: American Jewish Anxieties in Transition," *Annals of the American Academy of Political and Social Science*. 483 (July), pp. 75–88.

Coleman, James S., et al. 1966. *Equality of Educational Opportunity*. Washington, DC: U.S. Government Printing Office.

Coleman, James S., et al. 1982. *High School Achievement*. New York: Basic Books.

Collins, Randall. 1979. *The Credential Society*. New York: Academic Press.

Crossman, Richard (ed.). 1952. *The God That Failed*. New York: Bantam Books.

De Witt, Karen. 1992. "Survey Finds American Children Write Poorly," *New York Times*. (May 17), p. A12.

Douglass, Frederick. 1968. *Narrative of the Life of Frederick Douglass*. New York: Signet Books. (Originally published in 1845.)

Durkheim, Émile. 1961. *The Elementary Forms of the Religious Life*. Trans. Joseph Ward Swain. New York: Collier Books.

———. 1964. *The Division of Labor in Society*. Trans. George Simpson. New York: Free Press. (The Simpson translation originally published in New York: Macmillan, 1933.)

———. 1975. *Durkheim on Religion*. W. S. F. Pickering (ed.). Trans. Jacqueline Gedding and W. S. F. Pickering. London: Routledge & Kegan Paul.

Ebaugh, Helen Rose. 1991. "The Revitalization Movement in the Catholic Church: The Institutional Dilemma of Power," *Sociological Analysis*. 52 (Spring), pp. 1–12.

Economist. 1985. "Religious Schools: Dividing and Multiplying." 294 (February 23), p. 25.

Education for Democracy Project. 1987. "Education for Democracy: The Changes We Need to Make," *Education Digest*. 53 (October), pp. 10–13.

Eitzen, D. Stanley. 1992. "Problem Students: The Sociocultural Roots," *Phi Delta Kappan*. 73 (April), pp. 584–88+.

Epstein, Kitty Kelly, and William F. Ellis. 1992. "Oakland Moves to Create Its Own Multicultural Curriculum," *Phi Delta Kappan*. 73 (April), pp. 635–38.

Fields, Echo E. 1991. "Understanding Activist Fundamentalism: Capitalist Crisis and the 'Colonization of the Lifeword,'" *Sociological Analysis*. 52 (Summer), pp. 175–90.

Flynn, Charles P., and Suzanne R. Kunkel. 1987. "Deprivation, Compensation, and Conceptions of an Afterlife," *Sociological Analysis*. 48 (Spring), pp. 58–72.

Gallup, George, Jr., and Frank Newport. 1990. "More Americans Now Believe in a Power Outside Themselves," *Gallup Poll Monthly*. (June), pp. 33–38.

Gamoran, Adam. 1990. "Civil Religion in American Schools," *Sociological Analysis*. 51 (Fall), pp. 235–56.

Glasser, William. 1992. "The Quality School Curriculum," *Phi Delta Kappan*. 73 (May), pp. 690–94.

Goldberg, Milton, and James Harvey. 1983. "A Nation at Risk: The Report of the National Commission on Excellence in Education," *Phi Delta Kappan*. 65 (September), pp. 14–18.

Gracey, Harry L. 1977. "Learning the Student Role: Kindergarten as Academic Boot Camp," In Dennis H. Wrong and Harry L. Gracey (eds.), *Readings in Introductory Sociology*. 3rd ed. New York: Macmillan, pp. 215–26.

Gurley, John G. 1984. "Marx's Contributions and Their Relevance Today," *American Economic Review*. 74 (May), pp. 110–23.

Guth, James L., and John C. Green. 1988. "Grand Old Deity," *Psychology Today*. 22 (April), pp. 20+.

Hammond, Phillip E. 1985. "The Curious Path of Conservative Protestantism," *Annals of the American Academy of Political and Social Science*. 480 (July), pp. 53–62.

Hanline, Mary Frances, and Carola Murray. 1984. "Integrating Severely Handicapped Children into Regular Public Schools," *Phi Delta Kappan*. 66 (December), pp. 273–76.

Hinsberg, Thomas F. 1974. "The Church: Agent of Social Change," *Journal of Applied Behavioral Science*. 10 (Summer), pp. 432–37.

Hodgson, Godfrey. 1973. "Do Schools Make a Difference?" *Atlantic*. 231 (March), pp. 35–46.

Jackson, Philip. 1968. *Life in Classrooms*. New York:

Holt, Rinehart and Winston.

Jaynes, Gerald David, and Robin M. Williams (eds.). 1989. *A Common Destiny: Blacks and American Society.* Washington, DC: National Academy Press.

Johnson, Benton. 1992. "On Founders and Followers: Some Factors in the Development of New Religious Movements," *Sociological Analysis.* 53 (Supplement), pp. S1–S13.

Johnstone, Ronald L. 1975. *Religion and Society in Interaction.* Englewood Cliffs, NJ: Prentice-Hall.

Katz, Claudio. 1992. "Marx on the Peasantry: Class in Itself or Class in Struggle?" *Review of Politics.* 54 (Winter), pp. 50–71.

Kozol, Jonathan. 1991. *Savage Inequalities: Children in America's Schools.* New York: Crown.

———. 1992. "If Money Doesn't Matter, Why All the Savage Inequalities?" *Education Digest.* 57 (March), pp. 32–36.

Kuipers, Joan. 1992. "Not Yet a Mile in Their Moccasins and Already My Feet Hurt," *Phi Delta Kappan.* 73 (May), pp. 718–20.

Lewis, Sinclair. 1970. *Elmer Gantry.* New York: Signet Classics. (Originally published in New York: Harcourt, Brace, 1927.)

Lichtenstein, Peter M. 1985. "Radical Liberalism and Radical Education: A Synthesis and Critical Evaluation of Illich, Freire, and Dewey," *American Journal of Economics and Sociology.* 44 (January), pp. 39–54.

MacKinnon, Malcolm H. 1988a. "Part I: Calvinism and the Infallible Assurance of Grace: The Weber Thesis Reconsidered," *British Journal of Sociology.* 39 (June), pp. 143–77.

———. 1988b. "Part II: Weber's Exploration of Calvinism: The Undiscovered Provenance of Calvinism," *British Journal of Sociology.* 39 (June), pp. 178–210.

Marx, Karl. 1970. *Critique of Hegel's "Philosophy of Right."* Trans. Annette Jolin and Joseph O'Malley. New York: Cambridge University Press.

Meadows, B. J. 1992. "Nurturing Cooperation and Responsibility in a School Community," *Phi Delta Kappan.* 73 (February), pp. 480–81.

Mullins, Mark R. 1988. "The Organizational Dilemmas of Ethnic Churches: A Case Study of Japanese Buddhism in Canada," *Sociological Analysis.* 49 (Fall), pp. 217–33.

New York Times. 1989. "Senate Panel Hears Manley Tell of Learning Disability." (May 19), p. B17.

Oakes, Jeannie, and Martin Lipton. 1992. "Detracking Schools: Early Lessons from the Field," *Phi Delta Kappan.* 73 (February), pp. 448–54.

O'Dea, Thomas F. 1966. *The Sociology of Religion.* Englewood Cliffs, NJ: Prentice-Hall.

Oestereicher, Emil. 1982. "The Depoliticization of the Liberal Arts," *Social Research.* 49 (Winter), pp. 1004–12.

Parsons, Talcott. 1968. "The School Class as a Social System: Some of Its Functions in American Society," In Robert R. Bell and Holger R. Stub (eds.), *The Sociology of Education.* Revised ed. Homewood, IL: Dorsey Press. pp. 199–218.

Pike, Bob. 1992. "Why I Teach My Children at Home," *Phi Delta Kappan.* 73 (March), pp. 564–65.

Plutzer, Eric. 1991. "The Protestant Ethic and the Spirit of Academia: An Essay on Graduate Education," *Teaching Sociology.* 19 (July), pp. 302–07.

Power, Clark, and Lawrence Kohlberg. 1987. "Using a Hidden Curriculum for Moral Education," *Education Digest.* 52 (May), pp. 10–13.

Rossell, Christine H. 1988. "Is It Busing or the Blacks?" *Urban Affairs Quarterly.* 24 (September), pp. 138–48.

Scotch, Richard K. 1988. "Disability as the Basis or a Social Movement: Advocacy and the Politics of Definition," *Journal of Social Issues.* 44, pp. 159–72.

Silverman, William. 1989. "Images of the Sacred: An Empirical Study," *Sociological Analysis.* 49 (Winter), pp. 440–44.

Stake, Robert E. 1992. "The Teacher, Standardized Testing, and Prospects of Revolution," *Phi Delta Kappan.* 73 (November), pp. 243–47.

Stotsky, Sandra. 1992. "Academic vs. Ideological Multicultural Education in the Classroom," *Education Digest.* 57 (March), pp. 64–66.

Sullivan, Deidre. 1991. "Targeting Souls," *American Demographics.* 13 (October), pp. 42–46+.

Sweet, William Warren. 1950. *Story of Religion in America.* New York: Harper.

Taylor, Angela R. 1991. "Social Competence and the Early School Transition: Risk and Protective Factors for African-American Children," *Education and Urban Society.* 24 (November), pp. 15–26.

Thompson, Kenneth. 1991. "Transgressing the Boundary between the Sacred and the Secular/Profane: A Durkheimian Perspective on a Public Controversy," *Sociological Analysis.* 52 (Fall), pp. 227–91.

Thumma, Scott. 1991. "Negotiating a Religious Identity: The Case of the Gay Evangelical," *Sociological Analysis.* 52 (Winter), pp. 333–47.

Twain, Mark. 1973. "Bible Teaching and Religious

Practice," In Maxwell Geismar (ed.), *Mark Twain and the Three R's.* Indianapolis: Bobbs-Merrill, pp. 106–10.

U.S. Bureau of the Census. 1966. *Statistical Abstract of the United States: 1966.* 87th ed. Washington, DC: U.S. Government Printing Office.

U.S. Bureau of the Census. 1992. *Statistical Abstract of the United States: 1992.* 112th ed. Washington, DC: U.S. Government Printing Office.

Weber, Max. 1958. *The Protestant Ethic and the Spirit of Capitalism.* Trans. Talcott Parsons, in 1930. New York: Charles Scribner's Sons.

Wilson, John. 1978. *Religion in American Society.* Englewood Cliffs, NJ: Prentice-Hall.

Chapter 13

Almond, Gabriel A. 1991. "Capitalism and Democracy," PS. 24 (September), pp. 467–74.

Appelberg, Kirsi, et al. 1991. "Interpersonal Conflicts at Work and Psychosocial Characteristics of Employees," *Social Science & Medicine.* 32, pp. 1051–56.

Bailyn, Bernard, et al. 1977. *The Great Republic.* Lexington, MA: D.C. Heath.

Burstein, Paul. 1977. "Political Elites and Labor Markets: Selection of American Cabinet Members, 1932–72," *Social Forces.* 56 (September), pp. 189–201.

Cambridge Reports. 1976. *Cambridge Reports Trends and Forecasts*, p. 6.

Clines, Francis X. 1992. "At Site of 'Iron Curtain' Speech, Gorbachev Buries the Cold War," *New York Times.* (May 7), pp. A1+.

Dahl, Robert A. 1967. *Pluralist Democracy in the United States: Conflict and Consent.* Chicago: Rand McNally.

———. 1976. *Democracy in the United States: Promise and Performance.* 3rd ed. Chicago: Rand McNally.

———. 1982. *Dilemmas of Pluralist Democracy.* New Haven, CT: Yale University Press.

Deutsch, R. Eden. 1985. "Tomorrow's Work Force," *Futurist.* 19 (December), pp. 8–11.

DiGaetano, Alan. 1988. "The Rise and Development of Urban Political Machines: An Alternative to Merton's Functional Analysis," *Urban Affairs Quarterly.* 24 (December), pp. 242–67.

Domhoff, G. William. 1983. *Who Rules America Now?: A View for the Eighties.* Englewood Cliffs, NJ: Prentice-Hall.

———. 1990. *The Power Elite and the State: How Policy Is Made in America.* New York: Aldine de Gruyter.

Dugger, William M. 1988. "An Institutional Analysis of Corporate Power," *Journal of Economic Issues.* (March), pp. 79–111.

Edsall, Thomas Byrne. 1986. "Republican America," *New York Review of Books.* 33 (April 24), pp. 3–4+.

Gallup, George, Jr., and Frank Newport. 1991. "Confidence in Major U.S. Institutions at All-time Low," *Gallup Poll Monthly.* (October), pp. 36–40.

Garson, G. David. 1977. *Power and Politics in the United States.* Lexington, MA: D.C. Heath.

Gartner, Alan, and Frank Riessman. 1974. "Is There a Work Ethic?" *American Journal of Orthopsychiatry.* 44 (July), pp. 563–67.

Gerth, Hans, and C. Wright Mills (eds.). 1946. *From Max Weber: Essays in Sociology.* New York: Oxford University Press.

Gilpin, Robert. 1975. U.S. *Power and the Multinational Corporation: The Political Economy of Foreign Direct Investment.* New York: Basic Books.

Gorbachev, Mikhail S. 1992. "The Right of Time and the Imperative of Action," Excerpts in *New York Times.* (May 7), p. A14.

Grant, Alan R. 1979. *The American Political Process.* London: Heinemann.

Greenberg, Edward S. 1974. *Serving the Few.* New York: John Wiley and Sons.

Greider, William. 1992. "The Betrayal of Democracy." National Public Television (April 15).

Halal, William E., and Alexander I. Nikitin. 1990. "One World: The Coming Synthesis of New Capitalism and New Socialism," *Futurist.* 24 (November/ December), pp. 8–13.

Horton, Paul B., Gerald R. Leslie, and Richard F. Larson. 1991. *The Sociology of Social Problems.* 10th ed. Englewood Cliffs, NJ: Prentice-Hall.

Hosking, Geoffrey. 1992. "The Roots of Dissolution," *New York Review of Books.* 39 (January 16), pp. 34–38.

Hummel, Ralph P. 1990. "Bureaucracy Policy: Toward Public Discourse on Organizing Public Administration," *Policy Studies Journal.* 18 (Summer), pp. 907–25.

Humphries, Craig. 1991. "Corporations, PACs and the Strategic Link between Contributions and Lobbying Activities," *Western Political Quarterly.* 44 (June), pp. 353–72.

Kim, Jae-On, and Mahn-Geum Ohn. 1991. "A Theory of Minor-Party Persistence: Election Rules, Social Cleavage, and the Number of Political Parties," *Social Forces.* 70 (March), pp. 575–99.

Kohn, Melvin L. 1976. "Occupational Structure and Alienation," *American Journal of Sociology*. 82 (July), pp. 111–30.

Korpi, Walter. 1991. "Political and Economic Explanations for Unemployment: A Cross-national and Long-term Analysis," *British Journal of Political Science*. 21 (July), pp. 315–48.

Lee, Lee C. 1991. "The Opening of the American Mind: Educating Leaders for a Multicultural Society," *Human Ecology Forum*. 19 (Winter), pp. 2–5.

Leigh, J. Paul. 1991. "Employee and Job Attributes as Predictors of Absenteeism in a National Sample of Workers: The Importance of Health and Dangerous Working Conditions," *Social Science & Medicine*. 33, pp. 127–37.

Lindblom, Charles E. 1982. "Another State of Mind," *American Political Science Review*. 76 (March), pp. 9–21.

Lohr, Steve. 1992. "Fixing Corporate America's Short-term Mind-set," *New York Times*. (September 2), pp. D1+.

Manley, John F. 1983. "Neo-Pluralism: A Class Analysis of Pluralism I and Pluralism II," *American Political Science Review*. 77 (June), pp. 368–83.

Marx, Karl. 1932. "Manifesto of the Communist Party," In Marx, *Capital, the Communist Manifesto and Other Writings*. Trans. Stephen L. Trask. New York: Modern Library, pp. 315–55.

Merton, Robert K. 1968. "Manifest and Latent Functions," In Merton, *Social Theory and Social Structure*. 3rd ed. New York: Free Press, pp. 73–138.

Mills, C. Wright. 1959. *The Power Elite*. New York: Oxford University Press.

Morton, Herbert C. 1977. "A Look at Factors Affecting the Quality of Working Life," *Monthly Labor Review*. (October), pp. 64–65.

Navarro, Peter. 1988. "Why Do Corporations Give to Charity?" *Journal of Business*. 61 (January), pp. 65–93.

Neustadtl, Alan, and Dan Lawson. 1988. "Corporate Political Groupings: Does Ideology Unify Business Political Behavior?" *American Sociological Review*. 53 (April), pp. 172–90.

Nixon, Richard. 1992. "Yeltsin Needs Us. We Need Yeltsin," *New York Times*. (June 12), p. A25.

Ranney, Austin. 1966. *The Governing of Men*. New York: Holt, Rinehart and Winston.

Rice, Robert W., Douglas A. Gentile, and Dean B. McFarlin. 1991. "Facet Importance and Job Satisfaction," *Journal of Applied Psychology*. 76 (February), pp. 31–39.

Riegle, Donald W., Jr. 1982. "The Psychological and Social Effects of Unemployment," *American Psychologist*. 37 (October), pp. 1113–15.

Riordan, William L. 1963. *Plunkitt of Tammany Hall*. New York: E. P. Dutton.

Roelofs, H. Mark. 1967. *The Language of Modern Politics*. Homewood, IL: Dorsey Press.

Salomon, David, and Jules Bernstein. 1982. "The Corporate Thrust in American Politics," In Leonard Cargan and Jeanne H. Ballantine (eds.), *Sociological Footprints*. 2nd ed. Belmont, CA: Wadsworth, pp. 176–79.

Samuelson, Paul A. 1980. *Economics*. 11th ed. New York: McGraw-Hill.

Scheiberg, Susan L. 1990. "Emotions on Display: The Personal Decoration of Work Space," *Administrative Science Quarterly*. 33 (January), pp. 330–38.

Seligman, Adam B. 1991. "Charisma and the Transformation of Grace in the Early Modern Era," *Social Research*. 58 (Fall), pp. 591–620.

Sibbison, Jim. 1991. "In Poppy's Footsteps: Dan Quayle, Business's Backdoor Boy," *Nation*. 253 (July 29/August 5), pp. 141+.

Smith, Adam. 1930. *Inquiry into the Nature and Causes of the Wealth of Nations*. London: Methuen. (Originally published in 1776.)

Spector, Paul E., Daniel J. Dwyer, and Steve M. Jex. 1988. "Relation of Job Stressors to Affective, Health, and Performance Outcomes: A Comparison of Multiple Data Sources," *Journal of Applied Psychology*. 73 (February), pp. 11–19.

Stevenson, Richard W. 1992. "Keating Is Sentenced to 10 Years for Defrauding S & L Customers," *New York Times*. (April 11), pp. A1+.

Terkel, Studs. 1974. *Working*. New York: Pantheon Books.

Thomas, Michael M. 1991. "The Greatest-Ever Bank Robbery: The Collapse of the Savings and Loan Industry," *New York Review of Books*. 38 (January 31), pp. 30–35.

Tiglao, R. 1991. "March of Pluralism: Democracy Takes Routes Despite Hazards and Obstacles," *Far Eastern Economic Review*. 153 (September 5), pp. 550–55.

Tocqueville, Alexis de. 1966. *Democracy in America*. Trans. George Lawrence. New York: Harper & Row. (Originally published in 1835.)

Toffler, Alvin. 1981. *The Third Wave*. New York: Bantam Books.

Tolchin, Martin, and Susan Tolchin. 1972. *To the Victor. . . .* New York: Vintage Books.

542

Twain, Mark. 1973. *Mark Twain and the Three R's*. Indianapolis: Bobbs-Merrill.

U.S. Bureau of the Census. 1992. *Statistical Abstract of the United States: 1992*. 112th ed. Washington, DC: U.S. Government Printing Office.

Vallas, Steven Peter. 1988. "New Technology, Job Content, and Worker Alienation: A Test of Two Rival Perspectives," *Work and Occupations*. 15 (May), pp. 148–78.

Walker, Jack L., Jr. 1991. *Mobilizing Interest Groups in America: Patrons, Professions, and Social Movements*. Ann Arbor, MI: University of Michigan Press.

Wallerstein, Immanuel. 1974. *The Modern World-System: Capitalist Agriculture and the Origins of the European World-Economy in the Sixteenth Century*. New York: Academic Press.

Weber, Max. 1947. *The Theory of Social and Economic Organization*. Trans. A. M. Henderson and Talcott Parsons. New York: Free Press.

Wilensky, Harold L. 1966. "Work as A Social Problem," In Howard S. Becker (ed.), *Social Problems: A Modern Approach*. New York: John Wiley and Sons, pp. 117–66.

Wise, David. 1976. "Cloak and Dagger Operations: An Overview," In Jerome H. Skolnick and Elliot Currie (eds.), *Crisis in American Institutions*. 3rd ed. Boston: Little, Brown, pp. 88–101.

Wolfe, Alan. 1973. *The Seamy Side of Democracy*. New York: David McKay.

Worchel, Stephen, and Susan L. Shackelford. 1991. "Groups under Stress: The Influence of Group Structure and Environment on Process and Performance," *Personality and Social Psychology Bulletin*. 17 (December), pp. 640–47.

Yankelovich, Daniel. 1974. "The Meaning of Work," In J. M. Rosow (ed.)., *The Worker and the Job*. Englewood Cliffs, NJ: Prentice-Hall, pp. 19–47.

Chapter 14

Arkin, William M. 1992. "Little Nuclear Secrets," *New York Times*. (September 9), p. A21.

Armstrong, David. 1987. "Silence and Truth in Death and Dying," *Social Science and Medicine*. 24, pp. 651–57.

Bayer, Ronald, et al. 1988. "Toward Justice in Health Care," *Journal of Public Health*. 78 (May), pp. 583–88.

Becker, Howard S., and Blanche Geer. 1958. "The Fate of Idealism in Medical School," *American Sociological Review*. 23 (February), pp. 50–56.

Belkin, Lisa. 1992a. "In Lessons on Empathy, Doctors Become Patients," *New York Times*. (June 4), pp. A1+.

———. 1992b. "Frustrating Spate of New Rules for Clinics," *New York Times*. (August 30), pp. 33+.

Ben-David, Joseph. 1971. *The Scientist's Role in Society*. Englewood Cliffs, NJ: Prentice-Hall.

Bendzsel, Miklós, and István Kiss. "The Socio-ethical Dimension of Invention," *Impact of Science on Society*. 37, pp. 233–40.

Butterfield, Fox. 1992. "Universal Health Care Plan Is Goal of Law in Vermont," *New York Times*. (May 12), p. A17.

Cardy, Robert L., and Cathy Korodi. 1991. "Nurse Appraisal Systems: Characteristics and Effectiveness," *Social Science & Medicine*. 32, pp. 553–58.

Cleveland, Harlan. 1988. "Theses of a New Reformation: The Social Fallout of Science 300 Years after Newton," *Public Administration Review*. 48 (May/June), pp. 681–86.

Coe, Rodney M. 1978. *Sociology of Medicine*. New York: McGraw-Hill.

Economist. 1991a. "Money for the Boffins." 318 (February 16), pp. 15–16.

Economist. 1991b. "Will the Bangs End with a Whimper?" 321 (November 2), pp. 79–82.

Fox, Renee C. 1978. "Training for Uncertainty," In Howard D. Schwartz and Cary S. Kart (eds.), *Dominant Issues in Medical Sociology*. Reading, MA: Addison-Wesley, pp. 189–202.

Freidson, Eliot. 1970. *Profession of Medicine*. New York: Harper & Row.

———. 1978. "Colleague Relationships among Physicians," In Howard D. Schwartz and Cary S. Kart (eds.), *Dominant Issues in Medical Sociology*. Reading, MA: Addison-Wesley, pp. 228–37.

———. 1981. "Professional Dominance and the Ordering of Health Services: Some Consequences," In Peter Conrad and Rochelle Kern (eds.), *The Sociology of Health and Illness*. New York: St. Martin's Press, pp. 184–97.

Gray-Toft, Pamela, and James G. Anderson. 1981. "Stress among Hospital Nursing Staff: Its Causes and Effects," *Social Science and Medicine*. 15 (September), pp. 639–47.

Hugick, Larry, and Graham Hueber. 1991. "Pharmacists and Clergy Rate Highest for Honesty and Ethics," *Gallup Poll Monthly*. (May), pp. 29–31.

Jamal, Muhammad, and Vishwanath V. Baba. 1991. "Type A Behavior, Its Prevalence and Consequences among Women Nurses: An Empirical

Examination," *Human Relations*. 44 (November), pp. 1213–28.

Keith, Verna M., and David P. Smith. 1988. "The Current Differential in Black and White Life Expectancy," *Demography*. 25 (November), pp. 625–32.

Kornblum, William, and Joseph Julian. 1989. *Social Problems*. 6th ed. Englewood Cliffs, NJ: Prentice-Hall.

Larsen, Ulla. 1990. "Short-term Fluctuations in Death by Cause, Temperature, and Income in the United States, 1930–1985," *Social Biology*. 37 (Fall/Winter), pp. 172–87.

Levin, Sharon G., and Paula E. Stephan. 1991. "Research Productivity over the Life Cycle: Evidence for Academic Scientists," *American Economic Review*. 81 (March), pp. 114–32.

McNerney, Walter J. 1988. "Nursing's Vision in a Competitive Environment," *Nursing Outlook*. 36 (May/June), pp. 126–29.

Mallett, Karen, et al. 1991. "Relations among Burnout, Death Anxiety, and Social Support in Hospice and Critical Care Nurses," *Psychological Reports*. 68 (June), pp. 1347–59.

Markson, Elizabeth. 1971. "A Hiding Place to Die," *Trans-action*. 9 (November/December), pp. 48–54.

May, Marlynn L., and Daniel B. Stengel. 1990. "Who Sues Their Doctors? How Patients Handle Medical Grievances," *Law & Society Review*. 24, pp. 105–20.

Mechanic, David. 1978. *Medical Sociology*. 2nd ed. New York: Free Press.

Merton, Robert. 1973. *The Sociology of Science*. Chicago: University of Chicago Press.

Mitroff, Ian. 1974. "Norms and Counter-Norms in a Select Group of the Apollo Moon Scientists: A Case Study of the Ambivalence of Scientists," *American Sociological Review*. 39 (August), pp. 579–95.

Moravcsik, Michael. 1985. "The Ultimate Scientific Plateau," *Futurist*. 19 (October), pp. 28–30.

Najman, J. M., D. Klein, and C. Munro. 1982. "Patient Characteristics Negatively Stereotyped by Doctors," *Social Science and Medicine*. 16, pp. 1781–89.

Navarre, Bonnie Puckett. 1988. "Incentive Plans Needed for Nurse Administrators," *Nursing Management*. 19 (October), pp. 60–64.

Parkes, Katherine R. 1985. "Stressful Episodes Reported by First-Year Student Nurses: A Descriptive Account," *Social Science and Medicine*. 20, pp. 945–53.

Parsons, Talcott. 1951. *The Social System*. New York: Free Press.

Phillips, Gerald M., and J. Alfred Jones. 1991. "Medical Compliance: Patient or Physician Responsibility?" *American Behavioral Scientist*. 34 (July/August), pp. 756–67.

Pope, Kenneth S. 1990. "Ethical and Malpractice Issues in Hospital Practice," *American Psychologist*. 45 (September), pp. 1066–70.

Quint, Jeanne C. 1978. "Institutionalized Practices of Information Control," In Howard D. Schwartz and Cary S. Kart (eds.), *Dominant Issues in Medical Sociology*. Reading, MA: Addison-Wesley, pp. 87–99.

Reverby, Susan. 1981. "Re-forming the Hospital Nurse: The Management of American Nursing," In Peter Conrad and Rochelle Kern (eds.), *The Sociology of Health and Illness*. New York: St. Martin's Press, pp. 220–33.

Rifkin, Jeremy. 1980. "Recombinant DNA," In Rita Arditti, Pat Brennan, and Steve Cavrak (eds.), *Science and Liberation*. Boston: South End Press, pp. 145–56.

Ryan, William. 1976. *Blaming the Victim*. 2nd ed. New York: Vintage Books.

Siegel, Bernie S. 1988. *Love, Medicine and Miracles*. New York: Harper & Row.

Sirken, Monroe G., et al. 1987. "The Quality of Cause-of-Death Statistics," *American Journal of Public Health*. 77 (February), pp. 137–39.

Somers, Mark John, and Dee Birnbaum. 1991. "Assessing Self-Appraisal of Job Performance as an Evaluation Device: Are the Poor Results a Function of Method or Methodology?" *Human Relations*. 44 (October), pp. 1081–91.

Specter, Michael. 1991. "The Case of Dr. Gallo," *New York Review of Books*. 38 (August 15), pp. 49–52.

Street, Richard L., Jr. 1991. "Information-giving in Medical Consultations: The Influence of Patients' Communicative Styles and Personal Characteristics," *Social Science & Medicine*. 32, pp. 541–48.

Szasz, Thomas S., and Marc H. Hollender. 1956. "A Contribution to the Philosophy of Medicine: The Basic Models of the Doctor-Patient Relationship," A.M.A. *Archives of Internal Medicine*. 97 (May), pp. 585–92.

Trankina, Michele L. 1991. "Psychology of the Scientist: LXIV. Work-related Attitudes of U.S. Scientists," *Psychological Reports*. 69 (October), pp. 443–50.

Trinkaus, John. 1991. "Medications and Information for Patients: A Quick Look," *Psychological Reports*. 68 (June), pp. 911–14.

544

Turner, Bryan S. 1987. *Medical Power and Social Knowledge*. London: Sage.

Twaddle, Andrew C., and Richard M. Hessler. 1977. *A Sociology of Health*. St. Louis: C. V. Mosby.

University of California Nuclear Weapons Labs Conversion Project. 1980. "Livermore and Los Alamos Scientific Laboratories," In Rita Arditti, Pat Brennan, and Steve Cavrak (eds.), *Science and Liberation*. Boston: South End Press, pp. 93–112.

U.S. Bureau of the Census. 1984. *Statistical Abstract of the United States: 1984*. 104th ed. Washington, DC: U.S. Government Printing Office.

U.S. Bureau of the Census. 1986. *Statistical Abstract of the United States: 1986*. 106th ed. Washington, DC: U.S. Government Printing Office.

U.S. Bureau of the Census. 1992. *Statistical Abstract of the United States: 1992*. 112th ed. Washington, DC: U.S. Government Printing Office.

Watkins, Margaret, Sandra Lapham, and Wendy Hoy. 1991. "Use of a Medical Center's Computerized Health Care Database for Notifiable Disease Surveillance," *American Journal of Public Health*. 81 (May), pp. 637–39.

Williams, Robin M., Jr. 1970. *American Society*. 3rd ed. New York: Alfred A. Knopf.

Wolinsky, Frederic D. 1980. *The Sociology of Health*. Boston: Little, Brown.

Wolinsky, Frederic D., and Sally R. Wolinsky. 1981. "Expecting Sick-Role Legitimation and Getting It," *Journal of Health and Social Behavior*. 22 (September), pp. 229–42.

Wyngaarden, James B. 1984. "Science and Government: A Federal Agency Perspective," *American Psychologist*. 9 (September), pp. 1053–55.

Chapter 15

Adler, Robert W. 1991. "How We Use and Abuse Water," In Judith S. Scherff (ed.), *The Mother Earth Handbook*. New York: Continuum, pp. 120–34.

Alpern, David M. 1981. "Mr. Fixit for the Cities," *Newsweek*. 98 (May 4), pp. 26–30.

Barnet, Richard J. 1980. *The Lean Years: Politics in the Age of Scarcity*. New York: Simon & Schuster.

Bartlett, Robert V. 1990. "Comprehensive Environmental Decision Making: Can It Work?" In Norman J. Vig and Michael E. Kraft (eds.), *Environmental Policy in the 1990s*. Washington, DC: Congressional Quarterly Press, pp. 235–54.

Beck, Melinda. 1982. "The Decaying of America," *Newsweek*. 99 (August 2), pp. 12–17.

Brown, Lester R. 1978. *The Twenty-Ninth Day*. New York: W. W. Norton.

Caldwell, Lynton K. 1990. "International Environmental Politics: America's Response to Global Imperatives," In Norman J. Vig and Michael E. Kraft (eds.), *Environmental Policy in the 1990s: Toward a New Agenda*. Washington, DC: Congressional Quarterly Press, pp. 301–21.

Cockburn, Alexander. 1988. "Chemical Reaction," *Environment and Society*. 1 (August), pp. 18–19.

Commoner, Barry. 1972. *The Closing Circle: Nature, Man and Technology*. New York: Bantam Books.

Comp, T. Allan. 1991. "Earth Day and Beyond," In Theodore D. Goldbarb (ed.), *Taking Sides: Clashing Views on Controversial Environmental Issues*. 4th ed. Guilford, CT: Dushkin, pp. 11–14.

Cutler, Blayne. 1991. "The World's Choices for Birth Control," *American Demographics*. 13 (June), p. 14.

Dahmann, Donald C. 1985. "Assessments of Neighborhood Quality in Metropolitan America," *Urban Affairs Quarterly*. 20 (June), pp. 511–35.

Dreier, Peter, and W. Dennis Keating. 1990. "The Limits of Localism: Progressive Housing Policies in Boston, 1984–1989," *Urban Affairs Quarterly*. 26 (December), pp. 191–216.

Ehrlich, Paul R., and Anne H. Ehrlich. 1991. "Population Control: Necessary But Insufficient," In Judith S. Scherff (ed.), *The Mother Earth Handbook*. New York: Continuum, pp. 17–31.

Elliott, Osborn. 1991. "March on Washington," *Congressional Record*. 137 (October 17), pp. 1–4.

Exter, Thomas. 1991. "Please Stop at Nine Billion," *American Demographics*. 13 (April), p. 13.

Farnsworth, Clyde H. 1992. "Reichman Troubles Roil Canada," *New York Times*. (May 14), pp. D1+.

Feagin, Joe R., and Robert Parker. 1990. *Building American Cities: The Urban Real Estate Game*. 2nd ed. Englewood Cliffs, NJ: Prentice-Hall.

Gittell, Marilyn. 1985. "The American City: A National Priority or an Expendable Population?" *Urban Affairs Quarterly*. 21 (September), pp. 13–19.

Gottman, Jean. 1961. *Megalopolis: The Urbanized Northeastern Seaboard of the United States*. Cambridge, MA: MIT Press.

Graves, Robert. 1962. *Claudius the God*. New York: Vintage Books. (Originally published in New York: Harrison Smith and Robert Haas, 1935.)

Hagood, Susan. 1991. "Toxic Shock: The Pesticide

Fix," In Judith S. Scherff (ed.), *The Mother Earth Handbook*. New York: Continuum, pp. 177–92.

Hartmann, Betsy. 1987. *Reproductive Rights and Wrongs: The Global Politics of Population Control & Contraceptive Choice*. New York: Harper & Row.

Hoke, Franklin. 1991. "Spectrum," *Environment*. 33 (July/August), pp. 21–24.

Hopkins, Ellen. 1989. "The Dispossessed," In Jeffrey M. Elliot (ed.), *Urban Society*. 4th ed. Guilford, CT: Dushkin, pp. 82–87.

Hueber, Graham. 1991. "Americans Report High Levels of Environmental Concern, Anxiety," *Gallup Poll Monthly*. (April), pp. 6–12.

Jacobs, Jane. 1961. *The Death and Life of Great American Cities*. New York: Vintage Books.

Kaplan, Marshall. 1990. "Infrastructure Policy: Repetitive Studies, Uneven Response, Next Steps," *Urban Affairs Quarterly*. 25 (March), pp. 371–88.

Krauss, Clifford. 1992a. "Washington Marchers Demand Attention to the Cities," *New York Times*. (May 17), p. 22.

———. 1992b. "$2 Billion Accord Reached on Emergency Aid to Cities," *New York Times*. (June 6), p. 7.

London, Bruce, et al. 1986. "The Determinants of Gentrification in the United States: A City-Level Analysis," *Urban Affairs Quarterly*. 21 (March), pp. 369–87.

Lyman, Brad. 1992. "Urban Primacy and World-System Position," *Urban Affairs Quarterly*. 28 (September), pp. 22–37.

MacLeish, William H. 1992. "Water, Water, Everywhere, How Many Drops to Drink?" In John L. Allen (ed.), *Environment 92/93*. 11th ed. Guilford, CT: Dushkin, pp. 180–83.

Magnuson, John J., and Jennifer A. Drury. 1992. "Global Change Ecology," In John L. Allen (ed.), *Environment 92/93*. 11th ed. Guilford, CT: Dushkin, pp. 39–43.

Makhijani, Arjun, Amanda Bickel, and Annie Makhijani. 1991. "Still Working on the Ozone Hole," In John Allen (ed.), *Environment 91/92*. 10th ed. Guilford, CT: Dushkin, pp. 183–87.

Malthus, Thomas Robert. 1798. *First Essay on Population*: 1798. London: Printed for J. Johnson in St. Paul's Churchyard.

Mathews, Jessica Tuchman. 1991. "Rescue Plan for Africa," In John Allen (ed.), *Environment 91/92*. 10th ed. Guilford, CT: Dushkin, pp. 75–81.

Matthews, Tom. 1979. "Nuclear Accident," *Newsweek*. 93 (April 9), pp. 24–26+.

Meadows, Donella H., et al. 1972. *The Limits to Growth: A Report on the Club of Rome's Project on the Predicament of Mankind*. New York: Signet Books.

Mellor, John W. 1991. "The Intertwining of Environmental Problems and Poverty," In John Allen (ed.), *Environment 91/92*. 10th ed. Guilford, CT: Dushkin, pp. 69–74.

Miller, Alan. 1991. "Climate: Economic Models and Policy on Global Warming," *Environment*. 33 (July/August), pp. 3–5+.

Molotch, Harvey, and Serena Vicari. 1988. "Three Ways to Build the Development Process in the United States, Japan, and Italy," *Urban Affairs Quarterly*. 24 (December), pp. 188–214.

Mumford, Lewis. 1971. "Statement of Lewis Mumford, Author. Hearings before the U.S. Senate, Subcommittee on Executive Reorganization, Committee on Government Operations, April 21, 1967," In Ted Venetoulis and Ward Eisenhauer (eds.), *Up against the Urban Wall*. Englewood Cliffs, NJ: Prentice-Hall, pp. 431–56.

Njogu, Wamucii. 1991. "Trends and Determinants of Contraceptive Use in Kenya," *Demography*. 28 (February), pp. 83–99.

Odom, Anthony M. 1991. "Apprehending the City: The View from Above, Below, and Behind," *Urban Affairs Quarterly*. 26 (June), pp. 589–609.

Pagano, Michael A. 1988. "Fiscal Disruptions and City Responses: Stability, Equilibrium, and City Capital Budgeting," *Urban Affairs Quarterly*. 24 (September), pp. 118–37.

Palen, J. John. 1981. *The Urban World*. 2nd ed. New York: McGraw-Hill.

Petersen, William. 1975. *Population*. 3rd ed. New York: Macmillan.

Pfeiffer, John. 1989. "How Man Invented Cities," In Jeffrey M. Elliot (ed.), *Urban Society*. 4th ed. Guilford, CT: Dushkin, pp. 6–11.

Pollock, Cynthia. 1986. "The Closing Act: Decommissioning Nuclear Power Plants," *Environment*. 28 (March), pp. 10–15+.

Prokesch, Steven. 1992. "Developer Files for Bankruptcy for Huge London Office Project," *New York Times*. (May 28), pp. A1+.

Ridker, Ronald G., and W. D. Watson. 1980. *To Choose a Future: Resources and Environmental Problems of the United States*. Baltimore: Johns Hopkins Press.

Robertson, Ian. 1980. *Social Problems*. 2nd ed. New York: Random House.

Robertson, Kent A. 1990. "The Status of the Pedestrian Mall in American Downtowns," *Urban Affairs Quarterly*. 26 (December), pp. 250–73.

546

Robertson, Roland. 1992. *Globalization: Social Theory and Global Culture*. London: Sage.

Rohatyn, Felix. 1991. "The Case for a New Domestic Order," *New York Review of Books*. 38 (November), pp. 6+.

Schneider, Keith. 1991. "Ranges of Animals and Plants Head North," *New York Times*. (August 13), pp. C1+.

Schneider, Stephen H. 1991. "Cooling It," In John Allen (ed.), *Environment 91/92*. 10th ed. Guilford, CT: Dushkin, pp. 188–95.

Schwab, William A. 1982. *Urban Sociology*. Reading, MA: Addison-Wesley.

Silk, Leonard. 1986. "Modern Views of Population," *New York Times*. (July 9), p. D2.

Simmel, Georg. 1950. *The Sociology of Georg Simmel*. Trans. Kurt H. Wolff. Glencoe, IL: Free Press.

Sjoberg, Gideon. 1960. *The Preindustrial City: Past and Present*. Glencoe, IL: Free Press.

Spates, James L., and John J. Macionis. 1982. *The Sociology of Cities*. New York: St. Martin's Press.

Stahura, John M. 1988. "Changing Patterns of Suburban Racial Composition, 1970–1980," *Urban Affairs Quarterly*. 23 (March), pp. 448–60.

Stevens, William K. 1992. "Lessons of Rio: A New Prominence and an Effective Blandness," *New York Times*. (June 14), p. 10.

Stuart, Lettice. 1992. "Hines Renovating 2 Shell Towers He Built in 70's," *New York Times*. (February 16), sec. 10, p. 11.

Sullivan, Thomas, et al. 1980. *Social Problems*. New York: John Wiley and Sons.

Terry, Don. 1989. "In Week of an Infamous Rape, 28 Other Victims Suffer," *New York Times*. (May 29), p. 25.

Tönnies, Ferdinand. 1957. *Community and Society*. New York: Harper.

United Nations. 1985. *Demographic Yearbook, 1985*. New York: United Nations Publishing Service.

U.S. Bureau of the Census. 1989. *Statistical Abstract of the United States: 1989*. 109th ed. Washington, DC: U.S. Government Printing Office.

U.S. Bureau of the Census. 1992. *Statistical Abstract of the United States: 1992*. 112th ed. Washington, DC: U.S. Government Printing Office.

U.S. Congress. House. Committee on Agriculture. 1976. "Malthus and America (1974)," In Phillip Appleman (ed.), *Thomas Robert Malthus: An Essay on the Principle of Population*. New York: W. W. Norton, pp. 253–56.

Wald, Matthew L. 1989. "10 Years after Three Mile Island," *New York Times*. (March 23), pp. D1+.

———. 1992. "Nuclear Power Plants Take Early Retirement," *New York Times*. (August 16), sec. 4, p. 7.

Walton, John (ed.). 1985. *Capital and Labor in the Urbanized World*. London: Sage.

Wayne, Leslie. 1992. "New Hope in Inner Cities: Banks Offering Mortgages," *New York Times*. (March 14), pp. 1+.

Wirth, Louis. 1938. "Urbanism as a Way of Life," *American Journal of Sociology*. 44 (July), pp. 3–24.

Chapter 16

Barron, James. 1982. "Poison Worries Lead to Precautions for Halloween," *New York Times*. (October 28), p. B1.

Blumer, Herbert. 1975. "Outline of Collective Behavior," In Robert Evans (ed.), *Readings in Collective Behavior*. 2nd ed. Chicago: Rand McNally, pp. 22–45.

Brown, Michael, and Amy Goldin. 1973. *Collective Behavior*. Pacific Palisades, CA: Goodyear.

Cantril, Hadley. 1940. *The Invasion from Mars*. Princeton, NJ: Princeton University Press.

Chamberlain, Mariam. 1990. "The Emergence and Growth of Women's Studies Programs," In Sara E. Rex (ed.), *The American Woman, 1990–91: A Status Report*. New York: W. W. Norton, pp. 315–24.

Cuzan, Alfred G. 1990. "Resource Mobilization and Political Opportunity in the Nicaraguan Revolution," *American Journal of Economics and Sociology*. 49 (October), pp. 401–12.

———. 1991. "Resource Mobilization and Political Opportunity in the Nicaraguan Revolution: The Praxis," *American Journal of Economics and Sociology*. 50 (January), pp. 71–83.

Davies, James C. 1962. "Toward a Theory of Revolution," *American Sociological Review*. 27 (February), pp. 5–19.

Davis, Mike. 1992. "In L.A., Burning All Illusions," *Nation*. 254 (June 1), pp. 743–46.

Economist. 1991. "Wielding the Axe." 318 (February 16), pp. 3–10+.

Farley, John E. 1982. *Majority-Minority Relations*. Englewood Cliffs, NJ: Prentice-Hall.

Fields, Echo E. 1991. "Understanding Activist Fundamentalism: Capitalist Crisis and the 'Colonization of the Lifeworld,'" *Sociological Analysis*. 52 (Summer), pp. 175–90.

Fischer, Claude S., and Glenn R. Carroll. 1988. "Telephone and Automobile Diffusion in the United States, 1902–1937," *American Journal of Sociology*. 93 (March), pp. 1153–78.

Foy, Eddie, and Alvin F. Harlow. 1928. "Excerpt from *Clowning through Life*," New York: E.P. Dutton. In Ralph H. Turner and Lewis M. Killian. *Collective Behavior*. Englewood Cliffs, NJ: Prentice-Hall, 1957, pp. 104–13.

Freeman, Jo. 1979. "The Woman's Liberation Movement: Its Origins, Organizations, Activities, and Ideas," In Jo Freeman (ed.), *Women: A Feminist Perspective*. Palo Alto, CA: Mayfield, pp. 557–74.

Gamson, William. 1975. *The Strategy of Social Protest*. Homewood, IL: Dorsey Press.

Gibson, Jeffie Ann Pearson, and Lillian M. Range. 1991. "Are Written Reports of Suicide and Seeking Help Contagious? High Schoolers' Perception," *Journal of Applied Social Psychology*. 21 (September 16–30), pp. 1517–23.

Gurney, Joan Neff, and Kathleen J. Tierney. 1982. "Relative Deprivation and Social Movements: A Critical Look at Twenty Years of Theory and Research," *Sociological Quarterly*. 23 (Winter), pp. 33–47.

Hannigan, John A. 1985. "Alain Touraine, Manuel Castells and Social Movement Theory: A Critical Appraisal," *Sociological Quarterly*. 26 (Winter), pp. 435–54.

———. 1991. "Social Movement Theory and the Sociology of Religion: Toward a New Synthesis," *Sociological Analysis*. 52 (Winter), pp. 311–31.

Hueber, Graham. 1991. "Americans Report High Level of Environmental Concern, Anxiety," *Gallup Poll Monthly*. (April), pp. 6–12.

Kerbo, Harold R. 1982. "Movements of 'Crisis' and Movements of 'Affluence,'" *Journal of Conflict Resolution*. 26 (December), pp. 645–63.

Kerbo, Harold R., and Richard A. Shaffer. 1986. "Unemployment and Protest in the United States, 1890–1940: A Methodological Critique and Research Note," *Social Forces*. 64 (June), pp. 1046–56.

Killian, Lewis M. 1964. "Social Movements," In Robert E. L. Faris (ed.), *Handbook of Modern Sociology*. Chicago: Rand McNally, pp. 426–55.

Kimmel, Allan J., and Robert Keefer. 1991. "Psychological Correlates of the Transmission and Acceptance of Rumors about AIDS," *Journal of Applied Social Psychology*. 21 (October 1–15), pp. 1608–28.

Klandermans, Bert. 1984. "Mobilization and Participation: Social-Psychological Expansion of Resource Mobilization Theory," *American Sociological Review*. 49 (October), pp. 583–600.

Klein, Andrew L. 1976. "Changes in Leadership Appraisal as a Function of the Stress of a Simulated Panic Situation," *Journal of Personality and Social Psychology*. 34 (December), pp. 1143–54.

Lauer, Robert H. 1977. *Perspective on Social Change*. 2nd ed. Boston: Allyn & Bacon.

Le Bon, Gustave. 1952. *The Crowd*. London: Ernest Benn. (Originally published in 1896.)

Lenski, Gerhard, and Jean Lenski. 1982. *Human Societies*. 4th ed. New York: McGraw-Hill.

Linton, Ralph. 1973. "Discovery, Invention, and Their Cultural Setting," In Amitai Etzioni and Eva Etzioni-Halevy (eds.), *Social Change*. 2nd ed. New York: Basic Books, pp. 451–56.

———. 1982. "One Hundred Percent American," In Leonard Cargan and Jeanne H. Ballantine (eds.), *Sociological Footprints*. 2nd ed. Belmont, CA: Wadsworth, pp. 58–59.

McDonald, Douglas H., and Lillian M. Range. 1990. "Do Written Reports of Suicide Induce High-School Students to Believe That Suicidal Contagion Will Occur?" *Journal of Applied Social Psychology*. 20 (August), pp. 1093–1102.

Malcolm, Andrew H. 1980. "The 'Shortage' of Bathroom Tissue," In Reece McGee et al. *Sociology*. 2nd ed. New York: Holt, Rinehart and Winston, pp. 497–98.

Manegold, Catherine S. 1992. "Amid Wreckage, Survivors Tell Their Stories," *New York Times*. (August 25), pp. A1+.

Mann, Leon. 1981. "The Baiting Crowd in Episodes of Threatened Suicide," *Journal of Personality and Social Psychology*. 41 (October), pp. 703–09.

Marshall, S.L.A. 1947. *Men under Fire*. New York: William Morrow.

Mellor, John W. 1991. "The Intertwining of Environmental Problems and Poverty," In John Allen (ed.), *Environment 91/92*. 10th ed. Guilford, CT: Dushkin, pp. 69–74.

Monsivais, Carlos. 1990. "From '68 to Cardenismo: Toward a Chronicle of Social Movements," *Journal of International Affairs*. 43 (Winter), pp. 385–93.

Morrison, Denton E. 1973. "Some Notes toward Theory on Relative Deprivation, Social Movements, and Social Changes," In Robert R. Evans (ed.), *Social Movements*. Chicago: Rand McNally, pp. 103–16.

Murdock, George Peter. 1956. "How Culture Changes," In Harry L. Shapiro (ed.), *Man, Culture, and Society*. New York: Oxford University Press, pp. 247–60.

Nessel, Jen. 1992. "Images of the Surreal City," *Nation*. 254 (June 1), pp. 746–48.

New Haven Register. 1986. "Letterman's Flip Remark Prompts $1 Million Suit." (July 26), p. 14.

Nielsen, Francois. 1985. "Toward a Theory of Ethnic Solidarity in Modern Societies," *American Sociological Review*. 50 (April), pp. 133–49.

Oberschall, Anthony. 1973. *Social Conflict and Social Movements*. Englewood Cliffs, NJ: Prentice-Hall.

Orwell, George. 1946. *Animal Farm*. New York: Harcourt, Brace & World.

Reinhold, Robert. 1992. "A Terrible Chain of Events Reveals Los Angeles without Its Makeup," *New York Times*. (May 3), sec. 4, p. 1.

Rice, Berkeley. 1981. "Gourmet Worms: Antidote to a Rumor," *Psychology Today*. 15 (August), pp. 20+.

Rosnow, Ralph L. 1988. "Rumor as Communication: A Contextualist Approach," *Journal of Communication*. 38 (Winter), pp. 12–28.

———. 1991. "Inside Rumor: A Personal Journey," *American Psychologist*. 46 (May), pp. 484–96.

Ryder, Norman B. 1980. "The Future of American Fertility," In Arlene Skolnick and Jerome H. Skolnick (eds.), *Family in Transition*. 3rd ed. Boston: Little, Brown, pp. 51–66.

Shibutani, Tamotsu. 1966. *Improvised News: A Sociological Study of Rumor*. Indianapolis: Bobbs-Merrill.

Small, Gary W., et al. 1991. "Mass Hysteria among Student Performers: Social Relationship as a Symptom Predictor," *American Journal of Psychiatry*. 148 (September), pp. 1200–05.

Smelser, Neil J. 1963. *Theory of Collective Behavior*. New York: Free Press.

Stevenson, Richard W. 1992a. "Verdicts in Beating Case Produce Anger," *New York Times*. (April 30), pp. A1+.

———. 1992b. "Repairing Los Angeles: High Enthusiasm and Long Odds," *New York Times*. (May 10), sec. 4, p. 3.

Stiefel, Michael. 1982. "Soft and Hard Energy Paths: The Roads Not Taken," In John Allen (ed.), *Environment 82/83*. 3rd ed. Guilford, CT: Dushkin, pp. 49–50.

Tilly, Charles. 1978. *From Mobilization to Revolution*. Reading, MA: Addison-Wesley.

Turner, Ralph H. 1964. "Collective Behavior," In Robert E. L. Faris (ed.), *Handbook of Modern Sociology*. Chicago: Rand McNally, pp. 382–426.

Turner, Ralph H., and Lewis M. Killian. 1972. *Collective Behavior*. 2nd ed. Englewood Cliffs, NJ: Prentice-Hall.

Valocchi, Steve. 1990. "The Unemployed Workers' Movement of the 1930s," *Social Problems*. 37 (May), pp. 191–205.

Vander Zanden, James W. 1981. *Social Psychology*. 2nd ed. New York: Random House.

Weissman, Myrna M., et al. 1991. "A Reply to 'Increased Risk of Stroke in Patients with Panic Attacks: Real or Perceived?'" *American Journal of Psychiatry*. 148 (October), p. 1421.

Zupan, Mark A. 1991. "Paradigms and Cultures: Some Economic Reasons for Their Stickiness," *American Journal of Economics and Sociology*. 50 (January), pp. 99–103.

Photo Credits

Page 6 Tim Defrisco/Allsport;   Page 9 (top) Stock Montage/Historical Picture Service;   Page 9 (bottom) The Bettmann Archive;   Page 10 Brown Brothers;   Page 14 Texas Inprint;   Page 15 Angel Franco/NYT Pictures;   Page 24 Aneal Vohra/Unicorn Stock Photos;   Page 29 Gale Zucker/Stock, Boston;   Page 33 Benn Mitchell/The Image Bank;   Page 38 (top) Photofest;   Page 38 (bottom) ©1991 Capital Cities/ABC, Inc. (Ron Tom);   Page 43 (all) © 1965 by Stanley Milgram. From the film Obedience, distributed by the New York University Film and Video Library and Pennsylvania State University, PCR;   Page 50 Agence France Presse;   Page 53 Courtesy of AT&T Archives;   Page 57 The Forschner Group, Inc.;   Page 59 Victor Englebert/Photo Researchers;   Page 65 AP / Wide World Photos;   Page 69 Canapress / Paul Chiasson;   Page 73 Don Hogan Charles/NYT Pictures;   Page 80 Steve Satushek/The Image Bank;   Page 84 AP/Wide World Photos;   Page 87 Steve Castagneto/NYT Pictures;   Page 89 AP/Wide World Photos;   Page 93 Gale Zucker/Stock, Boston;   Page 97 Edna Douthat/Photo Researchers;   Page 100 (left) Spencer Grant/Stock, Boston;   Page 100 (right) Peter Menzel/Stock, Boston;   Page 108 AP/Wide World Photos;   Page 112 Elizabeth Crews/Stock, Boston;   Page 113 Jim Middleton/NYT Pictures;   Page 116 AP/Wide World Photos;   Page 119 Charlie Archambault/U.S. News & World Report;   Page 123 AP/Wide World Photos;   Page 124 Reuters/Bettmann;   Page 132 Susie Fitzhugh/Stock, Boston;   Page 137 David Hiser/Photographers Aspen;   Page 138 Frank Siteman/The Picture Cube;   Page 140 Elizabeth Crews;   Page 145 Peter Menzel/Stock, Boston;   Page 152 Nina Berman/SIPA Press;   Page 154 Miro Vintoniv/Stock, Boston;   Page 157 Jonathan Rawle/Stock, Boston;   Page 164 Robert Yager/Tony Stone Images;   Page 167 Mark Antman/Stock, Boston;   Page 171 Gale Zucker/Stock, Boston;   Page 177 AP/Wide World Photos;   Page 179 AP/Wide World Photos;   Page 181 SIPA Press;   Page 185 James L. Shaffer/Photo Edit;   Page 192 Suzanne Arms Wimberly/Jeroboam;   Page 200 J. Benser/Leo de Wys;   Page 204 Guy Le Querrec/Magnum;   Page 208 Michael Salas/The Image Bank;   Page 212 NBC;   Page 216 Michael Hayman/Photo Researchers;   Page 218 Costa Manos/Magnum;   Page 222 J. Berndt/Stock, Boston;   Page 232 Bob Daemmrich;   Page 237 (left) George Gardner/Stock, Boston;   Page 237 (right) Spencer Grant/Stock, Boston;   Page 241 Dan Walsh/The Picture Cube;   Page 246 Jason Laure/Woodfin Camp;   Page 250 Bob Kramer/The Picture Cube;   Page 252 N.R. Rowan/Stock, Boston;   Page 257 ©Kim Garnick/NYT Pictures;   Page 259 ©ELP Communications. All rights reserved. Courtesy of Columbia Pictures Television;   Page 270 AP/Wide World Photos;   Page 274 Jean Claude LeJeune/Stock, Boston;   Page 279 Jean Gaumy/Magnum;   Page 281 AP/Wide World Photos;   Page 285 Emile Mercado/Jeroboam;   Page 289 Martine Franck/Magnum;   Page 293 Ellis Herwig/Picture Cube;   Page 302 Richard Cartwright/CBS;   Page 305 Marc & Evelyn Bernheim/Woodfin Camp;   Page 307 Owen Franken/Stock, Boston;   Page 312 Amy Etra/PhotoEdit;   Page 315 David Sams/Texas Inprint;   Page 317 (left) Elizabeth Crews;   Page 317 (right) Elizabeth Crews;   Page 321 Paul Fortin/Stock, Boston;   Page 325 Jean Higgins/Unicorn Stock Photos;   Page 336 Bruce Flynn/Stock, Boston;   Page 339 Bob Daemmrich/Stock, Boston;   Page 341 Historical Pictures/Stock Montage;   Page 343 ©1992 Joel Gordon;   Page 349 Eugene Richards/Magnum;   Page 350 Susie Fitzhugh/Stock, Boston;   Page 355 Jeffrey Dunn/Picture Cube;   Page 358 Bob Daemmrich/Stock, Boston;   Page 366 Shelly Katz/Black Star;   Page 371 Tim Graham/Sygma;   Page 374 Joseph Koudelka/Magnum;   Page 378 AP/Wide World Photos;   Page 385 Mike Fiala/AFP Photo;   Page 388 Lee Gregory;   Page 393 AP/Wide World Photos;   Page 402 J. Berndt/Picture Cube;   Page 406 (top) Mary Evans Picture Library/Photo Researchers;   Page 406 (bottom) Lynn McLaren/Photo Researchers;   Page 412 Harold Sund/The Image Bank;   Page 417 AP/Wide World Photos;   Page 419 ©Steve McCurry/Magnum;   Page 420 David Sams/Texas Inprint;   Page 422 Susie Fitzhugh/Stock, Boston;   Page 424 Phil Huber/Black Star;   Page 434 David M. Grossman;   Page 438 Peter Menzel/Stock, Boston;   Page 440 Culver Pictures;   Page 443 Hank Morgan/Rainbow;   Page 448 Stephen Crowley/NYT Pictures;   Page 452 (left) Harry Crosby/Photo Researchers;   Page 452 (right) John Coletti/Stock, Boston;   Page 454 Agence France Presse;   Page 457 ©Santiago Lianquin/NYT Pictures;   Page 470 Ben Van Hook/Black Star;   Page 474 AP/Wide World Photos;   Page 477 Jan Sonnenmair/NYT Pictures;   Page 483 AP/Wide World Photos;   Page 488 Agence France Presse;   Page 491 David Young-Wolff/Photo Edit;   Page 495 Spencer Grant/Stock, Boston;   Page 498 AP/Wide World Photos;

Table and Figure Credits

Table 2.1 "Efforts to Reduce the Spread of Aids" from *The Gallup Poll Monthly*, November 1991. Reprinted with the permission of The Gallup Poll News Service.

Table 3.1 "How Humanity Was Created?" from *The Gallup Poll Monthly*, November 1991. Reprinted with the permission of The Gallup Poll News Service.

Table 4.1 "Community Crime and Safety" from article, "Public See Crime Up Nationally" from *The Gallup Poll Monthly*, March 1992 by Larry Hugick. Reprinted with the permission of the Gallup Poll News Service.

Figure 5.3 "A Sample of Lines in the Ach Experiment" from *Social Psychology*, by Dr. Solomon E. Asch. Copyright © 1952 and reprinted by permission of Dr. Solomon E. Asch.

Figure 6.1 "Media Use in the Last Twenty-Four Hours" from *The Gallup Poll Monthly*, February 1991. Reprinted with the permission of The Gallup Poll News Service.

Figure 7.1 "Support of Death Penalty for Individuals Convicted of Murder" from *The Gallup Poll Monthly*, June 1991. Reprinted with the permission of The Gallup Poll News Service.

Table 7.1 "The Five Modes of Adaptation in Merton's Anomie Theory," adapted with the permission of The Free Press, a Division of Macmillan, Inc., from SOCIAL THEORY AND SOCIAL STRUCTURE, Revised and Enlarged Edition by Robert K. Merton. Copyright © 1968, 1967 by Robert K. Merton.

Figure 9.1 "Approval of Interracial Marriage Over Time" from *The Gallup Poll Monthly*, April 1991. Reprinted with the permission of The Gallup Poll News Service.

Table 11.1 "Prejudice and Discrimination Against Emerging Minorities" from *The Gallup Poll Monthly*, October 1991. Reprinted with the permission of The Gallup Poll News Service.

Table 14.4 "The Medical Profession in Comparative Perspective" from *The Gallup Poll Monthly*, May 1991. Reprinted with the permission of the Gallup Poll News Service.

Table 15.1 "Outlook Toward Environmental Issues" from *The Gallup Poll Monthly*, April 1991. Reprinted with the permission of the Gallup Poll News Service.

Figure 16.1 "The J-Curve: Strain & Revolution" from *American Sociological Review*, February 1962, Volume 27, by James C. Davies. Reprinted with the permission of the American Sociological Association.

Name Index

Subject Index